Myres S. McDougal

TOWARD WORLD ORDER AND HUMAN DIGNITY

Toward World Order and Human Dignity

Essays in Honor
of Myres S. McDougal

Edited by
W. Michael Reisman
Burns H. Weston

Introduction by Harold D. Lasswell
Afterword by Eugene V. Rostow

THE FREE PRESS
A Division of Macmillan Publishing Co., Inc.
NEW YORK

Collier Macmillan Publishers
LONDON

The Free Press
A Division of Macmillan Publishing Co., Inc.
866 Third Avenue, New York, N.Y.   10022

Collier Macmillan Canada, Ltd.

Library of Congress Catalog Card Number: 75–36109

Printed in the United States of America

printing number

1 2 3 4 5 6 7 8 9 10

Library of Congress Cataloging in Publication Data

Main entry under title:

Toward world order and human dignity.

 "Bibliography of works by and relating to Myres S. McDougal as compiled by Frederick S. Tipson": p.
 Includes bibliographical references and index.
 CONTENTS: Jurisprudential perspectives: Morison, W. L. Myres S. McDougal and twentieth century jurisprudence. Higgins, R. Integrations of authority and control. Miller, J. C. Psychological aspects of systems analysis. Weston, B. H. The role of law in promoting peace and violence. Falk, R. A. The role of law in world society.--People: Caldwell. M. E. Well-being. Chen, L. Self-determination as a human right. Schwelb, E. The law of treaties and human rights.--Institutions: Bebr, G. Judicial policy of the Court of Justice in developing the legal order of the European Communities. Moore, J. N. The legal tradition and the management of national security. Raman, K. V. Customary prescription. Reisman, W. M. and Suzuki, E. Recognition and social change in international law. [etc.]
 1. International law--Addresses, essays, lectures. 2. McDougal, Myres Smith, 1906-   3. Jurisprudence--Addresses, essays, lectures. I. McDougal, Myres Smith, 1906-   II. Reisman, William Michael III. Weston, Burns H.
JX68.T68   341   75-36109
ISBN 0-02-926290-9

CONTENTS

ABOUT THE AUTHORS

GERHARD BEBR is Legal Advisor to the Commission of the European Communities in Brussels, Belgium. A former Lecturer in Law at the Yale Law School, his publications include *Judicial Control of the European Communities* (London: Stevens & Sons, 1962) and *Rule of Law Within the European Communities* (Brussels: Institut d'Études Européenes, 1965).

WILLIAM T. BURKE is Professor of Law at the University of Washington, Seattle. Coauthor (with Myres S. McDougal) of *The Public Order of the Oceans* (New Haven & London: Yale University Press, 1962), he is Vice-President of the Marine Technology Society and Editor-in-Chief of the *Ocean Development and International Law Journal*. A frequent consultant on Law of the Sea questions, Dr. Burke is also a member of the Board of Directors of the Law of the Sea Institute (University of Rhode Island), the Advisory Council to the Ocean Studies Program of the Woodrow Wilson Center for Scholars, the Ocean Policy Committee of the National Academy of Sciences, the Ocean Affairs Advisory Committee of the United States Department of State, and the Advisory Committee to the United States Interagency Task Force on the Law of the Sea.

MARY ELLEN CALDWELL is Professor of Law at the University of Florida, Gainesville. Coauthor (with Layman E. Allen) of *Communications Sciences and Law* (Indianapolis: Bobbs-Merrill, 1965), she is a member of the Executive Council of the American Society of International Law.

LUNG-CHU CHEN is Senior Research Associate at the Yale Law School. Coauthor (with Harold D. Lasswell) of *Formosa, China, and the*

United Nations (New York: St. Martin's Press, 1967), he currently is working in collaboration with Myres S. McDougal and Harold D. Lasswell on a comprehensive policy-oriented treatise entitled *Human Rights and World Public Order.*

RICHARD A. FALK is Albert G. Milbank Professor of International Law and Practice at Princeton University. A former Vice-President of the American Society of International Law, he currently is Co-Director of the North American Team of the World Order Models Project of the Institute for World Order, Co-Director of the Project on the Future of the International Legal Order, and a member of the editorial boards of the *American Journal of International Law, Foreign Policy Magazine, Alternatives—A Journal of World Policy,* and *International and Comparative Public Policy.* His books include *Law, War and Morality in the Contemporary World* (New York: Frederick A. Praeger, 1963), *Legal Order in a Violent World* (Princeton: Princeton University Press, 1968), *The New States and International Legal Order* (Leyden: A. W. Sijthoff, 1968), *The Status of Law in International Society* (Princeton: Princeton University Press, 1970), *This Endangered Planet* (New York: Random House, 1971), and *A Study of Future Worlds* (New York: Free Press, 1975).

ROSALYN HIGGINS, formerly of the Royal Institute of International Affairs, is presently a Barrister of the Inner Temple and a member of the faculty of the London School of Economics and Political Science. A past Vice-President of the American Society of International Law, she is a member of the editorial boards of the *American Journal of International Law,* the *British Yearbook of International Law,* and *International Organization.* Her books include *The Development of International Law Through the Political Organs of the United Nations* (London: Oxford University Press, 1963), *Conflict of Interests—International Law in a Divided World* (Charter Springs: Dufour Editions, 1965), and *The Administration of the United Kingdom's Foreign Policy through the United Nations* (Syracuse: Syracuse University Press, 1966). She also is completing a three-volume study entitled *United Nations Peacekeeping: Documents and Commentary* (New York: Oxford University Press), the first two volumes of which were published in 1969 and 1970.

DOUGLAS M. JOHNSTON is Professor of Law at Dalhousie University, Halifax, Nova Scotia, Canada. Coordinator of the Marine and Environmental Law Program at Dalhousie University, he also is Chairman of the Trilateral Commission Task Force on the Oceans and a Fellow of the World Academy of Art and Science. He is the author of *The International Law of Fisheries* (New Haven & London: Yale University Press, 1965), *Agreements of the People's Republic of China, 1949–67: A Calendar* (Cambridge: Harvard University Press, 1968), and the coeditor (with

James Barros) of *The International Law of Pollution* (New York: Free Press, 1974) and (with R. St. J. McDonald and G. Morris) *Canadian Perspectives on International Law and Organization* (Toronto: University of Toronto Press, 1974).

HAROLD D. LASSWELL is Ford Foundation Professor Emeritus of Law and the Social Sciences at the Yale Law School. He has been President of the World Academy of Art and Science, a fellow of the National Academy of Science, and President of both the American Society of International Law and the American Political Science Association. He is Co-chairman of the Policy Sciences Center in New York City. His many books include: *Psychopathology and Politics* (New York: Viking, 1930); *World Politics and Personal Insecurity* (New York, London: Whittlesey House, McGraw-Hill Book Co., 1935); *Politics: Who Gets What, When, How* (New York: Whittlesey House, 1936); *Power and Personality* (New York: Viking, 1948) (the Salmon Memorial Lectures, New York Academy of Medicine); as coauthor (with A. Kaplan), *Power and Society: A Framework for Political Inquiry* (New Haven: Yale University Press, 1950); as coauthor (with A. Kaplan), *World Revolution of Our Time* (Stanford: Stanford University Press, 1951); as coauthor (with R. Arens), *In Defense of Public Order* (New York: Columbia University Press, 1961); *The Future of Political Science* (Englewood Cliffs: Prentice-Hall, 1963); as coauthor (with M. S. McDougal and I. Vlasic), *Law and Public Order in Space* (New Haven: Yale University Press, 1963); as coauthor (with A. Rogow), *Power, Corruption and Rectitude* (Englewood Cliffs: Prentice-Hall, 1963); as coauthor (with D. Lerner), *World Revolutionary Elites: Studies in Coercive Ideological Movements* (Cambridge: MIT Press, 1966); and *A Preview of Policy Sciences* (New York: American Elsevier Publishing Co., 1971).

JAMES C. MILLER is Associate Professor of Psychology in the Department of Psychiatry in the Yale University School of Medicine. Chief Psychologist at the Connecticut Mental Health Center in New Haven, and a member of the Participating Faculty of the Yale Law School, he is the coauthor (with Myres S. McDougal and Harold D. Lasswell) of *The Interpretation of Agreements and World Public Order* (New Haven & London: Yale University Press, 1967).

JOHN NORTON MOORE is Professor of Law and Director of the Center for Oceans Law and Policy at the University of Virginia, Charlottesville. From 1973 to 1976, Professor Moore was Chairman of the National Security Council Interagency Task Force on the Law of the Sea and Deputy Special Representative of the President for the Law of the Sea Conference. A member of the Board of Editors of the *American Journal of International Law* and a member of the Council on Foreign Relations and the

Council of the Section of International Law of the American Bar Association, he is the author of *Law and the Indo-China Conflict* (Princeton: Princeton University Press, 1972) and the editor of *Law and Civil War in the Modern World* (Baltimore & London: The Johns Hopkins University Press, 1974) and of a three-volume collection entitled *The Arab-Israeli Conflict* (Princeton: Princeton University Press, 1974).

WILLIAM L. MORISON is Professor of Law at The University of Sydney, Australia. Currently, he is a Visiting Fellow in the Department of Law at The Australian National University, Canberra. His publications include a coauthored casebook (with R. L. Sharwood and C. L. Pannam) entitled *Cases on Torts* (2d ed., Sydney: The Law Book Company, Ltd., 1968) and a recent essay entitled "Frames of Reference for Legal Ideals," 2 *Dalhousie Law Journal* 3 (1975).

K. VENKATA RAMAN is a Fellow at the United Nations, Institute for Training and Research (UNITAR) in New York. Formerly a member of the Faculty of Law at Queen's University, Kingston, Ontario, Canada, his publications include *The Ways of the Peacemaker—A Study of United Nations Intermediary Assistance in the Peaceful Settlement of Disputes* (New York: United Nations Institute for Training and Research, 1975).

W. MICHAEL REISMAN, a coeditor of this volume, is Professor of Law at the Yale Law School. A member of the editorial boards of the *American Journal of International Law,* the *American Journal of Comparative Law,* and the *Journal of Conflict Resolution,* his books include *Nullity and Revision: The Review and Enforcement of International Judgments and Awards* (New Haven & London: Yale University Press, 1971), *The Art of the Possible: Diplomatic Alternatives in the Middle East* (Princeton: Princeton University Press, 1970), and *Puerto Rico and the International Process: New Roles in Association* (St. Paul: West Publishing Company, 1975).

EUGENE V. ROSTOW is Sterling Professor of Law and Public Affairs at the Yale Law School. Dean of the Yale Law School from 1955 to 1965, and Under Secretary of State for Political Affairs from 1966 to 1969, his books include *Planning for Freedom: The Public Law of American Capitalism* (New Haven & London: Yale University Press, 1959), *The Sovereign Prerogative: The Supreme Court and the Quest for Law* (New Haven & London: Yale University Press, 1962), *Law, Power and the Pursuit of Peace* (Lincoln: University of Nebraska Press, 1968), and *Peace in the Balance: The Future of American Foreign Policy* (New York: Simon & Schuster, 1972).

EGON SCHWELB is a former member of the faculty of the Yale Law School and presently a consultant to the United Nations Secretariat on international human rights and related matters, having served from 1947 to 1962 as Deputy Director of the Division of Human Rights in the United Nations Secretariat. Author of *Human Rights and the International Community* (Chicago: Quadrangle Books, 1964), his most recent publications include "The International Court of Justice and the Human Rights Clauses of the Charter," 66 *American Journal of International Law* 337 (1972), "Complaints by Individuals to the Commission on Human Rights: Twenty-Five Years of an Uphill Struggle (1947–1971)," in C. Boasson and M. Nurock, eds., *The Changing International Community* (The Hague: Mouton, 1973), and "Human Rights," in 8 *Encyclopaedia Britannica* 1183–89 (15th ed., 1974).

EISUKE SUZUKI is Assistant Professor of Law at the University of Houston. A University Consortium Fellow for World Order Studies at the Yale Law School, from which he received the degree of Doctor of Juridical Science in 1974, his doctoral dissertation was awarded the Yale Law School's Ambrose Gherini Prize. Dr. Suzuki is currently Editor-in-Chief of *Yale Studies in World Public Order,* a semiannual journal devoted to policy-oriented international legal studies.

FREDERICK SAMSON TIPSON is Assistant Director of the Center for Oceans Law and Policy and Lecturer in Law at the University of Virginia School of Law, Charlottesville. He currently is completing a doctoral dissertation on the American study of international law and the work of Myres S. McDougal and Harold D. Lasswell.

BURNS H. WESTON, a coeditor of this volume, is currently a Senior Fellow at the Institute for World Order in New York City and Director of the Institute's Transnational University Program. On leave from The University of Iowa, Iowa City, where he is Professor of Law and Director of the Center for World Order Studies, Dr. Weston is a member of the Board of Editors of the *American Journal of International Law* and a member of the Executive Council of the American Society of International Law and the Advisory Council of the Procedural Aspects of International Law Institute. The author of *International Claims: Postwar French Practice* (Syracuse: Syracuse University Press, 1971) and coauthor (with Richard B. Lillich) of *International Claims: Their Settlement by Lump Sum Agreements* (Charlottesville: University Press of Virginia, 1975), he has written extensively in the international property rights field, with emphasis on private foreign investment and Third World development.

Acknowledgments

Publication of this volume has been greatly facilitated by the generosity of the Yale Law School and Roger M. Blough, Samuel S. Cross, Lloyd N. Cutler, Sidney W. Davidson, Warren W. Eginton, Victor S. Johnson, Nicholas deB. Katzenbach, Cecil J. Olmstead, Stanley R. Resor, and Cyrus R. Vance. Eugene V. Rostow and Abraham S. Goldstein provided indispensable advice and support.

W. MICHAEL REISMAN
BURNS H. WESTON

INTRODUCTION

Harold D. Lasswell

Professor Myres S. McDougal is a transforming influence whose revolutionizing impact is partially exhibited in the present collection of distinguished articles in his honor. Appropriately enough the contributors focus on jurisprudence and international law, two areas in which Professor McDougal's distinctive and often disturbing mark is already deep.

Fortunately, his direct production is far from ended, as a glance at the bibliography, with its references to work in progress, abundantly shows. The scope of McDougal's jurisprudence is in no sense limited to international legal studies. He is perfecting an instrument that will undoubtedly be applied with telling effect to every phase of legal process at every level of jurisdiction. Eventually all the conventional fields of specialization will be covered (procedure, evidence, property, contract, tort, criminal law, constitutional law, corporations, tax, and so on). The fundamental approach will invite innovations in research and teaching, redraw boundaries, and generate new ways of looking at the interplay of law, man, and society.

Professor McDougal's orientation to law can be understood in part by scrutinizing his career with an eye to the principal sequences of development. If one begins with teaching—where he has always been a stellar performer—the sequence moves from "property" to "international law" and "jurisprudence." This is, however, an inadequate choice. Of seminal importance were the three years of legal history at Oxford under the direct and encouraging supervision of W. S. Holdsworth, a landmark figure in the punctilious and alert exploration of the past. It is not farfetched to assert that McDougal has spent the ensuing years of his professional life in a sustained effort to achieve intellectual mastery of the huge capital investment that he made in the details of history. Saturation in legal history set him apart from most contemporaries, especially in the United States.

At first McDougal applied his knowledge of the past to conventional purposes related to litigation. History was perceived as an inexhaustible mine of potential "precedents" in the never ending stream of controversy about the "authority" of "rules" invoked by advocates, judges, and commentators. More than this: History is a mine whose ore can be endlessly exploited for the fabrication of "distinctions." The simplest ploy is to locate a statement whose "manifest content" is a matter of applying logic ("syntactics") to propositions whose character is allegedly prescriptive. In further support of a distinction the skilled lawman uses historical knowledge to establish the "causes" and "consequences" of an ostensibly authoritative statement. If causes or consequences are shown to diverge from the contemporary situation, a distinction is born. In traditional perspective the procedures of affirmation and rebuttal culminate in the discovery of the "true" legal norm.

McDougal was emancipated from addiction to the conventional uses of history when he encountered a group of brilliant teachers at Yale whose approach exemplified "American legal realism." A partial caricature of the new viewpoint holds that since legal doctrines are hopelessly ambiguous, the skill of a legal craftsman can be measured by his success in justifying any specific claim in terms of any general doctrine. If this is so, what, if anything, could be said to account for such uniformities as appear in the response of courts?

The legal realists replied to this question by turning to the social and psychological sciences whose practitioners are accustomed to penetrate "justifications" or "rationalizations" and to demonstrate the influence of conditioning factors connected with culture, class, interest, and personality. McDougal was exposed to outstanding psychologists and social scientists as a member and a collaborator in "the cave of winds," a less than reverent name for the seminar in which Thurman Arnold used to acquaint himself and others with the emerging map of knowledge "beyond legal technicality." Frequent or occasional participants came from many specialties. At the time, Yale had a distinctive concentration of talent at the Institute for Human Relations. McDougal welcomed the comprehensive formulations of Bronislaw Malinowski, the "functionalist" in anthropology, and of other able figures in psychiatry and psychology.

This was an epoch—between World Wars I and II—when the American academic community was experiencing belated interest in the scientific approach to man and society. The Rockefeller Foundation was the principal source of leadership and money, and Yale was a principal center of excitement, conflict, and achievement. At one time the plan was to bring law into close physical proximity to the life sciences by moving the Law School to a new building at the heart of a complex that included medicine and all the biological and social sciences.

In the zestful and challenging environment of Yale, McDougal's command of history was a self-stabilizing factor that prevented him from going overboard for the social, psychological, or behavioral sciences then current. At the same time his grasp of historical knowledge—some of which was partly generalized—enabled him to recognize that new insights and methods were continually in the making.

McDougal became aware that several dimensions of the legal process were neglected by those who most exuberantly invoked the prestige of "science." It was a period when an ex-physicist like Walter Wheeler Cook was passionately committed to the view that law must be made into an empirical science by mimicking physics, chemistry, and other disciplines concerned with physical events. Legal researchers, it was said, must rely on "behavioral" indices of the conceptual categories employed in explanatory propositions. Scientists were supposed to eschew "preferential statements."

McDougal understood that lawyers and the institutions of legal process are too much involved with choice to ignore "preferences," "values," "biases," "goals" (or whatever corresponding label is used). Why should the lawyer become a "value-neutral" figure who relinquishes an "adult" role in shaping the future aims of legal and social systems? Could you, if you had ever known a philosopher, in good conscience leave the choice of value goals to him?

Issues of this kind permeate history, as McDougal well knew, where they complicate the professional historian's conception of his role. Should all historians "abdicate" moral judgment as well as scientific analysis? For the legal profession, too, such questions keep rising from the dead.

The "scientism" of the twenties and thirties left another trail of dissatisfaction in its wake. Owing in part to the need of an expanding corps of craftsmen to learn and improve their trade, the emphasis was highly methodological. The concentration of attention on "slicing" problems into "manageable bits" led to the specialists's famous predicament of knowing too much about too little.

Such specialism impressed McDougal, as many others have been impressed, as singularly myopic. It left out the significance of time and place and furnished no intellectual tools with which to discern the major features of past trends or to anticipate the direction of future development. And lawyers, at least, could not ignore the actual and potential structure of decisionmaking arenas. Lawyers ignore context and policy at their peril, and imperil the interests of clients who take their advice seriously.

As a young teacher of property law, McDougal was able from the start to make full and devastating use of his training in history and legal realism. His growing knowledge of the social setting and of the legal problems of public planning led to steadily evolving change in the treatment of conventional rhetoric, procedures, and instruments. McDougal threw his weight on the side of strengthening the intellectual and operational dimensions of metropolitan and regional planners. In these matters his most imaginative, informed, and cosmopolitan colleague was Maurice Rotival. On the institutional structures and functions of corporate property his principal colleague was William O. Douglas.

In short, McDougal was predisposed by professional training, insatiable curiosity, and unceasing concern for "relevance" in the domain of public policy to welcome and to collaborate in an approach to jurisprudence that is truly contextual, problem oriented, and multimethod. The collaboration between us began at a time when our interests were overlapping and convergent. I was in search of colleagues in various fields of knowledge who perceived the importance of a configurative approach and who were willing to develop the implications of a comprehensive working model of the social process. In particular I was on the lookout for a colleague learned in the law and highly motivated to execute the much-touted but little-realized aspiration toward a valid integration of "law and the social sciences." An associate was needed who could overcome the difficulties in delimiting the "authority" component of the power process. Colleagues in political science, for instance, felt as much at home as lawyers in the reiteration of nonoperational notions of law.

Stimulated by the fundamental issues posed by World War II and its aftermath, McDougal moved directly into international law and jurisprudence. So far as jurisprudence is concerned, the original plan was to go forward with an unannounced workshop in which we could collaborate "privately" in perfecting a systematic approach while generating material for use in regular courses. This strategy was abandoned in favor of a seminar-workshop on "Law, Science and Policy" (LSP), which self-chosen candidates for martyrdom survived as best they could. The change was in partial response to the challenge of enriching a new graduate program designed for law teachers, officials, and students who were admitted to the Law School on a limited quota basis (50 percent American, 50 percent other). LSP provided a kaleidoscopic view of whatever Professor McDougal and I were concerned about at the moment and produced among the survivors a battle-hardened corps of qualified permanent collaborators. For others LSP was a preview of LSD.

It would have been possible long since to have published an inclusive map of jurisprudence and to have relied on successive revisions to improve the original sketch. Such an alternative was incompatible with Professor McDougal's driving concern for comprehensiveness and with his acute awareness of the many questions that can validly be raised about meta-law (theories *about* law). Fortunately for the long-run impact, McDougal's early formation occurred in the "prerealist" world. During his first famous year at Yale as an advanced student fresh from Oxford, McDougal fought a rough-and-tumble tournament as a knight of conventional wisdom. When he was eventually convinced of the importance of much, at least, of the new realism, he was especially qualified to deal with the intellectual hang-ups of "natural lawyers," "historicists," "positivists," and the like.

McDougal's cognizance and mastery of the exacting criteria of legal craftsmanship, and his tendency toward "over-preparation," generated another "delay." He chose to use international law as a forum where the new jurisprudence could be at least partially exemplified. He therefore took the lead in selecting problems of great scholarly and policy interest such as "security," "space," and "sea." McDougal was, of course, suffering from no delusions about the immediate acceptance of a policy-oriented approach among colleagues in this country or abroad. In any case the experience of applying a comprehensive method could not fail to increase self-confidence in the approach if, in one's own terms, it succeeded. The feedback from experience would generate adaptations to the distinctive priorities of any problem cluster.

Looking back over Professor McDougal's intellectual evolution "within the system" many high points might be distinguished. For the most part they depend on the creative use of "communication theory." In delimiting "authority" it was essential to emphasize the significance of "perspectives" and "operations" and to clarify the potential use of composite "indicators" that employed "symbols," "signs," "deeds," and "resources." By insisting upon the significance of "expectation," "demand," and "identity" it became possible to overcome the exaggerators of "formalism," "verbalism," or "behaviorism."

A fruitful early step was to work out the full implications of the "normative ambiguity" of legalistic rhetoric, to distinguish "common" from "special" interests, and among common interests to identify the "inclusive" and the "exclusive." It became easier to elucidate "values" and "institutions" and to exemplify principles of "content" and "procedure" in performing the five intellectual tasks of problem-oriented jurisprudence. Other basic notions fell into line, especially "public order" and "civic order," and the "constitutive" process; likewise, the "observational standpoints" of the scientific ("contemplative") observer and the participant ("manipulative") observer.

A predisposing factor in McDougal's creative use of communication theory was his early training in the language and literature of classical Greece. His first appearance as a classroom teacher was in the role of an instructor in Greek, which furnishes a clue to his mastery of the complex sentence with its compelling conjuncture of the lucid and the evocative.

We have in no sense accounted for the many factors that made

McDougal what he is or his influence what it has been and will be. Presently available clues provide no more than a cloudy picture of the chain of motivation, aptitude, and circumstance that helps to explain either the tenacity and vision with which this formidable scholar has pursued his professional career, or the transformational stresses of an epoch in which Professor McDougal's jurisprudence can achieve a guiding impact.

I

Jurisprudential Perspectives

Chapter 1

Myres S. McDougal and Twentieth-Century Jurisprudence: A Comparative Essay

WILLIAM L. MORISON

According to Immanuel Kant, the human mind is capable of experiencing objects of thought only under certain very generally fixed categories.[1] However, even if it be true that the philosopher's theorizing is imprisoned within categories over whose selection he has no choice, it is otherwise with more specialized fields of inquiry, in particular with inquiry about law. It is fundamental to the thought of Myres McDougal [2] that, while in this area categorization continues to be essential for scholarly penetration, it is essential for the effectiveness of such penetration that the categories be deliberately and pragmatically chosen for the purposes in view.

In this general aspect, the thought has both critical and positive drives. On the critical side, it presents differently minded legal writers as hampering the achievement of their own objectives, whether they are professional lawyers and their academic imitators offering theories *of* law or scholars

3

attempting to analyze legal processes from a distance and offering theories *about* law.[3] On the positive side it rejects skeptical and eclectic solutions and itself offers a framework for, and of, legal inquiry.[4]

The controversy surrounding McDougal is partly attributable to the radical character of this critical aspect of his thought. If it were merely that he criticizes traditional approaches to jurisprudence for the narrowness of the categories they adopt, he at least might expect to find common ground with a considerable body of teachers who, beginning from the comfortable proposition that in the house of jurisprudence are many mansions, present their classes with numerous gems of thought about the various schools. McDougal's criticism of the approaches of most jurisprudential thinkers, however, is that they employ categories which are both too narrow and confused, that they lack both comprehensiveness and clarity. His description of a theory as inadequate refers to its failure to encompass and to identify the material sufficiently. He therefore sees the uncritical synthesist as having gone for inspiration to one after another thinker with bees in their bonnets and as having ended up with a swarm of bees in his own bonnet.

McDougal is not alone in his conviction of the positively damaging role of inadequate theory in hindering legal inquiry. For example, the perversion of commonsense notions by theorists who misunderstand the functions of language is a familiar theme of H. L. A. Hart's.[5] Yet, whereas a main source of Hart's interest in this aspect of legal theories derives from a general philosophical approach (and he concentrates in this part of his work on a particular source of trouble), McDougal's interest seems rather to be sparked by his observation of the ill effects of current approaches to the legal materials in which he has been specially interested (such as the law of property and, particularly, international law) and the jurisprudence of particular scholars with whom he has found himself from time to time in contact. His attack is therefore on every kind of inadequacy which stands in the way of achieving the scholarly tasks of legal analysis as he sees them.

There is no warrant in what has been said for giving a "historical" explanation of McDougal under the impression that by so doing one has disposed of him. There are reasons for predicting that theoretical inadequacy in McDougal's sense will persist into the indefinite future, both in professional theories of law and academic thinking about law. It is a trite observation that the nature of the professional lawyer's work in its various governmental or private fields is conducive to the formation and preservation of cults. Craft here slides easily into witchcraft. McDougal himself has been concerned to call attention to reasons why Jeremy Bentham's long-standing demand for "cognoscibility" in the law, with its continuing legacy in the shape of attempted codes and restatements, is doomed to continuing frustration associated with the sacrifice of values. In the absence of any simple solution of this kind to professional problems, a fertile field is likely to continue to exist for the preservation of professional mysteries to which only the "practical" man has access. Some academics, stung by their position on the outer fringes of the cult, are likely to continue to attempt to establish their position as members by imitating its more mysterious, and therefore possibly more insensate, ceremonies.[6] At the same time, a fertile field is likely to continue for exposures from an approach such as McDougal's, using carefully organized sociological categories of analysis. Approaches from narrow angles in more scholarly jurisprudence, with confusing aspiration to being universal solvents of legal problems, are not to be regarded as phenomena peculiar to the days of the Yale of Wesley Hohfeld and the realists. The persistent popularity of such approaches seems to be virtually assured by a kind of law of natural selection. An apparently simple line will always have a direct appeal which a more complex and refined set of recommendations for inquiry lacks. Moreover, admiration for the logical rigor with which a particular hypothesis is pursued to all its possible conclusions may render students attracted by it insensitive to limitations on its proper scope of application and the degree of its importance. In the field of academic jurisprudence, therefore, as well as professional legal theory, it may be anticipated that McDougal's specifications for inquiry into adequacy will continue to find employment in the interests of the future of such theory.

In the following sections of this essay, some impacts upon the work of other writers of McDougal's blueprint for inquiry into the adequacy of a legal theory will be discussed, as a means of developing, clarifying, and assessing his own framework for inquiry into law.

The "Where Am I?" Question: Observational Standpoints

Commonly accepted methods of teaching law induce the student to think of himself as a judge. For example, if a student is encouraged to analyze tort cases, in terms of the technical terminology which is to be found in the cases themselves, he is likely to enter upon an imitation of judicial reasoning habits, giving the judicial account of tort, adopting the judicial division of kinds of wrongs, analyzing each wrong into the elements going to the cause of action, and inquiring into what are the appropriate defenses, following judicial techniques in the handling of statutes, other cases, and in coming to conclusions. All this is likely to go on in a dramatic fashion, fostering in the student illusions of grandeur which are reinforced and complemented by the judges' habit of writing as if they were not judges, but students. The judge's account is likely to be presented as observation about the materials he is studying—about which propositions in the books are "right"—rather than as being something for which he personally bears responsibility. This habit of judicial thinking engenders delusions of grandeur of a different sort on the bench. Confusion between what is matter for observation of reality and what is matter for legal decision may reach the point that questions of the order of whether God exists are solved by manipulations of the decisions of courts which may be conceived to bear on the matter.

McDougal believes that intellectual clarity will require an observer to locate himself consciously in the social process. This is not merely a matter of passive examination of oneself and one's surroundings, but a matter of the conscious adoption of a social role in relation to those surroundings. McDougal is concerned, further, to make recommendations to students and scholars about what that role should be. The role of the scholarly observer of law is that of commitment to achieving an adequate focus of attention on law and performing the intellectual tasks in relation thereto which McDougal sees as scholarly.[7]

Communicated self-consciousness about the legal scholar's role and the procedures he ought to adopt seems more marked in the United States than elsewhere. Perhaps this is partly attributable to the reflections forced on the national law schools by the demands of students, from a variety of states with a variety of laws, but all seeking educations immediately relevant to their own situations. Elsewhere, scholars generally are less likely to think it necessary to spoil the literary impact of their work by elaborate explanations of their own role and procedures. They are more concerned to convince others of the correctness of their assertions about the matters in which they happen to be interested than in recommending to them what it might be best to do with their lives as legal scholars, relying perhaps on others' catching the flame of their scholarly interests through the interests of the material, rather than seeking to exercise influence in the matter by precept. McDougal's sympathies are more with many American jurists in this regard. On the other hand, he has a good deal of sympathy with European positivist criticisms of the theoretical confusions of some American jurists in their efforts to maximize the effectiveness of the role of scholars in contributing to legal development and propagating professional skill. On the matter of observational standpoints, McDougal thus differs with all the schools of thought, though the points of maximum divergence vary.

The European positivists make reference to distinctions which have at least a superficial similarity to distinctions made by McDougal in his account of the "Where am I?" question. Yet their question is not "Where am I?" but "What am I saying when I assert conventional legal propositions?" Positivism tends to maintain touch with, and derive a measure of its inspiration from, current philosophical theory; therefore the positivist is likely to begin with questions about law which current linguistic philosophy treats as significant.[8] McDougal's criticism arises when the positivist, incautiously or deliberately, assumes that he has answered the "Where am I" question incidentally to his own question.

The point may be illustrated by reference to the work of a number of contemporary positivists. Alf Ross says that "the nature of law" is the main problem of jurisprudence and that this problem is how to interpret the concept "valid (Illinois, California, common etc.) law" as an integral constituent of every proposition of the doctrinal study of law.[9] Ross' distinction between a proposition *of* law and a proposition *about* law involves the difference between a rule *D* appearing in an authoritative source and the proposition "*D* is valid law" appearing in a textbook of the law of that country. Ross signifies this difference in terms which McDougal uses for the distinct purpose of describing the difference between the observational standpoint of a lawyer dealing with law in conventional terms and the observational standpoint of a scholar dealing with law.[10] But when Ross proceeds to say that "every proposition in a textbook must be understood with the general proviso that the author is presenting the law in force within a specific legal system,"[11] he introduces the very distortion which McDougal has pointed up. Ross is now using language which suggests that his distinction serves generally to characterize the proper approach of scholarly studies of the law of a particular country rather than some particular propositions in them and that he has answered McDougal's question as well as his own. McDougal's criticism would be confusion and lack of comprehensiveness. Ross could not retort that this is not really what he meant to say, or would have meant to say if he had seriously thought about this aspect at this point of his discussion.[12] For this kind of confusion is exactly what is to be expected from Ross' general approach: the initial preoccupation with a general philosophical point actively fosters submergence of, and confusion about, the question of the appropriate standpoint of scholarly legal inquiries.

Hans Kelsen is concerned with the positivist question "What am I saying?" "We merely make explicit," he says, "what all jurists, mostly unconsciously assume, when they consider positive law as a system of valid norms and not only as a complex of facts and at the same time repudiate any natural law from which positive law would receive its validity."[13] He adds as to the basic norm, which he regards as the foundation of the legal thinking of any system, "[t]hat the basic norm really exists in the juristic consciousness is the result of simple analysis of actual juristic statements."[14] This is, of course, akin to the notion which Kant applied to general philosophical categories of understanding, namely, that we cannot really escape from them in any kind of thinking about law, even the sociological. The human mind cannot "understand" or "interpret" law unless it uses the implications of the conventional notions:

The domination which has, sociologically, the character of State presents itself as creation and execution of a legal order, that is, a domination which is interpreted as such by the rulers and the ruled. Sociology has to record the existence of the legal order as a fact in the minds of the individuals involved; and if sociology interprets the domination as a State organization, then sociology itself must assume the validity of this order. Even as an object of sociology, "State domination" is not a bare fact but a fact together with an interpretation. This interpretation is made both by the rulers and the ruled and by the sociologist himself who is studying their behaviour.[15]

But this is no more than assertion. For McDougal it is vital to the position of the legal scholar that he see himself *in his scholarly work* as distinct from the participants in the legal processes he is studying, and that he does not regard himself as in any way bound to adopt, for his theory about law, the categories of the conventional theories of the law he is studying, developed as they are for the carrying out in the social process of different roles from his own.

H. L. A. Hart states that his aim is to further understanding of law, coercion, and morality as different but related social phenomena, but to do so by a means which we can relate to Kelsen's procedure, in that his main book "is concerned with the clarification of the general framework of legal thought."[16] One of the chief means of clarification is to raise questions about the meaning of expressions used in that thought. In this connection, Hart distinguishes between "internal" and "external" points of view toward the legal "system." Among "internal" points of view, Hart distinguishes between the attitudes of those members of a group who accept its legal standards but have no authority to take decisions and the attitudes of those who have authority to take decisions.[17] Among "external" points of view, Hart distinguishes the attitudes of those observers who are interested only in the regularities of behavior and decision within the group, from those who seek to understand those regularities in behavior and decision within the group as well as the "internal" attitudes of that group to the decisions and regularities in behavior observed.[18]

Hart's distinction of points of view is therefore made for rather different purposes than is McDougal's distinction of observational standpoints, to elucidate different uses of language rather than primarily to indicate the appropriate role for the legal scholar. From McDougal's viewpoint, Hart's emphasis tends to foster a defensive attitude to conventional legal thought, which McDougal is especially concerned to criticize for scholarly purposes. While Hart would not be concerned, as Kelsen is, *to make sense of* conventional legal statements, he is concerned, by the nature of his approach, *to find the sense in them,* and in the result he emerges with a more conventional picture of legal perspectives than McDougal would find satisfactory (as will appear). Hart inclines to direct more criticism at the legal philosopher for misunderstanding the purport of conventional legal language than at that language itself. The most searching examination to which Hart subjects conventional legal statements themselves tends to be directed at their form, at the manner in which they purport to connect factual situations with legal consequences, at what might very roughly be called the *copula* in legal assertions, rather than at the *terms* in legal propositions which the copula relates to one another. While McDougal, especially in connection with the development of the notion of normative ambiguity, has himself been concerned to stress the importance of these problems, he has been concerned, perhaps more importantly, to stress the inadequacies in the manner in which the *terms* used in conventional legal propositions refer to social process events, whether observed, predicted, or demanded, that is, to the deficiencies of the "eye of the law." McDougal is not here concerned merely with such questions as Hart raises as to whether the terms used are ambiguous or have a core of meaning even if they have "open textures," but with the adequacy of the categorizations represented by the terms for the purpose of organization of scholarly activities. He would argue that even to understand the perspectives themselves in their relationship with their environment it is necessary to resort to a sociological, as distinct from currently conventional, organization of legal processes.

Lon L. Fuller's work exhibits the American emphasis on the importance of the jurist's having "a proper sense of role" in relation to his legal environment. This role emerges for Fuller out of the function of legal philosophy, the most useful definition of which is, he says, "that which conceives of it as attempting to give a profitable and satisfying direction to the application of human energies in the law."[19] Paradoxically, the insistence on the importance of an awareness of role is combined with an insistence, in effect, on the importance of *not* observing too closely the distinctions of observational standpoint which McDougal makes. Fuller seems to suggest that the driving force of legal development is morality, that the problems of which participants in decision processes partake are moral problems, and the only way for an observer to understand these problems is to sympathize, to think himself into the position of the professional participant.[20] For example, Fuller says that if we are to predict intelligently what courts will do in fact, we must ask what they are trying to do and participate vicariously in the whole purposive effect that goes into creating and maintaining a system for directing human conduct by rules.[21] McDougal would recognize the occasional usefulness for an observer of imagining himself in the role of a judge for the purpose of obtaining insight into judicial reactions. But the observer would need promptly to resume his observing role for the purpose of assessing properly the evidence obtained by the dramatic exercise. Even Holmes' "bad man," interested in predicting judicial responses for his own selfish purposes, surely would need to be aware that his own reactions, interested or not, might be very different from the judge's and therefore would need to be concerned with the reasons for such differences in utilizing the device. Deliberate confusion of the kind Fuller advocates could lead only to unreliability in the prediction.[22]

If, instead of taking the artificial model of the "bad man" posited by Holmes by way of example, we take the example of the man with whom we are centrally concerned, the legal scholar who is also a member of a community or communities the law of which he makes it his scholarly task to observe, then McDougal's point equally applies. As a member of the community, the scholar makes claim on its decisionmakers that they should clarify and implement common interests, and from this jumping-off point he might work out what he would do in the decisionmaker's place about a particular matter. But his estimate as a scholar of how realistic an index of the future course of decision this exercise might be would vary enormously with his appraisal of the functioning of the decision processes within the community. In any serious total estimate of community perspectives as part of legal processes or their background, his own perspectives ultimately would become an almost insignificant statistic. Nor would he, as a scholar performing the functions McDougal envisages, take the view that he might help the clarification of common interests by refusing to face the facts in this respect. The winning of desired decisions by claiming that the decision already has been made in the past would be regarded as a tactic of some decisionmakers which is as inimical to the fullest satisfaction of enlightened claims made upon decisionmakers as it is for appropriation by a scholar especially concerned with further enlightenment as a value.

We find among the sociologists of law a tendency to separate the appropriate standpoint for the student of legal norms from the standpoint of the legal sociologist, which McDougal would recommend should be observed consistently. Max Weber suggests that both are "valid" within their proper limits. Taking the legal point of view, he says, we ask: what is intrinsically valid as law? That is to say, what significance, or what *normative* meaning, ought to be attributed in correct logic to a verbal pattern having the form of a legal proposition. Taking the view of the sociologist of law, Weber says, we ask: what actually *happens* in a community owing to the probability that persons participating in the communal activity, especially those wielding a socially relevant amount of power over the communal activity, subjectively consider certain norms as valid and practically act according to them?[23] Weber justifies the fragmentation of legal studies involved in this scheme of division on the ground that "the juristic precision of judicial opinions will be seriously impaired if sociological, economic, or ethical argument were to take the place of legal concepts."[24] For McDougal, the supposition that precision and system in legal concepts can be achieved by purely formal operations directed at perspectives authoritatively stated in the form of legal propositions is false. He sees the result as a polyglot confusion of perspectives representing demands, the character and origin of which are not only obscure, but obscuring to the purposes of a scholar aiming at enlightenment about legal processes. And significantly, it is the social effect of this kind of tortured travesty of legal perspectives which Weber proposes to examine in his sociology of law.

Karl Renner states that "[w]e propose to examine only the economic and social effect of the valid norm as it exists, so long as the norm does not change."[25] He is thus concerned to give an account neither of the state processes which he supposes generate the norms nor of the activities of the subsidiary organs which are supposed to ensure their validity. The sociologist thus ceases to be a sociologist when he is examining the propositions in law books. Among the earlier sociologists of law, Eugen Ehrlich stands apart from this approach; yet some at least of what Ehrlich says about the observational standpoint of the sociologist may be regarded in this respect as aligning him with the natural lawyers against the positivists and, thus, as putting him more in the camp of Fuller, among American lawyers, than with McDougal. For Ehrlich, the professional judge and the legal scholar are both concerned with the creation of legal propositions out of the norms for decision which are the "living law" connected with the inner order of associations. This creation takes place for Ehrlich by a process of universalization from what exists in the popular consciousness, but the universalization does not itself exist in the popular consciousness. In universalizing the norms the jurist must therefore go beyond what actually exists and participate in legal development. In this process the standpoint of the scholar and the lawmaker are the subject of confusion, regarded as necessary by Ehrlich:

> It is true the basic function of the jurist is to give information about the norms that are already in existence; but how shall one teach what it is that has validity as a norm unless the content of that which is taught in turn also becomes a norm? Whom should we ask for instruction on the question of what norms are valid but him who teaches the norms? The line of demarcation between Normenlehre (the science of norms) and Lehrnormen (norms that are being taught) manifestly is so tenuous that it must needs be overlooked in actual life; and in this way the great antinomy of the law arises, which continuously converts doctrine into norms, but veils the process itself from those who are taking part in the process.[26]

There could scarcely be a more explicit invitation to neglect "in actual life" the very recommendation which McDougal makes to separate theory *of* law from theory *about* law, which in his view is the first step in fulfilling the sociologist's need to separate the materials he is to study from his own account of them. Ehrlich's different view seems to arise from a vested interest in preserving the status of the professor of law as a legal "authority," and seems to be rationalized on the basis that the traditional role of "scientific" juristic activity in straining legal propositions "always served the sole purposes of concealing a necessary social process from the eyes of busybodies."[27] This argument will scarcely recommend itself to those committed to the value of shared enlightenment.

Roscoe Pound does not always see jurisprudence as a body of thought to be distinguished from the more fundamental perspectives of decisionmakers themselves about their own activities. The results of jurisprudential approaches, Pound suggests, should be appraised in terms of their suitability to function as techniques for legal development in the hands of decisionmakers, as well as in terms of their aiding jurists in organizing the materials and laying out the course of the legal order.[28] The relation of jurisprudence to conventional legal development techniques is presented, at least in part, as a relation between more advanced and more primitive legal techniques which historically are continuous with one another. Legal science is regarded as in its early stages at least as the "artificial reason and judgment of the law"[29] to which Sir Edward Coke referred. This scientific treatment begins, Pound tells us, by drawing distinctions between cases or rules superficially analogous, and second, by seeking and formulating principles behind the distinctions.[30] From principles we proceed to theory as in the *jus naturale,* the "second step in the scientific development of law," where the law is developed by reference to an ideal body of principles serving as a standard of criticism.[31] Pound then goes on to relate the history of various kinds of jurisprudential theories down to the twentieth century and finishes with the proposition that "the twentieth century seeks to unite jurisprudence with the other social sciences through some form of social philosophy."[32] The term "philosophy" seems to be used in a homely sense, thus holding out the prospect that what will emerge is a sophisticated set of maxims capable of employment by decisionmakers as their fundamental maxims for action. Pound claims that it is the judge's standpoint which will be most comprehensive for the purpose of examining the law in the sense of "authoritative materials for guidance of judicial and administrative determination."[33] Admittedly, Pound is talking here about the most useful standpoint to look at law in only one of its meanings, and he recognizes others as legitimate.[34] But this merely reinforces the point that traditional legal sociologists do not observe the sociological approach, as McDougal would see it, with consistency.

Even in the camp which would describe itself as "realist," there are those who would not see the adoption of the standpoint of the scholarly sociological observer as satisfactory or characteristic of realism. Karl Llewellyn, for example, distinguishes the position of the lawyer from that of the sociologist; the sociologist addresses himself to the "comforting sweep of the decades," whereas his own major work on jurisprudence is addressed "to the individual case, such as you and I will be handling on Thursday next."[35] From this Llewellyn concludes that the task of the legal scholar is the propagation of professional skill rather than enlightenment. Says Llewellyn: "Refinement, therefore, must go not into analysis for professional students of behavior, but into communicable knowhow for practical application by men of law. That . . . is what realism calls for. That, to the best of my ability, is what I have done."[36] But this is not Llewellyn's only standpoint. In the *Cheyenne Way*[37] he does undertake an "analysis for professional students of behavior," while in his article on the problem of juristic method, he aims to develop sociological concepts to "bridge between sociology and the legal."[38] McDougal, in contrast, adopts the sociological approach as the one affording the comprehensive view for the scholar and hence recommends it at all times. For Llewellyn, the professional orientation of *The Bramble Bush* and *The Common Law Tradition* seems to represent the workaday approach, and *Cheyenne Way* and "The Normative, The Legal, and The Law-Jobs," the holiday frolics. In this respect he is at odds with other realists, such as Bingham,[39] whose view about the appropriate observational standpoint coincides with McDougal's.

It seems common to regard realism as a historical phase in American jurisprudence, representing various kinds of extremism in which particularly important points about law were ridden to death by overemphasis, after which jurisprudence returned to sanity through regaining balance, though perhaps not the same balance as previously. Llewellyn remained a realist to the end of his life in his constant stress, and possibly over-stress, on the overriding importance of predicting decisions. Predicting decisions as a basis for examination of the requirements of policymaking is part of McDougal's thought regarding the appropriate tasks of the legal scholar, but this recognition did not lead McDougal in the same direction as Llewellyn. For McDougal, the performance of the predictive task requires, in turn, prior acquittal of the task of examination of prior trends of decision as well as the "scientific" task of attribution of causes in accordance with the procedures of social science. Hence the importance of establishing the standpoint of the jurist as a detached scholarly observer. In Llewellyn's later work, the predictive task is made to depend on encouraging "reckonability" of decision by encouraging professional skill in those participating in decisions. The traditions of the common law will produce results which can be foreseen by participants and observers alike, if the participants can recapture the techniques which represent the true tradition. Thus we can see Llewellyn as representing a declining stage of realism—regaining "balance" by rationalizing an accommodation with the professional outlook. For McDougal, on the other hand, realism is not to be looked upon as a phase, but, to borrow from French political progressives, an unfinished revolution. The insistence on the appropriateness of a detached sociological standpoint as providing comprehensively for the tasks of the enlightenment-oriented scholar is seen variously to come into conflict with theories of law supposed to represent a return to balance, whether the resurgent positivism of Ross and Hart, the natural law of Fuller, the modern sociology of Pound, or the postrealism realism of Llewellyn.

The Focus of Attention: The "What Fields Shall I Conquer?" Question

Once a thinker has adopted the standpoint of an independent scholarly observer of the legal process, and therefore has rejected the wholesale incorporation of professional legal classifications, designed as they are for objectives among which enlightenment is not always foremost, he necessarily finds himself faced with the task of devising or adapting to this end a formidable list of definitional and classificatory conceptions. McDougal has accepted this responsibility, and the following represent some of the most general notions.

Law is conceived as a social process of authoritative and controlling decision.[40] Each of these legal predicates is in turn expounded. Thus, *social process* refers to interactions among participants in a context which maintain relatively stable, but not necessarily formally organized, patterns of value shaping and sharing.[41] *Decisions* are taken to be commitments attended by threats of severe deprivation or extremely high indulgence.[42] They are said to be *authoritative* when they are, in a stipulated degree, in accordance with community expectation about who is to make them, about the criteria in accordance with which they should be made, and about the situations in which, and the procedures by which, they are to be made.[43] They are said to be controlling when the outcome sought is in fact realized to a significant degree.[44]

This set of explanations leads to a further set of concepts to be explained and, in the explanation of the notion of an *interaction* as a pattern of the perspectives and operations of the participants in the process under examination,[45] we arrive at the first question McDougal is accustomed to ask of any theory of jurisprudence, namely, "What is the balance of emphasis upon perspectives and operations?"[46]

The Balance of Emphasis on Perspectives and Operations

Perspectives are taken to mean the subjectivities (subjective events) of the choosing process, sometimes sought to be communicated in "rules" or "principles," while operations are regarded as nonsubjective events which constitute the behavior in the process of choice.[47] Conventional approaches to law place heavy emphasis on rules and principles, perhaps regarding law as exhausting its whole subject matter by reference to some subdivision of them. The imbalance of emphasis may be increased in some approaches by confused reference to the rules and principles and by failure to refer to the context even sufficiently to see them *as* perspectives of participants in the social process. This is commonly associated with a misuse of the intellectual weapon of logical analysis of the content of rules and principles. If, on the other hand, rules and principles are seen as perspectives, the severely limited functions of logical analysis are obvious. If, for example, demands for expectations about the outcome of decisions relating to a particular subject matter are discovered to be contradictory, this means no more than that one or the other or both will be disappointed. Then, there is no warrant for the tortuous efforts at reconciliation which are sometimes encountered in legal writing, as if the content of perspectives from given sources represented necessary truths.

This kind of distortion is not confined to unsophisticated professional writing. On this score McDougal finds himself in conflict with sophisticated juristic colleagues.

Ross makes his two main branches of the study of law *separate* studies of what McDougal would call operations and perspectives. Ross calls the study of operations—or, as he puts it, "the branch which concerns itself with the law in action"[48]—sociology of law, and he calls the study of perspectives—"the norms of law"[49]—the doctrinal study of law. Despite Ross' assertion that "doctrinal study of law can never be detached from the sociology of law," he nevertheless asserts that it "directs its attention to the abstract idea content of directives, and ignores the realities of the law in action."[50] It is, moreover, on this latter branch that he proposes to concentrate mainly, though not exclusively, his jurisprudential analysis. Ross then uses notions of what is involved in philosophical empiricism in effect to surround the character of legal perspectives in mystery. He says that it is a principle of modern empirical science that a proposition about reality must imply that, by following a certain mode of procedure under certain conditions, certain direct experiences will result. The sum of verifiable implications is said to constitute the "real content" of the proposition.[51] Ross takes a very narrow view of what may constitute a direct experience, and much of what he says at least seems to imply that it is only operations which in the legal field may do so; the "real content" of doctrinal propositions of law refers to "the actions of the courts under certain conditions."[52] Hence, Ross' statements about legal norms come to contain a dualistic reference to perspectives and operations in which the reference to perspectives is made in such a way that statements concerning them can be regarded for testing purposes merely as logical hypotheses about operations, so that a "real content" is preserved for them. This, we suggest, is the explanation of the coupling of the terms "meaning" and "motivation" in Ross' statements, as in his proposition that "the legal norms, like the norms of chess, serve as a scheme of interpretation for a corresponding set of social acts, the law in action, in such a way that it becomes possible to comprehend those actions as a coherent whole of meaning and motivation and to predict them within certain limits."[53]

Ross comes into conflict with McDougal not only on the matter of clarity but also on the score of narrowness of focus. Ross concentrates primarily on judicial decisions, and then only on those judicial perspectives that can be related to the generally consistent framework of hypotheses about the actions of courts which he takes to constitute a legal system: "So far as the individual judge is motivated by particular, personal ideas, these cannot be assigned to the law of the nation."[54] Ross does not pretend that the "doctrinal study of law," which he has made his primary interest, offers us even a sufficiently broad framework for inquiry into the extent to which the perspectives involved in legal norms influence actual decisional outcomes, as distinct from providing "meaningful explanations" of the verbal formulations in judicial opinions. A great variety of notions exists, he tells us, as to the relation between the opinion and the judgment, "which, naturally, is what we really want to predict."[55] His own conclusion is that it is doubtful whether indeed it is at all possible to arrive at a true understanding of what happens when a judge makes a decision and to gain knowledge of how to predict the outcome of legal disputes. "At any rate," he writes, "these problems are properly the study objects of other disciplines than the study of law."[56] For McDougal, this is an abdication of a field central to legal study. Nor is Ross' main focus of attention wide enough to provide a framework for inquiry into change of perspectives about the bases of competence of community decisionmakers. Every system of enacted law, in Ross' view, is necessarily based on an initial hypothesis which constitutes the supreme authority.[57] Every change of the latter is "an extra-systematic phenomenon," a product of political forces "dominated by ideas which cannot be expressed rationally, but only in magical terms."[58] McDougal would be bound to reply that whatever may be said of this, it provides no warrant for failing in our theory to provide for systematic reference to them.

Hans Kelsen rejects from the law the infinite complexities of the actual patterns of perspectives and operations involved in community decision processes. Law is for him a coercive order.[59] This order is a body of norms or standards which are not actual human perspectives as such, even though such perspectives commonly correspond with them.[60] If we want to think of laws as commands, we have to think of them as depsychologized commands.[61] A norm for Kelsen is a rule expressing that someone ought to act in a certain way, but not implying that anyone wills the person to act in that way. Legislatures do not really "will" the legal content of statutes, and parties may enter into transactions which have the effect of creating law without willing that law. The "subjective meaning" of legal acts— what law-creating bodies or persons may have actually wished—must be distinguished from the "objective meanings" which constitute the actual laws created.[62] Thus laws are not perspectives and neither are they operations. Kelsen argues that if law simply represented what goes on, it would lose its character as a body of standards, by reference to which, what goes on is to be judged. There must always be a certain tension between actual behavior and the content of norms.[63] Thus, "legal rules are in no wise concerned with a psychological or bodily process, that is, with the sphere of being or empirical reality." [64] From McDougal's viewpoint, the conventional legal denial of the complexity and multiplicity of legal processes, involved in such notions as that one can regularly determine "the" rule and "the" legal effect, must be criticized and not made the basis of a retreat from the complexities of reality. Once the complexity is squarely faced, an adequate theory is seen to be one which can handle that complexity.

Assessment of the relationship between McDougal's and H. L. A. Hart's work, in the matter of the relative emphasis placed on perspectives and operations, is complicated by terminological and other differences. McDougal, as we have seen, appropriates the term "rule" to the field of perspectives and,[65] if Hart were adopting this use of language, his concept of law as "the union of primary and secondary rules" [66] would necessarily lead to McDougal's cataloguing him among those contemporary thinkers whose theories continue the traditional and professional heavy emphasis on perspectives. But in Hart's own view, there is more to rules than perspectives. For example, he says that the required distinction between the external and internal approaches to rules is not between a view of rules as regularities of behavior and a view of rules as feelings. It is a distinction between two radically different types of statements made when a social group conducts its affairs by rule. Group members use the internal type to criticize their own and each other's conduct by reference to the rules as regular patterns of behavior which they accept as standards, treating deviations as a reason for such reactions and demands for conformity as justified.[67] In this process, he says, there is involved a critical reflective attitude to certain patterns of behavior as a common standard which should display itself in criticism (including self-criticism), demands for conformity, and an acknowledgment that such criticism and demands are justified.[68] Hart's reference to a rule thus purports to be a complex social situation. Whether this object is consistently achieved is examined in the next section.

In one of its aspects law is defined by Fuller as "the enterprise of subjecting human conduct to the governance of rules." [69] He adds that "unlike most modern theories of law, this view treats law as an activity." [70] If an "activity" were to be understood as a pattern of perspectives and operations, Fuller's theory would resemble McDougal's. But Fuller's notions of an "enterprise" and an "activity" are both designed to carry out an exhortative function, as well as a purely descriptive one, to give effect to his view of law as "the life work of the lawyer," [71] and to encourage lawyers to see that life work "as that of reducing the relations of men to a reasoned harmony" rather than "as that of charting the behavior sequences of certain elderly state officials." [72] There is, further, a kind of proviso to Fuller's delineation of law which reinforces the infusion of values of the jurist himself into the delineation of the subject matter. The aspirational function of the definition is supplemented by a critical function through the proviso that before such an enterprise may be considered law it must have achieved a measure of success in observing requirements described as "the internal morality of law." [73] Hence, patterns of perspectives and operations of a community itself are excluded from consideration as part of the law "activity" unless they are in accordance, to a minimum degree, with Fuller's own demands. McDougal differs from Fuller in that he seeks in the interests of clarity first to fix the focus of attention on a field before proceeding to the performance of the intellectual tasks of the scholar, such as goal clarification. Fuller, on the other hand, throws out a challenge to the possibility of an objective focus on the pattern of subjectivities and operations involved in any social context. "Viewed 'objectively'," he says of perspectives, "the meaning of the individual is subject to reinterpretation by the observer; viewed 'subjectively' it is a fleeting posture of the mind which can never be wholly recaptured." [74] Of operations, he asks: "From the fact that we talk about 'actions' and 'behavior,' does it follow that we know what we are talking about?" [75] He continues: "Just what do we mean by a judge's actions as distinguished from his meaning and intentions? Is it a movement of the arms or of jaws? Is it a movement at all? If not, what is it?" [76] McDougal has taken the view that we have better prospects of knowing what we are talking about if we seek to settle our field of inquiry and devise appropriate terms initially.[77]

From McDougal's point of view, demands other than enlightenment have disturbed the objective focus on patterns of perspectives and operations in the work of the major sociologists of law also. To some extent, Weber appears to have supported a view of law as norms because he wished to preserve a science of legal dogmatics, which he supposed would function to preserve juristic precision[78] and to suggest "ideal types" of law which might be useful as theoretical models for sociological studies.[79] But it may also be connected with his desire to win an ideological battle with Karl Marx by showing that the subjectivities which in his view constitute law are not merely a reflection of the economic situation of the persons holding them.[80] The result is perhaps a rather unfortunate investment of time in working out the relationships of various general features of legal *ideas* to economics: the importance for economy and society of whether legal modes of thinking are rational or irrational, and if they are rational, whether they are formally so or substantively so.[81] For McDougal, the result is a concentration of focus on some general strategies involved in legal processes, to the neglect of other aspects.

In Ehrlich's case, the operative demand in this connection seems to have been to win back social significance for the law professor. Ehrlich is disappointed by the extent to which what he terms "state law" (norms for decision designed by the state to serve its purposes [82] as well as norms directing state agencies to proceed) [83] has supplanted in importance what he terms "juristic law" (a body of rules consisting largely of norms for decision formulated by jurists, including professors of law).[84] He defends the best products of the latter as superior because they are more closely in touch with the "living law" than is state law, which is rigid and immobile and too often lags behind.[85] Ehrlich finds the living law in those associations which in their mutual relations make up society, and for him it consists of those legal norms which determine their inner order: "The legal norm is the legal command, reduced to practice, as it obtains in a definite association, perhaps of very small size, even without any formulation in words." [86] Ehrlich conceives state law and juristic law as perspectives, but commentators have not found the position so clear with regard to the "living law." In any case, there is a rough one-to-one correspondence for Ehrlich between some uniformities of behavior in associations and the norms obtaining therein, for "a social association is a plurality of human beings who, in their relations with one another recognize certain rules of conduct as binding, and, generally at least, regulate their conduct according to them." [87] Thus, the observable patterns of conduct within associations are a "means of cognition" [88] of the norms. By this account, Ehrlich is enabled to suggest how the jurist may possess himself of standards of criticism of state law to which appeal may be made in the name of law, but this strategic advantage, from McDougal's point of view, is bought at considerable sacrifice to clarity in the focus of attention, since the pattern of social interaction may be much more complex than Ehrlich's special interest in the matter has led him to suppose.

Even in Pound's work, the emphasis on study of perspectives continues, perhaps again because it is thought a useful strategy for the exercise of academic influence on decisionmakers. Pound considers it possible to unify the science of law under three headings: (1) legal order, (2) authoritative materials for the guidance of judges and officials, and (3) the judicial and administrative process.[89] Pound particularly concentrates on authoritative materials, and here there is some common ground with McDougal insofar as Pound presses the examination of legal perspectives beyond precepts (McDougal's "formulae") to received ideals (McDougal's "doctrine"). But Pound's references to techniques[90] and his subsequent treatment of legal process [91] are verbal strategies; a systematic means of considering the patterning of perspectives and operations appears to be lacking.

Authority and Control

McDougal holds that a conception of law as a process of authoritative and controlling decision provides an adequate focus for carrying out the appropriate intellectual tasks of the lawyer. A decision is authoritative for him when there is a measure of conformity with community expectations about who is to make it, and about the criteria observed and the procedures to be followed in the situation.[92] A decision is said to be controlling when the outcome sought is in fact realized to a significant degree. No rigid stipulations are made concerning what minimum frequency of the relevant perspectives is required to render the decision authoritative or what degree of control is requisite.[93] Among more particular critical questions asked of any theory are whether the theory established authority by transempirical derivation or by reference to experience and whether, if the latter, authority is conceived as arising in a demand by the jurist or in a demand external to the jurist insofar as he avoids reference to his own preferences.[94] McDougal warns that conceptions in this context may be phrased in terms whose manifest content is empirical, yet which on contextual examination are disclosed as making disguised transempirical references.[95]

Kelsen explicitly distinguishes authority and control, explaining that the actual power of forcing others to a certain behavior does not suffice to constitute an authority. The individual who has authority must have received the right to issue obligating commands, so that other individuals are obliged to obey. Such a right or power, he says, can be conferred upon an individual only by a normative order.[96] From Kelsen's approach, nothing which is not authorized can be lawful in any circumstances, although authoritative prescriptions can be lawful, yet not controlling, in some circumstances. This occurs when the prescriptions in question are part of a normative order which is in general effective and, even then, only if and as long as the particular prescriptions are at least sporadically effective.[97] In Kelsen's theory, however, lawfulness does not arise out of a coincidence in decision of authority and control, as it does in McDougal's. The effectiveness of a system (on which and on the rules of which Kelsen focuses primarily, rather than on decisions, as McDougal does) is regarded only as a *condition* of validity in Kelsen's theory while, on the other hand, the *reason* for the validity of any part of a system is its dependence on the system. The norms are valid, not because the total order is efficacious, but because they are created in a constitutional way.[98] Kelsen, unlike McDougal, further reduces control in importance by saying that in assessing control we are primarily concerned only with whether the organ of the system executes the sanction provided by the system, not whether the subjects obey it.[99] This is not to say, of course, that Kelsen's theory cannot operate to support a regime of naked power, as it is commonly alleged to have done in the time of the Nazis, a result which is connected with its failure to incorporate reference to community values in this account of the system of authority, as we shall see.

Kelsen concentrates upon the means of demonstration of the authority of the norms of the legal system. He regards that authority as derived from the higher norms and ultimately from the basic norm, but treats this derivation as of a special kind. A legal system is, in his view, "dynamic." The inferior norms are not obtainable from the basic norm by inference from the general to the particular, but have to be created through acts of will by those individuals who are authorized under the system.[100] Positive law cannot be derived from the basic norm, but can be understood by means of it.[101] The difference between a basic norm for Kelsen and that of a static natural law system is, however, only in the character of the term which constitutes the subject of it. The derivations which are made from it proceed, *pace* Kelsen, in precisely the same formal way—by derivation from the general to the particular—as takes place with derivations from superior natural law norms to inferior ones.

A basic norm of the Kelsen type is in the form that what is prescribed by persons of a certain description in accordance with certain procedures ought to be implemented, whereas a natural law norm may be in the form that conduct having certain qualities ought to be followed. In a legal system, as Kelsen envisages it, the discovery that something has been prescribed, as required by the basic norm, leads to the conclusion that it ought to be carried out, while under a static natural law system the discovery that particular conduct possesses certain qualities referred to in a superior norm leads to the conclusion that it ought to be carried out. The difference in the terms means that until an observer is able to discover acts of "will" referring to particular behavior, he is not about to make deductions within a system of the kind Kelsen posits; once given these he can deduce inferior norms from superior norms. If there is any other way the observer can proceed from superior to inferior norms, Kelsen does not explain what it is. Indeed, there could be no other method within Kelsen's framework. In this major respect, the decisionmaker, who looks to the law, as Kelsen would, in order to find what he ought to do, is in no different position from the observer. We may therefore contest Kelsen's claim to have grasped, by his normative jurisprudence, "the specific meaning of the legal rules," "the sense with which these rules are directed to the individuals whose behavior they regulate," the sense which is "expressed by means of the 'ought'." [102] Kelsen's account of this sense is that the validity of an inferior norm is that the norm in question has been created ultimately in accordance with the basic norm. But if, as we have attempted to demonstrate, this "creation in accordance with" the basic norm is no more than an ordinary deduction, the reasoning must follow some such form as: "What the Constitution-maker prescribes immediately or mediately ought to be carried out (basic norm); this (particular context) is prescribed mediately or immediately by the Constitution-maker; therefore, this ought to be carried out." Such a deduction is valid only if the expression "ought to be carried out" bears the same meaning throughout; that is, if the "ought" of the inferior norm bears the same meaning as the "ought" of the basic norm; if this is so, then the sense of "ought" in the inferior norm is explained only if the sense of "ought" in the basic norm is explained. In Kelsen's theory it is not. The basic norm is "presupposed" and does not have validity in the sense of an inferior norm, while the explication of the sense of "ought" in the inferior norm is supposed to consist in its relation to the basic norm. Kelsen thus has not given an account of authority even according to his own chosen method of explaining the sense of "ought" in the system of norms which he envisages as conferring it. His failure only seems to be covered over by the ambiguity in ordinary language between validity in the sense of formal validity of a deduction, and validity in the sense of obligatoriness. His "ought" remains "self-acting" in McDougal's terms. It appears in other words, as an ultimate demand, the source of which never is given, either in empirical or transempirical terms, and the "binding" force of which is generated by nothing more than logical and terminological confusions. This fate, from McDougal's viewpoint, is dependent on Kelsen's deliberate refusal to give an account of authority in social terms.

From a cognitive-descriptive point of view, Ross regards it as impossible to distinguish between a "legal order" and a "regime of violence" because the quality of validity which should distinguish the law is not an objective quality of the order itself, but only an expression of the way in which it is experienced by the individual; what may be a "legal order" for one will be a "regime of violence" for another. Ross believes that people have "validity experiences" in relation to orders where there is a disinterested respect for them impressed by the social milieu. But limitation of law by reference to whether it received this kind of ideological approval from those subject to it would, in his view, bind the concept to a criterion difficult to work with in practice.[103] Definitions aside, however, Ross seems to concern himself mainly with perspectives of authority,[104] and it is difficult to see what part his definition plays in fixing his focus of attention. Hence, he discards it.

Hart's account of the conditions required for the existence of a legal system differs from Ross' in that it requires a coincidence of a degree of authority and control in relation to various aspects of the system. Hart specifies that those rules of behavior which are valid according to the system's ultimate criteria of validity must be generally obeyed. Rules of recognition specifying the criteria of validity and rules of change and adjudication must be effectively accepted as common public standards of official behavior by officials.[105] But obedience by officials is sufficient, and it is in this context that Hart introduces the notion of authority, although he treats the term as being obscure.[106] In his view, the elucidation required is by reference to the distinction between primary and secondary rules—in the combination of which he finds the concept of law—and especially in terms of the internal aspect of the rules.[107] As we have seen, the internal aspect of rules appears for Hart in a social group where the requirement is satisfied "that there should be a critical reflective attitude to certain patterns of behavior as a common standard, and that this should display itself in criticism (including self-criticism), demands for conformity and in acknowledgement that such criticism and demands are justified." [108] He states that an external statement often can be distinguished from an internal statement, in that in the former there is a reference to the context which the latter lacks. Thus, it would be an external statement to say that "in England they recognize as law . . . whatever the Queen in Parliament enacts," but an internal statement normally follows if one says, "It is the law that . . . ." [109]

Hart differs from McDougal in his primary reference to a system of rules rather than to decisions. Hart's definition envisages in the concept of law a high degree of system in the rules, instead of leaving this to be made a matter of investigation in each context. Moreover, Hart seems to accept that a number of distinctions which Kelsen makes in explaining authority are important and his reinterpretations of them do not always seem thoroughly to dispose of difficulties in Kelsen's position. We have seen that in dealing with the derivation of norms from the basic norm, Kelsen claims that a dynamic system like law is somehow radically different from ordinary deduction. There is perhaps a parallel in Hart's proposition that the peculiarity needing attention in the internal aspect of rules is not psychological, but logical.[110] Insofar as the claim of a special logic in statements appealing to rules is a claim that the significance of what is happening cannot be understood without resort to the social context, McDougal would applaud it provided the relation between the verbalizing and the social context is made clear. But Hart does not seem yet to have demonstrated how any amount of reference to the circumstances in which expressions are used can serve as a *substitute* for elucidation of the meaning of the expressions in the mouth of the subject observed or even of particular words in them, and the relation between the verbalizing and the social context is thus left unclear. Hart says that the rule of recognition, which in his theory takes the place of Kelsen's basic norm, is very seldom expressly formulated as a rule.[111] Rather, it is *used* by officials as a guiding rule.[112] This use is described as "applying to a particular rule of a legal system, an unstated but accepted rule of recognition." [113] If this were all that was involved, it would seem only to suggest that we have here an instance of the very common situation in daily life of a person making a deductive argument with a suppressed—unstated but understood—major premise. Hart goes on to assert that "we can indeed simply say that the statement that a particular rule is valid means that it satisfies all the criteria provided by the rule of recognition." [114] But he immediately adds, "this is incorrect only to the extent that it might obscure the internal character of such statements." [115] Even this proviso, however, does not really establish that there is any special logic different from deductive logic in using a recognition rule. For various purposes, people make deductive arguments in order to show that they are valid, yet they do not at the same time accept the premises or the conclusion. In one sense one could therefore say that a rule is valid—validly inferred—without accepting it. Such a statement would be distinguished from the "internal" statement of a person who accepted the premises and therefore accepted the conclusion.

From the point of view of ordinary deductive logic, the difficulty in Hart's system of derivation lies in its lack of explicit meaning for the term "law," which apparently would appear as the predicate of a rule of recognition were it fully stated. From examples that Hart gives,[116] it would appear that a recognition rule in any given system takes the form "*xyz* is law" or "*xyz* is to count as law," the matter represented by the symbol *xyz* varying from system to system. If the recognition rule were purely a definitional statement, asserting that "law" when we were speaking of that system was to mean *xyz,* no explanation of the term "law" in such a statement would be required. The function of a definitional statement is itself to give it. But the function of a recognition rule, as Hart sees it, is not to guide people's use of words but their conduct. Therefore, in terms of his theory, a recognition rule cannot be understood as a definition. So an explanation of the meaning to be given to "law" in such a recognition rule is required. Neither the rule itself nor Hart's own general concept of law as a system of rules within rules explains it. Nor, it seems, is Hart seeking to answer this question when he seeks to answer the question arising in relation to the British system "Is the rule that 'What the Queen enacts in Parliament is law' law?" [117] He is here concerned with answering a question about the term "law" appearing *outside* the single quotes, not about what the term means in the recognition rule itself. Perhaps he is making a remark which is relevant to our question when he says, at this point, that "we need to remember that the ultimate rule of recognition may be regarded from two points of view: one is expressed in the external statement of fact that the rule exists in the actual practice of the system; the other is expressed in the internal statements of validity made by those who use it in identifying the law." [118] But in Hart's view, statements of validity are made in relation to the inferior rules and the notion of validity is not used in characterizing the rule itself. So why approach so indirectly the question of what is meant by the "internal" understanding of the recognition rule? Unfortunately, the answer is clear if Hart is making the same error we have attributed to Kelsen. This error involves confusing the validity of the argument by which, in Hart's terms, a primary rule is identified via the recognition rule with the validity that is accorded the primary rule when so identified, that is, as being "law." Validity in the latter sense can in fact be explained only by reference to the meaning of law in the recognition rule itself; it cannot be generated out of the process of any ordinary argument proceeding by derivation from it. And if a meaning *is* to be given to the term "law," so appearing, it must be capable of being done without reference to the derivational arguments from the recognition rule. For McDougal, these difficulties do not arise because a perspective of authority simply predicates of its subject matter that the persons or strategies or values specified in that subject matter, in the circumstances specified therein, are expected by the community to be the decisionmakers' decisional strategies or objectives used in community decision. And this covers cases in which the person whose perspectives of authority are being investigated attributes his perspectives to some more fundamental perspective —in Hart's terms, to expressing a recognition rule (or other secondary rule) or some primary rule.

A theory such as Fuller's, with the emphasis it gives to the alleged "moral" aspects of law, is sensitive to the failure of positivist doctrine to give wholly satisfactory accounts of words like "ought" and "law" as they appear in the "basic norms" or "recognition rules" of positivist theory.[119] At times, his criticism marches along with McDougal's as, for example, when he claims that Hart is attempting throughout, with the aid of his recognition rule, "to give neat juristic answers to questions that are essentially questions of sociological fact." [120] But when Fuller goes on to suggest that positivists are really making confused reference to ethical questions,[121] he parts company with McDougal. Fuller's suggestion as to the impossibility of giving an account of perspectives of authority of members of a community without "ethical" assertions of the observer's goals would be regarded by McDougal as springing from a confusion of observational standpoints. Fuller's main procedure, far from providing a focus for law which enables McDougal's varying intellectual tasks to be *subsequently* carried out, is to attribute what Fuller himself regards as a fundamental goal which law should achieve to the concept of law itself, by definition. This goal is the reduction of human conduct to the governance of rules.[122] Hence arises the "internal morality of law" [123] and the demands which it makes upon "fidelity to law";[124] to the extent that notions of what is authoritative, and, more important for Fuller, what is not authoritative, can be deduced by the application in particular contexts of the requirements of the definition, notions of authority in those contexts thus arise by a *priori* necessity and not by actual investigation of the authority perspectives of the community involved. Investigation of what members of a community *do* expect tends to be overshadowed by arguments about what they *must* expect.

Ehrlich deprecates attempts to derive authoritative rules from higher level abstractions [125] and recommends instead scientific observation of society and induction therefrom.[126] For McDougal, this is a correct approach. Yet Ehrlich expects to find, by mere observation of society, not only the perspectives of authority of its members, but the goals of the observer himself, necessarily generated by his own observations. And the view or, rather, multiplicity of views of society which Ehrlich thus takes into account accommodates itself to this objective. From McDougal's viewpoint, therefore, Ehrlich confuses the objective of fixing the focus of attention on authority perspectives in a society in the interest of seeking to determine beforehand the result of the performance of later intellectual tasks. Ehrlich requires society to function as a source of authority in so many different ways that it becomes impossible for him satisfactorily to identify law within it.

In the first place, Ehrlich's notion of an empirical approach to social phenomena is to explain them "not by construing them juristically but by inferring from facts the modes of thought that underlie them." [127] Thus, he purports to discover, in a vast multiplicity of detailed social relationships, assumptions of the participants about their "rights"—"men generally assume that their rights arise not from legal propositions but from the relations of man to man, from marriage, contract, last will and testament." [128] Ehrlich does not seem to conceive of these assumptions about rights as being primarily related in the minds of the participants to their expectations about the criteria on which decisionmakers will proceed, but, rather, as being associated with a special feeling—the *opinio necessitatis*—concerning their binding character as between the participants.[129] But while, therefore, they apparently need not be perspectives of authority in McDougal's sense, Ehrlich himself regards them as proper, if not quite compelling, criteria for decision in all circumstances. He thus posits that social investigation will yield an enormous quantity of detailed criteria for decision in particular circumstances to satisfy the investigator of the existence of the perspectives of which he speaks, but since he does not espouse the use of such modern sociological techniques as the interview, he proposes to infer them from uniformities in operations in social groups—to use these operations as a "means of cognition" [130] by inferring from them "the modes of thought that underlie them." Ehrlich's theory as to the source of authority of the decisionmakers themselves is thus made to rest on "society."

But the kind of investigation that might be needed to locate the authorized decisionmakers in society apparently is not a matter to which Ehrlich devotes attention. State lawmakers, like juristic writers and teachers of law, act, in Ehrlich's view, as persons commissioned by society.[131] However, he makes no attempt to be precise about what society means in this connection, although he attributes purposes to it, as in the statement that "the enormous importance of the state for the law is based upon the fact that society avails itself of the state as its organ in order to give effectual support to the law that arises in society." [132] The truth seems to be that in his theory for proper empirical investigation of community perspectives as to who shall be the decisionmakers, and the general criteria by which they are to act, Ehrlich substitutes his own demands regarding the proper functions for those in positions of control, his own ideal picture of a society. Thus, the legal proposition "is an instrumentality in the hands of society whereby society shapes things within its sphere of influence according to its will," [133] and "if there is such a thing as correct law or to be more exact legal propositions they are those that advance the human race in the direction of its future development." [134] Thus, too, "our sense of justice is merely one of those great indefinite divinings of hidden interrelations in the vast scheme of things," [135] and "[h]e who shall be able to speak the last word on the subject of justice will thereby have found the law of the development of the human race." [136] In short, Ehrlich's society becomes, in McDougal's sense, metaphysical. McDougal points out that "conceptions [of authority] may be phrased in terms whose manifest content is empirical, yet which on contextual examination are disclosed as making disguised transempirical references (e.g., 'the inevitable future is thus and so')." [137] Ehrlich's recommendation for the finding of an authoritative answer to the most difficult questions facing decisionmakers is to arrive at propositions of this sort. And as it is with juristic law, so it is with state law. Society uses the state, which begins as a military association, as a lever of social development. Where it fails to measure up to these demands, its law "is not a match for the uninterrupted sway of elemental forces which have their life and being in the social associations." [138] These forces, then, are both authoritative and ultimately controlling—authoritative because they are ultimately controlling.

Weber, on the other hand, set out to give a general account of community processes which would reflect no value of his own other than intellectual integrity.[139] He thus developed concepts of authority and control within society such that an investigator would be able to locate them independently of any appeal to his own values. He distinguished *domination* from other kinds of exercises of power merely by reference to the notion of authority: "In our terminology *domination* shall be identical with *authoritarian power of command*."[140] For Weber, a person claims "authority" when he claims "submission" on the part of the persons dominated, without regard to the latter's own interests, and this is what distinguishes domination in the strict sense from the power exercised over people who are simply influenced to act because their own interests require it, that is, "domination by virtue of a constellation of interests."[141] The claim to authority is successful when it obtains continuing recognition on one of a number of bases of legitimation. There may be an appeal to a system of consciously made rational rules which may be agreed upon or imposed from above.[142] Or the domination may obtain recognition as legitimate as a personal authority founded either on the sacredness of *tradition* or the belief in *charisma,* actual revelation or grace resting in the person. The first of these three types of legitimation is typically expressed in bureaucracy, the second in patriarchalism, and the third in domination by a concrete individual.[143] Elsewhere Weber uses the word "legal," instead of "rational" or "bureaucratic," to describe the first kind of domination.[144] His definition of law is an order of norms guaranteed by the probability of coercion by a special staff.[145]

Differences between McDougal's and Weber's approaches thus spring from their different notions of what are satisfactory methods of focusing attention for investigation.[146] Legal domination is for Weber a kind of theoretical model exhibiting certain features in an extreme and uncluttered form—an "ideal type"—by comparison with which investigation is to proceed. McDougal seeks to make his connotation for law sufficiently comprehensive to mark out the field for investigation. Hence, Weber's specifications of the kind of authority perspectives to be described as legal make law for him a concept narrower than McDougal's. Moreover, from McDougal's viewpoint, Weber's notion of legal perspectives of authority is too close to that involved in conventional views of law to be really useful, even as a standard of comparison with reality. Used in this way, it would be calculated to halt the investigations of the inquirer at the point where he discovered that the perspectives of authority of decisionmakers and other members of the community reflected the confusions of conventional legal thinking. While a subject of investigation might readily accede to the proposition that he expected the criteria for community decision to be rules, it would be quite unsatisfactory, from McDougal's point of view, if inquiry did not persist with questions concerning what values the subject expected the rules to implement. Weber posits that a characteristic of legal perspectives of authority is that there is a devotion, particularly among officials, to rules as such.[147] For McDougal, however, this represents a confusion of thinking common to many legal and nonlegal philosophers. One of the functions of this confusion may be to enable the claims of authority of decisionmakers to obtain recognition without too close examination of them. But through the confusion, McDougal would expect to find the claims of decisionmakers to represent, at some level of consciousness, common interests related to substantive community values and expectations, and the clarification of common interests thus would enter into the criteria for decision.

Pound's work, for McDougal, constitutes a retrogression from Weber to Ehrlich because of its reintroduction of interstitial rather than explicit demand conceptions of authority. Taking the standpoint of the judge, Pound, in effect, winnows from the approaches of various schools of thought what he considers to be of value for the judge's guidance and adds glosses of his own to the same end. From the positivist or "legal" approach to authority, Pound purports to find the fact of legal existence of precepts in their receiving of "the guinea stamp of the state."[148] Pound does not seem to find any difficulty in going on to define the state, in one sense at any rate, as "the source of authority of tribunals,"[149] despite the circularity that an observer might think is involved. From McDougal's viewpoint, the analytical or legal theory of the state, as Pound presents it, reveals itself not as a factual or functional conception, but as an entity postulated in the "theory" of judges; Pound's assertion that this determines the "is" of legal authority is unjustified from a sociological approach. For Pound, it does not *require* justification since he is generally satisfied to take the judge's standpoint and to treat the content of general judicial perspectives as a "postulate of the science of law."[150]

Pound takes the same point of view when he moves from legal theory to the political theory of the state as the source of authority. Pound still purports to be in the realm of the factual. The political theory involves for him not the immediate but the ultimate practical source of the authority of legal precepts in actual fact. "For example," he says, "in legal theory of the British government we look only at King, Lords, and Commons. But the political theory perceives back of them, as the ultimate basis of authority, the body of electors."[151] From McDougal's standpoint, this statement still looks at questions of authority from the viewpoint of the conventionally minded judge accepting what the materials he regards as authoritative have to say about the formation of governments. From this perspective, Pound is entitled to say, as he does, that there is a confusion between legal and political approaches in the "eighteenth-century contractual theory of government as originating in and continuing by the consent of the governed, coupled with the theory of the individual reason or the individual conscience as the final arbiter as to the binding force of a legal precept."[152] Taking the standpoint of the observer, however, McDougal would not find it possible to dismiss the perspectives of authority of participants in a legal process as confused simply because they are confused for other participants. In effect, Pound is here espousing the claims to priority of some conventional notions of authority by failing to make clear that he is only working out the implications of those claims, rather than establishing the content of those claims as "facts." In other words, his account presents the typical features of a demand conception of authority. Pound never considers the criticisms which a theory providing a basis for investigation of sociological fact might make because he couples "philosophical" and sociological theories of law. The sociological type, as Pound sees it, is a more advanced philosophical theory which retains the characteristic of philosophical theories that do not properly purport to deal with what *is* of binding authority, but rather with what *ought* to be of binding authority. Modern sociological philosophical theory, in Pound's view, holds to the idea of common values as the social reality; it sees the state as only one organ of the community for promoting its common purposes, as well as individual interests.[153]

Once Pound has located authority firmly in the professional tradition, by accepting its claims and relegating perspectives that might otherwise be disturbing to different departments of thought, he imposes his own demands on the legal profession by reading them into the professional tradition. Among the sources of law, Pound lists Moral and Philosophical Ideas and Scientific Discussion. The official development of the law is seen as catching at the "truth" in juristic ideas, and since these truths generally are presented as truths about what is to be done, rather than about what is done, the truths in current social philosophy come to represent a series of demands Pound can render as authoritative for judges and legislators at the present time. For example, Rudolf Stammler is said to have led us to "see" some truths which are fundamental to the matters which "are to" guide the officials: "he led us to see that the ideals to which we are to make the body of authoritative precedents and application of them in the judicial process conform are the ideals of an epoch."[154] Likewise, one of Pound's major ideals of the present epoch, namely to "[s]ecure all interests so far as possible with the least sacrifice of the totality of interests or the scheme of interests as a whole," is presented as "a kernel of truth in the theories of the historical school."[155] Pound represents legal systems generally as going through progressive stages, in which official and juristic thought in each make a permanent contribution to the next. The most advanced systems in our own time are presented as having gone through (1) the stage of primitive law, (2) the stage of strict law, (3) the stage of equity and natural law, and (4) the stage of maturity of law.[156] The permanent contribution of primitive law is the idea of a peaceful ordering of the community;[157] of strict law, the ideas of certainty and uniformity in the ordering;[158] of equity and natural law, the idea of good faith and moral conduct attained by reason;[159] and of the age of maturity of law, "the idea of individual legal rights."[160] We are now, in Pound's view, in a fifth stage, and what we "are to do" clearly hinges for him on grasping the emerging characteristics of this fifth stage, with its emphasis on social interests.[161] Thus we come to Pound's own high-level goal for law as "the satisfaction of as much of human demand as we can satisfy with a minimum of friction and waste"[162]—a goal surrounded by this means of presentation with an aura of authoritative truth.

Scientific thinking about the end of law, in Pound's view, has undergone a similarly progressive development closely connected with the official one, and issuing in the same goal. Thinkers continually have gone beyond an idea of the past to a more inclusive one. At first, jurists thought of the end of law as keeping the peace. Then they realized that this keeping of the peace was for the purpose of maintaining the social order; thereafter, that the maintaining of social order was for the purpose of individual self-assertion; and, later still, that the purpose of individual self-assertion was the satisfaction of human wants, including more than freedom. Thus, "what we have to do in social control, and so in the local order, is to reconcile these desires, or wants, so far as we can, so as to secure as much of the totality of them as we can. Down to the present, that is the more inclusive order."[163] For McDougal, the whole procedure means that Pound, however unintentionally, sacrifices scholarly focus to the strategy of enabling the scholar to present his notions as having authority.

The Process of Decision

In developing a detailed categorization (or "map") of a process of authoritative decision by reference to which the scholar may carry out his tasks, McDougal recommends that "a process of authoritative and controlling decision, as an integral part of a more comprehensive process of effective power, be economically described in terms of participants, perspectives, situations (structures), bases of power, strategies (functions), outcomes and effects."[164]

By contrast, when Kelsen speaks of the legal process, he refers to the manner in which the superior norms he posits regulate their own execution and the creation and execution of inferior norms.[165] The phases in the process with which McDougal is concerned become relevant for Kelsen only to the extent that they are involved in this different process. For example, decisionmakers, among the participants McDougal identifies, come into focus for Kelsen to the extent that they are constituted by the norms and thus are organs of the legal order to create and execute, but only to the extent that those activities are norm-related. The outcome relevant for Kelsen is only the order made; its effect on the value positions of the immediate participants themselves and the long-run effects on the values of other participants are seen as irrelevant. The only further relevant effects are that the created norm may lead to the creation of further norms by way of its application. It is through this same eye of the law conceived as a norm-creating and norm-executing process that Kelsen categorizes with similar constricting effect what McDougal describes as the functions of authoritative and controlling decisions. In the interests of comprehensiveness and sharpness, McDougal substitutes for the conventional view of legislative, executive, and judicial structures of the legal process a division of functions: intelligence, promotion, prescription, invocation, application, termination, and appraisal.[166] By contrast, the conventional division is, in Kelsen's hands, reduced to two, the norm-creating and norm-applying functions.

Hart's concept of law, while it makes law entirely a matter of rules, seeks to locate rules in the social process and to incorporate references to the social process in the explanation of them. Moreover, Hart does not present his concept as a comprehensive definition of a field of study. And if, nevertheless, the concept invites *emphasis* in scholarly studies upon rules, one of Hart's answers is that this serves as a corrective to tendencies to underemphasize rules in some modern theories. McDougal claims, however, that positivist theories lack *clarity* of focus upon the legal process, and Hart's treatment of that phase of the decision process which McDougal terms "perspectives"—that is, demands, identifications, and expectations— may be taken by way of example. It appears that, for Hart, decisionmakers must have a conception of law that is in some sense a final set of demands made upon them which they recognize, not to be related back to some further or higher set of demands they recognize. Unless the totality of their objectives is to be comprehended within these "legal" objectives, which Hart does not suggest, the problem arises for him of defining the legal ones and of expressing their relationship to other objectives which decision-makers might adopt. Unlike Kelsen, Hart recognizes the possibility of decisionmakers' facing conflicts between sets of objectives he would class as legal and other sets of objectives which apparently might be equally "ultimate," such as the moral duties they recognize.[167] To think otherwise, Hart says, is to indulge the "romantic optimism that all the values we cherish ultimately will fit into a single system, that no one of them has to be sacrificed or compromised to accommodate another."[168] This applies for Hart to decisionmakers as well as others, for he says that "no human being is *just* a lawyer or *just* a moralist."[169] But this drives Hart back to distinguishing the legal from the other demands of decisionmakers on themselves by reference to whether the demands fall within a system the criteria for recognition of which, we have suggested earlier, are left undefined. McDougal, on the other hand, recommends within the legal process a comprehensive categorization of the objectives of decisionmakers, as of other participants in the decision process as a whole, by reference to the substantive values involved, organized according to a sociologically oriented scheme with a view to observing the working out of these values in the constitutive and public order processes.

Like McDougal, Fuller criticizes the positivists for their limitations in dealing with objectives. He condemns "a concentration by theory on formal structure to the neglect of the purposive activity this structure is assumed to organize."[170] He points out that his view, unlike most theories of law, treats law as an activity,[171] and his fictitious mouthpiece, Foster, J., is made to say that "the law is not something lying inert in statutes and precedents, but is instead a process."[172] This approach is not, however, in Fuller's case a preliminary to identification of the phases, functions, and structures within the decision processes in the way it is for McDougal. Since the activity or process is considered as a common human enterprise, Fuller is actively concerned to avoid pinpointing the decisionmakers in a way which might emphasize their perspectives or those of other participants at the expense of the observer's. In Fuller's notion that we can find uniformities in law only by reference to the constancy of our common human purposes, there seems to be a hint of the ancient Greek notion that the world of experience has a fluidity rendering it incapable of characterization by reference to categories which could be given empirical reference. Therefore, discourse requires reference instead to ideal categories of general human thought only imperfectly realized in the world of experience. McDougal's view is that our categories of thought must be adapted to deal with the fluidity by finding the pattern in it. His development of the notion of process is designed to do this. He is concerned to perceive the order that does in fact exist in imperfectly revealed experience.

The early sociologists, from McDougal's viewpoint, failed to appreciate and meet the requirement that, for the purpose of carrying out their investigation of the causal relationships between law and society, generally it is necessary to focus upon both, in common social terms, and to identify legal processes and other social processes by similar criteria. Thus, Renner thought it satisfactory to take the "valid norm" as a datum and to "examine only the economic and social effect of the valid norm as it exists so long as the norm does not change."[173] Weber's main work has a similar character, despite the foundations laid by his own work for a different approach based on social domination. In his major work, an exercise in the relationships between the structure of society and the kind of legal theory held in the society,[174] the necessity for a systematic account of phases of the legal process does not arise and is not given. The account of decision functions is as conventional as Kelsen's. Weber accepts in this respect "our contemporary modes of legal thought"[175] and describes judicial activity in terms of the distinction between creating and finding law.[176]

Among the earlier twentieth-century sociologists of law, Ehrlich admittedly stands apart in the respect that his account neither of law nor of society is a reflection of conventional notions. But his reference to both is so diffuse, as we have seen, that he provided himself with no basis for general categorizations of the phases or functions that exist within legal and other social processes. Although Ehrlich has a good deal to say about matters related to various of the decision functions with which McDougal is concerned, he does not develop tools of investigation whereby their location, in whatever social process context, can serve the cause of systematic scholarly enlightenment. Ehrlich's procedure is to identify various participants or situations rather unsystematically, and then to ask: what are the functions of these persons or transactions? While in answering these questions Ehrlich comes to consider many of McDougal's authority functions, sometimes differentiating between them and sometimes not, they are considered only in the contexts in which the questions were asked; for example, the function of the attorney, the function of the legal transaction, the function of the judge.[177]

Pound's orientation to the legal process still reflects in some degree the reluctance noticed in Renner and Weber to treat the relation between law and society as one between different social processes envisaged in common social terms. For Pound, the legal process is only a subordinate aspect of law, apparently arrived at by broadening the conventional distinction between substantive law and procedure and connecting the legal process with the latter. The legal process comes to be regarded as the *means* by which law achieves its objectives. Thus, he praises Justice Cardozo for "his setting off of the judicial process from other meanings to which the term 'law' has been applied, yielding an idea applicable also to the administrative process, and not only giving us a very useful term, but obviating a confusion between the regime, the process by which it is maintained, and the body of authoritative precepts governing or guiding the process."[178] For Pound, therefore, the "regime" is the most comprehensive conception—"the regime of adjusting relations and ordering conduct by the systematic and orderly application of the force of a politically organized society."[179] Law, in the sense of various authoritative materials, provides the system and orderliness in that the regime is "carried on in accordance with a body of authoritative precepts applied by an authoritative technique, on a background of received ideals";[180] law in the sense of the legal process requires consideration only because these authoritative precepts are applied "through a judicial and an administrative process."[181] *"Analysis of the judicial process,"*[182] Pound says, is "distinguished as the functions which are involved in the decision of a case according to law (1) finding the facts . . . (2) finding the law . . . (3) interpreting the precept or precepts to be applied . . . (4) applying the precept or precepts so found and interpreted to the case in hand."[183] The importance left to the legal process by this account perhaps may be not unfairly indicated by the manner in which consideration of the judicial process in action shares the fourth volume of Pound's jurisprudence with the analysis of general juristic conceptions. Thirty-six pages are devoted to the former (discussing the impossibility of devising a system of law capable of mechanical application and the problems of individualization of justice in a particular case) and 505 pages to the latter. This, then, is the result in Pound's work of "setting off" the judicial process from other meanings of the term "law." For McDougal this setting off does not reduce confusion as Pound claims. Instead, as Pound applies the notion, it invites confusion. For the objectives and strategies of participants in legal processes are discussed separately from the account of the processes themselves. This facilitates the characteristic of Pound's thinking whereby the professional tradition is discussed on such a level of abstraction that it reflects more of his own demands than may be found in actual legal processes.

The Legal Process and Social Processes

Once McDougal has analyzed the legal process in terms which can be applied equally to other social processes, he explores the various relationships of the legal process to others. For this purpose, the general social process of the community with which the inquirer is concerned—which McDougal sometimes calls the "process of interaction"—simply has first to be identified, and provision made for inquiry into the manner in which the process of decision arises out of it. And for this purpose, McDougal develops the notion of "Precipitating Events," leading to the involvement of decisionmakers,[184] and recommends that the claims process—the presentation of demands to decisionmakers—be distinctively recognized and made subject to inquiry. Hence, a student following McDougal's recommendations for the establishment of a comprehensive focus of inquiry for any legal study will find himself in the first place making a preliminary identification of the phases of the process of interaction with which he is concerned and a similar identification of the phases of the process of claim. The identification of the process of interaction is important for Mc-Dougal not only as a basis for developing the process of claim, but also, for example, for the development of inquiry into the immediate outcome and longer range effects of decision which his theory makes the penultimate and ultimate phases of the decision process itself, thus ensuring continuity of the inquiry.[185]

Positivism in its "purest" form regards social processes generally as outside the field of legal study. Kelsen denies legal existence to the participants in social processes except insofar as their conduct is related to norms. Thus, "the people—from whom the constitution [of the United States] claims its origin—comes to legal existence first through the constitution. It can therefore be only in a political, not in a juristic sense that the people is the source of the constitution."[186] For McDougal, on the other hand, it is of primary importance that we not have different first principles for dealing with law and society.

Other positivists' accounts of law and society lack Kelsen's rigidity of insistence upon doctrinal "purity." Yet Ross continues to distinguish the approach via legal doctrine and the sociology of law. From the angle of the first approach, Ross substitutes for McDougal's inquiry into precipitating events of legal processes an inquiry into a set of causes of judges' statements in their opinions under the heading "Sources of Law"—"the aggregate of factors which exercise influence on the judge's formulation of the rule on which he bases his decision."[187] But the doctrinal eye through which these causes are to be examined limits the extent of the examination. To the extent that doctrine on a subject is undeveloped, Ross stops short, saying, for example, that "objective conditions cannot be indicated for the motivating influence of custom, precedent, and 'reason' " and "the doctrine of the sources of law must, therefore, be limited to indicating in loose terms the role played by the various sources in a specific legal system."[188] Any further inquiry into social causes of decision requires the observer to assume the different role of legal politician.[189]

Hart's work does not allow special scientific *status* for statements of rules or statements about rules; his general work is confined by his special *interest* in these kinds of statements and the light they throw on law as a social phenomenon. But Hart would hardly contend that by using, in regard to such statements, "a sharpened awareness of words to sharpen our awareness of the phenomena,"[190] we should emerge with a general map of law in relation to the social process of the kind which it is McDougal's purpose to establish. Hart does not give priority to laying a general framework for systematic consideration of law in relation to society, although he engages in various specialist investigations within the field of such relationships.

Fuller has devoted a good deal of attention to the relation between law and other social processes within a community. Perhaps his notion of the proper categorization of social processes for study is best exemplified in a passage in which, discussing what he describes as a "pervasive problem of social design," he claims that it is shared by morals, law, economics, aesthetics, and science.[191] This list may be compared with McDougal's main categories of value to which institutions within society are regarded as specialized and by reference to which McDougal describes the flow of interaction.[192] McDougal's value-institution categories are power (government, law, politics), wealth (production, distribution, consumption), respect (social class and caste), well-being (health, safety, comfort, arrangements), affection (family, friendship circles, loyalty), skill (artistic, vocational, professional training and activity), rectitude (churches and related articulators and appliers of standards of responsible conduct), and enlightenment (mass media, research).[193]

McDougal thus resorts more to numerous general categories, whereas some of Fuller's references are to particular types of specialized institutions with which McDougal includes others. Fuller's more detailed work indicates, moreover, a different emphasis in the purposes for which the categories are posited. Whereas McDougal's emphasis is on using the categories to further intellectual tasks which involve attention to the interactions between the various processes, and especially between law as one institution specialized to the power process and other processes, Fuller's main interest has been to call attention to what he discerns as features which the legal process shares with others. He has sought to demonstrate that other processes are human "activities" like law, "particular directions of human effort"[194] in which fact and value cannot be clearly separated. Thus, he says that corresponding to the view that law is simply "the existence of public order" we may assert that "science exists when men have the ability to predict and control the phenomena of nature."[195] In Fuller's view, this fails to indicate the purposiveness of the activity involved; science would be better regarded as the direction of human effort toward the prediction and control of the phenomena of nature. Hence, "the calling of the scientist has its distinctive ethos, its internal morality"[196] as law does. It is the same with economics, and, as with law, according to Fuller, we can distinguish within the internal morality of economics, a morality of aspiration and a morality of duty, the former being represented by marginal utility economics and the latter by that constituent of it which deals with relationships of exchange.[197] In regard to the morality of aspiration, the economist is setting up an end for the consumer, the full explanation of which necessitates, in some sense, the participation of the economist-observer himself: "the economist may not care what the consumer wants, but he cannot be indifferent to the process by which the consumer reaches his decision as to what he wants. If he is to understand that process, the economist must be capable of participating in it vicariously."[198] The projection of the observer's demands is facilitated by Fuller's indefinite notion of utility as an "ultimate criterion that stands above books, food, clothing and all the other things and services for which men may spend their money,"[199] but which the "economist cannot describe"[200] except by reference to the very fact that it is "the principle by which we make the most effective allocation of the resources at our command in achieving whatever objectives we have set for ourselves."[201] From McDougal's viewpoint, this amounts to an undesirable sacrifice of clarity of focus upon the process under observation to the undesirable purpose, from the enlightenment aspect, of serving a demand theory of economics. There seems no necessity for positing utility as a value independent of the observed economic subject's actual preferences as between different material wants, the economic subject in this respect performing exactly the same functions as Fuller recognizes the market may do when he is discussing exchange economics. He says: "[i]t is only with the aid of something like a free market that it is possible to develop anything like an exact measure for the value of disparate goods."[202] In sum, McDougal's theory of what is involved in the establishing of a focus of attention on special processes generally involves him in parallel points of differences with Fuller to those concerning what is involved in focusing on the legal process in particular.

The aspiration to examine the relation of law to social processes is by definition characteristic of sociologists of law. Renner says, for example, that we can develop a complete theory of law only if we supplement positive legal analysis by an investigation of two adjoining provinces, the origin and the social function of law.[203] It is, however, on the function, or effects, of law on which Renner concentrates—and within this area, principally on economic effects, economics being conceived as production and distribution for consumption. Consumption is given a special technical meaning, namely, "preservation and reproduction of the species,"[204] which in turn involves "production of human beings, of labor power."[205] There is a tendency to introduce demand conceptions, to make "functions" and "proper functions" equivalent terms, so that Renner refrains from considering the effect of law on institutions specialized to a number of values other than wealth altogether, for they are regarded as outside its proper scope: "within them the individual is free and not subject to the control of the state. Here he is no longer a citizen of the state but simply a human being who enjoys freedom of thought and religion, freedom of convictions which the state may not touch."[206] Hence, Renner's work does not provide for the systematic and comprehensive mapping of the social process as a basis for the study of law and society.

The insistence on study of law in relation to community processes generally is justly regarded as the key to the reputation of Ehrlich's work. Ehrlich tells us that "the center of gravity of legal development lies not in legislation, nor in judicial decision, but in society itself."[207] He is especially concerned with the social causes of legal phenomena and condemns exclusive emphasis on economic factors in this respect. He stresses that "purely social"[208] forces are at work as well, such as the "element of human personality" and "the trends of justice."[209] Nevertheless, he fails to categorize social processes in a comprehensive manner. We already have referred to the somewhat amorphous and unsteady character of Ehrlich's references to society.[210]

Weber, too, focuses upon the relation of law to society beyond the economic field. He tells us that law guarantees, in addition to economic interests, diverse interests ranging from the most elementary of personal security to such purely ideal goals as personal honor or the honor of the divine powers. Above all, he adds, it guarantees political, ecclesiastical, familial, and other positions of authority, as well as positions of social preeminence of any kind, which may indeed be economically conditioned or economically relevant in the most diverse ways, but which are neither economic in themselves nor sought for primarily economic ends.[211] In this list may be found references bearing various degrees of explicitness and comprehensiveness to all of the value categories through which McDougal focuses on society, except skill and enlightenment. But Weber does not use them for this purpose. Beginning from the view, like McDougal, that society may be considered as a complex of interactions of human beings,[212] he nevertheless eschews the task of comprehensive categorization of social processes on the ground that the flow of events is too infinitely variable to permit its execution. Weber considers, therefore, that our categories of inquiry must be designed to select from this flow the relatively small amount of material that is of interest to us: "Only a small portion of existing concrete reality is colored by our value-conditioned interest and it alone is significant to us."[213] The recommendation is that we select for study those elements which are related to our values in either a positive or a negative way,[214] and Weber adds that the values of the inquirer determine only the direction of his interest, not the character of the truth he discovers.[215]

Had Weber's own value position been similar to McDougal's, and had his design for cultural investigation of society been comprehensively worked out in the light of such a value position, the result might not have been very different from McDougal's. For McDougal's value position is comprehensive in the sense that he seeks the widest possible shaping and sharing of the eight values he posits. And since McDougal regards all social interactions as value-oriented (men seeking values through institutions),[216] an account of society in terms of the processes which are related to his values in some positive or negative, direct or indirect manner has to be quite comprehensive. Neither condition is satisfied by Weber, however. He appears to accept the inevitability of the values of the inquirer as being limited and variable.[217] Moreover, he is prevented from explicitly carrying through his conception of a cultural analysis of society in terms of his own values for the time being because, as a social scientist, he does not consider it consistent with scholarly integrity to disclose them.[218]

McDougal's method is different. The value-oriented approach which he recommends for the identification of social processes, *i.e.*, a classification of values sought and realized in the objectives and outcome phases of the processes under investigation, is not specifically concerned with his own personal values. It is designed to satisfy the requirement that theory should provide a value framework comprehensive enough to permit description of all values being sought and those being realized in any society (McDougal's own included).

The virtue of Pound's approach from McDougal's standpoint lies in its separation of interests from rights as a means of distinguishing de facto demands made in society generally and the demands which are recognized in the workings of the legal process. Even at this point, however, there is some difference between the relevant distinction as Pound and McDougal would see it. This is attributable partly to the restricted view of the legal process taken by Pound (to which reference has been made)[219] and partly to a certain flavoring of the definitions of the descriptive terms with "philosophical" considerations which tend to relate the description to the demands of the observer. Pound defines interests as "claims or wants or desires . . . which men assert *de facto,* about which the law must do something if organized societies are to endure."[220] "Interests (*i.e.,* claims, demands, expectations of human beings) are ends which the legal order seeks to secure or to satisfy. Rights, as we know them in law . . . are a means by which it does this work of securing interests."[221] Pound's distinction between interests and rights is not therefore designed sharply to distinguish a characterization of social processes by reference to *their* objectives phases from a characterization of decision processes, in McDougal's more comprehensive sense, by reference to *their* objectives phases.

Nor is the matter corrected as the analysis proceeds, for Pound's discussion takes place in terms of abstract reference to various "interests in" outcomes variously described without regular specifications of who is seen to be making the demand in question upon whom. Pound's general classifications of interests are similarly abstract. His major scheme of division is into individual, social, and public interests, with major emphasis placed on the first two, although he recognizes the possibility of adding institutional or group interests[222] and civilization interests.[223] Pound tells us that individual interests are claims or demands or desires involved in, and looked at from, the standpoint of the immediate individual life—asserted in title of the individual life. Public interests are the claims or demands or desires asserted by individuals involved in, and looked at from, the standpoint of political life—life in politically organized society. They are asserted in title of that organization, as claims of a politically organized society. Social interests are claims or demands or desires thought of in terms of social life and generalized as claims of the social group. They are claims which are involved in the maintenance, the activity, and the functioning of society; the wider demands or desires asserted in title of social life in civilized society.[224] From McDougal's standpoint there is here a great variety of criteria for assigning interests to particular categories, presented as if they were equivalents. In one recurring theme, the criterion seems to be in terms of what social process participants the observer is focusing upon; in another, the particular higher level objective to which the participant relates his demand; and in still another, the particular higher level objective to which the observer relates the demand. The result of this unsteadiness in the purported criteria of classification of demands is that in fact they do not serve the purpose of precise identification of demands for Pound; what does identify a particular demand is only its content. Hence, the discussion of interests proceeds at a high level of abstraction from the phases of the processes in which they arise. This is illustrated by Pound's doctrine of the ready convertibility of demands from individual demands to general social demands.[225] The extent to which Pound satisfies the need for a map of the social process therefore depends upon the extent to which his detailed catalogue of interests within the broad categories which he posits fulfills this function.

The first of these in the department of social interests is the social interest in the general security "asserted in title of social life in civilized society and through the social group, to be secure against those forms of action and courses of conduct which threaten its existence."[226] Its different forms are the interest in general safety,[227] in general health (and general morals?),[228] in peace and public order,[229] and in the security of acquisitions and transactions.[230] In one context, McDougal has defined security as "full opportunity, free from violence and threats of violence, to pursue all values by peaceful, non-coercive procedures."[231] So regarded, the notion has relation to the strategies by which values of whatever kind are sought in all social processes. Pound's different procedure, of separating out as major divisions of interest those aspects of the social processes which are important for the existence or identity of society, has the disadvantage that the attempt to determine whether a particular demand falls under this heading raises questions of fact, degree, and meaning to which answers are more easily given by definitional exercises about what goes to the identity of society than by any other means. Moreover, the vagueness of what is involved tends to conduce more to emotive exercises in advocacy of the kind that "we must do this or the whole fabric of society will collapse" than to offer a useful focus for the scholar. It is obvious that it is only some aspects of health, some aspects of the security of transactions, and so on, among Pound's different forms of interest, which might be important enough to be relevant to the identity or existence of society, however broadly conceived; other aspects of those matters, according to Pound's approach, would have to be caught up elsewhere in his system of interests, or not treated at all. McDougal's analysis provides for the comprehensive detailed consideration of all demands within particular value processes, their outcomes, and their effects on other value processes within society, however extensive or minimal.

At the other end of his list of social interests, Pound places the social interest in the individual life, that all individual wants "be satisfied at least so far as is reasonably possible and to the extent of a human minimum."[232] He envisages the individual life as including individual self-assertion (including physical, mental, and economic activity), individual opportunity (political, physical, cultural, social, and economic), and individual conditions of life[233] such "that each individual shall have assured to him the conditions of at least a minimum human life under the circumstances of life in the time and place."[234] All of these subcategorizations are very general compared to the correlative values in McDougal's sense, but in the last case, especially specific in regard to their formulation. Hence, first, they are categories which are not designed to assist the inquirer in where to look to discover them, and, second, they might well exclude many demands which the inquirer does discover. They lack both specification and comprehensiveness, and they do this because they tend to be Pound's own high-level demands projected onto the social scene.

The conception of the social interest in the individual life is difficult to distinguish from Pound's interpretation of the fundamental goal of twentieth-century society and of Pound himself. We have seen that, in terms of Pound's goals, the relationship between maintaining the social order (which seems to convey a similar idea to the social interest in the general security) and individual self-assertion (one of the departments of the social interest in the individual life) is that the latter is perceived as a more inclusive interest, in the sense of the *reason why* the social order is to be maintained, while the satisfaction of human wants, to which the third department of Pound's interest in the individual life is clearly related, is a more inclusive interest still.[235] Pound's divisions of interests, even at this level, are not designed to represent different kinds of objectives pursued with at least some degree of independence, but different levels of generality or ultimacy in relation to Pound's goals. Other social interests he considers presumably represent intermediate levels in his hierarchy of values—"the social interest in the security of social institutions"[236] (including domestic,[237] religious,[238] and political [239] institutions, and "perhaps" economic institutions)[240] and the social interest in the conservation of social resources [241] (including the interest in the conservation of the human assets of society).[242] Finally, we may mention Pound's social interest in the general progress, which appears to be designed to ensure that we do not stop in our analysis with the general goals we have at present, but proceed to envisage even more inclusive ones, in the fields of economic, political, and cultural progress.[243]

Hence, in our search in Pound's work for categories which will divide the field of inquiry systematically for the purpose of an objective focus of attention, we are finally thrown forward to Pound's categories of individual interest. The division here is a threefold one into interests of personality ("the claims or demands involved in the individual physical and spiritual existence"), domestic interests ("the claims or demands involved in what has been called 'the expanded individual life' "), and interests of substance ("the claims or demands involved in the individual economic life").[244] In this scheme, the third subdivision corresponds to McDougal's wealth category, and the second subdivision to McDougal's affection category. The narrowing of this category means that Pound has to deal with "advantageous relations with others" except in the domestic field under the head of individual interests of substance,[245] which McDougal would regard as unsatisfactory since wealth may or may not be the main value involved. Pound's procedure leaves "interests of personality" as a broad residual category involving, from McDougal's viewpoint, values as diverse as respect, rectitude, enlightenment, well-being, power, and skill. Pound's interests of personality are (1) in the physical person (McDougal's well-being), (2) in the freedom of the will (which is a notion going to all eight values from McDougal's viewpoint), (3) in honor and reputation (McDougal's respect), (4) in privacy (another multivalued category from McDougal's viewpoint, but involving especially respect and well-being), and (5) belief and opinion [246] (crossing the boundaries of enlightenment and rectitude, from McDougal's approach).

The main point of difference between Pound and McDougal in the present connection is, thus, not about their disagreements, however considerable, over the most satisfactory categorizations of individual interests; it is in what is proposed to be done with them. Taking his standpoint with the judge and administrator, Pound proposes to convert the individual demands observed into "social interests," and thus enter immediately into the task of weighing them against general goals. McDougal proposes instead to identify the social processes by reference to them, and to identify similarly the processes of claim and decision.

Law in Different Communities form Local to Global

McDougal speaks of a world community because interactions and interdeterminations among human beings are on a global scale,[247] and sets his focus of attention to include inquiry into the interrelations of the different community processes (from local, through regional, to global) exhibited in the world arena [248] and into the interpenetration of processes of authoritative decision in the different communities.[249] He seeks to obtain an empirical account, by methods appropriate to the task, of the broader community processes as well as the narrower, paying special attention in the former to the rival systems of public order which are exhibited in them and the varying balance between inclusive and exclusive participation in decision.

Ross conceives that once the idea of law is freed of its emotional load it is of no particular interest what it covers, although he prefers to "reserve the term 'legal system' for normative orders which have the same essential characteristics as a well-developed, modern national law system."[250] McDougal's view is that the expression of a preference for a narrow definition of law always has a narrowing, though often unintended, effect on the inquirer's focus of attention. Moreover, the grounds on which the preference is expressed may show that there has been inadequate focus on decision processes beyond the state arena for the purpose of exercising the choice. From McDougal's viewpoint, for example, Ross' statement that "the sanction attached to a legal decision in international law has merely the character of a public disapproval of the losing party if it does not adjust its behavior according to the judgment"[251] indicates an unawareness of the variety of coercive strategies operative within processes of authoritative decision in the world arena. By his characterization of the arena of world politics as a military arena,[252] McDougal emphasizes the expectations of violence and other extreme forms of coercion in the world power process of which world processes of authoritative decision form a part. Again from McDougal's viewpoint, the exercise of a positivist preference to confine the term "law" to processes within municipal arenas often appears as influenced as much by a failure to focus sociologically on municipal arenas themselves as by a failure to focus on the world arena; hence, the comparison proceeds on a false basis.

This criticism applies not only to positivists who, like Ross, refuse to regard international law as law, but to positivists like Kelsen who are inclined to the opposite view. Kelsen does not ask whether we can identify world processes of authoritative decision within the world in the manner that we identify processes of authoritative decision within municipal power processes. Rather, analogizing from his own scheme of inquiry into municipal law, he asks whether the material which presents itself as law in the international field can be represented as a system of coercive norms: "If it is possible to describe the material which presents itself as international law in such a way that thě employment of force directed by one State against another can be interpreted only as either delict or sanction, then international law is law in the same sense as national law."[253] But in pursuing this inquiry, Kelsen is unable to develop a single normative jurisprudence representing the *necessary* presuppositions of legal thinking within the arena, as he purports to be able to do in the municipal field. After examining the perspectives of authority of international lawyers and statesmen, Kelsen comes to the conclusion that the international order "can be interpreted as an order according to which the coercive act is a monopoly of the community [though made largely a matter of self-help] and it is permissible to interpret the primitive social order in this way because the individuals subjected to the order themselves interpret it in this way."[254] But since this is not the only possible interpretation, Kelsen recognizes that he has not established international law according to his own "scientific" canons of demonstration of a normative order.[255] Hence, while he rejects the view that war is sometimes neither a delict nor a sanction, and consequently rejects the view that there is no international order, he regards this rejection as "not a scientific but a political decision."[256] Kelsen appears to regain some confidence in the view that the existence of international law is a necessary epistemological postulate [257] when he finds the idea necessarily presupposed in the assumption of modern lawyers of the continuity of national law and the legal identity of the state in spite of a violent change of constitution.[258] But Kelsen still finds it possible to "organize" in two ways to account for the relation between national and international law: an "objective hypothesis" of the primacy of international law and the dependence of state laws, or a "subjective hypothesis" whereby a jurist may proceed from the primacy of his own state order and the dependence of international law thereon.[259] The choice between them is thus for him a political question. But this really means that Kelsen's neo-Kantian approach to the examination of legal perspectives, seeking to discover the necessary preconditions of legal thought, has in this arena manifestly broken down, as McDougal would claim it does in other arenas. The only satisfactory approach to subjectivities for the descriptive observer in any arena is to recognize that they may conflict, whereupon he "has the task of recording which perspectives typically prevail during given time periods and are expressed in decision outcomes."[260]

Hart's work presents from McDougal's viewpoint a similar failure to focus adequately both on the world legal process and state legal processes. Hart disposes of certain questions, where McDougal would take issue with him, largely by assumption. Thus, for example, Hart uses the expression "rules for states" as a synonym for international law in the course of the assertion that "the absence of those institutions [legislature, courts, etc.] means that the rules for states resemble that simple form of social structure, consisting only of primary rules of obligation, which, when we find it among societies of individuals, we are accustomed to contrast with a developed legal system." [261] For McDougal, this amounts to shortchanging not only the question of the existence of a world community and the complex interactions of individuals and communities involved, but also the question of whether a world legal constitutive process, as well as a world public order system (Hart's primary rules of obligation), can be detected. For McDougal, the question, for example, of whether there are perspectives of authority in the international arena about who is to make decisions for the community in particular contexts is not disposed of to the extent that we are unable to discover general world legislatures and courts analogous to those in the municipal field. Hart is admittedly less dogmatic in denying the possibility that there may be general criteria by which decisions are expected to be taken than in denying that there are authoritative decision-makers (*i.e.,* less dogmatic, in his terms, in denying a "recognition rule" than in denying the existence of "rules of change" and "rules of adjudication"), although he finally submits that "there is no basic rule providing general criteria of validity for the rules of international law and that the rules which are in fact operative constitute not a system but a set of rules, among which are the rules providing for the binding force of treaties." [262] Still, McDougal would not expect to find perspectives of authority about the criteria by which decisions are to be taken organized as tightly as Hart's notion of a recognition rule implies in the international or the municipal arena.

The difference between the two scholars persists when, having tentatively disposed of the question of the existence, in McDougal's terms, of a world constitutive legal process, Hart goes on to consider whether there is an international public order system. Hart is prepared to accord the description law to the rules of primary obligation in this arena because "if rules are in fact accepted as standards of conduct, and supported with appropriate forms of social pressure distinctive of obligatory rules, nothing more is required to show that they are binding rules." [263] To the question of why this particular set of binding rules should be characterized as legal, Hart gives a series of answers. First, we distinguish international law from international morality in speech, and some rules of international law are of the "rule of the road" type and morally neutral. But this leaves the question of how the legal rules are to be identified as a group. Hart mentions that in the case of the legal rules there is an appeal to precedents, treaties, and juristic writings,[264] and says also that morality is supported by appeals to conscience, while law is supported by appeals to fear or threats of retaliation or demands for compensation.[265] Insofar as Hart is here associating international law with the world power process, he shares some common ground with McDougal. But differences remain. McDougal would regard this as an incomplete statement of the sanctions (high indulgences or severe deprivations) which are associated with the world decision process; for McDougal, the identification of an authoritative decision process within the world power process depends upon the identification of expectations of the participants of those high indulgences or severe deprivations in given circumstances. For the purpose of focusing upon the world legal process it is important to McDougal that inquiry be directed not merely into how far perspectives of authority are sanctioned by threats or appeals, which goes to the question of how far perspectives are controlling, but also into how far these are expected, which goes to the question of the identification of the perspectives of authority themselves.

Fuller has little to say of the global community, and though he recognizes that some of his principles of order are at times operative within it, this apparently does not include his principle of legitimated power. Thus he says that international treaties are an instance of contract acting as a significant force in the organization of men's activities where no principle of legitimated power is involved at all [266] and that the Nuremberg trial proved that "adjudication can function significantly and beneficially without the support of either a legitimated power (in this case a world super-state) or contract (an agreement of submission)." [267] McDougal would not regard the possibility of identification of global processes of authoritative and controlling decision as dependent on the existence of a world superstate, but would invite inquiry about how far other bodies, including nation-states, function as decisionmakers for the world community on the basis of expectations of individuals and organizations that they will do so in given contexts.

Renner appears to say nothing at all of international law in his major work, and although Ehrlich recognizes "jural associations" of human beings which are worldwide, in particular, worldwide economic systems,[268] and finds respect for life, liberty, and property to be principles of a universal living law,[269] he nevertheless regards a universal international law as but a dream of the noblest and best.[270] All this is far from offering a focus on global decision processes. Weber's interest in the bureaucratic features of some legal processes turned his interest from the global arena, and he appeals to precedent for excluding it from his focus of attention: "Time and again, international law has been said not to be 'law' because it lacks a supra-national enforcement agency. Indeed, our definition of law, too, would not apply to an order which is guaranteed merely by the expectation of disapproval and reprisals on the part of those who are harmed by its violation." [271] This comment is similar to Ross' and would call for the same answer from McDougal.

Pound conceives a "law of the world" [272] as a possible next stage of law. Since, however, he has in his general account of law associated it with the state, and since he wishes to challenge the view that the effectuating agency must be a politically organized society,[273] he is bound to shift his connotation for law in the present connection in a manner never precisely explained. We do not know what Pound is predicting may occur when he asks "[m]ay a general body of organized principles of adjusting relations and ordering conduct in internal activities of independent political organizations grow up and become a legal order?" [274] But he is, at any rate, prepared to specify what will be the nature of the "legal process," in Pound's restricted sense of a process,[275] through which the order must be put into effect. There must be an independent tribunal, with full notice to the parties, full opportunity to present evidence and argument to the tribunal, and an independent judgment according to law.[276] "Law as distinguished from laws" Pound claims, "grows out of such a tribunal." [277] The distinction to which he refers here is that between "principles, conceptions, standards" (law) and prescriptions of "definite detailed consequences to follow definite detailed facts" (laws).[278] The former, Pound believes, has to do with general situations of human relations and human conduct,[279] but this point is hardly substantiated. There seems no reason why greater generality of application to legal subject matter should be associated with suitability for wider application over a geographical area. Indeed, in his general jurisprudence Pound associates sets of such general conceptions with civilizations of a time *and place*.

Pound's notion of what the general character of this "law" may come to be in the international arena is elaborated in terms of a demand for a present-day adaptation of the Grotian approach. Grotius' theory, however, is the one which Pound describes in his general jurisprudence as leading to "confusion of extra-legal ideals with the ideal element in the positive law and of both with the precept element," [280] and he clearly is not advocating a return to natural law theory as such. Discussing Anglo-American criticisms of it, he says that Englishmen and Americans were right in demanding a better theory of international legal obligation, but wrong in believing that they could find it without the aid of philosophy.[281] More specifically, Pound claims that the basis of this philosophy must be found by "thinking of a great task of social engineering, as it were, whereby the conflicting or overlapping interests and claims and demands of the peoples of this crowded world may be secured or satisfied so far as may be with a minimum of friction and a minimum of waste." [282] What a "philosophy" of these matters might be, Pound does not tell us here, but elsewhere he says that while science is organized and verified experience, philosophy is organized and verified reason.[283] Once resort is had to the notion of verifiable reason as giving some kind of authority to projected rules, however, we are reintroducing the same kinds of confusion that Grotius exploited and which Pound himself criticized; the consequence is to hinder a focus on actual community perspectives of authority within the world arena, whether we apply this reason to the nature of man, as Grotius did, or to the subject matter of modern sociology and modern psychology, as Pound advocates. It seems to be because of the confusing variety of notions covered by reason that Pound is able to suggest that principles do not require sanctions, whereas rules do.[284] The fact that principles depend upon reason in the sense that they are more general than rules that are arrived at by induction seems to be converted into the suggestion that they have an inherent persuasiveness which renders resort to force perhaps unnecessary.

From McDougal's viewpoint, Pound is prevented from focusing on law as a global process of decision by the orientation of his vocabulary to nation-state-centered usage. He is prevented from focusing on actual perspectives of authority by his attempt to discover a high-level touchstone of authority in the propositions of an unintelligibly defined philosophy. And he is prevented from examining the process of coercion within the global community in its protean forms by his confining of the notion of sanctioning to "courts," so that he cannot see an international law without at least setting up a hypothetical general court, rather than focusing on the actual carrying out of application *functions* in the global arena. It is clear that, like McDougal, Pound feels himself to be a member of a global community and wishes to make demands on community decisionmakers for the clarification of the common interests of such a community and their realization through a more effective decision process. For McDougal, obscuring theory hinders these objectives as much as a clear focus on global decision processes now and in the past assists them.

The Intellectual Tasks of Jurisprudence

McDougal's policy-oriented approach identifies five tasks for jurisprudence within its proper focus of attention: the clarification of goal values, the description of trends, the analysis of conditions, the projection of future developments, and the invention and evaluation of alternatives.[285] The expectation is that all methods of thinking will be frequently used in seeking the solution of any problem and that the separation is to be made a matter of relative emphasis.[286]

Clarification of Goal Values

McDougal formulates for himself an overriding goal which relates to the place of law in the entire social context. That goal he terms human dignity, and he regards it as realized to the degree that value shaping and sharing is widespread, rather than narrowly restricted. The general goal is thus not given immediate semantic reference but is, rather, an envelope term given content through specifications of what is to be regarded as involved in the broadest participation in the shaping and the sharing of values in all of McDougal's eight value categories. Emphasis is laid on moving from the general statement to specifications having empirical reference rather than derivation of the general from transempirical sources, both because of the importance that is attached to clarity for the scholar and in order to facilitate cooperation with those who may accept a set of goals thus specified but who would derive them from, or ground them in, many different faiths, philosophies, and experiences.[287] While McDougal's general objective is not treated as open to modification through time, the detailed specifications are regarded as subject to the discipline of continuous performance of the other intellectual tasks in the widest possible variety of contexts.[288]

Ross does not recommend to scholars that they should seek as part of their jurisprudential tasks to clarify their own goals to themselves and to others. For him, these have nothing to do with the examination of the language of legal doctrine or with legal sociology; they are regarded as being a subsidiary task of jurisprudence: "The role of the lawyer as legal politician is to function as far as possible as a rational technologist. In this role he is neither conservative nor progressive. Like other technologists he simply places his knowledge and skill at the disposal of others, in his case those who hold the reigns of political power." [289]

Kelsen does not regard the clarification of goals as an intellectual task at all. He thinks of a person's goals as an emotional matter,[290] and he seeks to put us on our guard against those who represent their goals as having absolute validity. His normative jurisprudence is presented as objective, describing rather than prescribing, though its propositions are 'ought' propositions.[291] For McDougal, goals are a matter of personal choice for reasons already given, but in the case of the enlightenment-oriented scholar, to whom he addresses himself, they will be a matter of informed personal choice in the way indicated earlier. McDougal believes it is not feasible to specialize in elaboration of the "positive law" in the manner of the positivists and leave the goal task aside. A scholar who engages in the systematic elaboration of conventional legal propositions can scarcely escape involvement with the confusions between intellectual tasks which are commonly involved in those propositions themselves (their "normative-ambiguity" in McDougal's terms) and in the commonly accepted methods of their elaboration. The positivist's goals will be surreptitiously and perhaps unconsciously introduced into the exegesis, with resultant confusion. Hence, conventional legal exegesis is not recommended by McDougal as an intellectual task for the scholar at all.

The pioneer English positivists, Bentham and Austin, were utilitarians, which meant that their ethical theory represented the formulation of their own highest level goal and a description of that of others. They thought that all pursue their own happiness and, with the assistance of a simple mathematical fallacy, that all pursue the happiness of all. Hence they conceived there could really be no argument about the propriety of measuring any institution against the standard of "the greatest happiness of the greatest number." Hart correctly notes that the distinction which Bentham and Austin made between law and morals—as they saw it, between the law as it is and the law as it ought to be—was a "utilitarian distinction" [292] between two inquiries by men who were as interested in the second as the first. The matter has, however, become more complex for subsequent English positivists because of recognition of the weight of the theoretical objections to the classical version of utilitarianism.

Hart refers briefly and in apparently approving terms to these objections.[293] Hart approaches morality differently, by asking what concepts of morality are tolerated by linguistic usage and are at the same time enlightening in calling attention to distinctions between law and what might be described as morality.[294] He detects in the standard usage of the term "morality" in relation to the "morality of a society" and in the contexts of that usage a reference to nonlegal rules identifiable by their importance. And he detects their immunity from deliberate change by the fact that voluntariness is a prerequisite of offenses against them and by the fact that the social pressure exerted in favor of them normally consists in appeals to shame or guilt.[295] Hart does not consider that many of these rules could plausibly be defended on a simple utilitarian approach.[296] He argues, however, for the retention of the term "morality" in this context because it enables us to focus comprehensively on elements in a social structure that function in an identical manner, and he considers that the term should not be confined, to put the matter in McDougal's terms, to any set of specifications of the observer's goals.[297] Thus Hart himself emphasizes that his analysis of morality does not involve clarifying his own goals, and this continues to be true when Hart moves to consider the ideals (described in his view as moral by use of the term analogous to the standard one) that he sees existing side by side with moral duties which carry beyond the limited issue of which duty demands concern for others' interests or sacrifice of personal interests.[298] Finally, however, he considers moral criticism of society itself, in which context he finds a further use of the term moral analogous because it makes an appeal to values already recognized in society to some extent, or it rationalizes or generalizes on them.[299] Here he does consider it possible for philosophy to show that a morality which demands that a legal system must treat all human beings within its scope as entitled to certain freedoms is the only one not involved in some inner contradiction, dogmatism, or irrationality. Hence it has special credentials as the true morality.[300] Hart thus only envisages the possibility of some limited demonstration of goals, but he does not offer a demonstrated general criterion for criticism of law. McDougal's solution is not to await some philosophical demonstration of a general set of goals but to present a systematic statement of goals as his own and to recommend them to the like-minded. While the modern English positivist is undoubtedly in a better position than his predecessors to offer a more subtle and illuminating account of what Austin described as positive morality, Hart's adherence to the approach of his predecessors in criticizing law in terms of morality leaves him worse off in the sense that none of his versions of morality at present offers him a touchstone for comprehensive elaboration of his own goals, which the utilitarian touchstone at any rate purported to do.

Traditionally, natural law approaches to jurisprudence have placed emphasis on goals; but in this respect Fuller finds fault both with traditional natural lawyers and McDougal, whom he regards as repeating the mistake of the older natural law school in presenting a value-oriented philosophy, involving an overly sharp and inflexible distinction between ends and means.[301] It is clear that McDougal's goal of human dignity, specified to mean the broadest participation in the production (shaping) and consumption (sharing) of power, enlightenment, wealth, well-being, skill, affection, respect, and rectitude—which goal he does not expect to change, though he would expect change from time to time in concrete specifications within these limits—is more specific than Fuller's aim to release the energies of mankind in "purposeful and creative activity" [302] toward achieving not only "the basic requirements of social living" but also "the fullest realisation of human powers" [303] and "a rational human existence" [304] or "reasoned harmony" [305] based on "human nature itself." [306]

McDougal might first claim that any goals which were expected to release the energies of mankind would need to be more specific than these, since Fuller's statements here fail of themselves to give a direction to inquiry or activity of any sort. Fuller does indeed translate the demands of human nature into the principle of "the common need," [307] which means "the common need men would perceive and feel if they knew the facts." [308] But even at this point he does not seem to provide himself with a manageable program of inquiry into what would be specifically involved in his general notion since discovery of common need in these terms would seem to involve Fuller in first educating the entire community in order to ascertain their demands if they knew the facts and continued this education through time. McDougal's program for closer specification of his goals entails only that he undertake continuous education of himself. Fuller is reconciled to the position that we cannot know the common need as he envisages it, but we nevertheless know enough to continue to progress toward it and are thus able to be effective in spite of our lack of definition of our ultimate goal.[309] We can, he considers, know what is plainly unjust without committing ourselves to declare with finality what perfect justice would be like.[310] But this last proposition seems to be incapable of demonstration by the nature of it. For this purpose we would have to have at least some general notion of what justice would be like. Fuller's limited results in the area of goal clarification appear to be attributable to a characteristic which his theorizing shares with Hart's: to a large degree he assumes that the scholar's standards of criticism must be in terms of morality, yet he is not able to give an account of morality which offers sufficiently specific standards of criticism. So long as the scholar is prepared to commit himself to a general statement of his goals only or mainly on the basis that their validity in some sense be demonstrated, or that some demonstration is possible though he is not immediately able to offer it, the goals produced tend to be unmeaningful or limited and encumbered with dubious supporting arguments.

Such goals as Renner formulates emerge, as we have seen, in a confusion of the "functions" of a legal institution as between its actual effects and its proper effects,[311] so that there is no square attention paid to the task of the inquirer in clarifying his own objectives. Ehrlich's position is subject, from McDougal's viewpoint, to the same criticisms as Fuller's. Goals are expressed in terms of similar high-level abstractions supposed to be connected with the nature of man and society which, it is supposed, must in a degree remain wrapped in mystery. For Ehrlich, the object of the jurist is to serve "the legal needs of daily life,"[312] "social and economic needs,"[313] "the ends that men are endeavouring to attain through law,"[314] the "advance of the human race in the direction of its future development,"[315] "a goal which lies in the sunlit distance, which the human mind can divine but not know,"[316] "the idea of tomorrow which is growing out of the idea of to-day,"[317] "the unceasing development of the social law,"[318] and "the changing demands of life."[319] Ehrlich does not move from these high-level abstractions to more concrete specifications in any systematic way.

Weber drew a sharp distinction between value judgments founded on ideals of the scholar[320] and science limited to observation, description, and explanation.[321] In his capacity as a professor, indeed, he considered it his duty to suppress his own value judgments, this outlook being in part influenced by the conditions of his time: "In view of the fact that certain value-questions which are of decisive political significance are permanently banned from university discussion, it seems to me to be only in accord with the dignity of a representative of science *to be silent* as well about such value problems as he is allowed to treat."[322] In editing a social science journal, he adopted the different policy of permitting himself to express value judgments provided he kept the readers and himself sharply aware at every moment of the standards by which he judged reality.[323] This is in accord with the approach which McDougal has taken as a professor as well as a writer. Like McDougal, too, Weber is concerned with the relation of statements about goals to empirical reality. Weber refers to "[t]he belief which we all have in some form or other, in the metaempirical"—McDougal uses the term "transempirical"—"validity of ultimate and final values in which the meaning of our existence is rooted."[324] McDougal, on the other hand, makes no assumption to this effect. The difference between the two scholars in this respect may not be important since Weber does not make it one of his tasks as a social or legal scholar to enter into demonstrations of this validity, which he terms "speculation" and treats as the personal affair of the scholar holding the values: "it involves will and conscience, not empirical knowledge."[325] For McDougal, the intellectual task of goal clarification ends where the scholar has reported his goals in terms of references to projected events of the kinds that may occur in the empirical sphere.

With Pound there is a return to the encumbering of the task of specification of his goals with demonstrations of validity of various kinds. He seeks authority for his goals by connecting them with the received ideals of the legal system,[326] or with the course of development of society itself, or with the course of development of legal and social philosophy,[327] for which a high degree of unity of results is predicted.[328] The result is, as with earlier sociologists of law seeking to find a basis of demonstration of goals in an interpretation of the direction of legal and social development, that the general statement of goals which emerges is abstract and nebulous: "The immediate direction . . . seems to be toward seeking to satisfy the maximum of the wide scheme of human desires or expectations (or wants, or demands) so far as it may be done through the legal order without too much sacrifice."[329] This statement is on its face subject to the standard objections to the older utilitarian philosophy; the possibility of its being given empirical reference depends on the specification of some standard of quantification of demands on a common basis, which neither Pound's methods of classification of interests, to which we have referred,[330] nor his concept of moving from particular interests in any civilization to broader jural postulates [331] satisfactorily provides. In this aspect, his position runs into difficulties which do not face an approach like McDougal's—which recognizes the existence of different kinds of demands (value categories) and is prepared to confront the conflicting demands of each kind encountered in society with his own set of goals of the same kind and measure them in terms of their relationship to that set of goals in the course of performance of the various intellectual tasks.

Description of Past Trends of Decision

McDougal seeks to describe past trends of decision in a manner that moves between a specific category of events and the total context, and examines the whole in terms of movement toward or away from postulated goals. The first of these undertakings means that the inquiry is to be over the field and organized in the manner already indicated in describing McDougal's concept of the legal theorist's focus of attention. The second calls attention to the desideratum that the task should be related to the other intellectual tasks of lawyers.[332] This involves an organization of the inquiry itself, with an awareness of the character of the larger scheme of inquiry of which it forms part, and movement to the extent necessary between that task and the others in the scheme.

In Ross' view, statements of valid law at the present moment, upon which he chiefly concentrates his interest, do not refer to the past.[333] As a legal politician, he envisages the possibility that trend studies may assist the legislator. But he confesses himself uncertain of the extent to which we are able to set up a study of trends which will be useful at the present stage of development of the social sciences.[334] Similarly, Kelsen's normative jurisprudence focuses generally upon discrete decisions for their norm-creating and norm-annulling aspects only, and for this purpose observation of particular trends as such receives explicit attention only in connection with the question of whether a particular norm may have been annulled by disuse according to a norm so providing.[335] The trend of decision as a whole requires merely to be examined to determine whether effectiveness, the condition upon which the existence of the legal system depends, is satisfied.[336]

Hart's focus upon law as a system of rules would serve, in his own view, to provide some survey of what decisionmakers and others were doing in the legal field at a particular time, since he believes that rules identifiable by the system are observed with tolerable regularity.[337] However, although there would be issues between McDougal and Hart about the extent to which this is so, it is not to be supposed that Hart envisages that a statement of rules existing in any context at a given time would serve comprehensively as a substitute for the kind of trend study that McDougal envisages. Hart's primary theoretical interest is simply more special than that of McDougal, who contrasts positivist aims with those of the sociologist of law. Additionally, McDougal emphasizes the extent to which, in common practice, statements of rules confuse the intellectual tasks as McDougal sees them, the extent to which, in the eye of the ordinary professional user, they are likely to do duty as a statement of goals, a description of past trends of decision, a projection of future decisions, and a statement of policies with which the user identifies himself. The positivist has contributed to this confusion if, as we have suggested, he at once emphasizes the importance of legal rules and fails to explain their sense in major respects.[338]

From Fuller's position, the confusions which McDougal detects in the functions that statements of rules are made to serve are in some degree at least a virtue. We have noticed Fuller's recurring theme that a sharp separation of statements of fact and value is impossible and undesirable.[339] Since in the handling of rules in a conventional fashion a sharp separation of intellectual tasks is at any rate not usual, his concentration on rules in his study of the past provides him with material congenial to his main themes. In particular, this enables him to posit a much more immediate relationship between the description of past trends of decision and the specification of goals than McDougal would consider possible except by confused thinking. Fuller says that if the conditions of successful group living determine the rules we ought to apply to the group, then the rules already applied themselves determine in part what those conditions are. Man's nature, he continues, consists partly of what he has made of himself, and natural law, therefore, demands that we must, within certain limits, respect established positive law.[340] The apparent equation made here between what man has made of himself and positive law would itself be objectionable to McDougal as suggesting an inadequate method of setting out to describe past trends of decision in their context even if it were not for the confusions likely to arise between intellectual tasks from this focus which Fuller adopts.

Among the earlier sociologists of this century, Renner presents the closest points of contact with McDougal, for Renner at least undertook the task of describing the development of law in relation to the total social context through a series of stages which he was prepared to characterize as a whole. Other earlier sociologists failed to develop the concept of a comprehensive trend study of the development of law in relation to values sought in society, for differing reasons. Ehrlich's account of society was not oriented by reference to any classification of substantive values sought within it. Hence his preferred kind of legal history was not a chronicle of legal propositions but a history of the living law usages, contracts, possession, articles of association, testamentary and other declarations. He explained that "the aim of all history of law is to discover the original meaning of the legal propositions and the original significance of the legal relations."[341] The paucity of the results here anticipated would be from McDougal's viewpoint a condemnation of a sociological approach to past trends without value orientation, although in Weber's case, the lack of a concept of a study of past trends of decision in the whole context of the social process is rather due to the special character of his value orientation: "Only a small portion of existing concrete-reality is colored by our value-conditioned interest and it alone is significant to us."[342] Thus Weber saw only two historical tasks—that into the "primary historical object" (that "very valued cultural individual") and that into "secondary historical facts," the causes to which the valued characteristics of that individual are related in the causal regress.[343] In the latter kind of study, Weber emphasizes that in his view general causal laws can be only an *aid* in achieving the object of the study which is to account for the individuality of the phenomenon by discovery of *concrete* causal relations.[344] Weber's notion of a historical investigation, therefore, is one which envisages the discovery of various discrete relationships.

Pound recaptures the concept of characterizing comprehensively the past development of law in relation to the total social context and using these characterizations both for projecting the future and for characterizing that future in terms of his goals. As we have seen, however, these characterizations are made in very general terms,[345] and this applies particularly to his value characterization of society at particular stages. In his main *detailed* account of the legal system at the present time, which occupies the whole of the fifth volume of his major work on jurisprudence (following almost an entire volume devoted to general juristic conceptions), Pound does not organize the material on the basis of the general scheme of "interests" by which he has classified the social subject matter to which law relates, but on the basis of the classifications of "rights" suggested by positivist thinkers following conventional professional categorizations. This means, from McDougal's viewpoint, that Pound has not presented the responses of decisionmakers in a form which relates them to the tasks involved in the social engineering which Pound posits.

The Task of Analyzing Conditioning Factors

McDougal distinguishes among the intellectual tasks of the legal scholar the "scientific" task. Here, relatively greater emphasis is placed, than in tracing trends of decision, upon detecting causal relationships between decisions and other variables. In preparation for the performance of this task he gives attention, first, to the development of appropriate languages and to the general theory of what is involved. Under the former head, for example, he notes the need is to consider factors in any particular analysis as responses to environmental or predispositioning variables, and to clarify operative factors by reference to the culture, class, interest group, and personality of participants in relation to the various value categories at various levels of crisis. Under the latter, his most general proposition is the "maximization postulate," which is that all responses are a function of net value expectation within the limits of capability, limited by resource factors or coercion. McDougal also gives attention to what is involved in carrying out the task, such as the development of appropriate theoretical models as tools of inquiry and appropriate organization of methods for obtaining and processing data. As with the other intellectual tasks, weight is placed on the belief that actual execution of the task should be effected by consideration of its relationship to the other tasks, notably in giving priority to an examination of factors expected to be important to other tasks.[346]

Normative jurisprudence as envisaged by Kelsen does not make causal statements at all. In the kinds of proposition it makes, the subject and predicate are regarded as related in a different way—by imputation.[347] Causal statements are indeed regarded as legitimate, but set apart in the field of sociology of law, which Kelsen envisages as concerning largely the effect of ideas of justice.[348] From his purportedly empirical approach to the nature of legal rules, Ross regards statements concerning their validity as involving assertions about their causal efficacy in the decisions of judges or at least in influencing argument, and regards the manner in which they operate in this way as controlled to a degree by a set of more ultimate rules or ideological considerations designated the sources of law, which he considers can be expressed only in very loose terms.[349] Within the sociological field of causal inquiry, the basic knowledge which Ross suggests the lawyer should seek as "rational technologist" is in narrow compass by McDougal's standards; namely, "the legal-sociological knowledge concerning the causal connection between the normative function of the law and human behaviour, or, as we may also say, concerning the possibilities of influencing human action by the apparatus of legal sanctions."[350] This limitation of the inquiry is connected with Ross' limited view, as compared with McDougal's, of the legal politician's function of advising decisionmakers on the practicalities of implementing goals the formation of which the advisor bears no responsibility.[351]

Hart is not concerned to lay down a framework for general causal inquiry, though he is concerned to clarify some matters of importance regarding the significance of rules in such an inquiry. He stresses the point that no positivist ever has suggested that a body of rules provides information which will wholly account for the responses of judges to situations before them because of peripheral uncertainties in the application of legal terms, as well as other factors.[352] At the same time, Hart is concerned to establish that terms regularly have a core of settled meaning which judges can be expected to utilize with tolerable regularity,[353] a point that McDougal does not follow on the ground that any degree of abstraction in concepts carries with it a degree of uncertainty in application. Beyond this, in speaking of the "Minimum Content of Natural Law," Hart is concerned with certain necessary relationships between natural facts and legal or moral rules. He stresses, however, that this is a limited inquiry into "a distinctively rational connexion between natural facts and the content of legal and moral rules," for "it is both possible and important to inquire into quite different forms of connexion"[354] which "are for sociology or psychology like other sciences to establish by the methods of generalization and theory resting on observation and, where possible, on experiment."[355] McDougal recommends an initiative in the latter kind of matter for the legal theorist.

Fuller makes what is involved in the scientific task for the legal theorist a basic issue. Philosophically, he takes a middle course between what he sees as the extreme sociological position, which tends to regard man as an animal whose behavior is determined,[356] and what he sees as the extreme positivist position, that society is just what we choose to make it.[357] Fuller's principles are "(1) that men can choose to adopt one form of social order or another, (2) that the achievement of particular ends may require the choice of particular forms of order, the available forms being limited in number."[358] What Fuller appears to be suggesting is that if men were freewilling, in the sense that they might at any time do anything from caprice, there would be no regularities of social behavior at all, with the result that the performance of a scientific task would be impossible; but because there is a constancy in human nature, regularities are observable in the kinds of arrangements that will achieve certain kinds of ends. Priority is given to causal factors in human nature rather than in environmental circumstances because "[i]f man's 'nature' is shaped entirely by the 'cultural matrix' then when that matrix is disturbed or broken it would seem that man would disintegrate and there would be no telling which way the pieces would fall. If there are constancies and regularities that persist through a change in social forms these must reflect some constancy in the nature of man himself."[359] Fuller relates the possible principles of order (the common need, legitimated power, contract, adjudication) and their effectiveness in particular circumstances to what he observes of this nature. Thus, he offers such causal principles as that the effect of legitimated power depends on the grounds of its acceptance,[360] that the power of adjudication to produce harmony is adversely affected by its tendency to produce a combative atmosphere,[361] and that contracts become less effective as the face-to-face is lost through agency arrangements.[362] From McDougal's viewpoint, these conclusions indicate the limited results to be achieved by directing our focus upon a human nature conceived by Fuller in ideal moral terms, observable only in the limited articulation which it has achieved in its environment up to the time of observation. McDougal accounts for the regularities to be observed in society by his maximization postulate. This postulate makes no assumption that constancies must be due *either* to the nature of man *or* to the character of his environment, but supposes that human beings seek to maximize differing values while interacting with one another and with other environmental variables.

Like Fuller, Renner displays the same initial concern with the problem of the extent to which society exhibits causal regularities. Renner's solution is that animal society is held together by physiological and biological laws, the laws of nature. These laws of nature become rules of collective human activity as soon as man realizes that it is these laws which hold the tribe together and begins to act deliberately in the way the law of nature compels him to act. But with the transformation of the natural laws of preservation of the species into social conventions and eventually into a code of conduct, Renner conceives that the laws of society diverge from the laws of nature, which are regarded as evolving with society, while natural laws may remain static.[363] Hence, he develops various theses concerning causal relationships between law and society in which major causal efficacy is attributed to social laws within the economic field.[364] Renner splits broad cultural factors sharply into the material culture and ideological factors. Priority in causal importance is given to the first. The narrower factors involved in the "class" of participants and which in McDougal's scheme are examined in relation to all eight value categories are in Renner's scheme limited by a definition correlating class with the participant's relationship to the system of production. Also, McDougal's further narrower categorizations of participants by interest group and personality in the different value categories are ignored.

Ehrlich, like Renner, discusses causal laws in society at the most general and fundamental level in terms of the requirements of preservation of the species: "The doctrine of evolution is not merely this or that scientific truth; it is the basis of all modern thinking."[365] For him, the causes of human action are to be discovered in general forces above and beyond the will of the individual concerned: "[Social science] comes into being as soon as that which goes on in society is referred not to the will of the human being who is acting but to the forces which are acting independently of him in society."[366] Priority is given to social forces as causal factors over state law, for the state organization "is not a match for the uninterrupted sway of elemental forces which have their life and being in the social associations."[367] While Ehrlich stresses the importance of economic forces among these associations, he stresses that "purely social" forces are at work as well. From the social forces arise the "facts of the law," factual institutions which become legal relations by organization in the course of development, and which he regards as small in number—usage, domination, possession, declaration of will.[368] Usage represents the final equilibrium of forces in an association, especially associated with wealth, birth, and personal relations;[369] domination describes power over individuals by others associated with the economic usefulness of the latter to the former; possession arises out of demands of economic utilization of things; and declaration of will represents institutions such as agreements and wills, agreements being associated especially with the economic order and wills being more the product of purely social forces. The state law is utilized by society to preserve these institutions. From McDougal's point of view, Ehrlich's general scheme of causal analysis assumes one-way causal relationships between factors at higher and lower levels, where the focus should rather be on examining interactions within and between the different processes, free of theoretical presuppositions about the causal dominance of factors within social processes thought of as more fundamental than factors within the power process. Moreover, in moving from his more "elemental" social forces to "facts of law" dependent on them, Ehrlich loses comprehensiveness of focus on the range of variables to be considered and treats a limited range of legal institutions as if they comprehended the sum of independent variables important for decisional responses. This specialization is carried further in his plea for concentration on the study of modern business documents as a means of passing to the life which surrounds them.[370]

Weber, like Ehrlich, is concerned to establish the complexity of causal pluralism within society in opposition to the Marxist insistence on the predominance of economic factors. Like Ehrlich, too, he was led eventually to concentrate his interest in the working of causal factors in society in relation to law within one specialized field, *i.e.,* in accounting for the special formal rational way of legal thinking which he found to be characteristic of the Western civilization of his time. In this enterprise he directed his mind especially to the working of what in McDougal's scheme of causal analysis are described as cultural factors. Thus, Weber found "formally rational" modes of thinking in other fields of Western capitalist civilization than the legal; for example, in the economic sphere, the operations of the capitalist which were controlled rationally by a balancing of costs and returns in which all elements, including his own entrepreneurial services, were brought to book.[371] In the rectitude area, Weber found in Protestantism the notion of accounting rationally to God.[372] Rheinstein formulates the question which Weber asks himself as follows: "Has perhaps the rise of formal rationality in legal thought contributed to the rise of capitalism or has, possibly, capitalism contributed to the rise of logical rationality in legal thought?"[373] In comparing Western with other civilizations for this purpose, Weber at least set sociologists of law an example of an examination of the causal relationships of features of the law of a society and the general value patterning of processes within that society. In the course of this examination, Weber also is led to make some animadversions on "class" factors within society, as, for example, in his proposition that the lower classes are in general the enemies of formal rationalism [374] and that the growth of the modern wealth elite has been more an effect than a cause of the formal rationality of the law.[375]

Weber's notion of a class is, indeed, narrower than McDougal's, for he treats it as a group within what McDougal would term the wealth process;[376] whereas McDougal uses the notion to refer to diverse groupings in position, potential, and expectation with respect to each of his eight value categories. Weber, on the other hand, has more or less parallel terms to refer to groupings in some of the other societal value processes such as "status groups" within the sphere of distribution of "honor"[377] and, less parallel, "parties" within the "house of power."[378] Moving from factors associated with class position to more specialized interest groups within the various processes, Weber again offers material of importance, though he does not make "interest group" a formal category designed for the systematic orientation of causal analysis, as McDougal does. Thus, Weber, for example, devotes attention to the influence of trained lawyers [379] and bureaucracies [380] on formal rationality of law. And again, "personality" factors, though not made by Weber a special category designed for regular use in systematic causal analysis, are referred to in particular to make his point that "charismatic" individuals have been social and hence legal innovators.[381] Likewise, material is sometimes offered, though not as systematically as McDougal would recommend, on the importance of the level of crisis, especially war,[382] at which the various factors are operating.

Whereas Weber concentrated on particular causal problems for their theoretical interest, Pound finds common ground with McDougal in his conception of the scientific task as part of the work of the lawyer in social engineering. Thus, Pound calls for "study of the actual social effects of legal institutions, of legal precepts, and of legal doctrines,"[383] that is, study of what determines how judges, lawmakers, and jurists actually develop legal materials as grounds of decision,[384] what social effects the doctrines of law have produced and how they have produced them,[385] and how or how far the law of the past grew out of social, economic, and psychological conditions.[386] Pound calls in all this material for a multifactor analysis, giving therefore only guarded approval to the findings of religious and ethical interpretations of history,[387] and criticizing the findings of political, geographical, ethnological,[388] and economic [389] interpretations of legal history. However, he refrains generally from criticism of the "civilization interpretation"[390] of legal history, and this prepares us for the emphasis he places on general cultural factors and a corresponding lack of emphasis on conflicts arising out of class, interest group, and personality factors in relation to the general resource environment. We have noticed Pound's attempts to characterize a whole "civilization era" by a single concise expression [391] and that his "jural postulates," which are given something of the character of prime movers at any given time, are very general.[392] Pound sometimes rather readily dismisses the importance of class and interest group factors, as when he supposes that judicial ideals and techniques counteract any subservience to their group interest. He believes the same cannot be said of juries,[393] but that the ideal of a profession as a public service does protect the legal profession.

The Task of Projecting the Future Course of Decison

By the projection task, McDougal understands the extrapolation of the future course of decision in its social context on the assumption that there will be no effective intervention by the inquiring scholar. As with the other tasks, he gives attention to the formulation of appropriate methods for such projection and to the correlation of the performance of this task with the others in the general scheme of scholarly inquiry he recommends. Under the former head he emphasizes the usefulness of developmental constructs, in the sense of hypotheses that characterize the most salient features of a selected cross-section of past and possible future events, and of taking into account maximum and minimum estimates respecting any category of event. Under the latter head, priority is recommended to the projection of categories most or least in harmony with the overriding goal, to organization of trend projection in terms of appropriate categories for examination, to emphasis on conditioning factors which have had the greatest impact on responses, and to emphasis on projecting policies which have had the greatest success in the past in conditions similar to those projected for the future.[394]

Kelsen considers it largely impossible to predict the activities of the legislative body, in respect to the vast number of matters which are left undetermined by the constitution, and the activities of a court, in respect of matters which are largely undetermined by existing norms.[395] Ross' concern to understand rules as related to ordinary experience leads him to treat the statement of rule as itself a prediction. The "real content" of such a statement is for him a prediction about what will figure in judicial opinions subject to the supposition that an action will be brought on which the rule has bearing and that in the meantime there has been no alteration in the law, that is, in the circumstances which are understood to condition the assertion that the rule is valid law.[396] Also by contrast to Kelsen, Ross, as a legal politician as distinct from a doctrinal student of law, is prepared to encourage prediction on a comprehensive scale.[397] Nevertheless, the limited doctrinal prediction task is given priority only to show, from McDougal's viewpoint, that the narrow task cannot be realistically carried on independently.

Hart's main concern from his own positivist approach is to establish that Ross is wrong in thinking that statements about legal rules can be *adequately* described as predictions.[398] He nevertheless believes rules can be used as a basis for prediction, though the satisfactoriness of this basis is limited by *inter alia,* a phenomenon of language that Hart discovers: the terms of legal rules are open textured. Thus, "when the area of open texture is reached, very often all we can profitably offer in answer to the question: 'What is the law on this matter?' is a guarded prediction of what the courts will do."[399] But because Hart is occupied with the task of demonstrating that we are not always or even generally left in this position,[400] he does not at this point give extensive attention to the question by what means the prediction to which he refers may be arrived at, or to broader questions of prediction of decisions other than the judicial.

Fuller, concerning himself primarily with the prediction of judicial decisions, emphasizes the application of the sense of justice in the context of the rules as the only effective method, for attention to the reasons which are assumed will actuate the court will bring us immediately to an examination of the ethical foundations of the relevant rules.[401] Unless we have good grounds for assuming that some irrational or personal consideration will intrude upon the case, he considers it essential to assure the dependability of our prediction that we should entertain the presumption that the demands of justice will be met.[402] From McDougal's viewpoint, this sets up a false contrast, since McDougal does not regard decisions in conflict with goals which the inquirer might think reflect justice as necessarily either irrational or personal. His maximization postulate assumes that they will have some degree of rationality in relation to some goals of the subject of inquiry at some level of consciousness, goals which may be goals related to the individual's personality or to his interest group, class, or culture.

The work of the earlier twentieth-century sociologists of law reflects the same kind of assumption in Fuller's work that the future development of the law in its context will represent an evolving justice, the contrast lying in the greater emphasis on the social or economic character of the forces determining the direction of events as contrasted with the character of man.[403] In general, little attempt is made at this stage to develop sophisticated techniques of projection. Renner's work reflects the assumption of Marxist philosophy in the manner developed below, and Ehrlich is disposed to defer detailed analysis of the future pending fuller scientific knowledge: "meanwhile our sense of justice is merely one of those great indefinite divinings of hidden interrelations in the vast scheme of things, which, like religion, ethics and perhaps art, lead mankind to distant unknown goals."[404]

Weber stands apart in that he seeks to bring the analysis of the many factors he has explored in performing the scientific task to bear on the prediction of the kinds of future legal responses in which he is especially interested, the movements toward or away from formal rationality in the law. Among antiformal factors, he lists the demands of special "classes," such as the merchants, for the replacement of technical with freer procedures by special tribunals,[405] for freer evaluation of proof,[406] and for substantive rules giving effect to the requirement of trust and confidence in business.[407] Anticommercial interests, such as labor, he sees demanding a "social law" based upon "such emotionally colored ethical postulates as justice or human dignity."[408] Among more special groups, he notes that lawyers have attacked the "slot-machine" theory of law, partly in a bid for the increased power which free evaluation would give them.[409] He does not, however, expect these tendencies to overcome the well-nigh universal attitude of judges throughout history that they are mouthpieces of norms.[410] Thus, in the end, he believes that "inevitably the notion must expand that law is a rational technical apparatus, which is continually transformable in the light of expediential considerations, and devoid of all sacredness of content."[411] Weber's work in this respect may be regarded from McDougal's viewpoint as an exercise in the employment of one appropriate method of arriving at a projection, by utilizing a factor analysis, while at the same time the unreliability of the conclusion points to the need for supplementary techniques. There would be widespread agreement that, since Weber wrote, judicial procedures have been affected by demands for freer processes of reasoning which pay greater regard to substantive values.[412]

Pound, on the other hand, believes that the judicial system is and can be expected to be far more value rational, in Weber's terminology, than Weber credits. Pound deprecates the attempt to predict future judicial decisions by resort to rules because he believes judges will respond to the fact that "the circumstances of social life change continually and unforeseen and unpredictable situations arise continually and call for reshaping and readjustment and new applications of legal precepts."[413] Pound at least raises the question of whether, as an alternative approach to prediction, we might not attempt to project the shape of a future "civilization era" and work out its detailed implications from its "jural postulates" on which decisions could be expected to be based.[414] This conception recognizes that, if we are to think in terms of a marriage of law and the social sciences, then, as McDougal would claim, we must be ambitious enough to aim at projecting a *total* social context—a future course of society—and a future course of decision within it. Pound appears to have been deterred from immediate detailed implementation of such a project, however, by theoretical assumptions of a Hegelian kind about the general way in which a society develops, that periods of integration are succeeded by periods of transition or disintegration preceding a new period of integration. Regarding the present era as one of transition, Pound says that "jural postulates of an era of transition are not readily discovered and I have not tried to formulate them" and "until the change to a distinct civilization era is complete, formulation could hardly be profitable."[415] We have seen that in his focus on the next "civilization era," Pound appears to base his fore-cast of its character on the Hegelian assumption that it will represent a higher synthesis, a more rational development, of characteristics of the previous stable civilization era.[416] From McDougal's viewpoint, this is illustrative of the hindrance offered by suppositions of deeper unifying forces for society behind the causal complexity which we observe, em-pirically, to the effective carrying out of intellectual tasks.

The Invention and Evaluation of Policy Alternatives for Community Decision

This is the culminating intellectual task which McDougal recom-mends for the legal scholar. A scholar may inquire into his own goals for community decision (having regard to the widest purview he can undertake of the total social context and of the correlation of other tasks with it), may make the broadest study of past trends in decisions (with all available tech-niques), may analyze conditioning factors operative on a similar basis, may project future decisions by applying all techniques available to those trend studies and the conditioning factors discovered, and may arrive at preferred policies in light of all these considerations. The aim is to evolve particular strategies for the maximization of goal values organized in a unified pattern of such strategies.[417] Since policies must be invented before they may be evaluated, attention is given to what means of encouragement of inventiveness can be utilized by the scholar.[418] In the evaluation of a policy alternative, emphasis is placed on specifying alternatives through all the phases of the processes in which its working out would be involved,[419] having regard to the results of the performance of the other intellectual tasks, and utilizing available techniques for bringing these results to bear.[420]

The policy task is altogether beyond the field of Kelsen's normative jurisprudence. Hart's major relevant thesis, that the need for judicial policymaking has been overemphasized, and his notion of law "in a cen-trally important sense" are designed to emphasize that the judge's task is mainly to apply provisions applying clearly to the circumstances before him.[421] Hart is indeed concerned additionally, as we have seen, with the task of criticism of law in terms of morality [422] and justice, which latter he views as a segment of morality.[423] Hart says, however, that "it is folly to believe that where the meaning of law is in doubt morality always has a clear answer to offer."[424] No doubt he would make the same point where he conceives the law to be clear and the question is whether it is in ac-cordance with the dictates of morality. Hart does not seem to offer a sys-tematic program for dealing with policy questions where morality, on his different view of it from that of the pioneer positivists, does not provide a solution.

Ross approaches the policy task at the third stage of his program for legal political inquiry. The first stage is the discussion of the emotional premises (that is, from Ross' viewpoint, the values of the influential groups to which the legal politician undertakes to give advice).[425] The second stage is the description of the relevant social facts and the social causal correlations operative. And the third stage is the formulation of conclusions in the form of instructions to the legislator or judge.[426] Ross stresses that he is recommending that the legal politician undertake this third task in spite of the fact that is involves making an irrational jump involving a personal decision (which is perhaps caused by, but does not follow from, argumentation made to support it) and the weighing of different, mutually incommensurable considerations.[427] He criticizes McDougal for failing to see that the integration of these considerations "is an irrational act beyond the realm of science."[428] In part, Ross' criticism appears to rest on an attribution to McDougal of a view of the policy task which he does not hold. Strictly, its performance, in McDougal's terms, does not issue in "instructions." It issues in the form of propositions that the adoption of one specified alternative set of courses of action would move events closer to specified goals which the inquirer reports to be his own—future hypothetical empirical events—than would other specified alternatives at the focus of attention. But Ross would certainly consider that even this kind of assertion cannot "logically" be made because of the absence of any possible criterion of "closeness" where multiple considerations are involved. However, this obviously must depend upon the degree of particularity with which the goals are specified, and McDougal has undertaken the continuing task of the required specification within the framework of human dignity by continuing interrelated performance of the intellectual tasks.

Fuller's approach to the policy task concentrates upon those questions which can be related to the morality of the law enterprise. Thus, in the policy field, one of his main recommendations is that we occupy ourselves with the problems of "institutional design" for our time, with questions of how far we are to rely in differing circumstances on various principles of order.[429] In one major work, his argument terminates with pleas for avoidance of the overuse of legislative fiat and overresort to adjudication.[430] A related set of central policy considerations concerns the degree to which laws must be clearly expressed in general terms that are prospective in effect and made known to citizens,[431] and to what extent one can safely leave things to the emergence of standards by a case-to-case treatment.[432] In all the formulations of problems, there is a contrast with McDougal's emphasis on the relation of the policy task to the substantive goals of the inquirer. Fuller's different approach in terms of goals to be attributed to the law enterprise leads instead to an occupation with problems of the form of legal regulation.

For Renner, society in our time exhibits contradictions between the legal system and the economic substructure, shown in the frictions arising out of the capitalist appropriation of the surplus value of labor through the institutions of property and contract. But it is moving toward a new period of conformity between legal system and substructure through society's adaptation of legal institutions which previously served to complement and buttress property. Renner conceives that if his analysis is right "our only problem would be to burst the shell which still obstructs the new development; to set free the complementary and supplementary institutions and to use them straightforwardly in accordance with their present and real functions."[433] To McDougal, Renner's representation of the problem oversimplifies it. It seeks, on the basis of Hegelian assumptions about the law of social development, to solve all problems of social engineering on the basis of encouraging some current trends in the power and wealth processes. For McDougal the problem is to estimate current trends in all eight value processes he recognizes, and to perform all the other intellectual tasks before reaching final conclusions.

Ehrlich, like Renner, sees the policy task within the limits of functions of lawmaking, rendering it a handmaiden to all powerful environmental influences but with a focus on those social forces as diffuse as Renner's is specialized. Ehrlich believes the content of the legal proposition often is given by society and the jurist's task is merely to give it form; where this is not so, the jurist's task is to observe the trends of justice.[434] Within these limits, Ehrlich gives encouragement to the performance of the policy task and regards it as creative; but unlike McDougal, he believes that this creativity is best encouraged by leaving the development of methods to the individual investigator.[435] There are, thus, no detailed recommendations for its implementation.

Weber, who in view of his interest in method might effectively have supplied the omission in the armory of the social scientist, necessarily refrains from outlining what is involved in the policy task for the professor as such, for the reasons which induced him as a professor to refrain from stating his goals.[436] On the other hand, it is precisely what is involved in the performance of the policy task for the enlightenment-oriented scholar which constitutes McDougal's major emphasis in jurisprudence.

Pound's work exhibits both a lively sense of the importance of the policy task and a lively appreciation of its theoretical complexity. He attributes his tolerance of different schools of jurisprudence in part to his desire that the insights of every avenue of inquiry be available to "aid the legislator or judge toward the maintaining, furthering and transmitting of civilization." [437] He thinks of "analysis, history and philosophy as giving us, as one might say, important pieces of apparatus for making the legal order an effective agency of social control." [438] Yet, we should argue, in the light of criticisms made under the previous headings, Pound's work falls short of devising a system within which these various pieces of apparatus could be utilized. From McDougal's viewpoint a synthesis of the thought of the schools is bound to do so, having regard particularly to the extent to which the organization of scholarly legal thinking has amounted to polishing apparatus designed not for scholarly, but for professional, purposes. For McDougal, the culmination of Pound's major work in an extensive review of the system of law under positivist categories, even though with some sociological color, is a commentary on this. The contrast between this culmination of Pound's work and that of McDougal's in the delineation of the policy task serves to emphasize the continuing contribution to be made, despite all the contributions of the major figures of twentieth-century jurisprudence with which we have compared McDougal's views, by a jurisprudence which is consistently policy oriented. Pound, more than any other Anglo-American jurist, alerted us to the extent to which questions of policy are involved in legal contexts and taught us to focus on policy issues. What McDougal has done in general and particular contexts is to elaborate and demonstrate the sternness of the discipline of thought required if our recognition of the overriding importance of policy considerations is to be translated into inquiry of a systematic scholarly character.

Notes

1. I. KANT, CRITIQUE OF PURE REASON 91 (J. M. D. Meiklejohn transl. 1943):

> Now the question is, whether there do not exist *a priori* in the mind, conceptions of understanding also, as conditions under which alone something, if not intuited, is yet thought as an object. If this question be answered in the affirmative, it follows that all empirical cognition of objects is necessarily conformable to such conceptions, since, if they are not presupposed, it is impossible that anything can be an object of experience. . . . The whole aim of the transcendental deduction of all *a priori* conceptions is to show that these conceptions are *a priori* conditions of the possibility of all experience. Conceptions which afford us the objective foundation of the possibility of experience are for that very reason necessary.

2. The term "thought of McDougal" is here and elsewhere in this chapter used to refer to views to which McDougal subscribes and expresses. It is not intended to raise any question about whether McDougal, Harold Lasswell, other associates, or some earlier thinker thought of something first. Since McDougal has sought to make the formulation of a policy-oriented legal theory a cooperative effort of a number of associates and is committed to the widest possible shaping and sharing of values and, in particular, to the value of enlightenment, the question to what thinker a particular item of knowlegde might be allocated can be of no interest to him. Insofar as a comparison of McDougal's views with those of others is entered upon in this chapter, it is purely for the purpose of assisting clarity in regard to their subject matter and the formulation of appropriate theory.

3. For the distinction between formulations *about* and formulations *of* a given legal system, see Lasswell & McDougal, *Jurisprudence in Policy-Oriented Perspective,* 19 U. FLA. L. REV. 486 (1966–67).

4. > From a therapeutic perspective the proper role of systematic jurisprudence is to discover and disestablish the contradictions, confusions, errors and omissions of unsystematic conceptions of law. More comprehensively expressed, the constructive role of systematic jurisprudence is to delimit the frame of reference appropriate to the study of law, and to specifv

detail the intellectual tasks whereby the opportunities presented by the proper focus of inquiry can be seized. (*Id*. at 488.)

5. *See* Hart's account of some theoretical uses of definition:

[T]hough theory is to be welcomed, the growth of theory on the back of definition is not. Theories so grown, indeed represent valuable efforts to account for many puzzling things in law; and among these is the great anomaly of legal language—our inability to define its crucial words in terms of ordinary factual counterparts. But here I think they largely fail because their method of attack commits them all, in spite of their mutual hostility, to a form of answer that can only distort the distinctive characteristics of legal language. Hart, *Definition and Theory in Jurisprudence,* 70 LAW Q. REV. 37, 41 (1954).

6. The formation of cults is, of course, common in academic jurisprudence as well as among professional lawyers. Some students of McDougal perhaps show a tendency in this direction. This is probably associated with the special language, despite McDougal's insistence on the need to maintain a sense of balance about this. He says that "if confusions are to be kept at a minimum the prophylaxis is not the adoption of esoteric vocabularies (or, on the other hand, timidity in introducing new terms in order to sharpen distinctions which are dimly perceived in ordinary usage)." He goes on to argue that the appropriate strategy is to propagate intellectual skill. Lasswell & McDougal, *supra* note 3, at 487. Nevertheless the language offers a set of externals of the system which can be adopted by those in search of quick dividends on their intellectual investment without necessarily mastering either the language or the system.

7. The full significance of these recommendations does not of course become clear until an account is given of those aspects of McDougal's thought to which reference is involved in describing the recommended role. A further recommendation McDougal makes is that a scholar in systematically studying a topic should work back from completing the intellectual tasks in relation to it to reviewing his focus of attention and his observational standpoint, indeed that there should be a relatively continuous back-and-forth process in the development of the thought.

8. Thus, for example, Alf Ross begins his account of the nature of law with a "brief linguistic digression" in which utterances generally are classified. A. ROSS, ON LAW AND JUSTICE 6–8 (1958).

9. *Id*. at 11.

10. *See* Lasswell & McDougal, *supra* note 3.

11. A. ROSS, *supra* note 8, at 9.

12. Indeed, elsewhere Ross describes the typical content of doctrinal works as consisting not only of (1) cognitive assertions concerning valid law of a greater or lesser degree of probability, but also of (2) noncognitive directives and (3) cognitive assertions concerning historical, economic, and social facts and circumstances which act as argument for either (1) or (2). *Id*. at 46.

13. 1 H. KELSEN, GENERAL THEORY OF LAW AND STATE 116 (20th Century Legal Philosophy Series, 1961).

14. *Id*.

15. *Id*. at 188.

16. H.L.A. HART, THE CONCEPT OF LAW at vii (1961).

17. *See id*. at 98–99.

18. *Id*. at 86–87.

19. L. FULLER, LAW IN QUEST OF ITSELF 2 (1940).

20. L. FULLER, THE MORALITY OF LAW 106–07 (1964).

21. *Id*.

22. The character of Fuller's approach to questions of establishing an observational standpoint, and its fostering of what McDougal would see as confusion, are both

illustrated by the judgment of Fuller's alter ego, Foster, J., in the fictitious "Case of the Contract Signed on Book Day," in THE PROBLEMS OF JURISPRUDENCE 71 (L. Fuller ed. 1949). In it, the judges of Newgarth, directed by the relevant conflicts rule of their jurisdiction to apply the law of Outerclime, find that law to be unsettled on the vital point. Foster, J., proposes to discover the law of Outerclime by determining what justice requires on the matter. So long as that system of rules is stirred by a yearning for justice, says Foster, J., it will be a system that excludes from participation in its building no man who can contribute fresh insight and wisdom toward the achievement of its goals. While Foster, J., expresses his awareness that he holds no commission from the Republic of Outerclime, he rejects the view that the most offhand indication of the meaning of a law by one of Outerclime's officials has more weight than the considered judgment of scholars and philosophers. *Id.* at 89. This deemphasis of the importance of observational standpoints seems to expose itself to all the criticisms of Fuller's general position made in the text.

23. M. WEBER, MAX WEBER ON LAW IN ECONOMY AND SOCIETY 11 (M. Rheinstein ed., E. Shils & M. Rheinstein transls. 1954), *transl. from* M. WEBER, WIRTSCHAFT UND GESELLSCHAFT (1925).

24. *Id.* at 320.

25. K. RENNER, THE INSTITUTIONS OF PRIVATE LAW AND THEIR SOCIAL FUNCTIONS 55 (O. Kahn-Freund ed. 1949).

26. E. EHRLICH, FUNDAMENTAL PRINCIPLES OF THE SOCIOLOGY OF LAW 364 (1936).

27. *Id.* at 340.

28. 1 R. POUND, JURISPRUDENCE 286–87 (1959).

29. *See* R. POUND, OUTLINE OF LECTURES ON JURISPRUDENCE 104 (5th ed. 1943).

30. 1 R. POUND, *supra* note 28, at 32.

31. *Id.* at 37.

32. *Id.* at 51.

33. 2 R. POUND, *supra* note 28, at 129.

34. *Id.*

35. K. LLEWELLYN, THE COMMON LAW TRADITION 6 (1960).

36. *Id.* at 516.

37. K. LLEWELLYN & E. HOEBEL, THE CHEYENNE WAY (1941).

38. Llewellyn, *The Normative, the Legal and the Law Jobs: The Problem of Juristic Method,* 49 YALE L.J. 1355, 1356 (1940).

39. Bingham, *What Is the Law?,* 11 MICH. L. REV. 1 (1912–13).

40. Lasswell & McDougal, *supra* note 3, at 503.

41. *Id.* at 505.

42. *Id.* at 502.

43. *Id.* at 502–03.

44. *Id.* at 503.

45. *Id.* at 502, 505.

46. *Id.* at 502.

47. *Id.*

48. A. ROSS, *supra* note 8, at 19.

49. *Id.*

50. *Id.*

51. *Id.* at 39.

52. *Id.* at 40.

53. *Id.* at 29.

54. *Id.* at 36.

55. *Id.* at 43.

56. *Id.* at 44.
57. *Id.* at 83.
58. *Id.*
59. H. KELSEN, *supra* note 13, at 18–19.
60. *Id.* at 40.
61. *Id.* at 35.
62. *Id.* at 36–37.
63. *Id.* at 408–09.
64. *Id.* at 409–10.
65. Lasswell & McDougal, *supra* note 3, at 502.
66. H.L.A. HART, *supra* note 16, at 96.
67. Hart, *Scandinavian Realism,* 1959 CAMB. L. J. 233, 238.
68. H.L.A. HART, *supra* note 16, at 56.
69. L. FULLER, *supra* note 20, at 106.
70. *Id.*
71. L. FULLER, *supra* note 19, at 3.
72. *Id.*
73. L. FULLER, *supra* note 20, at 155. *See also id.* at ch. 2.
74. L. FULLER, *supra* note 19, at 56.
75. *Id.* at 56–57.
76. *Id.* at 57.
77. As to McDougal's concept of operations see Lasswell & McDougal, *supra* note 3, at 502.
78. M. WEBER, *supra* note 23, at 320.
79. M. WEBER, THE METHODOLOGY OF THE SOCIAL SCIENCES 42–43 (E. Shils & H. Finch transls. & eds. 1949).
80. *See* Rheinstein, *Introduction* to M. WEBER, *supra* note 23, at xxix–xxxii; M. WEBER, FROM MAX WEBER: ESSAYS IN SOCIOLOGY 62 (H. Gerth & C. Mills transls. & eds. 1948) [hereinafter cited as ESSAYS IN SOCIOLOGY].
81. *See* Rheinstein, *supra* note 80, at 1.
82. E. EHRLICH, *supra* note 26, at 367 (1962).
83. *Id.*
84. *Id.* at 38, 348, 450.
85. *Id.* at 401.
86. *Id.* at 38.
87. *Id.* at 39.
88. *Id.* at 449.
89. 1 R. POUND, *supra* note 28, at 12–15.
90. *Id.* at 12.
91. *See* pp. 33–34 *infra.*
92. Lasswell & McDougal, *supra* note 3, at 502.
93. *Id.* at 504–05.
94. *Id.* at 503.
95. *Id.* at 504.
96. H. KELSEN, *supra* note 13, at 383.
97. *Id.* at 118–20.
98. *Id.* at 119.
99. *Id.* at 62.

100. *Id.* at 112.
101. *Id.* at 436.
102. *Id.* at 164.
103. A. Ross, *supra* note 8, at 56 .
104. For a summary account by Ross of his view of a national law system see *id.* at 32–34.
105. H.L.A. HART, *supra* note 16, at 113.
106. *See id.* at 20, 95–96.
107. *Id.* at 96.
108. *Id.* at 56.
109. *Id.* at 99.
110. Hart, *supra* note 67, at 237.
111. H.L.A. HART, *supra* note 16, at 98.
112. *Id.* at 99.
113. *Id.* at 100.
114. *Id.*
115. *Id.*
116. *Id.* at 104.
117. *Id.* at 108.
118. *Id.*
119. *See* Fuller, *Positivism and Fidelity to Law—A Reply to Professor Hart,* 71 HARV. L. REV. 630, 639 (1958).
120. L. FULLER, *supra* note 20, at 141.
121. L. FULLER, *supra* note 19, at 75.
122. L. FULLER, *supra* note 20, at 146.
123. *See id.* at 41–44.
124. *See id.* at 39–41.
125. E. EHRLICH, *supra* note 26, at 9.
126. *Id.*
127. *Id.* at 36.
128. *Id.*
129. *Id.* at 165.
130. *Id.* at 449.
131. *Id.* at 197; *cf. id.* at 364.
132. *Id.* at 153.
133. *Id.* at 202–03.
134. *Id.* at 204.
135. *Id.* at 207.
136. *Id.* at 211.
137. Lasswell & McDougal, *supra* note 3, at 504.
138. E. EHRLICH, *supra* note 26, at 373.
139. M. WEBER, *supra* note 79, at 3.
140. M. WEBER, *supra* note 23, at 328.
141. *Id.* at 324.
142. *Id.* at 336.
143. *Id.* at 336–37.
144. ESSAYS IN SOCIOLOGY, *supra* note 80, at 79.
145. M. WEBER, *supra* note 23, at 5.

146. *Id.* at 320.
147. *Id.* at 13; ESSAYS IN SOCIOLOGY, *supra* note 80, at 299.
148. 2 R. POUND, *supra* note 28, at 163.
149. *Id.* at 289.
150. *Id.* at 311.
151. *Id.* at 290.
152. *Id.* at 315–16.
153. *Id.* at 295.
154. 1 R. POUND, *supra* note 28, at 147–48.
155. 3 R. POUND, *supra* note 28, at 334.
156. 1 R. POUND, *supra* note 28, at 366.
157. *Id.* at 406.
158. *Id.*
159. *Id.* at 421.
160. *Id.* at 427.
161. *Id.* at 431–32.
162. *Id.* at 432.
163. *Id.* at 544.
164. Lasswell & McDougal, *supra* note 3, at 505.
165. H. KELSEN, *supra* note 13, at 132–33.
166. Lasswell & McDougal, *supra* note 3, at 505.
167. Hart, *Kelsen Visited,* 10 U.C.L.A. L. REV. 709, 727 (1963).
168. Hart, *Positivism and the Separation of Law and Morals,* 71 HARV. L. REV. 593, 620 (1958).
169. Hart, *supra* note 167, at 726.
170. L. FULLER, *supra* note 20, at 113.
171. *Id.* at 106.
172. THE PROBLEMS OF JURISPRUDENCE, *supra* note 22, at 82.
173. K. RENNER, *supra* note 25.
174. *See* Rheinstein, *supra* note 80.
175. M. WEBER, *supra* note 23, at 59.
176. *Id.*
177. E. EHRLICH, *supra* note 26, at 341, 343, 345.
178. 1 R. POUND, *supra* note 28, at 338–39.
179. 2 R. POUND, *supra* note 28, at 104–05.
180. *Id.* at 105.
181. *Id.*
182. Pound's italics.
183. 4 R. POUND, *supra* note 28, at 5–6.
184. Lasswell & McDougal, *supra* note 3, at 505–06.
185. *Id.* at 506.
186. H. KELSEN, *supra* note 13, at 261.
187. A. ROSS, *supra* note 8, at 77.
188. *Id.* at 103.
189. *Id.* at paragraph 84 contains relevant material from the latter point of view.
190. H.L.A. HART, *supra* note 16, at vii (*quoting* Professor J. L. Austin).
191. L. FULLER, *supra* note 20, at 29.
192. Lasswell & McDougal, *supra* note 3, at 506.
193. *Id.*

194. L. FULLER, *supra* note 20, at 118.
195. *Id.* at 119.
196. *Id.* at 120.
197. *Id.* at 17.
198. *Id.* at 18.
199. *Id.* at 17.
200. *Id.*
201. *Id.* at 16.
202. *Id.* at 24.
203. K. RENNER, *supra* note 25, at 54.
204. *Id.* at 229.
205. *Id.*
206. *Id.* at 296.
207. E. EHRLICH, *supra* note 26, at xv.
208. *Id.* at 115.
209. *Id* at 213.
210. *See* pp. 25–27 *supra*.
211. M. WEBER, *supra* note 23, at 35.
212. ESSAYS IN SOCIOLOGY, *supra* note 80, at 55.
213. M. WEBER, *supra* note 79, at 76.
214. *Id.* at 81.
215. *Id.* at 84.
216. Lasswell & McDougal, *supra* note 3, at 506.
217. *See* M. WEBER, *supra* note 79, at 84, 110–11.
218. *Id.* at 3.
219. *See* pp. 33–34 *supra*.
220. 3 R. POUND, *supra* note 28, at 15.
221. 1 R. POUND, *supra* note 28, at 136.
222. *See id.* at 433; 2 R. POUND, *supra* note 28, at 341.
223. 3 R. POUND, *supra* note 28, at 5–6.
224. *Id.* at 23–24.
225. *Id.* at 329.
226. *Id.* at 291.
227. *Id.*
228. *Id.* at 292.
229. *Id.*
230. *Id.* at 292–93.
231. McDougal, *The Comparative Study of Law for Policy Purposes: Value Clarification as an Instrument of Democratic World Order*, 61 YALE L.J. 915, 916 (1952).
232. 3 R. POUND, *supra* note 28, at 316.
233. *Id.*
234. *Id.* at 321.
235. *See* pp. 39–40 *supra*.
236. 3 R. POUND, *supra* note 28, at 296.
237. *Id.*
238. *Id.* at 299.
239. *Id.* at 301.
240. *Id.* at 302.
241. *Id.* at 305.

242. *Id.* at 307.
243. *Id.* at 311.
244. *Id.* at 28.
245. *Id.* at 221.
246. *Id.* at 33.
247. Lasswell & McDougal, *supra* note 3, at 506.
248. *Id.* at 506–07.
249. *Id.* at 507.
250. A. Ross, *supra* note 8, at 59.
251. *Id.* at 60.
252. Lasswell & McDougal, *supra* note 3, at 507.
253. H. Kelsen, *supra* note 13, at 328.
254. *Id.* at 339.
255. *Id.* at 341.
256. *Id.*
257. *Id.* at 373.
258. *Id.* at 369.
259. *Id.* at 386–87.
260. Lasswell & McDougal, *supra* note 3, at 504.
261. H.L.A. Hart, *supra* note 16, at 269.
262. *Id.* at 230–31.
263. *Id.* at 229.
264. *Id.* at 223.
265. *Id.* at 222–23.
266. The Problems of Jurisprudence, *supra* note 22, at 712.
267. *Id.*
268. E. Ehrlich, *supra* note 26, at 44.
269. *Id.* at 81.
270. *Id.* at 82.
271. M. Weber, *supra* note 23, at 6.
272. 1 R. Pound, *supra* note 28, at 457.
273. R. Pound, A World Legal Order: Law and Laws in Relation to World Law 23 (1959).
274. *Id.* at 37.
275. *See* pp. 33–34 *supra.*
276. R. Pound, *supra* note 273, at 38.
277. *Id.*
278. *Id.* at 17.
279. *Id.*
280. 1 R. Pound, *supra* note 28, at 487–88.
281. Pound, *Philosophical Theory and International Law,* 1 Bibliotheca Visseriana 73, 83–84 (1923).
282. *Id.* at 89.
283. R. Pound, *supra* note 273, at 13.
284. *Id.* at 17.
285. Lasswell & McDougal, *supra* note 3, at 508.
286. *Id.*
287. *Id.*
288. *Id.* at 508–09.
289. A. Ross, *supra* note 8, at 377.

290. H. KELSEN, *supra* note 13, at 7.

291. *Id.* at 163.

292. Hart, *supra* note 168, at 597.

293. H.L.A. HART, *supra* note 16, at 162–63.

294. *See, e.g., id.* at 164–65.

295. *Id.* at 164.

296. *Id.* at 170.

297. *Id.* at 177.

298. *Id.* at 177–78.

299. *Id.* at 179.

300. *Id* .at 201.

301. Fuller, *American Legal Philosophy at Mid-Century,* 6 J. LEGAL ED. 457, 479 (1953–54).

302. L. FULLER, *supra* note 20, at 9.

303. *Id.* at 5.

304. *Id.* at 9.

305. L. FULLER, *supra* note 19, at 3.

306. L. FULLER, *supra* note 20, at 102.

307. THE PROBLEMS OF JURISPRUDENCE, *supra* note 22, at 694.

308. *Id.* at 699.

309. L. FULLER, *supra* note 20, at 11.

310. *Id.*

311. *See* p. 37 *supra.*

312. E. EHRLICH, *supra* note 26, at 246, 318.

313. *Id.* at 120.

314. *Id.* at 202.

315. *Id.* at 204.

316. *Id.* at 211.

317. *Id.* at 243.

318. *Id.* at 401.

319. *Id.* at 402.

320. M. WEBER, *supra* note 79, at 3, 59–60.

321. M. WEBER, *supra* note 23, at xxxviii.

322. M. WEBER, *supra* note 79, at 8.

323. *Id.* at 59.

324. *Id.* at 111.

325. *Id.* at 54.

326. *See* p. 26 *supra.*

327. *See* p. 30 *supra.*

328. 1 R. POUND, *supra* note 28, at 191, referring to Pound, *How Far Are We Attaining a New Measure of Values in Twentieth-Century Juristic Thought?,* 42 W. VA. L.Q. 81 (1936).

329. 1 R. POUND, *supra* note 28, at 543.

330. *See* pp. 39–40 *supra.*

331. 3 R. POUND, *supra* note 28, at 8.

332. Lasswell & McDougal, *supra* note 3, at 509–10.

333. A. ROSS, *supra* note 8, at 41.

334. *Id.* at 356–57.

335. H. KELSEN, *supra* note 13, at 116.

336. *See* p. 22 *supra.*

337. H.L.A. HART, *supra* note 16, at 134.

338. *See* pp. 22–24 *supra*.

339. *See* p. 25 *supra*.

340. L. FULLER, REASON AND FIAT IN CASE LAW 10 (1942) (reprinted in 59 HARV. L. REV. 376 (1946)).

341. E. EHRLICH, *supra* note 26, at 319.

342. M. WEBER, *supra* note 79, at 76.

343. *Id.* at 159.

344. *Id.* at 78, 151.

345. *See* pp. 52–53 *supra*.

346. Lasswell & McDougal, *supra* note 3, at 510–11.

347. H. KELSEN, *supra* note 13, at 163–64.

348. *Id.* at 174.

349. *See* p. 34 *supra*.

350. A. ROSS, *supra* note 8, at 328.

351. *See* pp. 48–49 *supra*.

352. Hart, *supra* note 168, at 607–08.

353. *Id.* at 607.

354. H.L.A. HART, *supra* note 16, at 189.

355. *Id.* at 190.

356. Fuller, *supra* note 301, at 476.

357. *Id.* at 477.

358. *Id.* at 475.

359. *Id.* at 481.

360. L. FULLER, *supra* note 172, at 725.

361. *Id.* at 729.

362. *Id.* at 733.

363. K. RENNER, *supra* note 25, at 69.

364. *See, e.g., id.* at 252.

365. E. EHRLICH, *supra* note 26, at 447.

366. *Id.* at 410.

367. *Id.* at 373.

368. *Id.* at 85.

369. *Id.* at 86.

370. *Id.* at 496.

371. ESSAYS IN SOCIOLOGY, *supra* note 80, at 68.

372. *Id.* at 332–33.

373. M. WEBER, *supra* note 23, at 1.

374. ESSAYS IN SOCIOLOGY, *supra* note 80, at 220–21.

375. M. WEBER, *supra* note 23, at 304–05.

376. ESSAYS IN SOCIOLOGY, *supra* note 80, at 181.

377. *Id.* at 194.

378. *Id.*

379. *Id.* at 85; M. WEBER, *supra* note 23, at 198.

380. ESSAYS IN SOCIOLOGY, *supra* note 80, at 216.

381. M. WEBER, *supra* note 23, at 22–23.

382. *Id.* at 91.

383. 1 R. POUND, *supra* note 28, at 351.

384. *Id.* at 353–54.

385. *Id.* at 354.

386. *Id.* at 355.

387. *Id.* at 205.

388. *Id.* at 225.

389. *Id.* at 231.

390. *Id.* at 227 and § 16.

391. *See* p. 30 *supra.*

392. *See* p. 52 *supra.*

393. 2 R. POUND, *supra* note 28, at 461.

394. Lasswell & McDougal, *supra* note 3, at 511–12.

395. H. KELSEN, *supra* note 13, at 168.

396. A. ROSS, *supra* note 8, at 41.

397. *Id.* at 355–56.

398. *See generally* Hart, *supra* note 67, at 233–40.

399. H.L.A. HART, *supra* note 16, at 143.

400. Not to McDougal's satisfaction. *See* pp. 31–32 *supra.*

401. L. FULLER, *supra* note 340, at 29.

402. L. FULLER, *supra* note 22, at 85.

403. *See* pp. 52–53 *supra.*

404. E. EHRLICH, *supra* note 26, at 27.

405. M. WEBER, *supra* note 23, at 301–03.

406. *Id.* at 305.

407. *Id.* at 306–07.

408. *Id.* at 308.

409. *Id.* at 309.

410. *Id.* at 320.

411. *Id.* at 321.

412. *See, e.g.,* K. LLEWELLYN, *supra* note 35, at 41, 158–59.

413. 1 R. POUND, *supra* note 28, at 97.

414. *See* p. 53 *supra.*

415. 3 R. POUND, *supra* note 28, at 14.

416. *See* p. 30 *supra.*

417. Lasswell & McDougal, *supra* note 3, at 512.

418. *Id.* at 513.

419. *Id.* at 512–13.

420. *Id.* at 513.

421. *See* pp. 8–9 *supra.*

422. *See* p. 50 *supra.*

423. H.L.A. HART, *supra* note 16, at 153.

424. *Id.* at 200.

425. A. ROSS, *supra* note 8, at 334.

426. *Id.* at 336–37.

427. *Id.* at 337.

428. *Id.* at 325, n.9.

429. L. FULLER, *supra* note 20, at 180–81.

430. *Id.* at 181.

431. *Id.* at 93–94.

432. *Id.* at 65–66.

433. K. RENNER, *supra* note 25, at 298.

434. E. EHRLICH, *supra* note 26, at 198–200, 203.
435. *Id.* at 472.
436. *See* p. 38 *supra*.
437. 1 R. POUND, *supra* note 28, at 287.
438. *Id.* at 292.

Chapter 2

Integrations of Authority and Control: Trends in the Literature of International Law and International Relations

ROSALYN HIGGINS

The notion of authority is central to international law. As Richard Falk his written: "Authority is such a fundamental coordinate of legal analysis that its treatment will be decisively shaped by an author's jurisprudential orientation."[1] Unfortunately, there is disagreement over whether lawyers are concerned only with authority, and not with power, and confusion over what "authority" and "power" mean. Indeed, the terms are sometimes used interchangeably, although the difference in meaning is crucial to our understanding of international law.

The term "authority" is used variously. To some, it is a reference to an elite or to an especially knowledgeable position within the community: thus, "he speaks with authority." At other times, "authority" is used to indicate jurisdictional competence: if a court has jurisdictional competence, its decision, it is assumed, necessarily will be authoritative. Furthermore, there is a tendency to use "authority" identically with "legally binding" in the technical sense; a Security Council decision under Article 25 of the U.N. Charter is said to be "authoritative," in contrast to a recommendation of the General Assembly.

Myres McDougal has persuasively shown that the notion of authority goes considerably beyond the passing of a binding decision in a jurisdictionally competent body. One cannot discuss authority without developing empirical references to the expectations of individuals, no matter what community is involved. McDougal writes:

> By authority is meant expectations of appropriateness in regard to the phases of effective decision processes. These expectations specifically relate to personnel appropriately endowed with decision-making power; the objectives they should pursue; the physical, temporal and institutional features of the situations in which lawful decisions are made; the value which may be used to sustain decision, and so forth. . . . Genuine expectations of authority are discerned by contextual examination of past decision as well as by utilization of all the techniques of the social sciences for assessing the current subjectivities of individuals.[2]

And as Michael Reisman has written, authority

> is a set of conditioned subjectivities shared by relevant members of a group; when operative, when tripped so to speak by outside events, these subjectivities provide the individuals concerned with an indication of appropriate behavior. Authority can be considered a significant determinant of individual or group behavior, not necessarily when it compels a certain course, but when it indicates that course with a degree of clarity sufficient to excite internal tension or psychic dysphoria if an incompatible course is followed.[3]

In the view of Myres McDougal and his associates, law must also be concerned with questions of power, or control. Control, notes Reisman, "refers to resources that can be employed to secure a desired pattern of behavior in others."[4] Tom Farer has correctly observed[5] that the insistence that law is basically the overlap between the qualities of authoritativeness and effectiveness, exhibited by decisions governing the distribution of values in a social system,[6] does not mean that there is a magical threshold which prescriptions must cross to become "legal." Rather, he notes, the point to remember is that for the McDougalites there is no brooding reality beyond those perceptions and expectations. "Law" is a reference to cases where the perceptions are fairly intense and uniform and the expectations are rather high.[7]

What people believe is the "right" way of doing things will not be followed unless it is supported by some effective power. For authority to sustain a system of law it must be sufficiently effective to sustain expectations of conforming decisions for the future. Thus, power and authority are closely related, but by no means identical, and if our putative decision-maker were to turn to scholarship for aid, he would discover that he must consult two separate and often mutually suspicious literatures: international law and international relations.

The jurisprudence of Myres McDougal and his colleagues has insisted on the need for a balanced emphasis on, and necessary integration of, authority and control. It has insisted that law meaningfully defined must take account of the dynamics of authority as well as the dynamics of power. McDougal's treatises contain formulas for integrating the disciplines of law, political science, and international relations as aids to decisionmaking and to legal scholarship.

If McDougal's writings are a constant assertion of the interplay of authority and power within the constitutive process of decisionmaking, the literature of international law and international relations does little, in the main, to support or extend this effort. Much of the recent literature continues to foster the received wisdom—imparted to generations of students —that law is concerned with authority (but not power) and that international relations is concerned with power (but not authority). Some few international lawyers, to be sure, are concerned with factors relating to power, and some international relations writers, with authority. But even so, there is remarkably little work being done, other than by McDougal and his associates (of those previously or presently identified with New Haven), positively to integrate focus on the interlocking components of authority and power.

This state of affairs itself merits investigation. It is instructive to see, in the context of concern with notions of authority and power, how the proponents of each discipline see themselves and to examine the extent to which shared perceptions across the disciplines have confirmed scholars in their view that there can be little useful cooperation between international relations and international law.

In the United States there is a greater intellectual interchange between international lawyers and international relations scholars than in the United Kingdom. The reasons are complex and to some extent interlocking and self-perpetuating. In Britain, law is an undergraduate degree. An undergraduate may take his law degree and acquire his professional qualifications without ever having taken a course in international relations. In some British universities there is cooperation between law and international relations departments, but it is ad hoc and limited.[8] American law students, on the other hand, receive a B.A. degree before proceeding to law school, and as their B.A. degree is not as specialized as the British equivalent, it has often included a course in international relations. Furthermore, it is not uncommon for American international relations departments to offer a course in international law.

Similar differences are to be found among the professional associations existing in the two countries. It is indicative of the closer natural relationship in the United States between the two disciplines that over the years such international relations specialists as Wright, Briggs, Garner, and Lasswell have all been influential in the American Society of International Law. At a meeting of a professional international law body in the United States, it is not uncommon to find representatives of related disciplines; moreover, men holding political office may participate in panels on the legal aspects of the problems with which they are concerned. Sometimes even a high political figure—perhaps the Secretary of State himself—will make a speech of broad policy interest after the concluding dinner. Comparable interchanges are unlikely in a British setting. The two disciplines rarely meet at conferences, and seldom is it assumed that the international lawyer and the international relations scholar will have much of value to say to each other. As for the high political figure, the British system of parliamentary "question time" and ministerial responsibility make functions of this sort unlikely forums for policy pronouncements on matters of substantive interest.

If the American and the British experience is not identical, however, some common considerations obtain. There is within the discipline of international relations a reluctance to assume a useful contribution from international law. The reasoning varies considerably. The majority of international relations scholars appear to regard international law as an ineffectual and irrelevant restraint—ineffectual in that states will act in accordance with their perceived national interests and irrelevant in that international law continues to enunciate rules that clearly are not applied in practice. This viewpoint is frequently expressed by nonlawyers who pride themselves on their "realism." A smaller minority regard international law, insofar as it impinges upon international relations at all, as positively harmful. George Kennan and Hans Morgenthau deplore the fettering of national discretion, while John Burton, of University College (London), believes that reference to international law distorts systemic behavior.

Many international lawyers also have reservations as to the nature of the relationship of international law with international relations. The overall importance of political power generally is acknowledged. Thereafter, as with the international relations scholars, the reasoning and motivation vary considerably. To some, international law operates only where there is no major clash with international politics, a view articulately expounded by Georg Schwarzenberger.[9] To others, international law seeks deliberately to avoid that which is "political," being a distinct discipline. The problem of the effectiveness and acceptability of rules of law is not, they believe, a task for lawyers. The most distinguished proponent of this view is Judge Sir Gerald Fitzmaurice.[10] Those who adhere to the World Rule of Law movement believe in a process which has as its goal the conversion of governments to the belief that the rule of law is in the common interest.

Each and every one of these sentiments reflects an unintegrated, indeed divergent, view of power and authority. It is this lack of integration —in contrast to McDougal's own carefully interrelated balance between power and authority—which leads to the use of such language as "rules," "restraint," "rule of law," and "power politics." These expressions, in turn, imply a perception of the conventional conception of international law.

The view that international law is a body of rules that fails to restrain states falls short on several counts. In the first place, it assumes that law is indeed "rules."[11] But the specialized social processes to which the word "law" refers include many things besides rules. Rules play a part in law, but not the only part. This outlook, to some extent supported by functionalists at Columbia University, but articulated most forcefully by the Yale Law School proponents of a policy-oriented approach to international law, I have described elsewhere:

> When, however, decisions are made by authorised persons or organs, in appropriate forums, within the framework of certain established practices and norms, then what occurs is *legal* decision-making. In other words, international law is a continuing process of authoritative decisions. This view rejects the notion of law merely as the impartial application of rules. International law is the entire decision-making process, and not just the reference to the trend of past decisions which are termed "rules." There inevitably flows from this definition a concern, especially where the trend of past decisions is not overwhelmingly clear, with policy alternatives for the future.[12]

McDougal and his associates, of course, have been particularly active in elaborating these policy alternatives.[13] If law were merely "rules," then international relations scholars in this era of change would be justified in their dismissal of the relevance of international law because international law would be unable to contribute to, and cope with, a changing political world. Rules do not change themselves. To be sure, international law has its own inbuilt methods for change (treaty revision, progressive development through the International Law Commission, codification, custom). These methods, however, are slow. Hence, to rely merely on accumulated past decisions (rules), where their context has changed and their content is unclear, is to encourage contempt among international relations scholars. (One might add that although international law is often thought of, and taught, as "rules" in England, it was not a view which Sir Hersch Lauterpacht ever supported. He rejected the notion that the judicial function was the finding of the appropriate "rule" in an impartial manner. The judge, he argued, does not "find rules"; but he "makes choices"—and choices "not between claims which are fully justified and claims which have no foundation at all but between claims which have varying degrees of legal merit."[14] Of course, the challenge is to go beyond this "legal realist" insight and to formulate principles of procedure and substance to guide those choices.)

Part of the resistance to rejecting international law as "rules" is that the choice-making to which this rejection leads necessarily involves policy considerations. This entry into the field of values, it is sometimes contended, allows the subjective preferences of the decisionmaker to be advanced under the guise of "international law." But these subjectivities already are present, no matter how much we allege that we are merely "applying the correct rule." McDougal's systematic method of inquiry provides a framework whereby choices may be made and appraised in favor of the community, rather than powerful individuals or nations whose values in this matter are not ignored. The matter is well stated by Richard Falk, who observes that a rejection of law merely as rules provides

> more obvious occasion for choice on the part of the decision-maker, and hence a greater need to ground choice upon some rational foundation that will promote the ends of men and reach a result that is regarded as authoritative. Insecurity among international lawyers has often led them to stress the technical dimension of their craft, thereby disguising the primitive social character of international law. . . . The New Haven Group carries forward the pioneering direction of inquiry initiated by such continental jurists as Huber, Schindler, and de Visscher. McDougal supplements their emphasis upon the social context of international law by working out a systematic method to bring extralegal considerations to bear upon the legal process.[15]

A very different attitude is to be found among those lawyers who insist upon international law's being kept distinct from international politics. The traditionalist school in Britain, Europe, and the old Commonwealth urges the lawyer to stick to his proper tasks and to avoid the political, to "find the correct law, and to apply it." This outlook presupposes that there is a "correct law" outside the social context to which it is to be applied. Others have replied that only the context will reveal which of several legal arguments has the most merit.[16] McDougal, however, has gone further in saying that there is no single "correct law" to be applied, but rather a series of matching pairs of complementary norms (aggression/self-defense; sovereignty/extraterritorial jurisdiction, etc.) between which the decisionmaker must make a choice in the light of the context and agreed upon objectives.[17] The distinction made by the traditionalists is between legal and nonlegal matters; into the latter category (and thus beyond the pale of the lawyer) fall political, social, humanitarian, and moral issues. The classical view, enunciated in the context of the judicial function, has been expounded by Judges Fitzmaurice and Spender in the South West Africa Cases in 1962:

> We are not unmindful of, nor are we insensible to, various considerations of a non-juridical character, social, humanitarian and other, which underlie this case: but these are matters for the political rather than the legal arena. They cannot be allowed to deflect us from our duty of reaching a conclusion strictly on the basis of what we believe to be the correct legal view.[18]

And again in 1966:

> Law exists, it is said, to serve a social need; but precisely for that reason it can do so only through and within the limits of its own discipline. Otherwise it is not a legal service that will be rendered.[19]

But these assertions beg the question for, as Wilfred Jenks has observed, they do not tell us what *does* constitute a "sufficient expression in legal form" or where *does* the law draw "the limits of its own discipline."[20] Reference to "the correct legal view" or "rules" never can avoid the element of choice (though it can disguise it), nor can it provide guidance to the preferable decision.[21] In making this choice one must inevitably have consideration for the humanitarian, moral, and social purposes of the law. Policy considerations, although they differ from "rules," are an integral part of that decisionmaking process which we call international law; the assessment of so-called extralegal considerations is *part of the legal process,* just as is reference to the accumulation of past decisions and current norms. A refusal to acknowledge political and social factors cannot keep law "neutral," for even such a refusal is not without political and social consequence. There is no avoiding the essential relationship between law and politics.

To be sure, there are international lawyers, other than McDougal and his associates, who recognize that law and politics are not to be divorced. The "classical" view is rejected by Schwarzenberger, who fully acknowledges the impact of international politics upon international law. He has developed a view of international law which is inductive, interdisciplinary, and relativist,[22] yet he, too, believes in the essential separateness of international law and international relations—of authority from power. Schwarzenberger sees law as severely hampered in its operation by the realities of power politics. Law, he argues, can operate modestly in areas where power politics do not hold sway. The lawyer should acknowledge this, says Schwarzenberger, for his function is not to promote a "cause" but to be realistic. But Schwarzenberger's assumption that "law" and "politics" are opposites is meaningful only when law is viewed as a system of restraints on effective power. Significantly, Schwarzenberger is not primarily concerned in his massive and important writings with the numerous nonrestraint functions of the law. Hence, he does not believe that systematic policy orientation should be built into the legal process, thus making a bridge to international relations.

Yet policy orientation is inescapable in the legal system, at each moment of choice, whether acknowledged or not. McDougal's great contribution has been not only to recognize this reality, but to formulate a method of inquiry to cause policy predispositions to be openly articulated, appraised, and harnessed in the common interest.

International lawyers themselves have thus contributed to the misconceived international relations view, and rejection, of international law as "rules." International relations scholars, when examining the relationship of international law to their own field of study, are also concerned that the "law of nations" establish a set of prohibitions which manifestly are ignored in "real life." This recurring perception of law as "prohibitions," or as primarily a restraint system, is the contribution of international lawyers.

Kelsen, of course, is the proponent par excellence of international law as a prohibitory set of rules, for breach of which sanctions must be applied. And while the strict application of Kelsenian doctrine [23] is not much in fashion today, there nontheless remains excessive emphasis on the central nature of sanctions. It is hard for international lawyers to break out of the intellectual straitjacket of thinking of law as a restraint system. As with the notion of "rules," the notion of "restraint" should have a part in, but not a monopoly of, one's perception of international law.

As Louis Henkin has observed, the claim that international law is ignored by states when their vital interests are affected is the beginning of the inquiry and not the end of it.[24] He points to the fact that so far as the mass of government actions is concerned, the law "works" daily; there is no major interest to be had in violating international law. A proper sense of perspective on the restraint violation problem is required. The more one sees law only as prohibitions, the less one perceives its daily effective operation in other important areas. Henkin makes this point well:

> With few, isolated, sporadic exceptions, nations daily live up to the obligations of thousands of treaties, to the responsibilities and duties of states under customary law, even when there might be substantial interest and substantial temptation to violate law or when, if there were no law, nations would freely act otherwise. Even when the Cold War was most bitter, the United States and the USSR left each other alone, respecting each other's territory, property, diplomats, nationals; they carried out numerous treaties, bilateral and multilateral; they lawfully pursued trade and other forms of intercourse.[25]

In sum, law observance is the daily habit of government officials, and deliberately to violate international law would require that the day-to-day machinery of government be stopped and specific difficult decisions taken.[26] This would seem to remain a generally correct observation notwithstanding that the publication of the so-called Pentagon Papers shows that in periods of prolonged and acute stress, a democratic government may, by its very indifference, effectively grant a wide permission for a broad category of illegalities. There are many restraints upon foreign policy which do not flow from centralized sanctions. As the quotation from Henkin makes clear, even the most powerful nations have learned that there are forces within their society and, even more, in international society, that limit the freedom of choice. Furthermore governments are aware that when a proposed act would substantially violate international law, there is a risk of reprisals or of undermining a particular legal norm which generally is regarded as advantageous. Inexorably, then, we return to lawyers' beliefs as to the purported nature of international obligation. While there have been many debates on this point, the advantages of reciprocity today may be seen to have pride of place. The theory of international obligation has undergone, and still is undergoing,[27] radical change. Notions of natural justice have been replaced by the notion of state consent (a conservative doctrine, rooted in traditional notions of state sovereignty and curiously appealing to scholars of international relations).[28] Consent gradually has been replaced by consensus,[29] and studies indicate that nations come to regard themselves as bound by norms to which they have not given their express consent, either because they were not party to the law-making agency or because they did not wish to approve the specific proposals. Custom, evidenced by repeated practice, is a law-creating source, and it has come to be widely accepted that international institutions have a particular law-developing role to play in this regard.[30] If consensus, often tacit and sometimes unenthusiastic, is the basis of international law, then that consensus comes about because states perceive a reciprocal advantage in cautioning self-restraint. It often is not in the national interest to violate international law, even though there may be strong short-term reasons for doing so. This is because, except on a very small range of issues, there is more to be gained by maintaining the reciprocal benefits of an international law system than by winning a short-term advantage in a particular case. International relations scholars, and lawyers, too, who fail to account for these dynamics cannot help but perpetrate a misconception of international law as ineffective or illusory.

We mentioned earlier a remaining category of international relations scholars who see any existing relationship with international law less as irrelevant or ineffectual than as harmful. There are those like Kennan and Morgenthau who see law as having exercised an excessively large and unfortunate restraint upon national foreign policymaking. Thus, Kennan writes that "I see the most serious fault of our past formulation to lie in something I might call the legalistic-moralistic approach to international problems."[31] Many of us would be surprised to learn of this "legalistic-moralistic" approach to international relations. The point is, however, that Kennan starts out from the position that law is a "system of legal rules and restraints which . . . inhibits this process of change by imposing a legal straitjacket upon it [and that] this legalistic approach to international relations is faulty in its assumptions concerning the possibility of sanctions against offenses and violations."[32]

But law is not merely a system of rules. If one views law as a decision-making process operating in a policy context, then the arguments about "straitjackets against the possibility of change" fall to the ground; Kennan's remark about sanctions may be meaningful to the Kelsenian lawyer, but to no one else. Similarly, when Morgenthau refers to the "iron law of international politics, that legal obligations must yield to the national interest," [33] he sets up a false dichotomy between law observance and national interest, "to treat their concurrence as coincidental and their opposition as common."[34] Save for a very, very few cases, the national interest is understood to lie in law observance, even if this entails a short-term loss. Henkin puts this well:

> The issue of law observance, I would suggest, is never a clear choice between legal obligation and national interest; a nation that observes law, even when it "hurts," is not sacrificing national interest to law: it is choosing between competing national interests. . . .[35]

A position that is similar in fact, though intellectually far removed, is that taken by Dr. John Burton. Two main themes permeate his writings: that dysfunctional conflict is the product of misperceived communications between international actors and that a reperception of goals is necessary to resolve such conflict. In this task he wants no part of international law:

> The remedy is not to introduce an outside agent or set of "normative laws" to control such behaviour, but to provide states with the theories, insights and rules that enable them to achieve their goals without running into the self-defeating conflicts inherent in non-systemic behaviour.[36]

So arguing, however, Burton engages in the game of setting up a strawman very effectively to knock him down. One is not obliged to view international law as a set of "rules" to "control" state behavior, and modern approaches to international law are not quite as devoid of theories and insights relevant to national behavior as Burton believes.[37] At the heart of Burton's misgivings about international law lies a view of international law as the imposition of outmoded and irrelevant solutions by third parties. In fact, third party adjudication today plays a very small role in the international legal process. International law is essentially a decentralized system in which foreign offices, international institutions, and regional agencies are the main actors.[38] International adjudication still depends upon consent.[39] By and large, adjudications occur only when the parties "agree" to the court's finding a solution. It may remain Burton's contention that, even so, states are mistaken in their agreement that adjudication is a satisfactory way to settle disputes and that disputes can be settled in the long term by the methods which he and his colleagues propose.[40] This is not the place to examine this contention (although there seems to be a lack of relevant empirical data). We need simply note that Burton equates "international law" with a very tiny fraction of what actually is involved in the international legal process.

The thrust of the preceding paragraphs has been to reject the claims of irrelevance, ineffectiveness, and harmfulness of international law made by international scholars. I do so on the grounds that each rests on assumptions that misunderstand the nature of international law and, in particular, the essential relationship between power and authority. If a high proportion of international relations scholars regard international law as "rules" and "prohibitions," regard the "lack of sanctions" argument as telling, and are impressed by the "vital national interest" point, then manifestly we international lawyers incur at least part of the responsibility for the wide purveyance of these false assumptions. Too often have we ourselves spoken of international law in this way or, more frequently, failed to address ourselves to these issues in any systematic way at all. On the other hand, some measure of blame must attach to the international relations scholars, for there is a vast legal literature at least in the United States of which many seem unaware. The works of Falk, Fisher, Frank, Friedmann, Henkin, Lasswell, McDougal, J. N. Moore, Reisman, Schachter, Weston, and others are not read, as they should be. There are few in international relations who go the necessary half way of interdisciplinary cooperation.

The lesson, then, seems to be this: international relations scholars and international lawyers must realize that the discipline does not describe the state of the discipline and that very considerable developments and movements are taking place in both international law and international relations. The question therefore arises: to what extent are viable alternatives emerging to Myres McDougal's approach, most particularly in the context of reintegrating authority and power in our perceptions?

Primarily in the United States—but also outside, in the work of Julius Stone and Jenks—there is now an acknowledgment of the decentralized character of the international community, of the need to identify new perimeters for international law, and of the need to examine the political context of legal decisions. The inquiry, in short, has shifted from "rules" to the social and institutional means available for their effective implementation.[41] "An international lawyer cannot afford to hold constant the context within which law is created and applied or within which legal controversy takes place."[42] A functionalist approach to international law has developed which is closely concerned with David Mitrany's central thesis and the revisions of Stanley Hoffmann, Ernst Haas, and J. P. Sewell.[43]

The main thrust of functionalism is of interest to the international lawyer, as is Hoffmann's evidence that functionalism does not necessarily ensure a beneficial effect in due course in the areas of "vital state interest" to a state and as is Haas' further variation on traditional functionalism, which contends that a political clash may in fact lead to precedent making. Lawyers such as Jenks and the late Wolfgang Friedmann may be said to be functionalists. Their particular contribution has been to turn away from rules and restraint, and to point to common areas of endeavor in which the prime role of law is to provide the technical means whereby certain commonly held objectives can be fulfilled. Post, health, telecommunications, safety, and other concerns are common objectives whose pursuit has been institutionalized by legal structures. The work of the International Bank and the IMF also is law creating in certain ways. Less institutionalized, but still relevant for the functionalists' purpose, are the limited cooperative regimes that have emerged in respect of outer space, Antarctica, joint international business ventures, and so forth. Jenks' particular ability has been to point out areas ripe for functionalist legal development, and to formulate agenda.[44] Friedmann was less of a "prophet," and though perhaps his rhetoric was less compelling, his substantive contribution was enormous in putting across the functionalist view.[45]

While Jenks is something of an "outsider" (albeit a respected one) in the European legal tradition, Friedmann's writings represent the mainstream in today's legal thinking in America—an acceptance of the relevance of the political and social context to the legal process, an emphasis on law as normative cooperation, an indication that this approach can be pursued pragmatically. As Falk has correctly said: "Functionalism is really not a coherent framework of inquiry in the manner of McDougal. It is instead only a jurisprudential orientation that generates a certain style of inquiry and concentrates on certain sorts of legal developments."[46] It is this very fact which has made someone like Friedmann acceptable to the traditionalists, his emphasis on policy notwithstanding. And equally, it is this fact which has caused both Jenks and Friedmann to be so severely attacked by those lawyers representing the policy science approach. To the latter, an acceptance of the essential relationship of law and international politics is not enough; the "halfway house" of functionalism is damaging in that it purports to deal with policy, but fails through its lack of a systematic structure. Falk in an earlier incarnation (I doubt that he would take this position now) attacked Jenks on this basis,[47] and McDougal, in co-reviewing Friedmann's *The Changing Structure of International Law,* dismissed it as an "unchanging theory for inquiry."[48]

Systems analysis, in its broadest sense, has been of particular interest to a very limited group of international lawyers in the United States. In *The Political Foundations of International Law,* Morton Kaplan and Nicholas Katzenbach sought successfully to show the systemic basis of legal norms. The advantage of the systemic approach is that it moves international law away from the traditional exclusive concern with states and acknowledges as actors in the international process individuals, regions, blocs, and a variety of other participants. Falk himself, in cooperation with his colleagues at Princeton, particularly Oran Young,[49] has developed an interest in the further application of systems analysis to international law. Specifically, in order to avoid veering all the way back to the traditionalists in his concern to find "neutral principles," Falk urges the assistance of systems analysis in providing a set of universal, rather than purely national, values for the decisionmaker. But whereas he points, with increasing frequency, to the signpost of systems analysis as a means of avoiding subjectivity, he has not yet made any use in depth of this international relations tool.

I regard as mistaken the view that systems analysis can help to avoid the value choice in the legal process. Whereas systems analysis can provide insights into the effective functioning of international law, I am less confident that Falk is right in supposing that it can point to universal values. It can help identify the values of subuniversal systems, of corporations, regions, organizations. The literature seems to indicate that the identification of a universal system remains a definitional question, depending on the criteria for a system, and that values which are truly universal, reflecting a definitionally agreed upon global system, have yet to be identified.[50] Systems analysis can illustrate how there is a clash of values between partial systems, but the problems of choice for the decisionmaker still remain.[51]

Contemporary systems analysis does have, of course, the considerable advantage that the concept of authority can be identified in terms of different systems, and not necessarily only the nation-state.[52] Both systems analysis and the policy science approach of McDougal can usefully emphasize the varying locus of participants in a process of authoritative decisionmaking.

Yet John Burton, who started from a systems analysis background, and whose main focus of inquiry is conflict resolution, still finds formidable the barriers between his own discipline of international law and that of international relations. The main hurdle of intellectual cooperation lies in his disapproval of the concern of the international lawyer with values. Lawyers, in his view, should provide the techniques and skills for harnessing agreements based on the values of the different systems which they serve. But this view, which is based on a deep distrust of the skills and the impartiality of the lawyer so far as values are concerned, takes no account of the fact that no matter what arena (system) the decisionmaker serves he will be faced with choices which necessarily bring the question of values in their wake. Of course, contemporary systems analysis does have the considerable advantage, as mentioned, of identifying the concept of authority with more than the nation-state system. But so does the policy science approach.

In the crucial area of integrating power and authority, therefore, McDougal's policy science approach continues to be a more useful and acceptable tool of analysis than any of the alternatives offered. Some further elaboration would be helpful, particularly in the area of third party adjudication: what are the preferred loci of what sorts of disputes for decisionmaking, and in what circumstances? Again, the authoritative allocation of competences (jurisdiction) is an area badly needing detailed inquiry. Those of us who have benefited so greatly from the scholarship and friendship of Myres McDougal hope that he will be able to undertake these tasks among the many demanding his attention.

Notes

1. R. FALK, THE STATUS OF LAW IN INTERNATIONAL SOCIETY 87 (1970).

2. McDougal, *The World Constitutive Process of Authoritative Decision,* 19 J. LEGAL ED. 253, 256 (1967) (with H. Lasswell & W. Reisman).

3. M. REISMAN, NULLITY AND REVISION 4 (1971).

4. *Id.* at 5.

5. Farer, *International Law and Political Behavior—Towards a Conceptual Liaison,* 25 WORLD POLITICS 430, 435 (1973).

6. Young, *International Law and Social Science: The Contributions of Myres S. McDougal,* 66 AM. J. INT'L L. 61 (1972).

7. Farer, *supra* note 5, at 435.

8. University College, London, is institutionally unusual in that its international relations department is part of the law department.

9. Inaugural address by Georg Schwarzenberger, "The Misery and Grandeur of International Law," Oct. 24, 1963. See generally G. SCHWARZENBERGER, POWER POLITICS (1964).

10. In a series of judicial decisions on the bench of the International Court of Justice. See also Fitzmaurice, *Judicial Innovation—its Uses and its Perils—as Exemplified in Some of the Work of the International Court of Justice during Lord McNair's Period of Office,* in CAMBRIDGE ESSAYS IN INTERNATIONAL LAW, ESSAYS IN HONOUR OF LORD MCNAIR (R. Jennings ed. 1965).

11. If the best-known proponent of this view is Fitzmaurice, it is present in the writings of many others. For an interesting example, see Johnson, *The Place of Policy in International Law,* 2 GA. J. INT'L & COMP. L. 15 (1972).

12. Higgins, *Policy Considerations and the International Judicial Process,* 17 INT'L & COMP. L.Q. 58, 62–63 (1968).

13. M. MCDOUGAL, STUDIES IN WORLD PUBLIC ORDER (1960); M. MCDOUGAL & F. FELICIANO, LAW AND MINIMUM WORLD PUBLIC ORDER (1961); M. MCDOUGAL & W. BURKE, THE PUBLIC ORDER OF THE OCEANS (1962); M. MCDOUGAL, H. LASSWELL & I. VLASIC, LAW AND PUBLIC ORDER IN SPACE (1963); M. MCDOUGAL, H. LASSWELL & J. MILLER, THE INTERPRETATION OF AGREEMENTS OF WORLD PUBLIC ORDER (1967).

14. H. LAUTERPACHT, THE DEVELOPMENT OF INTERNATIONAL LAW BY THE INTERNATIONAL COURT 399 (1958).

15. R. FALK, *supra* note 1, at 647.

16. *See, e.g.,* Falk, *On Treaty Interpretation and the New Haven Approach,* 8 VA. J. INT'L L. 323 (1968); Stone, *Fictional Elements in Treaty Interpretation,* 1 Sydney L. Rev. 334 (1954); Lauterpacht, *Restrictive Interpretation and the Principle of Effectiveness in the Interpretation of Treaties,* 26 BRIT. Y.B. INT'L L. 46 (1949).

17. For elaboration, see McDougal, *Some Basic Theoretical Concepts about International Law: A Policy Oriented Framework of Enquiry,* 4 J. CONFLICT RESOLUTION 337 (1960); M. McDOUGAL, *The Ethics of Applying Systems of Authority,* in THE ETHIC OF POWER 226–28 (1965).

18. South West Africa Cases, [1962] I.C.J. 466 (joint dissenting opinion).

19. South West Africa Cases, [1966] I.C.J. 34.

20. C. JENKS, LAW IN THE WORLD COMMUNITY 54 (1967).

21. Higgins, *supra* note 12, at 58.

22. *See* G. SCHWARZENBERGER, MANUAL OF INTERNATIONAL LAW (1967); also inaugural address cited note 9 *supra.*

23. H. KELSEN, PRINCIPLES OF INTERNATIONAL LAW (1966). See also his valuable volume STATE AND INTERNATIONAL LEGAL ORDER (1964).

24. L. HENKIN, HOW NATIONS BEHAVE: LAW AND FOREIGN POLICY 182 (1968).

25. *Id.* at 45–50.

26. *Id.*

27. The classical statement is to be found in J. BRIERLY, THE BASIS OF OBLIGATION IN INTERNATIONAL LAW (1958). *See also* Schachter, *Towards a Theory of International Obligation,* 8 VA. J. INT'L L. 300, 301–02 (1968); C. PARRY, SOURCES AND EVIDENCE OF INTERNATIONAL LAW (1963); R. HIGGINS, THE DEVELOPMENT OF INTERNATIONAL LAW BY THE POLITICAL ORGANS OF THE UNITED NATIONS (1963); I. DETTER, LAW MAKING BY INTERNATIONAL INSTITUTIONS (1965); Jennings, *Recent Developments in the International Law Commission: Its Relation to Sources on International Law,* 17 INT'L & COMP. L.Q. 385 (1965); McGibbon, *The Scope of Acquiescence in International Law,* 31 BRIT. Y.B. INT'L L. 143 (1954).

28. *See, e.g.,* James, Book Review, INT'L AFFAIRS, Apr. 1964, at 301.

29. C. JENKS, LAW, FREEDOM AND WELFARE 83–100 (1963).

30. R. HIGGINS, *supra* note 27; I. DETTER, *supra* note 27; ASAMOAH, THE LEGAL EFFECT OF DECLARATIONS BY THE GENERAL ASSEMBLY; S. BAILEY, *Making International Law in the United Nations,* 1967 PROC. AM. SOC'Y INT'L L.; R. FALK, *On the Quasi-Legislative Competence of the General Assembly;* 1966 PROC. AM. SOC'Y INT'L L.; Schachter, *The Relation of Law, Politics and Action in the United Nations,* 109 HAGUE RECUEIL 171 (1963).

31. G. KENNAN, AMERICAN DIPLOMACY 1900–1950, 95–98 (1951).

32. *Id.* at 98–99.

33. H. MORGANTHAU, IN DEFENCE OF THE NATIONAL INTEREST 144 (1951).

34. L. HENKIN, *supra* note 24, at 263..

35. *Id.*

36. J. BURTON, SYSTEMS, STATES, DIPLOMACY AND RULES (1968).

37. This is particularly true of the functionalist and policy science approaches, which are discussed below.

38. Professor Richard Falk has been particularly articulate in pointing to the consequences of this decentralization. See particularly THE ROLE OF DOMESTIC COURTS IN THE INTERNATIONAL ORDER (1963). This emphasis on different actions in a horizontal structure leads away from the traditional link between states and international law and acknowledges the relevance of systems other than sovereign states.

39. Article 36(2) of the Statute of the International Court of Justice provides that "The states parties to the present Statute may at any time declare that they recognize

as compulsory *ipso facto* and without special agreement, in relation to any other state accepting the same obligation, the jurisdiction of the Court in all legal disputes. . . ." Article 36(3) adds, "The declarations referred to above may be made unconditionally or on condition of reciprocity on the part of several or uncertain states, or for a certain time."

40. *See, e.g.,* Nicholson, *Tariff Wars and a Model of Conflict,* 1967 J. PEACE RESEARCH, No. 1; M. NICHOLSON, CONFLICT ANALYSIS (1970); M. Banks, A. Groom & A. Oppenheim, *Gaming and Simulation in International Relations,* 16 POLITICAL STUDIES, no. 1 (1968).

41. This point is made by R. FALK, *supra* note 1, at 449.

42. *Id.*

43. *See* E. HAAS, BEYOND THE NATION STATE, FUNCTIONALISM AND INTERNATIONAL ORGANIZATION (1964); D. MITRANY, A WORKING PEACE SYSTEM: AN ARGUMENT FOR THE FUNCTIONAL DEVELOPMENT OF INTERNATIONAL ORGANIZATION (1943); Hoffman, *The Role of International Organization: Limits and Possibilities,* 10 INT'L ORGANIZATION 365 (1956); J. SEWELL, FUNCTIONALISM AND WORLD POLITICS (1966).

44. *See particularly* C. JENKS, *supra* note 20.

45. *See* W. FRIEDMANN, THE CHANGING STRUCTURE OF INTERNATIONAL LAW (1964).

46. *See* R. FALK, *supra* note 1, at 463.

47. Falk & Mendlovitz, *Some Criticisms of C. Wilfred Jenks' Approach to International Law,* 14 RUTGERS L. REV. 1 (1959).

48. McDougal & Reisman, *"The Changing Structure of International Law" Unchanging Theory of Inquiry,* 65 COLUM. L. REV. 810 (1965).

49. I have relied particularly on O. YOUNG, A SYSTEMATIC APPROACH TO INTERNATIONAL POLITICS; J. ROSENAU, LINKAGE POLITICS; and sources cited therein.

50. On the question of values, see M. NICHOLSON, CONFLICT ANALYSIS 157–63 (1970); W. GOULD & M. BARKUN, INTERNATIONAL LAW AND THE SOCIAL SCIENCES 150, 216–19 (1970).

51. Interestingly, much of Jenks' work has been directed to finding a set of universal values; though I would contend that in his exploration Jenks relies too much on formality (common points among Islamic, Christian, and Judaic legal systems) and too little on the reality behind (the nonrelevance of the origins of the legal system in the light of contemporary claims made by states operating in a secular community).

52. *See* M. KAPLAN, SYSTEM AND PROCESS IN INTERNATIONAL POLITICS (1957; THE INTERNATIONAL SYSTEM (K. Knorr & S. Verba eds. 1967); C. MCCLELLAND, THEORY AND THE INTERNATIONAL SYSTEM (1966).

Chapter 3

Psychological Aspects of Systems Analysis

JAMES C. MILLER

Analysis of the structural properties of a social system is an integral part of the study of interaction processes.[1] In seeking to maximize values, participants in the interaction process form groups and systems to implement common aims. These values may be pursued rationally, with the aim of maximizing objectives across all values; or they may be pursued in a variety of compensatory ways, less affected by conscious analysis or feedback. Additionally, groups and systems may generate real and fantasied value needs which may or may not relate to original system values. The purpose of this essay is to outline some of the ways in which structural properties of an established system and other process variables may be expected to interact.

One obvious set of interactions occurs at the formation or reformation of a system. Another occurs around system maintenance.

Traditional explanations of group and system formation often tend to suggest that one set of variables is more important than any other, or that one set is definitive. Thus, some people assume that adult motivation for forming social systems results from the notion (archaic) that the lack of a protective social network has severe biological consequences. Another common view has been that, pursuant to principles of division of labor and development of skills in a complex economic system, groups form to allow their members to survive economically. Another version of this argument is that "man is essentially a social animal" and that he cannot survive psychologically without seeking out others of his species in group settings.

In support of these explanations, it is argued that these factors are, or once were, necessary conditions of living. Thus, the absence of a parent or parent surrogate in early childhood would in fact bring about the biological death of the organism. Similarly, failure to establish appropriate system structures to ensure economic viability ultimately would result in starvation. And finally, total social deprivation would indeed produce disorientations that would threaten the organism's survival. Of course, no one can deny that groups and systems are necessary for biological, economic, and social functions. An extended list of this sort might even constitute a "cause." It would be an overdetermined one, however. Similarly, the list of such conditions would change as the participants, purposes, strategies, and outcomes of the group or system changed. The reality is, in short, that people form systems under multiple conditions and for multiple causes, reasons, and justifications. People form systems like virtually anything else, namely, to achieve certain valued outcomes.

Harold Lasswell has provided a convenient reminder of the range of these values.[2] He argues that there are at least eight basic values that people pursue: power, wealth, enlightenment, skill, respect, rectitude, affection, and well-being. In any social process, people pursue any and all of these values in varying degrees. Thus, to answer the question "Why do people form and maintain groups and systems?" a value analysis of a specific system is necessary. There is no general answer to the question, except the schematic one that people form and maintain groups and systems in order to maximize values.

Descriptions of basic value categories can be found in Lasswell and Kaplan[3] and in McDougal, Lasswell, and Miller.[4] Briefly, the categories may be characterized as follows: *power*—an interest in becoming a decisionmaker with regard to others or to oneself; *wealth*—an interest in transactions involving goods or services; *enlightenment*—devotion to the clarification of goals through fact collection or conceptual analysis; *skill* —attempted utilization of available resources to make patterns or strategies of them; *respect*—pursuit of distinction, honor, or merit; *rectitude*—concern with meeting or breaking standards of personal or social responsibility; *affection*—an interest in friendship, or closeness of people with each other; *well-being*—concern with somatic safety and comfort, as well as psychological safety and comfort.

In analyzing a specific social process, one needs to assess a complex interplay of social and psychological variables, an interplay which frequently takes the form of a conflict between available resources and over-riding goals. The pursuit of any value may be facilitated or limited by physical or social realities, such as the availability of resources which for the most part remain unchanged despite a change in participants' values, as well as by psychological or attitudinal realities whose condition is closely tied to the developmental history and changing outlook of the participants. By definition, institutional goals and strategies in most systems center on the acquisition and maintenance of power associated with control over wealth. Around these values various psychological issues are oriented, and are used either to further power and wealth acquisition or to defend against or explain away failures. In this context, psychological variables are seen as contingent on social events. In a given value framework, however, many central events may be governed by attitudinal factors.

Individuals or groups may or may not be consciously aware of their own or others' values or the strategies they use to maximize them. From the standpoint of an outside observer, they may reach a stated goal but fail to experience the attainment. For example, they may obtain a desired friendship with someone, but feel for uncertain reasons that the offered friendship is not enough; they may establish the conditions for adult psychological well-being, but not feel well. In such instances, we can say that the continued value seeking becomes reparative or compensatory; that is, people pursue one value as reparation or compensation for the actual or fantasied deprivation of another.

Reparative Values

The hypothesis that people tend to maximize value choices assumes that all values are sought and that, within cultural variations, a balance, or equilibrium, is achieved. Reparative value seeking, on the other hand, necessarily involves an imbalance of values, a preemption of one value choice by another. If one looks at a social system in process, such value substitutions can be observed. A worker shifted to a lower paying job, for example, may develop a set of values which deemphasizes wealth and reparatively emphasizes good working conditions, short hours, and the like. A physician who fails to cure a patient may develop a belated interest in researching the disease. A nation losing a war may develop strong interests in peace and humanitarian objectives. Valued objects also may change reparatively while the value sought remains the same. From a static perspective, however, one must use other indices of reparative value seeking, such as the intensity and rigidity with which values are pursued or rejected, the security arrangements around value maintenance, and, in some cases, the lack of realism with which value choices are made.

Lack of realism in value choice is seen, in this perspective, as an aspect of reparation. Individuals who set unobtainable goals, or who pursue goals with self-defeating strategies, are attempting to gain reparation for past or present, real or imagined, value deprivations. We postulate that individuals ordinarily act to maximize values within available resources. When this process appears disrupted, as in the case of unrealistic goal or strategy choices, it is a reasonable hypothesis that reparative values are being sought. A corollary hypothesis is that lack of realism in value choice reflects the salience of real or imagined *past* value deprivations, aspects of which the individual is unaware. The earlier and more extensive the deprivation, the more intractable the lack of awareness and the more likely the pursuit will be unrealistic or self-defeating. Conversely, the more recent the deprivation, the greater the likelihood of individual awareness and the greater the likelihood of realistic, though still reparative, value pursuits. We assume that present rewards and deprivations potentially activate all levels of rational and reparative responses. The relative contribution of these responses is a matter to be determined in the individual case.

With respect to our initial question, "why do people form and maintain groups and social systems?" the answer is that they may be in pursuit of any value, either realistically or unrealistically, rationally or reparatively defined. The present concern is primarily with the latter, or the reparative side of value seeking in groups and social systems.

It seems clear that in many cases rational goal orientations establish the conditions both for the development and the control of reparative value seeking. Complex system outputs may necessitate the establishment of multiple group and intergroup relations whose functioning either may facilitate or may retard the attainment of system values. Difficulties in goal attainment may initiate reparative responses which acquire a life of their own.

Real value rewards and deprivations, stemming from such necessities as role and skill discriminations in task attainment, are integral to the functioning of any social system. It is characteristic of most systems that structures of real rewards and deprivations tend to arouse fantasies of total value change. The dynamics of system membership are such that they have a tendency to evoke a central archaic fantasy: total care or abandonment. Since social systems are the major vehicles through which adult values are realized, they provide adequate reality to collude with such fantasies.[5] This can give rise to a level of anxiety which must be dealt with by the individual or the system.

Social systems, as well as the individuals within them, normally have a wide variety of structures upon which to rely in limiting anxiety. The more common ones involve the pursuit, achievement, and maintenance of other values in viable group and intergroup structures. A group or a system, out of a threat to its own well-being, may pursue a wide variety of value outcomes (with multiple strategies) as a means of dealing with the anxiety associated with the threat.

In natural settings, it often is difficult to separate out relatively conflict-free functioning in the pursuit of values as opposed to defensive (reparative) conflict resolution. An example is given by Menzies[6] in her analysis of hospital nursing practices. Nursing duties frequently involve anxiety-arousing situations. They require constant contact with physically diseased or injured persons who frequently are in pain, unable to care for themselves, and often in imminent danger of dying. There can be many conflicting feelings about the patient: concern, guilt, resentment at the patient's dependent state, and envy of the attention given the patient. To defend against these conflicts, nursing organizations establish a variety of compensatory goals and practices. These include frequent shifts of personnel, rotating assignments of nurses to patients, routinization of the relatonship of the nurse to the patient, training in the denial of the significance of the individual, diffusion of task responsibility, and obscuring of authority structure. Even though these reparative practices may interfere with the goals of patient care, they bind anxieties at a minimal level sufficient to allow the provision of the service, however impaired, to continue.

Other system measures of reparation involve the degree to which attempts are made to establish levels of security around certain values. The most general form is the provision of security around the work position. This involves systems of seniority, tenure, guaranteed wage, and the like. Program specifications may carry the same security arrangement, whereby funds are guaranteed for projects on term or for duration, space is guaranteed, and overriding goals are clarified and stated to place a high value on the program in the future plans of the organization.

Whether such practices are adaptive or disruptive in relation to value outcomes will of course vary with the situation being studied. Disruptive aspects of security arrangements around job positions and job programs are perhaps the most frequent examples cited. The plight of the nonproductive employee, the outdated policymaker, or the archaic job specification is a fixed part of our organizational lore. It is perhaps more characteristic of human service organizations that such defenses tend to be disruptive because of the complexity and difficulty of the mandated task. Also, social system defenses tend to be most disruptive in periods of rapid transition within a social system, when the anxieties stemming from fantasies of abandonment or statelessness apparently are provided greater reality.

Individual, group, and intergroup relations within social systems are complex events with complex, and quite diverse, explanations. A thorough study of a specific system would require, among other things, identification of the individual and group participants, clarification of their perspectives (objectives), analysis of the specific situations in which they find themselves, the strategies they use to deal with those situations, the outcomes they wish to produce, and the effects they hope and expect these outcomes will have. It should be quite clear that all group situations are multivalue situations; that is, they affect most, if not all, values.

System Process

Given the range of values involved in system process, it seems initially surprising that psychologists have been so interested in social system functioning. While some approaches have for this reason been parochial, there is reason to believe that psychologists can contribute to the exploration of group and system process. The initial question is: "what processes constitute a group or integrated system of groups?" Or, "what processes develop for most, if not all, participants, tasks, and settings?"

All systems organize around a task or related set of tasks. Such organization implies leadership. While systems may differ in their need to specify, or their interest in specifying, "a leader," there always is a leadership function; a system identifies itself around it. The rational function of leadership is to organize groups of individuals for task accomplishment, and although the process of evolving leadership and task strategies is a complex one, with varied potential for conflict, the process occurs regardless of the realism of the values sought. Whether task needs or non-task-related human needs (E. J. Miller and A. K. Rice call the latter "sentient" needs)[7] motivate the search for leadership, the process itself may create difficulties which inhibit the satisfaction of either need. The initial experience of the individual in a system generally is one of diffuse anxiety and confusion. The brief experience of entry into this undifferentiated mass is, for most people, quickly dispelled. But that experience is the core motivating event for group life, namely, the fear of a loss of personal identity.[8] If, as in the modal case, the individual has difficulty in coping with these threatening fantasies, he looks for help. Responses to that search, in the group and intergroup setting, create leadership. The reparative exchange, from the individual's point of view, involves giving up some control over his thoughts or actions in exchange for the protection (fantasied or real) of his identity or personal integrity.

In *Group Psychology and the Analysis of the Ego,* Freud discussed leadership in terms of replacement of the ego ideal.[9] That is to say, the leader replaces the member's ego ideal and governs the ego in its place; it then feels appropriate for the member to be governed by a leader. A comparable but more economic view would be that the ego ideal is projected onto the leader. It is, thus, the *leader* who would be described in terms in which the member might otherwise describe the ideal self. Stated in this latter way, it is easier to see the advantages that would accrue to this projection. Leadership may be rationally necessary to accomplish a task, but its sentient parallels are equally necessary, namely, the need to see the leader as a person of superior powers. As projected ego ideal, the leader could be neither destructive nor could he abandon. He could only aid and ensure the task of survival.

Another apparent advantage gained by the projection of the ego ideal is that it partly frees the group member from his own burdens or responsibilities. He no longer reminds himself of the painful discrepancies between ideal and real; norms belong to the group. On the other hand, this "advantage" also constitutes a central paradox. In simplest terms, it reconstitutes the ideal as an object or set of objects and thereby makes it more likely that such objects will affect the projector, in fact or in added projective fantasy, in a variety of complicated ways. One such way is quite clear: the group or the leader is now invested with the individual member's superego. While group members may feel initially liberated by this discovery, there is nonetheless the fear that the ultimate ideals and sanctions of the group have been placed in hands no less arbitrary. Such projective objects tend to escalate projective mechanisms as demands on leadership change.

Paradoxes of Leadership

We have discussed the projection of the superego as a fundamental process that occurs in the acceptance of leadership, and this acceptance of leadership is what constitutes or defines a group. We also have suggested that the acceptance of leadership paradoxically creates the conditions for negative reactions to leadership. Clearly, we have only begun to explore all of these issues as they affect group functioning.

A group, according to Freud, is "a number of individuals who have put one and the same object in the place of their ego ideal and have consequently identified themselves with one another in their ego."[10] The present formulation would lead to a slightly different conclusion, namely, that a group is a collection of individuals who have projected their ego ideals onto the same object. In most respects these formulations are complementary, although projective notions, we may argue, explain a wider range of leadership phenomena. Particularly, they are more valuable in helping to understand some of the more complex aspects of leadership.

The central leadership paradox follows directly from the projection of the ego ideal. A group member, in order to realize his own goals (or power values), must overcome the group-defining object—*i.e.,* the leader. Once the ego ideal is objectified in the leader, attaining it means attaining leadership or replacing the leader. Thus, the conditions for group formation and the conditions for group conflict and distintegration are identical.

Paradoxes around leadership naturally are more complicated than those we have described in relation to the defining characteristics of groups. It should be obvious that once a leader is identified, he may become a preferred object for the projection of many positive and negative feelings. Thus, if the leader is a fitting object for the responsibilities projected onto him, so also should he be a fitting object for the unacceptable feelings and fantasies of the group in the service of protecting the individual, as well as the group. Feelings concerning conflicts among members may be thought to be safely "stored" with the leader. He may be said to be responsible for failures in a variety of tasks of the group. As head of the group and keeper of group morality, he may come to believe that he alone is free of the inhibitions he imposes on others by his morality.

If one adds to this picture the very real possibility of members' introjection of projected fantasies about the leader, one can begin to glimpse a further paradox of leadership. If the unfolding projective process includes, as one might expect, a mixture of acceptance and rejection of the leader, the prospect of totally incorporating the projective object should arouse a very primitive and disruptive form of anxiety. Although such fantasies may have been separated, in collusive group defenses, by time, task, or a variety of reality factors, the incorporation of the object could not be so separated. The individual would be forced to integrate highly conflicted and contradictory fantasies with no guarantee of group support.

To summarize, paradoxes around leadership relate to a constellation of potentially conflicting fantasies projected onto a single individual or group of individuals. This act of projection, which creates leadership, also establishes the conditions for its destruction. The act which we have argued establishes leadership—the projection of the ego ideal—also creates the conditions under which leadership can be replaced by the process of "becoming like" the leader. The act of objectifying the ego ideal in a leader gives that leader a power to gratify desires which members eventually wish to reclaim. Freud argued that the necessity of the death of the father of the primal horde arose from the fact that he held the horde in check by his symbolic possession of women as the primary value.[11] We have argued, in contrast, that leaders are given varying control over members with respect to any and all values and that their destruction will be guaranteed in proportion to the amount and intensity of reparative values sought by their followers. The effects of real rewards and deprivations may intensify or modulate reparative rewards and deprivations depending on a variety of factors in the group context.

As we have seen, projection in the group or system setting is not limited to projection of the ego ideal. Various aspects of a person's inner world may be projected onto the leader for various purposes. Unacceptable negative aspects of the self may be projected onto the leader in order to rid the members of responsibility for them; they may be projected in order to attack and destroy the leader. The line between ridding oneself of unwanted thoughts or feelings by projecting them onto a leader, on the one hand, and attacking the leader, on the other, is yet another feature of the paradox. Still, given the conditions of leadership, these two activities are inconsistent. Ultimately the projective object would be destroyed.

Fortunately for the individual, social systems (life) normally provide the individual with defensive structures which help with such conflicts. Depending on the circumstances, these structures can be either "harnessable" in the service of a rational task or, at the other extreme, exceedingly magical, simplistic, and ultimately destructive of the task. W. R. Bion has proposed one means of classifying such collusive structures.[12] As an observer of groups, Bion was extremely sensitive to the startling simplifications of emotional life to which groups seem to be vulnerable. He articulated three simplifying "assumptions" which regularly occurred in groups as a means of reducing anxiety around task and role fulfillment. These assumptions are shared distortions of realities that appear when individuals in groups are threatened by a loss of the identities, expectations, and values which characterize them as individuals. He called these basic assumptions *dependency, fight–flight,* and *pairing.*

Such assumptions, according to Bion, are shared patterns of "as if" behaviors. Thus, in a basic assumption dependency group, members behave as if they were collected together to obtain protection and security, rather than to pursue the announced task of the group. This assumption implies that the leader is a highly potent, if not omnipotent, provider, curer, and problem-solver. The group in this assumption presents itself as needy or sick in order to obtain the benefits to be dispensed by the leader. They are his family, with the attendant security, rivalries, and limited world view that this implies.

Any group that fantasies its leader as all-providing must continually defend against the obvious realities of his shortcomings in this respect. If one is to avoid falling back on the core anxiety concerning *self*-preservation, the assumption can emerge that the *group* has met to preserve itself; what threatens the organization of the individual is translated into a threat to the organization of the group. Both are painful and extremely regressive, but a united group working on the problem clearly is to be preferred to the efforts of the individual. The regressiveness of this basic assumption is clearly seen in the desperate way the group behaves in believing that it can survive only by fighting or running away. Just as the threatened individual feels that the only alternatives are to attack or to flee, the threatened group feels that the only alternatives are to attack or to flee. Thus, what Bion called the fight–flight basic assumption group is an impending disaster site, or perhaps a disaster-in-process site. Leaders are selected for their vigilance and their hatred of the enemy; thinking is rigidly limited to action-oriented modes of survival; and there is no tolerance of deviation of any kind, either in thought or in action. Fight and flight are complementary: if the fantasied destructive enemy cannot be successfully fought, one must flee from him in order to survive. In relatively sedentary groups, of course, flight primarily involves mental, not physical, abandonment. But the ultimate form of flight for any group involves first leaving the field as a group and, second, dissolving the group.

Basic assumption pairing, according to Bion, assumes that the group has met for the functions of courtship and reproduction. The chronic fantasy of the pairing group is that, at some time in the future, the reproductive pair will produce a Messiah, a hope for salvation. In clinical experience, the pairing group has a wish fulfillment quality to it, in which the only possible fantasy is that good fortune will prevail. Hopefulness pervades the group; it is led by the unborn leader and therefore by the future. It is important that the promised land remain just out of reach, so the pairing group makes an effort to avoid testing its salvation fantasies. Since the function of the unborn leader is to save the group from its feelings of abandonment, anger, and despair, it is often observed in times of transition in the group. Basic assumption group life tends to touch on pairing as a previous assumption terminates. For similar reasons, it is ubiquitous at times of prolonged separation or termination.

One characteristic common to all these basic assumptions is that they involve an attempt to find simple magical solutions to complex and difficult group problems. The dependency group would look, childlike, to the leader; the fight–flight group would attack or run from the task and its leadership; and the pairing group awaits the savior. In terms of our previous discussion, the simplifications constitute choices on one side or the other of the central destructive ambivalence toward authority. The collusive simplification of the dependency and pairing basic assumption groups is that the good leader is present, or shortly will be present, to solve all of the group's problems. The collusive simplification of the fight–flight basic assumption group is that the persecutory leader is present and must be destroyed or avoided. In either case, the goal is to avoid having to tolerate and understand a disorganizing ambivalence toward authority. In the case of dependency and pairing groups, favorable aspects of the self are projected onto a present or future benevolent, productive, or restorative leader. In the case of the fight–flight group, unacceptable aspects of the self are projected onto a malicious, destructive leader. The total effect is a simple temporal splitting of ambivalent attitudes toward the leader, on the assumption that it is impossible to integrate conflicting feelings about the leader. What makes this phenomenon so pervasive in groups, more so than in individuals, is the increased threat to the identity of the individual that is created by the group. What makes the resolution so effective is the presence of collusive group support. Groups, then, allow us to see deeply regressive experiences, and defenses against those experiences occur with astonishing speed and simplicity. Phenomena which in individuals would be considered psychotic are plausible in groups of "normal" individuals pursuing a realistic primary task.

As we have seen, in both group and system functioning individual concerns center on a loss of identity either through engulfment or abandonment. Systems projectively create a benevolent leader who will reassure them of the possibility of differentiating from the group mass (by their projection) and of their secure position in the group as his follower. There even may be a brief instant when the members will introject these "qualities" of the leader in this simplest phase of the projective process. Subsequent developments in the group will disappoint the initial assumptions the group has made about the leader and will produce the manifold reactions, described previously, of attack, withdrawal, self-depreciation, and the like. In open systems, however, these developments are not likely to be predictable without further information about the position of the group in the context of the social system in which it is functioning. This raises the important question of the functioning of groups in intergroup relations, or in the complex set of intergroup relations which constitute a social system.

Intergroup Relations

The issues initially faced by groups in social system functioning are similar to the issues the individual must face in joining a group, namely, questions of identity ("who are we?") and questions of level of functioning ("what are we to do?"). In light of our prior analysis, it is not surprising that these questions are similar: through various projections, the individual comes to see the group as an extension of himself. The dominant "we" replaces the dominant "I." Persons may be differentiated within "we" as parents, siblings, or relatives, but the "we" becomes, for purposes of relating the group to the outside world, a unit comparable to the individual in interpersonal relations. Furthermore, the state and quality of functioning within the group will to some extent determine the nature of the interactions of that group with other groups, just as the functioning of the individual shapes interpersonal interactions.

The creation of a group in a social setting has dynamic parallels with many other creative events. Most such events involve an attempt to change perceived chaos and experienced lack of structure into something orderly and meaningful. In the life of the individual, these events begin with very primitive attempts to order one's experience, and to help the person to develop over time into a more sophisticated, more complex, and hopefully more functional organism. Groups in social structures offer the promise of help in ordering the external and internal worlds of their members. The psychological dimension of group formation in an intergroup setting is, then, to be characterized by the group's efforts to reduce the threat of disorder and chaos mobilized in larger, more complex, and more confusing social structures.

Consistent with this view, the group in an intergroup setting is immediately faced with two tasks. One is to establish order through group organization. The most primitive, and at group inception the most common, means of reducing the experience of chaos is to assume that the location of the chaos is outside the group. What this involves is an establishment of a boundary around the group whereby, as a means of establishing order within the group, all negative attributes are projected onto outside groups. This projection establishes at one and the same time a conflict with the second task, which almost as immediately confronts the newly established group. This second task is that the group must relate to other groups. The result of the initial projection, however, is potentially, and in fact quite predictably, disruptive of such relationships. Indeed, one can predict that the greater the initial anxiety and the greater the need of the group to project chaos and violence outside, the more difficulty the group will have in subsequent transactions with the outside world.

The broader context of this process is that social systems require the continual formation and interaction of groups. Of course, they may form around a task, develop an internal structure and differentiation of membership, and begin to deal effectively with other groups in the pursuit of the system task. Maximization of group values requires that both the formation and interaction tasks be carried out effectively. Unfortunately, even at the most realistic value-seeking levels there are obvious complementarities in these tasks, complementarities which lead to conflict. The prototype of this conflict is the need to establish structure and definition within the group while at the same time permitting that structure and definition to be permeable enough to permit intergroup functioning. The internal work of the group may not coincide with the need to interact with other groups. Similarly, the identifications, expectations, and demands of the group may come into conflict with those of other groups. All of these contingencies are highly probable disruptive influences on group structure and intergroup relations.

Critical incidents in group life—particularly formation and major value shifts—are occasions for the dominance of dynamic or irrational factors. What is striking about these factors is that they tend to have an intransitive quality in a social system. Thus, the projective simplification of two groups into good–bad affects not only the quality of intergroup relations, but tends to predetermine the nature of the interactions within the salient group. In the extreme case, the need to maintain a common vigilance toward the destructive and disorganized outgroup necessarily implies that no one can differ within the group. If differentiations begin to develop within the group, the danger is that part of the disorganization rejected from the group might reappear. Such groups usually are limited to agreeing only on the point or set of points with which they have negatively identified. The fantasy is that everyone must be the same, and everyone must embrace the same negatively defined ideals. If the primary task of the organization requires leadership, and if the organization survives, its most rigid fantasy will involve the denial of the need for, or the reality of, such leadership.

Social systems order intergroup events through superordinate group leadership. Management is constituted to determine the status hierarchy and to regulate intergroup relations. Thus, one might expect that the conflicts, anxieties, and defenses characteristic of individuals in relation to group leadership should be experienced, at least at primitive levels, by groups in their relationships concerning management. One should expect that the range of individual projective mechanisms would also be available to the group. There are, of course, important differences. We have described the initial task of the group in a closed system as the projection of the ego ideal onto the leader. We have described the initial task in the formation of a group in an open intergroup network as the projection of destructive aspects of the group onto other salient groups. Both tasks are of course present in both settings. Open systems, therefore, simply make it more obvious that there are alternate mechanisms for the splitting of ambivalent attitudes toward the leader. They provide an unfortunate realism to an essentially magical solution to the leadership paradox. The idealization of the intragroup leader is facilitated by the projection of chaos onto outgroups. What frequently makes this kind of solution more durable is the greater likelihood of task support for this division of reparation among groups in a social system. Delays in system communications across group boundaries also retard questioning such solutions. Otherwise, the processes can be identical to those of closed system small groups. Small groups tend to make better use of *time* to separate incompatible responses to authority, whereas groups in intergroup relations make better use of space, technology, task, or division of function.

This discussion would suggest that the notion that projection of chaos and violence onto outside groups inhibits the development of internal leadership needs to be modified. The threat to the open system group would be rational task leadership around relations to other groups. For defensive purposes, certain types of leadership, *e.g.,* fight leadership, would be entirely acceptable to the group. The important dynamic of such leadership is its limited mandate; it would be mandated to carry out the basic assumption of the group vis-à-vis outside groups. A leader with such a mandate who wished to implement overriding rational goals would normally be coerced, at best, into manipulating the group assumption to that end.

System Boundaries

The position of group leadership in intergroup activity is neither so limited nor so stable as the foregoing analysis might indicate. The leader's power, as well as the precariousness of that power, stems from his position on what Miller and Rice term the "boundary" of the group he represents.[13] They define a boundary, in social systems terms, as having two components. One consists of a "differentiation of technology, territory or time"; the other refers to leadership regulation, or what they call an "interpolation of a region of control." The first of these two components is primarily descriptive: an observer might characterize a group or system in terms of the territory it occupies, the times it functions, and its identifying technology or similar institutional functions. The second component is primarily prescriptive: an observer might notice, for example, that a guard regularly stops people at system points of entry, that a foreman enforces work regulations for a segment of workers, or that an organizational chief hires and fires. Together, these two components constitute the boundaries of a system: the unique set of attributes and norms that characterize its functioning.

Discussions of system boundaries have produced a variety of uses in ordinary language. We usually associate boundaries with territorial prerogatives. A person or a group of persons is said to "own" or "occupy" a space which is defined by its boundaries. Thus, backyards and blocks, cities and nations all have a minimal necessary definition in terms of their territorial limits or boundaries. We normally think of buildings and rooms and the objects they contain in terms of volume. One is usually less concerned with dimensions such as density, texture, and movement. A sports field, for example, usually is defined in terms of its spatial dimension, and we usually refer to areas outside those dimensions as "out of bounds." Occasionally a boundary is defined as a region, as opposed to a point or plane. Thus, in international law, the maritime boundary is defined by some countries as a region three or more miles from a national coastline.

While the concept of a boundary has been primarily spelled out in spatial metaphors, we are accustomed in everyday usage to employ temporal metaphors as well. Linear time measurement has proven so useful in technological cultures that we now are accustomed to locating many nontechnical events in such terms. The major boundaries of the average person's day are time boundaries, and a highly developed sense of linear time often is used as an index of cognitive development of maturation in advanced cultures. An important index of a system's effectiveness involves the degree to which it is able to manage time boundaries successfully.

As temporal metaphors frequently suggest, the concept of a boundary also is used in relation to social and technical norms. We often say of both social and technical behaviors that they are either within or "out of bounds." Generally speaking, a person's behavior is "within bounds" if he is acting in accordance with the rules of a system or subsystem.

What seems obvious from these examples is that the concept of a boundary, far from being simply descriptive of territory, time, or behavior, is a predominantly prescriptive concept. The word "boundary" is only an apparently descriptive term that serves a variety of complex social purposes. The evidence is fairly straightforward: of all of the possible distinctions that one could draw on purely a descriptive basis in space, time, or behavior, the ones that we commonly call "boundaries" are *those which serve some social purpose and whose crossing effects some social change*. Thus, any territory could be divided in a very large number of ways for various purposes. It could be divided geometrically, or by type and color of vegetation, or by ground level, or by proximity to some object, or by the use of virtually an endless number of other criteria. For most social purposes, however, and certainly for those we wish to employ here, socially functional boundaries are most relevant. Thus, pathways become prescribed routes for walking, and deviation from these routes may incur sanctions. Areas containing particularly valuable objects may be roped off, with punishments administered to those who enter. Maintaining or crossing boundaries in sanctioned ways may of course lead to value gains.

One may conclude, therefore, that a boundary is a spatial, temporal, or behavioral event whose change has noticeable social effects. A more limited definition which nonetheless calls attention to the central function of a boundary is that it constitutes a *discontinuity in the decisionmaking process*. The crossing of a boundary always raises a kind of jurisdictional problem, concerning how decisions will be made, by whom, and for what purpose.

The concept of a group boundary as involving discontinuities in decisionmaking is useful in understanding intergroup processes. The individual in an intergroup setting will attempt to establish boundaries around his experience by seeking leadership both within and among groups. The primary task of the individual in this situation is to minimize the chances of being without group support, of being ostracized or abandoned. Group membership is an available, if sometime tenuous, remedy. Within the group, the initial goal is to establish real or fantasied decisionmaking procedures which will allow projection of the chaos outside the boundaries of the reference group. The goal is to make individual projective processes into group projective processes.

Groups typically form boundaries either by acting on their initial projection (through immediately establishing leadership and order and some mechanism for external vigilance) or by denying the need to act by further projecting supportive leadership functions onto a superordinate group. The first type of group evolves strong leadership, with clear, often impermeable group boundaries. The second type will see little need for leadership and may take an open-door, open membership approach to their own group boundaries. The difference lies in the locus of decisionmaking.

In the group's relating to other groups, the effects of initial attempts to set group boundaries are predictable. A group with rigid boundaries will interact reluctantly and, as a result, will be generally less well informed and less evenly motivated for intergroup activities. A group with inadequate boundaries will be unable to react to outsiders because of its weak leadership: no one will be able to speak for the group. Indeed, such a group frequently has difficulty arriving at a position on relevant issues. It is unable to process the information it receives.

Group boundaries are both a precondition for intergroup relations and a central source of difficulties. Similarly, group leadership in intergroup relations simultaneously defines the group and creates the conditions that threaten it. A leader constitutes the "boundary" of his group. Within that group his leadership is as secure as task and emotional fulfillment of the members dictate. But he also represents the group to the outside world. If he could be relied upon in that role to gratify members' wishes relating to protection, gratification, retaliation, or whatever, the multiple aspects of his role would create minimal conflict. In fact, it would only enhance the internal solution that has led to his leadership. Frequently, however, the primary task of an organization requires quite different behavior on the part of a leader. It may require him to compromise highly cathected values of his group, it may require him to sacrifice some values to the enhancement of others, or it may even require him to identify in whole or in part with another group. Quite aside from the primary task, the leader may be persuaded of different values, roles, or identities in his transactions with the outside world. In any and all of these changes in the leader, his role in his reference group may be drastically affected. He may be asked to reaffirm his allegiance or to leave the group; he may be replaced internally by a leader who functions as the group desires (while he is promoted to "front" for the organization); or he may be asked to "umpire" disputes between his group and others.

The success with which group boundaries can be crossed in intergroup relations usually is correlated with the success of that activity in achieving the primary task of the group or system. The "trust" that the group has in the leader generally will depend on its perception of his ability to satisfy a wide range of value expectations and demands. Success at the primary task is certainly no guarantee that he will succeed in satisfying these demands. The leader may have the authority to affect a wide range of values within the system, but he also runs the risk of not being able to do so. If he cannot, his role of relating the system to the outside world can be used as a means of extruding him from the organization.

In this circumstance, leadership, which appears to be the highest form of membership, can become a means of ostracism. The leader is in many ways the member least protected against the perils of statelessness.

At any time, however, the leader may decide to adopt a reparative or compensatory stance with respect to his group. He may choose or be forced to reemphasize his shared identity with his group at the expense of pursuing broader system goals, or even at the expense of pursuing rational work goals for his group. He may feel or correctly observe that if he does not adopt such reparative goals his leadership will be challenged or terminated. He will trade external for internal leadership and agree to limitations on his authority to speak and negotiate for his group.

In natural systems these dynamics often occur with such frequency, particularly in low value-involvement situations, that they come to be seen as a fixed part of the operation of the system. In complex project-oriented systems, wherein role definitions are potentially multiple, flexible, and rapidly changing, an individual may join or lead in several project groups simultaneously. This strategy may be maximal for both the individual and the system for several reasons: (1) the individual can reduce the parochialism and limited system involvement associated with single group membership; (2) the skills of the individual can be realized in several components of the system, rather than in one component, hopefully to the benefit of both the individual and the system; and (3) the individual's value to the system, and thus his own security within the system, can be enhanced by not limiting his participation to a single, possibly temporary, project. The drawbacks to multiple group membership are, however, equally impressive: (1) multiple membership tends to blur group boundaries in a manner conducive to conflict, where group functions begin to overlap and compete; (2) individuals with common skills who belong to several groups may themselves become a functional group in the system, thus blurring organizational structures and authority and creating further conflict; and (3) the individual in multiple conflicting groups will experience the conflict and may be unable to make use of group projective defenses onto other groups to which he belongs. Competing groups may also attempt to isolate the problem or conflict in such individuals. For cooperative groups, the bridging function which such individuals serve will be valuable; for competing groups, there may be a need to eliminate such a function.

Systems deal with these dilemmas in various ways through organizational structures which generally encourage a division of values. The principal division involves the identification of a superordinate group which is given control over the allocation of resources among groups in the system. System leadership is entrusted with the task of defining and policing membership, leadership, and other value sharing among task groups. It can aid in rational group boundary formation and in monitoring transactions across boundaries in ways designed to maximize system values. Of course, ability to understand and control this process will vary enormously. Even systems high in process and task monitoring and achievement tend to evolve toward some important divisions of reparative goals. In many systems, divisions of reparation parallel or contribute to system goals. In others, the need to translate reparative values into action leads to the system's or subsystem's being defined in terms of them, or heavily influenced by them, in ways which disrupt manifest goals. The mediating factors that determine whether or not disruption will occur are related to how effectively values are shaped and shared within the system. The more effectively these tasks are met, the less likely it is that disruptive interpersonal group and intergroup processes will dominate the system and threaten the accomplishment of the primary task.

Conclusion

The organization of human resources around group tasks implies a complex psychological process. In its simplest version, this process involves an accommodation (which the individual usually is more than willing to make) to collective goals. According to this view, individuals project regulatory functions onto a "leader" in exchange for real and fantasied offers of specific roles and identities in the work of the group. To the extent that this projection is a relatively simple act of objectifying personal goals or ideals in the leader, and to the extent to which the content of these projections remains relatively simple and related to the work task, leadership will remain stable and the group will be able to work to achieve real values. To the extent that these projections become more complex and less encompassable by the work task, and to the extent to which they serve reparative aims for members, leadership will become more problematic and more subject to frequent changes in the emotional life of the group. In an organizational setting, this picture will be magnified by the possibility that the same process may occur between members and the leader, as well as between the group and other groups, with a corresponding extension of available roles and functions.

Notes

1. For demonstration of this point, see M. McDougal, H. Lasswell & J. Miller, The Interpretation of Agreements and World Public Order (1967).
2. See H. Lasswell, The Political Writings of H. D. Lasswell (1951).
3. See H. Lasswell & A. Kaplan, Power and Society (1950).
4. See M. McDougal, H. Lasswell & J. Miller, supra note 1.
5. See generally H. Lasswell, World Politics and Personal Insecurity (1935).
6. See I. Menzies, A Case Study in the Functioning of Social System Defenses Against Anxiety (1961).

7. *See* E. MILLER & A. RICE, SYSTEMS OF ORGANIZATION 1 (1967).

8. *See generally* P. SLATER, MICROCOSM (1966).

9. S. FREUD, GROUP PSYCHOLOGY AND THE ANALYSIS OF THE EGO at 196 (standard ed.) (1955).

10. *Id.* at 61.

11. *Id.* at 122.

12. *See* W. BION, EXPERIENCES IN GROUPS (1959).

13. E. MILLER & A. RICE, *supra* note 7, at 5–13.

Chapter 4

The Role of Law in Promoting Peace and Violence: A Matter of Definition, Social Values, and Individual Responsibility

BURNS H. WESTON

Ours, we are told, is a government of laws, not of men. What John Quincy Adams and his forebears of the Enlightenment meant, of course, is that no person—prince or pauper—is or should be allowed to treat the law with untrammeled whimsy; and perhaps now even Richard Nixon would agree to that. But in a critical sense this famous dictum is misleading, therefore potentially harmful. On final analysis, all government is "of men," even if not always "*by* and *for* the people." The individual human being is, for

This essay, whose intellectual debt needs no explaining, is a revised version of a paper written for inclusion in the proceedings of a symposium series entitled "Perspectives on American Violence and Aggression," and is based on a symposium series presentation made at Clemson University on April 17, 1975. The symposium series was supported by the Clemson University College of Liberal Arts and the South Carolina Committee for the Humanities through the National Endowment for the Humanities. Copyright, 1976, Clemson University. Published by permission.

good *and* ill, the ultimate actor always; and to suggest or believe otherwise is to misconceive the governmental process—to misapprehend the true architects of social justice and injustice—and thereby to handicap the workings of political accountability. Government is not the symbol of some transcendental hand, somehow removed from ordinary mortals. "In the long-run," wrote Thomas Carlyle, if somewhat hyperbolically, "every Government is the exact symbol of its People, with their wisdom and unwisdom." [1]

Now what I have just said about government is true also of law, since the law is, to large degree, but a normative way of speaking about government. In the long run, to paraphrase Carlyle, all *law* is the symbol of its people, with their wisdom and unwisdom; and it is this theme I seek to clarify in these pages. My concern is to demythologize the law so as to reveal how it can be and in fact is both a peaceful and a violent influence in human affairs, and my perception is that this task requires dealing with matters of definition, social values, and individual responsibility.

A Matter of Definition

What do we mean by "law" and "peace" and "violence"? Surely it is necessary to come to grips with these key concepts if only to avoid misunderstanding. The need for definition, however, is yet more basic than this, and extends well beyond the intellectual delights that inhere in such an exercise. Definitions condition not only what we are willing to think about, but also how we go about inquiring into what we are willing to think about.

Take the concept "law." From early childhood, we are trained to think upon law as mainly, if not entirely, a peaceful influence in human affairs. Indeed, it is from precisely this viewpoint that I was asked to deliver the lecture upon which this essay is based. It was thought that I, a lawyer, might have something to say about law as an *alternative* to violence. Thus, to maintain that law can be, and in fact is, a violent as well as a peaceful influence in human affairs is to suggest, if not a heresy, at least a need for definition.

And what about "peace" and "violence"? Contrary to popular belief, these words, like so many others in our daily discourse, simply are not as obvious as at first they appear. Like the perspiring bodies of all living creatures, they are in constant motion and change, carrying from context to context a host of different—oftentimes contradictory—associations. It may be asked, for example, why it took the U.N. Special Committee on the Question of Defining Aggression over twenty-four years to reach agreement on the meaning of that central Charter term "aggression." Ralph

Waldo Emerson put it most eloquently: "Language," he said, "is a city to the building of which every human being brought a stone." [2]

But there is more to these terms "peace" and "violence" than simply their fluctuating character. Even when used in one discrete context by people of essentially common background and training, they can be highly ambiguous—and not least when their users are law students, practitioners, and even law professors! Another popular misconception, one which I suspect is more dearly held by lawyers than by laypersons, is that the legal profession is generally endowed with clear-minded expression. True, many lawyers toil successfully in the vineyards of clarity; but to generalize from this fact that most lawyers speak with unambiguous tongue would be serious error—and I am not referring to what McDougal has called the "squid function" of the law, the art of deliberate obfuscation. My point is that much of our legal vocabulary, including such terms as "peace" and "violence," not to mention "law" itself, is fraught with tautology and normative ambiguity, such that we refer to both fact and legal consequence simultaneously, indiscriminately *describing* and *prescribing* at the same time. And such muddleheadedness, it must be emphasized, can lead to pernicious judgments. This is why, for example, former President Nixon—a lawyer—received widespread criticism when at a news conference he referred to Charles Manson, *before* trial and conviction, as a "murderer."

Let us, then, hazard some definitions, and let us try to do so more in descriptive than prescriptive fashion. Otherwise, we risk the chance for ambiguity—not a desirable result, surely, as regards a topic that needs neither sponsor nor justification as among the most important of our time.

"Law"

The word "law" has, of course, several diverse applications. Yet despite this fact we use the term with relative everyday ease. With little conspicuous difficulty, we use it to refer to matters essentially outside human intervention, as when we speak of "the law of gravity" or "the law of supply and demand"; and we use it to refer to matters which are, conversely, the product of human intervention, as when we speak of "the law of contracts," "criminal law," "the law of torts," "property law," and all the other breadwinners of the legal profession. Similarly, within the context of human intervention, we use it to refer to those social patterns which evolve essentially without benefit of centralized decisionmaking mechanisms, as when we speak of "customary law" or "international law"; and we use it to refer to those social patterns which evolve from highly articulated command and enforcement structures, as when we speak of all those executive orders, legislative enactments, and judicial decisions we call "the law of Iowa" or "the law of the United States of America." The point is, of course, that none of these uses is incorrect. Fundamentally, each is proper. However applied, the concept "law" represents, in the end, a set of events whose common property is sanctioned regularity.

To most people, however, including many lawyers, this sanctioned regularity called "law," insofar as it pertains to social arrangements, is conceived largely as a body of rules affirmatively prescribed and enforced by the sovereign State, to the general exclusion of those regularities which, somehow mysteriously divorced from "the law," we are wont to call "customary morality." Except for the international lawyers and "juris- prudes" who take the challenge of defining "law" seriously, little attention is paid to those normative principles and practices which result from self-determinative interactions in the private sphere. Consider, thus, why Amy Vanderbilt's *New Complete Book of Etiquette,* manifestly descriptive of ordered social behavior in the absence of positive sovereign command, is not ordinarily considered relevant to law school study. Tenaciously wedded to the legal positivist tradition of nineteenth-century English jurist John Austin and his followers, we cling to the belief that law is entirely or almost entirely a function of government—that it bespeaks only what governments say and do—and that it has little or no relation to what evolves in the absence of governmental intervention. So narrow a concep- tion, I submit, is empirically unwarranted and socially detrimental, at least in the long run. It feeds the insidious notion that law is, or that it must be, as if some natural law of physics, only the expression of the will of the strongest.

But how, then, do we define "law" so as to avoid transforming the mere *characteristics* of the popular model into the *prerequisites* of a com- prehensive theory about law; so as to avoid the allegation that law is not, or that it cannot be, the expression of the will of all or most of the people? The answer: to think upon law in functional rather than institutional terms, and from this perspective to acknowledge its invention, its application, and its appraisal both within and beyond the formal corridors of power. Law does not live by executives and legislators and judges alone. It lives also by individual human beings such as ourselves, pushing and pulling through reciprocal claim and mutual tolerance in our daily competition for power, wealth, respect, and other cherished values. To turn a phrase, law is legiti- mized politics—a Hydra-headed process of social decision, involving per- sons at all levels and from all walks of public and private life who, with authority derived both explicitly and implicitly from community consensus or expectation, and supported by formal and informal sanction, effect those codes or standards of everyday conduct by which we plan and go about our lives.

And thereby hangs the beginning—and indeed the end—of my tale. To think upon law as an alternative to violence or as a promoter of peace is as correct or incorrect as it is to think upon ourselves as alternatives to violence or as promoters of peace.

"Peace" and "Violence"

Consider, next, the word "peace." Do we mean by this term simply the absence of war, or what recently among students of Peace Science has come to be called "negative peace"? Or do we mean something more— call it "positive peace"—including not just the absence of hostilities or other coercive strife but also the presence of "good will towards men," as embodied in such concepts as "brotherly love," "human dignity," and "social justice"? Can "peace" be read to mean not just a social state in which values are shaped and shared more by persuasion than by coercion, but also one in which there is sought "the greatest production and widest possible sharing, without discriminations irrelevant of merit, of all values among all human beings"? [3] To the oppressed black, Chicano, or white sharecropper who lives under conditions of "law and order," but who literally or figuratively crops more than he or she shares, clearly this larger frame of reference is the more meaningful. Indeed, I suspect it is more meaningful even to the shell-shocked soldier who bunkers down into his foxhole to find a kind of peace that perhaps is more starkly real than any known to Man. Surely a narrow reference, however pure, cannot be his definition of "peace" either.

And finally, what about the word "violence"? Must we limit its meaning simply to the conduct of military hostilities and lesser uses of physical force? Or can it, too, have larger meaning, to include what in the recent literature has come to be called "institutional" or "structural" violence, involving not just physical coercion, but also those many other kinds of indignities that compel us to speak generally of "Man's inhumanity to Man"? To be sure, a broad definition of "violence" liberates the socially victimized assassin to reply to his degraders that they, too, engage in violence. The rhetoric of the Symbionese Liberation Movement at the time Patricia Hearst first made front-page headlines is testimony to that. But to the everyday poor and downtrodden, whose basic commonwealth is political impotence, certainly a narrow definition has dubious significance.

My point is, obviously, that these words "peace" and "violence" are very elastic terms which cover a wide variety of definitions that are neither right nor wrong, but that are, rather, of potentially limited utility. Monochromatic expressions purporting to describe polychromatic realities, they represent many different judgmental points on a policy-charged continuum of constructive and destructive behavior, as measured idiosyncratically by our personal value systems. The definitional problem, in other words, is not really factual, but ethical and tactical; and the intellectual challenge is to recognize this fact just as we must for all the other words we use that are equally susceptible of both descriptive and prescriptive interpretation.

Still, if only to make some communicable sense out of our topic, it seems necessary to settle upon some definitions of "peace" and "violence" that will not unduly offend our disparate sensibilities. Of course, and as suggested, this quest for generally acceptable definition is no easy one. As opposite sides of the same theoretical or behavioral coin, each beset by conflicting value preferences, the concepts "peace" and "violence" pose severe difficulties regarding where precisely to draw the diacritical line. I would suggest, however, at least three points of departure where *not* to draw the line.

First, I would not draw it at the use of nonuse of physical force per se. It takes no ethical or tactical judgment to agree that the threat, as well as the actual use, of physical coercion often destroys without enhancing (especially when it is intense) and that consequently it, too, is open to the designation "unpeaceful" or "violent." And the same can be said of many of those intensely deprivative social conditions which directly and indirectly aid and abet—or are conducive to—the exercise of physical force, even when not involving the actual use or threat of physical force. No, the ethical and tactical judgments reside elsewhere, somewhere beyond the realm of physical force per se where, surely, differences of opinion are bound to arise. For example, however much he may prefer rule by reasoned persuasion, the public official concerned about effective government, while perhaps willing to label as "violent" his use of physical force, is seldom likely so to label either his threat of physical coercion or his threat or use of nonphysical coercion. He simply does not want to taint or otherwise subvert his efforts at ensuring compliance with public policy. Nor, as a general rule, does anyone living *comfortably* in a democratic, nontotalitarian society.

On the other hand, neither would I frame a generally acceptable distinction between "peace" and "violence" in terms of the legality or illegality of the behavior in question, and not just because such a litmus would contradict my starting premise that law can and does promote violence as well as peace. In the first place, physical force is no less violent or unpeaceful for being lawful. As suggested earlier, probably even the concerned public official would agree to that. And in the second place, as comfortably well off as many of us are, the evidence is everywhere—in the tyranny of one ethnic group over another, in the abject poverty of billions, in the desecration of our environment—that much of what passes for lawful nonforceful behavior, whether publicly or privately inspired, sooner or later does violate, directly and indirectly, the human body as well as the human mind and spirit. It was, I suspect, from this perspective that in 1905 George Bernard Shaw wrote that "[o]ur laws make law impossible; our liberties destroy all freedom; our property is organized robbery; our morality is an impudent hypocrisy; our wisdom is administered by inexperienced or mal-experienced dupes, our power wielded by cowards and weaklings, and our honor false in all its points."[4] Let us face facts. Whether turn-of-the-century Britain or contemporary America, it requires little or no definitional hair-splitting to see that there is a great deal of legalized violence all around us, as least if we are willing to look beyond the physical force garden-variety.

But all this said, there would seem no escaping a related, and here third and final, point of departure. However much we might agree with Shaw about the perversities of Western society, a generally acceptable division between "peace" and "violence" is unconvincing if it is based on the distinctions we typically venture between "social justice" and "social injustice"—unconvincing, that is, if we neglect to add, as is usually our custom, the elements of physical coercion or intensity of deprivation to the equation. The reasons are three. First, it would suffer from that normative ambiguity against which I warned previously. Second, it would raise the idiosyncratic problem of having to define extremely value-laden terms and consequently would risk nonuniversality across political boundaries and between different cultures. And finally, absent the elements of physical coercion or deprivational intensity, it would fly in the face of ordinary usage; there simply are too many observable instances of social injustice that are neither coercive enough nor intense enough to be called "violent" and still be faithful to everyday communication. Of course, this social justice/social injustice test does have a certain propagandistic or consciousness-raising appeal. It does cause the privileged few to consider realms of perceived or felt violence that ordinarily they never think about, let alone experience. But if this advantage is allowed to control, then none of us, to say nothing of our by now legendary public official, ever could escape violence or the charge of violence totally. The words "peace" and "violence" then would lose all common meaning.

So where do we draw the line? Is there a seam in this so far seamless web? Are there general meanings that are simultaneously inclusive and exclusive enough to satisfy our respective sensibilities and still be useful? I think so, and I think they can be posed without engaging the ambiguities noted so far and without resorting, further, to that other favorite but false discriminant: conflict versus nonconflict. Conflict is endemic to society and therefore in the nature of both peace and violence. Moreover, it probably is required for mental well-being, at least if social psychologist and psychoanalyst Rollo May and like-minded others are to be believed.[5] At any rate, I take as my guide the two Arabic words for peace: *sulah,* which means the end of hostilities or a truce; and *salaam,* which means an enduring peaceful relationship based on mutual respect. I do so, however, recognizing that there seldom exist any pure states of peace and violence and that therefore one must approach the problem of general definition in flexibly behavioral terms.

Thus I would say that *peace* (or peaceful behavior) constitutes the exercise of public or private power without resort to *any* physical coercion, and, in further service to mutual respect, without deliberate or tacit encouragement of *any* conditions plainly conducive to physical coercion. And of course, *violence* (or violent behavior) would be the reverse: the exercise of public or private power by resort to physical coercion, and, in further derogation of mutual respect, by deliberate or tacit encouragement of conditions plainly conducive to physical coercion. Conceived in terms of the minimum order that is required to maintain the simple human respect contemplated by the term *salaam,* i.e., the absence of physical coercion and of conditions plainly conducive to physical coercion, these proposed generalizations are relevant to all levels of human interaction—a desirable advantage, I believe, considering that interpersonal behavior can shape intergroup experience and vice versa. Of course, as generalizations, they naturally continue a certain seamlessness in the definitional web. But that is always the price we pay for remaining loyal to everyday communication. No completely satisfying definitions are possible until we deal in discrete issues of fact and policy.

A Matter of Social Values

With our proposed definitions in mind, especially that of "law" as a Hydra-headed process of legitimized politics, it is appropriate to turn to our central theme to which the remainder of this essay is addressed: the role of law in promoting peace and violence. In so doing, I look first to where the law has been in the past, and leave to later consideration where it might go in the future. The reason for this approach will become apparent as we proceed.

It is fair to say, I think, that most modern legal systems, whether autocratic or democratic, and including the international legal system, are in theory, if not always in practice, dedicated to the promotion of peace (or minimum order) in interpersonal and intergroup relationships. We see this in our national criminal laws, in the United Nations Charter, in the various domestic and foreign prescriptions against capital punishment, in the Nuremberg judgments, and so forth. Of course, bearing in mind that ours is a more-or-less and not an either–or world, we are obliged to admit that this dedication will vary from context to context *even in theory.* For example, in most societies, individual persons and elite groups are authorized to use force for reasons of self-defense and crime prevention—that is, paradoxically, to use violence to get peace. An "eye for an eye, a tooth for a tooth" is everywhere to some degree a legitimized politic or expedient;

and in this way, obviously, the theoretical dedication is mixed. The law can and does promote violence to fight violence. On balance, however, it remains an empirically viable proposition that contemporary legal processes —in the home, in the local community, in the nation, and in the world— are committed to the promotion of peace or minimum order at least in principle. Minimum order is, after all, the sine qua non of their existence, whether in the United States or the People's Republic of China.

To speak of theory, however, is not to speak of practice, and if we accept, as I believe we must, that law is what people do and do not do, as well as (or in combination with) what people say and do not say, then clearly we are faced with a much less positive state of affairs than the one I just have outlined. Simply put, the strength of the law's commitment to peaceful behavior in interpersonal and intergroup relationships leaves much to be desired. First and most obvious, there are the Nazi Germanys of this world whose theoretical commitment to peace is itself, to be generous, open to serious doubt. Indeed, recalling the last two decades of United States policy in Southeast Asia, similar doubts arise in respect of, regrettably, even our own country. Next, there are the many failures which, for lack of adequate resources and well-conceived priorities, public and private officials commonly encounter when seeking compliance with peace-oriented norms. Despite my own serious reservations with much of the "law and order" rhetoric to which we have been treated in recent years, the institutional weaknesses to which the "law and order" lobbies point must be understood for what they really are, namely, substantial indicators of the extent to which our legitimized politics system blinks at violent behavior. And finally, there are the many ways in which our interlocking public and private legal orders tolerate and thereby promote conditions conducive to physical violence, by default or by design. They are familiar to all of us even though ordinarily we do not think of them as outcomes of legal process.

Most conspicuous, of course, even if scandalously removed from public outrage, is the tolerance—indeed, the annual $5 billion hardware encouragement—given to that monstrous nuclear threat system we insanely label a problem of *foreign* affairs, deluded as we are by the "fail-safe" rhetoric of its military-industrial and academic sponsors. Also conspicuous, but the more scandalously removed from public outrage because it has at least the aura of being closer to home, is that pervasive resistance which tenaciously fights delaying actions against equitably effective gun control legislation, ostensibly (but, I submit, erroneously)on the strength of our Constitution's Second Amendent. And this resistance continues, sadly, despite the actual or attempted assassination of two presidents, two governors, two senators, three nationally known civil rights leaders, and countless others whose fame has been too small to stir reformist action.

Now as indicated, these examples of violence-prone tolerances (or normative conditions) are probably the most obvious I could mention. But

consider also the following—by no means exhaustive, but all of them interdependent parts of a life-reducing whole:

      our celebration of violence in the mass media, not least in our chil-
dren's Saturday morning television cartoons, and in sharp contrast to our X-rating of sexual love in our movie theaters;

      our multimillion dollar manufacture and marketplace support of war
games, killer toys, and other amusements of human destructive-
ness, often gloriously wrapped in the rugged anti-authority or
extra-authority individualism of such spectacular deputies of
violence as Jesse and Frank James, Billy the Kid, Pretty Boy
Floyd, Bonnie and Clyde, John Dillinger, the Godfather, and
James Bond;

      our extravagant merchandizing of physical combat and competitive
victory in our sports arenas and places, such as caused few to
wonder at Coach Vince Lombardi's remark that "winning is
everything," and far surpassing the cricket match that allegedly
inspired the Duke of Wellington to comment that "[t]he Battle
of Waterloo was won on the playing fields of Eton";

      our broad and deep acceptance, evident in our classrooms and
churches only slightly less than elsewhere, of that ethnocentric
"we/they–us/them" syndrome which seduces us into making
heroes out of warlords and honored citizens out of zealots whose
Manifest Destinies inhibit our seeing that others quite different
from ourselves just might have some legitimate claim to simple
human respect;

      our shocking indifference—shocking, that is, considering the chrome-
plated wealth and sheepskin-bedecked talent of our land—toward the anomic conditions and incendiary frustrations that are
inextricably bound up in the poverty, hunger, and disease of our
urban ghettos and rural slums, ticking like time bombs and wait-
ing to go off perhaps before we make it back to our suburban
bedrooms and magnoliad plantations.

And so forth and so on. These tolerances also are some of the normative
regularities we live by. These tolerances also constitute part of our legitimized politics. These tolerances also figure among the codes and standards which help to make up what we call our legal system. As Michel de
Montaigne once put it, "[t]he laws . . . are born out of custom; every man
holding in inward veneration the opinions and customs approved and
received about him."[6]

    In sum, the past role of law in promoting peace and violence offers
little room for comfort to anyone who is dedicated to the grand principles
of human dignity, at least in the United States. For all the good and noble

work that is being done by many concerned people, it is sad but true, as H. Rap Brown is reputed to have said, that "violence is as American as apple pie."[7] Ours is a "Pow!" "Crash!" "Ugh!" "Bang!" "Boom!" nation, in which a tingling pleasure is derived not least from violence that is found relatively unpainful or unserious.

But let us not delude ourselves. To speak of the past role of *law* in promoting peace and violence is to speak not of some "brooding omni-presence" beyond ourselves, but of *our* past role in promoting peace and violence. Like Thomas Carlyle's government, the law is our symbol, re-flecting our wisdom and unwisdom; and this is the simultaneously simple and hard lesson we have to learn. All law—whether of the nuclear family, the specialized organization, the municipality, county, state, or nation, the world, or, as is usually the case, an interpenetrating combination of all these arenas—necessarily depends for its progressive and retrogressive de-velopment on the total flow of explicit and implicit communications and acts of collaboration which create those behavioral expectations we identify as formal and informal "codes," "standards," and "rules." Law is no mere body of rules accompanied by convictions of duty or obligation. It is, rather, a constantly churning stream of authoritative *and* effective decision which, like that one of its main tributaries we call "social custom," finds its ultimate wellspring not in theoretical abstractions or mortar-and-brick institutions, but in the ethics—the socioeconomic and political values—of its many human constituents who both shape it and, in turn, are shaped by it. This is what lawyers and political scientists have in mind, consciously or unconsciously, when they talk about the interrelation of law and so-ciety. And this is what I have in mind when I argue that the past role of *law* in promoting peace and violence is *our* past role in promoting peace and violence. Regrettably, our track record is not a good one.

Which raises the question: can the law change—can *we* change—so as to promote more peace than violence in the future? The answer, I sub-mit, lies not in the stars but in ourselves. It is a matter of individual re-sponsibility.

A Matter of Individual Responsibility

What, then, are the possibilities for enhancing the role of law in service to peace in the future? As indicated, assuming law to be as I have defined and described it, this depends on the extent to which ordinary people, work-ing in individual and group capacity, are willing to assume responsibility for the peace-oriented values they claim to hold dear. To be sure, many knowledgeable people, including especially governmental officials and other leadership figures, would reject this individualistic perspective as hope-lessly naive. How, it may be asked, can the average citizen, in the face of all those well-known institutional constraints, really do anything truly effective short of attending law school, becoming a high-powered lawyer, and possibly running for significant political office? Is it really credible to maintain that any one of us can make a noticeable difference, that any one of us can have real impact? Is it not true that the law tends to favor the status quo and that any grass-roots movement toward progressive change is therefore doomed from the start?

There is, I concede, much validity to these kinds of questions, and for this reason they bear closer scrutiny than I give them in my concluding paragraphs. At the very least, they point to what all of us know to be true about fundamental social reform, namely, that there never are quick nostrums. For the moment, however, consider the possibility that if we can envisage a peaceful nation and world that is realistically attainable, as surely we can and must, we also can devise ways in which to help make that vision a reality. Great historical change is not the result of inexorable predestined forces alone (if at all). Fundamental reforms come about also because some inspired people are able to perceive and act upon the need for change.

In other words, despite our poor showing in the past, and despite all the negative trends that portend a grim global future, I have an abiding faith in the capacity of the human imagination and spirit. Convinced that all of us are, in our diverse spheres of influence, opinion shapers and decisionmakers to one degree or another, I deeply believe that at least together we can motivate many of the normative reforms that are necessary to bring about the peace at home and abroad that is so desperately needed. Such would seem to be the lesson, at any rate, of the civil rights movement, the antiwar movement, the women's liberation movement, and maybe what might be called the anti-Watergate movement. Provided we have the will, we can make a difference. And to this end I commend two distinct but interdependent starting-points—the clarification of our violent and nonviolent values, and the choosing of peace-oriented life-styles—followed by enlightened and progressive political action. All three of these pursuits are indispensable to the truly effective exercise of individual responsibility in the quest for peace.

Values Clarification

By "values clarification" I mean a conscious commitment to a better understanding of the extent to which any one of us is willing to favor violent over nonviolent means to achieve the social goals we believe essential to our lives. One would hope, of course, that in this commitment we would be guided by the truism that violence—especially intense violence—seldom enhances and usually destroys disproportionately; by which I do not mean, be it understood, that we should always opt for nonviolence. A pacifist I am not, and as a lawyer I respect the need sometimes for intensely coercive sanctions to secure compliance with authoritative community norms. Furthermore, I confess a certain sympathy, albeit somewhat reluctantly, for violent revolutionary strategies under very carefully defined and exceptional circumstances.

But this is not to say that each of us should not deliberately undertake the clarification and constant reclarification of our violent and nonviolent values. We have constantly to ask under what conditions we are willing to spank our children or strike out at some other we might wish to chastise. We have constantly to ask under what conditions we are willing to support ordinances, statutes, and other social prescriptions which call for the use of force or which legitimize those practices that are conducive to violence. We have constantly to ask under what conditions we are willing to turn the key that can unleash nuclear warfare (and it is a key, not a pushbutton, and one I never would turn). We have, in sum, constantly to search for and clarify the ways in which our personal values make us, as the saying goes, not part of the solution but part of the problem.

Put another way, conscious and enlightened commitment to the genuine clarification of our values can illuminate the choices that are open to us, can assist us in isolating those policies we are willing to recommend and for which we are willing to assume responsibility, and can therefore help us to win friends and influence people in that all-important process of consensus formation upon which all social reformations ultimately depend. On final analysis, there never has been, there is not now, and there never will be any getting around the fact that the law is the accumulation and expression of individual values and concerns. For all its special mumbo jumbo, and despite the current cybernetics revolution, the law never has, does not now, and never will provide a technical or scientific escape from those final creative choices that each of us, private citizen or public official, is sooner or later called upon to make.

Life-Style Choice

By "life-style choice" I mean a conscious commitment to the actual living out of our peace-oriented values in both our professional and personal endeavors. For just as the structures of peace and violence can be influenced by individuals, depending on their reappraisal and choice of values, so obviously can these structures be advanced or retarded by the extent to which individuals choose to practice what they preach. Concededly, it is possible that this injunction to practice the peace we preach is easier for those of us who have yet to settle into family and career than it is for those of us who already are fairly fixed in our ways. But surely not much easier. In either case it is a difficult injunction to follow, requiring as it does the rearranging of thought patterns and work habits that are very familiar, very comfortable. Whether it means choosing, modifying, or switching to careers different from the ones we have planned, or resisting the superior orders and powerful reward systems that hold sway within our chosen professions, or refusing to go along with what is popular in our avocational and marketplace pursuits, or recommitting our investment portfolios and charitable contributions, or simply demanding of ourselves and families a divorce from particular day-to-day negative behaviors, it means above all being willing to call a halt, as they say, to "business as usual."

This is the lesson of My Lai. This is the lesson of Watergate. How each person conducts his or her life fundamentally affects our nation and world and consequently makes a difference to the future. A genuine reorientation of individual life-styles toward a more peaceful vision of the future than has prevailed in the past is one of the most significant ways we have to reorient our national and world societies in relation to peace and violence. It is no easy task, as I have said, since it borders on something in the nature of an identity crisis for each of us. And certainly it is not a strategy that is capable of rapidly dramatic results. But by way of personal example we set new life-style trends, and such trends are the stuff of custom —which in turn, lest it be forgotten, is one of the main pillars of the temple we call "law." A conscious commitment to the actual living out of our peace-oriented values can make and shape the law.

Political Action

Finally, there is law reform through "political action," by which I mean, without wanting to belabor the obvious, a conscious commitment, after reconsideration of personal values and life-style choices, to all those essentially collaborative techniques of everyday political life through which public opinion is newly influenced, popular consensus newly reached, and controlling norms newly and consequently established. Far too often it is thought that lawmaking, including law reform, takes place only in the courts, the legislature, and similar agents of the formal legal system. Such thinking, however, is legalism of the worst sort. Misconceiving the scope, if not the very nature, of legal process by relegating the more or less informal or unorganized modalities of law creation to virtual extinction, it serves to anesthetize our capacity for self-determination. It induces within us a sense of impotence or futility or just plain disbelief as regards our ability to effect real dominion over our lives.

Now I do not minimize the difficult and often lonely business of fighting City Hall. Clearly this is something with which we have to reckon. It is just that I do not minimize either the patently observable fact that in the great chess game of life even mere pawns, especially when working together, can checkmate the king. For all that the conventional wisdom would have it otherwise, lawmaking and reform do not reside exclusively (or even always most successfully) in the organic divisions of Montesquieu. No, they reside also in the performance of all those basic functions of social decisionmaking which cut across the executive, legislative, and judicial branches, and which involve, consequently, every category of private citizen and governmental official working to transform political demands or values into authoritative and effective community norms:

> the *intelligence function,* through which we gather, process, and disseminate persuasive decisional data;
>
> the *promotion function,* through which we engage in both simple recommendation and active advocacy;
>
> the *prescription function,* through which we and our representatives project social policies under some title of authority;
>
> the *invocation function,* through which we appeal to alleged authoritative words and deeds to justify compliance with, or deviation from, claimed community norms;
>
> the *application function,* through which we seek the transformation, by ballot and otherwise, of authoritatively prescribed policies into controlling events;
>
> the *appraisal function,* through which we monitor and evaluate past decisions in terms of the degree to which they actually secure the community goals in whose name they were rendered; and
>
> the *termination function,* through which we press for the repeal of arrangements that have ceased to serve their purpose or become inequitable.

These decision functions, which Yale scholars Myres McDougal and Harold Lasswell have so perceptively culled from our otherwise imperfectly revealed experience,[8] are of course well known to students of law and political science. Indeed, precisely because they are derived from social experience, they are at least vaguely familiar even to the average citizen (albeit, obviously, not in the esoteric terms borrowed here). To a varying degree, each of us is party to, and hence generally acquainted with, one or more of these functions in our everyday lives. About this there can be no doubt.

What is doubtful, however, is whether most of us—lawyer, political scientist, or layperson—see clearly the nexus between these decision functions and legal reform, between political action and the forging of more strongly peace-oriented legal orders than those we tolerate today. My reason for doubt is of course the large degree to which we persist in maintaining an essentially Austinian conception about the interrelation of law and social process. Just as we cling to the belief that law is entirely or almost entirely a function of government, so also do we assume, with curious paradox, that law and politics are separate and distinct, their twain rarely, if ever, meeting. Nothing, however, could be further from the truth. While much ink has been spilled in trying to differentiate "law" from "politics," the fact is that, as coordinate dimensions of that greater whole we call "the power process," each undefinable without major reference to the other, the two are distinguishable more in theory than they are in practice. And the sooner we learn this undeniable fact the sooner we will comprehend that political action is central to legal process and therefore to the structuring of that minimum order we call "peace." In a very real sense, through performance of whichever one or more of the previously mentioned decision functions is best suited to our respective capabilities and talents, all of us are lawyers in the quest for the termination of violence and of conditions conducive to violence in human affairs.

*   *   *

Thus we return to where we began: the role of *law* in promoting peace and violence—past, present, or future—is the role *we* play in promoting peace and violence. Can we accept and act upon this basic self-determinative lesson? Surely we must; for if we do not, we feed the misconception that law and the possibilities for achieving peace and other cherished values are beyond the reach of ordinary men. Worse, in a thermonuclear age with potentials for destruction which defy almost all imagination, we risk our very survival. If, on the other hand, we can accept this fundamental teaching, then just possibly, recognizing that law is at least as much a "trickle up" as it is a "trickle down" process of decision, we can make a difference and maybe do some good. On final analysis, the law—symbol of our wisdom and unwisdom—will be as peaceful and violent as we are peaceful and violent.

All this said and done, however, there remains the allegation that my thesis is hopelessly naive because it grossly underestimates the capacity of the law, like other social institutions, to become "larger than life" and therefore resistant to change. The point is etched poignantly in a parable drawn from Franz Kafka's *The Trial:*

> "Before the Law stands a doorkeeper on guard. To this doorkeeper there comes a man from the country who begs for admittance to the Law. But the doorkeeper says that he cannot admit the man at the moment. The man, on reflection, asks if he will be allowed, then, to enter later. 'It is possible,' answers the doorkeeper, 'but not at this moment.' Since the door leading into the Law stands open as usual and the doorkeeper steps to one side, the man bends down to peer through the entrance. When the doorkeeper sees that, he laughs and says: 'If you are so strongly tempted, try to get in without my permission. But note that I am powerful. And I am only the lowest doorkeeper. From hall to hall keepers stand at every door,

one more powerful than the other. Even the third of these has an aspect that even I cannot bear to look at.' These are difficulties which the man from the country has not expected to meet; the Law, he thinks, should be accessible to every man at all times . . . ."[9]

Less engagingly put, all legal systems invariably achieve, though for reasons that are not always to be disparaged, a measure of autonomy that is resistant to popular pressure. The law can and often does operate to promote the status quo values of those who are most closely in control of the existing power structures.

Yet surely this is not to say that legal reform through popular demand is never possible or that the rascals never can be thrown out. As evidenced by recent Soviet and Chinese history, even totalitarian systems must be sensitive to grass-roots opinion and influence. Of course, one individual against all the rest is usually powerless. Acting in concert, however, with the values we prize, the life-styles we choose, and the diverse political actions we pursue all geared to a common positive purpose, we can promote that commanding normative consensus against which, almost by definition, no legal system can claim complete immunity. The real question is: have we the will? And the answer is, regrettably, problematic. As naturalist-poet Loren Eiseley has written, "[t]he hand that hefted the ax, out of some old blind allegiance to the past fondles the machine gun as lovingly. It is a habit man will have to break to survive. . ."[10]

As regards the Kafkaesque world in which we live, however, the distinctive and concluding point I want to make is this: to the extent that all or part of any legal system significantly limits the capacity of individuals to determine what should happen to their lives, the role of law in promoting peace—our role in promoting peace—must be directed first at opening the doors of effective political participation. *"Government* without the Consent of the *Governed,"* wrote Jonathan Swift, "is the very *Definition of Slavery"*;[11] and to this one should add that political slavery or political alienation is one of the most basic reasons why men rebel. Leading to social frustration, it leads to violence. A first and continuous task in the quest for peace, therefore, must be the performance of all those legal-political functions that can effectively countermand the curse of imposed political alienation. The ultimate violence just may be political degradation, the ultimate peace its absence, and our ultimate mission, therefore, its elimination whenever and wherever found.

Notes

1. T. CARLYLE, PAST AND PRESENT 260 (1904).
2. R. EMERSON, *Quotation and Originality,* in 8 THE COMPLETE WORKS OF RALPH WALDO EMERSON 189–90 (University ed. 1903).

3. McDougal, *Perspectives for an International Law of Human Dignity,* in M. McDougal & Associates, Studies in World Public Order 987 (1960).

4. B. Shaw, *Preface to Major Barbara,* in 3 Collected Plays with Their Prefaces 15, 59 (Bodley Head ed. 1971).

5. *See* R. May, Power and Innocence—A Search for the Sources of Violence chs. 7 & 11 (1972).

6. 1 M. de Montaigne, Les Essais 161–62 n.3 (H. Motheau & D. Jouaust eds., *c.* 1926) (my translation).

7. *Quoted in* M. Blumenthal, R. Kahn, F. Andrews & K. Head, Justifying Violence: Attitudes of American Men 1 (1972).

8. *See, e.g.,* Lasswell & McDougal, *Criteria for a Theory About Law,* 44 S. Cal. L. Rev. 362, 385–87 (1971).

9. F. Kafka, Parables and Paradoxes 61 (Schocken paperback ed. 1961).

10. L. Eiseley, The Immense Journey 140 (Vintage Books ed. 1959).

11. J. Swift, The Drapier's Letters to the People of Ireland 79 (H. Davis ed. 1935).

Chapter 5

The Role of Law in World Society: Present Crisis and Future Prospects

RICHARD A. FALK

There are a variety of indications that we are living through one of the great transitional upheavals of human history.[1] Old forms of political organization cannot cope with emerging technologies of destruction or communication, traditional political and religious belief systems are disintegrating, old sources of energy are being displaced by new sources, and prophets of doom include in their growing rank persons of eminence.[2] Such signs of the passing of the old system are bound to provoke a crisis of legitimacy, a failure of confidence, and a concerted effort to revive the old symbols of order, as well as stimulate interpretations of modern conditions that deny the magnitude of the challenge. As a consequence, periods of transition for any political order are bound to be filled with confusion and struggle that often lead to bloodshed.

This chapter examines this situation from a global perspective by considering the role of international law in facilitating and obstructing a response. Underlying this inquiry is my conviction that a satisfactory response to this crisis of transition necessarily centers upon a reorganization of the world political system. The nature of this reorganization can take a variety of governmental forms, but it will have to include substantial transfers of national sovereignty for large and modern states, especially in military, economic, and environmental affairs, as well as the growth of effective mechanisms of central guidance to deal with these critical subject matters.[3]

On this basis, we proceed to depict the principal pressures on the present world order system. Our interpretation of these pressures is central to the assertion that an acceptance of the state system as an adequate problem-solving and value-realizing framework for human affairs is as willfully obsolete as the belief in Christopher Columbus' era that the earth was flat. This next section develops the case for the earth's roundness and implies the dangerous consequences of a failure to begin the process of normative and institutional adjustment at the earliest possible time.

Data on the Obsolescent State System

The breakup of the oil tanker *Torrey Canyon* in the Atlantic Ocean off the Crown of Thorns near Cornwall, England, in 1967 generated a strong new set of world order concerns. Thoughtful people began to realize that the delicate balance between man and nature was being increasingly threatened by the scale and technological character of human activities. World society was awakened to the finite capacity of the earth in a context of rapidly growing world population and of increasingly devastating pollution associated with an ever-expanding industrial production. Many observers became alarmed by the interplay between population dynamics and economic goals. The population of the world has been growing at a rate of 2 percent per year, which means a doubling every thirty-five years. Increases in the gross national product have been prime national goals everywhere, and the GNP has been growing, on the average, at least twice as rapidly as population. How long can such patterns of growth continue?[4]

These basic trends produced a series of doomsday prophecies in the years after the *Torrey Canyon* incident. Other warning signs seemed to confirm these grave forebodings. Some species of birds and fish seemed endangered by man's polluting practices. The threat of extinction confronting the peregrine falcon and the blue whale began to be interpreted as foretastes of what was in store for mankind as a whole. The notion of growth was threatening in relation to the rediscovery of limits that established the conditions for man's tenancy on earth. A concern with scarcity emerged. Soon, it was contended, the earth would be faced with shortages of space and resources. The so-called energy crisis was seen as a further confirmation of this dismal conception of the future, and only the first of a series of world issues associated with shortages in critical resources. Crowding would intensify human problems, especially with respect to clean air and water, sanitation, hygiene, and mental health. These worries seemed justified by the smog around big cities and the ecological collapse of such large bodies of inland water as Lake Erie, Lake Constance, and Lake Geneva.

Alarmist sentiments were voiced by increasingly responsible and respected spokesmen of the human race. In 1969 the Secretary General of the United Nations, U Thant, declared that "Members of the United Nations have perhaps ten years left in which to subordinate their ancient quarrels and launch a global partnership to curb the arms race, to improve the human environment, to defuse the population explosion, and to supply the required momentum to development efforts." Even President Richard Nixon, not known as an opponent of the status quo, argued in his State of the Union Address of January 22, 1970, that "The great question of the seventies is, shall we surrender to our surroundings, or shall we make peace with nature and begin to make reparations for the damage we have done to our air, our land and our water?"

In January 1972 a prominent group of British scientists issued *A Blueprint for Survival,* and its opening words set the tone of the whole document: "The principal defect of the industrial way of life with its ethos of expansion is that it is not sustainable. Its termination within the lifetime of someone born today is inevitable—unless it continues to be sustained for a while longer by an entrenched minority at the cost of imposing great suffering on the rest of mankind."[5] The cautious British newspaper, the *Manchester Guardian,* called the publication of the blueprint a major event that was likely to have an impact on human destiny comparable to that of the *Communist Manifesto.* Also in 1972 *The Limits to Growth* was published amid major fanfare because it contained a study carried out by computer simulation under the direction of an MIT team of systems analysts that lent an aura of scientific objectivity to an alarmist view of the future of the human race. The study was widely disseminated under the aegis of the Club of Rome, an international group of prominent and energetic leaders of business and science who had organized themselves into a private association because of their conviction that the predicament of mankind had to be confronted outside the centers of governmental power.[6]

As might have been expected, this surge of concern produced a strong counterreaction. Allegations of exaggeration were hurled at the champions of the ecological cause. John Maddox, the editor of the British science magazine *Nature,* treats concern with the planet's future as if it were a cultural sickness by calling it a "doomsday syndrome."[7] Another skeptic, Carl Kaysen, director of Princeton's Institute for Advanced Study, condescendingly slaps the wrist of the Club of Rome study, *The Limits of Growth,* by writing of the "computer that spelled out W*O*L*F." [8] The new ecological breed of alarmists has been accused of being neo-Malthusian heretics who want to stop the clock of history and innovation at the very moment when breathtaking technological breakthroughs might finally alleviate human suffering. Since Malthus was wrong, or at least since he shouted wolf far too soon, this line of argument proceeds, there is similar reasons to discount the warnings today and get on with the real work of producing more goods and services for more people.

There is also a moral reaction among welfare liberals against the claims of planetary emergency. This reaction reflects the basic judgment that poor people within American society and in the world generally are more likely to be benefited by a continuing pattern of economic growth than by any other set of social policies and goals.[9] Without growth providing more for all, it would be necessary to take from some to give to others, which has usually meant bloodshed in history. There is also the suspicion that the rich and powerful—the tennis shoe conservationists—are more compassionate toward the peregrine falcon than toward their own human brethren, and that somehow the insistence of the ecological movement on limited prospects for further safe expansion is tied to an ideology of defending the social and economic status quo, while purifying the air and water of wilderness regions so as to promote the concerns of the rich.[10] In this spirit, black Americans and black Africans have sometimes regarded policies and proposals designed to reduce population growth as a form of genocide. This reaction reflects the view that there is a connection between population size and political potency. It does seem logical to suppose that the larger the relative size of a minority group, at least in a democratic society, the greater will be its share of influence on social policy, although the influence exerted by Jews in America or the Swiss in international affairs suggests that factors other than percentages of the whole are often more important.

Part of the ecological backlash also reflects conflicting priorities. A ban on DDT seemed sensible from the point of view of countries with no malaria problem and the wealth to substitute more expensive pesticides, but not at all prudent for tropical nations struggling to provide the minimum necessities of life and public health for their populations.

Such a global situation of complexity and inequality breeds controversy and confusion. As a consequence, a concept of adequate social policy has not crystallized around a consensus. A sense of apathy is tending to replace the anxiety that existed only a few short years ago, and there is a failure to organize the sort of positive response that will be needed to promote human progress. In one central respect the doomsday issue is a red herring. The important fact—above any reasonable quibble—is that we are managing life on this planet in a dangerous and obsolete fashion and that without beginning the process of planetary reorganization we have no basis for confidence that we can solve the great problems of mankind, let alone work toward more positive forms of human development on an individual and collective basis.

The first step toward a positive program of response is *to agree on an agenda of problem areas and on the need for an integrated strategy of response*. Such an agreement will lift us out of the paralyzing eddies of debate about whether or not the world is at or near the ecological brink. It will also establish the connections between seemingly separate public interest initiatives. The basis of hope for the future is to grasp the connectedness of people and their problems and to think, feel, and act accordingly.

To orient thinking it is essential to understand the links that join together four human problems—population pressure, war, poverty, and environmental decay—which are often treated as separable concerns. Initiatives intended to deal with any of the four depend, for their eventual success, upon what is being done about the other three. The most crucial recent development is a biospheric consequence of human crowding and waste on a planet that relies on violence to solve disputes at all levels of human interaction and that is administered by governments of sovereign states, most of which are obsessed with maximizing their own wealth, power, and prestige. This larger picture of state sovereignty and social want supplies the dynamic tension to the wider world drama.

Population Policy

At the present time there is not enough food to feed the approximately 4 billion people in the world. The most recent FAO report shows that developing countries need an annual increase of 4 percent in food production to maintain the present diet of their expanding populations.

In 1971 and 1972 world food production increased between 1 and 2 percent. Reportedly, 10 to 20 million people die each year from hunger and malnutrition, and many millions more are chronically undernourished to such an extent that their prospects for mental development are severely and permanently curtailed. Perhaps as many as two-thirds of all people alive today do not eat well enough even to acquire the basis for realizing their human potential.

By the end of the century, or perhaps a few years later—it hardly matters whether it is the year 2000, 2005 or 2020—the number of inhabitants on this planet will double. It does not require an alarmist disposition to anticipate the strain on resources arising from efforts to provide for the minimal needs of food, clothing, housing, and education for this doubled human population, even if the goal is no more ambitious than maintaining existing standards of inadequacy.

But matters are worse. Most of this population increase will be concentrated in poor and already crowded countries. These poor countries, in Asia, Latin America, and Africa, have very young populations; typically, close to 40 percent of the people are under fifteen years of age. Such an age structure means that the population will continue to grow even if birthrates should begin to fall rapidly in the years ahead. In most of these societies, however, large families are still desired. For instance, in India studies show that a majority of potential mothers continue to want four or more children, a preference pattern throughout much of the Third World that ensures that population growth will go on for a long time.

Population growth tends to be reduced by a demographic transition that accompanies the industrialization process. But there is every reason to believe that such a transition, if it will ever occur in the poor countries, is several decades away. At the same time, urban migration is proceeding at a rapid rate. Kingsley Davis, a Berkeley demographer, has made trend projections showing that if urbanization continues at its present rate, half the people in the world will live in cities by 1984, everyone will be a city dweller by 2023, and half of these cities will have populations of over 1 million people each." These trends are not predictions, but tendencies implicit in present patterns. In the 1950s urban populations in the underdeveloped countries increased by an estimated 55 percent, producing enormous sprawling slums generating severe new pressures as a consequence of high unemployment and crime rates. Many cities in the Third World are growing by 7 percent or more per year, which means they are doubling in population every decade. It hardly requires an exceptional political imagination to comprehend the strains caused by such a growth pattern.[11]

In many respects the overcrowding and strain on facilities at national parks and museums illustrates the overall impact of increasing population. With fixed facilities every additional visitor above a certain threshold aggravates the problem of overcrowding. When jobs, food, space, and resources are the fixed facility, then the scope of the problem begins to become apparent.

Even in high consumption societies, the prospects of economic growth are connected with an expanding population. Estimates suggest that in the United States during the last decade population growth accounted for about one-third of the increase in demand for goods and services, the other two-thirds are attributed to rises in the standard of living and shifts in taste and technology. Some critical sectors of the economy have a large stake in stimulating further population growth; the following table [12] suggests the percentage of sales increase per year attributable to increases in population:

	%
Food industry	65
Beverages	34
Clothing	30
Furniture	35
Medical care	24

Housing	27
Auto sales	16
TV, radio sales	8

It is no wonder that many thoughtful men have concluded that population pressure is the key to the world crisis. But it becomes more and more apparent that even if this is the key, in some sense, it cannot turn the lock. There is no way to isolate population dynamics from many other aspects of the world situation. Birth control technology is not helpful in any central sense until the average desired family size falls to replacement levels. On the basis of the European and North American experience, however, such a drop is not likely to occur until people foresee a healthy and reasonably hopeful future for themselves. Child rearing and family life provide some of the few real satisfactions of people at subsistence levels, especially in rural settings; anxiety about the survival of children and care in old age also sustains the impulse to have four or more children.

Furthermore, national leaders and the citizenry itself tend to see a young and growing population as a sign of vitality and potency. Considering St. Petersburg, Florida, or any other leisure village helps to make us understand our bias against an older population structure. Countries with rapid economic growth, for instance, Japan, often encounter shortages of skilled manpower and prefer to adopt pronatalist policies rather than to attract labor lifting immigration constraints. Forces of nationalism thus tend to reinforce a laissez-faire view of population dynamics.

In countries with a high GNP it is obvious that each additional birth adds an environmental strain of considerable magnitude, assessed as fifty to one hundred or more times the strain of each additional Indian or African. In recent years the American population has increased by about 2 million per year, compared to 13 million or so for India. If an ecological measure is used, however, the American increase is fifty times two, or 100 million per year, compared to India's 13 million. Therefore, from a world ecological perspective the problems of population overload arise primarily from the interplay between rather small rates of population increase and high rates of per capita consumption in the rich countries. For this reason some demographers have even argued that population is the wrong variable to focus upon if ecological jeopardy and resource depletion is the primary concern.

Environmental Policy

As people and standards of living increase there is—other things being equal—an expanding burden on the environment. There are ways to mitigate this burden, and we need desperately to use technology to protect us against the dangers caused by technology. But the extent of our capacity to protect mankind and the planet against environmental hazards is unclear. At the present time the best judgment seems to be that we do not know enough to assess the extent or character of the danger.

Certain tendencies, however, are very menacing. For example, our industrial development rests upon the discharge into the environment of ultratoxic materials which are accumulating at a fantastic rate.

The following table [13] enumerates the increased *per capita consumption* in the United States during 1964–68 of some materials that do environmental damage:

	%
Mercury	2,150
Plastics	1,792
Nitrogen fertilizer	534
Synthetic organic fertilizer	495
Aluminum	317
Detergents	300
Electric power	276
Pesticides	217
Wood pulp	152
GNP per capita increase	59

This table strengthens the argument that it is the technological character of our society, rather than either its demographic or GNP dimensions, which constitutes the main danger.

As technology advances in a high GNP society there tends to be a geometrical rise in environmental burden and threat. Such a trend is also evident with respect to the prospects for modernizing agricultural production in the Third World. The following table[14] shows the amount of pesticides needed to increase agricultural yield per acre on land under cultivation in Asia (other than China and Japan), Latin America, and Africa:

% Increase in agricultural production	Pesticide tonnage needed (metric ton)
—	120,000
10	150,000
20	195,000
30	240,000
40	285,000
50	342,000
60	402,000
70	475,000
80	558,000

| 90 | 640,000 |
| 100 | 720,000 |

To gain a twofold increase in food production it is necessary to have a sixfold increase in pesticide use. In such a context, the future prospect of large-scale contamination seems evident. In 1965 a U.N. World Population Conference estimated that to meet food needs in the future with only modest improvements in diet would require increasing the food supply 43 percent by 1970, 103 percent by 1980, and 261 percent by 2000. Expanding Third World populations and accelerating urban growth are placing tremendous stress on governments to employ the most capital-intensive methods of agriculture at their disposal. Capital scarcity and poverty make it imperative to use the cheapest available pesticides, which also happen to be the most environmentally damaging because of their persistent quality. DDT is four to five times cheaper than any available substitute at the present time.

We are also entering a period of increasing shift from fossil fuels to nuclear energy. The prospect of relying on fission technology to meet basic energy needs, at least during an interim period when fusion methods are perfected, is fraught with environmental danger and will increase the vulnerability of contemporary civilization. The projected accumulation of radioactive wastes in the United States gives some insight into this dimension of technological development:[15]

	1970	1980	2000
Installed nuclear capacity $MW(e)$	11,000	95,000	734,000
Liquid wastes			
annual production, gal/yr.	23,000	510,000	3,400,000
accumulated volume, gal.	45,000	2,400,000	39,000,000
Total fission products in megacuries	1,200	44,000	860,000
Accumulated fission products; tons	16	388	5,350

Qualitative dangers are more difficult to assess. How does one evaluate the vulnerability of a nuclear facility to a hijacker's threat to crash a plane at Oak Ridge? One expert suggested that if such a threat were successfully carried out, it could release radioactive fallout a thousand times greater than that of the Hiroshima blast. This much radioactive material could blanket an area the size of California.

The carriage of oil by ocean tankers is another important expression of the polluting consequences of high technology civilization, as is the exploitation of offshore oil reserves. It is conservatively estimated that 2 million tons of oil are dumped or spilled into the ocean each year. The size and number of tankers are increasing, as are the frequency of oil spills. These occurrences are symbolic expressions of the sorts of environmental pressures generated by increasing resource demands in a world of diminishing supplies.

We are already experiencing the consequences of a poisoned habitat. Dangerous concentrations of toxic substances such as carbon monoxide and sulphur oxides are found in the human body. City dwellers have concentrations that are on the average ten times as high as have country dwellers. And toxic levels are higher in the residential areas of the center city than in the suburbs. The incidence of lung cancer is 37 percent higher in cities of more than 1 million than it is in cities of between 250,000 and 1 million. Reports of deaths from respiratory diseases suggest a strong correlation with pollution levels. In Osaka, Japan, fifty students were overcome by nausea at a basketball game recently after failing to hear an air pollution signal warning. The Tokyo Environmental Research Institute reports that Tokyo residents may have to wear gas masks in ten years to obtain protection against bronchial diseases. Air filters are already a common sight in Tokyo.

There are increasing prospects of resource shortages in the future. The following chart gives some sense of the available resource reserves in a number of critical areas. Resource concentrations are politically significant. Recent estimates conclude that the United States, with 6 percent of the world's population, is consuming between 35 and 40 percent of the world's nonrenewable resources each year, while the 30 percent of the world's population living in the industrial portions of the world consume as much as 90 percent of the world's energy and mineral resources each year. This disproportionate resource use has to be coupled with both the increasing reliance upon high technology methods to satisfy resource and energy demands, and with the inverse correlation between the location of resources and the level of living standards. An explosive set of political possibilities seems locked into this structure of resource supply and demand.

Among world economic powers Japan and the United States are particularly dependent on resource imports, as compared to the Soviet Union and China. As an indication, one recent study shows that of the thirty-six minerals needed for industrial processes, the Soviet Union is self-sufficient in twenty-six, whereas the United States is self-sufficient in only seven.[16] Such a comparison is part of a pattern. It suggests that foreign policy will be guided, even if only unconsciously, by the impulse to retain assured access to the mineral resources needed to sustain an import-dependent economy.

Part of the environmental crisis revolves around the desirability of evolving a resource conservation program, as well as a sharing of new resources, such as the mineral wealth of the oceans. Only the space super-

Lifetimes of Estimated Recoverable Reserves of Mineral Resources
Population and Consumption Rates as of 1964
Known Deposits That Are at Present Feasible to Mine Commercially

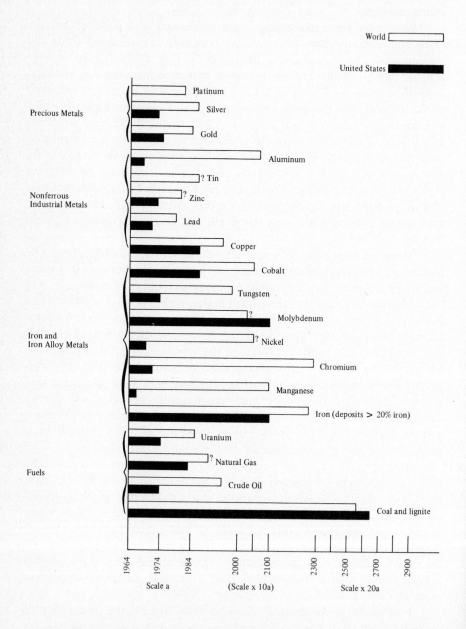

SOURCE: "Re-Visioning the Future of the Third World: An Ecological Perspective on Development," by Edward J. Woodhouse, *World Politics*, vol. XXV, no. 1 (copyright © 1972 by Princeton University Press: chart on p. 12). Reprinted by permission of Princeton University Press.

powers share the information obtained through satellite observation of mineral and geological formations, thereby accentuating inequality of access to the material wealth of the earth itself. It is a matter of considerable moment whether the technological superiority of the developed world maintains, or even increases, its nine-to-one edge in resource utilization when it comes to dividing up the wealth of the oceans. There are indications that the poor are getting poorer, in world terms, as a result of the increasing relevance of technological proficiency to economic growth and development. Therefore, the politics of world order seem regressive both from the perspective of environmental protection and in relation to goals of social and economic justice.

In opposition to this basic situation, some positive developments are underway, although their significance seems relatively minor. The 1972 Stockholm Conference on the Human Environment did manage to produce an agreed upon Declaration of Principles. Of greater practical relevance is the evidence of increased efforts by governments to cooperate in areas of environmental concern. One hopeful sign is that in 1972, ninety-one governments managed to successfully negotiate an Ocean-dumping Convention. However, as with other measures recently agreed upon by governments to protect environmental quality, successful implementation will continue to depend on the good faith and voluntary action of major governments; these are not reliable structures of authority if national goals diverge from international regulatory standards.

War

The horror of war has for centuries stimulated men of good will to search for a way to establish perpetual peace. In our era this search has intensified. World Wars I and II caused widespread death and destruction. The prospect of a third world war is almost too awesome to contemplate. The persistence of war as a social institution is evident from the occurrence of violent interstate conflicts in almost every portion of the world.

War planners in powerful countries inform political leaders that security in a strategic sense exists only when there is confidence in the capacity to inflict "unacceptable" damage on a potential enemy. In the context of the Soviet Union or the United States that means the assured capacity to kill tens of millions of people and substantially destroy the industrial sector. In 1967 Secretary of Defense Robert McNamara told Congress that damage would be "unacceptable" to the Soviet Union if it inflicted 20 to 25 percent "prompt" fatalities among the population and destroyed 50 to $66\frac{2}{3}$ percent of its industrial capacity. Our notions of national security continue to reflect this kind of calculation. There is an element of genuine bureaucratic madness. McGeorge Bundy, until recently a top national security adviser, has written that these calculations are not real choices for "sane men." In Bundy's words:

In the real world of real political leaders—whether here or in the Soviet Union—a decision that would bring even one hydrogen bomb on one city of one's own country would be recognized in advance as a catastrophic blunder; ten bombs on ten cities would be disaster beyond history; and a hundred bombs on a hundred cities are unthinkable. Yet this unthinkable level of human incineration is the least that could be expected by either side in response to any first strike in the next ten years. . . .[17]

Yet each year we grow still more reconciled to these "realities." As a consequence, we are locked within a dangerous and demeaning view of the world community. If "peace" remains dependent on the active threat of mass incineration, then sharp limits are placed on every effort to create an atmosphere of trust and cooperation in world affairs. And without the growth of trust there is no real prospect for the kinds of international cooperation needed to protect the environment and conserve the resources of the planet, let alone create an atmosphere that might help realize the human potential.

The war system is spreading throughout the world at an alarming pace. Over the decade between 1961 and 1970 GNP increased 8 percent per year. During this ten-year interval, military expenditures in the developed countries increased only 2.6 percent. These rates of increase calculated in constant dollars suggest military modernization as a priority development goal. Such a priority is alarming in a world of such massive social privation and great inequality in wealth, resources, and standards of living. While African and Asian armies are improving at breakneck speed (on an average doubling in quality every nine years), the basic indicators of human dignity are stationary or falling. There were 100 million more illiterates in the world in 1970 than there were twenty years earlier, and the prospects of infant mortality remain four times as great in a developing country as in an advanced country.

In the world as a whole, military expenditures increased from $119 to $216 billion between 1961 and 1970, with the developing countries' share tripling in that period from $10 billion in 1960 to an estimated $31 billion in 1971. In other words, it is apparent that governments, at least, continue to believe that there is no alternative to military establishments and arms races if they want to obtain national security and prestige. China's acceptance as a world power seems associated, in part, with her acquisition of nuclear weapons, a message received in Japan, India, Pakistan, and Indonesia. The ease of access to weapons materiel and know-how means that any threatened or ambitious government or any determined opposition group will be able to secure weapons of mass destruction within a decade or so.

The war system is linked in several ways with other world problems. For one thing, countries under external threat from large states associate their security with a growing population.

Military development requires scarce materials and highly skilled personnel. These resources satisfy no human needs and hence are withdrawn from productive uses. The war system also emphasizes the elements in human experience that divide people and, hence, makes it more difficult to evolve common policies or a shared ecological ethos. State sovereignty reinforces ideas of rivalry and encourages each state to maximize its own interests regardless of the effects on the world community as a whole. Maximizing self-interest in a world of scarce resources, including space, air, and water, generates intense conflict to obtain larger shares of the fixed stock, as well as inducing a steady deterioration in the quality of the resources.

Human Rights

In many countries, individuals are likely to be punished or even killed if they disagree too vigorously with the government. There are prisoners of conscience in almost every major country of the world. Reports of torture now come even from many societies with long traditions of toleration and stability. Severe forms of racial discrimination persist in southern Africa. Political repression is encountered in governments with orientations on the left and the right, in Czechoslovakia, Hungary, Cuba, and the Soviet Union on one side and Greece, Brazil, South Africa, and Spain on the other side.

Less extreme, but fundamental, limitations on human rights are found everywhere and are closely related to ethnic and economic status. Minority groups are subject to official harassment, particularly to the extent that they are mobilized to demand change and equity, and necessarily evolve patterns of pathological and paramilitary response to a situation of hoplessness and frustration.

Even a country with such strong constitutional traditions amid affluence as the United States seems to have been moving in dangerous directions with regard to individual liberties, as a consequence of an unpopular war and the dangers of anomic violence posed by dissatisfied minorities. There has been a series of political trials against antiwar leaders in the United States.

In main, the impulse to repress arises from the inability or unwillingness of a government to meet the real problems of its society in a humane and efficient way. Those who govern fear exposure of their bad will or impotence. This is the central message of the Watergate epic. Modern governments tend to fear disclosures to their own populations more than to potential foreign enemies. Indeed, given satellite flights and the importance of mutual reassurance with regard to nuclear weapons, it is normally beneficial to avoid international secrets in the security area. Nothing would be more dangerous to the stability of nuclear deterrence than unfounded suspicions about what the other side might be able to do or is intending to do.

In essence, many governments are run for the benefit of the dominant interest groups in their society, rather than for the welfare of their overall population.[18] It is, thus, possible for GNP and GNP per capita to rise rapidly without any improvement in the standard of living for the impoverished masses who compose 70 to 80 percent of the population of a country.

Brazil illustrates the compatibility of high rates of economic growth as measured in GNP accounts, an average of 10.8 percent per year over the last decade, with an actual worsening of economic conditions for the mass of the population. The architects of Brazil's "economic miracle" admit that their country's strategy rested on high technology investment and frozen wages. The admission that such a development path is "brutal medicine" is often coupled with the alleged need to take a relaxed view of social justice so as to promote the country's economic growth. Defenders of the Brazilian strategy also contend that an obsession with income distribution would lead to a "premature welfare state" which would ruin the economy.

Such an economic strategy in a country of mass privation virtually ensures political repression to sustain stability. It also embodies insensitivity toward the human consequences of social policy and is likely to be equally unconcerned about ecological dangers.

Indeed, it is significant that Brazil has taken the international lead among Third World countries in arguing that economic development should take precedence over environmental concerns. In a typical statement of the Brazilian outlook, Miguel Ozorio de Almeida, special advisor to the Foreign Minister and delegate to the 1972 Stockholm Conference on the Human Environment, argued on an *international stage* the exact opposite of what Robert Campos maintains and what the Brazilian economy exemplifies on the *domestic stage*. Ambassador Almeida relied on *per capita* income inequalities of about forty to one that arise when the population/product totals of the nine most developed countries are compared to those of the twenty-five most underdeveloped. According to Ambassador Almeida, "These major disproportions must be kept in mind in any discussion of the ability of countries to act in the environmental field." [19] Not surprisingly, Ambassador Almeida dismissed a plea for ecological equilibrium as tantamount to requiring man to accept a "pre-fire utilization stage." Even a return to the caves would not do, he alleged, as the dampness would require fire, which may affect the ecological balance in some measurable way, and so "nothing short of a chimpanzee society could be considered as fully integrated into ecological equilibrium." [20] Ambassador Almeida supplemented this caricature of the ecological perspective with a typical affirmation of technocratic optimism, contending that we do not know enough to be worried and that science has produced so much in the past that we are justified in relying upon "geo-chemical wizardry" to cope with whatever problems of scarcity and pollution do exist. As he put it:

> [T]he most important point I can make is that now, more than ever, we must not allow ourselves to be cheated of our opportunities, to be swept into a period of unnecessary panic. . . . We must not meet unjustifiable fears with dreary solutions; scarcity for all, reduction of population, and masochistic castigation of present and future generations through economizing on resources that are far from exhausted.[21]

Ambassador Almeida's views are significant because they so clearly illustrate the link between ecological irresponsibility abroad and political repression at home: the international position is vindicated by an appeal to the injustice of economic inequality between rich and poor countries, while the domestic repression arises from the refusal to narrow the gap between rich and poor citizens.

Conclusion

The international setting, then, is beset by the cumulative and inter-related pressures generated by population growth, environmental decay, the war system, and the denial of human rights. I believe that the impact of these pressures is already beginning to disintegrate the world order system of our time. It seems clear that the relevance of international law to the future will be directly proportional to its capacity to mitigate or overcome these pressures. Yet, international lawyers have not, by and large, shifted their focus from a concern with the legal dynamics of interaction within a stable and durable world order system constituted by sovereign states.

International Law as a World Order Variable

To what extent can international law and international lawyers help fashion a response to this unprecedented world order challenge? Does the role and perspective of law tend to maintain existing arrangements of power, wealth, and authority during periods of stress? Or can law be used to encourage progressive developments, given the present world order setting? It is in relation to this series of questions that Professor McDougal's work in conjunction with Harold Lasswell and others of the last decades becomes so profoundly relevant to the central issues of human destiny.

In approaching a discussion of these issues it seems useful to distinguish sharply among the role of international law in (1) the present world order system; (2) the transition process; and (3) in a future world order system that is projected as both desirable and attainable by some definite time.[22] These distinctions will be considered in relation to a world situation characterized by *crisis* and *transition*. Note that the transition to new organizational forms seems destined to take place in any event, through collapse and trauma, if not through conscious reconstruction, education, and peaceful political action. The international law specialist can help shape and facilitate a beneficial type of transition (or indeed can hasten the advent of traumatic transition), and his skills and influence are relevant.[23] The tradition of international law, despite all the shortcomings of law-in-action on a world level, provides the most sustained tradition of inquiry into the conditions of tolerable world order, the only disciplined inquiry that relies upon largely shared concepts and explicit goals,[24] and the most nearly universal language of discourse on the proper organization of mankind that is available. National actors, regardless of conflicts of ideology, culture, race, and stage of economic development, rely on international law to express their grievances in relation to the existing order or to support their adversary positions in disputes with one another. As such, the tradition of law in world affairs is a natural focus for initiating the collaborative work needed to ready the consciousness of man for the birth of a new system of world order.[25] Such a focus could provide an arena for the convergence of distinct, even antagonistic, perspectives regarding the future of world order and is not meant in any sense to imply a prediction of the automatic emergence, much less the inchoate existence, of a universal legal consciousness.[26]

Furthermore, such a focus should not be understood to imply a belief in the centrality of law in relation to the maintenance or transformation of world order systems. On the contrary, I believe that law in *any* social setting operates as a quasi-dependent variable that generally promotes the values and perceived interests of existing power/wealth arrangements; the more highly articulated the social order, the more likely it is that the legal system will achieve a measure of autonomy from immediate political pressures.[27] As international relations remain highly competitive and relatively decentralized, it is to be expected that the legal system has little distinct identity on vital matters and that it, therefore, reflects the values and perceived interests of the government leaders, especially those who act on behalf of powerful and rich states and who, in turn, reflect the values and interests of their most influential constituent groups. This dependent character of law will be accentuated whenever, as has been the case in world affairs since the Russian Revolution of 1917, there is a cleavage on fundamental goals and methods among the members of this leadership group.[28] During a period of transition, basic issues of peace and justice will be assimilated into the struggle for control. Under such circumstances law can generally perform only in a marginal capacity, providing a common framework for restraint and normative guidance. This tendency to assimilate legal issues into a larger political framework has been somewhat curtailed in recent decades by the efforts of principal governments to maintain normative guidelines in order to avoid large-scale, especially nuclear, military conflict.[29]

Furthermore, the focus upon international law as a world order perspective should also not be taken as an automatic endorsement of the *beneficial* role played by law. As will become evident in later sections, my analysis takes it for granted that to the extent that *change* rather than *stability* is of prime concern, law tends to function in a regressive fashion, insulating and rigidifying existing domains of control, obscuring and rejecting demands for change, sustaining privileged positions, exonerating and insulating structures of inequality and domination from formal challenge. The legal system also can and does function in a positive fashion; under appropriate circumstances it can facilitate concensus formation in a fragmented world community, but its negative impacts must be understood to avoid false postures of acquiescence or complacency.[30]

Finally, the focus on law as a variable should not be understood as eliminating the need for political action and movements. Law can contribute to the struggle for a new world order system only to the extent that it incorporates a positive vision of what is desirable and possible in the future. A new system of world order will not be achieved, to say the least, by mobilizing evidence, mounting persuasive arguments, and demonstrating the reasonableness of proposals.[31] It is legalism of the worst variety to disassociate proposals for drastic world order revision from the political process through which such proposals could be put into practice.[32] I envision a wide-ranging struggle against those who benefit from, and are affiliated with, the present economic and political structure of world society. The world order movement I favor is dedicated to the principles of nonviolence as a prime strategy (although I acknowledge a reluctant willingness to support coercive, and even violent, strategies under certain exceptional and carefully defined circumstances).[33] In this sense, it is important to work for a world order movement dominated by a Gandhian ethos, rather than one that accepts the inevitability of armed struggle and holy war. But such a commitment implies personal sacrifice, organized coercion, and the realignment of power.[34]

Perhaps it should be mentioned that the term "international law" is being used in the extended sense of world law to embrace all legal roles and relations on a global level. A reason to continue using the term "international law" is to emphasize continuity with the legal tradition of earlier periods, to acknowledge the persisting primacy of national governments as international actors, and to stimulate global discussion with minimum attention to terminological innovation.[35] But it should be clear that the new international law includes within its scope such important international actors as international institutions and multinational corporations.[36]

It is also important to introduce a distinction between international law and world order. By international law is meant the processes by which national governments and other actors stabilize and revise their interrelations through the assertion of claims and counterclaims about permissible behavior, and through the invocation of rules and procedures to justify their own behavior or condemn the behavior of other governments. Nonstate actors play a subordinate role in the claiming and rule-invoking processes; the description of international order as constituted by sovereign states remains generally accurate. By world order is meant the structure of power, authority, and beliefs that give human relations their specific shape on all levels of social interaction, ranging from the nuclear family to a world government. A world order *system* is a comprehensive description of the pattern of world order arrangements prevailing at a given historical period and some account of the ways in which its various parts interact to produce a whole. In this usage, world order is an analytic construct. The assessment of a given world order system's normative status as beneficial or detrimental is an entirely distinct matter, depending on positing values and assessing or testing their degree of realization, as well as on comparing the existing system with alternative systems of world order. The comparative study of systems of world order is an analytic process, but the selection of a particular system as more desirable than the present one is a matter of preference and judgment.[37] Both operations are important, but it is useful to keep them as distinct as possible, enabling an understanding of operations by analysis and of preferences by normative judgment.

A Metalegal Focus for Appraisal

In appraising the place and function of law in world order systems it is important to have clear and, to the extent possible, operational criteria for appraisal. It seems useful to rely on two kinds of criteria, normative goals and organizational imperatives.

1. *Normative goals.* The role of law in a social order is valued to the extent that it helps to achieve the realization of certain goals. These goals may vary from one historical period to the next, and from one type of political consciousness to another. We propose four normative goals: first, minimization of large-scale violence in the relations among states; second, maximization of human welfare, as conceived both in relation to minimum standards and with regard to distributive equity; third, maximization of social justice, as conceived in relation to removing barriers to individual and group autonomy and development; and fourth, the maximization of environmental quality. These goals are formulated in response to the salient world social pressures dealt with in the preceding section associated with population growth, the war system, repression, and environmental decay.[38] It is understood that these pressures are interrelated, and that the

effort to solve one may aggravate others, thereby raising central issues of trade-offs and weighting.[39]

2. *Organizational imperative.*   The role of law in the present world order system will also be considered in relation to its contribution (or lack thereof) to the development of a *central guidance system* capable of managing human affairs in a coherent fashion. Because we interpret these dangers as proximate and appreciable, we accord high priority to reorganizing the structure of power and authority on a world level. This assessment stems from a belief that the fragmented character of the present world order system and the preeminent role played by highly militarized and industrialized sovereign states preclude the generating of the drastic adjustments needed to cope with the buildup of these world pressures.

Central guidance is deliberately vague as an image of institutional adjustment.[40] The organizational imperative could be satisfied by an *imperial* consolidation of power and authority in a single center of national government or by some kind of *contractual* consolidation of power and authority through the voluntary agreement of existing centers of governmental decision. My preference is for contractual consolidation, but the quest for survival takes precedence over the political means to secure it. This same preference, and limitation upon it, exists in relation to the advocacy of nonviolence. International law needs to be assessed in relation to its capacity to support the rapid buildup of a world central guidance system, one capable of meeting the nuclear and ecological challenges, without relinquishing a capacity to alleviate human misery or infringements upon human dignity.

It seems evident, also, that the creation of a central guidance system is not a *guarantee* against the occurrence of catastrophe; it simply represents an *indispensable* change of organizational structure at this stage in human development. The movement toward imperial forms of central guidance might under certain circumstances actually increase the danger of catastrophe, and therefore the endorsement of this organizational imperative must be conditioned, to some extent, by continuous assessment of the specific dangers discerned in relation to actual power-consolidating trends.

Our metalegal point of appraisal takes account of these criteria. Available data do not permit very precise tests of adequacy for the international legal system and do little more at this stage of inquiry than orient the analysis toward these paramount questions. Such a reorientation is not trivial, however, for it tends to displace the implicit bias of present analysis, namely, the capacity of the international legal order to promote the security, wealth, and prestige of a particular national actor. These kinds of goals are generally conflict oriented, depending (except with regard to trade and alliance patterns) upon securing larger shares of limited stocks of power, resources, and leadership.[41] Hence, conflict remains the preeminent concern of those individuals entrusted with formulating policies for leading national governments; instrumentalities for cooperation exist, but in rudimentary form, and are relied upon, to date, mainly to deal with ancillary matters of functional necessity (postal unions, transoceanic cables, maritime safety signals), to discuss adverse positions with respect to matters of more serious consequence, and, perhaps, to help shape negotiated outcomes of violent or quasi-violent conflicts among states. Functional requirements for predictability and control at the national level are generating strong support for the establishment of international regimes in relation to ocean resources, the international economy, terrorism, and satellite broadcasting.

The Relevance of Law Within the Present World Order System: Routine Stabilization and Adaptation to the Pressures of Transition

The role of international law is largely determined by the persistence of the logic and structure of the Westphalia system, although recent functional and normative developments are placing the state system under increasing reformist pressure.[42] As is by now well known, and most creatively explicated by Myres McDougal and his colleagues over the past two decades, the limits of legal reform have been closely associated with the *shared perception* of *common interests* by *officials acting on behalf of national governments.* Common interests may involve *a joint concern* for reliable communications under normal circumstances (arrangements for international postal and cable contact) or under conditions of extreme emergency (the hot line between Washington and Moscow). Common interests may also support tacit or explicit norms, procedures, and institutions in conditions of *reciprocal interests,* where the alternative to agreement is an erosion, or even a general collapse, of standards (rules governing prisoners of war, according immunity to diplomats from foreign states, and fixing catch quotas for declining fishery stocks). International lawyers can play, and have played, an important role by formulating proposals responsive to common interests and yet sensitive to the differential capacity of governments to use their unequal economic, military, and diplomatic capabilities to uphold positions of privilege within the world system. That is, international law can develop along the axes of perceived common interests so long as such developments do not impair the imperatives of statecraft in a world system of unequal and rival governments with diverse ideologies, cultures, histories, national priorities, resources, and degrees of industrialization.

The *potential scope* of common interests can be extended by the impacts of various kinds of *interdependence,* and by an appreciation and acceptance of the declining and shifting utility of military power as a direct instrument of foreign policy.[43] With respect to interdependence, for instance, governments realize that territorial control is not sufficient to achieve national policy and that it is necessary to work out *cooperative* arrangements to uphold the mutual interests of sovereign states; such a conclusion has been most clearly demonstrated in recent years in the area of international economic policy and with respect to the general drift of technological innovation.[44]

Military power has been decreasingly used to enforce directly the claims of the rich upon the poor. As a result, more legally conceived regimes of mutual interest and informal penetration, based on reciprocity between the need for capital and assistance by the host country and the need for protection and stability by the investor/donor country, have been developed in various forms as substitutes or "covers" for cruder variants of "economic imperialism." The efforts of the English and the French in the Suez campaign of 1956 may represent the last assertion of explicit military claims to rectify economic grievances (in that instance, the confiscatory expropriation of the Suez Canal by Egypt in alleged violation of treaties).

The search for regimes embodying some arrangement for minimum world public order in situations of unresolved conflict is another aspect of legal reform in the present world order system. Military power, if relied upon by both sides of a struggle, leads to decisive outcomes—"victories" —in the present context of world relations only when strategic rivals are not centrally involved; otherwise, some form of stalemate is likely to result. However, a military stalemate may be exceedingly destructive and achieved only after enormous costs—human and material—as in Korea and Vietnam; hence, there are strong incentives to evolve settlement procedures that achieve political compromises without going through the agonies of war.

To resolve a conflict, as well as to end or suspend its military phase, requires a more fundamental approach to minimum order. Common interests of governments need to be identified in mutually convergent patterns, and forms for their implementation should be found. The war in Indochina and the conflict in the Middle East represent arenas in which it has been impossible over a period of many years either to resolve the underlying conflict by decisive action or to transmute the military struggle into a less destructive form of struggle.[45] The relevant actors hold such contradictory images of what would constitute a reasonable outcome that they cannot agree upon a regime of minimum public order; therefore, costly and unstable stalemates persist on a military level. The organized international community has been unable and reluctant to mobilize a consensus of sufficient specificity and strength to impose its vision of minimum public order, in part inhibited by the involvement of the Soviet Union and the United States on opposite sides. *Minimum order proposals*—those designed to prevent large-scale violence—depend on convergent intergovernmental perspectives as to the nature of a compromise. The parameters of compromise are difficult to establish in a revolutionary war without fixed boundaries (*i.e.,* Vietnam) or in a war of liberation where the stakes of struggle are the legitimacy of the target government (*e.g.,* Israel or South Africa). Every compromise that stabilizes the situation appears to be a covert resolution in favor of one side or the other; there is no way to divide the stake, no natural line of reasonable settlement. A cease-fire without political assurances leaves the established elite in exclusive control of the governmental machinery, whereas a proposal for a coalition government provides the revolutionary forces with a "Trojan Horse" inside the citadels of established and, perhaps, ineffectual authority.

Some efforts have been made to shift the terms of conflict by redefining the conditions of compromise. For instance, a neutral regime might promote a compromise in some situations,[46] whereas in others the exchange of security concessions for economic benefits might be negotiable. However, such means provide little prospect of adequately suppressing violence when governments are committed to ideological positions that defy renouncing political objectives, and when one side possesses ideological momentum while its opponent holds a military edge. Therefore, international conflicts can persist for many years—destructive, inconclusive and unpredictable, but extremely costly and damaging for the affected population and societies.[47]

In the realm of intense political conflict there is little present prospect of significant world order reform. The goals, rhetoric, and belief systems of opposing sides are too sharply contradictory, often asymmetries of power and legitimacy are too pronounced, and counsels of moderation tend to be looked upon with suspicion, regarded as seeking at the conference table what was not acquired on the battlefield. The upsurge of disruptive acts by countergovernmental elites in the form of hijackings, kidnappings, and bombings underscores the asymmetry of position and tactics in one type of struggle for control over authority structures in sovereign states. Occasionally, where the struggle is converted into an inconclusive internal war, minimum order can be established—at least temporarily—by acquiescing to a provisional partition of national territory, as between contending factions. But partition boundaries are often artificial and nonauthoritative and do not often provide for more than a respite. Given ideological schism, geopolitical rivalry, military technology, mobilization of political masses, and the tactics and absolution of revolutionary struggle, it does not seem likely that international lawyers can contribute very significantly to the capacity of the present world order system to compromise or resolve conflicts involving legitimacy issues, especially in any setting where there is a high degree of superpower involvement.

If the conflicting parties are more prudent or have more self-evident functional needs, then cooperative regimes might be agreed upon to replace unrestrained competitive processes. The nonproliferation treaty of 1967 is an attempt to implement primarily a bipolar consensus that further proliferation of nuclear weapons would be detrimental. The perceived interests of the United States and the Soviet Union generally converge on this matter and can be defined by reference to a tacit, but operative, set of rules of the game. The most difficult issue of compromise was between nuclear powers who were unwilling to renounce the nuclear option, and nonnuclear powers who were asked to renounce the nuclear option. The nuclear powers pledged in the treaty to help the nonnuclear states proceed rapidly to develop *peaceful uses of nuclear energy* and to continue the search for nuclear and general disarmament. In effect, nonnuclear governments were promised greater participation in the nonmilitary benefits of nuclear energy than could probably have been achieved by self-help, and were also given nominal assurances that the present nuclear powers endorsed the goals of denuclearizing interrelations. Is this a reasonable bargain? By whose test?[48] The practical prospects of the nonproliferation bargain depend on the extent to which it accords, now and in the future, with *perceived interests* of those governments that could otherwise proceed to develop nuclear weapons. It is too early to discern whether the nonproliferation treaty represents a successful bargain and whether the very terms of the bargain may not undermine its stability. It should be understood that the capacity for peaceful uses of nuclear energy enhances the capacity to develop military uses, especially by providing trained personnel and stockpiles of weapons-grade fissionable material (particularly plutonium).[49] The countermove to develop international safeguards against the diversion of fissionable material for forbidden uses does not yet provide a basis for assessing the stability of the NPT system.

The Seabed Proposals put forward by President Nixon in 1970 also exemplify the impulse to strengthen the cooperative side of the world order system.[50] These proposals compromise the interests of various categories of state interests in a very complex mix. The main sets of opposed interests arise from the relations between advanced and less developed countries, between coastal and landlocked countries, and between the community of nations and individual sovereign states. The Nixon proposals establish, in general, three zones of control: (1) *exclusive* coastal state control over ocean minerals out to a depth of 200 meters; (2) *trusteeship* for a coastal state over an intermediate zone up to 400 meters depth, in which revenue is shared with the international community and devoted to the development of poor countries; and (3) exclusive *international* administration of minerals beyond the intermediate zone for the benefit of mankind. Obviously these proposals seek to strike a bargain based on mutual interests of distinctly situated governments having diverse interests. Whether such a bargain can be struck depends both on the degree of convergence that can be achieved in relation to these proposals, and on whether domestic special interest groups prevent or facilitate the formation of a supportive national position even in the United States. What is a fair allocation scheme for ocean minerals? Should the exclusive zone be drawn instead at 100 meters depth? How can it be enforced? Protracted negotiations (which partly reflect powerful incentives to prevent or delay an agreed upon solution) help those domestic interest groups in the industrial countries that would benefit from a persistence of laissez-faire competition for ocean mineral resources. It remains uncertain whether trade-off regimes of this sort can be successfully established to moderate competition in newly developing frontiers of international activity. Moderation entails both some supervisory presence that stabilizes investment, inhibits detrimental side effects (*e.g.,* pollution), and serves welfare ends (*i.e.,* diverts some wealth to poorer countries).

If these reformist potentialities are successfully utilized, then there may be a series of incremental changes in international relations that are cumulatively significant:

1. Increasing realm of cooperative activity among governments in relation to significant subject matter;[51]
2. Increasing stake in the maintenance of the international system by different categories of states;
3. Increasing role and relevance of international administration and institutional actors;
4. Increasing importance of universal intergovernmental regimes in which nonparticipation or exclusion is damaging.[52]

The issued posed is whether the cooperative potentialities of the present world order system can be rapidly strengthened in response to the growing pressures in several distinct sectors of international life for some form of functional integration. Such integration rests upon the outcome of consensual procedures, which means that governments with very different positions, orientations, and priorities will have to be positively attracted by any given proposals, or influenced to acquiesce by pressures and/or payoffs. The alternative to rapid international institutional development will be either a persistence of laissez-faire permissiveness in a context of increasing interdependence or a further extension of sovereign and imperial notions of authority to new domains, and perhaps in new forms.[53] The disposal of nerve gas in the ocean by unilateral action is an example of the permissive style of unilateral self-determination of claims; the expansion of the zone claimed as territorial waters is an example of *sovereign* style; the use of reconnaissance overflight or outer space by superpowers for purposes of global surveillance is an example of *imperial* style.

In this reformist context, international lawyers have an opportunity to design international solutions that embody the convergent perspectives of the main international actors. The designing process makes it possible to move discussion up closer to the bargaining context by which divergent interests are identified and satisfied. The determinants of agreement are largely extralegal, reflecting whether governments on balance prefer normative and institutional stability to the free play of competitive forces, and whether, from their divergent perspectives, their leaders perceive the basis of compromise along convergent lines. In the disarmament setting, there is resistance on several levels of the national polity: an ambivalence about renouncing discretion over military policy, a tendency to view the position of the "other side" as unreasonable in the sense of being beyond the boundary of serious negotiability, a split between a particular national elite resulting from cross-cutting priorities; as well, powerful internal economic and institutional pressures sustain an arms budget and a military establishment. What remains uncertain is whether in such newly emerging areas as ocean mineral resources, weather control, satellite broadcasting, and environmental management, the process of negotiation will resemble the rigid framework surrounding issues of arms control and disarmament, or the more flexible and technical framework of postal regulations and maritime safety procedures.

In sum, world order reforms depend on achieving rapid institutional growth in a number of functional areas of considerable economic and political importance. This kind of reformism will not immediately involve the substantial transfer of sovereign control over matters of war and peace. However, if the consensual procedures operative in international life manage to generate a series of cooperative regimes and these regimes generally succeed in practice, then a process of confidence building may be initiated and help build the political basis for further reliance on internationalist approaches. Of course, experience with internationalist solutions is likely to be mixed in the years ahead, with no emergence of a clear trend line or unambiguous learning experience.

The Relevance of Law to the Future of World Order: Beyond Reform

Whether an obsolete social system can evolve within itself a new structure of authority is highly problematical. Most transitional contexts in human affairs have produced convulsive struggles between the forces of the old and new orders. There is no reason to suppose that international society can avoid this kind of bloody transition. And yet the terms of struggle seem so cataclysmic, and the prospects for triumph by forces associated with a preferable system of world order seem so dismal, that it may not even be rational to use violence to challenge existing arrangements, defective as these are. At the same time, the dangers of nuclear or ecological breakdown, possibly in an irreversible form, seem severe enough to make the risks of acquiescence even greater than the risks of challenging the world order status quo.

In such circumstances, can anything be expected of international lawyers? This is a difficult inquiry that concerns both vocational orientation and the role of law in stabilizing an obsolete state system. The craft of law involves the provision of norms, procedures, and advice that generally serve dominant groups who seek to perpetuate the existing political system. On an international level these groups do not share a common orientation toward most issues, except possibly a shared and reciprocal acceptance of the legitimacy of national governments. But on matters of substance, the potential realm of agreement is limited. Within some sectors of international life, inequality and dependency are so great that relations are determined by the dominant actor. Such a situation has existed in the past with regard to foreign investment and interventionary diplomacy. International law tends to be at the disposal of conservative forces, formalizing in normative terms the outcomes of inequitable bargaining or behavior. Peace treaties, after all, ratify the outcomes of war, however unjust the cause and combat tactics of the victor. Peace treaties, international concession agreements, and juridical confirmation of colonial status disclose settings wherein international law and lawyers have generally acted to legitimate the will of dominant governments in a system of formally equal states.

In more conflict-oriented circumstances, international law rationalizes existing patterns of international behavior. A government can always use legal language to rationalize aggressive conduct. Aggressive behavior can be characterized as "defensive," and the adversary's defensive moves can be characterized as "aggressive," and there are no international institutions of stature and capability to transcend the exchange of self-serving pronouncements. The divisions in international society and the weakness of the political organs of the United Nations mean that there is no global consensus that can take precedence over adversary claims. Besides, the complexity of conflict situations often gives a certain plausibility to contradictory lines of justification, even if these justifications seem entirely selfserving from a third party perspective.

Given the pervasive inequality in international life, international law functions largely as an opiate. In war/peace settings, legal mechanisms are generally able neither to identify the wrongdoer nor to provide an authoritative framework for decision, or even guidance. Rather, the international lawyer mainly performs as an adjunct to state diplomacy, an argumentative presence that disarmingly steps forward to confuse or disable the opposition by rationalizing claims of right. Lyndon Johnson, Robert McNamara, and Dean Rusk relied on *legal justifications* to win public support for the war in Vietnam, but analytic discussions of the American involvement in Vietnam by policy advisors or throughout the Pentagon Papers pay virtually no attention to the legal dimension.[54] It is evident that international law may facilitate the *public presentation* of a complicated and controversial decision, but that it rarely shapes the decisionmaking process itself, and therefore is not often worthy of notice by those who are concerned with explicating the actual wellsprings of diplomacy.[55]

In these respects international law may, despite its pretensions, have a damaging net impact. Its invocation may disguise the extent to which the war system serves the imperial needs of the powerful, rather than the community needs of order, restraint, and guidance. Of course, such a regressive law role is inherent in every social system, but it is more serious in the international system because it is both highly unjust and quite vulnerable to collapse. In such circumstances, legality and legitimacy conflict. To stabilize the routine may improve the daily ordering of international transactions, but it hardly comes to terms with the main agenda of world order reform, let alone advances the case for a world order system change.

International law as a perspective on world order also suffers from its tendency to neglect the influence of domestic public order systems. The significance of domestic factors cannot be fully assessed by reference to *values* and *ideological predisposition,* as has been done so creatively by McDougal and Lasswell, but depends as well on matters of *actor role* within the *world power and wealth structure, on realities of bureaucratic momentum, and on demands of the domestic polity.* An explicit ideology of world order may be quite progressive and enlightened, but if it becomes *in fact* associated with maintaining *domestic employment and profits through arms spending or with the support of repressive governments abroad,* then the objective character of a given actor's world order position is negative. Such a distinction is important because it relates to the preeminent position played by the United States in the world system, a position that is obscured to the extent that international lawyers uncritically accept formulations of explicit ideology based on a liberal democratic creed, without exposing the real bases of American behavior with respect to the use of overt and covert violence in foreign countries. Even conservatives have argued that a more objective accounting of motivation by the United States is necessary for the effective protection of selfish interests.[56] Liberal expositions of policy in world order rhetoric—the Wilsonian tradition in foreign affairs—tend to overgeneralize America's world role, as well as to distort its essential character.[57] A focus on the linkages among domestic political perspectives, national bureaucratic orientations, and the world roles of particular states would improve our understanding of why certain international actions are undertaken and others are not.

In this regard, international lawyers operating outside the realms of power have three principal functions: first, to expose one-sided self-serving legal rationalizations in order to neutralize the efforts by governments to disguise the motives of their actions, especially when they concern matters of war and peace; second, to design alternative world order systems that are more responsive to normative goals; and third, to evolve tactics and strategies for world order reform and transition. What seems needed at all levels of social and normative imagination are concepts of world order that rekindle hope in the future of human society and that favor reconstituting international life along more equitable and durable lines. This plea includes a call for the rebirth of utopian thought, but in a context guided by the practical wisdom of an engineering and futurist perspective.[58] We need *utopian engineering* to provide a vision and to discover ways to foster its realization. International lawyers have a major contribution to make by combining their skill in depicting comprehensive authority structures with their interest in procedures of implementation. Myres McDougal has cleared this path; it is time now for more international lawyers to choose it.

Separate commitments to specialized constituencies cannot mobilize the energies necessary to create a new politics of survival and progress for our country or our planet. What is needed now is an appreciation of the extent to which human prospects depend on achieving a dynamic ecological equilibrium and genuine social equity, *i.e.,* providing for the needs and wants of the human race within the real carrying capacity of the planet, on the basis of prudence about the future as well as a positive attitude toward modern science and technology as a source of adjustment as well as jeopardy, and with an understanding of the dynamic needs for change and adaptation by man as an evolving species.

We believe these goals are possible and that they imply important tactical consequences for those who are now primarily concerned with a particular part of our four-sided challenge. It is desirable to shape personal commitments in response to vivid attractions and repulsions; it is desirable that each of us be motivated by insight into the symbolic and inherent costs associated with the danger to animal species such as the blue whale, or by a sense that the crowding of the earth is the fundamental fact, or that ecological costs of the high technology life-styles are the basic danger, or that war is the central jeopardy of our era. Such responses are each genuine and helpful, but only if connected with a wider appreciation of what must be changed in general to bring about particular results.

Zero Population Growth, to take just one example, is a constructive idea to the extent that it mobilizes particular energies in relation to specific action. However, it may also have harmful effects to the extent that it conveys the belief that voluntary action by socially responsible citizens can meet the basic problems of the modern world. Such inhibitions on reproductive behavior may actually do damage if they cut down the size of families among those groups in the society which have the most highly developed ecological conscience.

The strength of the movement to deal with our four-sided challenge will depend ultimately on its ethical and political cohesiveness. Can it provide the foundation for a new humanistic vision, can it help engender a process of creative adjustment this side of catastrophe?

Of course, such a change-oriented enterprise requires very fundamental shifts in values throughout the world. The sooner we gain a clear vision of how to peacefully and effectively encourage these shifts, the better are our chances of rescuing ourselves and our children from our current desperate slide into despondency. By beginning to work out a coordinated strategy among those already alerted to some aspect of the danger we can signal our refusal to be bound by the predicted future of *A Clockwork Orange*.

On a level of immediate action we have to form networks and links to permit cooperation among those who seek to work for this future in distinct ways. We need to have both the format and the plan that makes our action today meaningful in relation to our dreams and hopes for tomorrow. This is a profoundly human mission as there is a widely shared realization that man must carry out these projects alone, in the belief that we are each responsible, in some minute way, for the spiritual evolution of the human species, the incompleteness of which is a marvelous source of openness and hope, a challenge that recreates the opportunity possessed by some early ancestors to work for harmony among men and between man and nature.

By loosening the fourfold knot we may be able to recover a sense of the future that is worth cherishing, that draws on the vision of men like Dag Hammarskjöld, Sri Aurobindo, Teilhard de Chardin, Pope John XXIII, who believed that man was moving through biological and cultural time toward ideals of human unity and harmony, toward the spiritualization of nature and politics, and toward a new higher stage of biological evolution in which our present problems would be regarded by future generations as part of a painful, but necessary, adolescence in the history of the human race.

Notes

1. This position has been developed in a variety of ways. For representative statements, see C. YOST, THE INSECURITY OF NATIONS (1968); A. D. SAKHAROV, PROGRESS, COEXISTENCE AND INTELLECTUAL FREEDOM (rev. ed. 1970); R.B. FULLER, UTOPIA OR OBLIVION: THE PROSPECTS FOR HUMANITY (Bantam ed. 1969); C. P. SNOW, THE STATE OF SIEGE (1969); J. FORRESTER, WORLD DYNAMICS (1971); Z. BRZEZINSKI, BETWEEN TWO AGES: AMERICA'S ROLE IN THE TECHNITRONIC ERA (1970); E. KAHLER, THE MEANING OF HISTORY (1964). *See also* Owen, *Foreign Policy Premises for the Next Administration,* 46 FOREIGN AFFAIRS 699, 699–702 (1968); Hoffmann, *International Organization and the International System,* 24 INT'L ORGANIZATION 389 (1970). For an optimistic interpretation of this transitional situation, see P.T. DE CHARDIN, THE PHENOMENON OF MAN (1959).

2. *See* references cited note 1 *supra;* A. SZENT-GYÖRGI, THE CRAZY APE (1970). My interpretation of this situation is developed in R.A. FALK, THIS ENDANGERED PLANET: PROSPECTS AND PROPOSALS FOR HUMAN SURVIVAL (1971).

3. Among the great transitions that occurred earlier in human experience are those from food gathering to settled agriculture, from rural-dominated patterns of existence to urban-dominated patterns, from the feudal principalities of the Middle Ages to the system of states characteristic of the modern age; a central tension presently exists between forces of ecological and nuclear disintegration of human society and those social, economic, and political forces working toward global unification. The breakup of the old order confirms the reality of an era of transition; it cannot answer the question as to whether the new system of world order that emerges will represent a successful or unsuccessful response to the mounting challenges of the present period.

4. The two sides of the limits to growth debate can be grasped by considering the following materials: D.H. MEADOWS, D.L. MEADOWS, J. RANDERS, & W.W. BEHRENS III, THE LIMITS TO GROWTH (1972); TOWARD A STEADY STATE ECONOMY (H. Daly ed. 1973); Heilbroner, *Growth and Survival*, 51 FOREIGN AFFAIRS 139 (1972); P. PASELL & L. ROSS, RETREAT FROM RICHES: AFFLUENCE AND ITS ENEMIES (1973).

5. EDITORS OF THE ECOLOGIST, BLUEPRINT FOR SURVIVAL 3 (1972).

6. *See* references cited note 4 *supra*. The substance of this debate should be distinguished from the appraisal of the Club of Rome as a transnational actor comprised of a small number (about seventy-five) of high status individuals located in a large number of countries. This kind of actor which exerts pressure in relation to a world interest, rather than any sectoral interest, is an exciting development of great significance. The present orientation of the Club of Rome seems benevolent, and yet somewhat technocratic and elitist; as an actor on the world stage its presence is clearly to be welcomed at this moment of historical crisis. Amelio Peccei, an Italian industrialist, is the founder and has been the driving force of the Club of Rome; his thinking is outlined in A. PECCEI, THE CHASM AHEAD (1969).

7. J. MADDOX, THE DOOMSDAY SYNDROME (1972).

8. The phrase is the title of a usefully critical essay directed at the limits to growth study. Kaysen, *The Computer that Printed Out W*O*L*F*, 50 FOREIGN AFFAIRS 660 (1972).

9. "[I]t is difficult or even impossible to conceive of continued economic growth in the poor countries in general taking place in a context of economic stagnation in the industrialized world." Kaysen, *supra* note 8, at 667.

10. *See* R. NEUHAUS, IN DEFENSE OF PEOPLE (1971); this position is also argued in PASSELL & ROSS, *supra* note 4.

11. As reported in *Meetings*, 163 SCIENCE, No. 3865, at 408 (1969).

12. These figures are based on an article in U.S. NEWS & WORLD REP., Sept. 28, 1970, at 81.

13. Table adapted from G.T. MILLER, JR., REPLENISH THE EARTH at 118–19 (1972).

14. Table from MAN'S IMPACT ON THE GLOBAL ENVIRONMENT, Report of the Study of Critical Environmental Problems (SCEP), at 282 (C. L. Wilson & W. H. Matthews, eds. 1970).

15. Table adapted from *Id.* at 301.

16. Ewell, *U.S. Will Lag U.S.S.R. in Raw Materials*, 48 CHEM. & ENG'R. NEWS, Aug. 24, 1970, at 42; for a discussion of this observation and a wider presentation of related issues, see this important article by Nazli Choucri, with the research assistance of James P. Bennett, *Population, Resources, and Technology; Political Implications of the Environmental Crisis*, 26 INT'L ORGANIZATION 175 (1972).

17. Bundy, *To Cap the Volcano*, 48 FOREIGN AFFAIRS 1 (1969).

18. The overall logic of repression in this kind of characteristic Third World context is vividly portrayed in the Costa-Gavras film *State of Siege*.

19. Almeida, *The Confrontation between Problems of Development and Environment*, INT'L CONCILIATION, No. 586, at 37, 41 (1972).

20. *Id.* at 44.

21. *Id.* at 56.

22.   I have been associated with two projects devoted to these issues. At Princeton University under the auspices of the Center of International Studies a study of incremental changes in world order has been proceeding for the last five years and has involved scholars at many universities drawn from a large number of countries. Some of the output of the project is found in four published volumes: 1–4 THE FUTURE OF THE INTERNATIONAL LEGAL ORDER (C.E. Black & R.A. Falk eds. 1968–72). The second project is organized under the auspices of the Institute for World Order, formerly the World Law Fund, with Saul H. Mendlovitz supplying the principal initiative; this venture has been named the World Order Models Project. It, too, involves scholars from many countries working in collaboration, although the mission of the World Order Models Project is to develop models for achieving overall and drastic improvements in the quality of world order by the end of the century. Each of eight groups of scholars (*i.e.,* representing North America, Europe, Latin America, the Soviet Union, India, Japan, South America, and a transnational perspective) is developing its own program for world order reform based on its particular national, regional, or ideological perspectives and priorities. There has been no effort to achieve any consensus beyond a common definition of the problem. The directors have been meeting twice a year to review and criticize work in progress. These kinds of efforts are seeking, along with much other work under way (*e.g.,* Club of Rome), to develop a climate receptive to the peaceful emergence of new orientations toward world order within the main national centers of power and authority of the present system. For recent publications under the auspices of the World Order Models Project, see R. FALK, A STUDY OF FUTURE WORLDS (1975); R. KOTHARI, FOOTSTEPS INTO THE FUTURE: DIAGNOSIS OF THE PRESENT WORLD AND A DESIGN FOR AN ALTERNATIVE (1975); A. MAZRUI, A WORLD FEDERATION OF CULTURES: AN AFRICAN PERSPECTIVE (1976); and S. MENDLOVITZ ed., ON THE CREATION OF A JUST WORLD ORDER (1975). For a forthcoming publication in the same series, see J. GALTUNG, THE TRUE WORLDS: A TRANSNATIONAL PERSPECTIVE.

23.   I would mention here, merely in passing, that it is important to establish a new field of study entitled "Comparative Systems of World Order" which will evolve more rigorous conceptions of world order alternatives. These systems of world order can be designed to reflect historical evolution up to the present, futurist extrapolations from the present, utopian projections of the future, and analytic depictions of distinct arrangements of power/authority.

24.   No one has contributed more significantly to this overall enterprise than has Myres S. McDougal. His corpus of work calls upon the legal specialist to include the functions of appraisal, recommendation, and invention in his definition of vocational duty. To the extent that such an orientation now seems normal, rather than exotic, it can be attributed to McDougal's powerful influence upon how we as international lawyers approach our scholarly undertakings.

25.   For some evidence of this potentiality, see C.W. JENKS, THE COMMON LAW OF MANKIND (1958); F.S.C. NORTHROP, THE MEETING OF EAST AND WEST (1944); F.S.C. NORTHROP, THE TAMING OF NATIONS (1952). *But see* Myres S. McDougal and Harold D. Lasswell's cautious approach to the prospects for a universal system of world order, based on their sense that the recognition of diverse national systems of public order that were antagonistic to one another in both normative and ideological terms would place realistic limits on the prospects for a unified system of world law or structure of world society. MCDOUGAL & ASSOCIATES, STUDIES IN WORLD PUBLIC ORDER 3–41 (1960). *See also* A.B. BOZEMAN, THE FUTURE OF LAW IN A MULTICULTURAL WORLD (1971).

27.   For some important efforts to emphasize changes in human consciousness as the critical variable in altering prospects for political and legal reform, see C. REICH, THE GREENING OF AMERICA (1970): G. FEINBERG, THE PROMETHEUS PROJECT (1968). *See also* KAHLER, *supra* note 1.

28.   Indeed, the transitional character of the present world order system accentuates conflict at all levels of human existence, from the family to the world. There are many arenas of confrontation between "old" and "new" values in the modern world, as well as between vested and revisionist interests. On an international plane

these confrontations involve a variety of issues of wealth, power, and dignity and are often discussed in the rhetoric of international law.

29. I have depicted this position as one intermediate in concept and effect between that held by McDougal (verging on a fusion of law and policy) and that espoused by Kelsen (verging on a rigid separation of law and policy). *See* R.A. FALK, THE STATUS OF LAW IN INTERNATIONAL SOCIETY 41–59 (1967); *cf. also* Falk, *The New States and International Legal Order,* 2 RECUEIL DES COURS 7 (1966).

30. There are several significant considerations of the impact of global fragmentation upon the quality of world order. Kissinger, *Domestic Structure and Foreign Policy,* 1966 DAEDALUS, Spring, 503; Hoffmann, *International Systems and International Law,* in THE INTERNATIONAL SYSTEM 205–37 (K. Knorr & S. Verba eds. 1961); A.J. MAYER, WILSON VS. LENIN: POLITICAL ORIGINS OF THE NEW DIPLOMACY (1959); A.J. MAYER, POLITICS AND DIPLOMACY OF PEACEMAKING: CONTAINMENT AND COUNTERREVOLUTION AT VERSAILLES 1918–1919 (1967); H.F. PETERSON, POWER AND INTERNATIONAL ORDER (1964).

31. Values and interests, not evidence, orient and shape policy; evidence and reasoning may have a marginal impact within the agreed "paradigm" of prevailing thought, but evidence and reasoning that emanate from (or propose) counterparadigms are excluded from serious consideration, just as their proponents are excluded from access to positions of responsible leadership.

32. An appropriate understanding of the political character of world order reform underlies Wagar's *The City of Man. See* W.W. WAGAR, THE CITY OF MAN (1967). For valuable related analyses of why world order reform has failed in the past, see W.C. SCHIFFER, THE LEGAL COMMUNITY OF MANKIND (1954). *See also* F.H. HINSLEY, POWER AND THE PURSUIT OF PEACE (1963).

33. The search for social change and human dignity in southern Africa seems to depend on some recourse to violence by dissatisfied groups. If such recourse is responsible, that is, if there is due regard to the links between means and ends, then I would support it for the following reasons: existing regimes are intolerable, extreme, and unwilling to pursue negotiated solutions; the pursuit of nonviolent strategies has already been attempted at great sacrifice by the aggrieved peoples and appears to be futile; the ruling groups have relied upon the most blatant and persistent kinds of violence to discourage even peaceful forms of opposition. I would also expect a good chance that violence would lead to a successful outcome; a maximum effort to minimize the ambit, duration, and intensity of violence; and a clear commitment to work for a just solution in a postviolence setting. Militant nonviolence is almost always necessary as a prelude to fundamental social change, and it may have to vindicate its threat by recourse to actual violence in order to induce entrenched groups to abdicate or seek a voluntary accommodation. For a careful and persuasive discussion of "civil disobedience" as a nonviolent strategy of extreme opposition to state action, see L.C. VELVEL, UNDECLARED WAR AND CIVIL DISOBEDIENCE 183–250 (1970); for a more passionate defense of nonviolent militance, see the writings of and about Daniel and Phillip Berrigan. *See,* in particular, D. BERRIGAN, THE CATONSVILLE NINE (1970).

34. I have taken this position in R. FALK, LEGAL ORDER IN A VIOLENT WORLD 8–38 (1968).

35. I concede that the opposite case for a new more globalist terminology is almost as persuasive. Such a case rests on the growing importance of nongovernmental actors, the reality of globalist patterns of thought, action, and aspiration, and the need to convey the breakup of the old order by the adoption of new symbolic forms of expression. My final judgment however, is that the persistence of the Westphalia system is still sufficiently pronounced to make it desirable to emphasize the continuity, however anachronistic, of the present world order system. To shift the focus from international law to world law still seems premature, and possibly sentimental, claiming a discontinuity that would be unconvincing to some, while disguising for others the work that remains to be done.

36. In this regard Johan Galtung provides stimulating overemphasis on the prospects for a new world order system emerging out of the activities of transnational

actors. His contributions to the World Order Models Project (*supra* note 23) have developed this theme in considerable detail and with great ingenuity. *See* Galtung, *The Future of the International System,* in MANKIND 2000 12–41 (R. Jungk & J. Galtung eds. 1969).

37. Of course, the forecasted future, a feasible future, and a preferred future are interconnected in the mind of the analyst as well as in the actualities of the processes by which the present becomes the future.

38. My own explication of these values is set forth in R. FALK, A STUDY OF FUTURE WORLDS (1975), especially ch. 1.

39. Professors McDougal and Lasswell have evolved a distinct set of eight values which provide them with a systematic basis for dealing normatively with the world order issues. For one convenient formulation see McDougal & ASSOCIATES, *supra* note 26, at 31–36.

40. It is a phrase intended to avoid statist or governmental connotations and yet to suggest the overriding need for a degree of global oversight and coordination. Ideally, the buildup of a central guidance mechanism in human affairs might be accompanied by a breakdown of state-centered bureaucracies. Therefore, the new world order would be more efficient in relation to global management, and yet less intrusive with respect to the dynamics of individual and group existence.

41. In a sense, we are formulating the limits to growth argument in geopolitical terms; the basic need is to change the structure of international transactions and aspirations in such a way that governments do not grow or improve their position at the expense of one another.

42. For a detailed presentation of the Westphalia system, see R.A. Falk, *A New Paradigm for International Legal Studies: Prospects and Proposals,* 84 YALE L.J. 969 (1975).

43. Some aspects of this process are considered in K. KNORR, ON THE USES OF MILITARY POWER IN THE NUCLEAR AGE (1966); R. OSGOOD & R.W. TUCKER, FORCE, ORDER, AND JUSTICE (1967). *See also* S. HOFFMANN, THE STATE OF WAR (1965).

44. *See* R.N. COOPER, THE ECONOMICS OF INTERDEPENDENCE: ECONOMIC POLICY IN THE AMERICAN COMMUNITY (1968); E.B. Skolnikoff, The International Imperatives of Technology, 1972 (Institute of International Studies, University of California at Berkeley).

45. For an eloquent argument advocating reliance on legal mechanisms to mute or resolve what has appeared to be an irreconcilable conflict in the Middle East, see M. REISMAN, THE ART OF THE POSSIBLE: DIPLOMATIC ALTERNATIVES IN THE MIDDLE EAST (1970).

46. For one attempt to develop this theme, see C.E. BLACK, R.A. FALK, K. KNORR & O.R. YOUNG, THE POLITICS OF NEUTRALIZATION (1968).

47. Also, the dynamics of the competition lead each side to act either to maintain its advantage or overcome its disadvantage. The interplay of rival perceptions, accentuated by bureaucratic considerations, sustains "the arms race" despite its high potential for mutual loss by way of expenditure and danger. *See* H. YORK, RACE TO OBLIVION: A PARTICIPANT'S VIEW OF THE ARMS RACE (1970).

48. McDougal's stress on reasonableness as a test of claims and expectations emphasizes the need for "configurative analysis" of the relevant feature of each specific context of decision. *See* McDougal, Lasswell & Reisman, *Theories About International Law: Prologue to a Configurative Jurisprudence,* 8 VA. J. INT'L L. 188 (1968).

49. *See generally* NUCLEAR PROLIFERATION: PROSPECTS FOR CONTROL (B. Boskey & M. Willrich eds. 1970).

50. For a discussion of these proposals and some alternatives, see W. FRIEDMANN, THE FUTURE OF THE OCEANS (1970). *See also* E.M. Borgese, The Ocean Regime, Oct. 1968 (An Occasional Paper, Center for the Study of Democratic Institutions).

51. For analysis and evidence, see Wallace & Singer, *Intergovernmental Organization in the Global System, 1815–1964: A Quantitative Description,* 24 INT'L ORGANIZATION 239 (1970); Angell, *An Analysis of Trends in International Organization,* 3 PEACE RESEARCH SOC'Y INT'L PAPERS 185 (1965). *See also* Galtung, *supra* note 37.

52.   On sanctions, see Friedmann, *supra* note 51, at 81–95; Reisman, *Sanctions and Enforcement,* in 3 THE FUTURE OF THE INTERNATIONAL LEGAL ORDER, *supra* note 23, at 273–335.

53.   *See* Henkin, *Arctic Anti-Pollution: Does Canada Make—Or Break—International Law?,* 65 AM. J. INT'L L. 131 (1971).

54.   *See, e.g.,* C. COOPER, THE LOST CRUSADE: AMERICA IN VIETNAM (1970); T. HOOPES, THE LIMITS OF INTERVENTION: AN INSIDE ACCOUNT OF HOW THE JOHNSON POLICY OF ESCALATION WAS REVERSED (1969); in this regard, the absence of concern with legal justification is particularly striking throughout the Pentagon Papers.

55.   In routine contexts of international relationship, international law probably does provide a generally reliable guidance and grievance framework which contributes in a very critical way to the stability that we take for granted in many areas of international life.

56.   For a particularly astute statement along these lines, see H.W. BALDWIN, STRATEGY FOR TOMORROW (1970).

57.   I have made such an analysis in THE STATUS OF LAW IN INTERNATIONAL SOCIETY, *supra* note 30, at 570–90; one very typical formulation of the neo-Wilsonian tradition is Rostow, *The Great Transition: Tasks of the First and Second Postwar Generations,* 56 STATE DEP'T BULL., Mar. 27, 1967, at 491.

58.   The rising interest in futurism and in a systems approach appears to be an effort to fulfill this need. The orientation is promising, but early results were often disappointing and uneven. *See, e.g.,* Bell, *Toward the Year 2000: Work in Progress,* 1967 DAEDALUS, Summer, 639; H. KAHN & A.J. WIENER, THE YEAR 2000 (1967); for a more exciting perspective on the future, see W.I. THOMPSON, AT THE EDGE OF HISTORY (1971).

II
People

Chapter 6

Well-Being: Its Place Among Human Rights

MARY ELLEN CALDWELL

>   *The fundamental question is a moral one: How can we learn to base our policies and action on love, rather than hate, hope instead of fear? I would claim that we in the United States will not long be able to retain our own humanity and decency, the mutual trust that makes democracy possible, in a world in which one-third of human beings get too much to eat and two-thirds are starving. Such a world will brutalize all its inhabitants. Even from the narrow point of view of our own short-range interests, it is clear that wherever poverty and misery exist, political instability and chaos are likely to arise. The only way we can be assured of a stable world in which the United States can live peaceably is to work for a diminution of poverty and misery everywhere.[1]*
>   —*Roger Revelle*

History chronicles man's survival as a species; the most urgent contemporary issues turn on whether and under what conditions man will continue to survive. An ever-growing thermonuclear capacity makes it possible for man to bring *Homo sapiens* to an abrupt end. Existing patterns of wanton resource exploitation may make the earth uninhabitable in the foreseeable future. And, in our dismal movement toward one or both of these ends, inequitable distributions of health and wealth among contemporary peoples portend social conflict. In this context, decisions affecting survival must be made. On the one hand, conflicts must be resolved peacefully, since violence is capable of unleashing the vicious arsenals of atomic, biological, or chemical weaponry. On the other hand, if violent conflicts are avoided by the rapid transmission of wealth and industrial skills to the world's disadvantaged poor, the ecological impacts on the air, soil, and water may be devastating.

It is in this context that we are asked to consider whether well-being is an international human right. As a strictly biological matter, it is obvious that some minimal level of health and welfare is necessary for survival and reproduction. It is equally apparent that, on a personal level, people always have aspired to the highest attainable standards of physical, mental, and social well-being, and at the expense, if need be, of their fellow human beings. Do these facts support the assertion that well-being is a human right? Does it serve any useful purpose to broaden this inquiry in the context of international human rights?

Admittedly, the questions thus posed involve symbol manipulation. Their referent is a political-legal system that is capable of ensuring access to, and the production of, conditions that afford the highest possible levels of individual well-being. By phrasing claims for community action and protection in terms of "morally justifiable human rights," it is possible to influence policy toward particular aspirations. More important, however, is the significance that such symbol manipulation bears for policy implementation. Once community decisionmakers are committed to the protection of a "right" (or value), manipulation of appropriate symbols and action help to transform that policy into positive community responses, responses which entail a variety of decisions relating to the allocation of resources and other uses of community power to vindicate particular claims relating to well-being.

An *aspirational* right to health and welfare, already inscribed in national constitutions and international agreements, is rapidly being implemented on an ever-broadening scale.

The bills of rights of older national constitutions, following the eighteenth-century models of the United States and France, enunciate certain rights against governmental interference with life and the general conditions of physical, mental, and social well-being. The newer national constitutions, incorporating twentieth-century safeguards for human rights, guarantee a number of additional "rights" directly related to health and welfare. Labor rights, social insurance, and specific protection for mother and child are stated as programmatic goals in those fundamental charters. In the international arena, the United Nations Charter, Article 55, states that

> with a view to the creation of conditions of stability and well-being which are necessary for peaceful and friendly relations among nations . . . the United Nations shall promote . . . .

b. solutions of international economic, social, health and related problems.

Article 56 pledges the members "to take joint and separate action in cooperation with the organization for the achievement of the purposes set forth in Article 55." The states parties to the Constitution of the World Health Organization have proclaimed the enjoyment of the highest attainable standard of health and welfare as one of the fundamental rights of every human being and have declared that "governments have a responsibility for the health of their peoples which can be fulfilled only by the provision of adequate health and social measures." Article 13 of the Covenant on Economic, Social, and Cultural Rights recognizes the right of everyone to the enjoyment of the highest attainable standard of physical and mental health. Implementing steps to be taken by the parties to that Covenant are specified in detail: (1) the provision for the reduction of the stillbirth rate and of infant mortality and for the healthy development of the child; (2) the improvement of all aspects of environmental and industrial hygiene; (3) the prevention, treatment, and control of epidemic, endemic, occupational, and other diseases; and (4) the creation of conditions which would assure to all medical service and medical attention in the event of sickness. Other rights, intimately related to the promotion of well-being, also are recognized in this Covenant. Among them are the right of everyone to be free from hunger, the right to an adequate standard of living (including adequate food, clothing, and housing), the right to work and to the enjoyment of favorable conditions, rest, leisure, and reasonable limitation of working hours, and the right to social security (including social insurance).

Such aspirational assertions reflect a universal preference for health and welfare and the conditions required for their realization. Most lawyers would agree, of course, that the general expression "right to health" does not state a claim that will be protected in authoritative decisionmaking arenas. Nevertheless, an interesting question remains: by what processes do widely shared demands for health and welfare become transformed into legal claims?

Recognizing that legal systems always have given some measure of protection to health and welfare and that such legal protection is today more comprehensive than ever before, it must be concluded that a great number of *aspirational* claims to health and welfare already have become *justiciable* rights. Analysis of this transformative process and its projection into the future cannot be done in a legalistic vacuum, however. First, it is essential to recognize that the demand for well-being is a characteristic of all living matter. Second, it is necessary to undertake a broad survey of the responses of legal systems to particular well-being needs and claims. And third, on the basis of the foregoing analysis, it is necessary to assay the most likely future developments and to appraise the alternative procedures available for ensuring that well-being, if not presently an international human right, soon will emerge as an effectively recognized and politically protected fundamental goal of optimum world order.

The Place of Well-Being Among Human Values

Well-Being: A Goal of Living Matter

Living organisms share two distinctive attributes: adaptive behaviors designed to effect self-preservation and mechanisms for reproduction. The former usually is viewed as an individual trait and the latter as a species characteristic that facilitates perpetuation of the group as a whole. It would be erroneous to assume, however, that one type of behavior invariably has priority over the other. In some organisms, such as the amoeba, the reproductive act at once negates the identity of the reproducing parent, with the contradictory result that reproduction both preserves the species and destroys the original unit. In other life forms, notably insects, copulation is simultaneously the death dance of the male. And among still other groups, the reproductive instinct is carried far beyond conception and the birth of the young to patterned protection of helpless offspring even when the protective action poses a grave threat to the life of the defending parent.

For reasons not yet clearly understood, many forms of animal life exhibit behaviors that entail great risk to individual survival. These patterns often are described in anthropomorphic terms that suggest motive. Individual members of various species risk life itself in the defense of a mate or of a territory or of the collective security of the group. Male members, in a struggle for power, battle the leader of the herd. Whoever prevails establishes recognizable patterns of deference from the females and other males. These examples suggest that, while both defensive and offensive actions are employed to protect individual and group survival, they are used to attain other values as well.

So, too, it is with man. Instincts for self-preservation and procreation are powerful influences on human behavior, but in some contexts life and safety are risked willingly in the pursuit of other values. Political history is peopled with the heroes and traitors who gambled with their lives in contests for power. Scholars and men of science have faced death in the search for knowledge. Adventurers have placed the hope of success far above physical security in their explorations of seas, jungles, mountains, caves, and outer space. For money and other forms of wealth, men have endured fantastic hardships and threats to bodily integrity in a wide assortment of enterprisory activities. For affection, generations of men and women have breached social norms whose sanction is the violence of the jealous lover or group outrage. To maintain respect in the community, both suicide and the hazardous traditions of the feud and vendetta have been the custom in many societies. Martyrdom, in the name of a religious or ethical imperative, has placed death for a cause well above biological impulses toward life, reproduction, and self-preservation. Finally, the pursuit of well-being itself often has claimed the lives of those in search of new therapies and cures. Thus, despite the urge to live and the apparent *will* of living matter to replicate itself, species man is quite capable of subordinating well-being to other values, including power, enlightenment, skill, wealth, affection, respect, and rectitude.

There is no question, of course, that in matters relating solely to well-being most people prefer corporeal integrity, vitality, minimal anxiety, and harmonious social relations over sickness, mental illness, and the contempt of their fellow beings. Choices favoring the positive value of well-being over its disvalues, however, rarely are made in isolation, and this fact, given that the same can be said of the choice of well-being over other values, provides the basis for the first inquiry: what is the place of well-being among human values?

Well-Being and Technological Innovation

The answer, if indeed one can be given, must be sought in the context of received perspectives and institutional priorities operating in a limited resource environment. All three of these elements are subject to change. Attitudes shift, institutions modify, and resource bases transform. At any given point in time, human value preferences and choices are made in such a context.

Perspectives that may or may not reinforce human demands for life and good health are shaped by the teachings of religion, literature, philosophy, and political ideology. The homely language of the New Testament teaches that life is more than food, the body more than clothing. Tragic themes in literature are the lonely isolation of power, the poverty of wealth, and the sorrow of knowledge gained. Philosophers have pondered the nothingness of being and the absurdity of existence itself. In times of crisis, political sloganeers have called for guns instead of butter and have demanded that everyone be willing to lay down his or her life for the homeland or for the freedom of the people.

The priorities given to the positive value of well-being by political, educational, scientific, industrial, familial, and religious institutions not only reflect past value choices relating to health and vitality, but also help shape future demands. If, in allocating resources, governments place a low priority on the health of the public at large, the impacts of such decisions are felt throughout the community. If the production of wealth entails high health risks to producers and consumers, it can be inferred that wealth institutions have placed low priority on well-being. If religious teachings are interpreted as denigrating the body as sinful or unclean and as preferring life in the hereafter to the wholesome nurturing of life on earth, there results an unfortunate brake on the promotion of well-being as an acceptable human goal. These are but a few examples of institutional practices that qualify the place of well-being as a human value.

The state of the resource environment also affects human choices among competing values. In all probability, *Homo sapiens* evolved from hominids that were predatory carnivores. Many of man's early years were spent in the use of his agility and weapons to obtain a diet of animal protein and to avoid becoming animal protein for other creatures. As his skill increased, so did his numbers. And as his numbers increased, man became more dependent upon his skills and his imagination in his exploitation of the environment.

In this context of received perspectives and institutional priorities operating on a limited resource environment, it is important to note that one of the principal uniformities to emerge from man's history is the continuous transformation of technological possibilities into human necessities (a uniformity that has its parallel, interestingly enough, in the development of human rights). Before expanding on this point, however, it is helpful to detail, through a brief review of the broad outlines of human history up to the beginnings of modern industrialization, the interrelation of technological innovation and the demand for well-being.

In his progressive shift from hunter-gatherer to city-builder, man incorporated into his social structure some basic technological innovations. The fist axe, the chipped flint, the plow, the irrigation ditch, the sewage system, the fortification, the ship, and all the sophisticated descendants of these technologies were worked into man's social organization in ways to protect his enhanced dominion over nature and his defenses against attacks by his enemies. The result was a gradual rise in his numbers and the level of his well-being.

As human communities began to grow, their dependence upon technological supports for food production and other resource exploitation increased. Each increment of knowledge, each organizational modification, and each technical invention that produced the resource base for larger numbers of peoples and diminished rates of community mortality and morbidity created social perspectives that viewed new knowledge, inventions, and institutional forms as indispensable. From a contextual point of view, man's evolving skills in political organization, in the creation and application of knowledge, in the management and distribution of resources, and in the development of norms demanding respect for life and human dignity were interdependent. Only the present magnitude of his numbers under conditions of intensely specialized divisions of labor makes it difficult to perceive the singularity of the overall thrust of human effort to attain the highest possible level of individual and collective health and welfare.

Once community leaders developed appropriate skills for influencing large groups to work together to feed and defend their collective members, effective political institutions became necessary instruments for the survival of such communities. At the same time, because protected communities grew in size, it became necessary to study ways and means for ensuring the continued flow of food and other resources into densely populated areas. Elaborate defense works were established to protect the urban communities as well as their hinterlands. In addition, new techniques in agriculture and animal husbandry emerged to intensify the productivity of food sources. It also was necessary to deal with the problem of urban effluents and other biological hazards accompanying the aggregation of large numbers of people in relatively small areas. Waste disposal, maintenance of water purity, and counteractive measures against disease and pestilence became the object of research and the target of many technological applications. Massive programs involving the development of transportation systems and the provision of water and power supplies demanded the application of engineering skills and the accumulation of large amounts of capital. These needs, in turn, created new manpower requirements. The labor force, skilled in the primary agricultural and extractive enterprises, had to be supplemented by specialists trained in mechanics, engineering, and management.

The proliferation of functions to be served in urbanized communities transformed the educational process. It was necessary to provide training in the elementary skills of reading, writing, and mathematics, supplemented by education in the fundamental sciences. At the beginning of the modern age of science, the ancient professions of medicine, law, and theology still attracted a large number of elite students, but many who might otherwise have pursued these fields turned to the practical arts and applied sciences from which they emerged to manage and expand an industrializing urban society. Whether or not it was fully comprehended at the beginning of industrialization, it is now clear that complex technologies—material and social—could not have been possible without a substantial infusion of basic science and research. The necessary conditions for the production of applied science and technology were twofold: a literate population in which the fundamental assumptions of the scientific method were broadly shared and the commitment of substantial community resources for basic scientific research. The former condition was met by the expansion of compulsory education. Basic science, on the other hand, was promoted as an elitist preoccupation of an educated minority, rapidly translated into useful applications in technologically oriented industry.

Technology and World Health

There emerges from this sketch of the interrelation of well-being and technological innovation a clear pattern of development. Once human inventions—material and intellectual—are incorporated into community practice, they become the necessary conditions of group survival unless and until they are replaced by newer innovations still more efficient in promoting human health and welfare.

This dependence of groups upon their own inventions accounts, at least in part, for migrations and for the development of transportation networks. Societies dependent upon chipped flint, iron, or other such materials rarely retained simpler redundant capacities for sustaining their numbers, and often they were obliged to seek out new sources of essential materials. The phenomenon is exemplified in the trade patterns of shipbuilders in pursuit of proper timber, of spice merchants in search of food preservatives, and of financiers in quest of precious metals. These patterns of dependence can be traced in the development of overland and maritime transportation networks that interlinked diverse parochial communities throughout the globe. These networks had profound impacts upon the well-being of all the peoples associated with their development and use.

Modern science has made the point that isolated, endogamous human groups exhibit both positive and negative biological characteristics. The members of such groups often show remarkable adaptations to peculiar climatic-resource environments in which they thrive. At the same time, they commonly are found to be vulnerable to a number of biological threats when placed in foreign environments or in contact with persons from different zoologic backgrounds. Because all living organisms serve as hosts and transporters for an indeterminate number of pests, parasites, bacteria, and viruses and because, additionally, they carry genetic endowments that may or may not be suitably mixed with those of foreigners, the increased tempo of social contact had significant impacts on all of the human communities involved in the expanding transportation network.

History thus records that global migration and social intercourse produced both positive and negative effects on human health. It also indicates that the pursuit of well-being was only one of a number of the motivations for such contacts. Political leaders seeking more land and peoples over whom to exercise dominion and to levy tribute, merchants searching for raw materials or markets, religious zealots determined to visit holy places or to convert unbelievers, scientists and teachers desiring to learn or to disseminate "the truth"—these and countless other forces provided the biological links in a network that transmitted health and disease, well-being and death, among disparate human groups. Industrialization brought all peoples into a global transportation system, and the technologies of the scientifically advanced countries accelerated the distribution of life-saving skills. Ironically, modern technology also made it possible, even probable, for these connecting links to be equally suitable for the dissemination of death-dealing skills as well. Of course, a complete record of past trends would reflect more, not fewer, contradictions and ambiguities in the human pursuit of well-being.

The act of declaring well-being a "universal human right" forces all mankind to reassess these hard facts. In one sense, it is a verbal defiance of the biological laws that govern other forms of life, and the implications for the future ordering of human social relations are, as a result, profound. If all men share a right to well-being, then the health and welfare of other human beings cannot be regarded as expendable. A meaningful realization of that right demands that the resources and skills required to attain the highest possible level of well-being will be made available to each individual without discrimination. The claim of a "right to well-being" will require the termination of all human activities that bring about conflicting outcomes.

These reflections on the biological and cultural history of human survival make it difficult to assign well-being a particular niche in a hierarchy of human values. Life-protecting commands apparently are programmed in our genes. It is altogether "natural" that each individual should claim for himself social protection of his biological purpose and goal. It also is "natural" that this claim should be made not solely for the benefit of individuals, but also in the name of the species as a whole.

Trends in the Legal Protection of Well-Being

The preceding discussion of the relationships between technology and the growth of the human family pointed up the continuous transformation of useful innovations into human necessities. A parallel trend is evident in the conversion of aspirations for well-being into moral and legal rights, although the latter process is dependent, of course, upon an institutional and technological capacity to fulfill well-being demands.

A study of past trends in the legal protection of health requires a clear delineation of the well-being process and the claims arising therefrom. The responses to those claims by authoritative decisionmakers will reveal the extent to which the demand for well-being is vindicated as a legal right or remains a mere aspirational social goal. The principal characteristics of the well-being process which has crystallized in patterns of preference and practice, however, have not materially changed in the past two centuries. A simplified model of the process by which human communities seek to protect and enhance well-being is set forth in the following table.

People	aspiring to the highest attainable standards of physical, mental, and social well-being
in an	
Environment	including the resources for positive well-being as well as natural and manmade pathogens
using	
Well-Being Institutions	consisting of manpower, facilities, and techniques specialized to well-being
and invoking	

Community Decisionmakers	authorized to determine claims and to allocate resources for the protection and enhancement of well-being
in a	
Social Context	of competing demands upon the resource base which may or may not be compatible with the attainment of high levels of well-being
producing	
Outcomes or Responses (domestic/international)	affecting individual and group well-being

The model is useful because it helps us to organize and analyze the needs and preferences that comprise the demand for well-being.

People in an Environment

In a biological world, where birth, life, and death are integral phases of interaction with other animate and inanimate matter, well-being is a relative concept. There are no absolute standards by which to measure physical, mental, or social well-being. At any given point in time it is possible only to compare among various social groups such matters as mortality, morbidity, life expectancy, and other well-being indicators. Where differences appear, as they continue to do, an observer must turn to the social and environmental context in an effort to account for these differences.

The first global effort to assess the well-being of the human family occurred in the 1950s, when the World Health Organization (WHO) published *The First Report on the World Health Situation*.[2] Periodically thereafter, WHO issued the second and third reports in its continuing effort to monitor changes in the well-being situation of peoples around the world.[3] The statistical indicators used in these reports are now generally accepted as basic standards by which well-being can be measured.

The most broadly used indicator is the death rate. Gross mortality data shed no light on the causes of death. They do indicate, however, which populations are least advantaged in the fundamental business of staying alive. Morbidity statistics provide more detailed information about the incidence and prevalence of illness and incapacitation. Among the health problems reported in analyses of morbidity are the occurrence and distribution of parasitical, contagious, and chronic degenerative diseases. Where the data are available, morbidity statistics also include birth defects, malnutrition, addiction, mental illness, accidents, and losses suffered in disasters.

Most of the recording procedures in the formulation of well-being indicators do not identify the environmental conditions that may account for particular disabilities and death. For example, mortality and morbidity indicators rarely reflect the threats to well-being occasioned by domestic or international violence. If a person dies of acute malnutrition, statistical reports do not reveal whether this condition may have been brought about by the actions or omissions of other people. Yet for the purposes of protecting and improving the health of peoples it is essential that health indicators reflect many other elements of the context that account for negative well-being.

Therefore, in addition to the indicators already cited, an inventory of environmental factors that are relevant for a comprehensive understanding of the well-being process should include the identification of (1) natural phenomena over which man presently has no technological control (*e.g.,* climate, weather, earthquakes, and certain epidemics); (2) parasitical and contagious diseases for which effective eradication and immunization techniques have not been perfected; (3) diseases that can be attributed to ineffectively applied techniques of prevention and eradication; (4) diseases that are related to human activities (*e.g.,* exposure to manmade sources of radiation, DDT poisoning, ingestion of pathogenic food additives, and an assortment of other ills currently attributed to environmental pollution); and (5) injuries and disabilities caused by defective or improperly used materials (*e.g.,* automobiles) or hazardous environments (*e.g.,* mines, manufacturing establishments, homes). This list naturally could be expanded to include the negative well-being impacts of peculiar social practices such as abortion, infanticide, physical mutilation, food taboos, and the use of some drugs.

Also it is essential that the well-being process be examined with a view to identifying "preventable" and "nonpreventable" causes of morbidity and mortality. The former category includes those causes for which there are both technological and institutional means of prevention. If malaria can be prevented by eradication of an identifiable mosquito, it becomes a "preventable" disease only when eradication techniques can be effectively applied in a target territory. If smallpox, rubella, or poliomyelitis can be prevented by mass immunization, they become preventable diseases when immunizing agents are available and can be administered effectively among target populations.

Between the two extremes of preventable and nonpreventable "causes" of human death and disability lies a third category. It consists of those that are technically or technologically controllable, but not controlled because the existing social institutions are unable or unwilling effectively to apply the control technologies. Cases in point are proposed bans on the use of DDT and phosphate detergents, the installation of air pollution abatement equipment in factories and internal combustion engines, and the implementation of "safe" methods of solid waste disposal. Competing economic interests and competing demands upon a limited resource base force institutions to elect priorities and those elections often result in a demotion of well-being to third or fourth place among human values.

In sum, it is clear that the well-being process is susceptible of description by some of the accepted health indicators, supplemented by an accounting of other environmental-institutional factors that are directly related to the state of well-being in any given community. The model of that process demands, however, that explicit consideration also be given to those institutions that are specialized to the lessening of negative well-being.

Using Well-Being Institutions

An analysis of the effectiveness of the health professions in dealing with human ills demands an answer to the following compound question: who, with what purposes or goals, supported by what other interested entities, engages in what practices, using what resources and techniques, under what standards of responsibility, with what effects? I shall not attempt here to analyze each element of this question seriatim; rather, a brief review of the kinds of issues involved may be illustrated in summary form.

The origins of health specialists are lost in prehistory. Evidence suggests that from his first appearance as a distinct species man has engaged in preventive and therapeutic health practices. There is clear anthropological proof that prehistoric brain surgeons enjoyed some successes; a few of their patients survived long enough to discuss their operations. Before the rise of the modern scientific era, however, there is little evidence that prescientific healers played a large role in the miracle of man's survival as a species. Among some groups, it is possible that sanitary rituals and food taboos had the effect of reducing the incidence of certain ailments, and modern scientists occasionally are astonished to find in folk medicine some chemical or other agents that are effective in the treatment of disease. For all practical purposes, however, modern medicine and health care, as well as most of *materia medica,* are no older than the industrial revolution.

Although the literature still contains references to the "healing arts," institutions specialized to well-being are scientific and increasingly technological. Thus, in matters relating to well-being, technological innovation rapidly is being transformed from the *possible* to the *necessary.* Quarantine, immunization, sterile procedures in childbirth and surgery—these and other preventive and curative practices have evolved in the scientifically oriented West from the technically possible and medically advisable to the accepted routine of the medically necessary and required.

Few areas of the world remain unexposed to the basic tenets of modern Western medicine, but the scientific "germ theory" approach to disease is not uniformly accepted. Folk or traditional methods, wholly unrelated to scientific medicine, still are preferred by many of the world's peoples. Even among those societies that share the fundamental assumptions of modern medical science there exist some basic differences. In countries where the private sector is primarily responsible for the delivery of health care, public sector services often are regarded as inferior. The same may not be true in states where the public sector is the primary provider of health services. Among those countries in which some form of "socialized medicine" is the norm, there appears to be a more flexible approach to the problem of professionalism and accreditation and a greater receptivity on the part of healer and patient to the special but limited qualifications of the paraprofessional.

These observations on the very recent emergence of modern medicine and the pluralism currently exhibited by health systems around the world are quite relevant to an inquiry into the role of well-being institutions in the shaping of world health. Whether the health care delivery system is essentially private or public is a critical factor in matters affecting manpower recruitment and training, the establishment of research and treatment facilities, and the support of basic and applied research in the furtherance of medical skills.

Both the deliverers and the receivers of health care, in every system of medical or economic organization, are active claimants in the general community decision process. Their interests, often compatible, sometimes antagonistic, are placed at issue in the context of other competing community demands for protection and support. As a prelude to the discussion of the legal protection afforded well-being, it is essential to examine that decision process and the claims made upon it in the name of the highest standards of physical, mental, and social well-being.

Invoking Community Decisionmakers in a Social Context

This element in the well-being process is a crucial one, including as it does all those political-legal entities competent to receive and act upon— in the name of the community—claims relating to the protection of well-being. Some of these entities clearly are specialized to matters of human health and welfare. Others are general purpose and their function is to weigh competing claims to a limited resource base and to allocate resources in conformity with value priorities prevailing in the community at large. Thus, governmental agencies whose jurisdictions touch upon health matters have primary responsibility for the articulation of community health demands into official community policy. All such agencies, however, are subject to the dictates of executive, legislative, and judicial entities charged with the responsibility of balancing well-being claims against competing political, economic, and other social interests.

Typical of the contemporary issues presented to community decisionmakers are the following: how much coercion will be employed to enforce universal immunization against certain communicable diseases? how much financial and advisory support will be given to public education in matters relating to individual and community health? how much money will be allocated to manpower training in the health professions? to what extent will pollution abatement claims be decided in terms of acceptable levels of negative well-being? in what ways will the legal system be modified to promote a preferred population policy? under what conditions will the world community effectively renounce all forms of atomic-biological-chemical warfare? And so forth.

Realism requires, of course, that all special claims be considered in the context of competing demands upon a finite resource base. Those who press for an absolute, 100 percent protection against oil pollution of the high seas are confronted by vested interests in the exploitation and transportation of a fuel that is vital to an industrialized community. Responsible decisionmakers must weigh the social gains of continuing exploitation of this valuable source of energy against the admitted risks of loss to human and other animate populations if trafficking in petroleum entails irreparable damage to the biosphere. Indeed, even those whose principal interest is human health cannot always agree on major issues. Defenders of continued use of DDT point to the plight of millions who will contract malaria if its use is halted. Those who would ban this pesticide claim that DDT contamination of the food chain threatens the life and health of the entire human race. Proponents of contraceptive drugs believe that impending overpopulation places the species in grave danger. Opponents fear that the chemicals in these drugs may cause grave physical and genetic harm to the users and their offspring.

Community Responses to Well-Being Claims

By its very nature, well-being is a local community concern. If an individual suffers illness or disability, his negative well-being has local community impacts. Those who would respond to claims for prevention, cure, and rehabilitation must make that response effective in the immediate environment of the claimant's home community. For this reason, the delivery of health services and the administration of public health measures take place at the local level. However, for reasons noted earlier, increasing mobility and improved modes of transportation make it necessary for local communities to protect themselves from the contaminations that accompany migration and foreign commerce. Thus, by laws, treaties, and decrees originating in the capitals often far removed from the average citizen's home environment, both national and international decisionmakers have assumed responsibility for protecting health and welfare at the local level. Among the earliest examples of such action were the quarantine regulations by which travelers and cargoes were segregated for a time to determine whether they carried communicable diseases or pests. Even before the causes of leprosy, plague, cholera, and other contagious diseases were known, governments initiated many sound epidemiological measures requiring the reporting of certain diseases, relegating those affected to special hospitals, disinfecting the premises occupied by patients, and requiring special procedures in the disposal of the dead. The first genuinely international cooperation in the protection of well-being related to such measures. At the Sanitary Conference of 1851, twelve nations first met together in an attempt to improve their methods for handling the problem of epidemic disease.[4]

Out of this background, there arose two major types of scientific and legal response to individual claims for health. One was directed toward improving the quality and distribution of medical services. The other was directed toward maintaining a healthful environment. As the sciences developed more knowledge about the causes and cures of disease and disability, the more effectively communities could act.

Public action has developed on three levels: local, national, and international. It has been coercive-corrective, regulative, supervisory, and enterprisory. The goals of community action have been prevention, cure, rehabilitation, compensation, and, in some situations, reconstruction of the entire context in which responsibility for well-being has been conferred on policemen, licensed health professionals, public health officers, educators, scientific advisors, regulatory agencies, insurers, courts, and countless others. Both coercive and persuasive means have been employed for implementing health policy. It would be a gigantic task to outline the developments in the legal protection of claims for well-being in such systematic terms. A few examples suffice to illuminate the degree to which "the right to health" is currently protected by community legal systems, and to suggest ways in which that right might be further protected in the future.

Domestic Protection of Well-Being

In conventional terms, the principal modes of community response to value claims has been by way of the criminal law, administrative regulation, the allowance of civil remedies in courts empowered to hear private claims in contract or tort, and the public undertaking of proprietary or enterprisory functions. In the following functional analysis of trends in well-being protection, these four types of community action are examined. Each of these modes of legal response deals in some measure with target populations (*i.e.,* the infirm and those likely to be exposed to sickness or death), health specialists and institutions, and particular social practices that affect the environmental context of human well-being.

Coercive-Corrective Protection For centuries, threats to individual and community health have been treated by the imposition of severe social sanctions. Primitive peoples regarded the sick and the dead as unclean menaces to the health of the group. Ostracism, expulsion, and incarceration in pesthouses were a few of the means employed to separate the ailing from the well. Those unfortunate enough to be afflicted with an especially contagious or odious disease were immediately segregated from society under conditions as severe as those imposed by the criminal law. Similarly, ritualistic taboos in the handling and disposition of the dead were calculated to protect the living from evil matter and spirit.

Early laws also imposed harsh sanctions upon those who attempted to treat the sick. The Code of Hammurabi, for example, prescribed that if a free man died as the result of an operation, the surgeon's right hand should be cut off. Today, in many jurisdictions, a physician who performs an unlawful abortion is subjected to severe criminal penalties. Laws prohibiting "mercy killings" fall within the ambit of criminal law and serve to deter actions that would shorten a patient's terminal agony. Criminal penalties also attach to a doctor's dispensing addictive drugs, except in the course of treating a patient. In these and a number of other instances, the community may execute or imprison those whose principal function is the treatment and cure of the sick.

The main purpose of criminal law, however, is to maintain minimum public order. By the use of capital punishment, imprisonment, and fines, the community attempts to protect itself from human behavior that takes life altogether (murder, manslaughter, and negligent homicide), puts life in jeopardy (attempted killings and assaults with intent to kill), impairs corporeal integrity (assault and battery, and mayhem), imperils sexual privacy (rape and carnal knowledge of a child), and restricts personal liberty (kidnapping, abduction, and involuntary servitude). In addition, communities also have endeavored to guarantee security of possessions against the misappropriation of those things which are necessary for living well (robbery, larceny, burglary, and arson). All these crimes, while directly against the individual citizen's well-being, are considered to be public wrongs which the whole community seeks to prevent.

There are, however, crimes which threaten the community directly and undermine the security which is necessary for securing and maintaining well-being. Stringent sanctions are prescribed for those who provoke and engage in riots and insurrections. The declaration of a state of emergency or of martial law enhances the repressive powers of community authorities. This escalation of community coercion is a direct response to the escalation of threats to group and individual well-being. The penalties imposed on those found guilty of treason are similarly justified in the name of community survival and welfare.

In combination with some civil regulatory sanctions, the criminal law also is employed to protect environmental conditions necessary to support human life and health. Fines and imprisonment are frequently used to induce compliance with laws directed against the producers and processors of unsafe consumer products, to ensure the maintenance of sanitary water and sewage disposal systems, and to guarantee minimum standards of safe and wholesome housing and working conditions.

Regulative Procedures and Sanctions   In order to differentiate regulatory techniques from those involving coercive-corrective sanctions, it is necessary to make some important observations. The first is to note that, however coercive the effects, involuntary commitment of the ill is a civil, not a criminal, procedure. The second is the recognition that a number of severe sanctions are employed by regulatory agencies, but conventional law does not regard them as "criminal," with the result that they do not ordinarily carry the social stigma of criminality. These sanctions may include the denial, suspension, or revocation of a person's privilege to engage in a particular occupation or enterprise, or they may involve large civil fines. In either case, the economic sanction may be more damaging than some of the lesser penalties imposed by criminal law. The principal focus, of course, is upon means for protecting community well-being by way of public regulation.

Regulatory laws generally are not directed toward patients. Nevertheless, communities often seek to regulate the sick and certain other populations that may become ill. The leprosarium, the tuberculosis sanitorium, the insane asylum, the quarantine island, the isolation ward, and the "poorhouse" are among the major institutions designed to segregate and regulate the ill and infirm. Regulations also are used to prevent the occurrence or spread of contagious disease among special populations. Medical inspection of school children is an example, since immunization against certain diseases is often required as a condition of entry into the school system. In communities that make education compulsory, this "health regulation" is collaterally supported by the sanctions imposed by the education law upon parents.

Just as the criminal law provides some protection of the public against certain practices by the medical profession, the regulatory laws also are designed to regulate health professionals. Licensure to engage in professional employment is the principal regulative medium. The maintenance of express standards of training and practice are enforced by license denials or suspensions, together with a variety of civil fines and other noncriminal sanctions to secure compliance.

The principal targets of government regulation, however, are persons whose activities affect the environment of community health. Comprehensive regulatory schemes have been adopted to ensure safe food, housing fit for human habitation, pure water, and adequate systems of waste disposal.

Agricultural regulations are designed to prevent and control diseases among food plants and animals. The objective is twofold: to minimize the threat to human health from diseases transmitted by food animals, and to protect the supply of food required to fulfill existing nutritional demands of the community. These regulations are supplemented by food inspection procedures. Directed toward processors and distributors, food inspection seeks to guarantee that food products be wholesome and free from bacteriological or chemical contaminants that might cause human illness. Regulatory procedures are enforced by a number of sanctions, including condemnation and destruction of products found to be unwholesome and the suspension of the privilege to engage in food processing and distribution.

Building and housing codes provide the means for ensuring freedom from dampness, adequate lighting, ventilation, drainage, sanitary waste disposal, and fire safety in accommodations intended for human habitation and employment. In industrial communities, health and safety regulations are imposed upon employers to protect employees, and upon all of those enterprises whose activities tend to pollute the community's air, soil, or water.

Supervision of Individual and Group Claims for Legal Protection of Well-Being   The corrective-coercive and the regulative sanctions employed to protect health and well-being involve legal initiatives by community authorities. Prosecuting authorities, inspectors, and regulatory agencies have the responsibility for applying community prescriptions in particular cases. Quite a different function is served by "supervisory" entities empowered to decide claims made by private persons for the protection of a well-being interest. The principal areas of traditional law involved in such claims are tort and contract, and claimants under both theories seek to prevent threatened injuries or to receive compensation for harm inflicted by others.

The laws of tort and contract recognize a wide variety of interests in individual well-being. They demand that people conduct their affairs with prudence and care for the safety of others. If a person is physically harmed by the negligent acts or omissions of another, then the injured party may demand that the culpable person compensate for the injury. Although legal systems long have resisted claims for protection against mental, as distinguished from physical, injuries, in recent years medical science has been able to prove that fright, shock, grief, anxiety, rage, and shame also are "physical" injuries causing marked changes in the body. As a consequence, where medical proof is available, courts have begun to broaden the range of the right to health to include compensation for genuine mental disturbance.

Whether such actions to prevent or to compensate for injury are phrased in terms of negligence or breach of contract, they are essentially compensatory in their effects. But supervisory sanctions, like criminal and regulatory sanctions, also are intended to prevent harm or its recurrence.

None of these three systems, however, requires the positive provision of health services. An example is the present state of the laws affecting physicians. For the most part, the law does not require a doctor to accept a patient for treatment even though the physician may have a moral or professional obligation to do so under certain circumstances. The professional's liability to a patient generally is limited to wrongful and harmful acts committed in the course of practice. As harsh as it may sound, this particular formulation is intimately related to the degree to which the community has assumed an enterprisory responsibility for the direct provision of health services.

The protection afforded individuals against harms directly inflicted by others and against malpractice by those charged with their professional health care is further supported by the allowance of a number of other claims against persons whose activities create dangerous and unwholesome environments. Thus, those who deal with explosives, flammable liquids, and other "inherently" hazardous substances and processes are held to very strict liability for the injuries threatened or inflicted. Manufacturers are increasingly being held liable for injuries caused by their defective products. Industrial establishments may be made to compensate large numbers of claims to sickness and physical disability as a result of industrial pollution of community air and water supplies. Quite apart from the regulatory sanctions that may be applicable to such enterprises, private citizens still have available the injunctive remedies as well as damages in tort or contract to force compliance with private claims.

Enterprisory Protection of Well-Being As the term suggests, this type of protection involves the assumption of governmental responsibility for certain enterprises to provide community health and environmental services. Examples are public hospitals and health services, public housing, public water, power, and sanitation systems, and fire and police protection. Community assumption of these and other health protection enterprises depends in large measure upon the underlying political and economic theories embraced by that community. Diverse patterns of governmental activity in providing such services reflect the complex set of priorities set by the community's decisionmakers.

INTERNATIONAL PROTECTION OF WELL-BEING

Even in an interdependent world where life processes are perceived as global, local communities continue to exercise a great deal of autonomy in the use of power and in the allocation of resources for the protection of well-being. It is clear, however, that complete autonomy at either the local or the national level is both undesirable and impossible. It is undesirable because local decisionmakers are incapable of taking action to prevent the negative well-being effects produced by their equally autonomous neighboring communities—pandemics, air and water pollution, and atmospheric radiation are cases in point. It is impossible because the groups that experience intense apprehension of acute well-being deprivation are likely to take actions against offenders that, in turn, threaten or disrupt the local well-being processes. To avoid the dire internal consequences of an effective economic quarantine or other coercive action, local communities may find it necessary to cooperate with their neighbors in matters relating to health. One needs only to recall that when conflicting quarantine measures employed by nation-states in the early 1800s seriously impaired international commerce, a few European commercial powers met together to cure their ailing economies by designing effective reciprocal epidemiological methods for protecting domestic community health.[5] In more recent times, demands for control of nuclear technology have been intended primarily to attain international agreements to protect local communities from the health effects of autonomous national decisions about both peaceful and military uses of nuclear energy.

On the most fundamental level, all past efforts to prevent the scourge of war, including the numerous international agreements declaring the permissible limits in the treatment of war prisoners and noncombatants, were directed toward the protection of human well-being. Local, national, and even regional efforts in the name of health and welfare do not always proceed on the assumption that there exists for everyone a fundamental right to health and welfare. Yet as nations move toward global consensus on matters relating to human survival and well-being, the clearer it becomes that international responses to well-being claims should be species protective.

In examining the protection presently given by the international community of nations to claims for well-being, it is essential to take into account the activities of international organizations. The World Health Organization is the principal international agency devoted exclusively to the universal protection and improvement of human well-being. However, other international agencies also are intimately involved in the attainment of global health. For example, the Food and Agriculture Organization (FAO) is concerned on a worldwide basis with nutrition. The International Labor Organization (ILO) has addressed itself to matters of industrial hygiene and social insurance. The International Civil Aviation Organization (ICAO) cooperates in applying the International Sanitary Regulations to prevent the spread of disease in international air transport. The United Nations Children's Fund (UNICEF) distributes funds for the improvement of maternal and child welfare. The World Meteorological Organization (WMO) and the International Telecommunications Union (ITU) provide data and communications media for assembling and broadcasting epidemiological information. The United Nations Economic and Social Council (UNESCO) has assumed joint responsibilities with WHO in rural sanitation and hygiene, school health, and health training for teachers. The International Atomic Energy Agency (IAEA) is concerned with peaceful uses of atomic energy and the protection of human populations from dangerous radiation. The Universal Postal Union (UPU) assists in the regulation of transportation of dangerous goods. The efforts of these and other international governmental agencies are assisted, moreover, by nongovernmental organizations. WHO alone has official relations with over seventy such groups, among them the League of Red Cross Societies and international councils or committees in such diverse fields as health education, nursing, midwifery, sanitary engineering, microbiology, brain research, social work, housing and planning, planned parenthood, pharmacy, and veterinary medicine. Not one of these organizations, however, is endowed with the legal competence to impose coercive-corrective sanctions, to regulate individual or group activities, to hear and decide individual claims for the protection of well-being, or to engage in health and welfare enterprises at the national or the local level. Although serving the goals of world health in very important ways, they are limited in their functions to gathering, analyzing, and disseminating essential health information, and providing advice, technical assistance, and funds for health-related programs to countries that request such aid. Their decisionmaking activities affect the allocation of knowledge, skills, trained personnel, and money among the state-claimants for help in achieving higher standards of physical, mental, and social well-being among their citizens.

The Place of Well-Being in the Future World Order

If there is to be world order, even minimum world order, there must be peace and a broader sharing of human values across national boundaries. The same may be said of achieving high levels of well-being. Far from having fewer demands than present generations for adequate wholesome food and comfortable housing, the next half century will be witness to still larger and more insistent demands for greater health protection. As the communications media continue to engender expectations among the world's poor and infirm, desires for more healthy and rewarding lives will increase. It is altogether reasonable to predict, therefore, that the demand for well-being will grow and spread.

Just as the attainment of the highest possible standard of health will continue to be a primary human goal, man's dependence upon technology to sustain his present numbers will also persist. Cities are now wholly dependent upon elaborate networks for transporting people and goods. The "green revolution" of the 1960s involved the adoption of a new technology upon which those saved from famine are now totally dependent. There is every reason to believe that the future will bring an intensification of that dependence. Few redundancies are retained in a technologically based social system. Therefore, when any one portion does not function, it poses an immediate threat to the well-being of the entire community. Natural disasters, power failures, and strikes remind everyone of the fragility of the technological system on which we rely for continued health and welfare.

People in the Future Environment

The future portends some change in the principal health indicators. Mortality rates will continue to decline unless the effects of overpopulation suddenly result in widespread famine and disorder. Morbidity caused by parasitic and contagious diseases will also decline as the medical sciences develop effective means for prevention and cure.

However, the incidence of chronic ailments that affect the mature and aging and of diseases caused by manmade pathogens is not likely to diminish soon. The very prolongation of life will increase enormously the number of people peculiarly susceptible to these types of illnesses, and no one seriously expects a sudden and effective "technological fix" for either the causes or the cures. Furthermore, nutritional deficiencies will persist among the majority of the world's people for decades to come. Technologies for providing new sources of protein are well under way, and the difficulties lie not in technology, but in human ignorance, in resistance to change of food habits and in inefficient methods of distributing the food that is available.

The unifying causative element in all these problem areas is population increase. Produced by effective death control, the so-called population explosion now accounts for most of the health problems of the foreseeable future. For a number of reasons the population is aggregating in urban areas at unprecedented rates. This aggregation has produced in the past twenty-five years enormous metropolitan slums in which health conditions are abominable. The expansion of industrial production spurred by this growing consumer market accounts for most of the environmental contamination observed around the world.[6]

Still, even though population and pollution have emerged as macroproblems of world health, there is some reason for guarded optimism about the future. Evolving technologies may provide the means for preventing a number of health hazards that presently defy human control. Epidemiological reporting, supported by quick-reaction immunization laboratories, have made it possible in recent years to curb periodic influenza epidemics, and these programs will be expanded. The world "weather watch" is developing storm warning systems which, if rationally observed, will reduce the human toll from hurricanes and tornadoes. Seismologists and engineers are improving earthquake warning procedures and techniques for earthquake prevention to bring this type of natural disaster under some degree of human control. Widespread public interest in health and safety will probably intensify in the future. The consumer movement could bring about more effective institutions to control human activities that threaten public health.

Well-Being Institutions

The health professions of the future will continue to be specialized and dependent upon sophisticated health technology. The number of significant advances in the life sciences during the past twenty-five years is unprecedented, and those predicted for the future are even more remarkable,[7] but the principal problems of the future are institutional, not technological. For example, it is already possible, by means of computer-assisted diagnostic procedures, to survey the individual state of health for hundreds of people within a few hours. On the basis of information provided, doctors can recommend appropriate medical action. However, neither the technology nor the techniques are presently used on a large scale because health systems do not have the personnel and facilities to perform all the tasks that the diagnosticians recommend. The most critical need of future well-being institutions, if health-protecting skills are to be broadly shared, are health care systems capable of handling increasing demands for their services.

Probable Future Well-Being Claims

The most likely developments in future decisionmaking relating to well-being will involve radical reorganization of health-protecting agencies, revised priorities at the national and local levels, and more international cooperation in program implementation and effective sanctioning processes.

At the national level, among the more fascinating questions likely to be faced by decisionmakers everywhere are those arising out of emerging technologies. The ethics of human experimentation and organ transplantation already have been put at issue in the legal forum. What disposition should be made to claims that, where necessary, the health service system should provide the following to all persons, irrespective of their ability to pay:

Genetic counseling and remedies, where indicated, for the correction of congenital defects

Cyborg technology

Chemotherapy for control of fatigue, memory, mood, and personality

Therapeutic rejuvenation and delay of aging

Painless means of voluntary cessation of life in cases of terminal illness

From quite another standpoint, consideration should be given to individual rights if consensus determines that the state has the "right" to require the following for the protection of individual and group health:

Periodic physical and mental examinations accompanied by compulsory therapy as indicated

Limitations on the number of permissible live births per person

Preventive detention of persons likely to cause harm to other individuals or to groups

How can individuals engaged in political dissent effectively protect themselves from involuntary incarceration on the grounds that they suffer from mental illness and have the right to be treated by the health system, which has the correlative duty to provide such treatment? If effective robots or other mechanical means are available, should human beings have a right to demand that hazardous work be performed mechanically? Conversely, should the state forbid the use of humans in experiments or enterprises that pose unusual threats to corporeal or mental integrity?

Individual claims for equal access to competent health care, regardless of ability to pay, and the corresponding pressures generated by health professionals for financial support will present national decisionmakers with some hard choices in resource allocation. In the international arena, arms control and peacekeeping machinery are essential, but so are matters affecting optimum order. The population question and environmental pollution already are on the agendas of the United Nations and its affiliated organizations. Stimulated in part by international pressures, the leaders of the polluting industrialized countries are beginning to set standards and to enforce stringent sanctions upon industries and enterprises whose practices endanger health. Bilateral and regional undertakings to clean up international rivers and other shared waters and to restore air quality in contiguous zones have laid the groundwork for parallel arrangements in other areas of the world. A reorientation of development assistance to focus on pollution prevention and population control will affect almost all of the present and future international assistance programs.

These are only a few of the well-being claims likely to be raised in the future. If a human right is something which is owing to every human being simply because he is human, how many of the foregoing can be given the label "human right"?

Future Community Responses to Well-Being Claims

Present verbal deference in constitutional charters and international agreements to human well-being, accompanied by corroborative practice, indicate that a right to health and welfare is increasingly recognized by community decisionmaking processes.

Nationally and internationally, the content of that "right" has changed over time, largely in response to the changing patterns of human dependency on the technology required for maintaining preferred levels of health. The particular ways in which the right is vindicated in an individual's immediate environment are determined by the prevailing political and economic institutions and their attendant social and cultural perspectives. In his encyclical *Pacem in Terris,* the late Pope John XXIII declared that

> Man has the right to life. He has the right to bodily integrity, and to the means necessary for the proper development of life, particularly food, clothing, shelter, medical care, rest, and finally, the necessary social services. In consequence, he has the right to be looked after in the event of ill-health; disability stemming from his work; widowhood; old-age; enforced unemployment; or whenever through no fault of his own he is deprived of the means of livelihood.[8]

For years to come, there will be enormous differences among human communities in the ways by which they attempt to give effect to these asserted rights.

Local community decisionmakers will continue to assign duties and responsibilities in the public and private sectors in varying patterns. Care of the ill, widowed, aged, and unemployed may be lodged, as in the past, primarily with the family, or it may become a duly recognized responsibility of government. Existing mixed patterns of social legislation exhibit enormous variety in the ways that these kinds of protection may be afforded.

The overall resource environment, mediated by the prevailing technology, will set limits on what is an attainable level of health. As technology advances, the specific content of the right to life, to bodily integrity, and to the means necessary for the proper development of life may take on an entirely different character than that existing today. However broadly shared well-being becomes in the future, the discrepancies between goals and levels of achievement will continue to shape new demands. In such a context, it is highly improbable that aspirational expressions of a right to health and welfare will be narrowed or deleted in national charters or international agreements of the future. Indeed, they may be broadened to include "rights" not yet dreamt of as justifiable claims.

Cynics have observed that with few exceptions countries which declare the constitutional right to health in the most elaborate detail enjoy lower standards of well-being than their neighbors. What value, therefore, are mere words on a sacred parchment? Clearly they serve little purpose if either resources or the will to implement such declarations is lacking. At least three positive purposes are served, however, for nations that genuinely seek to promote the well-being of their peoples. In the first place, the declaration of a right to health operates as a constitutional curb on governmental or private activities which are contrary and inimicable to the enunciated constitutional goal. Second, such a declaration provides the jurisdictional justification for practical implementation on legislative and administrative levels. Finally, it serves the important function of assuring international assistance agencies of the basic national commitment to well-being goals.

In the international arena, a first order priority for the future is the attainment of minimum world order. Decisionmakers everywhere must condemn and renounce all future uses of atomic, biological, and chemical means for conducting war. In addition, they must reach immediate agreement on safe disposal procedures for existing ABC weapons, stockpiles, and wastes. In the interests of optimum world order, at least four opportunities for positive action lie ahead in the immediate future.

The first involves the control of both intentional and accidental sources of manmade environmental pollution. Even though the use of certain biocides, detergents, and food additives and the industrial discharge of substances that cause air, soil, and water pollution have no warlike purpose, the effects upon others are so destructive that continued use and discharge must be regarded as intentional wrongs. On the local and national levels, the legal processes can punish, regulate, or hold liable in civil damages offending individuals and groups. Internationally, states that fail to assume their international responsibilities in one or another of these ways should be held liable to strict standards of liability for losses suffered by other states as a consequence of unrestrained domestic activities.

A second response might follow the recommendations made by C. Wilfred Jenks to subject to international supervision and settlement all scientific experimentation and tests, and all schemes of development likely to affect adversely the natural environment of another state.[9]

A third legal response to global claims for improved conditions of well-being could be brought about by the creation of an operational world health program. As presently constituted, WHO, its affiliated organizations, and the several multilateral and bilateral assistance agencies are capable of acting only at the invitation of host countries. If, for example, a nation-state abandons its international commitment to eradicate a certain disease-bearing vector, with the result that other countries become infested or re-infested, the exposed populations presently have recourse only to the conscience of the reneging state. An operational world health agency, endowed with jurisdiction to deploy, say, an international eradication team within the offending state, would be able to protect countries threatened by infestation. Such a mechanism would shift the responsibility for positive action to an agency beyond the parochial control of the nation-states. If such a solution is not immediately feasible, then the aggrieved peoples in reinfected areas should be able to seek in international tribunals redress and indemnification for the tortious actions of their neighboring states.

A fourth response of the world community to world health needs could be met by the creation of a genuinely international science capacity. Progress in basic research is currently dependent upon the fluctuations in resource commitment by national decisionmakers. Recent retrenchments in United States appropriations for health-related research, for example, will retard the global advance in fundamental scientific knowledge and technology. An independent scientific research establishment, financed through a world tax or by revenues derived from earth–space areas not subject to the sovereignty of nation-states, would be able to redress the world imbalances that occur in science enterprises under national dominion.

Summary and Conclusion

Three major developments point to the emergence of an effective, but limited, international commitment to well-being as a universal human right: (1) international agreements designed to protect specific well-being claims; (2) international organizations chartered to promote optimum levels of physical, mental, and social well-being; and (3) human rights covenants the terms of which pledge signatories to implement well-being goals by taking specified domestic legal action.

From the standpoint of some observers, these grand arrangements among nation-states exempt from the coercive process of an international police force do not constitute international legal recognition of an individual right to well-being. Such a view overlooks, unfortunately, the effective power of expectations of reciprocity. International commitments to well-being are entered into primarily because states comprehend the need for global cooperation in the protection of their respective peoples. Treaties and other agreements that purport to ban or regulate specified practices in international war are conceived as self-protective and are subscribed to in the expectation that cosigners will be equally jealous of the health and safety of their respective populations. International arrangements for the sharing of epidemiological information do not provide coercive means for obtaining information from reluctant parties; but the effectiveness of cooperative knowledge sharing resides in the mutual benefits which are derived from the exchange of critical data about the local and international health situation at any given time. Similarly, commitments to apply WHO sanitary regulations, to engage in eradication of disease vectors, and to inoculate vulnerable populations, serve both domestic and international demands for health protection. Those who do not cooperate can be expected to be quarantined (economically and/or militarily), to suffer the internal consequences of epidemic and death, or ultimately to experience direct intervention by threatened neighbors who may view the domestic health crisis as "a matter of international concern."

International disaster relief operations attest to the fundamental interest of peoples everywhere in lessening pain and suffering among their fellows. International expressions of ethical norms, such as those in the Genocide Convention embodying the deferential values of love, respect, and responsibility for other human beings, are effective on the principle of the "Golden Rule." The fact that the world's conscience occasionally is unaffected by atrocious behavior within a nation-state is, of course, unfortunate. Nevertheless, such expressions do represent the high valuation placed upon human well-being by an increasing number of people throughout the globe.

International arrangements for financial and technical assistance and for trade agreements that will promote the economic development of less developed nations are not devoted exclusively to wealth objectives; they have significant health impacts as well. The enormous strides taken by developing countries in the past few decades in lowering mortality rates, in providing sanitary water supplies, in increasing food production, and in improving health care delivery systems would not have been possible without generous amounts of external capital and technical aid.

There is every reason to believe that technological and institutional skills will continue to evolve in ever-inventive ways. Whatever the long-range future portends, it is likely that human populations will continue to increase in numbers too large to be afforded optimum levels of health and welfare. Indeed, all indicators suggest a widening gap between "haves" and "have-nots" in the foreseeable future. All of these trends will be unfolding in an earth environment which presently promises little by way of new and renewable resources to sustain current levels of health and welfare however inequitably shared among the world's peoples today. In all of this the most fascinating question is how human beings will resolve the apparently contradictory demands for individual and species well-being. Roger Revelle invoked love and hope.[10] Stephen Gorove has said:

> If we intend to create a lasting and workable system of "world" or "half-world" organization, be it in the near or in a somewhat more distant future, it will have to be built on corresponding supranational standards and loyalties. If "respect" for the individual human being is considered a "goal and condition for the harmony of interpersonal relations," a wider sense of belonging to the world community, a "loyalty to mankind" is equally a goal and a condition for the wider harmony of human relations.[11]

The striking oddity of it all is that the flowering of eighteenth-century Enlightenment into twentieth-century Superscience seems to have brought us around full cycle to appeals to rectitude. Human dignity—an international human right to well-being, to respect and deference, simply because we are human—seems wholly dependent upon our willing it to be so and our collective acceptance of some of the somber consequences entailed in the exercise of that will. The call seems to be to use our brains, talents, resources, influence, esteem, good will, ethical norms—indeed, our lives—in the promotion of those aspirations which, if deemed good for us individually, must be deemed good for all.

Notes

1. HOUSE COMM. ON SCIENCE AND ASTRONAUTICS, 90TH CONG., 2D SESS., CAN THE POOR COUNTRIES BENEFIT FROM THE SCIENTIFIC REVOLUTION? 521 (1968).

2. WORLD HEALTH ORGANIZATION, FIRST REPORT ON THE WORLD HEALTH SITUATION (1959).

3. In 1963 and 1967, respectively.

4. WORLD HEALTH ORGANIZATION, THE FIRST TEN YEARS OF THE WORLD HEALTH ORGANIZATION 3 (1958).

5. *Id.*

6. *See* Caldwell, *Population,* in THE FUTURE OF THE INTERNATIONAL LEGAL ORDER (C.E. Black & R.A. Falk eds. 1972).

7. *See* H. KAHN AND A.J. WIENER, THE YEAR 2000 (1967).

8. *Pacem in Terris,* Part I, para. 11.

9. Jenks, *The New Science and the Law of Nations,* 17 INT'L & COMP. L.Q. 327 (1968). *See also* Caldwell, *The U.N. and Science: Past and Future Implications for World Health,* 64 PROCEEDINGS AM. SOC'Y INT'L L. 172 (1970).

10. *See* note 1 *supra.*

11. Gorove, *Towards World Loyalty,* 23 MISS. L.J. 164 (1952).

Chapter 7

Self-Determination as a Human Right

LUNG-CHU CHEN

The new era of self-determination is symbolized by Biafra and Bangladesh. As former colonial people and territories substantially disappear, the focus of attention has begun to shift from colonial to noncolonial contexts as far as claims of self-determination are concerned. The principle of self-determination has played a leading role in accelerating the emancipation of millions and millions of people from former colonial shackles. But as decolonization comes to an end, will the principle of self-determination be interred? Is it a doctrine with limited historical application or one with universal applicability?

Claims to self-determination by groups within established nation-states, old or new, are beginning to be pressed with ever-increasing urgency. As Professor Van Dyke puts it:

> Obviously, for many governments and political leaders, the word *self-determination* has become a weapon, used in political struggles simply because it has appeal, whether or not it is apt. And those who try to derive

The author gratefully acknowledges the criticism and comments of his colleagues, Myres S. McDougal, Harold D. Lasswell, and W. Michael Reisman.

advantage from the world's appeal are inclined to read into it whatever meaning serves their purposes.[1]

And in the words of Professor Rupert Emerson:

[W]hile the concept lends itself to simple formulation in words which have a ring of universal applicability and perhaps of revolutionary slogans, when the time comes to put it into operation it turns out to be a complex matter hedged in by limitations and caveats.[2]

The fashionable question today is whether self-determination includes the right of secession, and "how small is small" for the purposes of self-determination.[3] Two recent statements neatly contrapose the issues. The late Secretary-General U Thant said:

So, as far as the question of secession of a particular section of a Member State is concerned, the United Nations' attitude is unequivocable. As an international organization, the United Nations has never accepted and does not accept and I do not believe it will ever accept the principle of secession of a part of its Member State.[4]

In sharp contrast, Conor Cruise O'Brien has written:

There is no tidy formula for determining what is to be done in a secession situation. Certainly the "right to self-determination" does not provide such a formula, since it bogs down in mysticism about what a nation is, and in dogmatic, contradictory and unprovable assertions about the claim to nationhood of the seceding group. But it may be safely predicted that if the international community evolves toward a rule of law, the principle which it will increasingly seek to have applied through arbitration in secession disputes will be that of consent of the governed, not the present implicit doctrine: "no secession at any price anywhere."[5]

So long as mankind continues to give deference to human dignity and human rights—at least in rhetoric—self-determination will continue to be invoked and reinvoked. For, as will be shown, the principle of self-determination is deeply rooted in the notion of human dignity and human rights.[6] The demands of mankind for achieving as much freedom and sharing of power as possible have been made under a variety of legalistic labels and contexts. Self-determination may be invoked singly or in combination with other labels such as sovereignty, independence, and nonintervention. In every situation where claims for forming an independent body politic are made, the problems of recognition, self-determination, and protection of minority groups are in some measure involved and interrelated.[7] Generally speaking,[8] when the group demanding independence has effective power to secure a factual separation, the doctrines invoked are those of "recognition."[9] When the group does not have sufficient effective power and needs external support to secure factual separation, the doctrines invoked are primarily those of self-determination. When the group cannot effect, or secure enough external assistance to effect, factual separation, what it demands is mostly special protection.[10]

The focus of inquiry in this essay will be on the second situation. Our concern will be claims to form a new entity. These always will be countered by a demand for "unity," which may or may not be accompanied by a concession for special protection to certain groups. What is fundamentally at stake is the shaping and sharing of power and other values within the different entities and the larger communities of which they are a part, and all options in general community decision must be appraised in terms of their potential impacts upon the different entities and communities.

Discussion about self-determination has too often proceeded in terms of highly technical, normatively ambiguous legal concepts which purport to make simultaneous references to varying factual contexts, to claims made to authority, and to responses by authoritative decisionmakers. As a result, the performance of the intellectual skills appropriate to any rational problem-solving has been impaired. Given the complexity of the problem, a configurative approach is called for, an approach that is contextual, problem oriented, and multimethod.[11] To use this approach effectively, a systematic and disciplined performance of a series of distinguishable but interrelated intellectual tasks should be undertaken. These include: (1) clarification of goals and policies of the community; (2) description of the trend toward or away from the realization of these goals; (3) analysis of the constellation of conditioning factors that appear to have affected past decision; (4) projection of probable future developments; and (5) formulation of particular alternatives that would contribute, at minimum net cost, to the realization of preferred goals.[12]

A comprehensive agenda of inquiry would thus proceed with a careful delimitation of the problem, underlining the significant features of the process of interaction, the process of claim, and the world constitutive process of authoritative decision. The second stage of examination would be a clarification of the fundamental community goals and policies, giving both high-level abstraction and concrete specification, followed by a survey of trend of past decisions with regard to all past and prospective types of controversy, ascertaining the degree of approximation toward recommended policies, and analyzing factors conditioning past decisions. Finally, the inquiry would conclude with appraisals in terms of past inadequacies and future promise, and a recommendation of alternatives contributing to optimal realization of human dignity.

The Process of Interaction

Self-determination is an integral part of a more comprehensive social process in which groups and individuals employ strategies, affecting resources, through institutions to attain their goals. For resolving the issues about separation, unity, or special protection, it is necessary to look in minute detail at the features of interactions which are most peculiarly relevant: the degree to which power is shared and the degree to which people who identify themselves as a distinct group are subordinate to, or free from, the other groups in the making of their own choices. It is the freedom of participation in different value processes which is fundamentally at stake. As in other contexts, this process can be described in terms of the participants, their perspectives, the situations of their interaction, the base values at their disposal, the strategies employed, and the outcomes and effects achieved.

Participants

The participants in the more comprehensive process of interaction are groups and individuals. Groups, territorial or functional, include nation-states, international governmental organizations, transnational political parties and political orders, pressure groups, and private associations.

Despite the conspicuous rise of transnational organizations, both governmental and nongovernmental, and despite the increasing role played by private business associations in recent years, the nation-state continues to be the most important wielder of effective power and plays the most prominent role. This has been vividly highlighted as the older empires of the European powers disintegrated and many former colonial territories have rushed into statehood. With the rapid multiplication of nation-states, the membership of the United Nations has more than doubled.[13] Nation-states vary tremendously in terms of size, population, resources, and stage of development measured by science and technology.[14] In an arena in which the superpowers coexist with intermediate powers, small states, and ministates and territories, the world is far from monolithic.

Nation-states display a great deal of diversity in terms of demographic composition, structures of power shaping and sharing, and public order system demanded and projected. Ethnic factors, though deliberately or otherwise downplayed, have made their impact widely and keenly felt.[15] With exceptional cases, most of them contain different ethnic, linguistic, cultural, and religious groups within their national boundaries.[16] They differ in recent history in terms of colonial relationships, scope of exposure to the transnational interactions, and development in wealth and other value-institution sectors.

People also live in territorial communities other than nation-states or component parts of nation-states, including trust territories, non-self-governing territories, and territories under military occupation such as the Arabs under the Israeli occupation.[17]

Groups may be cohesive territorially or dispersed throughout a particular territory. Concentration or dispersity of the population is an important factor. Within a territorial community the level of enlightenment and skill of a particular group may be superior, equal, or inferior to that of the rest of the community. Comparable analyses can be made for other values.

Consideration should also be given to the present distribution of population and groups on the global scale. Note especially the position of a particular group in relation to other territorial and functional groups in the contemporary world and the scope of its contribution to the production of values.

Perspectives

Account should be taken of the intensity and distribution pattern of demand in a population, in terms of what values are demanded and with what intensity, particularly the degree of power sharing demanded.

The prevailing identification of all groups in a territory cannot be assumed to be uniform: while some groups may demand and insist upon separate identity and development, others may be opposed. Contrast, for example, the demands of the Greek Cypriots with those of the Turkish Cypriots. The demand for separation may or may not be widely shared by many groups in the population of a territory. The degree of support, when carefully observed, may be confined only to the elite, or may extend to the rank and file.

The expectations of people about the conditions under which demands can be achieved may exhibit varying degrees of realism. They may or may not perceive the degree of freedom they enjoy. They may or may not share a long history of being persecuted and oppressed. They may or may not share a distinctive pattern of expectations about the past, present, and future. A most widely shared expectation today is that unless a people are "free to determine their own destiny" their demands for the wide shaping and sharing of values would be utterly impossible.[18]

Situations

The interactive situations relate to geographical features, temporal features, degree and kind of institutionalization, and levels of crisis.

Regarding institutionalization, structures of authority in terms of colonial or noncolonial relation are particularly significant. The degree of monopoly and stratification in the structure of authority is crucial. The dependency relationship between the ruling elite and the rank and file may be highly institutionalized and rigidified or may exist simply as a fact of ordinary political life.

Concerning geographical factors, note should be taken of the proximity of a territory to other communities (landlocked or a remote island) and of patterns of concentration or dispersal of population. Opportunities for internal lines of communication are significant. The territory may be separated by open sea from the mother country, or it may remain relatively remote and isolated from other communities. The physical separation of former East Pakistan and West Pakistan by 1,000 miles of Indian territory is in marked contrast to the contiguity of Biafra and the rest of Nigeria.

The importance of "territorial imperative" has recently received wide attention in the popular literature.[19] Though political systems are sometimes based on blood or tribal links, the prevailing pattern is based on territorial units. In the contemporary world the concepts of statehood and territoriality are inexorably linked; for a polity to exist meaningfully, control over some territory is absolutely essential. In a sense, the establishment of a body politic involves the delimination of its territorial boundaries. In the prevailing system of the nation-state, location has served the function of directing one's primary loyalty.[20] In many of the newly independent states, physical boundaries are often artificial and imprecise, legacies of former colonial empires. The intensity of emotional attachment to these boundaries varies and can become or generate a source of tension.

In terms of temporal factors, the length of time people have inhabited a particular territory is important. Also important is the length of time over which diverse elements in a territory have been integrated.[21]

And, of course, the crisis features may exhibit many differing degrees in intensity of expectation. Crises of war and the aftermath of wars, affecting the existing structural stability, often provide opportunities for aspiring groups to assert themselves aggressively.

Base Values

Attention should be given to the aggregate base values available in a community and to the relative resources at the disposal of different groups. Different groups may be differently situated in terms of possession of values indispensable to forming and maintaining a viable community. Sometimes groups may have the resources to "go it alone" without injury to other groups; in other contexts, both the new group and the old entity may be disastrously affected by secession.

Strategies

The use of strategies, persuasive or coercive, should be assessed against the backdrop of those persecution and oppression situations which are deemed human rights deprivations. Use of coercive strategies by the counterelite may simply be a response to provocative deprivations of the ruling elite. A most important factor is whether continued unity or separation can be achieved by persuasive or coercive measures. Another important dimension refers to the probable impact of separation or continued unification upon the future employment of strategies of persuasion and coercion.

Outcomes

The degree of protection or deprivation of human rights, as a culminating outcome in interaction, can be observed in terms of all eight values.[22] Aggregate consequences can be measured in relation to each of the various groups in a territorial community.

Important outcomes are in terms of the degree to which different groups are deprived of their freedom and the consequence of this deprivation for the shaping and sharing of human dignity values. The relevant factor is the degree to which different groups are deprived of, or subordinate to, other groups for the shaping and sharing of values—particularly power.

Effects

Changes in the status and affiliation of groups, territorial and functional, have important continuing impacts not only on the community directly concerned, but also on the larger community of which it is a part and with which it interacts. The degree of impact, of course, depends on context. Hence, an appropriate description of the effect on different communities would require a contextual analysis.

The Context of Conditions

The contemporary world has witnessed the ever-rising demand of peoples for freedom in the sense of wider and more secure participation in power processes and all other value processes which we consider essential to human dignity. The rising demand for self-determination—"power to the people"—is a part of this overall demand. While colonialism was once praised as "a civilizing mission," the peoples of the world have, with minor exceptions, a keen perception of the evils inherent in a relationship in which a group of people is dominated and exploited by an alien group. This perception has become keener as the pace of decolonization accelerates. Equally important in the context of modern inquiry and communication, peoples' perceptions of their interdependences have become more pervasive and realistic.[23]

These rising demands are intermingled with the conflict of identities, particularly global identity and national identities. The trend toward greater identification with the larger community is tempered, and often over-whelmed, by the trend toward the parochial syndrome in which nation-states or lesser identities predominate. Nationalism in the broadest sense remains a most powerful driving force.[24]

Given the growing expectations of a world of limited resources, the burgeoning population, and unceasing deprivations, expectations of violence both in external and internal arenas remain high. In a system conditioned by such an expectation of violence, the pervasive anxiety for personal and group security shows no sign of abatement. Violence is generally accepted as a fact of life, and not infrequently viewed by oppressed groups as indispensable to attaining survival, freedom, and justice.[25]

The Process of Claim

The focus in this section is upon the process by which some participants make claims to freedom and separation while others insist on continuing unification; each seeks the prescription and application of community policies that serve their own ends. It is convenient to consider briefly the claimants, their objectives, specific types of claims, and the conditions peculiarly affecting these claims.

Claimants

Both groups and individuals make claims of self-determination to established decisionmakers, particularly groups characterized by distinct ethnic, linguistic, cultural, and other features.

Groups with a territorial base, *i.e.,* territorial communities, are most important. These territorial communities are either nation-states or component parts of a naton-state, including trust territories, non-self-governing territories, and territories under military occupation.

Among those who have recently claimed the right to self-determination are the Germans, Koreans, Vietnamese, the Biafrans or Ibos,[26] the South Sudanese,[27] the Baltic peoples, the Formosans (Taiwanese),[28] the Somalis,[29] the Kurds[30] and Armenians, Germans of Rumania,[31] Scots in Scotland, the Catalans and the Basque people in Spain,[32] the Bangalis,[33] Catholics in Northern Ireland,[34] French Canadians in Quebec,[35] the Welsh people,[36] the Lebanese people,[37] Croats in Yugoslavia,[38] the Tibetan people,[39] and many former colonial people in Asia and Africa who have only recently achieved independence.

The group which claims self-determination may occupy a relatively well-defined territory that might be separated from the state of which it allegedly forms a part, such as Bangladesh, Biafra, Nagaland, and the South at the time of the American Civil War. Or the group may intermingle with

the dominant majority, such as the Chinese in the Southeast Asian countries, blacks in the United States, and Asians in East Africa.

Perspectives

The most general objective of claimants in invoking the processes of
authoritative decision in controversies about self-determination is to employ
authority as a means of establishing a new entity. Claimants seek to ensure
that authority supports their claim for separation or continuing unification.

The range of values demanded, the sense of realism, and the intensity
with which claims are pressed vary according to context, particularly the
degree to which groups are dominated or subordinated.

The demand to establish a new body politic may or may not be widely
shared by many groups in the population of a territory. It may simply be a
demand by the elite, or it may also command the support of the rank and
file of a population. While components of a group may demand to establish
a new entity, other components in the same territory may oppose this position.

Claims to self-determination are generally put forward by claimants
for themselves. But sometimes claims to self-determination are put forward
on behalf of other peoples—by a third state against other states. Examples
include the Pakistan claim against India about Kashmir, the Greek claim
against the United Kingdom about Cyprus, the competing claims of Indonesia and the Netherlands against each other with respect to West Irian
(formerly Dutch New Guinea), and the Moroccan claim against France
about Mauritania. Sometimes claims to self-determination are put forth
simply in the name of humanity and human rights.

The expectations of a people vary about conditions under which demands can be achieved. Though all groups in a territory may share a long
history of being persecuted and oppressed, they may not share a distinctive
pattern of expectations about the past, present, and future. Members of the
aspiring group generally share the expectation that the territory in which
they reside should be the one on the basis of which they organize and develop as a separate national entity and to which they give primary loyalty.

Specific Types of Claims

Self-determination is a multireferential doctrine which has been invoked in diverse situations. Comprehensively formulated, claims to self-
determination can be divided, as we have suggested previously, into two
basic categories:

1. Claims involving establishment of a new entity—claims by a group
    within an established entity to form a new entity from part of the pre-
    existing entity;

2. Claims not involving establishment of a new entity:
   a. Claims of an entity to be free of external coercion;
   b. Claims of a people to overthrow their effective rulers and establish a new government in the whole of an entity;
   c. Claims of a group within an entity to special protection (*e.g.,* autonomy).

A most comprehensive study of self-determination would need to address itself to all these claims. In a restrictive sense, category 1 is usually associated with claims to self-determination. For the present purpose, we shall concern ourselves only with category 1, *i.e.,* claims of a group within an established entity to form a new entity from part of a preexisting entity, colonial or otherwise. Such claims to self-determination can further be subdivided into two kinds: claims in the "colonial contexts," invoked by a colonial people against a colonial power, and claims in the noncolonial contexts. The former category is generally grounded on the relevant provisions of Chapters XI through XIII of the U.N. Charter.[40] As to the latter, in addition to Article 1(2), which refers to "respect for self-determination of peoples," other grounds such as "maintenance of international peace and security" (Article 1 (1)), "sovereign equality of states" (Article 2(1)), and "non-intervention in the domestic affairs" (Article 2(7)) are also invoked. At times, however, the interplay of "colonial" and "noncolonial" elements is by no means clear.

The Context of Conditions

The same features that significantly affect the process of interaction have a significant bearing on the process of claim.

The emancipation and awakening of millions and millions of people in the Third World have profoundly changed the context of world politics. Traditional or primitive societies that several decades ago could still be bought, sold, or traded in the chancelleries of Europe are today fiercely asserting a right to control their own destinies. Resentful of traditional colonial methods, they have not only sought to resist foreign domination but also have learned to question "foreign values."

As the rigid bipolar world has developed into a world which is "militarily bipolar but politically multipolar," nonsuperpowers, including intermediate and small states, find room for survival and development. Tempered and disciplined by cold and hot wars in a dynamic power-balancing world, the leaders of the newly independent African-Asian states have distinguished themselves by adopting the policy of nonalignment in world affairs. Nonalignment, in their view, is not isolation. Rather, it means a more or less independent position without long-range commitment to either side in the East–West confrontation of ideologies. Though the continuing need to rely on foreign aid, often with strings attached, has made the pursuit of nonalignment difficult, these leaders are quite skillful in taking advantage of their marginal position in their relations to the superpowers. A pluralistic international environment has indeed contributed tremendously to the continuing emergence and multiplication of new national entities.

The Constitutive Process of Authoritative Decision

The process of authoritative decision to which claimants may turn for resolution of controversies about self-determination is the comprehensive constitutive process of the world arena.[41] The features of this process, peculiarly relevant to self-determination, may be noted briefly in terms of decisionmakers, perspectives, arenas, base values, strategies, outcomes, and effects.

Decisionmakers

International government organizations, particularly the United Nations, are among the most important decisionmakers in dealing with controversies relating to self-determination.[42] To a lesser degree, regional organizations such as the Arab League, O.A.U. (Organization of African Unity), and the O.A.S. (Organization of American States) also have their role to play. From its inception the Arab League has aided in the national independence movements of Arab states living under foreign domination. The O.A.U. Charter projects the liberation and independence of the remaining African colonies as a major purpose of the Organization.[43]

The position of the nation-state continues to be of unique importance, acting either as a member of international governmental organizations or on its own behalf. The resolution of controversies about self-determination in the noncolonial context depends in large measure upon a flow of unilateral decisions by each of the existing nation-states. The important role played by colonial powers themselves is not to be overlooked. For instance, almost the entire French colonial empire has been transformed into a network of independent states, practically without direct participation on the part of the United Nations.

Perspectives

The specific goals of self-determination are maintained in an ongoing constitutive process that projects and sustains a minimum public order of security and an optimum public order in which all values are abundantly shaped and widely shared.

The objectives are most explicitly stated in the United Nations Charter, the International Covenants on Human Rights, and various resolutions adopted by United Nations organs, especially the Declaration on Decolonization of 1960.[44]

These instruments represent a set of widely shared expectations that the realization of self-determination for all peoples—especially in the colonial context—is a matter of "international concern" and not the exclusive "domestic jurisdiction" of a particular territorial community.[45]

Arenas

Within the United Nations, the General Assembly and, to a lesser extent, the Security Council are uniquely relevant. It is usually in these bodies that claims are first lodged. Of particular importance are the Trusteeship Council, the Fourth Committee of the General Assembly, and the Special Committee of Twenty-Four on Decolonization.[46]

The Secretary-General of the United Nations plays a significant role in connection with controversies relating to self-determination. For instance, in 1963, he verified the will of the people of Sabah and Sarawak to join Malaysia;[47] in 1969, he performed the supervisory function over "the act of free choice" of West Irian in deciding to remain a part of Indonesia;[48] and in 1970, he was entrusted with the task of ascertaining the wishes of the people of Bahrain at the request of the United Kingdom and Iran.[49]

Base Values

The grants of authority to the United Nations in regard to colonial territories, including trust territories and non-self-governing territories, are explicit, elaborate, and comprehensive, as provided in Chapters XI to XIII of the U.N. Charter. This is a particularly happy example of authority serving as a base of power. Authority conferred by the U.N. Charter is most frequently invoked here. On the other hand, in the noncolonial context, the authority of the United Nations is very general. The impressive achievement of the United Nations in connection with decolonization, as compared to the limited role it has played in regard to noncolonial controversies about self-determination, is in no small part related to this basic difference.

Control over enlightenment, skills, wealth, well-being, loyalties, rectitude, and military forces by the United Nations is rather limited as compared to the aggregate base values at the command of the nation-states.[50] However, the great reserve of effective base values under the exclusive command of nation-states is potentially available in support of self-determination.

Strategies

Because of their limited resources, international governmental organizations have tended to emphasize the use of diplomatic and ideological instruments. Most of the activities have been in the form of discussion in newly established arenas. The potential relevance of recourse to economic and military strategies is, however, underlined by cases such as the Congo and Cyprus, and by the sanctions invoked against South Africa and Southern Rhodesia.

Outcomes

Outcomes exhibit both the honoring of demands for self-determination as well as the outright rejection of claims for self-determination. All seven functions of decision—intelligence, promotion, prescription, invocation, application, termination, and appraisal—are performed.[51] Prescriptive efforts on the part of the United Nations are particularly impressive: the relevant provisions of the United Nations Charter, the Declaration on the Granting of Independence to Colonial Countries and Peoples of 1960, the self-determination clause (Article 1) embodied in both International Covenants on Human Rights, and the principle of self-determination embodied in the Declaration on Principles of International Law Concerning Friendly Relations and Co-operation among States in accordance with the Charter of the United Nations adopted by the General Assembly in October 1970.[52]

The emergence of some sixty independent states after the end of World War II is testimony to the importance of the applying function of nations in regard to self-determination.

Clarification of Community Policies

The observer identifying with the whole of humankind commences with the preference that every people be free to shape its own destiny and that every viable identity group enjoy as much freedom as possible. Self-determination of peoples is an expression of human dignity and is deeply rooted in the concept of human dignity.[53] By human dignity we include both minimum order, in the sense of prevention of unauthorized coercion, and optimum order, in the sense of the widest possible shaping and sharing of values.[54]

The recommended test in granting or rejecting a demand for self-determination is not whether a given situation is "colonial" or "noncolonial," but whether granting or rejecting the demands of a group would move the situation closer to goal values of human dignity, considering in particular the aggregate value consequences on the group directly concerned and the larger communities affected. In other words, the basic question is whether separation or unification would best promote security and facilitate effective shaping and sharing of power and of all the other values for most people. In a world of ever-increasing interdependence, a proper balance between freedom of choice and the viability of communities must be maintained.

For achieving the indispensable information, it is vital to employ a systematic contextual approach. It is essential to examine alternative consequences of either granting or rejecting claims for separation or unity. Specific consideration should be given to the following: (1) the degree to which the demanding group can form a viable entity, both in terms of its internal processes and its capacity to function responsibly in its relations with other entities; (2) the probable consequences of independence (separation) for the remaining people in the entity of which it has been a part; and (3) the consequences of demanded independence (separation) or unity (unification) for the aggregate pattern of value shaping and sharing for the peoples of the surrounding communities and for the world at large.

It is all these probable consequences that must be ascertained and tested in a given context by a careful analysis of contextual factors: participants, perspectives, situations, base values, strategies, outcomes, and effects. The special features of any particular context, including both the empirical manifestations of each feature and the configuration of all features, may affect the aggregate outcome.

The following questions should focus attention on the specific components of our major goal statement. The three major components of perspectives are demand, identification, and expectation. It is of utmost importance to ascertain the intensity of demands either for separation or unity and the distribution pattern of demands in a population, observing the degree of support on the part of the elite and the rank and file respectively. Not only the demands of those associated with the aspiring groups, but also of those associated with antagonistic groups, as well as those sectors of the population who identify with neither, are relevant. Beyond the simple question of separation or unification, proper attention should be given to specific value demands regarding power, respect, enlightenment, wealth, and so on. The greater the intensity and the more inclusive the shared demand, the greater would be the weight to be accorded the demand.

Self-determination being a search for, and the maintenance of, the self, identifications are of crucial importance, especially the intensity and inclusivity of identification with a territorial community and the range and degree of identification with regional and global communities. Hence, it is vital to ascertain: (1) the degree to which the elite and the rank and file of the aspiring group identify with an existing or projected territorial community; (2) the extent to which members of the aspiring group associate themselves with all members of an existing or projected territorial community; (3) the degree to which members of the aspiring group identify with a single class or ethnic or linguistic group; (4) the degree of territorial inclusivity; and (5) the range and degree of identification with regional and global communities and the degree of conformity to regional and global public policies. The demand for separation is to be taken seriously when it is put forth by those who share a distinct identity.

Another component is the world views about the past, present, and future entertained by the different participants. The complex of matter-of-fact expectations tends to affect, consciously or unconsciously, the attention frame of participants. Hence it is important to explore in which direction and to what extent alternative courses of action will affect these expectations. Those who share a distinctive pattern of expectations about the past, present, and future—particularly a long history of glory or of persecution and oppression—are to be accorded a presumptive deference.[55]

In terms of participation, attention should be directed to observation of how a particular group that makes a demand for separation fits in with the territorial and functional groups in the contemporary world, and to compare what changes in participation are being sought by demanders and by those who oppose the demand. Separation is favored when it would increase the widest possible participation with responsibility at all levels. The emphasis is to achieve a level of effective participation by the individual, especially participation in the power process, and not just receipt of welfare. Effective power shaping and sharing, as distinguished from participation in other value processes, is crucial, for there should be enough bases of power to keep the entity viable.

The state of enlightenment and skill cannot be overlooked. Answers to the following questions should be sought: Do the people concerned actively participate in making the demand? In the past what different choices were available to these people? What choices would be open to them in the future? Would granting the demand lead to significant value shaping and better distribution of values? Would participation in the relevant value processes be effectively widened? Note that acting together in the sense of participation in forming a new entity is quite different from a situation in which people already have substantial access to power.[56]

Regarding situations, compare the present and proposed structures of authority, both functional and territorial, and ascertain the degree of sharing of a common destiny in reference to the larger community. Note the length of time over which previous factors have been integrated and consider alternative time intervals for future integration and consolidation, e.g., the degree and pace of integration of the new community under a new order. Appraise the intensities of demand for change, as measured by the magnitude and direction of values involved, for all who are implicated in the situation—those who are making claims and those who would be affected.

With regard to base values, consideration should be given to consequences of accepting or denying a particular demand in terms of values. What are the present distributions of values of different groups? What changes are demanded in terms of authority and controlling values? What are the available alternatives and their consequences for people, territory, institutions, and resources?

We favor separation when the new pattern of distribution of base values would yield aggregate results for the most individuals closer to our preference in terms of persons, resources, and institutions. Needless to say, a presumption is ordinarily in favor of groups pursuing their goals by persuasive, rather than coercive, means. However, in contexts in which deprivations of human rights are extreme and in which persuasion is of obvious futility, use of violence as a last resort to achieve freedom and human dignity is perforce to be condoned.

In terms of viability of a political community, inquiry can be directed to three major aspects: security, power, and wealth and other values.

In a world wherein expectations of violence remain high, the military capability of an entity has been unduly overemphasized. A deemphasis on military capability is in order. It is difficult, under contemporary conditions, even for nuclear powers to insure their own defense. The defense of external security of separate entities is of necessity becoming an inclusive function of the larger community. In an interdependent world in which nation-states of different sizes coexist, the critical element in a state's security lies less in its self-sufficient military strength than in development of an inclusive authority in a world public order system in which unauthorized coercion is minimalized. Note, for instance, the increasing demands for nonnuclear zones in many regions of the world.

There is no simple answer to the question of whether a larger country can operate more efficiently. A great deal depends upon other factors such as economy, education, the level of living and literacy, and, more generally, the political culture of a community. In fact, in a compact community with an average population size of, say, 10 million, people can participate more effectively in the political process. In a vast country, there is a tendency toward a high degree of bureaucratization whereby the government takes on a life of its own.[57] In a highly bureaucratized society, the people may develop many inhibitions against the wide shaping and sharing of power by the general population.

In terms of economic viability, bigness per se does not provide all the answers. Overbureaucratization is as much a problem in the economic sphere as in the power sector. In an increasingly interdependent world in which functionalism regularly transcends national boundaries, wealth and other value activities have increasingly become transnational in scope and impact. Yet, the capacity of a new entity to develop itself cannot be overemphasized. No less important is its capacity to act responsibly in its interactions with other participants in the world arena. Nor can the implication of the existence of a new entity for the surrounding communities and the global community be overlooked.

The most important of all these features is of course the outcomes in terms of impact upon different values expected to attend each option, for the aspiring group, the old entity to which the aspiring group belongs, and the larger surrounding communities, including the global community. Hence, the critical test in considering a claim to self-determination is to evaluate the aggregate value consequences for all those communities, potential as well as existing, in honoring or rejecting the claim, and to honor the option that will promote the largest net aggregate of common interest by fully estimating the relative costs and benefits of the different options for each of those communities.

Trends in Decisions and Conditioning Factors

Community Prescriptions

The modern principle of self-determination originated in the seventeenth century when the nation-state system emerged.[58] Deeply rooted in the concept of nationality, the principle was then divorced from considerations of human rights or democracy. Prolonged religious wars made the position of many minority groups acute, but the problem was viewed as a matter that solely concerned a sovereign and his subjects. As the degree of interdependence grew, the problem of minority protection began to assume an international dimension: a third state occasionally demanded self-determination on behalf of minority groups lying within the jurisdiction of other nation-states.[59] Self-determination was seen as a manifestation of collective rather than individual will. With the introduction of the concepts of democracy and the sovereignty of the people following the French Revolution, the plebiscite was employed to determine the public will of the people in territorial disputes.[60]

At the end of World War I the principle of national self-determination took new shape under the championship of President Woodrow Wilson:

> No peace can last, or ought to last, which does not recognize and accept the principle that governments derive all their just powers from the consent of the governed, and that no right anywhere exists to hand people about from sovereignty to sovereignty as if they were property.[61]

Though self-determination guided the settlement of territorial disputes between nations as well as within states, it was assumed to be applicable only in European contexts. The colonial possessions of the European powers in Asia and Africa were outside the scope of its application. According to the Covenant of the League of Nations, "the wishes of the populations" were the major consideration in selecting the mandatory power for class A mandates; [62] but, in practice, this provision was virtually ignored, to say nothing of classes B and C mandates.[63] The network of the new mandates system was not directed to the task of preparing dependent peoples for ultimate self-government. From the outset the system was crippled as a universal set of arrangements because it applied only to the territories of the *defeated* powers. Consequently, in the post–World War I period, the application of the principle of self-determination was confined to the "unsettled areas of Eastern Europe and the Near East."[64]

During World War II, the principle of self-determination was included in the Atlantic Charter of August 14, 1941.[65] Whatever the reluctance of old colonial powers to apply it to themselves, self-determination had now acquired a universal appeal akin to that of the concept of human dignity and was correlated with the maintenance of world public order.

In 1945, at San Francisco, the world community formally recognized this principle as essential to peace and security, as well as to human rights, and upheld its application to all "peoples," regardless of geographical or racial factors.[66] Aside from Article 55[67] and the relevant provisions concerning the non-self-governing territories and the international trusteeship system, the Charter identifies as one of its major purposes to "develop friendly relations among nations based on respect for . . . self-determination of peoples." [68]

Though the Universal Declaration of Human Rights is silent on the question of self-determination, both International Covenants on Human Rights—the International Covenant on Civil and Political Rights and the International Covenant on Economic, Social, and Cultural Rights—accord a prominent position to this matter.[69] In identical words, both Covenants proclaim the right of self-determination of all peoples in their first article: [70]

1. All peoples have the right of self-determination. By virtue of that right they freely determine their political status and freely pursue their economic, social and cultural development.

*   *   *

3. The States Parties to the present Covenant, including those having responsibility for the administration of Non-Self-Governing and Trust Territories, shall promote the realization of the right of self-determination, and shall respect that right, in conformity with the provisions of the Charter of the United Nations.

In 1950, the General Assembly called upon the Economic and Social Council to request the Commission on Human Rights "to study ways and means which would ensure the right of peoples and nations to self-determination." [71]

By its resolution 545 (VI) of February 5, 1952, the General Assembly decided that the Covenants on Human Rights should include an article on the right of self-determination of peoples:

This article shall be drafted in the following terms: "All peoples shall have the right of self-determination," and shall stipulate that all States, including those having responsibility for the administration of Non-Self-Governing Territories, should promote the realization of that right, in conformity with the Purposes and Principles of the United Nations, and States having responsibility for the administration of Non-Self-Governing Territories should promote the realization of that right in relation to the peoples of such territories.[72]

The Commission on Human Rights completed the drafting of two International Covenants on Human Rights at its tenth session, held from February 23 to April 18, 1954. Thereupon the text of the two Covenants as drafted by the Commission was transmitted to the Economic and Social Council and the General Assembly in 1954.

The text of Article 1 as drafted by the Commission on Human Rights [73] reads:

1. All peoples and all nations shall have the right of self-determination, namely, the right freely to determine their political, economic, social and cultural status.

2. All States, including those having responsibility for the administration of Non-Self-Governing and Trust Territories and those controlling in whatsoever manner the exercise of that right by another people, shall promote the realization of that right in all their territories, and shall respect the maintenance of that right in other States, in conformity with the provisions of the United Nations Charter.

3. The right of peoples to self-determination shall also include permanent sovereignty over their natural wealth and resources. In no case, may a people be deprived of its own means of subsistence on the grounds of any rights that may be claimed by other States.

In the course of consideration by the Commission on Human Rights, attention was immediately directed to the question of whether self-determination was a "political principle" or a "legal right."[74] It was held that self-determination could have a place on the Covenants on Human Rights only when it was a "right." Despite assertions to the contrary and despite suggestions for treating self-determination under a special declaration or a separate covenant, the Commission proceeded to prepare a draft article on self-determination.

The wording of the first clause in paragraph 1 of the Article, "All peoples and all nations shall have the right of self-determination," was meant to be universal. "Peoples" was meant to refer to peoples in all countries and territories, whether independent, trust, or non-self-governing. The insertion of "all nations" was intended to emphasize the universal character of the right of self-determination.[75]

Suggestions were made that the right of self-determination should be given concrete expression by including the right to "establish an independent State," to "choose its own form of government," to "secede from or unite with another people or nation." These suggestions were rejected, because, it was thought, an enumeration of this kind was apt to be incomplete; a formulation in general terms was considered preferable.[76]

In 1955, the Third Committee devoted considerable time to a consideration of Article 1 of the two draft Covenants. It proceeded in the following sequence: holding a general debate; submitting various amendments to the text as drafted by the Commission on Human Rights; establishing a Working Party to redraft a text; submitting of amendments to the text proposed by the Working Party; considering two draft resolutions relating to procedure; and adopting the text of Article 1 by the Committee.[77]

A focal point of debate at the Third Committee was whether the Covenants should include an article on self-determination. Both the pros and cons were voiced in very sharp terms. Those opposed to the inclusion of the article argued that it would reduce the number of states willing to accept the Covenants; the provisions of the U.N. Charter regarding self-determination are phrased in general and vague terms, not susceptible of precise application; self-determination is referred to as a "principle," not a "right," and hence is devoid of authoritative effect. Even Chapters XI and XII concerning the non-self-governing territories and trust territories do not mean immediate independence and self-government for the peoples of these territories. Self-determination, extremely complex in international practice, involves the problems of minority protection and the right of secession. As self-determination is not essential to human rights, the Universal Declaration on Human Rights contains no provision on self-determination.[78]

Those who insisted on the inclusion of a self-determination article contended that the "right" of self-determination was a prerequisite to the protection and enjoyment of all other human rights by individuals and hence must be prominently placed in the Covenants. This is a right embodied in the U.N. Charter; its incorporation in the Covenants was previously decided by the General Assembly in its Resolution 545 (VI).[79]

Though there had been considerable debate about the meaning of "peoples" and "nations," the word "nations" was deleted from paragraph 1 of the Working Party's text [80] on the ground that "peoples," as used in the Preamble to the U.N. Charter, was more comprehensive. When put to vote before the Third Committee in 1955, the words "All peoples have the right of self-determination" were adopted by a roll-call vote of forty-one to none, with seventeen abstentions.[81]

The text of Article 1 of both draft Covenants as adopted by the Third Committee reads as follows:

1. All peoples have the right of self-determination. By virtue of the right they freely determine their political status and freely pursue their economic, social and cultural development.

2. The peoples may, for their own ends, freely dispose of their natural wealth and resources without prejudice to any obligations arising out of international economic cooperation, based upon the principle of mutual benefit, and international law. In no case may a people be deprived of its own means of subsistence.

3. All the States Parties to the Covenant, including those having responsibility for the administration of Non-Self-Governing and Trust Territories, shall promote the realization of the right of self-determination, and shall respect that right, in conformity with the provisions of the United Nations Charter.[82]

This text, with minor syntactical refinements, was adopted in 1966 as the first article of the two International Covenants on Human Rights.

The landmark Declaration on the Granting of Independence to Colonial Countries and Peoples, unanimously adopted in 1960 by the General Assembly,[83] proclaims, *inter alia,* that:

1. The subjection of peoples to alien subjugation, domination and exploitation constitutes a denial of fundamental human rights, is contrary to the Charter of the United Nations and is an impediment to the promotion of world peace and co-operation.

2. All peoples have the right to self-determination; by virtue of that right they freely determine their political status and freely pursue their economic, social and cultural development.

3. Inadequacy of political, economic, social or educational preparedness should never serve as a pretext for delaying independence.

4. All armed action or repressive measures of all kinds directed against dependent peoples shall cease in order to enable them to exercise peacefully and freely their right to complete independence, and the integrity of their national territory shall be respected.

5. Immediate steps shall be taken, in Trust and Non-Self-Governing Territories or all other territories which have not yet attained independence, to transfer all powers to the peoples of those territories, without any conditions or reservations, in accordance with their freely expressed will and desire, without any distinction as to race, creed or colour, in order to enable them to enjoy complete independence and freedom.[84]

As the most frequently invoked resolution in the United Nations, this Declaration has been reaffirmed annually by the General Assembly and has contributed tremendously to the accelerating tempo of decolonization in the recent years.[85]

The principle of self-determination is also embodied in the Declaration on Principles of International Law concerning Friendly Relations and Co-operation among States in accordance with the Charter of the United Nations adopted by the General Assembly in 1970.[86] As a compromise between the African-Asian states and the Western states, an express reference to the 1960 Declaration on Decolonization was omitted, but its essence was incorporated. This Declaration states:

> By virtue of the principle of equal rights and self-determination of peoples enshrined in the Charter of the United Nations, all peoples have the right freely to determine, without external interference, their political status and to pursue their economic, social and cultural development, and every state has the duty to respect this right in accordance with the provisions of the Charter.
>
> Every state has the duty to promote, through joint and separate action, realization of the principle of equal rights and self-determination of peoples, in accordance with the provisions of the Charter, and to render assistance to the United Nations in carrying out the responsibilities entrusted to it by the Charter regarding the implementation of the principle, in order:
> (a) To promote friendly relations and cooperation among states; and
> (b) To bring a speedy end to colonialism, having due regard to the freely expressed will of the peoples concerned;
> and bearing in mind that subjection of peoples to alien subjugation, domination and exploitation constitutes a violation of the principle, as well as a denial of fundamental human rights, and is contrary to the Charter.[87]

It appears from the foregoing that community prescriptions regarding self-determination are sufficiently clear and impressive.

Competence to Apply Policy

While the basic community policy of self-determination is projected in unequivocal language by the Charter and other related documents, its application in concrete circumstances is not unchallenged. The most common challenge, as in many other contexts, is based on the claim of "domestic jurisdiction" in order to repudiate the competence of the United Nations.[88]

Article 2(7) of the United Nations Charter, the well-known "domestic jurisdiction clause," provides that

> Nothing contained in the present Charter shall authorize the United Nations to intervene in matters which are essentially within the domestic jurisdiction of any state or shall require the Members to submit such matters to settlement under the present Charter; but this principle shall not prejudice the application of enforcement measures under Chapter VII.

Article 2(7) is frequently invoked to reject United Nations competence to deal with particular disputes, including controversies involving self-determination. Needless to say, there are matching counterclaims, as is to be expected from the doctrinal polarities that characterize a legal system. But the "domestic jurisdiction" formula has so much appeal in a nationalistic era that it has figured prominently in the debates of the U.N.

Article 2(7) of the Charter derives from Article 15(8) of the Covenant of the League of Nations, which reads as follows:

> If the dispute between the parties is claimed by one of them, and is found by the Council, to arise out of a matter which by *international law is solely within the domestic jurisdiction of that party,* the Council shall so report, and shall make no recommendation as to its settlement (emphasis added).

The Permanent Court of International Justice interpreted the provision this way:

> The question whether a certain matter is or is not solely within the domestic jurisdiction of a state is an essentially relative question: it depends upon the development of international relations.[89]

That is to say, the concept of "domestic jurisdiction" can be made meaningful only by reference to the context of world conditions at a given time.

The legislative history of Article 2(7) has frequently been invoked by competing claimants. However, the records of the San Francisco Conference offer no conclusive answer. The framers of the U.N. Charter neither saw fit to deprive or curtail the United Nations of the necessary authoritative competence essential to the effective performance of its tasks, nor wished the organization to "pry into" matters generally considered to be within the exclusive domain of individual nation-states.[90] Where or how was the line to be drawn?

Concepts in international law are definite to the extent that they are uniformly understood in content and procedure. Expectations about content are by nature somewhat vague, as the contingent circumstances to which they refer are phrased in general terms. Hence the importance of procedure, in terms of who is authorized to act, and how to apply prescription to concrete situations. To discover the structure of assumptions underlying the doctrine of "domestic jurisdiction," an examination of the U.N. record is in order.

Whenever a dispute involving self-determination is brought before the organization, Article 2(7) of the Charter usually receives initial attention, except in some clear-cut cases. The contention regarding U.N. authority is generally juxtaposed. No monopoly of a single power, the doctrine of domestic jurisdiction has been asserted by many states, large and small alike.

While it may be simple to ascertain the manifest objectives sought by competing claimants who repudiate or accept U.N. authority in a given dispute, it is far from easy to detect the latent objectives of these claimants. Even the attitudes of a single state do not remain consistent: its position is often dictated by the degree of "involvement" and "interest" perceived in a given dispute.

From the outset, the Indonesian question dramatized the issue of self-determination in the United Nations.[91] Despite Dutch opposition, the Security Council dealt with the case and facilitated the final settlement by reference to the principle of self-determination. Claims to self-determination often arose in contexts where the charge of infringement of "sovereignty" and "independence" was made by one state against another, *e.g.,* in the Greek question of 1946,[92] the Iranian complaint against the U.S.S.R. in 1946,[93] the Czechoslovakian question in 1946,[94] the Hyderabad issue in 1948,[95] the Yugoslavian complaints in 1951,[96] and the Hungarian question of 1956.[97] Claims to self-determination were occasionally pressed by a third state against other states, such as the Pakistan claim against India about Kashmir,[98] the Greek claim against the United Kingdom about Cyprus,[99] the competing claims of Indonesia and the Netherlands against each other with respect to Dutch New Guinea (West Irian),[100] and the Moroccan claim against France about Mauritania.[101] Most common claims arose, of course, in contexts where colonial and dependent peoples were demanding self-determination. The list is long, including the disposition of former Italian colonies,[102] the Palestine question,[103] the Togoland question,[104] Cameroons,[105] Ruanda-Urundi,[106] Southern Rhodesia,[107] Namibia,[108] and the territories under Portuguese rule.[109]

In opposing claims for decolonization, the colonial powers have often resorted to Article 2(7) of the Charter in order to perpetuate their rule in the dependent territories. Despite persistent objections of states, such as Portugal and South Africa, it is now well established that the United Nations has the authoritative competence to deal with disputes relating to self-determination. The U.N. action in regard to the Namibia case is the most instructive recent example.[110] In cases relating to "colonial territories," it is crystal clear. Not only has the United Nations accelerated the political independence of the trust territories and the non-self-governing territories, it has also contributed mightily to the economic, educational, and social welfare of the peoples in these territories. On the other hand, the United Nations has been extremely cautious in dealing with the question of self-determination for people who do not reside in "colonies or trust territories." The limited success of the United Nations in this latter category does not imply a lack of formal authority, but reflects a sense of realism and caution necessitated by the actual base values at its disposal.

Yet, when a serious dispute involving the demand for self-determination is current, the decisionmakers are generally able to relate the seriousness of the dispute to the task of maintaining world public order.[111] And when peace and security are perceived as threatened, the United Nations is often able to make a move.

In sum, responses to claims of domestic jurisdiction seem to have been shaped by reference to the major purposes of the organization in the light of the contextual factors perceived as relevant to a given dispute. Such an approach is the only sensible way of operating in an inordinately complicated and dynamic world situation. Claims to domestic jurisdiction are dismissed whenever an important dispute involves genuine demands for self-determination and a significant degree of threat to world peace and security.

Claims to self-determination on the part of the people in a colonial territory, once established, are given almost conclusive presumption for recognition of the claims. On the other hand, when a particular claim to self-determination is found to be "noncolonial" in nature, a strong presumption is against recognition of the claim. Hence the importance of (1) the criteria to decide which territory is a colony and (2) the competence to decide which territory is a colonial territory.

What are colonial territories? Colonialism is a loaded term.[112] As Professor Ved Nanda points out, "Colonialism as traditionally defined has been a political-economic relationship between a dominant Western nation and a subservient non-Western people."[113]

In United Nations practice, colonial territories refer to both trust territories and non-self-governing territories. Under Chapters XII and XIII of the Charter, the United Nations established an international trusteeship system to administer and supervise trust territories placed under it by individual agreements. This system applied to: (1) territories then held under mandates established by the League of Nations; (2) territories detached from the Axis Powers as a result of World War II; and (3) territories voluntarily placed under the system by states responsible for their administration.[114]

The major objective of the trusteeship system is

> . . . to promote the political, economic, social, and educational advancement of the inhabitants of the trust territories, and their progressive development towards self-government or independence as may be appropriate to the particular circumstances of each territory and its peoples and the freely expressed wishes of the peoples concerned, and as may be provided by the terms of each trusteeship agreement.[115]

The administration of trust territories is supervised by the Trusteeship Council.[116]

A total of eleven territories was placed under the international trusteeship system: Togoland under French administration; Togoland under British administration; Cameroons under French administration; Cameroons under British administration; Tanganyika under British administration; Ruanda-Urundi under Belgian administration; Western Samoa, administered by New Zealand; Nauru, administered by Australia on behalf of Australia, New Zealand, and the United Kingdom; New Guinea under Australian administration; and Somaliland under Italian administration.[117] Finally, the trust territory of the Pacific Islands, also known as Micronesia —consisting of the former Japanese-mandated islands of the Marshalls, Marianas (excluding Guam), and Carolines—is known as a strategic territory under United States administration according to an agreement approved by the Security Council in April 1947. All these territories, except the Pacific Islands,[118] have now realized goals of the trusteeship system, either as independent states or as part of independent states.[119]

Unlike trust territories, non-self-governing territories are dealt with under Chapter XI of the United Nations Charter. Non-self-governing territories refer to "territories whose peoples have not yet attained a full measure of self-government."[120] Member states administering non-self-governing territories are required

> . . . to transmit regularly to the Secretary-General for information purposes . . . statistical and other information of a technical nature relating to economic, social, and educational conditions in the territories for which they are respectively responsible . . . .[121]

Since the Charter was silent on who was to decide which territories fell into this category, it was done on a voluntary basis, in the first years of the United Nations. In 1946, for example, eight member states—Australia, Belgium, Denmark, France, the Netherlands, New Zealand, the United Kingdom, and the United States—enumerated the territories under their administration which they considered to be non-self-governing and proceeded to furnish information on them to the United Nations. This practice was resisted by Spain and then Portugal when they became members of the United Nations in 1955.[122] It was only at the fifteenth session of the General Assembly in 1960, following the adoption of the Declaration on the Granting of Independence to Colonial Countries and Peoples, that criteria for determining whether a particular territory was non-self-governing began to crystallize and gain clarity.

The principles embodied in General Assembly Resolution 1541 (XV) of December 15, 1960, have since become the classic standards for determining what constitutes a non-self-governing territory (colony) in contemporary practice. They have become the essential guidelines for the Special Committee of Twenty-Four in its work.[123]

The Resolution states that Article 73(e) of the Charter imposes an obligation to transmit the required information, an obligation which ceases as soon as the territory concerned has achieved a "full measure of self-government." A prima facie case for a non-self-governing territory is one which is "geographically separate and is distinct ethnically and/or culturally from the country administering it."[124] Once such a prima facie case is established, other elements such as administrative, political, jurisdictional, economic, and historical factors can be considered. If "the relationship between the metropolitan State and the territory concerned" is of such a nature that the latter is placed "in a position or status of subordination," the presumption that such a territory is non-self-governing under Chapter XI of the Charter is confirmed.[125]

Independence is not considered to be the only mode to terminate the colonial status, for the Resolution indicates that a non-self-governing territory is considered to have achieved self-government by "(a) Emergence as a sovereign independent State; (b) Free association with an independent State; or (c) Integration with an independent State."[126] Since its inception, an important task for the Special Committee on Decolonization has been to establish a list of territories to which the Declaration on the Granting of Independence to Colonial Countries and Peoples applies and which it oversees. As of 1971, for example, there were, in addition to southern Africa, forty-one territories scattered around the globe that remained on the agenda of the Special Committee.[127] Many of them were quite remote, and most of them were small in size and population. Several of them have since emerged to independence, but none engaged international attention and efforts to the extent of southern Africa.

But the competence of the United Nations to define criteria for determining non-self-governing territories and to apply them did not go unchallenged. As a rule, objections were based primarily on the argument of domestic jurisdiction, *i.e.,* that U.N. actions interfere with the internal constitutional relationship between a metropolitan power and its overseas territories. The United Nations has rejected these objections, particularly after the Special Committee on Decolonization came into operation.

Normative Content

Colonial or noncolonial, it is no secret that the normative quality and content of the principle of self-determination remain controversial. Though it may seem to be academic to many, the question whether the principle of self-determination is a legal right in international law continues to be raised. Note, for example, the following observation by Profesor L. C. Green:

> It would appear from the above that, despite the statements of politicians or of partisan commentators, there is still no right of self-determination in positive international law, although since 1966 there may be one *in nascendi.* It is insufficient for a non-binding document to declare that the right is inherent when practice shows that has never been regarded as the case.[128]

Professor Rupert Emerson, an expert on the subject of self-determination, counseled caution in drawing positive conclusions in view of the persistence of doubt and opposition.[129]

On the other hand, the popular view holds that self-determination has become a legal norm in international law. Take, for instance, Dr. Rosalyn Higgins' view:

> It therefore seems inescapable that self-determination has developed into an international legal right, and is not an essentially domestic matter. The extent and scope of the right is still open to some debate.[130]

In her view,

> [I]t seems academic to argue that as Assembly resolutions are not binding nothing has changed, and that "self-determination" remains a mere "principle," and Article 2(7) is an effective defence against its implementation. To insist upon this interpretation is to fail to give any weight either to the doctrine of *bona fides*, or to the practice of states as revealed by unanimous and consistent behaviour.[131]

As manifested in United Nations practice, the principle of self-determination has been affirmed and reaffirmed, applied and reapplied. It is beyond any reasonable doubt that this principle "had exercised and would continue to exercise a profound influence upon the creation and existence of states and upon the relation between them."[132] In terms of both prescription and application, the right of all peoples to "freely determine their political status and freely pursue their economic, social and cultural development"[133] has become a basic principle of international law. No principle of law is ever given "unlimited application," however.

A meaningful inquiry should strive to contextualize the trend of past decisions in terms of "who gets what, when, and how."

The U.N. Charter stipulates "self-determination of 'peoples,' " and hence leaves room for arguments over "who" is an eligible "national unit," entitled to self-determination. It is often assumed that the basic unit for self-determination is "nation" and that only a people constituting a nation are entitled to self-determination.[134] The opposing view is that the very concept of nation, as symbolized by nationalism, is extremely ambiguous and controversial and that it is highly debatable whether a nation makes a state or a state makes a nation.[135]

The controversy cannot be solved by definitional exercises. After World War I, the principle of self-determination found expression in the European territorial settlements, involving notably the peoples in eastern Europe, the Balkans, and the Middle East as a result of the defeat or disintegration of the German, Russian, Austro-Hungarian, and Turkish empires. The peoples involved were primarily ethnic communities, nations or nationalities distinguished by language and culture crisscrossing the existing political entities.

Following World War II, the disintegration of the overseas empires has opened up the era of decolonization. Political boundaries inherited from the colonial era are accorded utmost deference, while diversity in ethnicity, language, and culture often is ignored. The peoples, formerly haphazardly grouped and administered as a political unit by the colonial power, emerge as newly independent entities based on the preexisting colonial administrative boundaries, however diverse or heterogeneous the population composition may be. The ethnic element is either ignored or played down.

No neat formula emerges: in ascertaining the basic unit of "nation" or "peoples" to exercise self-determination, the sociological, geographical, historical, psychological, and political factors of a social context have been recognized as relevant.[136] There is generally reference to the distinct features of the population concerned in terms of race, language, religion, or cultural heritage, and to the extent to which the territory involved is an identifiable territory or sufficiently contiguous to constitute one geographic unit. The United Nations Charter provides that in the administration of colonies "due account should be taken of the political aspirations of the people,"[137] and the United Nations has stressed the importance of the "freely expressed views of the people concerned."[138] The perspectives of the people—their demands, expectations, and identifications—are commonly accorded great weight. The opposition to Katanga's secession was in large measure based on the judgment that it was something engineered by outside interests and implemented by outside mercenaries, and not a popular demand or movement supported by the indigenous population.[139] In practice, the willingness manifested by the population concerned "to consider themselves as one people" is given special attention.

While no single test is considered conclusive, the United Nations has been particularly cautious in ascribing weight to assertions based on historical considerations. It is thought that attempts to change the status quo on the ground of past historical ties tend to ignore existing political realities, including the contemporary expectations of a people. Once historical issues are injected, it is extremely difficult to decide on how far back to trace the history. While a colonial power is apt to invoke the "civilizing" history of colonial rule, the competing claimant may base his claim on the centuries or millenia prior to colonial control. The point was made in the cases of the Franco-Moroccan dispute over Mauritania [140] and the Dutch–Indonesian dispute over West Irian (Dutch New Guinea).[141] In the controversy over self-determination for the Palestinians, the question of cutoff date is a focal point of contention.[142] It appears that the member states of the United Nations were more inclined to address themselves to existing political realities and to give greater weight to recent historical considerations. The underlying consideration is obviously to stabilize community expectations on the basis of "current history." The decisionmakers of the United Nations seem firmly disposed toward the position that a genuine exercise of self-determination is best achieved by respecting the shared demands and expectations of the people within an identifiable territory, whose sense of distinctive identity is based on a relatively common and unique political experience.

In practice the United Nations has also shown deference to the "territorial integrity" and the "established boundaries" of existing nation-states. Thus, the Declaration on the Granting of Independence to Colonial Countries and Peoples states that

> [a]ny attempt aimed at the partial or total disruption of the national unity and the territorial integrity of a country is incompatible with the purposes and principles of the Charter of the United Nations.[143]

Similarly, the Declaration on Principles of International Law Concerning Friendly Relations and Co-Operation among States in accordance with the Charter of the United Nations concludes the section on self-determination with the following statement:

> Nothing in the foregoing paragraphs shall be construed as authorizing or encouraging any action which would dismember or impair, totally or in part, the territorial integrity or political unity of sovereign and independent states conducting themselves in compliance with the principle of equal rights and self-determination of peoples as described above and thus possessed of a government representing the whole people belonging to the territory without distinction as to race, creed or colour.
>
> Every state shall refrain from any action aimed at the partial or total disruption of the national unity and territorial integrity of any other state or country.[144]

Understandably, member states of the United Nations, particularly newly independent states, are ordinarily reluctant to acknowledge that any component part of a nation-state is entitled to break off by the direct exercise of self-determination. As Van Dyke aptly stated:

> [T]he United Nations would be in an extremely difficult position if it were to interpret the right of self-determination in such a way as to invite or justify attacks on the territorial integrity of its own members.[145]

Incumbent elites of the world want to defend and perpetuate the existing state system, and the United Nations, knowing that its power bases derive principally from the support of the member states, is extremely cautious so as not to make decisions inimical to the incumbent elites. This explains why, despite the massive human tragedies and a protracted struggle for nearly three years, only five states formally recognized the Biafran claim to self-determination, while the United Nations and the Organization of African Unity were silent.[146] In the case of the Congo, the United Nations even waged an organized effort to frustrate Katanga's claim to secession from the Congo.

However, the claim to self-determination in the form of secession is as old as the history of the nation-state. The lack of support for Biafra has not precluded the birth of the independent state of Bangladesh.[147] While nation-states are understandably cautious in tackling problems of self-determination in "noncolonial" settings, it cannot be assumed that they have altogether lost the capacity—and the willingness—to appreciate and recognize the merit of each idiosyncratic case for self-determination.

After a provisional identification of "who" is entitled to self-determination, decisionmakers have to decide when and under what conditions self-determination is to be realized. While the "colonial people" typically demand an immediate and unconditional exercise of self-determination, the colonial or administering powers no less typically call for the fulfillment of certain preconditions. In the view of the colonial powers, the U.N. Charter requires that the development of self-government in the dependent or trust territories be effected "according to the particular circumstances of each territory and its peoples and their varying stages of development."[148] They often assert that since their presence or administration was at the invitation, or with the consent, of the colonial people, they simply cannot betray their sacred trust by abandoning these people before they are "ready" to manage their own affairs. To do otherwise would thus be in contravention of the Charter policy.[149]

Prior to 1960, at no time did the United Nations characterize the exercise of self-determination as "unqualified" or "unconditional." What it took was an exploratory, developing approach, under which not all colonial peoples were granted self-determination at the same time or to the same extent. But in 1960 a sweeping policy change took place. In its landmark resolution, the Declaration on the Granting of Independence to Colonial Countries and Peoples,[150] the General Assembly, stressing the "necessity of bringing to a speedy and unconditional end colonialism in all its forms and manifestations," declared that "[i]nadequacy of political, economic, social or educational preparedness should never serve as a pretext for delaying independence," and urged that

> [i]mmediate steps shall be taken, in . . . all . . . territories which have not yet attained independence, to transfer all powers to the peoples of those territories, without any conditions or reservations, in accordance with their freely expressed will and desire.

While the practical application of this sweeping policy must be related to the special conditions surrounding each case, as shown in the work of the Special Committee of Twenty-Four,[151] the Declaration did affirm the basic community policy in unequivocal language.

Assuming that the requirements for exercising self-determination are understood, an intriguing question is whether a blank timetable should be set for all territories or for some specific territories, or whether all problems of timing should be decided case by case. Setting a definite timetable, it is maintained, would have a constructive effect on the perspectives and operations of the people concerned. Though the majority of member states favor self-determination for all people without undue delay, they seem to agree that cases differ too much from one another to warrant the adoption of "blanket" timing.

Another question of decision strategy is the procedure to implement an exercise of self-determination. Shall implementation of the principle be left to the discretion of the states in effective control, to international organizations, notably the United Nations, to consultation between ruling authorities and the people, or simply left to armed revolt? While claimants for self-determination favor international participation, the colonial powers tend to insist on exclusive implementation procedures. Thus far the United Nations has rejected the claim that the administering authorities have exclusive competence. With respect to trust territories, the United Nations has borne direct responsibility in facilitating the realization of self-determination. In the case of nontrust territories, if genuine demands for self-determination are believed to be at stake, the United Nations generally does not hesitate to step in.

Claims to self-determination in the World War II era have not always been confined to contexts of acute controversy and a high expectation of violence. In fact, many controversies have been worked out without fanfare between the administering authorities and the people concerned. If the participants directly involved appear capable of resolving their mutual differences in a satisfactory manner, the United Nations prudently abstains from intervention. The United Nations has insisted that such a direct consultative procedure not be used as a pretext. Therefore, it seems that the U.N. tends to become involved whenever it appears that no just settlement can reasonably be expected from negotiation between the immediate parties.[152]

Of various modalities for giving expression to self-determination, the plebiscite has appeared to be the preferred instrumentality. In international law and practice, the plebiscite has come to denote a referendum of a significant number of the local population concerning proposed changes in the status of their territory.[153] Its basic postulate of the consent of the indigenous population as the component of sovereignty can be traced back to ancient natural law roots. Plebiscites were increasingly favored after the emergence of full-fledged political doctrines of popular sovereignty, accompanied by the renunciation of wars of conquest, after the French Revolution. In a number of instances, it was put to use as a practical procedure to determine the "public will" of the people concerned in territorial disputes.

Maintaining that no change of sovereignty should be made without the consent of the people concerned, the French Constituent Assembly initiated in 1790–91 a plebiscite in the ninety-eight communes of the papal territory of Avignon and the Comtat-Venaissin before annexation.[154] Subsequently, plebiscites were held in connection with the annexations of Savoy (1792),[155] Nice (1793), [156] the Belgian Communes (1793),[157] and the Rhine Valley (1793).[158]

During the era of Napoleon and the Congress of Vienna, the plebiscite was consigned to a state of oblivion. Not until the resurgence of nationalism and democracy in 1848 was the practice of plebiscites revived. The plebiscite was utilized by the Italian patriots to further unification [159] and by Prussia and the Germanic Confederation to solve the Schleswig question.[160] It was reaffirmed in the case of Moldavia and Wallachia at the Conference of Paris in 1856.[161] Subsequently it was employed by Great Britain in ceding the Ionian Islands to Greece;[162] it was also incorporated in the Treaty of Prague of 1866 between Austria and Prussia.[163] Thus, "by 1866 the method of appeal to a vote of the inhabitants, either by plebiscite or by representative assemblies, especially elected, bade fair to establish itself as a custom amounting to law."[164]

The Prusisan annexations of Schleswig in 1867, in defiance of the Treaty of Prague, and of Alsace-Lorraine in 1871, dealt a severe blow to the practice of the plebiscite. Subsequently, the Congress of Berlin completely ignored the plebiscite, due in large measure to the general attitude of deprecation toward non-European "native populations." This new state of oblivion lasted until World War I.

Before World War I the plebiscites manifested varying structural and procedural characteristics. Informal and unilateral, the plebiscites of the French Revolution and the Italian votes of 1848–70 were formulated and implemented by an elite with effective control and often involved no more than a general assessment of the popular mood. On the other hand, the plebiscites in Savoy and Nice,[165] Moldavia and Wallachia,[166] and in the Ionian Islands,[167] St. Bartholomew, the Danish West Indies,[168] and Norway [169] were executed—through formal agreements to which both parties, or states representing their interests, were signatories. Whether or not there was a formal agreement, all these plebiscites were carried out by only one party, which, in most instances, was still exercising military occupation over the area concerned. In the informal and unilateral plebiscites, the state which stood to benefit by the cession controlled the process. In those plebiscites involving formal agreements, the participant ceding the area possessed the control. Hence, these plebiscites, while reinforcing the basic principle of self-determination, fell short of developing adequate procedures.

The case of Moldavia and Wallachia was significant in that for the first time some degree of international supervision was present in the plebiscite procedure. The plebiscite was administered by Turkish officials, but the regulations for implementation were drafted in concert with the ambassadors of Austria, France, Great Britain, Prussia, Russia, and Sardinia, as well as the consultative European Commission.[170]

After World War I, important procedures developed. With one exception, the plebiscites were prescribed in the peace treaties as an integral part of the peace settlement.[171] Renunciations of sovereignty over territories by the defeated powers were made contingent on the outcome of these consultations. In marked contrast to pre–World War I practice, these postwar plebiscites were all held under formal international administration and by secret ballot. Plebiscites were conducted in Schleswig (1920),[172] Allenstein and Marienwerder (1920),[173] the Klagenfurt Basin (1920),[174] Upper Silesia (1921),[175] Sopron (1921),[176] and the Saar (1935).[177]

In United Nations practice, the plebiscite has become a useful device in the implementation of international trusteeships. Article 76(b) of the Charter requires that the progressive development of the inhabitants of the trust territories be guided by "the freely expressed wishes of the peoples concerned." Though the provision is not specific on how these wishes are to be ascertained, the plebiscite has become a popular and preferred mode for determining the future status of trust territories. Thus, plebiscites were held in British Togoland (1956),[178] French Togoland (1958),[179] British Cameroons (1959 and 1961),[180] Western Samoa (1961),[181] and Ruanda-Urundi (1961).[182] All of the plebiscites held in these trust territories were conducted by the administering authority, but under United Nations supervision.

The first U.N. plebiscite was in British Togoland, which took place on May 9, 1956. A vote of 93,095 favored union with an independent Gold Coast and 67,492 favored temporary continuation of the U.N. trusteeship pending an ultimate settlement.[183] Upon the formal termination of the trusteeship agreement by the General Assembly, British Togoland joined with the Gold Coast to form the new independent state of Ghana on March 6, 1957.[184]

As practically all the trust territories have assumed a new status following the formal termination of the trusteeship agreements, the plebiscite has also been adapted to non-self-governing territories as one means of implementing self-determination. The United Nations no longer distinguishes the status of trust from other colonial territories for the purpose of self-determination.

The United Nations has also rendered indirect assistance in assessing popular wishes in other situations. Elections held in South Korea were observed and reported by United Nations commissions.[185] Representatives of the Secretary-General were instrumental in ascertaining the wishes of the people in Malaysia (1963) [186] and in Bahrain (1970),[187] via consultation with their political and community leaders. The United Nations oversaw the elections held in the Cook Islands in 1965,[188] and, to a lesser extent, in Equatorial Guinea in 1968.[189]

In West Irian (West New Guinea), a plebiscite of sorts was carried out under United Nations supervision, though its unfortunate procedural defects were condemned. The question of West Irian was considered by the General Assembly from 1954 to 1957, and again in 1961.[190] The Netherlands proposed a U.N.-supervised plebiscite to assess the wishes of the people in West Irian, over which it retained jurisdiction after the rest of the former Netherlands Indies was transferred to the Republic of Indonesia in 1949. Indonesia rejected the proposal on the ground that the territory was an integral part of Indonesia. As Sukarno and his associates phrased it, the issue was not a new act of self-determination for the people of West Irian, who were already members of Indonesia, but their liberation from the yoke of the Dutch colonial rule. When fighting erupted between Dutch and Indonesian forces in the West Irian area, both sides were urged by the United Nations to seek a peaceful solution. With the good offices of the then Acting Secretary-General, U Thant, an agreement providing for the transfer of the administration of West Irian and for the ultimate self-determination of its people was signed on August 15, 1962, by the representatives of Indonesia and the Netherlands. The quick ratification of the agreement by both parties on September 20, 1962, was followed by the General Assembly's approval the next day.[191] Under the terms of the agreement, a United Nations Temporary Executive Authority (UNTEA) was to administer the former Netherlands dependency as of October 1, 1962, for an interim period of seven months, pending administration by Indonesia. Meanwhile, Indonesia would make arrangements by the end of 1969 to enable the 700,000 Papuans of the territory to decide whether they wished to retain or sever their ties with Indonesia. The Secretary-General would, at the invitation of Indonesia, appoint a representative to discharge his responsibilities to "advise, assist and participate" in arrangements for the "act of free choice." A number of U.N. designated experts were to remain in the territory when full administrative authority was transferred to Indonesia.

After the transfer of full administrative control from UNTEA to Indonesia on May 1, 1963, the United Nations performed no supervisory, political, or administrative function whatsoever for the territory. The United Nations experts, though designated, were barred from entry into West Irian by President Sukarno. Shortly afterwards, Indonesia withdrew from the United Nations.[192] Hence no U.N. personnel were present in West Irian from May 1, 1963, to August 23, 1968. The second phase of the agreement had never been implemented.

In was only on August 23, 1968, that the Secretary-General's representative, Ambassador Fernando Ortiz-Sanz, and his mission arrived in West Irian.[193] He soon discovered that the Papuan people had not been given adequate information regarding the forthcoming act of free choice and that their rights of free speech, freedom of movement and of assembly, as guaranteed by the agreement, had been and continued to be violated. It appeared that the people of the territory were at all times under the tight political control of the Indonesian administration.[194] Rejecting Ortiz-Sanz' proposal of "one man, one vote" for urban areas, the Indonesian government insisted on *musjawarah,* democracy *à la* Indonesia.

The consultation proceeded in eight consultative assemblies, involving a total representation of 1,025. Under the practice of *musjawarah,* all the members of each of the eight assemblies were required to stand up to signify approval of the consensus reached—*i.e.,* to remain a part of Indonesia. In the absence of individual secrecy, intimidation by surveillance could hardly fail to blunt freedom of choice. The outcome, not surprisingly, was unanimous in favor of retaining the ties with Indonesia.[195] In his report to the Secretary-General, Ambassador Ortiz-Sanz concluded with some subtlety that

> with the limitations imposed by the geographical characteristics of the territory and the general political situation in the area, an act of free choice has taken place in West Irian in accordance with Indonesian practice, in which the representatives of the population have expressed their wish to remain with Indonesia.[196]

When this report was transmitted to the General Assembly in November 1969, bitter criticism was voiced by many African states.[197] It was pointed out that the method and procedure used in the act of free choice were inadequate and that the people of West Irian could not be considered to have exercised their right of self-determination, as envisioned by the 1962 agreement. In their view, the argument that the people of West Irian were too primitive to have a general ballot was untenable, for the method of "one man, one vote" had been successfully practiced by the same so-called undeveloped people in Australian Papua (East New Guinea). The representativeness of the consultative assemblies was open to question because they had been filled with members either handpicked by the Indonesian government or elected, through *musjawarah,* for favoring the retention of ties with Indonesia. It was feared that this gross departure from the prevailing "international standards of free elections" could set a dangerous example, particularly for southern Africa.

Thus, the representative of Ghana went so far as to propose that the people of West Irian be accorded a further opportunity meaningfully to express their "free choice" by the end of 1975. While this proposal failed passage, it did obtain considerable support. Even supporters of Indonesia took pains to stress that the method and procedure used in this particular instance could be considered appropriate only for the special circumstances of West Irian and should in no way constitute a precedent.[198] In sum, the general view seems to be that the West Irian case is an unwarranted departure from an important international norm.

The question of Algeria was brought before the United Nations annually while the Algerian people were fighting for independence.[199] In 1960, the First Committee of the General Assembly proposed a U.N.-conducted plebiscite in order to carry out the right of self-determination of the Algerian people. The proposal fell short of the necessary two-thirds majority vote in the Assembly. Subsequently, a plebiscite was held in Algeria in July 1962, after the long negotiations between the French government and Algerian leaders; the plebiscite, administered by France, resulted in Algeria's independence.

Attempts have been made to use the plebiscite to solve the Kashmir question, but without success.[200] Kashmir was first brought to the attention of the Security Council on January 1, 1948. India accused Pakistan of aggression by assisting the invading tribesmen in western Kashmir; Pakistan countered that the accession of Jammu and Kashmir to India was illegal. From the outset India had claimed sovereignty over Kashmir, while Pakistan maintained that Kashmir belonged neither to India nor to Pakistan, pending the exercise of the right of self-determination by the people in the disputed territory. When both governments accepted proposals, including provision for a free and impartial plebiscite submitted by the United Nations Commission for India and Pakistan in November 1948, a cease-fire was ordered as from January 1, 1949. On January 5, 1949, the Commission adopted a formal resolution incorporating the proposals. In March 1949, the Secretary-General nominated Fleet Admiral Chester W. Nimitz, of the United States Navy, as plebiscite administrator subject to formal appointment by the government of Jammu and Kashmir after a formal truce. But the situation worsened and the plebiscite contemplated in January 1949 has not materialized.

International plebiscites also have been conducted without U.N. involvement. A case in point is the plebiscite held in Outer Mongolia shortly after World War II.[201] In the exchange of notes signed on August 14, 1945, at the conclusion of the Sino-Soviet treaty of friendship and alliance, the government of the Republic of China agreed to recognize the independence of Outer Mongolia on the condition that the desire for independence often expressed by the Outer Mongolian people be confirmed by a plebiscite. When the plebiscite took place in Outer Mongolia on October 20, 1945, more than 283,000 participating Mongols voted 100 percent in favor of independence from China.[202] The Vice-Minister of the Interior of the Republic of China was personally present in Ulan Bator to observe the plebiscite. The independence of the Mongolian People's Republic was hence recognized by the government of the Republic of China on January 5, 1946, and later by the People's Republic of China on October 6, 1949.[203]

In summary, the plebiscite has been repeatedly employed to ascertain the most fundamental political demands of the people of a territory. Occasional deviations or defects in plebiscite implementation are inevitable in any legal institution, but do not seem to negate the ostensible usefulness of the plebiscite modality. The crucial challenge, as shown by the trend of past practice, is to refine the methods and techniques of the plebiscite so as to ensure free expression of the true wishes of the people concerned in each idiosyncratic case.[204] In the clear absence of such prospect, the plebiscite is not only meaningless, but also may be harmful. The very absence of a real possibility for free choice in Namibia has been an important reason for rejection of the plebiscite modality there by the world community.[205]

The importance of effective and impartial international supervision of every phase of the plebiscitary process cannot be gainsaid. However, the implementation of the plebiscite is to a considerable extent dependent upon the good will and cooperation of the administering power concerned. When such good will and cooperation are obviously unattainable, the oppressed group would not—and could not be expected to—wait "patiently" forever, like a sitting duck at the complete mercy of the ruling elite. Hence the preferability of the plebiscite does not and cannot preclude resort to other strategies.

No serious champion of world public order denies that self-determination should be given effect without violence, for violence is inimical to the very notion of human dignity. In a world community stricken with many injustices, however, insistence on nonviolence can under certain circumstances be tantamout to perpetuation of those injustices. Indeed, recourse to violence may at times be the only alternative open to an oppressed people. In a global system preoccupied for the most part with national affairs, it is to be conceded that, on occasion, the use of violence may be the only practical strategy for dramatizing the cause of a people struggling for self-determination.[206] Claimants who resort to violence are quick to express their preference for a nonviolent solution, but contend that local conditions of repression and world inattention have left them with no other alternative. In Algeria, Indonesia, Hungary, and Angola violence flared on a substantial scale. The United Nations, while expressing regret for the fact of violence, did not seem to have condemned its use by the oppressed. However, the United Nations took a different position in the case of Katanga. Such a difference is evidently attributable to its basic judgment about the soundness of the respective claims to self-determination.

The Declaration on Principles of International Law Concerning

Friendly Relations and Co-operation among States in Accordance with the Charter of the United Nations provides:

> Every state has the duty to refrain from any forcible action which deprives peoples referred to above in the elaboration of the present principle of their right to self-determination and freedom and independence. In their actions against, and resistance to, such forcible action in pursuit of the exercise of their right to self-determination, such peoples are entitled to seek and to receive support in accordance with the purposes and principles of the Charter.[207]

This paragraph was formulated with particular adroitness, leaving it sufficiently vague so as to gain acceptance by those who believe third states have an obligation to provide all necessary support, including military force, and those who believe third states are required to render only moral and political support. In the course of the drafting debate, a number of delegates emphasized that peoples subjected to colonial rule have the right to achieve freedom and independence by all necessary means, including the use of force.[208]

Although the interpretation remains controverted, we are inclined to the position that the United Nations does not disavow self-determination by revolution under all circumstances, especially when an oppressed people who are capable and genuinely identified with one another are blocked from access to the channels of world attention.[209]

In terms of outcomes, although self-determination is commonly equated with "independence," it is not necessarily so. Arrangements other than independence, when freely chosen by the people concerned, are also acceptable. Viewed from United Nations practice and the context of world politics, self-determination does encompass alternatives ranging from considerable self-government inside an existing state, through an autonomous status within an established state, to complete independence. Thus, the Declaration on Principles of International Law Concerning Friendly Relations and Co-operation among States provides:

> The establishment of a sovereign and independent State, the free association or integration with an independent State or the emergence into any other political status freely determined by a people constitute modes of implementing the right of self-determination by that people.[210]

The differences in these outcomes can be classified by reference to the degree of participation in external as well as internal decision processes. "Self-government" involves either "assimilation of people" or "integration of territory." Under the assimilation formula, the people concerned become, on an individual and nonterritorial basis, full citizens of the state to which they choose to give allegiance. In the case of "integration of territory," the people of the territory concerned participate in the internal processes of the larger state, having varying degrees of benefits and burdens, as agreed upon. Moving a step further, "autonomy" makes no distinction between "assimilation" and "integration." Though the people exercise more comprehensive control over their internal decision processes, they lack independent competence to participate in the external processes. "Independence," as well known, means that people form themselves into a new body politic, possessing complete authority and control over its people, resources, territory, and institutional practices; it is endowed with the authority to participate independently in the international arena of formal authority.

In the post–World War II period, the overwhelming choice in exercising self-determination has been independence, which hardly is surprising in this age of nationalism and decolonization. However, objections have sometimes been voiced against associations based on "self-government" or "autonomy," which, as indicated, fall short of full and independent participation in the world arena.[211] This view is unnecessarily restrictive of choice. It overlooks the point that while in most instances independent statehood is the most desirable and practicable option, in some situations the scope of effective influence is perceived to be greater within the framework of a large state rather than in the formalistic grandeur of a microstate. In any event, the fundamental requirement inherent in the concept of self-determination is a *procedure,* not a preset outcome. Whether the choice in a particular case is "independence" or otherwise is less important than whether it is genuinely and freely made by the people concerned. If the freedom of choice of the people is sustained, the policy objective of self-determination is fulfilled. The decisions of the United Nations manifest the flexibility that is realistically adapted to the contextual complexities of world affairs.

Viewing United Nations practice as a whole, it appears that the world community has as much interest as the people directly concerned in seeing that solutions to self-determination problems will be beneficial to all.[212] Hence, in dealing with a claim to self-determination, the United Nations is concerned with: (1) the prospect of the territory or people concerned of becoming a viable state; (2) the present stage of advancement; and (3) the effect of granting or refusing the exercise of self-determination. It is considered essential that the people directly concerned have a reasonable prospect of becoming a viable entity—politically, economically, and so on—in this increasingly interdependent world. The community concern for a viable and self-sustaining economy is abundantly shown by the stress on "economic sovereignty," as embodied in the Declaration on Permanent Sovereignty over Natural Resources.[213] The shared expectation is that a new state should be capable of managing its own affairs and becoming a responsible member of the world community. While the new state is not expected to contribute substantially to world public order in the immediate future, it is expected to possess at least minimum political unity and strength so as not to become an immediate source of world insecurity. The degree of advancement of the people concerned is generally assessed by reference to the educational, political, and other value institutions and practices of a given territory. Some minimum standard in these sectors is considered essential to a meaningful exercise of self-determination.

Thus, no major value consequences of self-determination are regarded as irrelevant by U.N. decisionmakers in dealing with concrete problems of application.[214] In the case of Cyprus, for instance, since a substantial Turkish minority was involved, the United Nations did not see fit to let the majority group, the Greek Cypriots, dictate the outcome of self-determination, which would have meant a merger of the island with Greece.[215] In regard to the Congo, allowing the secession of the resources-rich province of Katanga would have been disastrous for the remainder of the Congo.[216] Though the passionate demand of the Ibos for separation was noted widely, the outside support was weak, presumably because of the deep concern that its separation would have had disastrous consequences for the rest of Nigeria, and beyond.[217] Such an implication was less apparent in the case of Bangladesh.[218]

It is worth noting that both colonial and noncolonial powers are apt to link their claims with the concept of world public order, though from different perspectives. While the colonial powers assert that the weakness displayed by a chaotic internal situation is tempting to big or neighboring powers, the anticolonial powers argue that the continuation of a dependency relation perpetuates an inherent instability that invites outside "intervention." These potential security implications have not escaped the United Nations in its response to claims of self-determination. Thus, while the United Nations has neither "endorsed" nor "condoned" colonialism in any form, it has been sufficiently sensitive to probable adverse effects on world order that would result from a premature and inadequate application of self-determination. This particular concern was amply manifested in the cases of Libya and Eritrea. The final decision not to partition Libya[219] or to form Eritrea as a separate entity[220] was due in large measure to considerations of minimum order. Similar considerations led to the different treatment accorded to former British Togoland and Cameroons.[221]

The recent multiplication of "ministates," "mini" with population, territory, and/or resources, has sharpened the debate on the viability of a new entity.[222]

Immediately before the French Revolution, Europe was composed of many tiny states, notably those loosely associated within the Holy Roman Empire. With the rise of Germany and Italy in the mid-nineteenth century and the high tide of empire-building and colonial expansion, it was generally assumed that national units would be quite substantial in terms of people, territory, and resources, and that the lesser peoples would either be assimilated or fade into the background. Following World War I, the eruption of several relatively small states from the Hapsburg and Tsarist empires brought about the "Balkanization" and further fragmentation of national units.

The accelerating pace of decolonization in the post–World War II era has brought about the radical multiplication of many more smaller units—now called ministates—and caused a great deal of international concern about the viability of the extant ministates and the desirability of adding potential ministates. The issue was highlighted in 1967, when Anguilla, a Caribbean island with 6,000 people, demanded independence from the United Kingdom.[223] In the introduction to his annual report in September 1967, Secretary-General U Thant, while conceding the right of even the smallest territories to attain independence through self-determination, underlined the desirability of distinguishing "the right to independence" from "the question of full membership in the United Nations." [224] A study conducted by the UNITAR in 1969 indicated that a total of seventeen U.N. member states have a population of less than 1 million, and a number of others have a population bordering on that figure.[225]

While no formula has been worked out to determine "how small is small" for the purposes of self-determination, the point that a new entity should be capable of developing itself as a viable entity and capable of acting responsibly in the external arena is widely appreciated. For it is increasingly recognized that the very existence and function of a new entity have value consequences far beyond its own borders.

Projection of Probable Future Developments

As decolonization gradually comes to an end, the principle of self-determination will decrease in importance in the colonial context. However, this does not mean that questions of self-determination will no longer arise. From time to time, people who do not think of themselves as "colonials" are bound to assert a political identity separate from the dominant element in the nation-state in which they are incorporated. While increasing global and regional cooperation can be expected, nationalism will in all likelihood remain highly appealing as a means of expressing dissatisfaction with a disadvantaged territorial position.[226] Hence the principle of self-determination will be of continuing significance in international affairs.

In the contemporary world community, attaining independence does not mean an end to the search for statehood. Rather, it signifies the commencement of a new task, the vital task of nation-building. Nation-building is multidimensional in nature: it involves all aspects of national life, all principal value institutions of a body politic, and its external as well as internal relations. An ongoing process of value accumulation and growth, the road to nation-building is beset with difficulties and hazardous.[227]

In the struggle for independence, there was an identifiable common enemy, the colonial ruler, against whom the rank and file were readily mobilized. Once the common enemy disappears, however, the internal solidarity of preindependence days is all too often replaced by factions representing diverse interests and competing demands. The "demogogic" elite can no longer hold the people together by mere appeal to emotion, and it finds that the "rising expectations" of the people become "rising frustrations" amid the manifold of complex problems. Hence assertion by discriminated and oppressed groups for a separate destiny.

A pessimistic construct would be that the established elites around the world would hold onto the now classic distinction between colonial claims and noncolonial claims (in the sense that when a group of non-Western people is subjected to the foreign rule of Westerners, it constitutes colonialism), recognizing demands for self-determination only for the former. As Professor Rupert Emerson points out:

> Despite the fact that the self-determination of the World War I peace settlement seems clearly to have involved secession, and that it is nonsense to concede the right to "all peoples" if secession is excluded, the customary verdict has been that self-determination does not embrace secession, at least as any continuing right.[228]

He further observes:

> If the right of secession is eliminated and the maintenance of the territorial integrity of states takes priority over the claims of "peoples" to establish their own separate political identity, the room left for self-determination in the sense of the attainment of independent statehood is very slight, with the great current exception of decolonization.[229]

In other words, according to this construct, the only room left for self-determination in the foreseeable future would be in the "reactionary" beachheads of southern Africa. The prevailing system of the nation-state would be so rigidified that no drawing of new boundaries would be tolerated by the extant elites, even in the name of human dignity. The world community would become a rigid caste system of the established nation-states, in which established national elites come to each other's rescue to suppress demands of new groups and perpetuate the interests of the elites in power.

An optimistic construct would reverse this gloomy prospect. The reaffirmation of basic community policies in regard to decolonization has crystallized into a set of perspectives that render it hypocritical to deny a voice to more advanced participants in the universalizing culture of science and technology. The diffusion of this common civilization, despite inner conflicts of view, has also spread the democratic theory that the consent of the governed is essential to human dignity. Deeply rooted in the ultimate goal of human dignity, self-determination would continue to serve as a ringing doctrine and symbol for group formation and identification, a symbol for the perpetual search of the collective self. Groups would be allowed to break away from established nation-states when it would help promote abundant production and the wide sharing of values for the group directly concerned, without causing undue hardship to the remaining community of which it was a part and without its having a serious disruptive impact on the public order both regionally and globally. Self-determination would be the guiding principle by which individuals would form a new territorial community and identify and associate with the community to maximize all the values they pursue. The history of the world will continue to be a history of humankind, grouping and regrouping, guided by the invisible hand of the maximization postulate.

This probable course of development need not be adversely affected by the changing configuration of world politics—from bipolarity to triangular power relations, or to multiple power centers.

Granted the strength of the trend toward a few power centers, we must not lose sight of the counterforces that modify the rate of movement in this direction, and call an eventual halt to the swallowing up of intermediate and small states in the process. In the present epoch of nationalism, many newly independent states, emerging from centuries of oblivion, have only recently found their collective identity. The people of these states cherish dearly their new status of independence, and their leaders are often able to take advantage of the opportunities of marginal position in relation to the superpowers to veer toward alignments or nonalignment that can defend a new-found position in the community of nations. Smaller states contribute to world security by modulating the confrontations of the major powers with one another.

It is no novelty that organized groups of contrasting size and potency do establish and maintain a balance of power that is stable for long periods. For instance, the rise of giant corporations in many markets does not destroy all the competing units. Rather, a familiar pattern of market economy commonly includes a few superunits, several intermediate units, and a multitude of lesser entities. It is frequently perceived that common interests are best served by defending the essential integrity of a system in which the tendencies toward a single imperial organization or a completely bipolarized or tripolarized pattern are successfully resisted within the new equilibrium of forces. It is by no means farfetched to expect that the future public order could be worked out within the framework of the present international system and that minimum security could come about in gradual fashion.

As hyperdestructive weapons become more accessible, the strategic dangers involved in their deployment will be more widely and deeply appreciated in military, diplomatic, and lay circles throughout the world. If coercions are effectively minimized, a growing sense of security can add to the frequencies of pluralizing and decentralizing modes of collective action. The superpowers themselves may be gradually modified as the permanent alertness generated by the arms race is lessened or superseded. The overcentralizing tendencies of superpowers themselves can in some measure be modulated or reversed not by the use of force but through the stimulation and cultural distinctiveness of intermediate and small nation-states.[230]

In sum, in the foreseeable future, the present international system will continue, a system in which nation-states of differing size and influence coexist and interact.

Appraisal and Recommendations

While the trend of past decisions indicates that the United Nations, in dealing with issues relating to self-determination, stresses the basic distinction of colonial and noncolonial issues, this distinction need not be conclusive, particularly when colonialism is narrowly understood to be the domination by whites over nonwhites. The essence of self-determination is human dignity and human rights. Underlying the concept of human dignity is the insistent demand of the individual to form groups and to identify with groups that can best promote and maximize his pursuit of values both in individual and aggregate terms. The formation and reformation of groups are ongoing processes.

Legal doctrines operate in pairs of complementarity,[231] here exemplified by the interplay between self-determination and territorial integrity. Is the seeming conflict between "territorial integrity" and self-determination irreconcilable? Territorial integrity for what? When the principle of territorial integrity is stretched too far, "the room left for self-determination in the sense of the attainment of independent statehood is very slight, with the great current exception of decolonization." [232] Too often, international crimes have been committed and perpetuated under the cloak of "territorial integrity." The concept gains support because we are living in a world of the state system in which established elites share vested interests in seeking to prolong their power position. If blind adherence to "territorial integrity" results only in massive deprivations of human rights in that territory, the regime has already lost its raison d'être. Without the allegiance of the people living in the territory, "territorial integrity" is hollow and empty.

Not unnaturally, established elites look to their own backyards when they are seized with a particular issue for self-determination. The nation-states, as they exist today around the globe, are mostly heterogeneous in demographic composition, and thus the established elites are, as a rule, highly sensitive to possible implications whether to support or reject a claim for self-determination for their own community. In other words, their primary frame of reference is problems at home. For individuals to get together and form a political community that would best promote their welfare and deference values and for an individual to identify with a particular body politic and show allegiance to it is as old as the history of humankind. This is what political process is about. The prevailing state system can be justified and sustained only when, in the final analysis, it would serve the interests of the people. When it fails to do so—and particularly when it becomes oppressive of people's demands for human dignity—change is in order and indeed imperative.

Those who are opposed to the concept that self-determination includes the right of secession do not state it in categorical and absolute terms. On the other hand, those who consider the right of secession inherent in the right of self-determination do not advocate an arbitrary and unrestricted application. It would seem that the possibility for claiming and exercising the right of self-determination by a group within an established nation-state is still a viable component of community expectation.

Until the successful birth of Bangladesh as an independent state in December 1971, it was widely assumed that there is no room for secession, meaning for a group to break off from an established nation-state, in the contemporary world, an assumption that is readily echoed by members of the United Nations. The following statement by U Thant typifies this line of thinking: "As an international organization, the United Nations has never accepted and does not accept and I do not believe it will ever accept the principle of secession of a part of its Member State." [233]

The success of Bangladesh has begun to change people's expectations. It has inspired immediate response and a rethinking of the subject of secession, as seen, for example, by O'Brien's timely article on "The Right of Secession." [234] It has increasingly become apparent that the absolute adherence to territorial integrity is no virtue—rather, it is self-defeating—when the people who demand freedom are subject to systematic deprivations on a vast scale. The principle of territorial integrity must not serve as a shield for tyrants, dictators, or totalitarian rulers; it must not become a cloak behind which human deprivations are justified, condoned, and perpetuated. Today the world is too interdependent, humankind is living too closely together, to permit the doctrines of domestic jurisdiction or territorial integrity to become an instrument of oppression and deprivation.

On the other hand, it is too often assumed that small nation-states are militarily vulnerable, politically weak, and that smaller national units, constrained by small national incomes and markets, are economically in a disadvantageous position to function effectively and develop rapidly. On this assumption, fragmentation of an existing body politic into smaller units is commonly opposed. As previously indicated, the underlying assumption is not to be taken for granted.

It can be said that although governments are generally reluctant to support self-determination in a noncolonial context (if colonialism is given the connotation of subjugation of a people by an elite with which they do not identify) for understandable reasons, they obviously do not rule it out completely. Again, there is room for groups to break away from established states and this prospect actually will be of increasing significance in the years to come; the critical test is to judge each case by its merit.

The essential point for the future, as for the past, is to provide workable criteria in reference to both content and procedure. While principles of content guide the choice of subject matter relevant to evaluating the policy alternatives open to a decisionmaker, principles of procedure offer agendas and techniques for bringing pertinent content to the focus of attention of a decisionmaker.

It is of course assumed that all available private remedies (persuasive means) have been explored and exhausted before a case is brought to inclusive community decisionmakers. To facilitate a rational and systematic decision, the decisionmaker should, as in other contexts, (1) employ procedures appropriately designed to bring all relevant content in its proper context of the focus of attention; (2) adjust the time and facilities for decisionmaking to the importance of the values at stake and to community policies involved; (3) focus provisionally on the manifest, articulated demands of the parties themselves; (4) explore as objectively as possible both precipitating events and context, and characterize relevant facts and prescriptions; (5) observe trends in past experience in terms of the degree of approximation to general community policies; (6) observe realistically both the predispositional and environmental factors that have affected past decisions; (7) construct alternative future probabilities and estimate the relative costs and gains of the different options; and (8) relate all options to basic general community policies and identify the alternative that will promote the largest net aggregate of common interest.[235]

Empires rise and fall; nation-states come and go. But the demands of humankind for freedom and human dignity will remain strong.

An ongoing process in the search of the self, self-determination is profoundly associated with the very notion of human dignity. Sharing of power is of paramount importance. The crucial test in granting or rejecting a claim for self-determination is greater approximation to the goals of human dignity, considering the value impact not only upon the aspiring group directly involved, but also upon the existing entity of which it is a part and the surrounding larger communities, including the global community. When decisions regarding self-determination are rationally and adequately made, they will greatly contribute to the maintenance of both minimum and optimum public order.

Notes

1. V. VAN DYKE, HUMAN RIGHTS, THE UNITED STATES, AND WORLD COMMUNITY 81 (1970).

2. Emerson, *Self-Determination,* 65 AM. J. INT'L L. 459, (1971).

3. *Id.* at 469.

4. Press conference by U Thant, Secretary-General of the United Nations, in Dakar, Senegal, Jan. 4, 1970, in *Secretary-General's Press Conference,* 7 U.N. MONTHLY CHRONICLE, No. 2, at 34, 36 (1970).

5. N.Y. Times, Dec. 30, 1971, at 25, col. 5.

6. *See* authorities cited notes 53–54 *infra* and accompanying text.

7. Other legalistic labels include domestic jurisdiction, equality of states, etc.

8. The following is a very rough characterization. Of course, we recognize that the process of interaction is dynamic and, as changes occur, different legal doctrines become relevant.

9. On the doctrine of recognition, see H. LAUTERPACHT, RECOGNITION IN INTERNATIONAL LAW (1947); T. CHEN, THE INTERNATIONAL LAW OF RECOGNITION (1951); 2 DIGEST OF INTERNATIONAL LAW (M. Whiteman ed. 1963); Blix, *Contemporary Aspects of Recognition,* 130 HAGUE RECUEIL 587 (1970); Lachs, *Recognition and Modern Methods of International Co-operation,* 35 BRIT. Y.B. INT'L L. 252 (1959).

10. On the question of minority protection, see I. CLAUDE, NATIONAL MINORITIES, AN INTERNATIONAL PROBLEM (1955); UNITED NATIONS, PROTECTION OF MINORITIES (1967); H. JUNCKERSTORFF, WORLD MINORITIES (1962); M. MOSKOWITZ, THE POLITICS AND DYNAMICS OF HUMAN RIGHTS 155–73 (1968); V. VAN DYKE, *supra* note 1, at 85–91; J. LADOR-LEDERER, INTERNATIONAL GROUP PROTECTION (1968); J. LAPONCE, THE PROTECTION OF MINORITIES (1960); UNITED NATIONS, DEFINITION AND CLASSIFICATION OF MINORITIES (1950); Bruegel, *A Neglected Field: The Protection of Minorities,* 4 HUMAN RIGHTS J. 413 (1971).

11. For an introduction to this approach, see McDougal, *Jurisprudence for a Free Society,* 1 GA. L. REV. 1 (1966); Lasswell & McDougal, *Jurisprudence in Policy-Oriented Perspective,* 19 U. FLA. L. REV. 486 (1967). *See also* Moore, *Prolegomenon to the Jurisprudence of Myres McDougal and Harold Lasswell,* 54 VA. L. REV. 662 (1968); Feliciano, Book Review, 68 YALE L.J. 1039 (1959); Falk, *Some Thoughts on the Jurisprudence of Myres S. McDougal,* in R. FALK, THE STATUS OF LAW IN INTERNATIONAL SOCIETY 642–59 (1970).

12. The principal books applying this approach are listed below: W. REISMAN, NULLITY AND REVISION: THE REVIEW AND ENFORCEMENT OF INTERNATIONAL JUDGMENTS AND AWARDS (1971); B. WESTON, INTERNATIONAL CLAIMS: POSTWAR FRENCH PRACTICE (1970); M. McDOUGAL, H. LASSWELL & J. MILLER, THE INTERPRETATION OF AGREEMENTS AND WORLD PUBLIC ORDER (1967); L. CHEN & H. LASSWELL, FORMOSA, CHINA, AND THE UNITED NATIONS (1967); B. MURTY, THE IDEOLOGICAL INSTRUMENT OF COERCION AND WORLD PUBLIC ORDER (1967); D. JOHNSTON, THE INTERNATIONAL LAW OF FISHERIES (1965); M. McDOUGAL, H. LASSWELL & I. VLASIC, LAW AND PUBLIC ORDER IN SPACE (1963); M. McDOUGAL & W. BURKE, THE PUBLIC ORDER OF THE OCEANS: A CONTEMPORARY INTERNATIONAL LAW OF THE SEA (1962); R. ARENS & H. LASSWELL, IN DEFENSE OF PUBLIC ORDER (1961); M. McDOUGAL & F. FELICIANO, LAW AND MINIMUM WORLD PUBLIC ORDER: THE LEGAL REGULATION OF INTERNATIONAL COERCION (1961); M. McDOUGAL & ASSOCIATES, STUDIES IN WORLD PUBLIC ORDER (1961).

13. The rapid emergence and multiplication of African-Asian states can be seen from their participation in the international arena. Of the fourteen states participating in the Conference of Berlin in 1885, none was Asian-African. Five Asian states (China, Japan, Persia, Siam, and Turkey) were among the twenty-seven participants in the First Hague Conference of 1899. The number of the African-Asian participants remained the same at the Second Hague Conference of 1907, while the total of participants increased to forty-three. When the League of Nations was founded in 1920, only five of its original forty-five members were Asian (China, India, Japan, Persia, and Siam), and the only African member was Liberia (not counting South Africa). Turkey, Iraq, Ethiopia, Afghanistan, and Egypt joined the League subsequently. When the United Nations was created in 1945, eleven of its fifty-one original members were African-Asian. As of this writing in November 1972, of the 132 member states of the United Nations, 72 were African-Asian, excluding South Africa and Israel.

14. For statistical comparison, see B. RUSSETT, H. ALKER, K. DEUTSCH & H. LASS-WELL, WORLD HANDBOOK OF POLITICAL AND SOCIAL INDICATORS (1964) [hereinafter cited as B. RUSSETT]; C. TAYLOR & M. HUDSON, WORLD HANDBOOK OF POLITICAL AND SOCIAL INDICATORS (2d ed. 1972).

15. See ETHNICITY: THEORY AND EXPERIENCE (N. Glazer & D. Moynihan eds. 1975); Connor, Nation-Building or Nation-Destroying, 24 WORLD ˘POL. 319 (1972); Possony, Nationalism and the Ethnic Factor, 10 ORBIS 1218 (1967).

16. As reported by Walker Connor:

> Of a total of 132 contemporary states, only 12 (9.1 per cent) can be described as essentially homogeneous from an ethnic viewpoint. An additional 25 states (18.9 per cent of the sample) contain an ethnic group accounting for more than 90 per cent of the state's total population, and in still another 25 states the largest element accounts for between 75 and 89 per cent of the population. But in 31 states (23.5 per cent of the total), the largest ethnic element represents only 50 to 74 per cent of the population, and in 39 cases (29.5 per cent of all states) the largest group fails to account for even half of the state's population. Moreover, this portrait of ethnic diversity becomes more vivid when the number of distinct ethnic groups within states is considered. In some instances, the number of groups within a state runs into the hundreds, and in 53 states (40.2 per cent of the total), the population is divided into more than five significant groups. (Connor, supra note 15, at 320.)

17. Namibia (South West Africa) presents a unique situation. See Advisory Opinion on Legal Consequences for States of the Continued Presence of South Africa in Namibia (South West Africa) notwithstanding Security Council Resolution 276 (1970), [1971] I.C.J. 16; Advisory Opinion on Admissibility of Hearings of Petitioners by the Committee on South-West Africa, [1956] I.C.J. 23; Advisory Opinion on Voting Procedure on Questions Relating to Reports and Petitions Concerning the Territory of South-West Africa, [1955] I.C.J. 67; Advisory Opinion on the International Status of South-West Africa, [1950] I.C.J. 128.

So does Taiwan (Formosa). See Chen & Reisman, Who Owns Taiwan: A Search for International Title, 81 YALE L.J. 599 (1972).

18. As Hans Kohn put it:

> In the age of nationalism people wish no longer to be objects of a history made by others but wish to feel themselves active agents of their own history. They will accept no longer their traditional positions as unchangeable. They wish to improve their positions in their own lands and to improve the positions of their countries in relation to other countries. (Kohn, Changing Africa in a Changing World, 41 CURRENT HISTORY 193, 194 (1961).)

In this connection, see an interesting study: D. GORDON, SELF-DETERMINATION AND HISTORY IN THE THIRD WORLD (1971).

19. Recent discoveries of the so-called territorial nature of certain animal species

by scientists of animal behavior have received a good deal of attention. The work of K. LORENZ, ON AGGRESSION (M. Wilson transl. 1966) is a pioneer in the field. The theory of biologists has also been expounded by popularizers. *See, e.g.,* R. ARDREY, THE TERRITORIAL IMPERATIVE: A PERSONAL INQUIRY INTO THE ANIMAL ORIGINS OF PROPERTY AND NATIONS (1966). They have vividly described how animals of different types (fish, birds, mammals, etc.) stake out their "own" area, fix their boundaries, and defend against outside instrusion. The underlying motivation is said to be their "territorial instinct."

20. *See* Pye, *Identity and the Political Culture,* in CRISES AND SEQUENCES IN POLITICAL DEVELOPMENT 101–34 (L. Binder & L. Cindor eds. 1971).

21. The case of Palestine provides a vivid example in which the question of a cutoff point is much debated. *See* Bassiouni, *'Self-Determination' and the Palestinians,* 65 AM. J. INT'L L., No. 4, at 31 (1971).

22. The reference is to power, respect, enlightenment, well-being, wealth, skill, affection, and rectitude. For definition of these concepts, see H. LASSWELL & A. KAPLAN, POWER AND SOCIETY 55–58 (1950); Lasswell & Holmberg, *Toward a General Theory of Directed Value Accumulation and Institutional Development,* in COMPARATIVE THEORIES OF SOCIAL CHANGE 12–58 (H. Peter ed. 1966).

23. *See generally* M. McDOUGAL, H. LASSWELL & I. VLASIC, *supra* note 12, at 134–37; R. FALK, THIS ENDANGERED PLANET (1971); C. JENKS, LAW, FREEDOM AND WELFARE 71–82 (1963); Brown, *The Interdependence of Nations,* 212 HEADLINE SERIES 1 (1972).

24. Literature on nationalism is vast. For bibliography, see B. SHAFER, *Bibliographical Essay,* in FACES OF NATIONALISM 491–513 (1972); K. DEUTSCH & R. MERRITT, NATIONALISM AND NATIONAL DEVELOPMENT: AN INTERDISCIPLINARY BIBLIOGRAPHY (1970).

25. *See generally* THE RHETORIC OF REVOLUTION (C. Katope & P. Zolbrod eds. 1970). For such struggle in the context of Africa, see R. GIBSON, AFRICAN LIBERATION MOVEMENTS (1972); K. GRUNDY, GUERRILLA STRUGGLE IN AFRICA (1971).

26. *See generally* C. AGUOLU, BIAFRA: ITS CASE FOR INDEPENDENCE (1969); J. OYINBO, NIGERIA: CRISIS AND BEYOND (1971); N. AKPAN, THE STRUGGLE FOR SECESSION, 1966–1970 (1972); U. ELEAZU, NIGERIA, BIAFRA AND THE ORGANIZATION OF AFRICAN UNITY: SELF-DETERMINATION VERSUS TERRITORIAL INTEGRITY (1969); F. FORSYTH, THE BIAFRA STORY (1969); A. KIRK-GREENE, CRISIS AND CONFLICT IN NIGERIA (1971); A. NWANKWO & S. IFEJIKA, THE MAKING OF A NATION: BIAFRA (1969).

27. *See* M. BESHIR, THE SOUTHERN SUDAN: BACKGROUND TO CONFLICT (1968); G. MORRISON, THE SOUTHERN SUDAN AND ERITREA: ASPECTS OF WIDER AFRICAN PROBLEMS (1971); Gray, *The Southern Sudan,* 6 J. CONTEMPORARY HISTORY 108 (1971); Kilner, *Better Outlook for Sudan,* THE WORLD TODAY, Apr. 1972, at 181; N.Y. Times, Mar. 24, 1972, at 1, col. 4; *id.,* Dec. 6, 1972, at 13, col. 1.

28. *See* L. CHEN & H. LASSWELL, FORMOSA, CHINA, AND THE UNITED NATIONS: FORMOSA IN THE WORLD COMMUNITY (1967); Chen & Reisman, note 17 *supra. See also* M. PENG, A TASTE OF FREEDOM: MEMOIRS OF A FORMOSAN INDEPENDENCE LEADER (1972); W. BUELER, U.S. CHINA POLICY AND THE PROBLEM OF TAIWAN (1971); L. CHEN, TAI-WAN E TOK-LIP KAP KEN-KOK (The Independence and Nation-Building of Taiwan) (1971); D. MENDEL, THE POLITICS OF FORMOSAN NATIONALISM (1970); G. KERR, FORMOSA BETRAYED (1965); FORMOSA TODAY (M. Mancall ed. 1964).

29. *See* J. DRYSDALE, THE SOMALI DISPUTE (1964); S. TOUVAL, SOMALI NATIONALISM (1963); Brown, *The Ethiopian-Somali Frontier Dispute,* 5 INT'L & COMP. L.Q. 245 (1956); Lewis, *Developments in the Somali Dispute,* 66 AFR. AFFAIRS 104 (1967).

30. *See* Edmonds, *Kurdish Nationalism,* 6 J. CONTEMPORARY HISTORY 87 (1971).

31. *See* Castellan, *The Germans of Rumania,* 6 J. CONTEMPORARY HISTORY 52 (1971).

32. *See* Payne, *Catalan and Basque Nationalism,* 6 J. CONTEMPORARY HISTORY 15 (1971); N.Y. Times, Sept. 24, 1972, at 2, col. 3; *id.,* Dec. 7, 1972, at 15, col. 1; *id.,* Dec. 13, 1972, at 4, col. 3.

33. *See* THE I.C.J. SECRETARIAT, THE EVENTS IN EAST PAKISTAN, 1971 (1972); W. BARNDS, INDIA, PAKISTAN, AND THE GREAT POWERS (1972); *Hearings on S. Con. Res. 55, S. Con. Res. 58 & S. Res. 242 on Recognition of Bangladesh Before the Senate Comm. on Foreign Relations,* 92 Cong., 2d Sess. (1972); Nanda, *Self-Determination in International Law: The Tragic Tale of Two Cities—Islamabad (West Pakistan) and Dacca (East Pakistan),* 66 AM. J. INT'L L. 321 (1972); *East Pakistan Staff Study,* 8 REV. INT'L COMM'N JURISTS 23 (1972); *The War in Bengal: India Attacks,* NEWSWEEK, Dec. 6, 1971, at 30; *India and Pakistan: Poised for War,* TIME, Dec. 6, 1971, at 28.

34. *See* H. JACKSON, THE TWO IRELANDS: A DUAL STUDY OF INTERGROUP TENSIONS (1971); THE LONDON SUNDAY TIMES INSIGHT TEAM, NORTHERN IRELAND: A REPORT ON THE CONFLICT (1972); Beckett, *Northern Ireland,* 6 J. CONTEMPORARY HISTORY 121 (1971); *Ulster: Britain Takes Over,* NEWSWEEK, Apr. 3, 1972, at 32; Buckley, *Double Troubles of Northern Ireland—A Visit with the Protestant Militants,* N.Y. Times, Dec. 10, 1972, §6, at 35 (Magazine).

35. For general background, see P. TRUDEAU, FEDERALISM AND THE FRENCH CANADIANS (1968); Spry, *Canada: Notes on Two Ideas of Nation in Confrontation,* 6 J. CONTEMPORARY HISTORY 173 (1971); Guidon, *Two Cultures: An Essay on Nationalism, Class, and Ethnic Tension,* in CONTEMPORARY CANADA 33–59 (R. Leach ed. 1967); Johnson, *The Dynamics of Federalism in Canada,* 1 CAN. J. POL. SCI. 18 (1968); McCrae, *The Constitutional Protection of Linguistic Rights in Bilingual and Multilingual States,* in HUMAN RIGHTS, FEDERALISM, AND MINORITIES 211–27 (A. Gotlieb ed. 1970).

36. *See* Morgan, *Welsh Nationalism: The Historical Background,* 6 J. CONTEMPORARY HISTORY 153 (1971).

37. *See* Salibi, *The Lebanese Identity,* 6 J. CONTEMPORARY HISTORY 76 (1971).

38. *See* Singleton, *The Roots of Discord in Yugoslavia,* THE WORLD TODAY, Apr. 1972, at 170; N.Y. Times, July 18, 1972, at 3, col. 1; *id.,* Aug. 30, 1972, at 4, col. 4; *id.,* Oct. 1, 1972, at 15, col. 1; *id.,* Oct. 18, 1972, at 16, col. 1; *id.,* Oct. 26, 1972, at 3, col. 3.

39. *See* S. DHYANI, CONTEMPORARY TIBET: ITS STATUS IN INTERNATIONAL LAW (1961); INTERNATIONAL COMMISSION OF JURISTS, THE QUESTION OF TIBET AND THE RULE OF LAW (1959); INTERNATIONAL COMMISSION OF JURISTS, LEGAL INQUIRY COMMITTEE ON TIBET, TIBET AND THE CHINESE PEOPLE'S REPUBLIC: A REPORT (1960); H. TU, HSI TSANG FA LU TI WEI CHIH YEN CHIU (A Study of the Legal Status of Tibet) (1966); Anand, *The Status of Tibet in International Law,* 10 INT'L STUDIES 401 (1969); Bradsher, *Tibet Struggles to Survive,* 47 FOREIGN AFFAIRS 750 (1969); Sinha, *How Chinese Was China's Tibet Region?,* TIBETAN REV., Apr. 1968, at 9.

40. These are: Chapter XI: Declaration Regarding Non-Self-Governing Territories; Chapter XII: International Trusteeship System; Chapter XIII: The Trusteeship Council.

41. *See* McDougal, Lasswell & Reisman, *The World Constitutive Process of Authoritative Decision,* in 1 THE FUTURE OF THE INTERNATIONAL LEGAL ORDER 73 (C. Black & R. Falk eds. 1969).

42. For a brief account, see *The Role of the United Nations in the Demise of the Colonial System,* 3 OBJECTIVE: JUSTICE, No. 2, at 8 (1971). *See also* Y. EL-AYOUTY, THE UNITED NATIONS AND DECOLONIZATION: THE ROLE OF AFRO-ASIA (1971). For the role played by the specialized agencies and other international institutions affiliated with the United Nations, see Implementation of the Declaration on the Granting of Independence to Colonial Countries and Peoples by the Specialized Agencies and the International Institutions Associated with the United Nations, U.N. Doc. A/8314 (1971) (Report of the Secretary General).

43. Charter of the Organization of African Unity art. 2(1) reads as follows:
The Organization shall have the following purposes:
. . . .
    (c) to defend their sovereignty, their territorial integrity and independence;
    (d) to eradicate all forms of colonialism from Africa. (479 U.N.T.S. 39, 72 (1963).)

44. *See* authorities cited notes 69–85 *infra* and accompanying text.

45. *See* authorities cited notes 88–111 *infra* and accompanying text.

46. The Special Committee of Twenty-Four is the shorthand for the Special Committee on the Situation with regard to the Implementation of the Declaration on the Granting of Independence to Colonial Countries and Peoples, which was created under G.A. Res. 1654 (XVI), 16 U.N. GAOR Supp. 17, at 65, U.N. Doc. A/5100 (1961). Originally consisting of seventeen members, it was enlarged to twenty-four by G.A. Res. 1810 (XVII), 17 U.N. GAOR Supp. 17, at 72, U.N. Doc. A/5217 (1962). In 1972, with the withdrawal of the United States and the United Kingdom from the Committee, Sweden was the only Western power in the Committee. As of May 1, 1972, other members of the Committee were Afghanistan, Bulgaria, China, Czechoslovakia, Ecuador, Ethiopia, Fiji, India, Indonesia, Iran, Iraq, Ivory Coast, Mali, Sierra Leone, Syrian Arab Republic, Trinidad and Tobago, Tunisia, U.S.S.R., United Republic of Tanzania, Venezuela, and Yugoslavia. On the work of the Special Committee, see Khol, *The "Committee of Twenty-Four" and the Implementation of the Declaration on the Granting of Independence to Colonial Countries and Peoples,* 3 HUMAN RIGHTS J. 21 (1970); Report of the Special Committee on the Situation with regard to the Implementation of the Declaration on the Granting of Independence to Colonial Countries and Peoples, U.N. DOCS. A/7623 and addenda (1969); U.N. Doc. A/8314, note 42 *supra.*

47. 20 U.N. GAOR, Annexes, Agenda Items Nos. 90 & 94, at 44, ¶¶320–21, U.N. DOC. A/5694 (1965).

48. *See* authorities cited notes 190–98 *infra* and accompanying text.

49. U.N. Doc. S/9772 (1970).

50. The 1972 budget of the United Nations was $213 million. N.Y. Times, Dec. 2, 1972, at 13, col. 4. In the U.N. diplomatic circle, the U.N. budget is compared to that of the Fire Department of New York City. According to Professor Karl W. Deutsch's estimate, as based on data in B. RUSSETT, *supra* note 14, at 56–68, the total governmental expenditures (governments at all levels—national, state or provincial, and local) of nation-states are approximately between one-quarter and one-third of the GNP of the non-Communist countries. On the other hand, the total expenditures of all the international organizations are roughly 1 percent of the GNP of these same countries. Deutsch, *The Probability of International Law,* in THE RELEVANCE OF INTERNATIONAL LAW 60 (K. Deutsch & S. Hoffmann eds. 1968).

51. For an elaboration of the seven functions of decision, consult McDougal, Lasswell & Reisman, *supra* note 41, at 131–54. *See also* H. LASSWELL, A PRE-VIEW OF POLICY SCIENCES 85–97 (1971).

52. *See* authorities cited notes 65–87 *infra* and accompanying text.

53. Read, for instance, the following statement:
Self-determination might indeed be regarded as implicit in the idea of democracy; for if every man's right is recognized to be consulted about the affairs of the political unit to which he belongs, he may be assumed to have an equal right to be consulted about the form and extent of the unit. (E. CARR, CONDITIONS OF PEACE 39 (1942).).
Commenting on the significance of the international systems of mandates and trusteeship, Professor Elihu Lauterpacht observed: "These revealed the emergence of the principle that territories and peoples are not mere chattels to be acquired and disposed of by and for the benefit of the proprietary state, but are instead the

heritage of those who dwell within them." Lauterpacht, *Some Concepts in Human Rights.* 11 How. L. J. 264, 271 (1965).

Cf. also J. MOORE, LAW AND THE INDO-CHINA WAR 83–114 (1972).

54. For more detailed development, see McDougal, Lasswell & Chen, *Human Rights and World Public Order: A Framework for Policy-Oriented Inquiry,* 63 AM. J. INT'L L. 237 (1969). *See also* McDougal, *Human Rights and World Public Order: Principles of Content and Procedure for Clarifying General Community Policies,* 14 VA. J. INT'L L. 387 (1974); McDougal, Lasswell & Chen, *The Protection of Respect and Human Rights: Freedom of Choice and World Public Order,* 24 AM. U. L. REV. 919 (1975); McDougal, Lasswell & Chen, *Human Rights for Women and World Public Order: The Outlawing of Sex-Based Discrimination,* 69 AM. J. INT'L L. 497 (1975).

55. The nation-building history of the Jewish people is instructive in this context.

56. Take Algeria, for instance. Having fought the long agonizing war of independence, the Algerian people emerged strongly consolidated as a national entity, much more so than a state carved out with accidental colonial boundaries that had independence thrust upon it without much struggle and sacrifice on the part of its population. Actual struggle in the defense of one's identity and territory is indeed vital to the birth and growth of nationhood in the contemporary world.

57. Even Chairman Mao Tse-tung was quoted as saying that more decentralization would be desirable in China in order to further political participation of the people.

58. For a historical survey of the principle of self-determination, see A. COBBAN, THE NATION STATE AND NATIONAL SELF-DETERMINATION (1970); 1 S. WAMBAUGH, PLEBISCITES SINCE THE WORLD WAR 1–45 (1933).

59. *See* I. CLAUDE, *supra* note 10, at 1–15.

60. *See* authorities cited notes 153–58 *infra* and accompanying text.

61. Address by President Woodrow Wilson, U.S. Senate, Jan. 22, 1917, in 54 CONG. REC. 1741, 1742 (1917).

62. LEAGUE OF NATIONS COVENANT art. 22, para. 4.

63. Under the League system, the mandate territories were divided as follows (the states in parentheses were the mandatory powers): (1) A mandates: Iraq, Trans-Jordan, Palestine (Great Britain), Syria and Lebanon (France); (2) B mandates: Cameroons (Great Britain and France), Tanganyika (Great Britain), Togoland (Great Britain and France), Ruanda-Urundi (Belgium); (3) C mandates: North Pacific Islands (Japan), Nauru (Great Britain, New Zealand, and Australia, with the latter acting), New Guinea (Great Britain, New Zealand, and Australia, with the latter acting), Western Samoa (Great Britain, Australia, and New Zealand, with the latter acting), and South West Africa (Great Britain and South Africa, with the latter acting).

64. Concerning the League mandate system, see N. BENTWICH, THE MANDATES SYSTEM (1930); D. HALL, MANDATES, DEPENDENCIES, AND TRUSTEESHIPS (1948); Q. WRIGHT, MANDATES UNDER THE LEAGUE OF NATIONS (1930). An important case concerning self-determination in the nonmandate context was the Aland Islands question involving Finland and Sweden. For a comprehensive study, see J. BARROS, THE ALAND ISLANDS QUESTION: ITS SETTLEMENT BY THE LEAGUE OF NATIONS (1968). *See also* L. CHEN, STATE SUCCESSION RELATING TO UNEQUAL TREATIES 71–73, 206–08 (1974).

65. The declaration, jointly made by President Franklin D. Roosevelt and Prime Minister Winston S. Churchill, included the following principles:

>First, their countries seek no aggrandizement, territorial or other;
>Second, they desire to see no territorial changes that do not accord with the freely expressed wishes of the peoples concerned;
>Third, they respect the right of all peoples to choose the form of government under which they will live; and they wish to see sovereign rights and self-government restored to those who have been forcibly de-

prived of them. (A DECADE OF AMERICAN FOREIGN POLICY: BASIC DOCU-MENTS, 1941–49, at 1 (1950).)

66. *See* U.N.C.I.O. DOCS. 296, 455 (1945); R. RUSSELL, A HISTORY OF THE UNITED NATIONS CHARTER 810–13 (1958); L. GOODRICH, E. HAMBRO & A. SIMONS, CHARTER OF THE UNITED NATIONS: COMMENTARY AND DOCUMENTS 29–31 (3d & rev. ed. 1969). During the Big Four consultation at San Francisco, the Soviet Union first proposed that the principle of equal rights and self-determination of peoples be included among the purposes of the world organization. R. RUSSELL, *supra,* at 810.

67. U.N. CHARTER art. 55 reads:

> With a view to the creation of conditions of stability and well-being which are necessary for peaceful and friendly relations among nations based on respect for the principle of equal rights and self-determination of peoples, the United Nations shall promote:
> a. higher standards of living, full employment, and conditions of economic and social progress and development;
> b. solutions of international economic, social, health, and related problems; and international, cultural and educational cooperation; and
> c. universal respect for, and observance of, human rights and fundamental freedoms for all without distinction as to race, sex, language, or religion.

68. *Id.* art. 1, para. 2.

69. The text of these Covenants appears in G.A. Res. 2200A (XXI), Annex, 21 U.N. GAOR Supp. 16, at 49–60, U.N. Doc. A/6316 (1966). The text can also be found in UNITED NATIONS, HUMAN RIGHTS: A COMPILATION OF INTERNATIONAL INSTRUMENTS OF THE UNITED NATIONS 3–18 (1967); BASIC DOCUMENTS ON HUMAN RIGHTS 199–236 (I. Brownlie ed. 1971). The two Covenants came into effect in 1976 after thirty-five States had ratified or acceded to them.

For background reading on international protection of human rights, see A. ROBERTSON, HUMAN RIGHTS IN THE WORLD (1972); INTERNATIONAL PROTECTION OF HUMAN RIGHTS: CASES AND MATERIALS (L. Sohn & T. Buergenthal eds. 1973); A. DEL RUSSO, INTERNATIONAL PROTECTION OF HUMAN RIGHTS (1971); J. CAREY, UN PROTECTION OF CIVIL AND POLITICAL RIGHTS (1970); V. VAN DYKE, HUMAN RIGHTS, THE UNITED STATES, AND WORLD COMMUNITY (1970); HUMAN RIGHTS, FEDERALISM, AND MINORITIES (A. Gotlieb ed. 1969); INTERNATIONAL PROTECTION OF HUMAN RIGHTS (A. Eide & A. Schou eds. 1968); M. MOSKOWITZ, THE POLITICS AND DYNAMICS OF HUMAN RIGHTS (1968); UNITED NATIONS, THE UNITED NATIONS AND HUMAN RIGHTS (1968); THE INTERNATIONAL PROTECTION OF HUMAN RIGHTS (E. Luard ed. 1967); E. SCHWELB, HUMAN RIGHTS AND THE INTERNATIONAL COMMUNITY (1964); H. LAUTERPACHT, INTERNATIONAL LAW AND HUMAN RIGHTS (1950).

70. G.A. Res. 2200A, Annex, *supra* note 69, at 49, 53. Para. 2 of Article 1 embodies what is known as "economic self-determination":

> All peoples may, for their own ends, freely dispose of their natural wealth and resources without prejudice to any obligations arising out of international economic co-operation, based upon the principle of mutual benefit, and international law. In no case may a people be deprived of its own means of subsistence. (*Id.*)

71. G.A. Res. 421, 5 U.N. GAOR Supp. 20, at 43, U.N. Doc. A/1775 (1950).

72. G.A. Res. 545, 6 U.N. GAOR Supp. 20, at 36–37, U.N. Doc. A/2119 (1951).

73. U.N. Doc. 2573, Annex 1 (1954).

74. Annotations on the text of the draft International Covenants on Human Rights, 10 U.N. GAOR, Annexes, Agenda Item No. 28, U.N. Doc. A/2929, at 13 (1955).

75. *Id.* at 14.

76. *Id.* at 15.

77. U.N. Doc. A/3077 (1955).

78. *Id.* paras. 28–34.

79. *Id.* paras. 35–44.

80. U.N. Doc. A/C.3/L.489 and Corr. 1 & 2 (1955).

81. U.N. Doc. A/3077 (1955).

82. *Id.* para. 77.

83. Though the resolution was adopted by a formally unanimous vote, nine states —Australia, Belgium, Dominican Republic, France, Portugal, South Africa, Spain, United Kingdom, and the United States—abstained. This resolution was orginally proposed by Premier Nikita Khrushchev of the Soviet Union when he addressed the General Assembly on September 23, 1960, urging "the complete and final liberation of peoples languishing in colonial bondage." Amid the ensuing bitter exchanges between the East and the West, the African-Asian delegates followed up the Soviet initiative, culminating in the adoption of this historical resolution. It was pointed out that the principles embodied in this Declaration had previously been expounded in the 1955 Bandung Conference and other African-Asian conferences.

84. G.A. Res. 1514, 15 U.N. GAOR Supp. 16, at 66, 67, U.N. Doc. A/4684 (1960).

85. *See, e.g.,* G.A. Res. 1654, 16 U.N. GAOR Supp. 17, at 65, U.N. Doc. A/5100 (1961); G.A. Res. 1810, 17 U.N. GAOR Supp. 17, at 72, U.N. Doc. A/5217 (1962); G.A. Res. 1956, 18 U.N. GAOR Supp. 15, at 8, U.N. Doc. A/5515 (1963); G.A. Res. 1970, 18 U.N. GAOR Supp. 15, at 49, U.N. Doc. A/5515 (1963); G.A. Res. 2105, 20 U.N. GAOR Supp. 14, at 3, U.N. Doc. A/6014 (1965); G.A. Res. 2189, 21 U.N. GAOR Supp. 16, at 5, U.N. Doc. A/6316 (1966); G.A. Res. 2326, 22 U.N. GAOR Supp. 16, at 4, U.N. Doc. A/6716 (1967); G.A. Res. 2465, 23 U.N. GAOR Supp. 18, at 4, U.N. Doc. A/7218 (1968); G.A. Res. 2548, 24 U.N. GAOR Supp. 30, at 5, U.N. Doc. A/7630 (1969); G.A. Res. 2708, 25 U.N. GAOR Supp. 28, at 7, U.N. Doc. A/8028 (1970); G.A. Res. 2878, 26 U.N. GAOR Supp. 29, at 16, U.N. Doc. A/8429 (1971); G.A. Res. 2908, 27 U.N. GAOR Supp. 30, at 2, U.N. Doc. A/8730 (1972).

86. G.A. Res. 2625 and its Annex, 25 U.N. GAOR Supp. 28, at 121, U.N. Doc. A/8028 (1970). At its seventeenth session, the General Assembly decided to undertake, in accordance with Article 13 of the Charter, a study of the principles of international law concerning friendly relations and cooperation among states in accordance with the Charter of the United Nations with a view of their progressive development and codification. G.A. Res. 1815, 17 U.N. GAOR Supp. 17, at 66, U.N. Doc. A/5217 (1962). Among the seven principles listed by the Resolution was the principle of equal rights and self-determination of peoples. For the purposes of studying these principles, the General Assembly decided to establish a Special Committee on Principles of International Law concerning Friendly Relations and Co-operation among States (G.A. Res. 1966, 18 U.N. GAOR Supp. 15, at 70, U.N. Doc. A/5515 (1963), which subsequently came to be known as the "1964 Special Committee."

Beginning in 1962, the item "Consideration of principles of international law concerning friendly relations and cooperation among States in accordance with the Charter of the United Nations" was dealt with by the General Assembly at its seventeenth through twenty-fourth (excluding the nineteenth) sessions. The item was included in the agenda of the Assembly in 1970 (twenty-fifth session) and assigned to the Sixth Committee. As a basis for its consideration, the Committee had before it the report of the 1970 session of the Special Committee on Principles of International Law concerning Friendly Relations and Co-operation among States, which contained a draft Declaration on Principles of International Law concerning Friendly Relations and Co-operation among States.

The Sixth Committee considered this item at its 1178th and 1184th meetings on the 23, 24, 25, and 28 of September 1970. For the summary records of these meetings *see* U.N. Doc. A/C.6/SR.1178–84 (1970). At the 1183d meeting, a draft Resolution cosponsored by sixty-four delegations (U.N. Doc. A/C.6/L.973 and Corr. 1

(1970)) was introduced. At the following meeting, this Resolution was adopted without objection. *See* Report of the Sixth Committee, U.N. Doc. A/8082 (1970). It was the consensus of the Committee that the title of the Declaration should read: Declaration on Principles of International Law Concerning Friendly Relations and Co-operation among States in accordance with the Charter of the United Nations.

As a result of these discussions, the General Assembly adopted, *inter alia*, G.A. Res. 1815, *supra;* G.A. Res. 1966, *supra;* G.A. Res. 2103, 20 U.N. GAOR Supp. 14, at 91, U.N. Doc. A/6014 (1965); G.A. Res. 2181, 21 U.N. GAOR Supp. 16, at 96, U.N. Doc. A/6316 (1966); G.A. Res. 2327, 22 U.N. GAOR Supp. 16, at 83, U.N. Doc. A/6716 (1967); G.A. Res. 2364, 23 U.N. GAOR Supp. 18, at 89, U.N. Doc. A/7218 (1968); G.A. Res. 2533, 24 U.N. GOAR Supp. 30, at 106, U.N. Doc. A/7630 (1969); G.A. Res. 2625, *supra.*

The Special Committee considered the principle concerning equal rights and self-determination of peoples at its 1966, 1967, 1968, and 1969 sessions. An account of the consideration of the principle of equal rights and self-determination of peoples by the Special Committee at its 1966, 1967, 1968, and 1969 sessions appears respectively in the following documents: 21 U.N. GAOR, Annexes, Agenda Item No. 87, U.N. Doc. A/6230, at 91–99 (1966); 22 U.N. GAOR, Annexes, Agenda Item No. 87. U.N. Doc. A/6799, at 29–37 (1967); 23 U.N. GAOR, Annexes, Agenda Item No. 87, U.N. Doc. A/7326, at 52–68 (1968); 24 U.N. GAOR Supp. 19, at 48–68, U.N. Doc. A/7619 (1969); 25 U.N. GAOR Supp. 18, at 41–52, U.N. Doc. A/8018 (1970).

See also Rosenstock, *The Declaration of Principles of International Law Concerning Friendly Relations: A Survey,* 65 AM. J. INT'L L. 713 (1971); Houben, *Principles of International Law Concerning Friendly Relations and Co-operation among States,* 61 AM. J. INT'L L. 703 (1967); McWhinney, *Friendly Relations and Co-operation among States: Debate at the Twentieth General Assembly, United Nations,* 60 AM. J. INT'L L. 356 (1966).

87. G.A. Res. 2625, Annex, *supra* note 86, at 123–24.

88. On the doctrine of domestic jurisdiction, see McDougal & Reisman, *Rhodesia and the United Nations: The Lawfulness of International Concern,* 62 AM. J. INT'L L. 1 (1968); Ermacora, *Human Rights and Domestic Jurisdiction (Articles 2, 7 of the Charter),* 124 HAGUE RECUEIL 371 (1968); R. HIGGINS, THE DEVELOPMENT OF INTERNATIONAL LAW THROUGH THE POLITICAL ORGANS OF THE UNITED NATIONS 58–130 (1963); M. RAJAN, UNITED NATIONS AND DOMESTIC JURISDICTION (2d ed. 1961); V. VAN DYKE, *supra* note 1, at 105–56; H. LAUTERPACHT, INTERNATIONAL LAW AND HUMAN RIGHTS 166–220 (1950); Fawcett, *Human Rights and Domestic Jurisdiction,* in THE INTERNATIONAL PROTECTION OF HUMAN RIGHTS 286–303 (E. Luard ed. 1967); CORNELL LAW SCHOOL, THE STATUS OF DOMESTIC JURISDICTION, PROCEEDINGS OF THE FOURTH SUMMER CONFERENCE ON INTERNATIONAL LAW (1962).

89. Tunis–Morocco Nationality Decrees, [1923] P.C.I.J., ser. B, No. 4, at 23–24.

90. *See* 6 U.N.I.C.O. DOCS. 436–40, 486–89, 494–99, 507–08 (1945); L. GOODRICH, E. HAMBRO & A. SIMONS, *supra* note 66, at 60–66; R. RUSSELL, *supra* note 66, at 463–64.

91. *See* UNITED NATIONS, EVERYMAN'S UNITED NATIONS 122–24 (8th ed. 1968); YEARBOOK OF THE UNITED NATIONS 1946–47, at 338–41 (1947) [hereinafter cited as Y.B.U.N.]; Y.B.U.N. 1947–48, at 362–87 (1949); Y.B.U.N. 1948–49, at 212–37 (1950).

92. *See* Y.B.U.N. 1946–47, at 360–75 (1947).

93. *See id.* at 327–36.

94. *See* Y.B.U.N. 1947–48, at 451–58 (1949).

95. *See id.* at 458–60.

96. Y.B.U.N. 1951, at 337–39 (1952).

97. *See* Y.B.U.N. 1956, at 67–96 (1957).

98. *See* EVERYMAN'S UNITED NATIONS, *supra* note 91, at 109–21. *See* M. CHAGLA, KASHMIR 1947–1965 (1965); J. KORBEL, DANGER IN KASHMIR (1966); P. LAKHANPAL, ESSENTIAL DOCUMENTS AND NOTES ON KASHMIR DISPUTE (1965); A. LAMB,

CRISIS IN KASHMIR (1966); Potter, *The Principal Legal and Political Problems Involved in the Kashmir Case,* 44 AM. J. INT'L L. 361 (1959).

99.   *See* Y.B.U.N. 1954, at 94–96 (1955).

100.   *See* authorities cited notes 190–92 *infra* and accompanying text.

101.   *See* Y.B.U.N. 1960, at 140–42 (1961).

102.   *See* EVERYMAN'S UNITED NATIONS, *supra* note 91, at 161–63.

103.   *See id.* at 91–97. *See also* M. REISMAN, THE ART OF THE POSSIBLE (1970); Leonard, *The United Nations and Palestine,* 454 INT'L CONCILIATION 601 (1949).

104.   *See* Y.B.U.N. 1955, at 316–24 (1956); Y.B.U.N. 1958, at 355–60 (1959).

105.   *See* Y.B.U.N. 1958, at 346–55 (1959).

106.   *See* Y.B.U.N. 1960, at 455–69 (1961); Y.B.U.N. 1961. at 484–94 (1962).

107.   *See* UNITED NATIONS, A PRINCIPLE IN TORMENT: I. THE UNITED NATIONS AND SOUTHERN RHODESIA (1969); McDougal & Reisman, *supra* note 88; Cefkin, *The Rhodesian Question at the United Nations,* 21 INT'L ORG. 649 (1968); Robinowitz, *U.N. Sanctions and Rhodesia,* 7 VA. J. INT'L. L. 147 (1967); Zacklin, *Challenge of Rhodesia,* 575 INT'L CONCILIATION 1 (1969).

108.   *See* UNITED NATIONS, A PRINCIPLE IN TORMENT: III. THE UNITED NATIONS AND NAMIBIA (1971). For a collection of documents and rich bibliography regarding Namibia since the League of Nations era, see L. Sohn & T. Buergenthal, *supra* note 69, at 337–504.

109.   *See Chapter X: Territories under Portuguese Administration,* in Report of the Special Committee on the Situation with regard to the Implementation of the Declaration on the Granting of Independence to Colonial Countries and Peoples, U.N. DOC. A/8723/Add.3 (1972); UNITED NATIONS, THE UNITED NATIONS AND DECOLONIZATION 25–30 (1965).

110.   *See* THE UNITED NATIONS AND NAMIBIA, *supra* note 108; Advisory Opinion on Legal Consequences for States of the Continued Presence of South Africa in Namibia (South West Africa) Notwithstanding Security Council Resolution 276 (1970), [1971] I.C.J. 16. For response to I.C.J.'s 1971 Opinion on Namibia, *see, e.g.,* Lissitzyn, *International Law and the Advisory Opinion on Namibia,* 11 COLUM. J. TRANSNAT'L L. 50 (1972); Dugard, *Namibia (South West Africa): The Court's Opinion, South Africa's Response, and Prospects for the Future, id.* at 14.

111.   *See* U.N. CHARTER chs. VI–VII, particularly art. 34, which provides:

> The Security Council may investigate any dispute, or any situation which might lead to international friction or give rise to a dispute, in order to determine whether the continuance of the dispute or situation is likely to endanger the maintenance of international peace and security.

Note, also, the proviso of Article 2(7) of the Charter, which states that the principle of domestic jurisdiction "shall not prejudice the application of enforcement measures under Chapter VII."

112.   For a succinct account, see Emerson, *Colonialism: Political Aspects,* 3 INT'L ENCYC. SOC. SCI. 1 (1968).

113.   Nanda, *supra* note 33, at 321.

114.   U.N. CHARTER art. 77, para. 1.

115.   *Id.* art. 76(b).

116.   *See id.* art. 87.

117.   *See* Marston, *Termination of Trusteeship,* 18 INT'L & COMP. L.Q. 1 (1969); R. ASHER, THE UNITED NATIONS AND PROMOTION OF THE GENERAL WELFARE 934–96 (1957); J. MURRAY, THE UN TRUSTEESHIP SYSTEM (1957); C. TOUSSAINT, THE TRUSTEESHIP SYSTEM OF THE UNITED NATIONS (1956).

118.   After this writing, plans were made in 1975 to create a commonwealth of the northern Mariana Islands in political association with the United States. The Committee of Twenty-Four expressed regret about the plans and urged the United States "to continue, in consultation with the Micronesian people, to encourage national unity

in all districts" of the Trust Territory of the Pacific Islands. *Decolonization Committee Ends Work for 1975; Chairman Says Liberation Process Irreversible,* 12 U.N. MONTHLY CHRONICLE, No. 8, at 22, 27 (1975).

119. *See id.* at 22–29.

120. U.N. CHARTER art. 73, para. 1.

121. *Id.* art. 73(e).

122. Their arguments were based on the familiar ground that the colonial territories under their respective administration were not colonies at all, but were in fact integral parts of their own metropolitan territories.

123. On the work of the Special Committee of Twenty-Four, see note 46 *supra.*

124. G.A. Res. 1541, Annex, Principle IV, 15 U.N. GAOR Supp. 16, at 29, U.N. DOC. A/4684 (1961).

125. *Id.* Principle V.

126. *Id.* Principle VI.

127. *See* Report of the Special Committee on the Situation with regard to the Implementation of the Declaration on the Granting of Independence to Colonial Countries and Peoples, U.N. DOC. A/8423 and Add. 1–8 (1971).

128. Green, *Self-Determination and Settlement of the Arab–Israeli Conflict,* 65 AM. J. INT'L L., No. 4, at 40, 46 (1971).

129. Emerson, *supra* note 2, at 460–62. Viewing the right of self-determination as one aspect of the right of revolution, Professor Emerson concluded that "all people do *not* have the right of self-determination: they have never had it, and they never will have it." R. EMERSON, SELF-DETERMINATION REVISITED IN THE ERA OF DECOLONIZATION 64 (1964). In his view, success is its own justification.

130. R. HIGGINS, *supra* note 88, at 103.

131. *Id.* at 101–02.

132. 7 U.N. GAOR, 3d Comm. 157, U.N. DOC. A/C.3/SR.443 (1952) (remark of British delegate).

133. Art. 1, para. 1 of the International Covenant on Civil and Political Rights and of the International Covenant on Economic, Social, and Cultural Rights. *Supra* note 69, at 53, 49.

134. For instance. Cobban defines self-determination as "the right of a nation to constitute an independent state and determine its own government for itself." A. COBBAN, *supra* note 58, at 104. According to his further elaboration, "any territorial community, the members of which are conscious of themselves *as* members of a community, and wish to maintain the identity of their community, is a nation." *Id.* at 107.

135. For a summary account of the developing concepts of nation, see Rustow, *Nation,* 11 INT'L ENCYC. SOC. SCI. 7 (1968).

136. *See* T. Mensah, Self-Determination Under United Nations' Auspices, August 1963, at 288–329 (unpublished J.S.D. dissertation in Yale Law Library).

137. U.N. CHARTER art. 73(b).

138. *Id.* art. 76(b).

139. *See* J. GERARD-LIBOIS, KATANGA SECESSION (R. Young transl. 1966); E. LEFEVER, CRISIS IN THE CONGO: A UNITED NATIONS FORCE IN ACTION (1965); C. O'BRIEN, TO KATANGA AND BACK (1962).

140. *See* Y.B.U.N. 1960, at 140–42 (1961).

141. *See* authorities cited notes 190–98 *infra* and accompanying text.

142. *See* Bassiouni, note 21 *supra.*

143. G.A. Res. 1514, *supra* note 84, para. 6, at 67.

144. G.A. Res. 2625, Annex, *supra* note 86, at 122, 124.

145. V. VAN DYKE, *supra* note 1, at 102.

146. After the formal declaration of independence on May 30, 1967, 6 INT'L LEGAL

MATERIALS 679–80 (1967), Biafra was first recognized by Tanzania on Apr. 13, 1968, followed by Gabon (May 8, 1968), Ivory Coast (May 14, 1968), Zambia (May 20, 1968), and Haiti, 95 TIME, No. 4, at 21 (1970). France supported the cause of Biafra, but did not grant formal recognition. On January 12, 1970, Biafra formally surrendered. *See* Ijalaye, *Was "Biafra" at Any Time a State in International Law?*, 65 AM. J. INT'L L. 551 (1971).

147. For a brilliant analysis, *see* Nanda, note 33 *supra*.

148. U.N. CHARTER art. 73(b).

149. Note, for instance, the following statement:

> A substantial number of British territories had voluntarily placed themselves under British protection. The United Kingdom Government could not betray the trust imposed in the treaties with the peoples concerned, nor transfer its responsibilities. (2 U.N. GAOR, 3d Comm. 163 (1947) (remark of British representative).)

150. G.A. Res. 1514 (XV), note 84 *supra*.

151. *See* Khol, note 46 *supra;* UNITED NATIONS, THE UNITED NATIONS AND DE-COLONIZATION (1965).

152. *See* T. Mensah, *supra* note 136, at 402–33.

153. The account concerning plebiscites here draws upon Chen & Reisman, note 17 *supra*. The pioneering work on plebiscites was done by Sarah Wambaugh. *See* S. WAM-BAUGH, A MONOGRAPH ON PLEBISCITES (1920) [hereinafter cited as WAMBAUGH, MONOGRAPH]; S. WAMBAUGH, PLEBISCITES SINCE THE WORLD WAR (2 vols.) (1933) [hereinafter cited as WAMBAUGH, PLEBISCITES]; S. WAMBAUGH, THE SAAR PLEBISCITE (1940). Dr. Wambaugh, an American national, served in the League of Nations permanent Secretariat and was appointed as one of the three experts who drafted regulations for the Saar plebiscite in 1935. *See* Hinton, *She Specializes in Plebiscites: Dr. Sarah Wambaugh*, N.Y. Times, Feb. 17, 1946, § 6 (Magazine), at 24. *See also* H. JOHNSON, SELF-DETERMINATION WITHIN THE COMMUNITY OF NATIONS (1967); J. MATTERN, THE EMPLOYMENT OF THE PLEBISCITE IN THE DETERMINATION OF SOV-EREIGNTY (1920); DeAuer, *Plebiscites and the League of Nations Covenant*, 6 TRANS-ACTIONS OF THE GROTIUS SOC'Y 45 (1921); Jones, *Plebiscites*, in 13 *id*. 165 (1928).

154. *See* WAMBAUGH, MONOGRAPH, *supra* note 153, at 33–40, 173–268.

155. *See id.* at 41–43, 269–96.

156. *See id.* at 43–45, 296–301.

157. *See id.* at 45–51, 302–58.

158. *See id.* at 51–55, 302–58.

159. *See id.* at 58–101, 370–725; J. MATTERN, *supra* note 153, at 80–96.

160. *See* WAMBAUGH, MONOGRAPH, *supra* note 153, at 132–49, 864–944.

161. *See id.* at 101–22, 726–837.

162. *See id.* at 122–32, 838–63.

163. *Id.* at 935–37.

164. *Id.* at 1.

165. *See id.* at 41–45, 269–301.

166. *See id.* at 101–22, 726–837.

167. *See id.* at 122–32, 838–63.

168. *See id.* at 155–56, 977–84.

169. *See id.* at 165–69, 1051–72.

170. *See id.* at 101–22, 726–837.

171. *See* 1 S. WAMBAUGH, PLEBISCITES, *supra* note 153, at 3–45; J. MATTERN, *supra* note 153, at 128–50.

172. *See* 1 S. WAMBAUGH, PLEBISCITES, *supra* note 153, at 46–98; 2 *id.* at 3–47.

173. *See* 1 *id.* at 99–141; 2 *id.* at 48–107.

174. *See* 1 *id.* at 163–205; 2 *id.* at 124–63.

175. *See* 1 *id.* at 206–70; 2 *id.* at 163–261.

176. *See* 1 *id.* at 271–97; 2 *id.* at 261–69.

177. *See* 1 *id.* at 411–41; 2 *id.* at 491–527; S. WAMBAUGH, THE SAAR PLEBISCITE (1940); THE ROYAL INSTITUTE OF INTERNATIONAL AFFAIRS, THE SAAR PLEBISCITE (1934).

178. *See* Y.B.U.N. 1956, at 354–56, 368–71 (1957).

179. *See* Y.B.U.N. 1956, at 356–58, 372–76 (1957); Y.B.U.N. 1958, at 355–60 (1959).

180. *See* Y.B.U.N. 1959, at 361–71 (1960); Y.B.U.N. 1960, at 47–77 (1961).

181. *See* Y.B.U.N. 1960, at 480–81 (1961); Y.B.U.N. 1961, at 484–94 (1962).

182. *See* Y.B.U.N. 1960, at 455–69 (1961); Y.B.U.N. 1961, at 475, 495–98 (1962).

183. Y.B.U.N. 1956, at 368 (1957). Elsewhere, in another U.N. publication, the figures recorded are 93,365 for union with Gold Coast and 67,422 for separation. UNITED NATIONS, EVERYMAN'S UNITED NATIONS 374 (8th ed. 1968).

184. Y.B.U.N. 1957, at 315 (1958).

185. EVERYMAN'S UNITED NATIONS, *supra* note 183, at 126.

186. *Id.* at 141–44.

187. UNITED NATIONS, EVERYMAN'S UNITED NATIONS: A FIVE-YEAR SUPPLEMENT 46 (1971); U.N. Doc. S/9772 (1970).

188. *See* Y.B.U.N. 1965, at 570–74 (1966); Y.B.U.N. 1964, at 427–28 (1965); 20 U.N. GAOR, Annexes, Agenda Items Nos. 23 & 24, U.N. Doc. A/5962 at 2–56 (1965).

189. Y.B.U.N. 1968, at 737–42 (1969).

190. *See* Y.B.U.N. 1961, at 51–55 (1962); Y.B.U.N. 1957, at 76–80 (1958); Y.B.U.N. 1956, at 125–27 (1957); Y.B.U.N. 1955, at 61–63 (1956); Y.B.U.N. 1954, at 56–60 (1955).

191. Y.B.U.N. 1962, at 124–28 (1963).

192. By letter dated January 20, 1965, the Deputy Prime Minister and Minister of Foreign Affairs of Indonesia informed the United Nations Secretary-General that the government of Indonesia, in protest of the seating of "neo-colonialist Malaysia" as a member of the Security Council, had decided to withdraw from the United Nations. U.N. Doc. A/5857; *id.* S/6157 (1965). Subsequently, on September 19, 1966, the Ambassador of Indonesia to the United States sent a telegram to the Secretary-General, informing him that the Indonesian government "has decided to resume full co-operation with the United Nations and to resume participation in its activities starting with the Twenty-First Session of the General Assembly." U.N. Doc. A/6419; *id.* S/6498 (1966). For further background and a discussion of the legal issues raised, see Schwelb, *Withdrawal from the United Nations: The Indonesian Intermezzo,* 61 AM. J. INT'L L. 661 (1967).

193. Report by the Representative of the Secretary-General in West Irian, submitted under article XXI, paragraph 1, of the Agreement between the Republic of Indonesia and the Kingdom of the Netherlands Concerning West New Guinea (West Irian), 24 U.N. GAOR, Annexes, Agenda Item No. 98, U.N. Doc. A/7723, Annex I, at 5 (1969).

194. *Id.* at 7–8.

195. *See id.* at 9–20.

196. *Id.* at 20. For the version of the Indonesian government, see 24 U.N. GAOR, Annexes, Agenda Item No. 98, U.N. Doc. A/7723, Annex II (1969).

197. U.N. MONTHLY CHRONICLE, Dec. 1969, at 42.

198. *Id.*

199. *See generally* Y.B.U.N. 1960, at 132–36 (1961); Y.B.U.N. 1961, at 97–101 (1962); M. ALWAN, ALGERIA BEFORE THE UNITED NATIONS (1959); E. BEHR, THE

ALGERIAN PROBLEM (1962); J. KRAFT, THE STRUGGLE FOR ALGERIA (1961); G. TIL-LION, ALGERIA: THE REALITIES (1958).

200.   *See* authorities cited note 98 *supra.*

201.   During the twelfth and thirteenth centuries, parts of Russia and China were brought under Mongol control. The Mongol Empire declined as their dynasty in China was overthrown in 1368. After the Manchus conquered China in 1644, Outer Mongolia came under Manchu suzerainty in 1691, while the Khalkha Mongol nobles swore an oath of allegiance to the Manchu emperor. The Mongol rulers of Outer Mongoiia thus enjoyed autonomy under Manchu formal sovereignty. This oath of allegiance has become the basis of all successive Chinese claims of title to Outer Mongolia, subsequent to the overthrow of the Ch'ing (Manchu) dynasty and the establishment of the Republic of China.

As Russia expanded eastward, confronting both Japan and China, Mongol leaders received support from Russia. The Mongols declared their independence from Manchu rule in December 1911, following the successful Chinese revolution which established the Republic in October. By the agreements with Russia in 1913 and 1915, China accepted Mongolian autonomy under continued Chinese suzerainty.

In the agreement signed between the U.S.S.R. and China, on May 31, 1924, Outer Mongolia was referred to as an "integral part of the Republic of China." In November 1924, the great People's Hural met and declared the establishment of the Mongolian People's Republic (M.P.R.), calling itself "independent" in the new constitution. Shortly afterward, in March 1925, the Soviet Commissar for Foreign Affairs clarified its position toward the M.P.R. in these words: "We recognize the M.P.R. as part of the Chinese Republic, but we recognize also its autonomy in so far-reaching a sense that we regard it as not only independent of China in its internal affairs, but also as capable of pursuing its foreign policy independently." U.S. DEP'T OF STATE FACT BOOK OF THE COUNTRIES OF THE WORLD 455 (1970).

About Mongolia, see C. BAWDEN, THE MODERN HISTORY OF MONGOLIA (1968); G. FRITERS, OUTER MONGOLIA AND ITS INTERNATIONAL POSITION (1949); O. LATTI-MORE, NATIONALISM AND REVOLUTION IN MONGOLIA (1955); G. MURPHY, SOVIET MONGOLIA (1966); R. RUPEN, MONGOLS OF THE TWENTIETH CENTURY (1966); A. SANDERS, THE PEOPLE'S REPUBLIC OF MONGOLIA (1968).

202.   U.S. DEP'T OF STATE FACT BOOK, *supra* note 201, at 455. According to another source, 97.8 percent, not 100 percent, of the votes cast were in favor of independence. R. WINTER, BLUEPRINTS FOR INDEPENDENCE 209–10 (1961).

203.   U.S. DEP'T OF STATE FACT BOOK, *supra* note 201, at 455.

204.   For some proposed methods of improvement, see 1 S. WAMBAUGH, PLEBISCITES, *supra* note 153, at 485–507; H. JOHNSON, *supra* note 153, at 183–99. For a detailed proposal of an internationally supervised plebiscite for Taiwan, see Chen & Reisman, *supra* note 17, at 666–69.

205.   The International Court of Justice dismissed South Africa's proposal to hold a plebiscite in Namibia, reasoning that "the Mandate was validly terminated and that in consequence South Africa's presence in Namibia is illegal and its acts on behalf of or concerning Namibia are illegal and invalid, it follows that it cannot entertain this proposal." Advisory Opinion on Legal Consequences for States of the Continued Presence of South Africa in Namibia (South West Africa) Notwithstanding Security Council Resolution 276 (1970), [1971] I.C.J. 16, 58. For a scholarly proposal of plebiscite for Namibia made in the light of the Court's opinion, see Dugard, *supra* note 110, at 48–49.

206.   As colonialism is widely viewed as inherently illegitimate, it is considered permissible to employ all necessary means, including the use of force, to eradicate any vestiges of colonialism.

207.   G. A. Res. 2625, *supra* note 86, Annex, at 124.

208.   Report of the Special Committee on Principles of International Law Concerning Friendly Relations and Cooperation among States, 25 U.N. GAOR Supp. 18, at 43, 50–51, U.N. DOC. A/8018 (1970); 24 U.N. GAOR Supp. 19, at 59–60, U.N. DOC.

A/7619 (1969); 23 U.N. GAOR, Agenda Item No. 87, at 63–64, U.N. Doc. A/7326 (1968).

209. Most recently the General Assembly, while voting overwhelmingly to condemn colonialism, gave explicit recognition of the "legitimacy" of anticolonial armed struggle. G.A. Res. 2908, 27 U.N. GAOR Supp. 30, at 2, U.N. Doc. A/8730 (1972). *See also* U.N. MONTHLY CHRONICLE, Nov. 1972, at 12; N.Y. Times, Oct. 5, 1972, at 10, col. 1.

210. G.A. Res. 2625, *supra* note 86, Annex, at 124. *Cf.* W. REISMAN, PUERTO RICO AND THE INTERNATIONAL PROCESS: NEW ROLES IN ASSOCIATION (1975).

211. To many members of the Special Committee of Twenty-Four, any outcome falling short of independence should be subject to subsequent reversal because in their view, only when the ultimate status of independence is attained can the right of self-determination be considered to have been genuinely exercised.

212. *See* authorities cited notes 53–57 *supra* and accompanying text.

213. G.A. Res. 1515, 15 U.N. GAOR Supp. 16, at 9, U.N. Doc. A/4684 (1960); G.A. Res. 1803, 17 U.N. GAOR Supp. 17, at 15, U.N. Doc. A/5217 (1962). *See* UNITED NATIONS, I. THE STATUS OF PERMANENT SOVEREIGNTY OVER NATURAL WEALTH AND RESOURCES; II. REPORT OF THE COMMISSION ON PERMANENT SOVEREIGNTY OVER NATURAL RESOURCES (1962); Gess, *Permanent Sovereignty over Natural Wealth and Resources,* 13 INT'L & COMP. L.Q. 398 (1964); Halperin, *Human Rights and Natural Resources,* 9 WM. & MARY L. REV. 770 (1968); Hyde, *Permanent Sovereignty over Natural Wealth and Resources,* 50 AM. J. INT'L. 854 (1956); Schwebel, *The Story of the United Nations Declaration on Permanent Sovereignty over Natural Resources,* 49 A.B.A.J. 463 (1963).

214. Note, for instance, the following statement: "Self-determination (does) not mean that a people has the right to sever association with another Power regardless of the economic effect upon both parties, or of the effect upon their internal stability and security. . . ." 7 U.N. GAOR, 3d Comm. 175, U.N. Doc. A/C.3/SR.447 (1952) (remark of United States delegate).

215. As the British representative put it: "But supposing that *enosis* (union), which is the whole claim, were to take place. . . . Does anyone believe that the Turkish ethnic group would be given the right to determine its own future? Of course not." 9 U.N. GAOR 53 (1954).

216. *See* G.A. Res. 1474 (ES–IV), 4th Emergency Special Session, U.N. GAOR Supp. 1, at 1, U.N. Doc. A/4510 (1960). Katanga's secession was proclaimed on July 11, 1960, and ended on January 14, 1963. On the eve of the declaration of independence, Katanga, with its 1,654,000 inhabitants, represented 12.5 percent of the total population of the Congo, while its mining production amounted to 75 percent of Congolese mining production, and its contribution to the total resources of the Congo was approximately 50 percent. J. GERARD–LIBOIS, *supra* note 139, at 3–5.

217. *See* U. UMOZURIKE, SELF–DETERMINATION IN INTERNATIONAL LAW 265–68 (1972); Nixon, *Nigeria and Biafra,* in CONFLICT IN WORLD POLITICS 281, 294–300 (S. Speigel & K. Waltz eds. 1971).

218. *See* Nanda, *supra* note 33. But, unlike Biafra, Bangladesh was in fact successful in attaining independence, which has of course made all the difference. As has been pointed out: "Had Biafra succeeded, it would have been hardly worthwhile arguing that it ought not to have succeeded, just as it is hardly worthwhile to maintain now that it ought not to have been crushed." U. UMOZURIKE, *supra* note 217, at 266.

219. The demands of the various sections of Lybia, notably Tripolitania, Cyrenaica, and Fezzan, for separate independence were denied.

220. The General Assembly decision to let Ethiopia incorporate Eritrea was said to take into consideration the "interests of peace and security in East Africa," the "rights and claims of Ethiopia . . . including in particular Ethiopia's legitimate need for adequate access to the sea." G.A. Res. 390, 5 U.N. GAOR Supp. 20, at 20, U.N. Doc. A/1775 (1950).

221. As previously noted in authorities cited notes 183–84 and accompanying text,

when the first U.N. plebiscite was held in British Togoland in May 1956, 93,095 persons voted in favor of union with an independent Gold Coast and 67,492 persons voted for an alternative choice. Since the southern half of the territory was considered too small to be viable and its people were against union with the neighboring French Togoland, the solution was to let the whole British Togoland join with the Gold Coast, with which they had had a long association, to form the new independent state of Ghana. In the case of Cameroons under British administration, separate plebiscites were held in February 1961 in both the Northern Cameroons and Southern Cameroons. While a majority of the voters in the Southern Cameroons wished to join the neighboring French Cameroons, the majority choice in the Northern Cameroons was for association with the independent Federation of Nigeria. Unlike British Togoland, their respective choices were honored by the United Nations: the Northern Cameroons became part of the Federation of Nigeria and the Southern Cameroons joined the Republic of the Cameroon.

222.   The problems confronting ministates and miniterritories are recently highlighted by a comprehensive UNITAR study. UNITED NATIONS INSTITUTE FOR TRAINING AND RESEARCH, SMALL STATES AND TERRITORIES: STATUS AND PROBLEMS (1971). *See also* P. BLAIR, THE MINISTATE DILEMMA (1967); PROBLEMS OF SMALLER TERRITORIES (B. Benedict ed. 1967); S. DE SMITH, MICROSTATES AND MICRONESIA (1970); Emerson, *supra* note 2, at 469–73; Fisher, *The Participation of Microstates in International Affairs,* 1968 PROCEEDINGS AM. SOC'Y INT'L. L. 164 (1968).

223.   *See* W. BRISK, ANGUILLA AND THE MINI–STATE DILEMMA (prepared under the auspices of the Center for International Studies, New York University, CIS #5, undated).

224.   22 U.N. GAOR Supp. 1A, at 20, U.N. DOC. A/6701/Add. 1 (1967).

225.   UNITAR, *supra* note 222, at 75–76.

226.   Walker Connor observed that:
       There is, moreover, considerable reason to expect a further proliferation of self-determination movements. For most people, ethnic consciousness still lies in the future. National consciousness presupposes an awareness of other culture-groups, but, to a majority of the world's population, the meaningful world still ends with the village. If the past and present are instructive, it can be expected that cultural and political consciousness will spread with increased communications and that the ethnic hodgepodges that are Asia and Africa will produce a host of new demands for the redrawing of political borders. (Connor, *Self-Determination: The New Phase,* 20 WORLD POL. 30, 46 (1967).)

227.   The literature on nation-building is vast. A valuable guide is a series of publications, "Studies in Political Development," sponsored by the Committee on Comparative Politics of the Social Science Research Council and published by Princeton University Press. COMMUNICATION AND POLITICAL DEVELOPMENT (L. Pye ed. 1963); BUREAUCRACY AND POLITICAL DEVELOPMENT (J. LaPalombara ed. 1963); POLITICAL MODERNIZATION IN JAPAN AND TURKEY (R. Ward & D. Rustow eds. 1964); EDUCATION AND POLITICAL DEVELOPMENT (J. Coleman ed. 1965); POLITICAL CULTURE AND POLITICAL DEVELOPMENT (L. Pye & S. Verba eds. 1965); POLITICAL PARTIES AND POLITICAL DEVELOPMENT (J. LaPalombara & M. Weiner eds. 1966); L. BINDER, CRISES AND SEQUENCES IN POLITICAL DEVELOPMENT (1971). Most of these contain comprehensive and useful bibliographies. *See also* G. ALMOND & J. COLEMAN, THE POLITICS OF DEVELOPING AREAS (1960); D. APTER, POLITICS OF MODERNIZATION (1965); C. BLACK, THE DYNAMICS OF MODERNIZATION (1966); NATION-BUILDING (K. Deutsch &. W. Foltz eds. 1963); I. HOROWITZ, THREE WORLDS OF DEVELOPMENT (2d ed. 1972); S. HUNTINGTON, POLITICAL ORDER IN CHANGING SOCIETIES (1968); DEVELOPMENT AND SOCIETY (D. Novack & R. Lckachman eds. 1964); COMPARATIVE THEORIES OF SOCIAL CHANGE (H. Peter ed. 1966).

228.   Emerson, *supra* note 2, at 464.

229.   *Id.* at 465.

230.   On the role of small states in international affairs, see D. VITAL, THE SURVIVAL

OF SMALL STATES (1971); D. VITAL, THE INEQUALITY OF STATES (1967); Leff, *Bengal, Biafra & the Bigness Bias,* 3 FOREIGN POLICY 129 (1971).

231. *See* McDougal, *The Ethics of Applying Systems of Authority: The Balanced Opposites of a Legal System,* in THE ETHICS OF POWER: THE INTERPLAY OF RELIGION, PHILOSOPHY, AND POLITICS 221–40 (H. Lasswell & H. Cleveland eds. 1962).

232. Emerson, *supra* note 2, at 465.

233. Secretary-General's Press Conference, *supra* note 4, at 36.

234. O'Brien, *The Right to Secede,* N.Y. Times, Dec. 30, 1971, at 25, col. 3.

235. These principles have recently been reformulated by the World Public Order Studies group led by Professors Myres S. McDougal and Harold D. Lasswell at Yale Law School. For a comprehensive earlier formulation, see M. MCDOUGAL, H. LASS-WELL & J. MILLER, THE INTERPRETATION OF AGREEMENTS AND WORLD PUBLIC ORDER: PRINCIPLES OF CONTENT AND PROCEDURE (1967).

Chapter 8

The Law of Treaties and Human Rights

EGON SCHWELB

This essay deals with an area where two fields of public international law meet: the law of treaties and the law of the international protection of human rights. Myres S. McDougal has made signal contributions to each of these fields. For present purposes, it is sufficient to mention in regard to the law of treaties, his coauthorship of *The Interpretation of Agreements and World Public Order,*[1] his constructive participation in the Study Panel on the Law of Treaties of the American Society of International Law, and his membership in the United States delegation to the first session of the United Nations Conference on the Law of Treaties in 1968. McDougal's essay, with Gertrude C. K. Leighton, on *The Rights of Man in the World Community: Constitutional Illusions versus Rational Action,*[2] first published in 1949, was a pioneering enterprise in the field of the law of human rights. Its authors were among the first to investigate, contemporaneously with Lauterpacht's writings on the subject, the legal force and potential of the human rights provisions of the U.N. Charter. They de-

An article based on this contribution was published in ARCHIV DES VÖLKERRECHTS, Band XVI, Heft I (1973).

262

molished the arguments presented then, and ever since, by spokesmen for the American Bar Association and others against the United States' becoming a party to international instruments in this field. It remains both a work of brilliant scholarship and, at the same time, a call to arms. More recently, McDougal—together with Harold Lasswell and Lung-chu Chen—has undertaken "a policy-oriented inquiry" on the subject of human rights and world public order.[3]

In the pages that follow, three meeting points between the Vienna Convention on the Law of Treaties and the law of human rights will be examined.

The Principle of Universal Respect for, and Observance of, Human Rights and Fundamental Freedoms and the Vienna Convention on the Law of Treaties

In the sixth paragraph of the preamble to the Vienna Convention on the Law of Treaties,[4] the states parties assert that they have agreed on the Convention

> [h]aving in mind the principles of international law embodied in the Charter of the United Nations, such as the principles of the equal rights and self-determination of peoples, of the sovereign equality and independence of all States, of non-interference in the domestic affairs of States, of the prohibition of the threat or use of force, and *of universal respect for, and observance of, human rights and fundamental freedoms for all.*[5]

The italicized words were added to the draft Preamble submitted to the plenary meeting of the Vienna Conference [6] on the proposal of the Netherlands and Costa Rica since the Drafting Committee had not included the principle expressed therein because the Committee felt it had no special link with the Convention.[7] In introducing the amendment, the representative of the Netherlands said that there seemed to be no need to stress the growing importance of human rights in interstate relations and as a subject matter of international conventions.[8] Respect for human rights was one of the main foundations of peace and justice. After listing some of the major recent human rights instruments, the representative stated that the unanimous adoption of the two Covenants on Human Rights by the General Assembly was a milestone in the efforts of the United Nations to ensure universal respect for human rights. He went on to say that the European Convention on Human Rights had become a living reality in intra-European relations. The international community was becoming increasingly aware that effective respect for human rights must be ensured in state practice; it was coming increasingly to consider itself entitled to judge whether states were respecting the norms of the most fundamental rights. Here, above all, the representative of the Netherlands continued, the area which, under Article 2(7) of the Charter, was essentially within the domestic jurisdiction of states was progressively narrowing.

Thus, according to the Netherlands representative, the importance of the relationship among the codification of human rights, their progressive development, and the law of treaties scarcely needed stressing. As certain human rights did indeed belong to the notion of *jus cogens,* he emphasized, the Conference would expose itself to justifiable criticism if it were not to embody in the Preamble to the Convention the principle of respect for human rights. It also should be borne in mind, he said, that the Conference had adopted the Swiss amendment to Article 57 (now Article 60, paragraph 5, of the Vienna Convention), the effect of which was that the provisions of that Article concerning the right to invoke a breach as a ground for terminating a treaty or suspending its operation did not apply to treaties of a humanitarian character.

In the debate on the Netherlands–Costa Rican amendment, the representative of Spain observed that the purpose of that amendment was to complete the list of the principles and rules of a *jus cogens* character enumerated in the sixth paragraph of the Preamble.[9] The new example given was an excellent one.

The representatives of Ecuador, Bulgaria, the United States, Brazil, Iraq, Bolivia, and Czechoslovakia also spoke in favor of the amendment by the Netherlands and Costa Rica.[10] The delegations of Uruguay, the U.S.S.R., Cuba, and Poland supported the reference to human rights but favored using the wording of Article 2(3) of the Charter *"promoting and encouraging* respect for human rights," etc., rather than the phraseology of the Netherlands–Costa Rican text, which was based on Article 55(c) of the Charter (*"universal respect for, and observance of,* human rights," etc.).[11] The representative of the Netherlands pointed out that in setting forth a principle of international law it would be inappropriate to speak of "promoting and encouraging." He also quoted from what was then the draft of the Declaration on Principles of International Law concerning Friendly Relations and Co-operation among States in accordance with the Charter of the United Nations, wherein it was declared that "States shall co-operate in the promotion of universal respect for and observance of human rights and fundamental freedom for all." That language, he said, had been accepted by all the members of the Special Committee on Principles of International Law concerning Friendly Relations and Co-operation among States, *including the U.S.S.R.* The representative of the U.S.S.R. did not insist on his suggestion for a different wording and said he would be prepared to vote on the language of the amendment as it stood.[12] Thereupon the Netherlands–Costa Rican amendment was adopted by ninety-three votes to none, with three abstentions.[13]

The representatives of Sweden and Argentina explained that they had abstained in the vote on the amendment by the Netherlands and Costa Rica not because their delegations were against the principle of universal respect for, and observance of, human rights and fundamental freedoms for all, but because they did not think that the principle of human rights was directly covered in the Convention. The other principles enumerated in the sixth paragraph of the Preamble were in their opinion more closely related to some of the principles embodied in the Convention.[14]

Now it is a well-established rule of interpretation that every word and part of a treaty is presumed to have a meaning and to produce some legal effect. It is the normal function of a preamble to provide an expression of the objects of a treaty.[15] These propositions are now supported and confirmed by Article 31 of the Vienna Convention itself, which provides that a treaty shall be interpreted in good faith in accordance with the ordinary meaning to be given to the terms of the treaty *in their context* and in the light of its object and purpose. The *context* for the purpose of the interpretation of a treaty comprises, in addition to the *text, including its preamble and annexes,* certain other instruments (which are not relevant for our present purpose). It follows that, in interpreting the Vienna Convention, recourse may be had to the statement in the Preamble of the principle of universal respect for, and observance of, human rights and fundamental freedoms for all. A provision of the Vienna Convention, the interpretation of which will be facilitated by this statement of the Preamble, is paragraph 5 of Article 60, as will be shown subsequently.[16] The reasoning of the representatives of Sweden and Argentina that there was no connection between the Vienna Convention and human rights,[17] which led them to abstain in the vote on the Netherlands–Costa Rican amendment, was therefore not fully convincing. The addition of the principle relating to human rights to paragraph 6 of the Preamble is of importance because it contributes to a certain equilibrium among the various Charter principles which are recited there.

Apart from its use as an aid in interpreting other provisions of the Vienna Convention, the reference to human rights in the Preamble will not add to the existing obligations of member states of the United Nations which become parties. The Charter itself provides for a stronger obligation of member states in this field. It does not set forth only a "principle" but contains, in Article 56, the pledge of all members to take joint and separate action in cooperation with the organization for the achievement of the purposes set forth in Article 55.

In the case of states nonmembers of the United Nations, which are eligible to become parties to the Vienna Convention (Article 81), the Preamble will bring about their general commitment to the principle of respect for, and observance of, human rights. In the case of two prominent nonmembers, however, there will be no addition to their international commitments. The Federal Republic of Germany is a party to the European Convention on Human Rights and to the International Convention on the Elimination of all Forms of Racial Discrimination.[18] The Preamble to the latter Convention incorporates the pledge to promote and encourage respect for, and observance of, human rights. Also, the Federal Republic and Switzerland are members of the Council of Europe, whose aims include the maintenance and further realization of human rights and fundamental freedoms. Every member of the Council must accept the principle of the enjoyment by all persons within its jurisdiction of human rights and fundamental freedoms.[19]

The Status of the Individual in the Law of Treaties

Lord McNair has pointed out that in the general rule *pacta tertiis nec nocent nec prosunt* and in the expression *pactum in favorem tertii* the *tertius* is a state and not an individual.[20] When, at its sixteenth session in 1964, the International Law Commission considered what subsequently became Articles 34 to 38 of the Vienna Convention on the Law of Treaties (which deal with treaties and third states), it had before it the proposal by the Special Rapporteur, Sir Humphrey Waldock, to include in the draft Convention a provision on the "application of treaties to individuals."[21] The draft Article submitted by the Special Rapporteur (Article 66) read as follows:

> Where a treaty provides for obligations or rights which are to be performed or enjoyed by individuals, juristic persons, or groups of individuals, such obligations or rights are applicable to the individuals, juristic persons, or groups of individuals in question:
> (a) through the Contracting States by their national systems of law;
> (b) through such international organs and procedures as may be specially provided for in the treaty or in any other treaties or instruments in force.

In his commentary on his draft, Sir Humphrey Waldock said that there was no need for the Commission to become involved in the controversial questions of whether and to what extent an individual may be regarded as a subject of international law. The application of treaties with respect to individuals under the existing rules of international law appeared to be fairly well defined. In general, they are applied to individuals through the contracting states and through the instrumentality of their respective national legal systems. However, there are a number of well-known examples of treaties which have provided special international tribunals or procedures for applying to individuals rights or obligations arising under treaties. Sir Humphrey mentioned the Convention of 1907 setting up the

Central American Court of Justice, which, subject to certain conditions, gave that Court jurisdiction over cases between a government and a national of another state; Article 304 of the Peace Treaty of Versailles and similar provisions of the other post–World War I peace treaties, which provided for the establishment of Mixed Arbitral Tribunals to which individuals were to have direct access; the Upper-Silesian Arbitral Tribunal created under the German–Polish Convention of 1922; Article 87(b) of the United Nations Charter dealing with petitions relating to trust territories; and the right of petition under the European Convention on Human Rights of 1950. The Special Rapporteur referred also to the Charters of the International Military Tribunals of Nuremberg and Tokyo which were intended to establish international machinery for dealing with the international obligations of individuals.[22] Additionally, he drew attention to the Advisory Opinion No. 15 of the Permanent Court of International Justice on the Jurisidiction of the Courts of Danzig (1928). The effect of this decision, in Waldock's view, was, *inter alia,* that it was no longer possible to appeal, with any chance of success, to an alleged principle of the impossibility of individuals' acquiring rights directly under a treaty, an interpretation not shared by McNair.[23] In the course of the debate in the International Law Commission, one of its members[24] mentioned, in addition, the 12th Hague Convention of 1907 relative to the Establishment of an International Prize Court (not subsequently ratified) giving individuals whose cargo had been seized the right to appeal to that Court.[25]

Since the International Law Commission's 1964 session, at least three more international treaties providing for access to international authorities by individuals claiming the violation of their rights have come into being: the International Convention on the Elimination of All Forms of Racial Discrimination;[26] the Optional Protocol to the International Covenant on Civil and Political Rights;[27] and the American Convention on Human Rights, Pact of San José, Costa Rica.[28]

Sir Humphrey Waldock's proposal for the Article on the application of treaties to individuals met with considerable opposition in the International Law Commission. As it has been one of the main tenets of Soviet legal doctrine that the individual is not, and cannot be, a subject of international law, it is not surprising that the then Soviet member of the Commission, Mr. Tunkin, said that he "had come to the conclusion that [the article] was not indispensable and should be dropped." "[T]he main purpose of the article," he contended, "was to ensure the observance of treaty obligations affecting individuals; but the Commission had already approved an article embodying the principle *pacta sunt servanda*[29] under which States were bound to observe treaty obligations, the manner in which that was to be done being left to them." In Mr. Tunkin's opinion, "the statement made in subparagraph (a) of Waldock's draft added nothing to the provisions already adopted and there hardly seemed to be any need for the provision in subparagraph (b) even if the existence of such exceptions were admitted—a matter about which he had serious doubts."[30]

The strongest opposition to the inclusion of the Article came from Mr. Ago, then Chairman of the Commission. His opposition was based on the allegation that "one of the most controversial theoretical problems of internationalist doctrine" was involved. It was open to question whether rights and obligations deriving from a treaty really existed for individuals. The examples given in the literature and by the Special Rapporteur himself showed, in Mr. Ago's opinion, that different interpretations were possible in support of either thesis:

> None of them settled the question whether subjective international rights and international obligations of individuals really existed, whether such rights and obligations were really international or rather internal in character, whether they derived from the treaty itself or from action taken by States or by other bodies in pursuance of the rights and obligations created by treaty, or whether those bodies themselves were international or national in character . . . . If the Commission acknowledged that an international treaty had effects on third parties, and if, when speaking of third parties, it referred to individuals, it would be implicitly admitting that individuals could possess international rights or obligations and were consequently subjects of international law . . . . Mr. Ago could not subscribe to an article that took a positive view on the international personality of the individual at that stage in the development of international law.[31]

In reply to Mr. Ago, Sir Humphrey Waldock pointed out that he could hardly conceive of the European Commission on Human Rights as a municipal tribunal and it applied a Convention through international machinery; he believed the view expressed by the Chairman (Mr. Ago) on that point to be in contradiction with the existing practice.[32]

Mr. Paredes was of the opinion that

> [W]hen two or more States agreed to guarantee certain rights for individuals, those individuals were not given the capacity to plead before an international court, but duties were agreed between the contracting parties, of which the individuals were the beneficiaries. The obligation was established between the States and it was for them to ensure that it was fulfilled and to demand its fulfillment in case of default. In the case of an agreement on human rights, for instance, if one of the parties violated the agreement on its own territory and with respect to its own nationals, they could not bring an action before an international court, but could only act through one of the contracting parties, which would assume the role of protector of the individuals concerned and demand fulfillment of the obligation in its own name.[33]

(In regard to this statement it is appropriate to point out that in addition to subscribing to the international procedures existing in 1964, to which the Special Rapporteur had referred, the speaker's own country, Ecuador, subsequently, on April 4, 1968, signed and on March 6, 1969, ratified the Optional Protocol to the International Covenant on Civil and Political Rights.[34] Furthermore, on November 22, 1969, Ecuador signed the American Convention on Human Rights.)[35] Mr. Paredes also

> thought it would be extremely dangerous to attack the jurisdiction of the State on the pretext of providing international protection for the individual citizen, by creating yet another court in addition to those already established under municipal law of every country. In Ecuador, for example, litigants were protected by three courts (even four, if actions for damages were taken into account).[36]

It therefore would not be advisable to prolong litigation by introducing yet another—international—court.

Of course, no proposal to establish such an international court was before the Commission. What was involved was the codification of the existing state of affairs which makes it possible for states to provide by treaty for international organs and procedures. The members of the Organization of American States, including Ecuador, had for many years been considering the conclusion of an Inter-American Convention on Human Rights, the establishment of an Inter-American Commission and Court of Human Rights, and the Commission's right to receive petitions. They had been in the process of the very action to which sovereign states are entitled under the lex lata, the codification of which the Special Rapporteur proposed in his draft Article,[37] activities which eventually culminated in the adoption and signature of the American Convention on Human Rights.

In support of his opposition to the Article, Mr. Jiménez de Aréchaga invoked "drafting difficulties." The proposed text, he said,

> adopted an Anglo-Saxon common law approach identifying rights with remedies. The way in which it had been formulated would not be appropriate for continental systems of law, under which rights were regarded as coming into existence before remedies. Under those systems it could not be stated, as proposed, that a right was "applicable to the individuals through . . . international organs and procedures."[38]

However, Sir Humphrey Waldock's text did not seem to identify rights with remedies. In the introductory part of the draft Article it referred to (substantive) rights and obligations and, in subparagraph (b) in particular, it intended to codify the rule that international remedies, "through . . . international organs and procedures," may be provided for. No conflict between common and civil law systems appears to have been involved.

It was difficult for the members of the Commission to deny that the Charter of the United Nations guaranteed the right of petition under the trusteeship system. Mr. Lachs tried to distinguish this fact by saying that it was limited to "a step in the direction of full self-determination."[39] Even if this were so, however, the right of petition has been exercised, and accepted by the General Assembly and the Trusteeship Council, also in matters concerning the rights of individual inhabitants of trust territories far removed from the issues of self-determination and independence. Mr. Elias suggested that the Article should be deleted or at least left aside because "some of the problems the article set out to solve were so complex that even with the most ingenious drafting, he feared it would be impossible to devise an acceptable text."[40] Mr. Briggs "was unable to see what purpose the article was intended to fill. Presumably the sense in which it talked of rights being applicable to individuals was through the contracting parties by their systems of law. . . . The article could be dropped."[41]

Several members of the Commission agreed that states were perfectly free to conclude treaties directly conferring rights on individuals, but not all of them were convinced of the necessity or the desirability of including the draft Article.[42] Mr. Rosenne[43] said that a provision on the question dealt with in the draft Article was necessary, if only because of the definition of a "treaty" adopted by the Commission.[44] Mr. Yasseen agreed that there was nothing to prevent states from stipulating in a treaty that the treaty was directly applicable to individuals. He said that the Commission certainly should propose a solution in its draft, but the article should be differently drafted; it should stress the tendency, supported by international case law, to consider the treaty itself as the basis of the solution.[45] The Special Rapporteur stated that

> [A]s the general feeling seemed to be against including the article, he wished to put on record his view that sub-paragraph (b) dealt with a phenomenon which already existed in international law and the extent and importance of which had perhaps not been sufficiently recognized during the discussion . . . . In general he would much regret the deletion of sub-paragraph (b) since it would not accord with the high importance attached by the Charter and by modern international law generally to human rights and freedoms.[46]

The Article was withdrawn. Mr. Bartoš said that he supported the idea expressed in the Article and regretted its withdrawal from the draft.[47] Earlier in the debate he had emphasized that

> in a draft convention prepared with a view to the progressive development of international law, it was the Commission's moral and intellectual duty to recognize that rights could be directly conferred and obligations directly imposed on individuals, juristic persons, or groups of individuals.[48]

Mr. Bartoš' regret was shared by Messrs. Yasseen, Tsuruoka,[49] Ruda,[50] and Reuter.[51] Mr. Reuter added that he could not accept any interpretation which cast doubt on the fact that the principles laid down in the Charter were intended to benefit individuals.

In its report on its sixteenth session, the International Law Commission reported on its proceedings relating to the draft Article in the following terms:

> The Commission also considered the application of treaties providing for obligations or rights to be performed or enjoyed by individuals. Some members of the Commission desired to see a provision on that question included in the present group of draft articles, but other members considered that such a provision would go beyond the present scope of the law of treaties, and in view of the division of opinion the Special Rapporteur withdrew the proposal.[52]

When the report of the International Law Commission was considered in the Sixth Committee at the twentieth session of the General Assembly in 1965, the representative of the United Kingdom said that his delegation believed that a minimum provision of the nature of the Special Rapporteur's proposal was well supported by contemporary international law and practice, particularly in respect of human rights.[53] Accordingly, he regretted that the Commission had not incorporated a draft article dealing with that point. The Netherlands representative concurred.[54] The representative of Finland suggested that the Commission reconsider its decision to exclude from the scope of the draft Articles a provision concerning the rights and obligations of individuals. International law should recognize present-day technical and social developments and seek to regulate the rights and obligations of those individuals for whose acts states were responsible.[55]

No action along these lines was taken by either the General Assembly or the United Nations Conference on the Law of Treaties. As a consequence, the Vienna Convention does not contain a provision expressly dealing with the problem raised in the International Law Commission by the Special Rapporteur.

In my view, the noninclusion of the Article on the application of treaties to individuals is of no practical importance, for it cannot possibly affect the validity of existing treaty provisions concerning rights and obligations of individuals, nor can its noninclusion prevent new ones from being concluded. On the other hand, a provision along the lines of that proposed would have been desirable in the interest of the completeness of the work of codification. The insertion by the Vienna Conference of the reference to human rights in paragraph 6 of the Preamble to the Vienna Convention confirms that the retention of the draft Article proposed by Sir Humphrey Waldock would have been appropriate.

More generally, under the Charter of the United Nations, "the progressive development of international law and its codification," on the one hand, and, on the other hand, "promoting international cooperation in the economic, social, cultural, educational, and health fields, and assisting in the realization of human rights and fundamental freedoms for all without distinction as to race, sex, language or religion," *i.e.,* Article 13(1)(a) and (b), are two different and separate operations. The former comes within the direct jurisdiction of the General Assembly and of subsidiary organs which it may establish for that purpose (as, *e.g.,* the International Law Commission); whereas jurisdiction as to the latter is shared among the General Assembly and, under the General Assembly's authority (Article 60), the Economic and Social Council (Article 62) and the latter's subsidiary organs (Article 68). As a consequence, the organizational arrangements made for questions of international law and for economic and social questions (including questions of human rights) are separate on all levels: in the Main Committees of the General Assembly (*i.e.,* the Second, Third, and Sixth Committees); in the subsidiary organs (*i.e.,* the subsidiary organs of the General Assembly under Article 22 and the commissions of the Economic and Social Council in economic and social fields, and for the promotion of human rights under Article 68); and in the Secretariat (*i.e.,* in the Office of Legal Affairs on the one side and the Department of Economic and Social Affairs and the Division of Human Rights on the other).

The organizational merits of the dichotomy between legal affairs, on the one hand, and economic and social (including human rights) matters, on the other, need not be discussed here. But no organizational logic can have moved the authors of the Charter to the extreme of intending that what was being done in economic, social, and human rights matters should be and remain terra incognita for the organs working in the field of international law and vice versa.

The Protection of Humanitarian Conventions Against Termination or Suspension Because of Their Breach

Proceedings of the International Law Commission

Subparagraph 2(b) of Article 57 of the 1966 draft Articles on the law of treaties,[56] entitled "Termination or Suspension of the Operation of a Treaty as a Consequence of its Breach," provided that a material breach of a multilateral treaty by one of the parties entitled "a party specially affected by the breach to invoke it as a ground for suspending the operation of the treaty in whole or in part in the relations between itself and the defaulting State."[57] As drafted, the provision applied to all multilateral treaties. At the second part of the seventeenth session of the International Law Commission in January 1966, several members expressed misgivings about this provision in its application to general multilateral treaties such as the Geneva Conventions on the Law of the Sea and the Vienna Convention on Diplomatic Relations, and, in particular, with regard to its effect on humanitarian conventions.[58]

Mr. Bartoš said that the Article was perhaps too liberal to be applicable to treaties of that kind and that it did not take into account the evolution of international law as embodied in the judgments of the Nuremberg International Military Tribunal. The humanitarian conventions formed part of the legal conscience of nations; it was inconceivable that a state should be free to suspend the application of such conventions just because another state had ceased to apply them. A very serious question was involved, he maintained, and the substance should prevail over the form.[59]

Mr. de Luna said that when a treaty of a humanitarian character was violated, suspension should not be made too simple, for the treaty was necessary to, and in the interests of, the entire international community.[60] He explained, however, that he had mentioned multilateral humanitarian conventions mainly to satisfy his own conscience and not to suggest any change in the proposed draft.[61]

Sir Humphrey Waldock said that it clearly would serve no good purpose for the injured state to suspend the operation of a particular clause of a humanitarian convention with respect to nationals of the defaulting state since the effects of the illegality would then be visited on innocent persons. In such cases, the only effective remedy probably would lie in other forms of reprisal or counteraction outside the treaty itself. Even so, he argued, it might be going too far to forbid the injured state to suspend the operation of the treaty vis-à-vis the defaulting state.[62]

The Commission referred the Article to the Drafting Committee for reconsideration in the light of the discussion. In its 1963 draft the Commission had given the right to invoke the breach to "any other party."[63] The governments of the Netherlands[64] and the United States[65] had proposed the wording "Any other party, *whose rights or obligations are adversely affected* by the breach." In his fifth report, the Special Rapporteur had suggested that, in lieu of this phrase, it might be preferable to say "any other party *whose interests are affected* by the breach."[66] The Drafting Committee proposed the text eventually adopted, under which only "a party *specifically affected* by the breach" is entitled to invoke it as a ground for suspending the operation of the treaty.[67]

To take account of the concern expressed by members of the Commission, that the termination or suspension of general multilateral treaties should not impair the duty to fulfill any obligation embodied in the treaty to which a party was subjected under another rule of international law, the Special Rapporteur also prepared a new article for the Drafting Committee, which, as draft Article 40, was approved by the Commission and which, with some changes by the Committee of the Whole of the Vienna

Conference, became Article 43 of the Vienna Convention, entitled "Obligations imposed by international law independently of a treaty." The Article provides, in part, that the termination of a treaty or the suspension of its operation "as a result of the application of the present Convention or of the provisions of the treaty, shall not in any way impair the duty of any State to fulfil any obligation embodied in the treaty to which it would be subject under international law independently of the treaty."[68]

In an earlier study, this writer expressed the view that the Commission did not altogether avoid the danger to multilateral humanitarian conventions of which its distinguished members had clearly been aware.[69] In the text of Article 57 recommended by the Commission and as a consequence of the new Article 40 (now Article 43 of the Vienna Convention) just referred to, the danger was lessened, but not completely removed. The requirement that the party intending to have recourse to a bilateral suspension under subparagraph 2(b) must be *specially affected* by a breach would considerably reduce the incidence of such suspensions of humanitarian conventions, but it would not eliminate them altogether. Peremptory rules of international law cannot be evaded by the suspension of the operation of the treaty, and as the new Article 40 (now Article 43) confirmed, rules of customary law existing independently of the treaty remain binding. Still, there remain many cases where, in Waldock's phrase, the effects of the illegality committed by one state could be visited on innocent persons. This writer recommended, therefore, that further attempts should be made to protect general multilateral treaties, in particular, humanitarian conventions, against the adverse effect which subparagraph 2(b) and possibly also subparagraph 2(c) might have on their integrity.[70]

Proceedings of the Vienna Conference

THE FIRST SESSION (1968)

When the Committee of the Whole of the Vienna Conference (first session, 1968) considered draft Article 57, the representative of Switzerland expressed concern lest the rule stated in Article 57 disturb a whole series of conventions relating to the protection of the human person.[71] Although the Geneva Conventions for the protection of war victims prohibited reprisals against the protected persons and were virtually universal, they still were the subject of some doubts and reservations. Encouragement was given to the conclusion of bilateral or partial agreements or the registration with a neutral intermediary of concordant declarations by states which were not parties to the Conventions, but which expressed the wish to observe some of their principles or essential provisions. Such agreements, the Swiss delegation felt, should not be exposed to termination or suspension that would endanger human life. In addition, there were conventions of equal importance concerning the status of refugees, the prevention of slavery, the prohibition of genocide, and the protection of human rights in general. Even a material breach of those conventions by a party should not be allowed to injure innocent people. That idea, to which the Swiss delegation attached particular importance, could be expressed in a paragraph 5 to be added to Article 57, which might read:

> The foregoing rules do not apply to humanitarian conventions concluded with or between States not bound by multilateral conventions for the protection of the human person which prohibit reprisals against individuals. Agreements of this kind must be observed in all circumstances.

This Swiss oral amendment was of a limited scope. It would have exempted from the application of draft Article 57 only "humanitarian conventions concluded with or between States not bound by multilateral conventions for the protection of the human person which prohibit reprisals against individuals." It would not have afforded protection, at least not complete protection, to such instruments as the International Covenants on Human Rights, the International Convention on the Elimination of All Forms of Racial Discrimination, the European Convention on Human Rights, or the European Social Charter. These instruments, as has been held concerning the European Convention on Human Rights, establish a specific *ordre public,* in the European case an *"ordre public* of the free democracies of Europe." Such an *ordre public* means more than just the prohibition of reprisals.[72]

The representative of Italy supported the Swiss amendment.[73] There were conventions to which the general principle—that a party was not bound to apply a treaty with respect to another party which did not do so itself—could not be applied. These conventions must be observed by the parties even if another party failed to observe them. As examples, he gave the Geneva Conventions of 1949 and the 1961 Vienna Convention on Diplomatic Relations.

The representative of Denmark also supported the Swiss amendment.[74] Even if the inclusion would not be absolutely necessary from a legal point of view, the Danish delegation believed that the principle was of such fundamental importance that it should be stated in Article 57 in any case.

The Swiss amendment seemed unnecessary to the representative of the Ukrainian S.S.R.[75] Without giving an example, he said that many treaties prohibited denunciation even in the event of a breach. Furthermore, Article 57, paragraph 4 reserved the rights of the parties under any provision in the treaty applicable in the event of a breach.

Sir Humphrey Waldock, who had been the Special Rapporteur on the Law of Treaties of the International Law Commission and who participated in the proceedings of the Vienna Conference as Expert Consultant, commented:

> Every delegation must sympathize with the proposal made by the Swiss representative during the discussion for a new paragraph excluding certain categories of humanitarian conventions from the application of article 57. He was bound, however, to draw attention to certain difficulties in connexion with that proposal. Many of the humanitarian conventions in question, and notably the Geneva Conventions, contained clauses permitting their denunciation merely by giving notice without stating any reason; it might therefore seem strange to exclude any possibility of suspension or termination as a reaction to a material breach. The question of breaches of humanitarian conventions of that kind raised very delicate moral and legal issues. He doubted whether those issues could easily be resolved in the context of the rules regarding the rights arising from breach. The Commission had sought to cover problems of that kind rather in article 40, under which the termination or suspension of a treaty did not in any way impair the duty of any State to fulfil any obligation in the treaty to which it was subject under any other rule of international law. Rules in the treaty which were also obligatory under customary international law and which were rules of *jus cogens* would thus continue to be binding even in the event of a treaty termination or breach.[76]

The Swiss representative had expressed the hope that the Drafting Committee would take his proposal into consideration. However, the Drafting Committee submitted the Article to the Committee of the Whole without change.[77] No action on the Swiss proposal was taken at the 1968 session.

THE SECOND SESSION (1969)

When the Vienna Conference at its 1969 session considered in plenary meeting draft Article 57 as prepared by the International Law Commission and as recommended by the Committee of the Whole, the Swiss delegation submitted a written amendment—to add to Article 57 a new paragraph 5, reading as follows:

> The foregoing paragraphs do not apply to provisions relating to the protection of the human person contained in conventions and agreements of a humanitarian character, in particular, to rules prohibiting any form of reprisals against protected persons.[78]

In support of this new version of the proposal, the representative of Switzerland repeated the substance of what the Swiss delegation had said in support of its oral amendment of 1968:

> His delegation had already urged in the discussion on article 50[79] that conventions relating to protection of the human person should be

sacrosanct. Its amendment to article 57 was based on a number of considerations. First, the 1949 Geneva Conventions, which were virtually universal and, in his delegation's view, formed part of the general law of nations, prohibited reprisals against the persons protected. Second, in the spirit of those Conventions, encouragement was given in certain circumstances to the conclusion of *ad hoc* bilateral agreements expressing the wish of States not yet parties to the Geneva Conventions to observe some of their basic principles, including the prohibition of reprisals against the persons protected. Lastly, there were other equally important conventions, concerning the status of refugees, the prevention of slavery, the prohibition of genocide and the protection of human rights in general, and in no event should their violation by one party result in injury to innocent people.

Consequently, his delegation thought it necessary to put a curb on the harmful effects which the provisions of article 57, paragraphs 2(b) and 3(b), could have on individuals. The absence of a proviso on the fundamental rules for the protection of the human person would be dangerous. The Swiss delegation therefore proposed that the Conference should adopt an additional paragraph for article 57, which would simply be a saving clause to protect human beings. If the Conference accepted the principle of such a clause, he would ask for paragraph 5 to be referred to the Drafting Committee, which had not so far considered the proposal in writing.[80]

The representatives of Costa Rica, Denmark, Brazil, Ecuador, Israel, Finland, Greece, Iceland, Italy, and El Salvador supported the Swiss amendment, and the representative of India said it was acceptable in principle.[81]

The representative of Ecuador found the idea of "reprisals" too narrow. He suggested that there should be a reference to a broader notion, as well as to "reprisals." The passage might read: "in particular, to rules prohibiting any form of persecution and reprisals against protected persons." The representative of Greece recalled the proviso in Article 40 (now Article 43 of the Vienna Convention) reserving the general rules of international law. Since many of the provisions of conventions of a humanitarian character formed part of general international law, Article 40 (43) already safeguarded a number of those conventions. But, he noted, the conventions in question, and particularly the Geneva Conventions, went further, and it was precisely in their case that the Swiss amendment was sound and necessary. The Greek representative also suggested that the drafting of the new provision should be such as not to repeal provisions under which a treaty can be denounced without a special reason being given.

The representative of the United Republic of Tanzania opposed the Swiss amendment.[82] He said that if a party which violated a humanitarian treaty knew that the other parties would apply its provisions to its nationals, it might perhaps be encouraged to violate the treaty, believing itself to be protected against any sanction. He also criticized the drafting of the Swiss amendment as vague and asked what was meant by the expressions "conventions and agreements of a humanitarian character" and "rules prohibiting any form of reprisals against protected persons."

The representative of Switzerland recognized the force of the Greek representative's argument concerning the application of Article 40 (43), but thought that even something which was self-evident had better be stated. With regard to the Greek comment about the possibility of a denunciation of a humanitarian convention, the Swiss representative pointed out that some time might elapse between the performance of an act which provoked reprisals and the time when the denunciation could take effect. He went on to say that the point raised by the Tanzanian representative had been considered by the 1949 Geneva Conference, which had concluded that reprisals against war victims should be entirely prohibited; moreover, if the dangerous path of reprisals were followed, serious consequences might quickly ensue.[83]

As the suggestions regarding the Swiss amendment referred to points of drafting, the President thought that the Conference should take a decision on the principle underlying the amendment and then refer it to the Drafting Committee for modification in the light of the suggestions put forward during the discussion. The Conference adopted the principle embodied in the Swiss amendment by eighty-seven votes to none, with nine abstentions.[84] Subsequently, the Drafting Committee presented a slightly redrafted text for the paragraph to which the Conference agreed, now paragraph 5 of Article 60 of the Vienna Convention. It reads as follows:

> Paragraphs 1 to 3 do not apply to provisions relating to the protection of the human person contained in treaties of a humanitarian character, in particular to provisions prohibiting any form of reprisals against persons protected by such treaties.

The Scope of the Protection of Humanitarian Treaties

Paragraph 5 of Article 60 of the Vienna Convention prohibits the application of the provisions authorizing the suspension or termination of treaties as a consequence of their breach to provisions which (1) relate to the protection of the human person and (2) are contained in treaties of a humanitarian character. The term "protection of the human person" should be interpreted with due regard to the last phrase of paragraph 6 of the Preamble, which has been considered in the first part of this essay; that is, in accordance with the commitment of the states parties to respect and observe human rights and fundamental freedoms for all. Any provision of a treaty of a humanitarian character which implements this principle is protected by paragraph 5. The question might be raised as to whether "the protection of the human person" is a concept different from "the protection of human rights." There is, certainly, a difference between the two phrases insofar as there exist provisions relating to the protection of the human person which do not always establish an enforceable *right* of the persons whose protection they serve. Examples are provisions of maritime conventions as regards standards of safety at sea or provisions of some International Labor Conventions obligating states to maintain standards of industrial health and safety. On the other hand, it may be argued that "the protection of the human person" is narrower than "protection of human rights" because, on first sight, it does not appear to cover the protected person's property. It is submitted, however, that it would not be justified to draw this general conclusion from the difference in the wording.

Article 46 of the Hague Regulations respecting the Laws and Customs of War on Land of 1907[85] provides that "family honor and rights, individual life, *and private property,* as well as religious convictions and worship, must be respected. *Private property may not be confiscated.*" Under Article 47, "pillage is expressly forbidden." Plunder of public *or private* property is a war crime under Article 6(b) of the Charter of the International Military Tribunal for the Trial of German Major War Criminals.[86] And Article 18 of the Geneva Convention of 1949 [87] relative to the Treatment of Prisoners of War provides that all effects and articles of personal use and for their clothing or feeding shall remain in the possession of prisoners of war. The Article contains provisions in regard to sums of money and articles of value carried by prisoners of war which, if taken from them for reasons of security, must be returned at the end of the prisoners' captivity. Similar provisions are contained in Article 97 of the Geneva Convention of 1949 relative to the Protection of Civilian Persons in Time of War.[88] There can be hardly any doubt that all these relate to the protection of the human person notwithstanding that they deal with property.

Furthermore, when Article 14 of the International Covenant on Civil and Political Rights and Article 6 of the European Convention on Human Rights entitle everyone to a fair and public hearing by a competent independent and impartial tribunal in the determination of his rights and obligations in a suit at law, what is involved in most cases is the property of the litigants. This right to fair civil proceedings is a right of the human person. In Article 11 of the International Covenant on Economic, Social, and Cultural Rights, the states parties recognize the right of everyone to an adequate standard of living for himself and his family, including adequate food, clothing, and housing. These rights clearly require that the protected person have and retain material objects of personal and, in some form or other, real property or the right to the use thereof. In order to delimit (for the purposes of Article 60, paragraph 5) the concept of "the protection of the human person" in regard to the person's property, one might accept the formulation of the American Declaration of the Rights and Duties of Man of 1948 (Article XXIII), which states that "every person has a right to own such private property as meets the essential needs of decent living and helps to maintain the dignity of the individual and of the home."[89]

To be protected against termination or suspension on the ground of breach, a provision relating to the protection of the human person must be contained in a treaty of a humanitarian character. The legislative history makes clear what the authors of the amendment and the delegates who voted for it had in mind when they resorted to the term "treaties of a humanitarian character": instruments such as the Geneva Conventions for the protection of war victims of 1949 and bilateral agreements supplementing them; the "conventions concerning the status of refugees," a phrase which covers the Convention on the Status of Refugees of 1951, the 1966 Protocol thereto, and the Convention on the Status of Stateless Persons of 1954; conventions for the prevention of slavery, a term which includes the Slavery Convention of 1926, the 1953 Protocol amending it, and the Supplementary Slavery Convention of 1956; the Convention on the Prevention and Punishment of the Crime of Genocide of 1948; and conventions for the "protection of human rights in general." The latter term includes, of course, the great number of instruments relating to human rights which have been concluded within or under the auspices of the United Nations and of Specialized Agencies [90] and through the instrumentality of regional organizations.[91]

The treaties to which express reference was made in the proceedings of the Vienna Conference need not, however, exhaust the scope of "treaties of a humanitarian character." The Preamble to the Constitution of the International Labor Organization refers to the "failure . . . to adopt *humane* conditions of labor" and recalls that the High Contracting Parties were moved by sentiments of justice *and humanity* when they agreed to the Constitution. It would seem to follow that International Labor Conventions are "treaties of a humanitarian character." Conventions concluded to guarantee standards of safety at sea or the safety of air traffic are, it is submitted, also of a humanitarian character.

Provisions prohibiting any form of reprisals against protected persons are specially mentioned. The four Geneva Conventions on war victims of 1949 prohibit reprisals against protected persons expressly[92] and come within the terms of the exception also for this reason. There are many treaties in existence which prohibit reprisals without using this specific term. When the states parties to the International Covenant on Civil and Political Rights undertake to respect and to ensure to *all individuals within their territory* and subject to their jurisdiction the rights recognized in the Covenant without distinction of any kind [Article 2(1)], they commit themselves not to apply reprisals against persons so protected. This proposition is not affected by the right of states parties to derogate from their obligations in time of public emergency (Article 4). The same is true under the European Convention on Human Rights (Articles 1 and 15). Nor do the Slavery Conventions, the Genocide Convention, the International Convention on the Elimination of All Forms of Racial Discrimination, and similar instruments lend themselves to an interpretation which would permit the nonobservance of their provisions on the ground of the taking of reprisals.

The Limits of the Scope of Article 60(5)

Paragraph 5 of Article 60 protects a treaty of a humanitarian character only against denunciation or suspension by virtue of paragraphs 1 to 3 of the Article, that is, against termination or suspension as a consequence of its breach. In particular, it does not affect the termination of, or withdrawal from, a treaty under its provisions or by consent of the parties. Its application to treaties which contain no provision regarding termination, denunciation, or withdrawal raises specific problems. These contingencies are regulated by Articles 54 and 56, respectively, of the Vienna Convention. Some examples of cases coming under Articles 54 and 56 are given in the paragraphs that follow.

Surprising as it may seem in a period when talk about peremptory rules of international law abounds, most treaties "for the protection of the human person" or "treaties of a humanitarian character" provide that they may be unilaterally denounced or withdrawn from. This applies to the Genocide Convention (Article XIV), of which the International Court of Justice has said that the principles underlying it "are principles which are recognized by civilized nations as binding on States, even without any conventional obligation."[93] A state party to the International Convention on the Elimination of All Forms of Racial Discrimination may denounce it by written notification to the Secretary-General, and the denunciation takes effect one year after the date of receipt of the notification (Article 21). Other examples are the Slavery Conventions of 1926 and 1956, the Convention for the Suppression of the Traffic in Persons and of the Exploitation of the Prostitution of Others of 1949, the Abolition of Forced Labour Convention of 1957, the Discrimination (Employment and Occupation) Convention of 1958, and the Convention against Discrimination in Education of 1960. The European Convention on Human Rights of 1950[94] and the American Convention on Human Rights of 1969 also can be denounced (Articles 65 and 78, respectively). All these Conventions require a period of notice, usually six months or one year.

The four Geneva Conventions of 1949 all contain denunciation clauses which, after stating that the denunciation shall take effect one year after notification, provide as follows:

However, a denunciation of which notification has been made at a time when the denouncing Power is involved in a conflict shall not take effect until peace has been concluded, and until after operations connected with release and repatriation of the persons protected by the present Convention have been terminated.[95]

After providing that the denunciation shall have effect only with respect to the denouncing Power, the articles go on to say that:

It shall in no way impair the obligations which the Parties to the conflict shall remain bound to fulfill by virtue of the principles of the law of nations, as they result from the usages established among civilized peoples, from the laws of humanity and the dictates of the public conscience.[96]

These provisions are inspired by the well-known Preamble to the 1899 and 1907 Hague Conventions concerning the Laws and Customs of War on Land, the so-called Martens Clause. Sir Humphrey Waldock has, as he says, drawn inspiration from the denunciation clauses of the Geneva Conventions of 1949 in proposing what eventually has become Article 43 of the Vienna Convention on the Law of Treaties (obligations imposed by international law independently of a treaty).[97] The denunciation of a treaty does not in any way impair the duty of the denouncing state to fulfill an obligation embodied in the treaty to which it would be subject under international law independently of the treaty. For this rule to apply it is not necessary that the obligation involved derive from a peremptory norm of international law. It applies also when the rule involved is a norm of *jus dispositivum,* an ordinary, not peremptory, norm of customary international law. A state which is bound by a rule of customary international law existing independently of a treaty cannot free itself from its obligation to abide by that rule by denouncing a treaty which happens also to contain that rule.

While paragraph 5 of Article 60 does not permanently deprive a state of the right to denounce a humanitarian treaty which, in conformity with its own terms, can be terminated or withdrawn from, it nevertheless protects the treaty from immediate termination or suspension for the duration of the period of notice which the treaty requires.

The International Covenants on Human Rights Cannot Be Denounced or Withdrawn From

Neither of the two Covenants adopted by the General Assembly in 1966 contains a provision regarding its termination. Neither is subject to denunciation. According to Article 56 of the Vienna Convention, a treaty which contains no provision regarding its termination and which does not provide for denunciation or withdrawal is not subject to denunciation or withdrawal unless:

(a) it is established that the parties intended to admit the possibility of denunciation or withdrawal; or

(b) a right of denunciation or withdrawal may be implied by the nature of the treaty.

In regard to (a), it cannot be established that the General Assembly or the parties to the Covenants intended to admit the possibility of denunciation or withdrawal. In the nineteen years during which the draft Covenants were considered by various organs of the United Nations (between 1947 and 1966), no suggestion to this effect was made. Moreover, the "context for the purpose of the interpretation" of the Covenants and an *argumentum a contrario* derived from it prove conclusively that neither denunciation nor withdrawal is permitted. By the same resolution by which the General Assembly adopted the two Covenants which do not provide for denunciation,[98] it adopted also the Optional Protocol to the International Covenant on Civil and Political Rights, Article 12 of which is to the effect that any state may denounce the Protocol at any time, the denunciation to take effect three months after the date of receipt by the Secretary-General of the notification.

In regard to subparagraph (b) of Article 56(1) it is clear that by no stretch of the imagination can a right of denunciation or withdrawal be implied by the nature of the Covenants, by the adoption of which the General Assembly completed one of the major tasks with which it was charged by Article 13(1)(b) of the Charter, *i.e.,* to assist "in the realization of human rights and fundamental freedoms for all without distinction as to race, sex, language, or religion."[99]

Annex

The Convention on the Law of Treaties
Done at Vienna on May 23, 1969[100]

The States Parties to the present Convention,

Considering the fundamental role of treaties in the history of international relations,

Recognizing the ever-increasing importance of treaties as a source of international law and as a means of developing peaceful co-operation among nations, whatever their constitutional and social systems,

Noting that the principles of free consent and of good faith and the *pacta sunt servanda rule* are universally recognized,

Affirming that disputes concerning treaties, like other international disputes, should be settled by peaceful means and in conformity with the principles of justice and international law,

Recalling the determination of the peoples of the United Nations to establish conditions under which justice and respect for the obligations arising from treaties can be maintained,

Having in mind the principles of international law embodied in the Charter of the United Nations, such as the principles of the equal rights and self-determination of peoples, of the sovereign equality and independence of all States, of non-interference in the domestic affairs of States, of the prohibition of the threat or use of force and of universal respect for, and observance of, human rights and fundamental freedoms for all,

Believing that the codification and progressive development of the law of treaties achieved in the present Convention will promote the purposes of the United Nations set forth in the Charter, namely, the maintenance of international peace and security, the development of friendly relations and the achievement of co-operation among nations,

Affirming that the rules of customary international law will continue to govern questions not regulated by the provisions of the present Convention,

Have agreed as follows:

*   *   *

Article 56

Denunciation of or withdrawal from a treaty containing no provision regarding termination, denunciation or withdrawal

1.   A treaty which contains no provision regarding its termination and which does not provide for denunciation or withdrawal is not subject to denunciation or withdrawal unless:

   (a) it is established that the parties intended to admit the possibility of denunciation or withdrawal; or

   (b) a right of denunciation or withdrawal may be implied by the nature of the treaty.

2.   A party shall give not less than twelve months' notice of its intention to denounce or withdraw from a treaty under paragraph 1.

*   *   *

Article 60

Termination or suspension of the operation of a treaty as a consequence of its breach

1.   A material breach of a bilateral treaty by one of the parties entitles the other to invoke the breach as a ground for terminating the treaty or suspending its operation in whole or in part.

2.   A material breach of a multilateral treaty by one of the parties entitles:

   (a) the other parties by unanimous agreement to suspend the operation of the treaty in whole or in part or to terminate it either:

      (i) in the relations between themselves and the defaulting State, or

      (ii) as between all the parties;

   (b) a party specially affected by the breach to invoke it as a ground for suspending the operation of the treaty in whole or in part in the relations between itself and the defaulting State;

   (c) any party other than the defaulting State to invoke the breach as a ground for suspending the operation of the treaty in whole or in part with respect to itself if the treaty is of such a character that a material breach of its provisions by one party radically changes the position of every party with respect to the further performance of its obligations under the treaty.

3. A material breach of a treaty, for the purposes of this article, consists in:
    (a) a repudiation of the treaty not sanctioned by the present Convention; or
    (b) the violation of a provision essential to the accomplishment of the object or purpose of the treaty.

4. The foregoing paragraphs are without prejudice to any provision in the treaty applicable in the event of a breach.

5. Paragraphs 1 to 3 do not apply to provisions relating to the protection of the human person contained in treaties of a humanitarian character, in particular to provisions prohibiting any form of reprisals against persons protected by such treaties.

Notes

1. M. McDougal, H. Lasswell & J. Miller, The Interpretation of Agreements and World Public Order (1967). For a sympathetic review and synopsis by one of the editors of this volume, see Weston, Book Review, 117 U. Pa. L. Rev. 647 (1969).

2. 14 Law & Contemp. Prob. 490 (1949), *reprinted in* 59 Yale L.J. 60 (1949) and *in* M. McDougal & Associates, Studies in World Public Order 335 (1960).

3. For preliminary clarification, see McDougal, Lasswell & Chen, *Human Rights and World Public Order: A Framework for Policy-Oriented Inquiry*, 63 Am. J. Int'l L. 237 (1969).

4. U.N. Doc. A/Conf. 39/27 (1969), in 63 Am. J. Int'l L. 875 (1969), and in 8 Int'l Legal Materials 679 (1969) [hereinafter cited as Vienna Convention].

5. *Id.* (emphasis added).

6. In accordance with traditional legislative practice, the Vienna Conference dealt with the Preamble to the Convention only on May 20, 1969, *i.e.,* toward the end of its second (1969) session, which concluded on May 22, 1969. At the first meeting of its second session on April 9, 1969, the Conference, acting on a recommendation from the Secretary-General, had decided that the drafting of the Preamble should be entrusted to the Drafting Committee, which would submit the text not to the Committee of the Whole, but directly to he plenary. *See* United Nations Conference on the Law of Treaties, 2 Official Records 2, Second Session, 7th plenary meeting, para.- 13, U.N. Doc. A/Conf. 39/11/Add.2 (1969) [hereinafter cited as Official Records]; Memorandum by the Secretary-General on "Methods of Work and Procedures of the Second Session of the Conference," para. 7, U.N. Doc. A/Conf. 39/12 (1969).

7. Mr. Alvarez (Uruguay), 2 Official Records, *supra* note 6, at 172, 31st plenary meeting, para. 32.

8. Mr. Heuben (Netherlands), *id.* at 169, paras. 11–15.

9. Mr. Castro (Spain) (now a judge of the International Court of Justice), *id.* at 173, para. 47.

10. Mr. Alcivar-Castillo (Ecuador), *id.* at 170, para. 22; Mr. Koulichev (Bulgaria), *id.* at 5, para. 45; Mr. Kearney (United States), *id.* para. 56; Mr. Nascimento e Silva (Brazil), *id.* para. 65; Mr. Yasseen (Iraq), *id.* para. 66; Mr. Romero Loza (Bolivia), *id.* para. 79; Mr. Němecek (Czechoslovakia), *id.* at 176, 32d plenary meeting, para. 7.

11. Mr. Alvarez (Uruguay), *id.* at 172, 31st plenary meeting, para. 34 (emphasis

added); Mr. Khlestov (U.S.S.R.), *id.* at 174, para. 72; Mr. Alvarez Tabio (Cuba), *id.* at 176, 32d plenary meeting, para. 5; Mr. Nahlik (Poland), *id.* para. 12.

12. *Id.* paras. 16–20. The draft to which the representative of the Netherlands referred was contained in the Report of the Special Committee on Principles of International Law concerning Friendly relations and Co-operation among States, 22 U.N. GAOR, Annexes, Agenda Item No. 87, para. 161, U.N. DOC. A/6799 (1967), as expressing the consensus of its Drafting Committee. It now appears without change in the final text of the Declaration as adopted on October 24, 1970, by G.A. Res. 2625 (XXV), under the heading "The duty of States to co-operate with one another in accordance with the Charter." The full text of the principle reads:

> States shall co-operate in the promotion of universal respect for, and observance of, human rights and fundamental freedoms for all, and in the elimination of all forms of racial discrimination and all forms of religious intolerance. (G.A. Res. 2625 (XXV), 25 U.N. GAOR Supp. 28, at 123, U.N. Doc. A/8028.)

13. 2 OFFICIAL RECORDS, *supra* note 6, 32nd meeting, para. 21.

14. Mr. Blix (Sweden), *id.* para. 32; Mr. de la Guardia (Argentina), *id.* para. 34.

15. "That the preamble forms part of a treaty for purposes of interpretation is too will settled to require comment." C. Rousseau, *Principes généraux de droit international public* 717–19 (1944), quoted by Sir Humphrey Waldock in his Third Report on the Law of Treaties [1964] 2 Y.B. INT'L L. COMM'N 57. As Special Rapporteur of the International Law Commission, Sir Humphrey, and the Commission itself in its 1964 Report to the General Assembly, pointed out that the I.C.J. had more than once had recourse to the statement of the objects and purpose of a treaty in the preamble to interpert a particular provision, e.g., in the *United States Nationals in Morocco Case,* I.C.J. Reports, 1952, pp. 196 and 199, [1964] 2 Y.B. INT'L L. COMM'N 56 and 203, 19 U.N. GAOR Supp. 9, at 27 (1964).

16. *See* the third part of this essay.

17. *See* note 14 *supra.*

18. Adopted by General Assembly Resolution 2106 A (XX) of Dec. 21, 1965, opened for signature on Mar. 7, 1966, in force since Jan. 4, 1969. The Federal Republic of Germany was admitted to the United Nations in 1973.

19. Articles 1(b) and 3 of the Statute of the Council of Europe, 1949, 43 AM. J. INT'L L. 162 (1949).

20. A. McNAIR, THE LAW OF TREATIES 307 (1961).

21. H. Waldock, Third Report on the Law of Treaties, *supra* note 15.

22. *Id.* at 46. For references to the instruments listed in the text, see *id.* nn. 221–25.

23. *See* H. LAUTERPACHT, THE DEVELOPMENT OF INTERNATIONAL LAW BY THE INTERNATIONAL COURT 173 (1956); A. McNAIR, *supra* note 20, at 336–39.

24. Mr. Verdross (Austria), [1964] 1 Y.B. INT'L L. COMM'N 114, para. 22.

25. Final Act of the Second Peace Conference held at the Hague in 1907 and Conventions and Declarations annexed thereto. Misc. No. 6 (1908). Cd. 4175, H. M. Stationary Office 101; J. SCOTT, THE HAGUE CONVENTIONS AND DECLARATIONS OF 1899 AND 1907, at 188 (1915).

26. *See* note 18 *supra.*

27. Adopted and opened for signature, ratification, and accession by G.A. Res. 2200A (XXI) of Dec. 16, 1966.

28. Signed at the Inter-American Specialized Conference on Human Rights, San José, Costa Rica, Nov. 22, 1969, OAS Official Records OEA/Ser. K./XVI, Doc. 65, Rev. 1; 9 INT'L LEGAL MATERIALS 99 (1970).

29. Now Article 26 of the Vienna Convention.

30. Mr. Tunkin (U.S.S.R.), [1964] 1 Y.B. INT'L L. COMM'N 117–18, paras. 55–56.

31. Mr. Ago (Italy), *id.* at 116–17, paras. 44–50.

32. Sir Humphrey Waldock (United Kingdom) (now a judge of the International Court of Justice), *id.* at 118, para. 60.

33. Mr. Paredes (Ecuador), *id.* at 115, paras. 30–31.

34. Report of the Secretary-General on the Status of, *inter alia,* the Optional Protocol to the Covenant on Civil and Political Rights, 25 U.N. GAOR, Agenda Item 59, Annexes, U.N. Doc. A/8071, Annex (1970).

35. Final Act of the Inter-American Specialized Conference, *supra* note 28.

36. *See* authority cited *supra* note 33.

37. Final Act of the Fourth Meeting of the Inter-American Council of Jurists, Santiago, Chile, 1959.

38. Mr. Jiménez de Aréchaga (Uruguay) (now a judge of the International Court of Justice), [1964] 1 Y.B. INT'L L. COMM'N 117, para. 53.

39. Mr. Lachs (Poland) (now a judge of the International Court of Justice), *id.* at 118–19, paras. 69–70.

40. Mr. Elias (Nigeria), *id.* at 117, para. 51.

41. Mr. Briggs (United States), *id.* at 117, para. 52.

42. Mr. Verdross (Austria), *id.* at 114, paras. 21–23; Mr. Castren (Finland), *id.* paras. 24–25; the late Mr. Amado (Brazil), *id.* at 116, paras. 38–40; the late Mr. de Luna (Spain), *id.* at 116, paras. 40–41; Mr. Liu (China), *id.* at 117, para. 54; Mr. El Erian (United Arab Republic), *id.* at 118, para. 57.

43. Mr. Rosenne (Israel), *id.* at 115, para. 32.

44. Now Article 2(1)(b) of the Vienna Convention.

45. Mr. Yasseen (Iraq), [1964] 1 Y.B. INT'L L. COMM'N 114–15, paras. 26–28.

46. *Id.* at 118, paras. 60–61.

47. Mr. Bartoš (Yugoslavia), *id.* para. 63.

48. *Id.* at 116, para. 44.

49. Mr. Tsuruoka (Japan), *id.* at 118, para. 65.

50. Mr. Ruda (Argentina) (now a judge of the International Court of Justice), *id.* para. 66.

51. Mr. Reuter (France), *id.* para. 68.

52. Int'l L. Comm'n, Report, [1964] 2 Y.B. INT'L L. COMM'N 176, U.N. Doc. A/5809 (1964).

53. Mr. Sinclair, General Assembly, 20th session, Sixth Committee, 843rd meeting, Oct. 7, 1965, at 24, para. 26.

54. Mr. Tammes, *id.,* 847th meeting, Oct. 12, 1965, at 47, para. 14.

55. Mr. Manner, *id.,* 850th meeting, Oct. 13, 1965, at 47, para. 14.

56. Reports of the International Law Commission on the second part of its 17th session and on its 18th session (1966), [1966] 2 Y.B. INT'L L. COMM'N 253, U.N. Doc. A/6309/Rev.1 (1966).

57. Corresponding to Article 60 of the Vienna Convention and article 42 of the 1963 draft.

58. Mr. Tunkin, [1966] 1 Y.B. INT'L L. COMM'N PART I 63, para. 72; *id.* at 65, para. 9.

59. Mr. Bartoš, *id.* at 66, para. 22.

60. Mr. de Luna, *id.* at 63, para. 68.

61. *Id.* at 66, para. 26.

62. Sir Humphrey Waldock, *id.* para. 23.

63. Report of the International Law Commission Covering its 15th Session (1963), 18 U.N. GAOR, Supp., 9 U.N. Doc. A/5509 (1963), [1963] 2 Y.B. INT'L L. COMM'N 204, draft art. 42.

64. [1966] 2 Y.B. INT'L L. COMM'N, *supra* note 56, at 318. (Emphasis added.)

65. *Id.* at 354.

66. Waldock, Fifth Report on the Law of Treaties, [1966] 2 Y.B. INT'L L. COMM'N 35, art. 42. (Emphasis added.)

67. [1966] 1 Y.B. INT'L L. COMM'N PART I, *supra* note 58, at 127–28, para. 2.

68. *Id.* at 129, 131–32, paras. 32, 71–78; Conference Records, *supra* note 4, at 227–28, 463, First session, 40th and 78th meetings of the Committee of the Whole, paras. 70–77, 3–5.

69. Schwelb, *Termination or Suspension of the Operation of a Treaty as a Consequence of its Breach,* 7 INDIAN J. INT'L L. 320 (1967). The article was based on a memorandum which the writer prepared as Rapporteur of the Study Group on the Law of Treaties of the American Society of International Law in September 1966.

70. For a detailed presentation of the dangers which Article 57 as prepared by the International Law Commission would have involved for humanitarian conventions, see Schwelb, note 69 *supra.*

71. Mr. Bindschedler (Switzerland), 1 OFFICIAL RECORDS, *supra* note 6, at 354, 61st meeting of the Committee of the Whole, paras. 12–13.

72. *See* Schwelb, *supra* note 69, at 323–25.

73. Mr. Maresca (Italy), 1 OFFICIAL RECORDS, *supra* note 6, at 358, 61st meeting, para. 62.

74. Mrs. Adamsen (Denmark), *id.* para. 67.

75. Mr. Korshak (Ukrainian S.S.R.), *id.* at 355, para. 19.

76. Sir Humphrey Waldock, *id.* at 359, para. 76. Because the Swiss proposal had not been introduced in writing, as required by the rules of procedure, the Chairman of the Committee of the Whole asked the Committee what action it wished to take on the matter. *Id.* para. 80. The Austrian representative said that despite the difficulties to which the Expert Consultant had referred, his delegation was in favor of adopting the Swiss proposal. Mr. Verosta (Austria), *id.* para. 81. The representative of the United Kingdom said he thought most of the members of the Committee were in favor of the Swiss delegation's proposal. It seemed very difficult, however, to find a satisfactory definition of the type of treaty concerned. It would be easy to use the word "humanitarian," of course, but to what treaties would that description properly apply? The representative of the United Kingdom suggested that instead of an amendment to Article 57, the Swiss delegation might perhaps consider submitting a resolution on the subject in plenary. Sir Francis Vallat (United Kingdom), *id.* para. 83. The Swiss representative asked whether it might not be possible to instruct the Drafting Committee to examine the question. An alternative would be to authorize the Swiss delegation to submit a draft of a new article, and while the idea was not easy to express, it would be desirable for it to appear in the convention. The Swiss delegation could also accept the suggestion made by the United Kingdom representative. Mr. Ruegger (Switzerland), *id.* para. 84.

77. Mr. Yasseen, Chairman of the Drafting Committee, *id.* at 478, 81st meeting, para. 23.

78. U.N. DOC. A/Conf. 39/L.31 (1969).

79. Now Article 53 of the Vienna Convention (treaties conflicting with a preemptory norm of general international law *(jus cogens)).*

80. 2 OFFICIAL RECORDS, *supra* note 6, at 112, 21st plenary meeting, paras. 21–22.

81. Mr. Redondo-Gómez (Costa Rica), 2 OFFICIAL RECORDS, *supra* note 6, at 112, 21st plenary meeting, para. 26; Mrs. Adamsen (Denmark), *id.* para. 27; Mr. Nascimento e Silva (Brazil), *id.* para. 32; Mr. Escudero (Ecuador), *id.* para. 33; Mr. Rosenne (Israel), *id.* para. 38; Mr. Castren (Finland), *id.* para. 42; Mr. Eustathiades (Greece), *id.* paras. 43–44; Mr. Andersen (Iceland), *id.* para. 49; Mr. Maresca (Italy), *id.* para. 51; Mr. Galindo-Pohl (El Salvador), *id.* para. 60; Mr. Jagota (India), *id.* para. 47.

82. Mr. Seaton (Tanzania), *id*. para. 57.

83. *Id*. paras. 65–67.

84. *Id*. paras. 64, 68.

85. Final Act of the Second Peace Conference held at the Hague in 1907 and Conventions and Declarations annexed thereto, Misc. No. 6 (1908) Cd. 4175, at 59. (Emphasis added.)

86. U.S. DEP'T OF STATE, PUB. No. 2461 at 45 *et seq.* (Executives Agreement Series no. 472, 1946).

87. 75 U.N.T.S. 972.

88. 75 U.N.T.S. 973.

89. FINAL ACT OF THE NINTH INTERNATIONAL CONFERENCE OF AMERICAN STATES, BOGOTÁ, 1948, *reprinted in* [1948] U.N. Y.B. ON HUMAN RIGHTS 440–42.

90. The United Nations and Specialized Agencies instruments referred to in the text are reprinted in Human Rights. A Compilation of International Instruments of the United Nations, U.N. Doc. ST/HR/1 (1973), U.N. Publication Sales No. E.73.XIV.2.

91. *See*, e.g., European Convention on Human Rights, 1950, with Protocols, *supra* note 18; European Social Charter, 1961, European Treaty Series, No. 35, *reprinted in* [1961] U.N. Y.B. ON HUMAN RIGHTS 442; American Convention on Human Rights, 1969, *supra* note 28.

92. Art. 46 of the Geneva Convention for the Amelioration of the Condition of the Wounded and Sick in Armies in the Field of 1949, 75 U.N.T.S. 970; art. 47 of the Geneva Convention for the Amelioration of the Condition of Wounded, Sick and Shipwrecked Members of Armed Forces at Sea of 1949, 75 U.N.T.S. 971; art. 13 of the Prisoners of War Convention and art. 33 of the Civilians Convention, 75 U.N.T.S. 973.

93. Advisory Opinion on Reservations to the Convention on Genocide, [1951] I.C.J. Reports 23.

94. On December 12, 1969, the government of Greece denounced the European Convention on Human Rights. The denunciation took effect on June 13, 1970. The obligations of Greece under the Convention continued until that date. Note verbale of the permanent representative of Greece to the Secretary General of the Council of Europe of December 12, 1969, and note verbale of the Secretariat General of the Council to the permanent representative of Greece of December 17, 1969, [1969] 12 Y.B. EUR. CONV. HUMAN RIGHTS 79–85; letter from Secretary General of the Council of Europe to the Ministers of Foreign Affairs of Member States of June 24, 1970, [1970] 13 Y.B. EUR. CONV. HUMAN RIGHTS 4–5. On November 28, 1974, Greece became again a party to the European Convention on Human Rights.

95. Arts. 63, 62, 142, & 158, respectively.

96. *Id*.

97. [1963] 1 Y.B. INT'L L. COMM'N 131, 693rd meeting, para. 31. On Article 43 of the Vienna Convention see also text at notes 68 and 70 *supra*.

98. G.A. Res. 2200A (XXI), *supra* note 27.

99. The conclusion presented in the text to the effect that no right of denunciation or withdrawal may be implied by the nature of the two Covenants on Human Rights does not require strengthening by the following observation, which is presented here only for the sake of completeness:

> Sub-paragraph (b) of article 56 does not represent the codification of *lex lata*. One of its supporters praised it by saying that it "made a positive contribution to the progressive development of international law by curbing the abusive practice of perpetual treaties, the purpose of which was to impose a policy enabling the strong to dominate the weak." (Mr. Alvarez Tabio (Cuba), 2 OFFICIAL RECORDS, *supra* note 6, at 109, 21st plenary meeting, para. 86.)

The amendment inserting subparagraph 1(b) of Article 56, U.N. Doc. A/Conf. 39/

C.1/L.311, had been adopted in the Committee of the Whole of the first session (1968) of the Conference by a vote of twenty-six to twenty-five, with thirty-seven abstentions. 1 OFFICIAL RECORDS, *supra* note 6, at 343, 59th meeting of the Committee of the Whole, May 8, 1968, para. 54. Pending the entry into force of the Vienna Convention it is not yet the law and does not apply to the Human Rights Covenants (Article 4 of the Vienna Convention, "Non-retroactivity of the present Convention").

100.   U.N. Doc. A/Conf. 39/27; see *supra* note 4.

III
Institutions

Chapter 9

Judicial Policy of the Court of Justice in Developing the Legal Order of the European Communities

GERHARD BEBR

The legislative and administrative powers of the European Communities have an integrating effect which, in the long run, may make for some degree of legal unity. The numerous regulations in the field of agriculture, of free movement of labor, of competition, etc., indicate and generate new patterns of integration. The case law of the Court of Justice reveals a similar integrating pattern, though perhaps in a less apparent manner. This effect results from the Court's interpretation of the Community law, on the one hand, and from the development of legal notions proper to the Community legal order, on the other. The present study explores, through selected examples, the integrating impact of the Court's case law on the development of the Community legal order.

The views expressed herein are strictly those of the author and in no way reflect, interpret, or advocate any official policy of the European Communities. This essay was completed in December 1972.

Compared with the constitutions of traditional intergovernmental international organizations, two features of the Communities are immediately striking. First, the Treaties establishing the European Communities confer rights and impose obligations on member states and individuals alike.[1] Second, they create Community institutions with powers more or less independent of the member states.[2] These two features reveal the independent and autonomous character of the Community legal order. As a necessary and logical corollary, an independent Community judiciary— the Court of Justice of the European Communities—has been established.[3]

Within the Community legal order, the Court performs three essential functions. It ensures: (1) the legal exercise of Community powers by Community institutions on an action of a member state, an individual, or a Community institution, as the case may be;[4] (2) the respect and execution of Community obligations by member states or individuals;[5] and (3) the uniform interpretation of the provisions of Community law by national courts of member states.[6] The potentialities and limits of this integrating impact are to be seen within its realistic context. On the one hand, the EEC Treaty sets forth, to a large extent, general principles which are to be implemented by the Community institution. This offers ample room for a judicial policy which promotes integration by way of interpretation, and this policy is further facilitated by the fact that the Treaty deals primarily with economic, social, and fiscal matters, which are dynamic by their very nature. On the other hand, the degree of political cohesion within the Communities—or, more precisely, the limits of such cohesion—restricts this law-creating function of the Court, a point which should serve as a stern warning against hasty conclusions drawn from the experience of matured federations.[7]

The integrating impact of the Court's judicial policy may be particularly well observed in its case law dealing with the rights of individuals and member states within the Community legal order (see the first two parts of this essay). This impact is no less pronounced in the Court's case law promoting effective operation of the Community (see the third part of this essay). Moreover, the case law has an integrating impact on the national courts applying Community law, an aspect to be examined in the last part of this essay.

The Individual in the Community Legal Order

The Court has shown particular concern for the judicial protection of individuals within the Community legal order. This protection has two different aspects: one is directed against illegal acts on the part of Community institutions, the other against a member state's failure to execute its Community obligations.

Individuals may bring before the Court of Justice an action for annulment against allegedly illegal acts of Community institutions.[8] The Court always has stressed that the provisions concerning the judicial protection of individuals are to be interpreted extensively, and it has further enhanced its competence by developing a wide notion of a binding Community act. By such means the Court has facilitated the access of individuals to the Community jurisdiction, and the importance of this integrating factor may be fully appreciated if it is realized that only the Court may review the legality of Community acts.

As the EEC Treaty assures no protection for the individual against a member state's failure to respect and execute its Community obligations, the Court itself has created and developed such protection. By extensively interpreting Treaty provisions deemed "directly applicable," the Court has enabled individuals to invoke such provisions before national courts. This is one of the most conspicuous—if not the most conspicuous—examples of the integrating force which the Court's case law has so far developed.

Protection Against Illegal Acts of the Community

LIBERAL ACCESS TO THE COURT

According to Article 173, section 2 of the EEC Treaty, an individual may bring an action against a decision addressed to a third party if he is directly and individually affected in his interests. Only under these conditions does the Court admit an appeal. In the *Plaumann* case, the Court ruled that because of the silence of the Treaty these requirements may not be interpreted restrictively.[9] The *Cement* case strongly confirmed this ruling, maintaining that "silence of the provision with regard to a matter affecting the legal guarantees of individuals cannot be interpreted in a manner most unfavorable for them.[10]

NOTION OF A BINDING COMMUNITY ACT

Under specific conditions, individuals may appeal binding acts of Community institutions. The Treaty, however, fails to define the essential elements constituting a binding act, a vital requirement on which the admission of an action depends.

The *Cement* case[11] dealt with this question in the field of competition. Acting on Article 85(1), which prohibits agreements among enterprises which purport to or actually prevent, restrain, or distort competition within the intrastate trade, the EEC Commission, in a preliminary examination, found an agreement likely to violate this prohibition. The competent Directorate General of the Commission informed the concerned enterprises that the agreement could no longer benefit from the provision of Article 15(6) of Regulation No. 17, according to which agreements duly notified to the EEC Commission are exempted from the imposition of possible fines. The enterprises were informed that fines may be imposed in the future should the agreement ultimately be found in violation of Article 85(1).

Article 15(6) of Regulation No. 17, according to which such a benefit may be withdrawn, requires that the concerned enterprises be informed by the Commission accordingly. In the given instance, the action of the enterprises against the legality of such a communication of the Commission concerned primarily its legal character. If this communication had been considered as a mere information lacking any binding force, the action would not have been admissible. But the Court evidently wished to avoid this result. Following its well-established policy of favoring liberal access of individuals to its jurisdiction, the Court considered the communication to be a binding decision, admitted the action, and heard the case. In the opinion of the Court, the EEC Commission communication deprived the enterprises of a temporary benefit as offered by Article 15(6) of Regulation No. 17:

> Thus this measure affects the interests of the enterprises. . . . [I]t brings about a definite change in their legal situation. By means of the disputed act the Commission, in an unequivocal manner, issued a measure producing legal effects on the interests of the enterprises concerned and imposing obligations on them. This act, therefore, is not merely an opinion, but a decision.[12]

According to the case law of the Court, it is the material content and not the form of an act which predetermines its legal nature.[13] The *Cement* case advances this jurisprudence further insofar as it relates the binding force of an act to the possible consequences for the parties concerned, irrespective of its formal appearance.

DUE PROCESS OF LAW

According to Article 85(3) of the EEC Treaty, enterprises may request, under specific conditions, an exemption from the restraint of competition prohibition of Article 85(1). Such a request must, of course, be substantiated. In one instance, a decision of the Commission was appealed which refused to grant such an exemption because the concerned enterprise had failed to prove that the required conditions had been met. The Court dismissed this argument of the Commission, maintaining that the concerned enterprises had a right to "adequate examination" of their request by the Commission. "The Commission may not simply confine itself to asking the enterprise to prove that the conditions required for the exemption are fulfilled," observed the Court, "but must contribute to the establishment of relevant facts and circumstances in accordance with administrative principles and the means available to it."[14]

Protection Against Member States' Failure to Execute
Community Obligations

COMMUNITY PROVISIONS "DIRECTLY APPLICABLE"

The Court's policy of assuring effective and wide judicial protection of individuals is clearly articulated in the case law declaring some Treaty provisions "directly applicable." According to the EEC Treaty, member states have, in general, two kinds of obligations. First, they are to abstain from introducing measures which would interfere with the pursuit of Community objectives and which are, therefore, prohibited. Thus, member states may not introduce any new customs duties or equivalent charges on importation or exportation,[15] or any new quantitative restrictions.[16] Second, member states must modify or abolish, within a determined period, measures existing at the time the Treaty entered into force which are considered incompatible with Community obligations, as, for example, quantitative restrictions or charges having equivalent effect.[17]

Member states execute these and other Community obligations under the control of the Court upon an action of the EEC Commission. If a member state fails in one of its obligations, the Commission, according to Article 169 of the EEC Treaty, may bring an action against such an allegedly defaulting state, before the Court of Justice, with a view to having such a violation determined. The member state must comply with the Court's judgment and repeal or modify its legislation in order to make it conform with Community obligations. Ultimately, individuals may benefit from a member state's compliance with the Court's judgment. This procedure, however, is time-consuming, and its initiation, moreover, is at the discretion of the Commission.[18] This drawback has prompted the Court to innovate means for more effective and immediate protection of individuals against violation of Community obligations by member states. It has recognized the right of individuals to invoke Treaty provisions before the competent national court of the member state acting in violation.[19] But this right of individuals is not unlimited; the Court admits it only if the Treaty provisions establishing the obligation of the member states are directly applicable. Hence, this individual protection depends on the nature and extent of a Treaty provision deemed "directly applicable," as interpreted and developed by the Court.[20]

The procedure of Article 169, initiated by the EEC Commission, and the procedure of Article 177, under which the Court may declare a Treaty provision "directly applicable," are independent and parallel and were conceived to serve two different purposes.[21] The procedure of Article 169 seeks to assure the execution of Community obligations by member states. The envisaged purpose of the procedure of Article 177 has been to ensure a uniform interpretation of Community law by national courts.[22] Declaring the Treaty provision "directly applicable," the Court has in fact widened the purpose of this procedure. It has utilized the procedure of Article 177 to secure immediate indirect protection of individuals against a member state's failure to respect Community obligations.[23]

The significance and function of a "directly applicable" provision for the protection of individuals becomes evident if the procedures of Articles 169 and 177 are briefly contrasted. According to Article 169, the EEC Commission may bring an action against an allegedly defaulting member state. In this instance of an adversary proceeding, the Court not only interprets but applies the Community law. Under Article 177, in contrast, a national court, in a pending litigation, may ask the Court for an interpretation of a provision of the Community law;[24] the request also may concern interpretation of the legal nature of a Community provision and its legal consequences. Under this procedure, the Court merely interprets a provision of the Community law in binding manner; its application rests with the national court concerned. But by declaring a Treaty provision "directly applicable," the Court seeks in fact to assure the application of a Community provision by a national court, notwithstanding a contrary provision of a national law. In this instance, the Court recognizes Community rights of individuals which national courts are to respect.

In the *Tariefcommissie* case,[25] the Court declared that Article 12 of the EEC Treaty, which prohibits member states from introducing new customs duties, was "directly applicable" in the sense that individuals might invoke the prohibition before national courts.[26] In the concrete case, this means that the national court must respect and apply the Community prohibition and abstain from applying a national law contrary to Article 12. This remarkable ruling calls for some observation. Article 12 speaks explicitly in terms of an obligation of member states. If the traditional rule of interpretation of international courts were strictly followed, the formulation of this obligation alone would have exercised a strong presumption against its direct application. Deliberately disregarding so narrow an interpretation, the Court took instead the legal nature of the Community legal order as the starting point of its reasoning. Characterizing it as a new order, to which individuals as well as member states are subject, the Court stressed the effect the operation of the Common Market may have on individuals.[27] Individuals enjoy rights not only when explicitly provided for by the Treaty, reasoned the Court, but also in instances in which member states or Community institutions are obliged to act.[28]

The Court does not, of course, consider every Treaty provision establishing an obligation on member states to be "directly applicable"; it has developed criteria for determining the direct applicability of Treaty provisions only gradually. Generally, a Treaty provision is "directly applicable" if it is clear in its meaning,[29] unconditional, and one which re-

quires for its application no further action either by the Community institution or by a member state.[30] This doctrine was first elaborated in cases
in which a member state violated its obligation to refrain from prohibited
measures, where it was relatively easy for the Court to determine the
nature of the obligation.

But the Court has gone still further. In the *Lütticke* case,[31] it found
"directly applicable" even the Treaty provision of Article 95(3), which
requires *positive* measures on the part of member states. According to
this provision, member states were to amend or abolish, as of January
1962, those internal fiscal charges imposed on imported products which
were higher than those imposed on similar domestic products. In the case
of a member state's obligation to take positive action, the Court considers
such a Treaty provision "directly applicable" only if the states have practically no discretion in executing them.[32]

The question of the direct application of a provision also may be
raised with regard to various binding Community acts. Community institutions have at their disposal three kinds of binding acts whose content and
legal effects differ. According to Article 189, a "regulation" has a general
application. It is binding in every respect and "directly applicable" in each
member state; it is a Community act whose application requires no further
measures on the part of the member states. In contrast, a "directive" binds
the concerned member state only as to the objectives to be obtained; choice
as to the form and means of achieving them is left to the discretion of the
state. A "decision" is binding "in every respect" on the addressee—be the
addressee a member state or an individual.

Direct application of a regulation is thus explicitly assured by the
Treaty itself. As to the direct application of a directive or a decision addressed to a member state, however, the Treaty is silent. Literally, Article
189 seems to exclude their direct application; yet the Court has not hesi-
tated to extend its case law on "directly applicable" Treaty provisions to
provisions of directives and decisions. Hence, individuals may invoke them
before national courts.[33] "Admittedly, according to Article 189, regulations
are 'directly applicable' and may, therefore, because of their legal nature,
discharge immediate effects. However," the Court reasoned, "one may not
deduce from this that the other categories of acts mentioned in this article
could never discharge similar effects."[34] This fundamental ruling of the
Court may well mark a new turning point in the development of "directly
applicable" provisions. It suffices to recall the increasing number of directives and decisions addressed to member states to understand the far-
reaching consequences of this ruling for the promotion of the protection
of individuals.

The intent of promoting the protection of individuals and, at the same
time, of assuring respect for Community obligations by member states
has evidently prompted the Court to exploit the provisions of Article 189.

These two vital considerations seem to have carried greater weight with the Court than the mere formal wording of this Article. Note, for example, the Court's revealing remark that in the case of a decision of the Community institutions obliging one or all member states to take a certain measure "its useful effect [*effet utile*] would be weakened if nationals of the State concerned could not invoke it and if national courts could not consider it as a part of Community law."[35] In the given instance, the Court dealt primarily with a direct application of a decision. Its reasoning was based almost exclusively on the nature of a decision which is "binding in every respect," to whomever it may be addressed. This, it seems, considerably facilitated the Court's task in declaring a provision of a decision addressed to a member state "directly applicable." In a later case, the Court did not hesitate to declare "directly applicable" a provision of a directive determining an earlier deadline for the execution of a specific Treaty obligation.[36] However, its reasoning seemed strongly influenced by the fact that the relevant Treaty provisions had been considered "directly applicable" as well.

But the Court imposes two restrictions on a possible direct application of a decision or directive: first, only specific provisions and not entire acts will be recognized as "directly applicable"; second, only those provisions of a decision or directive which meet the criteria already developed by the Court will be "directly applicable."[37] Three factors account for the powerful integrating effect implicit in a "directly applicable" provision, be it of the Treaty or of a binding Community act. First, an individual may invoke such a provision before a national court, even if the national law which the member state failed to repeal or modify is contrary to it; the national court must set aside the national law and apply the Community law instead. Second, an individual derives rights from a "directly applicable" Community provision which national courts must respect. And third, a "directly applicable" Treaty provision enjoys the same legal force throughout the Community.[38] National courts of all member states must consider and apply it in the same manner.

A provision of the Community law which is characterized as "directly applicable" is a subtle and flexible judicial instrument for fostering and consolidating the Community legal order. At the moment, it is perhaps the most powerful instrument of integration the Court has at its disposal.

MATERIAL COMMUNITY RIGHTS OF INDIVIDUALS

The interpretation of the material rights of individuals also reflects the integrating impact of the Court's case law. Its case law dealing with the free movement within the Community of workers who are nationals of member states, as provided for by the EEC Treaty, well illustrates the Court's policy of broadening these rights.[39] The free movement of goods and services within the Community is, in the view of the Court, as much the "foundation" of the Community as the free movement of workers across national boundaries,[40] and to promote the Community the Court has interpreted broadly some provisions of Regulation Nos. 3 and 4. Particularly noteworthy is its opinion according to which the concept of a migratory worker is one of Community law and not national law.[41] This ruling has had far-reaching consequences. By declaring the concept to be one of Community law, the Court reserves for itself the ultimate competence to interpret it and to give it Community meaning. Since this notion forms a part of the Community law, no member state may modify or change it, as it could if it had remained part of individual national legal orders.[42] By widely interpreting the meaning of a migratory worker, the Court has thus enhanced the right to free movement. Moreover, specific provisions of the Regulations were applicable, according to the Court, to persons who could not qualify as migratory workers in the technical sense.[43] The Court even found some provisions of the Regulation applicable to a visitor from another member state.[44]

To assure free movement of workers, Article 48 of the EEC Treaty prohibits discrimination based on nationality between workers of the member states, as regards "employment, remuneration and other working conditions." The Treaty requires equal treatment of the nationals of member states as to the application of the labor law by the receiving member state. In one instance, the Court expressly confirmed the right of a national of a member state to claim certain social benefits accorded by a law of the receiving member state to its own nationals:[45] "The social law of the Community law," the Court observed, "is based on the principle that the legal system of each member State must ensure for nationals of the other member States working within its territory all the legal rights that it grants to its own nationals."[46]

Although these examples indicate the tendency of the Court to strengthen the Community rights of individuals, their importance should not be overestimated. At the moment, their significance lies in the fact that the trend has emerged at all.

The Member States in the Community Legal Order

The integration of the member states into the Community legal order is, in view of traditional prerogatives, a delicate and difficult task. The Treaties contain practically no explicit Community clause defining Community matters, nor do they always clearly allocate the judicial and legislative competences between the Community and the member states. The Court, however, has begun to clarify this vital issue.

In the judicial field, the Court encountered no particular difficulty in delimiting the respective competences for review of the legality of Community acts and interpretation of provisions of the Community law (the Treaty and the Community acts). The exclusive competence of the Court in reviewing the legality of Community acts is clearly established by the Treaties themselves. But the competence of the Court to interpret provisions of Community law, as set forth in Article 177 of the EEC Treaty, is vague on a few points. According to this provision, any national court may—if it is a court of last instance, it must—request an interpretation of a Community provision by the Court, provided its intepretation is decisive for the outcome of the litigation pending before that national court. Acting under this jurisdiction, the Court has decided two different questions.

First, it has delimited its competence with regard to national courts. Repeatedly and emphatically, the Court has stated that under this procedure it merely interprets provisions of Community law—not national law—in an abstract manner;[47] the competence of national courts over national law remains intact.

Second, the Court has had to define the legal force of its preliminary rulings interpreting provisions of the Community law. Although the EEC Treaty makes no provision in this connection, the purpose of its Article 177 of assuring uniform interpretation and application of the Community law by national courts has prompted the Court to declare its interpretation to be binding on the national court concerned.[48] Thus, the Court has developed the preliminary ruling into a convenient instrument of integration. The impact of this ruling increases proportionally with the growth of Community legislation. This, in turn, widens the scope for judicial integration.

> The transfer by the States, from their internal legal systems over to the Community legal order, of rights and obligations to reflect those set forth in the Treaty . . . entails a definite limitation of their sovereign rights, against which a subsequent unilateral act that would be incompatible with the Community concept cannot be asserted. . . .[49]

This rather general principle has been refined by the Court in several cases dealing with the extent of continuing competence of member states in sectors over which the Community has enacted regulations.[50] The question has been whether a member state implementing the regulations could amend or complete the Community-prescribed tariff positions. The Court has categorically denied such competence, stressing the exclusive competence of the Community in this matter. As the regulations are directly applicable in all member states, they may not "take measures in execution of the regulations which would modify their scope of application or amend their provision. . . ."[51] Furthermore, "to the extent the member States have transferred legislative powers to the Community in the field of tariff matters, so as to assure the operation of the common agricultural market, they may no longer pass normative acts within this field."[52]

Following this line of argument, the Court has reasserted the exclusive competence of the Community in its external relations, even in those instances not explicitly provided for by the EEC Treaty.[53] In the Court's view, the competence of Community institutions within the Community implies their competence also in external relations, provided the Community institutions had acted within the Community. Such competence logically follows from the Treaty provisions and the Community acts regulating certain fields within the Community; it is impossible, reasons the Court, to dissociate the provisions governing intra-Community matters from those necessary for the Community's external relations.[54]

The implications of these precedents are far-reaching. The Community legislative and treaty-making powers, as determined by the Treaty, preclude national legislation and treaty-making powers within specific areas.[55] This transfer of powers to the Community implies the supremacy of Community law over national law, as will be shown subsequently.

The nature of the Community obligations of member states corresponds to the new legal order of the Community. As the Treaty makes no provision to this effect, one might consider them as mutual obligations of the states parties to the treaties. In one instance, a member state tried to justify its alleged violation of its Community obligation, arguing that the Council of Ministers itself disregarded it.[56] Dismissing this argument, the Court pointed out that the EEC Treaty created more than a mere mutual commitment among the various subjects of the Community legal order; it established a new legal order, the violation of which is to be determined by Community procedures. "[E]xcept for cases expressly provided for," the Court ruled, "the Treaty basically prohibits the member States from being their own judges."[57]

Promotion of Community Objectives

Two essential considerations have guided the Court in promoting Community objectives. The Court has persistently interpreted the Community provision in the light of fundamental Treaty objectives, thereby endorsing their Community function. Also, the Court always has advanced an interpretation promoting an effective operation of the Community.[58]

Aside from Articles 5 and 189, the EEC Treaty contains no explicit and formal "supremacy" clause. The Court has been fully aware, however, of the need for such supremacy as a prerequisite for effective operation of the Community. In the bold and remarkable ruling of the *ENEL* case, the Court stated that "it would be impossible legally to assert any internal text whatsoever against the law created by the Treaty . . . without robbing it of its Community nature and without jeopardizing the legal foundation of the Community itself. . . ." [59] The Court deduced the supremacy of the

Community law from the legal character of the Community legal order, from the transfer of limited state powers to the Community, and from the wording and spirit of the Treaty.

> This incorporation into the law of each member country of provisions of a Community origin, and the letter and spirit of the Treaty in general, have as a corollary the impossibility for the States to assert as against a legal order accepted by them on a reciprocal basis a subsequent unilateral measure which could not be challenged by it.[60]

Such a conflict, reasoned the Court, could not be resolved in the traditional manner on the basis of the respective constitutional provisions of member states. This would lead to different results, depending on the various constitutional provisions of the member states, and would violate Article 7 of the EEC Treaty, which prohibits "any discrimination on grounds of nationality." The Court found an additional ground for the supremacy of the Community law in the provisions of Article 189, which makes regulations "binding in every respect and 'directly applicable' in each member State."

The Court confirmed this law-creative judgment in the *San Michele* case.[61] Although this decision does not refer to the *ENEL* case, its reasoning is even more persuasive and more forceful and leaves no doubt about the supremacy of Community law. All the member states became parties to the Treaty "under the same conditions, definitely and without exception," the Court observed.[62] The ratification law, therefore, may not introduce a discrimination which is prohibited by the Treaty itself. If the relation of Community law were determined according to the various national laws, concluded the Court, this would necessarily create a discrimination contrary to the "public order" of the Community.[63]

In the *Internationale Handelsgesellschaft* case, the Court did not hesitate to uphold the supremacy of Community law even over national constitutional law.[64] In the strong words of the Court:

> The uniform validity of Community law would be impaired if a decision reviewing the validity of Community acts of the Community institutions would apply norms or principles of national law. The validity of Community acts may be reviewed in the light of Community law only. . . .[65]

Consequently, reasoned the Court,

> no provisions of national law, of whatever nature they may be, may prevail over Community law . . . lest it be deprived of its character as Community law and its very legal foundation be endangered. The validity of a Community act or its application in a member State remains, there-

fore, unimpaired, even if it is charged that the basic rights . . . or the national constitution were violated.[66]

In the *Lück* case,[67] the Court dealt with the legal consequences of the supremacy of the Treaty. According to the Court, Article 95, considered "directly applicable," precludes *application* of national provisions contrary to its prohibition.

Compared with the *ENEL* case, the other cases appear less spectacular. Nevertheless, they have an important bearing on the effective pursuit of Community objectives.

The Court interprets Treaty provisions concerning the elimination of state barriers and obstacles to the free movement of goods along the same line. Articles 9 through 12 of the EEC Treaty prohibit member states from introducing new customs duties or equivalent charges, but they do not define them. The Court has concluded that the *actual* effect that the customs duties or their equivalent may have on the free movement of goods is decisive.[68]

The Court has developed a similar view of charges equivalent to customs duties, *i.e.,* charges which restrain the free movement of goods across national boundaries. It also has excluded measures in place of the prohibited customs duties which could restrict such free circulation of goods. Such charges include "not only those measures which openly take on the classic customs form, but also those which, presented under other names, or introduced through other routes, would have the same discriminatory or protectionist effect as customs duties."[69] A charge has this effect "regardless of . . . the manner in which it may be levied. . . ."[70] But these charges were deemed equivalent to a customs duty only if they had the discriminatory or protectionist effect of a customs duty. A charge having no such effect would not be prohibited even though it might interfere with the free movement of goods. This is merely the consequence of relating these charges to the primary function of a customs duty. Nevertheless, the Court's extensive interpretation of charges equivalent to customs duties was impaired by this limitation, and, wishing to assure the freest movements of goods, the Court finally dropped it. Its new consideration as to the potential harmful effect of such charges was clearly stated in the *Diamond* case:

> [A]ny pecuniary charge, however slight, which is imposed unilaterally on national or foreign goods by reason of the fact that they cross a national border, and which is not stricto sensu a customs duty, is a tax of equivalent effect within the meaning of Articles 9 and 12 of the Treaty . . . even if its proceeds are not paid over to the State, even if it has no discriminatory or protective effects and even if the product so taxed does not compete with any similar product of national manufacture.[71]

Even the permitted temporary exemptions to the fundamental Treaty obligations of the member states have been interpreted restrictively. According to Article 226 of the EEC Treaty, a member state can take safeguarding measures during the transitory period, provided such measures previously were authorized by the EEC Commission. The Court has insisted on strict observation of a member state's obligation to obtain this prior authorization by the Commission, requiring them not to take these measures on their own.[72]

In violation of Article 226, a member state took safeguarding measures without prior Commission authorization. When a case was lodged by the Commission, the member state attempted to have it suspended, meanwhile requesting the Commission to approve the safeguarding measure already taken. The Court dismissed the request. "If it were possible to arrest the application of Article 169 by means of a request for an approval of safeguarding measures," the Court concluded, "such a provision would lose all its effectiveness." [73]

The Court also has interpreted Article 36 restrictively. According to the Court, member states may, for reasons of "public morality, public order, public safety," etc., restrict or prohibit importation, exportation, or transit.[74] However, in addition to the elimination of state barriers to the free movement of goods, the Court has been concerned with obstacles to interstate trade which private parties may maintain or establish by way of agreement.[75] These obstacles, of course, are different from state barriers, as are the conditions and extent to which they are prohibited by the Treaty. Article 85(1) of the EEC Treaty prohibits agreements or concerted practices among enterprises which are "likely to affect trade among the member States" and which, furthermore, have "as their object or result the prevention, restriction or distortion of competition. . . ."

The concept of interstate trade likely to be affected can serve as a convenient vehicle for promoting integration. For the Court, the purpose of this concept is "to separate the respective fields of application of Community law and of national law in the matter of cartel law."[76] It is thus a concept establishing the competence of the Community. The Court first examines whether the agreement is likely to affect interstate trade and then proceeds to examine its harmful effect on competition, interpreting Article 85(1) extensively—an interpretation which is supported by its very wording, "likely to affect." Thus, not only an actual but a potential influence on interstate trade is sufficient, in the view of the Court, to establish the competence of the Community.[77] The Court weighs the actual or potential effect of an agreement or concerted practice on interstate trade against the realization of the Common Market among the member states. What is decisive is "whether the agreement directly or indirectly, actually or potentially is capable of jeopardizing freedom of trade between the member States in such a manner as to prejudice the realization of the objective of a single market between States."[78] In *Maschinenbau Ulm,* the Court stressed the point emphatically, observing that the prohibition of an agreement depends on whether or not "it is capable of partitioning the market in certain products between member States and of thus rendering the economic interpenetration sought by the Treaty more difficult."[79] However, the fact that an agreement is likely to affect interstate trade is not in itself sufficient ground for its prohibition.[80] Therefore, to be prohibited, the agreement must have "the object or result [of] the prevention, restriction or distortion of competition within the Common Market," being "merely alternative conditions."[81] If the purpose of the agreement is evident, an examination of the harmful effects on competition is not necessary, and if its purpose cannot be inferred from the agreement, its actual effects must be examined.[82] "[I]f, however, an analysis of these [agreement] clauses does not reveal a sufficient degree of injury to competition, then the effects of the agreement must be examined."[83]

The Court views restraint or distortion of competition broadly. The prohibition of Article 85(1) applies to horizontal and vertical agreements alike,[84] and restraints or distortions of competition are examined with regard to the parties to the agreement, as well as to third parties.[85] Also, seeking to ensure effective competition in the interstate trade, the Court has been more concerned with economic realities than with the formal legal personality of the enterprises involved. In the *Dyestuff* case,[86] the Court upheld a decision of the EEC Commission imposing fines on Swiss and British companies (companies whose registered offices were outside the Community) for having participated, together with other enterprises of the member states, in a concerted practice by means of which the sales price for certain dyestuff was uniformly increased within the Common Market. On the order or instruction of the Swiss and British parent companies, the subsidiaries located within the Community, partly or wholly owned by these companies, but having their distinct legal personality, carried out the increase of the sales price. Dealing with the plaintiff's argument which challenged the Commission's competence to impose sanctions on third state companies, the Court, after realistic examination of the facts involved, refused to attach any significance to the formal legal separation of the companies within and outside the Community. The Court took the economic ties existing between the subsidiary and parent company as a starting point for its consideration, and thereafter concluded:

> The fact that the subsidiary has a distinct legal personality does not suffice to dispose of the possibility that its behaviour might be imputed to the parent company. . . . In view of the unity of the group thus formed, the activities may, in certain circumstances, be imputed to the parent company. . . . Thus it is indeed the applicant which carried out the concerted practice within the Common Market.[87]

Under the EEC Treaty, the sanction for violating the prohibition of Article 85(1) is that the offending agreement "was to be null and void." The *Grundig* case introduced a more flexible and differentiated approach.[88] The Court nullified only that part of the agreement which fell under the prohibition of Article 85(1); its remaining parts rest valid. The entire agreement becomes null, it would seem, only if the prohibited part of the agreement may not be severed from the whole.

Impact of the Case Law of the Court on National Courts

National courts interpret and apply the provisions of the Community law, but frequently they follow interpretations given by the Court in other cases. They are not bound to do this, since a preliminary interpretative ruling of the Court technically binds only the national court which requested it. In practice, however, such rulings carry much greater weight. In several decisions, national courts have referred, explicitly or implicitly, to the fundamental rulings of the Court upholding the supremacy of Community law or declaring a Treaty provision "directly applicable."

Supremacy of the Community Law

Several German courts, facing a conflict between German law and Community law, have upheld the latter. Their decisions have been based on the ruling in the *ENEL* case.

A decision of the Finanzgericht (Financial Tribunal) of the Saar is typical.[89] The case concerned the application of Article 95 of the EEC Treaty, which provides for equal treatment of imported products and identical or similar domestic products insofar as internal fiscal charges are concerned. Explicitly referring to the *ENEL* case, the tribunal upheld the supremacy of the provisions of Article 95 over the *subsequent* German law which modified the law on turnover tax. In a previous request for a preliminary ruling of the Court, the tribunal had considered the Treaty as an ordinary law,[90] basing its supremacy over prior national law on the traditional principle *lex posterior derogat*. Referring to the decision of the Court in the *ENEL* case, the Tribunal repudiated its earlier traditional view and concluded that Treaty provisions deemed "directly applicable" could not be assimilated to provisions of an ordinary law because in such an instance the subsequent national law would prevail over the Community law. That solution could not do justice to the pursuit of Community objectives.

A decision of the *Verwaltungsgericht* (Administrative Tribunal) of Frankfurt also echoes the ruling of the *ENEL* case.[91] Dealing with a conflict between an agricultural regulation of the Council and a subsequent regulation of the German Federal Minister of Agriculture, the tribunal upheld the supremacy of the Council's regulation. In its view, the Council's regulation was

> a higher legal norm than the federal regulation and therefore prevails . . . . This higher legal status of the Community regulation may be deduced from its legal nature as a norm of the Community legal order . . . . According to the prevailing doctrine and case law . . . the Community law prevails, in principle, over an ordinary national law.[92]

In considering the effect of supremacy of Community law on national law, the tribunal has said that

> the autonomy of the Community law prohibits its explicit or implicit derogation by the member States . . . . The objective of the EEC Treaty . . . to create, within a specific sector, a uniform law binding on all member States, would be endangered if they could modify this uniform law.[93]

A decision of the *Bundesverfassungsgericht* (Federal Constitutional Court) also illustrates the impact of the Court's case law.[94] A constitutional complaint had been brought before the constitutional court against two Community regulations, charging that their provisions violated certain fundamental rights as guaranteed by the German Constitution. Referring to the *ENEL* case, the constitutional court declared that Community law and national laws of the member states represent two different legal orders. The Community legal order, being autonomous, provides for its own system of judicial protection, the constitutional court observed, and considering the legal nature of the Community, its acts are not acts of German public authorities. Hence, the constitutional complaint was held inadmissible. Because autonomous and independent powers of the Community were created, the constitutional court continued, its acts need not be approved or ratified by the member states, and member states may not repeal them. In a 1971 decision, the constitutional court was even more explicit, as it maintained that "directly applicable" Community provisions prevail and displace contrary national law.[95]

The Court's case law has influenced similar developments in other member states. In a 1964 judgment, the Italian Constitutional Court declared that the EEC Treaty, once ratified by an ordinary law, acquired the force of an ordinary law as well.[96] In this case, the constitutionality of the Italian nationalization law, adopted after the Treaty entered into force, was contested as being contrary to some Treaty provisions. The constitutional court dismissed the charge on the ground that the case raised no constitutional issue. In its view, the case did not concern the relation of the EEC Treaty to the Constitution, but merely the relation of a law ratifying the Treaty to a subsequent law. In case of a conflict between the two laws, the Court concluded the latter had to prevail.

In its *San Michele* decision, however, the constitutional court, influenced by the *ENEL* case, seems to have abandoned its previous view and adopted a more subtle stand.[97] The constitutionality of the judicial powers of the Court of Justice under the ECSC Treaty was contested on grounds that certain provisions of the ECSC Treaty,[98] which establish an exclusive review jurisdiction of the Court over the legality of Community acts and their execution by national courts, violated specific Italian constitutional provisions requiring that the judicial function be exercised by regularly appointed judges.[99] The constitutional court dismissed these charges as unfounded and upheld the constitutionality of the challenged Treaty provisions. It availed itself of the *ENEL* decision's characterization of the Community legal order as an autonomous, independent legal order; national constitutional provisions are not applicable within the independent and autonomous legal order of the Community.

The Tribunale Civile of Brescia has ruled in similar vein, observing that "it is unanimously recognized . . . that a conflict between Community and national norms must be resolved in favour of the principle of supremacy as provided for by article 189. . . ."[100] In 1972 this view was confirmed *more explicitly* by the same tribunal, even with regard to subsequent national law contrary to Community law.[101]

Inspired by the *ENEL* case, a 1971 decision of the Belgian Cour de Cassation, the highest Belgian court, showed the same tendency, recognizing the supremacy of the Community law.[102]

Treaty Provisions "Directly Applicable"

In rulings which have had considerable impact on national courts, the Court has declared several EEC Treaty provisions "directly applicable" as a means of protecting individuals before national courts.[103] For example, the rulings of the Court declaring the provisions of Article 95 "directly applicable" have exercised a significant impact on the fiscal competence of member states. Because of the sacrosanct competence of the member states in this particularly sensitive field, national courts might have been expected to oppose such far-reaching rulings, the Treaty notwithstanding. But the contrary is true, as an inquiry into Article 95 shows.

Article 95 commits member states in two ways. Member states are to treat imported products on an equal basis with identical or similar domestic products as far as fiscal charges are concerned. Thus, member states may not introduce any new fiscal charges which would discriminate against imported products. Furthermore, member states must "abolish or amend," as of January 1, 1962, those provisions which existed at the time the

Treaty entered into force and which are contrary to the principle of equal treatment, as stated by Article 95(1). Both obligations of the member states, according to the Court, are "directly applicable."

A 1969 decision of the Bundesfinanzhof, the highest German tribunal in tax matters, followed this ruling of the Court.[104] The case concerned the rate of a compensatory tax imposed on an imported agricultural product for a member state. The high tribunal found the rate to have violated the nondiscrimination prohibition of Article 95(1), arriving at this conclusion because "a national court must, in case of a provision of the EEC Treaty which is 'directly applicable,' afford a judicial protection to the individual, as the Court of Justice decided in the case No. 57/65 concerning the effect of article 95. . . ."[105]

The protective function of a "directly applicable" Treaty provision, which has been stressed by the Court in its preliminary rulings, is particularly well demonstrated by a 1968 decision of the Finanzgericht (Financial Tribunal) of Münster.[106] In this instance, the tribunal had to deal with the direct application of Article 95(3), which obliges member states to abolish or amend existing discrimination against imported products insofar as internal fiscal charges are concerned. Here, the member state failed to amend its legislation. Following the preliminary ruling the Court of Justice in the *Molkerei-Zentrale* case, the tribunal held this obligation "directly applicable," so that individuals could invoke its violation: "If a national judge finds a conflict between a national provision and article 95 of the EEC Treaty, an individual may request from the national court to be placed in such a position as if the member State had fulfilled its Treaty obligations to legislate. . . ."[107]

Conclusion

Without the unceasing support of its Court of Justice, the Community legal order, envisaged as a uniform body of law, might have remained static at best. At worst, the Community Treaties might have degenerated into traditional international treaties interpreted and applied in accordance with traditional principles of international law, becoming more diverse in each national arena. From the outset the Court has prevented such a development. Inspired and guided by Community objectives, the Court has set out to orient the development of Community law in an entirely new direction. Quite pragmatically, it has linked the development of the Community legal order to the objectives sought. The great emphasis the Court always has placed on the new legal character of the Community or on the nature of the Community obligations of the member states are persuasive examples of this policy. Of course, it certainly would be misleading to overestimate the potential inherent in the integrating force of the Court's case law. But it would be equally misleading to ignore the steady and inconspicuous two-pronged approach of the Court toward integration.

Within the Community legal order itself, the Court has helped to promote and consolidate the development of a uniform law and to further its effectiveness by interpreting the provisions of the Community law extensively. The integrating effect is even more strongly reflected in the Court's decisions concerning the penetration of the Community law into the legal systems of the member states and its supremacy over national law. A uniform intepretation of material provisions of the Community law certainly is of considerable importance for its development.

Of vital and even greater importance, however, is the determined supremacy of Community law which enables the Community to function properly by excluding the application of a national law contrary to it. While Community law prevails only if its provisions are "directly applicable," its supremacy is implicit in a provision deemed "directly applicable" (for which purpose the Court developed the notion). It is particularly in this field that the Court may be expected to carry on the process of legal integration, for the Court has related its development to the actual growth of Community law.[108] From this perspective, a Court decision which determines direct application of some provisions of a decision addressed to a member state [109] assumes particular importance, anticipating, as it does, a case law which strengthens the process of integration. There are at least three doctrines which the Court could utilize for this purpose.

First, while there are other specific Treaty provisions prohibiting discrimination in various fields,[110] Article 7, prohibiting any discrimination based on nationality, is comparatively general. The field of possible application of Article 7 is thus wide. Should an occasion present itself, the Court could well declare this prohibition "directly applicable," although it might not entirely satisfy the requirements of a provision "directly applicable" so far developed.

Second, the expiration of the transitional period also may have some important bearing on this problem.[111] Some Treaty provisions may become "directly applicable" by the mere fact that the transitional period expired, provided they meet the requirements of a provision deemed "directly applicable."

Third, a judgment of the Court declaring a member state in violation of its Community obligations could serve as a particularly powerful integrating factor, an aspect which has thus far gone rather unnoticed. According to Article 171, a member state must implement such a judgment, but this implementation may sometimes require a considerable length of time, depending on the nature of the violation and on the measures to be taken by the member state. Could the judgment meanwhile be devoid of effect within the national legal system of that state, and will national courts continue to apply a national law which the Court already has found to be contrary to the Community obligations?[112] Such a judgment could have direct and immediate effect in concrete instances, analogous to that of a "directly applicable" provision—provided, of course, that the obligation of the member state derived from the judgment met the requirement the Court has established for a "directly applicable" provision.

Assuming that the Court finds a charge imposed by a member state to have violated Article 12 or, to cite another example, finds a law contrary to Article 48 insofar as it contains discriminatory provisions against nationals of other member states regarding employment or remuneration, the prohibitions themselves are clear and unconditional and, therefore, capable of being held "directly applicable" in national courts. Is there any reason why such a judgment of the Court, finding a violation of such a prohibition, should have no direct and immediate effect, so that individuals could invoke it long before a member state took the necessary measures?

In its judgment of July 13, 1972, the Court extended the principle of direct application of provisions of Community law even to its judgment, rendered pursuant to Article 169 of the Treaty, finding a member state in violation of its Community obligations.[113] The prolonged delay of the member state in executing such a judgment might have convinced the Court of the necessity for such a bold decision.[114] In this judgment, the Court firmly rejected the argument of the Italian government, which maintained that a violation of a "directly applicable" provision could be terminated only by a national measure repealing or modifying the national law, as required by constitutional provisions. In the Court's opinion, such a view would imply a subordination of the application of Community provisions to the law of the member states; a Community provision could not be applied as long as the national law contrary to it were not repealed or modified. To ensure the pursuit of Community objectives, the Court argued, the provisions of the Community law must be "directly applicable" and, moreover, must have the same legal force throughout the Community. Thus, no member state may invoke any obstacle to the application of the provisions of the Community law. "[I]n the given instance," the Court reasoned, "it follows from the force of the Community law, as validly determined for the Italian Republic, that national authorities are, at once, prohibited to apply provisions of national law contrary to it." National courts of the member state concerned must apply the Community provisions notwithstanding the still formally valid national law conflicting with it.

This judgment is a logical extension of the Court's persistent judicial policy seeking to ensure the supremacy of Community law and its effective operation. Two outstanding and closely related features characterize this policy, one seeking to promote the judicial protection of individuals, the other, closely related to the first, seeking to ensure an effective and rapid execution of Community obligations by member states.

The Court has gradually developed the concept of "directly applicable" provisions in the sense that individuals may invoke them before national courts—and even against their own state. In the Court's view, such provisions of the Community law create rights for individuals which national courts must safeguard against contrary national law. The Court is even inclined to develop, by its case law, *Community* rights of individuals,[115] a development which could appreciably foster the Community legal order.

The trend of the Court's judicial policy is no less remarkable in the case of the execution of its judgments by the member states. At present, it is inconceivable that the Court would declare as "unconstitutional" a law of a member state which conflicts with the Community law. The Treaty provides no legal basis for such a jurisdiction, since the Court may merely determine a violation of the Community obligations by a member state which must execute the judgment. But out of necessity, the Court has had to search for a subtle intermediary solution, a tendency well reflected in the various stages of development of its case law.

In the *Humblet* case,[116] the Court took a rather reserved stand on this point, maintaining that it may merely determine a violation of the Community law; the execution of the judgment, the Court held, rests with the member state concerned. In the *Van Gend & Loos* case,[117] however, the Court took a more flexible stand—due, presumably, to its experience with the rigid and time-consuming procedure of Article 169. In a preliminary ruling pursuant to Article 177, the Court recognized a direct application of certain provisions of the Community law in a specific instance, excluding the *application* of provisions of national law conflicting with it. Thus, the application of a provision of Community law is assured in a concrete instance, although the Court has rendered no judgment finding a violation of Community obligations by a member state.

The Court has introduced the third stage of this development by its judgment declaring charges on exports of objets d'art to violate Article 16 of the EEC Treaty.[118] This judgment prohibits *all* member state national authorities, be they judicial or administrative, from applying the national law found at the Court to be contrary to the provision deemed "directly applicable," and irrespective of whether the member state executed the judgment. A failure of the national legislature or administration to comply with the judgment *cannot* prevent an *immediate* application of the provisions of the Community law of the member state concerned. Of course, the *Objets d'art* case does not go so far as to declare the national law "unconstitutional," for which the Court lacks jurisdiction. Yet the Court has practically found the national law conflicting with the Community law inapplicable, thus assuring the application and supremacy of the provisions of the Community law. In the long run, this may be a satisfactory solution for effective operation of Community law, while formally respecting the legislative powers of the member states; it excludes possible delays and minimizes the constitutional difficulties a member state may encounter in executing a judgment.

Seen in these lights, it may be stated that the Court of Justice of the European Communities has perhaps played a greater role in developing the Community legal order than originally it was assumed or expected to do. It has reinforced the position of individuals within the Community legal order while delimiting the powers of the member states. In so doing it has more than assured "the observance of law and justice in the interpretation and application of [the EEC] Treaty" as required by its Article 164.

Notes

1. Molkerei-Zentrale Westfalen-Lippe v. Hauptzollamt Paderborn, 14 Recueil de la Jurisprudence de la Cour [hereinafter cited as Rec.] 212, 226 (Cour de Justice de la Communauté européenne 1968); Costa v. ENEL, 10 Rec. 1143, 1159 (1964); Van Gend & Loos v. Administration fiscale néerlandaise, 9 Rec. 3, 23 (1963).

2. *See, e.g.,* the Treaty establishing the European Economic Community, Mar. 25, 1957, 298 U.N.T.S. 11 [hereinafter cited as EEC Treaty], arts. 145 and 155 in connection with art. 189.

3. Treaty establishing the European Coal and Steel Community, Apr. 18, 1951, 261 U.N.T.S. 140, 1 EUR. Y.B. 359 [hereinafter cited as ECSC Treaty], art. 31; EEC Treaty art. 164; Treaty establishing the European Atomic Energy Community, Mar. 25, 1957, 298 U.N.T.S. 167, 5 EUR. Y.B. 455 [hereinafter cited as Euratom Treaty], art. 136.

5. ECSC Treaty arts. 88, 65(4), 66(5), 92; EEC Treaty arts. 169, 87 (in connection with the Council's Reg. No. 17, art. 15), 172.

6. EEC Treaty art. 177; Euratom Treaty art. 150. ECSC Treaty Article 41 provides only for a review of the validity of the Community acts, not for an interpretation of the Treaty. Unless otherwise indicated, the present study deals with the case law of the Court concerning the EEC Treaty and acts of the European Economic Community. Also, while the objectives and procedures under the respective jurisdictions of the Court differ, for the purpose of this essay such differences are treated as largely irrelevant.

7. Thus, one author proposed in 1963, only ten years after the Court was established and with a disarming ignorance of Community law, "a comparative study, historically [*sic*] and contemporaneously, of the Court of Justice and the United States Supreme Court," Miller, Book Review, 24 U. PITT. L. REV. 670, 672 (1963).

8. ECSC Treaty art. 33; EEC Treaty art. 173; Euratom Treaty art. 146. For a recent discussion of this problem see, *e.g.,* Bebr, *Recours en annulation et carence,* in DROIT DES COMMUNAUTES EUROPEENNES 309–20 (Ganshof van der Meersch ed. 1969).

9. Plaumann v. Commission CEE, 9 Rec. 199, 222 (1963). *See also* Bock v. Commission, 17 Rec. 897, 908 (1971).

10. Société Anonyme Cimenteries CBR v. Commission, 13 Rec. 94, 118 (1967). Unless otherwise indicated, the English translation used is taken from *CCH Common Market Reporter* (CCH COMM. MKT. REP.). *See also* Humblet v. Etat belge, 6 Rec. 1125, 1150 (1960).

11. Société Anonyme Cimenteries CBR v. Commission, 13 Rec. 94 (1967).

12. *Id.* at 116–17.

13. *E.g.,* Confédération nationale des Producteurs de Fruits et Légumes v. Conseil CEE, 8 Rec. 903, 918 (1962); Société Nouvelle des Usines de Pontlieue v. Haute Autorité, 7 Rec. 103, 142 (1961).

14. Consten et Grundig v. Commission, 12 Rec. 430, 501 (1966).

15. EEC Treaty art. 12.

16. EEC Treaty art. 31.

17. EEC Treaty arts. 32 & 33.

18. Thus, for example, Commission v. République Italienne, 14 Rec. 618, 625 (1968).

19. *E.g.,* Van Gend & Loos v. Administration fiscale néerlandaise, 9 Rec. 3, 24–25 (1963), forcefully confirmed by Molkerei-Zentrale Westfalen-Lippe v. Hauptzollamt Paderborn, 14 Rec. 212, 227 (1968).

20. For a detailed discussion of this problem, see Bebr, *Directly Applicable Provisions of Community Law: Development of a Community Concept,* 19 Int'l & Comp. L.Q. 257 (1970).

21. *See* Molkerei-Zentrale Westfalen-Lippe v. Hauptzollamt Paderborn, 14 Rec. 212, 227 (1968).

22. Besides a uniform interpretation of the EEC Treaty and of Community acts, the Court, according to Article 177, may also review the validity of Community acts on a request of a national court before which the act was challenged.

23. It is not quite correct to consider this procedure as a means of judicial protection of individuals, as this protection depends on the willingness of a national court to submit such a question to the Court. Individuals have no right to do so on their own behalf.

24. According to EEC Treaty Article 177(3), it must do so if it is a court of last instance.

25. *See* Van Gend & Loos v. Administration fiscale néerlandaise, 9 Rec. 3 (1963).

26. *Id.* at 25.

27. *Id.* at 23.

28. *Id.*

29. *Id.* at 24 as to art. 12; SACE v. Ministère des Finances de la République italienne, 16 Rec. 1213, 1223 (1970) (as to arts. 9 & 13(2)); Eunomia v. Ministère de l'Instruction Publique de la République italienne, 17 Rec. 811, 816 (1971) (as to arts. 9 & 16); Costa v. ENEL, 10 Rec. 1143, 1162, 1164 (1964) (as to arts. 53 & 37(2), respectively); Lütticke v. Hauptzollamt Saarlouis, 12 Rec. 294, 302–03 (1966) (as to arts. 95(1) & (3)); Fink-Frucht v. Hauptzollamt München, 14 Rec. 328, 341–42 (1968) (as to art. 95(2)); Salgoil v. Ministère du Commerce Extérieur de la République italienne, 14 Rec. 662, 673 (1968) (as to arts. 31 & 32(1)).

30. *E.g.,* Salgoil v. Ministère du Commerce Extérieur de la République italienne, 14 Rec. 662, 673 (1968); Fink-Frucht v. Hauptzollamt München, 14 Rec. 328, 341–42 (1968); Molkerei-Zentrale Westfalen-Lippe v. Hauptzollamt Paderborn, 14 Rec. 212, 226 (1968); Lütticke v. Hauptzollamt Saarlouis, 12 Rec. 294, 302 (1966); Costa v. ENEL, 10 Rec. 1143, 1162, 1164 (1964); Van Gend & Loos v. Administration fiscale néerlandaise, 9 Rec. 3, 24 (1963).

31. Lütticke v. Hauptzollamt Saarlouis, 12 Rec. 294 (1966).

32. *Id.* at 302. *See also* Salgoil v. Ministère du Commerce Extérieur de la République italienne, 14 Rec. 662, 674 (1968), in which case the Court refused a direct application of Articles 32 and 33 on the ground that these provisions leave a certain discretion to member states.

33. Grad v. Finanzamt Traunstein, 16 Rec. 825, 838 (1970).

34. *Id.* at 838 (author's translation).

35. *Id.* at 838–39 (author's translation).

36. SACE v. Ministère des Finances de la Republique italienne, 16 Rec. 1213, 1233–24 (1970).

37. Grad v. Finanzamt Traunstein, 16 Rec. 825, 838 (1970).

38. Molkerei-Zentrale Westfalen-Lippe v. Hauptzollamt Paderborn, 14 Rec. 212, 228 (1968); Salgoil v. Ministère du Commerce Extérieur de la République italienne, 14 Rec. 662, 675, (1968). *See also* Leonesio v. Ministère de l'Agriculture et des Forêts de la République italienne, 18 Rec. 287, 296 (1972); Wilhelm v. Bundeskartellamt, 15 Rec. 1, 15 (1969).

39. For further discussion of this development, see Séché, *The Revision of Regulations Nos. 3 and 4 (Social Security of Migrant Workers) in the Light of their Interpretation by the Court of Justice*, 6 Comm. Mkt L.R. 170 (1969).

40. Unger v. Bestuur der Bedrijfsvereniging voor Detailhandel, 10 Rec. 349, 362 (1964).

41. *Id.* at 362.

42. *Id.* at 363.

43. *Id.*

44. Hessische Knappschaft v. Singer, 11 Rec. 1191, 1199 (1965).

45. Württembergische Milchverwertung-Südmilch v. Salvatore Ugliola, 15 Rec. 363 (1969).

46. *Id.* at 369. English text 9 Comm. Mkt L.R. 194, 201 (1970).

47. *E.g.* Deutschmann v. République Fédérale d'Allemagne, 11 Rec. 602, 607 (1925); Albatros v. Société des Pétroles des Combustibles Liquides, 11 Rec. 1, 8 (1965); Da Costa v. Administration fiscale néerlandaise, 9 Rec. 59, 76 (1963).

48. Milch-, Fett- und Eierkontor v. Hauptzollamt Saarbrücken, 15 Rec. 165, 180 (1969). It is erroneous to consider a preliminary ruling of the Court having binding force as a mere advisory opinion, as maintained by A. GREEN, POLITICAL INTEGRATION BY JURISPRUDENCE 55 (1969).

49. Costa v. ENEL, 10 Rec. 1143, 1160 (1964).

50. Norddeutsches Vieh- und Fleischkontor v. Hauptzollamt Hamburg-St. Annen, 17 Rec. 49 (1971); Hauptzollamt Hamburg-Oberelbe v. Bollmann, 16 Rec. 70 (1970); Hauptzollamt Bremen v. Waren-Import-Gesellschaft Krohn, 16 Rec. 451 (1970); Deutsche Bakels v. Oberfinanzdirektion München, 16 Rec. 1001 (1970). *See also* Ipsen, Note, 5 EUROPARECHT 246 (1970).

51. Hauptzollamt Bremen v. Waren-Import-Gesellschaft Krohn, 16 Rec. 451, 459 (1970) (author's translation).

52. *Id.* (author's translation).

53. Commission v. Council, 17 Rec. 263 (1971).

54. *Id.* at 275. For comments on this important decision, see, *e.g.*, Gansshof van der Meersch, *Les relations extérieures de la CEE dans le domaine des politiques communes et l'arrêt de la Cour de Justice du 31 mars 1971*, 8 CAHIERS DE DROIT EUROPEEN 127 (1972); Louis. *Compétence internationale et compétence interne des Communautés*, 7 CAHIERS DE DROIT EUROPEEN 479 (1971); Raux, *La Cour de Justice et les relations extérieures de la CEE*, 76 REVUE GENERAL DE DROIT INTERNATIONAL PUBLIC 36 (1972); Sasse, *Zur answärtigen Gewalt der Europäischen Wirtschaftsgemeinschaft*, 6 EUROPARECHT 208 (1971).

55. For example, in the field of customs duties, quantitative restrictions, common customs tariffs, free movement of workers, and so forth.

56. Commission v. Grand-Duché de Luxembourg et Royaume de Belgique, 10 Rec. 1219, 1232 (1964).

57. *Id. See also* Commission v. République française, 17 Rec. 1003, 1018 (1971).

58. The *ENEL* case, upholding the supremacy of Community law over a national law of the member states, is certainly the most striking example. Costa v. ENEL, 10 Rec. 1143, 1158–60 (1964). For discussion of this case, see *e.g.*, Stein, *Towards*

Supremacy of Treaty Constitution by Judicial Fiat: On the Margin of the Costa Case, 43 MICH. L. REV. 491 (1965). *See also* Bock v. Commission, 17 Rec. 897, 909 (1971); Grad v. Finanzamt Traunstein, 16 Rec. 825, 838 (1970); Sociaal Fonds Diamantarbeiders v. Brachfeld & Chougol, 15 Rec. 211, 222 (1969); Wilhelm v. Bundeskartellamt, 15 Rec. 1, 15 (1969); Gouvernement de la République italienne v. Haute Autorité, 6 Rec. 665, 668 (1960); Compagnie des Hauts Fourneaux et Fonderies .de Givors v. Haute Autorité, 6 Rec. 503, 523 (1960); Fédération Charbonnière de Belgique v. Haute Autorité, 2 Rec. 291, 305 (1955–56).

59.   Costa v. ENEL, 10 Rec. 1143, 1160 (1964).

60.   *Id.* at 1159.

61.   Acciaierie San Michele v. Haute Autorité, 13 Rec. 35 (1967).

62.   *Id.* at 37.

63.   *Id.* at 38. *See also* Eunomia v. Ministère de l'Instruction Publique de la République italienne, 17 Rec. 811, 816 (1971); Politi v. Ministère des Finances de la République italienne, 17 Rec. 1037, 1048 (1971).

64.   Internationale Handelsgesellschaft v. Einfuhr- und Vorratsstelle für Getreide und Futtermittel, 16 Rec. 1125 (1970).

65.   *Id.* at 1135 (author's translation).

66.   *Id.*

67.   Lück v. Hauptzollamt Köln, 14 Rec. 359, 369–70 (1968).

68.   Commission v. Grand-Duché de Luxembourg et Royaume de Belgique, 8 Rec. 815, 827 (1962).

69.   *Id.*

70.   *Id.*

71.   Sociaal Fonds voor de Diamantarbeiders v. Brachfeld, 15 Rec. 211, 222 (1969) (English text 8 Comm. Mkt L.R. 335, 350–51 (1969). *See also* Commission v. République italienne, 15 Rec. 193, 201 (1969).

72.   Commission v. République italienne, 7 Rec. 635, 656 (1961).

73.   Commission v. Grand-Duché de Luxembourg et Royaume de Belgique, 8 Rec. 815, 825 (1962).

74.   Commission v. République italienne, 14 Rec. 618, 628 (1968).

75.   Consten et Grundig v. Commission, 12 Rec. 430, 494 (1966).

76.   *Id.* at 495.

77.   *Id. See also* Völk v. Vervaecke, 15 Rec. 295, 302 (1969); Société Technique Minière v. Maschinenbau Ulm, 12 Rec. 338, 359 (1966).

78.   Consten et Grundig v. Commission, 12 Rec. 430, 495 (1966).

79.   Société Technique Minière v. Maschinenbau Ulm, 12 Rec. 338, 359 (1966) (English text 5 Comm. Mkt. L.R. 372, 375 (1966).

80.   Not every restraint on competition necessarily violates Article 85(1). *See* Société Technique Minière v. Maschinenbau Ulm, 12 Rec. 338, 356 (1966). In the *Grundig* case, the Court stated, *inter alia,* that it was not necessary to examine the harmful effects of the exclusive dealership agreement on competition because its object to prevent and restrict competition was clearly established. Consten et Grundig v. Commission, 12 Rec. 430, 492–93 (1966). These decisions have sometimes been misunderstood. It may hardly be assumed that the Court intended to imply that, in general, an examination of the *degree* of such an examination was unnecessary. It does not seem to mean that an agreement which purports to restrain or prevent competition would be prohibited even though it may have a potentially merely negligible effect on competition. Thus, for example, the *Maschinenbau* case, *supra,* at 359–60. *See also* Völk v. Vervaecke, 15 Rec. 295, 302 (1969).

81.   Société Technique Minière v. Maschinenbau Ulm, 12 Rec. 338, 356 (1966); Consten et Grundig v. Commission, 12 Rec. 430, 492–93 (1966).

82. Société Technique Minière v. Maschinenbau Ulm, 12 Rec. 359 (1966); Consten et Grundig v. Commission, 12 Rec. 430, 496 (1966).

83. Société Technique Minière v. Maschinenbau Ulm, 12 Rec. 338, 359 (1966).

84. *Id.* at 356; Consten et Grundig v. Commission, 12 Rec. 430, (1966) 492–93.

85. Consten et Grundig v. Commission, 12 Rec. 430, 493 (1966); République italienne v. Commission, 12 Rec. 564, 591–92 (1966).

86. Imperial Chemical Industries v. Commission (not yet published) (1972) (English text 11 Comm. Mkt L.R. 617 (1972)); Geigy and Sandoz v. Commission (not yet published) (1972) (English text 11 Comm. Mkt L.R. 637 (1972)).

87. 11 Comm. Mkt L.R. 617, 629, 637, 640 (1972). For further discussion of this problem, see, *e.g.,* Mann, *The Dyestuff case in the Court of Justice of the European Communities,* 22 INT'L & COMP. L.Q. 35 (1973); Messen, *Der räumliche Anwendungsbereich des EWG-Kartellrechts und das allgemeine Völkerrecht,* 8 EUROPARECHT 18 (1973; Steindorff, *Annotation on the Decisions of the European Court in the Dyestuff Case of July 14, 1972,* 9 Comm. Mkt L.R. 502 (1972).

88. Consten et Grundig v. Commission, 12 Rec. 430, 498 (1966).

89. Judgment of Nov. 15, 1966, 15 Entscheidungen der Finanzgerichte [hereinafter cited as EFG] 76 (Finanzgericht Saar 1967). For a more detailed discussion of this problem, see Bebr, *How Supreme is Community Law in the National Courts,* 11 Comm. Mkt L.R. 3 (1974).

90. 14 EFG 73 (1966).

91. Judgment of Nov. 26, 1965 (Verwaltungsgericht Frankfurt) (unpublished).

92. *Id.* (author's translation).

93. The citation is taken from the case cited note 91 *supra.*

94. Judgment of Oct. 8, 1967, 13 Aussenwirtschaftsdienst des Betriebs-Beraters 477 (Bundesverfassungsgericht), 21 NEUE JURISTISCHE WOCHENSCHRIFT 348 (1968). For comments on the case see *e.g.,* Ipsen, Note, 3 EUROPARECHT 137 (1968); Frowein, 5 Comm. Mkt L.R. 484 (1968).

95. Judgment of Jun. 9, 1971, 17 Aussenwirtschaftsdienst des Betriebs-Beraters 418, 419 (Bundesverfassungsgericht).

96. Judgment of Mar. 7, 1964, 19 Foro Padano IV. 9 (Giurisprudenza) (1964) (English text 3 Comm. Mkt. L.R. 430 (1964)). For discussion of the case, see, *e.g.,* Bravo, *Observations: L'issue de l'affaire Costa v. ENEL devant le conciliatore de Milan,* 3 CAHIERS DE DROIT EUROPEAN 200, 204–17 (1967).

97. Société Acciaierie San Michele v. European Coal and Steel Community, 61 Foro Amministrativo 569 (1965) (English text 4 Comm. Mkt L.R. 81 (1966). For further discussion of this case, see, *e.g.,* Berri, *Note critique a l'arrêt No. 98/65 du 27 decembre 1965 (Soc. Acciaiarie San Michele v. European Coal and Steel Community) de la Cour Constitutionnelle Italienne,* 4 Comm. Mkt L.R. 238 (1966).

98. ECSC Treaty arts. 33(2), 41, 91.

99. ECSC Treaty arts. 102, 103.

100. Sandrini v. Ministero dell'Agricoltura e Foreste, 97 Foro Italiano I. 1388 (Tribunale Civile de Brescia 1972).

101. Amministrazione delle Finanze dello Stato v. SACE, 97 Foro Italiano I. 3264 (Tribunale Civile de Brescia 1972).

102. Etat belge v. Fromagerie Franco-Suisse "Le Ski," 86 Journal des Tribunaux 460 (Cour de Cassation de Belgique 1971).

103. *See* authority cited note 29 *supra.* For an exhaustive discussion of this problem, see Pescatore, *L'application directe des Traités européens par les juridictions nationales: la jurisprudence nationale,* 5 REVUE TRIMESTRIELLE DE DROIT EUROPEAN 697 (1969).

104. Judgment of Jan. 15, 1969, 95 Sammlung der Entscheidungen und Gutachten des Bundesfinanzhofs 67 (1969).

105.   *Id.* at 74 (author's translation). In several decisions, the German Finanzgerichte followed the preliminary rulings of the Court declaring Article 95 directly applicable. *E.g.,* Judgment of Nov. 26, 1969, 18 EFG 198 (Finanzgericht Hamburg 1970) (as to a direct application of art. 95(3), with reference to the Court's ruling in Lütticke and Fink-Frucht); Judgment of Oct. 15, 1968, 15 Aussenwirtschaftsdienst des Betriebs-Beraters 77 (Finanzgericht Düsseldorf 1969) (with reference to the ruling in Molkerei-Zentrale); Judgment of Feb. 14, 1967, 15 EFG 159 (Finanzgericht Düsseldorf 1967) (referring to the ruling in Lütticke); Judgment of Dec. 12, 1966, 43 Zeitschrift für Zölle und Verbrauchsteuern 61 (Finanzgericht Bremen 1967) (referring also to the ruling in Lütticke). *See,* however, the decision of the Finanzgericht Baden-Württemberg, Mar. 21, 1967, 15 EFG 240 (1967), which refused to follow the ruling of the Court in the *ENEL* case (upholding the supremacy of the Community law) and in the *Lütticke* case (declaring Article 95 directly applicable).

106.   Judgment of Nov. 6, 1968, 17 EFG 160 (Finanzgericht Münster 1969).

107.   *Id.* (author's translation).

108.   Molkerei-Zentrale Westfalen-Lippe, 14 Rec. 212, 230 (1968).

109.   *See* authority cited note 33 *supra.*

110.   *E.g.,* EEC Treaty arts. 37(1); 40(3); 48(2); 65; 67; 79.

111.   EEC Treaty art. 8(7). For a further discussion of this problem, see Rambow, *The End of the Transitional Period,* 6 Comm. Mkt L.R. 434 (1969).

112.   Two recent decisions of national courts illustrate this problem quite clearly. *See* Fromagerie Franco-Suisse "Le Ski" v. Etat belge, 85 JOURNAL DES TRIBUNAUX 413 (Cour d'Appel Bruxelles 1970) (English text 9 Comm. Mkt L.R. 219 (1970)); Detry v. Etat belge (Tribunal de Bruxelles 1967) (unpublished).

113.   Commission v. République italienne, 18 Rec. 529, 534–535 (1972).

114.   The background of the present case makes this clear. In December 1968, the Court found Italy in violation of Article 16 of the Treaty by imposing charges on exports. Commission v. République italienne, 14 Rec. 617, 629 (1968), a judgment Italy failed to comply with. A subsequent preliminary ruling of the Court rendered at the request of an Italian court dealing with a conflict between Article 16 and the Italian law imposing export charges, declared the prohibition of Article 16 "directly applicable." Eunomia v. Ministère de l'Instruction Publique de la République italienne, 17 Rec. 811, 816 (1971). As Italy failed to execute the 1968 judgment, the Court rendered, on an action of the Commission, a judgment for violating Article 171. *Cf.* authority cited note 113 *supra.*

115.   Internationale Handelsgesellschaft v. Einfuhr und Vorratsstelle, 16 Rec. 1125, 1135 (1970).

116.   Humblet v. Etat belge, 6 Rec. 1127, 1145–46 (1960).

117.   Van Gend & Loos v. Administration fiscale néerlandaise, 9 Rec. 3, 23, 25 (1963).

118.   *See* authority cited note 113 *supra.*

Chapter 10

The Legal Tradition and the Management of National Security

JOHN NORTON MOORE

The role of law in the management of national security has been an issue throughout American history. Traces of the debate may be found as long ago as 1793 in the exchange between Hamilton and Jefferson about the relative importance of "interests" and "morality" in deciding whether the United States should support France in the war with England.[1] Jefferson found an obligation to support France under the 1778 Treaty of Alliance and urged that the treaty obligation was morally binding on the nation.[2] Hamilton countered that there was no obligation, but that, even if there were, "good faith does not require that the United States should put in jeopardy their essential interests. . . ."[3]

At the turn of the century the debate achieved clearer focus in the writings of Alfred Thayer Mahan,[4] the great sea power strategist, and Elihu

This essay was written prior to the author's association with the Department of State and the National Security Council and does not necessarily reflect the views of the United States Government or any agency thereof. A much condensed version of this essay has been published as *Law and National Security*, 51 FOREIGN AFFAIRS 408 (1973).

Root, Secretary of State and a distinguished American jurist.[5] The core of the debate was the importance of arbitration as opposed to traditional diplomacy for the resolution of international conflict. Root and other jurists urged greater resort to arbitration and techniques of third party conflict resolution. Mahan countered that law, while sometimes useful, was inelastic and therefore incapable of dealing with moral questions or questions of national expediency.

In the aftermath of World War II the debate was resumed more sharply and with a broadened focus. On one side were distinguished international relations theorists such as Hans J. Morgenthau[6] and George F. Kennan,[7] who saw only a small role for international law and even warned of the dangers of a "legalistic-moralistic" approach in dealing with national security issues. On the other side were equally distinguished jurists such as Myres S. McDougal,[8] Philip C. Jessup,[9] and Hardy C. Dillard,[10] who warned that the "realists" had an incomplete understanding of the role of international law and that their misconceptions about legal process could, if influential, be costly for American foreign policy.

The realists have had, throughout the debate, an important message to convey. Overreliance on international law can be a prescription for disaster in a loosely organized and intensely competitive international system. If the disappointments with arbitration and universal disarmament schemes during the interwar years did not bring the message home, the Cold War certainly did.[11] The very strength of this message, however, has carried with it an overly broad attack on the international legal tradition. In turn, the popular success of the attack has been a factor contributing precisely to the dangers of which the jurists warned. For while we have been preoccupied with purging the dangers of a legalistic-moralistic strain in American foreign policy, we have failed to see that the national security process is poorly structured to take legal perspectives into account. Time and again this failure has been costly for American foreign policy. Accordingly, it is time to set aside the traditional debate and to recognize that, as with most debates, there are valid points to be made in both camps. As a nation we will be that much stronger if a variety of traditions, including the legal tradition, is adequately represented in the national security process, and we will be that much weaker if any one tradition is excluded.

A Brief History of the Debate Between the Realists and the Jurists

Aside from the early exchange between Hamilton and Jefferson, the debate between the foreign policy realists and the international jurists can be usefully divided into three principal phases (though with the inevitable artificiality of such divisions). Each merits brief examination.

The first phase centered from slightly before the turn of the century through the 1930s, a period characterized by vigorous growth both in theories of national interest and power and in theories of arbitration, conciliation, and other juristic techniques for the peaceful resolution of international disputes. Alfred Thayer Mahan's *The Influence of Sea Power Upon History 1660–1783*[12] burst upon the scene in 1890 and soon became a bible for advocates of national power. Paradoxically, in the same year Congress passed a resolution calling for greater use of arbitration in the settlement of international disputes,[13] which, together with the Hague Conferences and the ill-fated "cooling-off" treaties negotiated by Secretary of State William Jennings Bryan, illustrated the dynamism of the juristic school. It was perhaps inevitable that two such dynamic traditions would clash. A brief look at a principal statement by the most eloquent spokesman for each camp—Secretary of State Elihu Root for the juristic perspective and Admiral Mahan for the national power perspective—may illustrate the early focus of the debate.

In an address delivered in 1908 at the Second Annual Meeting of the American Society of International Law, Root urged that international opinion was a powerful sanction for international law. He also supported demands for international arbitration as a useful way to mobilize this opinion when the factors in the underlying dispute were complicated or doubtful and when, therefore, the force of public opinion could not be brought to bear directly on the dispute itself. There is scant focus in Root's address on any limitations of arbitration inherent in the international system. Similarly, there is no focus on the inadequacies of the international legal system in prescribing and applying legal norms. Given the trying international events to come, the tone is overoptimistic.[14]

Three years later, in a series of articles written for the *North American Review,* Mahan discussed what he felt to be the deficiencies of law as an instrument of international adjustment. He refused to accept a characterization of the debate as one of law versus armaments or war and instead characterized it as law versus diplomacy. He went on to urge that while international arbitration was useful for the solution of many controversies, it could not provide a solution for all classes of disputes since, in many situations, law is inelastic and rigid and, as such, incapable of dealing with moral questions or questions of national expediency such as the Monroe Doctrine.[15] Though Mahan was surely right that international arbitration is not the panacea for dispute settlement, his reasons therefor were as surely wrong. For the most part, states do not avoid arbitration because they fear its rigidity. They avoid it because, in addition to their sensitivity to the cost of continued conflict, they fear they may lose, and their estimate of the probability of losing rightly or wrongly outweighs their estimate of the probability of winning. Moreover, they know that there are a variety of juristic techniques for third party dispute settlement which permit explicit references to extralegal considerations.[16] Also, Mahan made a confused and dangerous argument for the legitimacy of power as a technique of international settlement. He urged, in an adaptation of social Darwinism, that

> [n]ational power is surely a legitimate factor in international settlements; for it is the outcome of national efficiency, and efficiency is entitled to assert its fair position and chance of exercise in world matters, not restricted unduly by mere legal tenures dependent for their existing legality upon a prior occupancy, which occupancy often represents an efficiency once existent but long since passed away.[17]

Few would doubt that power is a factor in international settlements or that there is anything per se legitimate or illegitimate in the exercise of power. But when it is hinted, without strong qualification, that power as a surrogate for national efficiency (in itself a large assumption) *ought to be* a normative standard for the appraisal of state conduct, one is not far from the power-national-merit mystique of the Third Reich.

Perhaps the most interesting point about this first round in the debate is that, like so much of the debate, it was largely a debate without dialogue. Without being inconsistent, one can agree with many of the points made by both sides, yet nevertheless recognize that the model presented by each is simplistic and incomplete. The jurists were overoptimistic about arbitration as a technique for resolving fundamental clashes of national interest, and the realists underestimated the role of authority in influencing state interests and behavior. Both were better at perceiving the strengths of their tradition than its weaknesses.

It seems probable that the international legal tradition had its greatest influence on American foreign policy up to and through this first phase of the debate. As George F. Kennan reports:

> [T]he United States Government during the period from the turn of the century to the 1930's, signed and ratified a total of ninety-seven international agreements dealing with arbitration or conciliation, and negotiated a number of others which, for one reason or another, never took effect.[18]

Additionally, the interwar years witnessed major efforts at multilateral arrangements for disarmament, the growth of the League of Nations (albeit without United States participation), and the Kellogg-Briand Pact. Another, although more impressionistic, indication of the influence of the legal tradition during this period is found in a comparison through time of the interrelation of influential governmental decisionmakers and the American Society of International Law. When the Society was founded in 1906, Elihu Root, then Secretary of State, was elected its first President, and the twelve Vice-Presidents included the Chief Justice of the United States, two Associate Justices of the Supreme Court, two former Secretaries of State, and William Howard Taft, then Secretary of War.[19] Though the work of the Society has continued to attract top governmental and non-governmental leaders, at no time since World War II has this early extraordinary interrelation been matched.

In the aftermath of World War II—the beginning of the second phase of the debate—the sudden national awareness of real security needs precipitated by Pearl Harbor, the enormously heightened international responsibility thrust upon the United States, the awesome nuclear condition, the clashes of national interest reflected in the Cold War, and a variety of other changes in the international system shifted the focus from law and idealism to power and national interest. The shift was one of emphasis only and was never total. Thus, until about 1960 the United States utilized the United Nations as a major cornerstone of foreign policy.[20] But the effect of the shift on the thinking of those charged with the management of national security was profound. If there had been an excessive reliance on the legal tradition prior to World War II, the stage was now set for an excessive swing in the opposite direction.

The second phase of the debate began at the height of the Cold War as an offensive by international relations theorists against what they regarded as costly errors in foreign policy induced by the legal tradition. The principal generals in this offensive were Morgenthau and Kennan. They inveighed against a characteristic legalistic-moralistic approach which, they asserted, was a major intellectual error running through American foreign policy. As Kennan put it:

> I see the most serious fault of our past policy formulation to lie in something that I might call the legalistic-moralistic approach to international problems. This approach runs like a red skein through our foreign policy of the last fifty years. It has in it something of the old emphasis on arbitration treaties, something of the Hague Conferences and schemes for universal disarmament, something of the more ambitious American concepts of the role of international law, something of the League of Nations and the United Nations, something of the Kellogg Pact, something of the idea of a universal "Article 51" pact, something of the belief in World Law and World Government. But it is none of these, entirely. Let me try to describe it.
>
> It is the belief that it should be possible to suppress the chaotic and dangerous aspirations of governments in the international field by the acceptance of some system of legal rules and restraints. This belief undoubtedly represents in part an attempt to transpose the Anglo-Saxon concept of individual law into the international field and to make it applicable to governments as it is applicable here at home to individuals.[21]

This thesis was immediately challenged by Myres S. McDougal in an article in the *American Journal of International Law* which took Morgenthau and Kennan severely to task for fundamental misconceptions about the nature of law.[22] McDougal demonstrated that the realists' attack failed to focus on "the role that law presently plays in the world power process and the role that, with more effective organization, it could be made to play in maintaining the values of a free, peaceful, and abundant world society."[23] He also pointed out that law and morality entered into the determination of the national interest and that, far from being impermissible, normative appraisal of state conduct is inescapable. His reply to Kennan on this latter point bears repeating:

> [Mr. Kennan's] major emphasis, that the "greater deficiency" is "the carrying over into the affairs of states of the concepts of right and wrong, the assumption that state behavior is a fit subject for moral judgment," approaches, and, but for other sad examples, would achieve, the incredible. How "states" alone of man's institutions can be immunized from rational evaluation in terms of the purposes they serve, or how a consequential morality can be made to stop short of appraising group behavior, is nowhere explained. With both law and morality eliminated, one can only wonder by what criteria Mr. Kennan proposes to settle disputes between states "on their merits."
>
> It is urgently to be hoped that attacks upon law and morality which so profoundly misconceive law, morality, and power, and their interrelations, will not cause many of us to mistake the real choice that confronts us. . . . The choice we must make is not between law and no law, or between law and power, but between ineffective and effective law.[24]

Hardy C. Dillard, later to become a judge of the International Court of Justice, wielded the cudgel effectively again in his Hague lectures of 1957.[25] Putting aside the moral problem in judging state behavior, Dillard demonstrated that the realists failed to focus on the relation between law and the national interest and that they misconceived " 'law' as somehing 'static' which binds states to a rigid set of rules—a conception which derives little authority from the fact that it is widely shared."[26] In the meantime, Covey T. Oliver, a jurist, and Raymond Aron, an international relations theorist, had independently questioned the Morgenthau–Kennan thesis that legalism and idealism had been a principal cause of error in American foreign policy, and both had found it wanting. Oliver noted that the Kennan thesis "is one hundred eighty degrees out of phase with those who have had the idea that the past errors may have resulted, at least in part, from a lack of law and its organized application, rather than from overdoses of 'legalistic-moralistic' thinking." [27] He then analyzed systematically each of the examples given by Kennan in support of his thesis and concluded that "Mr. Kennan has not made his case. . . ."[28] In a briefer analysis, Aron found that both excessive realism and excessive idealism could be a source of error and that "[t]he mistaken idealism of inapplicable abstractions, the mistaken realism which makes one sacrifice lasting interests to superficially shrewd deals, both result from a common error: intellectual error."[29]

Morgenthau and Kennan had a valid point, though they painted with too broad a brush and, as McDougal, Oliver, and Dillard have convincingly demonstrated, with too little paint as well. Both were validly concerned about an idealism and a moralism neither rooted in, nor tempered by, the often harsh realities of the international system. The point, though now obvious, is not trivial. There was and still is a significant group of lawyers and nonlawyers who might be termed legal idealists or "world peace through law" adherents for whom the Morgenthau–Kennan message has meaning.[30] But the realist attack was largely uninformed about the theories describing the subtle interrelations between law—particularly the authority component of law—and power which had been developed by international legal jurists (particularly those following the approach developed by McDougal and Harold Lasswell). Also, the realist attack ignored the relation between law and the national interest, egregiously underestimated the importance of normative appraisal of state conduct, and overstated the responsibility of legalist thinking as a causative element in past failures of American foreign policy. The realist attack also failed to realize that, at least since World War II, the mainstream of the international legal tradition was made up of "legal realists" who already were acutely conscious of the interrelation between law and power.

To sum up this second phase of the debate, the realists made a contribution in pointing out the dangers of an excessively idealistic or legalistic approach to foreign policy. The principal thrust of their argument, however, had little relevance for the intellectual mainstream of the international legal tradition, and the breadth of their offensive threatened to obscure the real utility of an international legal approach. Finally, it was by no means clear that, as a tradition, idealism or legalism had been in fact any more detrimental to American foreign policy than realism. Whether cause or effect, the realist tradition soon became, and has remained, the principal intellectual tradition of American foreign policy planners.

The third phase of the debate between the realists and the jurists began during the late 1950s and has continued to the present. Though it continues to demonstrate concern with phase two issues, the scope and modalities of the debate have been substantially broadened. The emphasis now is on inquiry as to the interrelation between theories of international law and theories of the international system, empirical inquiry about the role of law and lawyers in the foreign policy process, and controversy about conflicting approaches to international law. Where phases one and two of the debate were largely characterized, respectively, by a limited focus on the utility of international arbitration and other third party settlement techniques and on the nature and role of international law, phase three has spawned a variety of additional inquiries.

In 1961 Morton Kaplan and Nicholas Katzenbach published their seminal study, *The Political Foundations of International Law*,[31] which explored the importance of the international milieu in shaping international law. Similarly, in a series of important articles, Stanley Hoffmann has explored the limiting effect of the present revolutionary international system on the role which can be successfully played by international law.[32] Conversely, McDougal, Lasswell, and Michael Reisman have set about systematically to describe the global process of authoritative decision and its interrelation with the effective power process.[33] Other scholars have undertaken empirical studies of the role played by international law in warpeace crises,[34] and of the role of international law from the perspective of the social sciences,[35] and have attempted a redefinition of the importance of law and lawyers to the conduct of foreign relations.[36] Phase three, if not "Consciousness III," has provided a variety of data and insights which, when integrated, provide a useful overview of the utility and limitations of international law as a tool for conflict management.

Complete exegesis of the phase three debate between the realists and the jurists would require focus on the wide variety of issues involved. What do we mean when we speak of international law and, as a corollary, what is the scope of our inquiry as to the role of international law? What similarities and differences demarcate domestic and international legal systems and what is their significance for our inquiry? What is the impact of the international system on the development of international law and the significance of that impact? How does international law moderate or otherwise influence other features of the international system of which it is a part? What is or should be the role of international law in national security decisions? How should the national security process be structured to take an international legal perspective effectively into account? And last, what are the merits of competing approaches to international law, and how would the predominance of one or another approach influence answers to each of the preceding questions? Elsewhere I have sought briefly to develop the full range of these issues.[37] Since, however, the purpose of this essay is to focus on the international legal tradition and the management of national security, the next sections will focus, in turn, on persistent misperceptions about the utility of the international legal tradition for the management of national security, the utility and dangers of the international legal tradition in dealing with national security decisions, some examples of national security decisions in which more adequate consideration of the international legal tradition could have strengthened American foreign policy, and, finally, proposals for change in the structure of the national security process to take an international legal perspective more adequately into account.

Persistent Misperceptions About the Utility of the Legal Tradition for the Management of National Security

There are at least five persistent misperceptions about the utility of the legal tradition for national security decisions. Each obscures balanced appraisal of the strengths and weaknesses of that tradition.

The first and most persistent is the assumption that the most pertinent question, *i.e.,* the ways in which the legal tradition is useful or detrimental to the management of national security, is not worthy of attention. But focus on this question is important because it may be that the legal tradition can play a useful role in the formulation of foreign policy whether or not international law plays a controlling role in the present international system and whether or not the legal tradition plays a significant role in the present national security process.

The important points are two: first, the specific strengths and weaknesses of the legal tradition in the management of national security are just as deserving of attention as other issues in the realist–jurist debate; second, the existing utilization of the legal tradition may not be optimal for either national or international goals. These points are important because there is a persistent theme running through the literature that on issues of vital national interest states have not been constrained by international law and internationl legal inputs are therefore but window dressing.[38] Though there is doubtless substantial truth in the premise, in many instances this conclusion conceals both the costs of violation of international law and the ways in which an international legal perspective could have aided the national security process in optimizing national goals. Research on the role of international law in security decisions has been enormously oversimplified by focusing largely on the extent to which national security managers perceive international law to be a factor or use international legal rhetoric.[39] Since national security managers usually are not international lawyers, such research may be simply a self-fulfilling prophecy.

A second misperception is to confuse the relation between international law and the national interest, even to the point of assuming that international law and the national interest are opposing fundaments. There is more than a hint of this confusion in the writings of Morgenthau.[40] But the "national interest" is not a self-defining concept, and as given content by most theorists it would include a strong interest in the stability and quality of the international milieu. As Aron puts it:

> In these troubled eras no great power ever limits its objectives to the national interest, in the sense a Mazarin or a Bismarck would have given to this expression. In such periods a great power is defined by its capacity to show to humanity a perspective of stabilization and peace. When humanity

is racked by the devastations of war and revolutions, the idea of a great power is not so much a certain conception of social relationships or of a better economic and social system, as it is the promise of order before and above anything else. . . . [T]he West must stand for an idea of an international order. The national interest of the United States, or even the collective interest of the Anglo-Saxon minority, will not win over any country nor will it cause any loyalties if it does not appear to be tied to an international order—the order of power as well as the order of law.[41]

International law, then, may suggest the national interest in its resolution of competing values in a variety of operational settings. For example, it is strongly in the national interest to comply with the internationally established laws of war. Not to comply is to risk breakdown in army discipline, brutalization of combatants (with its associated social costs on the return of servicemen to civilian life), unnecessary escalation and continuation of conflict, reciprocal mistreatment of allied combatants and noncombatants, domestic loss of support, and unnecessary human suffering. Focus on these costs and the resolution of competing military and humanitarian considerations are most fully provided by the international legal tradition.

Thus, there is no necesary conflict between international law as a system of international constraints and the national interest. The real conflict, if any, is between any benefits of an illegal policy (such as United States assistance to insurgents in the Bay of Pigs invasion) and the short- and long-run costs of such policies, particularly national authority deflation and the undermining of international legal constraints contributing to the stability of the international milieu. There may also be a conflict between simplistic versions of international order and more meaningful formulations. For example, an overreliance on the text of the SEATO Treaty when it no longer reflects power realities might be in conflict with the national interest. In any event, both realms of genuine difficulty in arriving at the national interest are clarified by encouraging dialogue about international legal perspectives, not by excluding international lawyers from the deliberations. My own assessment is that, as a nation, we consistently undersell the importance of a powerful and consistent vision of world order as a component of the national interest and that the underrepresentation of international lawyers in the national security process is one major cause.

A variation on this second misperception is mechanically to assume that an internationally lawful action is in the national interest. It does not follow that a particular policy option is in the national interest solely because it is lawful. There is a wide variety of inputs concerning national goals, capabilities, projected costs and benefits, and the availability of alternative policies which also should enter into any decision. Conversely, though it is highly likely that illegal action is not in the national interest, this does not follow as a matter of logic, but only from the importance to national interests of encouraging long-run adherence to law and of avoiding the short- and long-run costs associated with law violation. The same may be said of the reverse of each of these equations, *i.e.,* that a policy is lawful because it is in the national interest or that a policy is not lawful because it is not in the national interest. Both are, simply, sophistries which, conscious or not, may commit the vice of national or personal chauvinism. Neither has any merit for analysis other than as a danger to be avoided.

International law frequently embodies notions of international morality and experience which serve to delimit the international common interest. Both as a matter of moral ought, as well as long-run national strategy, such considerations should be embodied in the national interest. For example, it would be a widely shared moral judgment that the United States ought not forcibly to appropriate Middle Eastern oil reserves at the expense of the indigenous communities, even if possession gains would outweigh long- and short-run costs associated with international law violation and the appropriations were otherwise feasible, a hypothesis which is dubious on both counts. The important points are that a decision as to illegality does not as a matter of logic decide the national interest and that, despite this lack of logical necessity, adherence to law is, for a variety of both selfish and altruistic reasons, a strong component of the national interest. Rather than simply assert that it is against the national interest to violate international law, international lawyers would better serve the ideal of fidelity to law by pointing out why it is important. A useful technique for avoiding confusion in the relation between international law and the national interest is to focus on the costs and benefits of compliance and noncompliance with international law, rather than on whether international law is or is not "controlling." "Realist" approaches which neglect such factors in costing alternative national policies are in reality only partially realistic. Similarly, government legal advisors would do well to articulate the costs and benefits flowing from pertinent international legal considerations, as well as to advise on legality or illegality.

A third misperception obscuring the utility of the legal tradition concerns incomplete or erroneous theories about the nature of law and the international legal system. Perhaps the most pervasive of these is the underestimation of the role of authority in the global power process and, particularly, the importance of community expectations about authority as a source of power. There is a functioning international constitutive process which creates, maintains, and modifies community expectations about the authoritativeness of national actions. That the process is less centralized than the domestic constitutive process does not make it any less real, only harder to describe. Just as in the domestic arena, community perceptions about authoritativeness flowing from this international process are translated into power realities in a number of meaningful ways. For example, an action such as the Korean War, in which perceptions as to the authoritativeness and legitimacy of the action are high, is likely to result in more allies than less clearly authoritative actions such as the Indochina war or unauthoritative actions such as the Anglo-French invasion of Suez. Similarly, it seems likely that one factor which tended to persuade Premier Khrushchev to comply with the Cuban quarantine was the increased authoritativeness of the action obtained by approval of the Organization of American States. Moreover, if perceptions about the nonauthoritativeness of national actions are intense and widespread, there may be a significant and lasting loss of national influence. Such costs seem to have been paid by the Soviet Union in the invasions of Hungary and Czechoslovakia, by France and Great Britain in the Suez adventure, and by the United States in the Dominican intervention. Perceptions about authority may also have important domestic impacts translatable into votes or other support for policy. Similarly, they may influence votes in international organizations such as the United Nations Security Council or the O.A.S. Council of Ministers. Of course, the influence of attitudinal factors on foreign policy is by its nature difficult to abstract and quantify. Difficulty in measurement, however, should not be confused with unimportance. Everything we know about the behavior of men and nations suggests that ideas and ideology play a significant motivational role. Attitudes about the authoritativeness of actions, rooted in community experience and common interest, have a peculiar force of their own which should not be dismissed as mere public opinion.

A second erroneous approach to the nature of law is to view law in Austinian terms as solely a restraint system. Law performs a variety of roles in addition to constraining deviant behavior.[42] Thus, international law provides techniques for conflict avoidance, for example, as in compulsory arbitration clauses and in the treaties prohibiting nuclear weapons in space and on the seabeds. To focus exclusively on the difficulties of international law in constraining state behavior is to miss the creative opportunities which law provides for conflict avoidance and promotion of all national interests.

A third error concerns the nature of legal rules. One argument is that since international lawyers always seem able to argue both sides of any case, there are no international legal norms or at least none sufficiently definite to offer guidance on critical national security issues. William P. Gerberding forcefully articulates this common complaint in his study of the role of international law in the Cuban missile crisis:

> It follows from the expediential character of most of the governmental pronouncements and even scholarly discourses on the blockade, from the susceptibility of documents and alleged "norms" and "principles" to almost any interpretation, and from the absence of authoritative and legitimate institutions to create, interpret, and enforce the "law" that it can be and is used in whatever manner governments choose to use it. It does not have a valid life of its own; it is a mere instrument, available to political leaders for their own ends, be they good or evil, peaceful or aggressive.

International law is, in sum, a tool and not a guide to action. . . .
[G]iven the amorphous character of international law, can or should
governments or lawyers or anyone else really summon up more concern
for it than for "reasons of state"? Skilled legal advocates and apologists
never face this problem, because for every "reason of state" they can find
or create a corresponding international legal norm. But surely this merely
reconfirms the irrelevance of international law in major political disputes.
Since it can mean nearly anything, it means almost nothing.[43]

Gerberding is right to call attention to the lack of centralized prescriptive and adjudicative competence in the international system as factors
contributing to the indeterminacy of legal norms. But he is wrong to conclude that all international law is amorphous. International law has areas
of clarity and areas of uncertainty, and in this respect international law is
not as qualitatively different from national law as the layman might suspect.
For example, it is virtually undisputed among international lawyers that
the United States role in the Bay of Pigs invasion and the Soviet role in
the Czechoslovakian invasion were violations of Article 2(4) of the United
Nations Charter, which proscribes "the threat or use of force against the
territorial integrity or political independence of any state. . . ." Also, it is
widely acepted that the Allied intervention in the Korean conflict was a
lawful exercise of collective defense under Article 51 of the Charter and
that the North Vietnamese mistreatment of Allied prisoners of war was in
violation of the 1949 Geneva Conventions and the customary international
law of war. Many other examples of reasonably definite legal conclusions
about war–peace issues could be given. On the other hand, it also is true
that the actions of the United States in the Cuban missile crisis, the 1965
Dominican intervention, and the Indochina war have been more controversial. Gerberding has fallen into the trap of generalizing about all international law on the basis of one of the more indeterminate issues.

It seems probable that one of the principle reasons contributing to a
cynacism about the determinacy of international legal norms is, as Gerberding has noted, that on many war–peace issues international legal experts do make opposing arguments.[44] However, one should not equate the
existence of a legal or any other argument with its validity. Since authority
is a source of power, it is likely that adversary legal arguments will be employed on important political issues. Merely because a good or even a bad
advocate can make a legal argument does not mean that the argument is
valid; subsequent adversary debate may create an appearance of greater
indeterminacy than actually exists. Moreover, the mere invocation of authority presupposes and reinforces its authoritativeness. Thus, adversary
argument presupposes and reinforces international law. Finally, even
if international legal norms were completely indeterminate on national security issues, it still would be a mistake to conclude that
they are irrelevant. For law, as a source of authority, is a base of
power which nevertheless would retain significant relevance on decisions

concerning implementation and justification of policy. Interestingly, the argument made by Mahan as to the principal weakness of international law is almost the exact reverse of the presently fashionable indeterminacy argument. Mahan felt that law was limited precisely because of its rigidity and inability to reflect political and moral factors.[45] Both arguments reflect a lack of sophistication about the nature of rules in any legal system, national or international. Mahan's theory reflected the extreme Blackstonian rule rigidity of his day (and apparently of the layman in every historical period), and the present indeterminacy argument reflects the rule skepticism of the extreme legal realist.[46] Legal rules and principles need be neither frozen doctrine divorced from policy nor contentless floating abstractions.

A fourth misperception obscuring the utility of the legal tradition involves the assumed unimportance of normative appraisal of national conduct. The Stafford Little Lectures delivered by Kennan in 1954 provide an example. Though Kennan somewhat restricted his earlier indictment of international law,[47] he still expressed skepticism that the purposes of nations "are fit subjects for measurement in moral terms."[48] Thus, he urged:

> Morality, then, as the channel to individual self-fulfillment—yes. Morality as the foundation of civic virtue, and accordingly as a condition precedent to successful democracy—yes. Morality in governmental method, as a matter of conscience and preference on the part of our people—yes. But morality as a general criterion for the determination of the behavior of states and above all as a criterion for measuring and comparing the behavior of different states—no. Here other criteria, sadder, more limited, more practical, must be allowed to prevail.[49]

The difficulty with Kennan's position is that the selection of goals for the appraisal of policies is inescapably part of any process of decision, including foreign policy planning,[50] and in selecting the national interest as the standard for appraisal, a normative choice has been made. Moreover, this choice and the implicit reasons in support of it have been concealed by the argument that moral choice is impermissible. An assertion of national interest may reflect either common or special interests.[51] To the extent that it permits justification of special interests it may be neither worthy of our support nor a persuasive basis for influencing the actions of others. Such an assertion may also be counterproductive for the real national interest in reinforcing common interests and disallowing special interests. In short, the selection of the "national interest" as the sole standard for appraisal may ignore the inevitability of normative appraisal, provide license for special as opposed to common interest, beg the question as to what is the national interest, and obscure the reasoning by which the normative standard of "the national interest" is selected as the standard for appraisal.

These criticisms of Kennan's position are neither new nor novel. Among moral philosophers, Reinhold Niebuhr has criticized Kennan's emphasis upon national "egoism" as a standard for appraisal and has pointed out "that any kind of prudence which estimates common problems from the perspective of a particular interest will define the interest too narrowly."[52] Similarly, David Little urges Kennan's lack of moral candor in implicitly making moral choices without explanation: "Kennan's most serious problem is that he has made all sorts of moral assumptions about the national interest but will not let anyone else in on why he has made these assumptions or what their full implications are for international relations."[53] In reflecting on such moral choice, the international legal tradition is a rich source of normative insight based on community common interest rather than the interests of any one nation. To the extent that we ignore the legal tradition, the moral judgments that we inescapably will make are likely to suffer accordingly.

The fifth principal misperception obscuring the utility of the legal tradition involves thinking of the legal tradition only in terms of international law. In fact, there may be a variety of national law consequences of security decisions which are an important component of planning. For example, the decision to use the armed forces abroad has important constitutional dimensions which are neglected only at great risk to the ability to continue the action. Similarly, as was demonstrated in the *Calley* case, international law is for many purposes incorporated into domestic law. If the legal tradition is not adequately represented in the national security process, these domestic law aspects of national security planning may also suffer.[54]

It seems likely that a principal cause of the continuing persistence of these and other misperceptions about the legal tradition is the lack of dialogue between international lawyers and international relations theorists. In ending these misperceptions and perhaps in ending misperceptions which international lawyers may harbor about the realist tradition it would seem useful to encourage a variety of proposals aimed at increasing the dialogue. These might include interdisciplinary conferences between international lawyers and international relations theorists, seminars for policy planners to consider the role of international law in national security decisions, and increasing the teaching of international relations in law schools and international law in international relations departments.

The Uses and Abuses of the Legal Tradition in the Management of National Security

A major shortcoming of the realist–jurist debate is that it has proceeded at a high level of abstraction about the potential of arbitration or the nature of international law rather than specifying the uses and abuses of the legal tradition in the management of national security. Focusing first on uses, they include:

Long-Range Planning

1. International law, with its focus on the long-run stability and quality of the international milieu, is useful in determining national interests, goals, and priorities.
2. International law is useful as an instrumental device for the solution of international problems before they mature into conflict.
3. International law is useful in planning for the control and moderation of conflict.

Crisis Management

4. International law is useful in decisions concerning all aspects of crisis management:
   a. Are the goals consistent with the national interest?
      (1) Has international law been taken adequately into account as one source of insight concerning whether the goals are morally sound and deserving of national action?
      (2) If the credibility of the national willingness to act is one element of the national interest, what are the international legal rights, privileges, powers, and immunities which make the situation more or less like other important situations?
      (3) Has the national interest in supporting common as opposed to special interests adequately been considered?
   b. Are the goals realizable through the proposed policy at a cost–benefit ratio which makes their pursuit consistent with the national interest?
      (1) Has the anticipated effect of the policy on the stability of the international system and on the loosening of legal constraints been taken adequately into account?
      (2) If the proposed policy is in violation of international law, have the international and domestic costs of authority deflation and other costs associated with international legal violation been taken adequately into account?
      (3) Have the international legal perspectives of target and third states and international organizations been adequately assessed in estimating probable response to the proposed policy?
   c. Are preferable policy alternatives available to achieve the same or similar goals at a more favorable cost–benefit ratio?
      (1) Has the full range of options and strategies associated with

the international law of conflict management been adequately canvassed?

(2)   In implementing the action, has international law been adequately utilized to structure action which maximizes benefit and minimizes cost to national authority and the international system?

(3)   In implementing the action, has international law been adequately utilized to structure action which maximizes the cost of unwanted target and third state response?

(4)   In implementing the action, has international law been adequately canvassed for assistance in communicating intention and avoiding unintended escalation?

(5)   Have the national law aspects of the proposed policy adequately been considered and structured?

d.   Are communications concerning the reasons for the action adequately presented?

(1)   Have international legal considerations been taken adequately into account in preparing private and diplomatic communications?

(2)   Have international legal considerations been taken adequately into account in preparing public justification?

(3)   Has the full range of forums suggested by international law been adequately considered as arenas for communication?

Continuing Review

5.   The international legal tradition provides oversight of the national interest in internally operationalizing adherence to international agreements.

6.   International law provides a normative basis for assessing the international conduct of one's own and other states.

The diversity of roles indicated by this rather impressionistic outline suggests that the legal tradition is an important tradition in the management of national security. It may be helpful briefly to illustrate each of these roles.

Long-Range Planning

First, international law, with its focus on the long-run stability and quality of the international milieu, is useful in determining national interests, goals, and priorities. One example is the importance of efforts to strengthen the United Nations as an effective mechanism for conflict management. An international legal perspective may assist in focusing on the importance and feasibility of long-run United States efforts to achieve this goal. The Nixon doctrine concerning the limits of United States military assistance in settings of internal conflict is another example of a general foreign policy precept about which there is a very substantial expertise in the international legal literature.[55] Access to such expertise might serve to refine and clarify this precept.

Second, international law is useful in long-range planning as an instrumental device for the solution of international problems before they mature into conflict. One example is the important efforts currently being made within the Third United Nations Conference on the Law of the Sea to reach agreement on the breadth of the territorial sea, unimpeded transit through straits, fisheries and other resource rights, an international regime for the deep seabed, and many other oceans issues. A second example is the 1967 Treaty for the Prohibition of Nuclear Weapons in Latin America.[56] Efforts to reach agreement on international obligations in case of airline hijacking, similar efforts concerning the kidnapping of diplomats and the spread of terrorism to third countries, and the international concern over pollution, population, and resource depletion are additional examples. Each of these problems contains the seeds of serious international conflict, and efforts to defuse them in advance are highly useful.

Third, international law is useful in long-range planning for the control and moderation of conflict. Current efforts to reach agreement prohibiting the manufacture, stockpiling, and use of biological weapons and efforts to agree on more effective laws of war and regimes for the protection of prisoners of war offer examples. Since expertise in these areas tends to be rather specialized, the feasibility and importance of such initiatives may be easily overlooked in the absence of an international legal input in the national security process.

Crisis Management

Fourth, international law adds a useful perspective in decisions concerning all aspects of crisis management. At a first stage of complexity in selecting and evaluating any national policy, at least four questions must be answered: Are the goals consistent with the national interest? Are the goals realizable through the proposed policy at a cost–benefit ratio which makes their pursuit in the national interest? Are preferable policy alternatives available to achieve the same or similar goals at a more favorable cost–benefit ratio? And finally, are communications concerning reasons for the action adequately presented?[57] These issues are inescapable whether one's perspective is realist or legalist. Yet even when the issues are phrased in *realpolitik* terms, an international legal perspective is relevant in a variety of important ways.

On the question of whether the goals are consistent with the national interest, international legal perspectives may play a variety of roles. First, international morality does and should play a role in defining the national interest, and international law frequently is a helpful index to the normative aspect of international conduct. Second, international law may provide guidance as to whether one situation is analogous to another, that other situation being one which may be helpful in a variety of ways in defining the national interest. For example, if credibility of national willingness to take action is one interest, international law may provide guidance as to whether the situation in question is like other important situations. The *Forrestal Diaries* indicate that Forrestal, President Truman, Royall, and Lovett discussed "the controlling legal rights and undertakings" as a starting point for policy in the Berlin crisis of 1948[58] One function of such a starting point may have been to clarify the extent to which the case of Berlin was like that of the rest of West Germany in terms of American commitment. Third, international law also may help to clarify the national interest in terms of distinguishing special from common interests. For example, there is a common interest in preserving the territorial integrity and international jurisdictional authority of every nation. Since these interests also are shared by the United States, it is in the national interest to support them.

International law may be even more important in decisions concerning whether the goals are realizable through the proposed policy at a cost–benefit ratio which makes their pursuit consistent with the national interest. Thus, the anticipated effect of the policy on the stability of the long-run international milieu may be critically important. It seems probable that the cost to the United States in loosening legal consraints in the abortive and unlawful Bay of Pigs invasion was quite high. Similarly, one of the long-run milieu costs of the Bay of Pigs operation was to lessen the authority of United States protests at the subsequent Soviet invasion of Czechoslovakia. Since a powerful and consistent vision of world order ought to be part of long-range national policy, the costs of action inconsistent with this goal should be taken into account. Similarly, illegal action may result in short-run costs. One such cost is the generalized loss of influence associated with the authority deflation which results from blatant law violation. In the case of the British and French Suez intervention in 1956, such authority deflation may have made the difference between United States silence and its active opposition, a variable which was critical for the success of the action.[59] Such authority deflation is also translatable into power realities in terms of allied military support in a war effort, votes in the United Nations and regional organizations, or even domestic political support. Also, in evaluating costs of a policy, it is important to estimate probable responses from target and third states and international organizations. In this regard international law can provide a useful indicator of the extent to which the action will be perceived as tolerable or intolerable. Thus, it seems likely that the ambiguities surrounding the 1954 Geneva

Settlement for Vietnam may have been a factor in encouraging the war by contributing to mutually inconsistent legal perceptions by North Vietnam and the United States.[60]

International law also plays a useful role in decisions concerning whether there are preferable policy alternatives available to achieve the same or similar goals at a more favorable cost–benefit ratio. This may be seen in at least five ways.

First, the international legal tradition focuses on a range of options and strategies for conflict management which may provide useful alternatives. The effective utilization of the O.A.S. machinery in the Honduras–El Salvador population pressures war is one example. Similarly, United States support for United Nations peacekeeping actions in Cyprus and the Congo provides a further example.

Second, international law can play an important role in structuring national action to maximize benefits and minimize costs to national authority and the international system. It may have been a costly omission in the joint United States–South Vietnamese Cambodian incursion not to have vigorously protested to the Security Council the ongoing North Vietnamese actions in Cambodia to lay a groundwork for the action, as was done in the 1948 Berlin crisis. Not to have done so may have unnecessarily lessened the authority position of both the United Nations and the United States. Along the same lines, it probably would have been possible and preferable to have obtained advance Cambodian assent to take proportional action on Cambodian territory against a prior illegal breach of neutral territory by North Vietnamese belligerent activities. Such a narrowly drawn advance agreement would have strengthened both domestic and international support for the action and would have contributed to the development of an important legal principle.[61]

Third, international law can assist in structuring action which maximizes the cost of unwanted target and third state responses. For example, President Nasser might have increased the chances of successfully closing the Strait of Tiran to Israeli shipping without triggering the Six Day War had he promulgated a narrowly drawn "defensive quarantine" of strategic shipping through the strait, requested UNEF withdrawal, if at all, only from Sharm-el-Sheikh, refrained from troop movements into Sinai and bellicose statements against Israel, and publicly proclaimed willingness to submit the lawfulness of the "quarantine" to the International Court of Justice. Such actions would have had the potential of greatly increasing the international legal costs of possible Israeli and third state military responses to the move.

Fourth, international law can aid in communicating intention and avoiding unintended escalation. Perhaps the classic example is the careful replacement of the word "blockade," possibly signifying an act of war, with the more indeterminate "defensive quarantine" at the urging of Leonard Meeker, Deputy Legal Adviser of the Department of State during the Cuban missile crisis.[62]

Finally, it is important that the national law aspects of security decisions not be overlooked. For example, in any case involving the use of the armed forces abroad there are constitutional issues presented which, if overlooked or poorly structured, may give rise to significant unnecessary costs. The controversy surrounding President Truman's decision not to seek explicit congressional authorization for the Korean War and the similar controversy surrounding the Tonkin Gulf Resolution provide instructive examples.[63]

International legal perspectives also play an important role with respect to adequate presentation of reasons for national action. There is a tendency to downplay the role of international law in justifying national actions or even to cite such justifications as proof of the importance of international law. The real issue, however, is whether international law is considered in the full range of decisions, including definition of the national interest, the costing of policy alternatives, policy implementation, and policy justification. The presentation of reasons for national action is an important and legitimate function. In fact, encouraging national decision-makers to provide international legal justifications for their actions will be desirable in terms of promoting both the national interest and the long-range health of the international legal system. Unhappily, the lack of systematic representation of the international legal tradition in the national security process frequently results in diplomatic and public communication devoid of explicit reference to fundamental legal justifications. President Nixon's address to the nation at the time of the Cambodian incursion, for example, has been criticized as failing to provide explicit international legal justification for the action.[64] Though hardly a break with tradition, the presentation of what I believe was a strong case could have been substantially strengthened by explicit incorporation of the international legal basis for the action. In view of the general failure adequately to consider the legal tradition, immediate justifications for national actions by highly placed policymakers tend to be both legally unpersuasive and generally less persuasive than if the legal tradition were taken adequately into account. President Johnson's overly broad pronouncement in the Dominican intervention about the impermissibility of another Communist government anywhere in this hemisphere is a case in point.[65] Moreover, international legal perspectives may play a valuable role in suggesting the full range of forums for communicating the reasons for national action. At a most elementary level there is an international obligation under Article 51 of the United Nations Charter to report to the Security Council actions taken in individual or collective defense. Though this obligation is seemingly evident, there was an unnecessary delay of some five days in reporting the Cambodian incursion under this provision.[66] In addition, an international legal perspective may offer greater sensitivity to the uses of the various United Nations and regional forums.

Continuing Review

A fifth major role for the legal tradition is to provide continuing supervision of the national interest in internally operationalizing adherence to international agreements. Several examples illustrate the need. Thus, although the United States is committed to the 1949 Geneva Conventions, efforts at field implementation during the Indochina war have lacked the vigor so strongly called for by the national and international interest. It seems likely that such policing would have been pursued more vigorously and imaginatively had the international legal tradition, which is specialized to the issues, been more adequately represented in the national security process. A second example is that of the Lithuanian defector, Simas Kudirka, who was hastily returned to Soviet custody in November 1970 from the United States Coast Guard cutter *Vigilant* in violation of the United Nations Protocol Relating to the Status of Refugees.[67] The incident might have been prevented if the Protocol had been previously operationalized in Coast Guard regulations by prohibiting immediate return of defectors pending subsequent determination of status, as required under the 1951 Convention Relating to the Status of Refugees which is incorporated by the Protocol.[68]

Lastly, international law is helpful in continuing review by serving as a normative basis for assessing the international conduct of one's own and other states. International law is specialized to normative assessment of state conduct. With respect to a wide variety of international conduct, it provides a more complete and thoughtful normative assessment of what state conduct ought to be than does any other discipline. Such conduct includes the use of force in international relations, human rights in armed conflict, the law of the sea, international jurisdiction, and a wide variety of other important issues. Not to have access to this rich tradition is needlessly to impoverish standards of judgment.

This sketchy series of illustrations of the utility of the legal tradition in the national security process is not intended to be exhaustive. It is intended, rather, as an impressionistic but, it is hoped, thought-provoking survey of the diverse roles which international law sometimes does and always ought to play.

To complete the picture of the uses and abuses of the legal tradition in dealing with national security issues, however, it is helpful to attempt to specify the principal potential dangers of abuse of the tradition. In doing so, I include several dangers which might be said to inhere in overly idealistic approaches to international relations, approaches which are by no means the exclusive domain of international lawyers:

1. Equating general goals with specific policies without assessing the effectiveness of those policies in implementing the goals (for example, arguments that since we wish a warless world we should unilaterally disarm);
2. Preoccupation with long-run milieu interests (or more simplistically, preoccupation with legal rhetoric) at the expense of more complete assessment of national interests and capabilities, both short and long term;
3. Pursuit of policies which are unrealistic in the present international system, particularly overemphasis on judicial process (for example, advocacy of submission of the Arab–Israeli or Indochina conflict to the International Court of Justice);[69]
4. Equating the lawfulness of a course of action with action in the national interest;
5. Overreliance on the deterrent effect of international law or on formal legal arrangements divorced from context or power realities (for example, reliance solely on international law for the protection of the *Pueblo* despite demonstrated North Korean willingness to violate international law; a second example might be overreliance on the text of the SEATO Treaty without assessment of its current political viability);
6. Overzealous adherence to "legalism" or premature efforts to strengthen the international system when such adherence or efforts would damage the system (for example, a too insistent pursuit of the Article 19 loss of vote for arrears in financial contributions when continued insistence would damage the United Nations more than noncompliance with Article 19);
7. Reliance on conceptions of international law which conceive of law as a static body of rules or which overemphasize the patterns of control available for enforcement of authoritative community norms; and
8. Indulgence of perceptions (or misperceptions) concerning international legal rights the effect of which is to inflame or sustain conflict, as for example when each side perceives the other as an aggressor and the conflict becomes one for vindication of international law.

Most of the foregoing dangers are suggested by a sympathetic reading of Mahan, Kennan, Morgenthau, Acheson,[70] Kissinger,[71] and Hoffmann, and they undoubtedly have substance. In fact, some recent writing continues to exhibit many of these tendencies. The important point, which the realists have not made, however, is that none of these defects, with the possible exception of the last, is inherent in a reasonably sophisticated legal approach as is characterized by the mainstream of the legal tradition in the present postlegal realist period. They are simply dangers in unsophisticated application of an international legal, or overly idealistic, approach to international relations. On the other hand, as an antidote to the temptation to ascribe intellectual error solely to the legal tradition, it is helpful to note also a comparable range of errors which may be committed by an unsophisticated realist approach. These would include:

1. Preoccupation with short-run possession goals at the expense of more complete assessment of national interests, including long-run interests in a stable world order (for example, it seems likely that the Bay of Pigs decision inadequately considered the cost of establishing a precedent for military assistance to exile groups);
2. Inadequate focus on authority in the global power process and a concomitant overemphasis on naked power;
3. Inadequate conception of the global constitutive process as a source of authoritative community norms;
4. Reliance on conceptions of international law which present law either as inherently indeterminate or as a static body of rules, which present law solely as a restraint system, and which underemphasize the patterns of control available for enforcement of authoritative community norms;
5. Viewing international law and the national interest as opposing fundaments;
6. Sacrificing lasting interests to superficially shrewd deals (the first error is a special case of such a sacrifice);
7. Reacting to events rather than basing foreign policy on long-range planning in the service of a coherent world view;[72] and
8. Inadequate focus on the morality of national action and the relation between morality and the national interest.

Interestingly, lists of intellectual errors in unsophisticated legalist and realist approaches to international relations suggest that realist and legalist traditions complement one another; each offsets the extreme tendencies of the other. Where the legal tradition may be overidealistic, the realist tradition may be insufficiently concerned with the morality of national action. Where the realist tradition may be preoccupied with naked power, the legal tradition may be preoccupied with processes of authority. And where the legal tradition may focus principally on milieu goals, the realist tradition may focus principally on possession goals. As such, a mix of traditions would seem healthier than the dominance of any one tradition over the other.

Some Examples of National Security Decisions in Which More Adequate Consideration of the Legal Tradition Might Have Strengthened American Foreign Policy

There are notable examples of national security decisions in which the legal tradition has played a highly useful role; chief among them are the Berlin crisis of 1948 [73] and the Cuban missile crisis of 1962.[74] More frequently, however, national security decisions seem to be made, implemented, and justified with an insensitivity to legal considerations, which in its cumulative impact has been costly for American foreign policy.

One example is the Bay of Pigs invasion. There is no evidence that the decision to initiate the abortive invasion was preceded by assessment of the cost to the United States of the illegality of covert assistance to the insurgents. It might be that a successful invasion would have been in the national interest in replacing the Castro regime with a non-Communist government, but it should have been evident that the effort, successful or unsuccessful, would establish a precedent for external assistance to exile insurgent forces which would work against the national interest when transferred to Korea, Indochina, the Middle East, or Latin America generally. Although it probably would overstate the case to say that the abortive invasion would not have taken place if an international legal tradition had figured prominently into the national security process, it seems fair to suggest that it would have been less likely in the face of candid articulation of the international legal costs of the action.

The 1965 Dominican intervention offers a second example. There is substantial international legal authority that intervention for the protection of nationals can, if carefully restricted, be lawful.[75] Though the protection of nationals was the announced purpose of the first phase of the United States action in landing 400 Marines, the action was neither implemented nor justified with legal authority in mind. Similarly, although there is considerably greater controversy about the lawfulness of the second phase of the Dominican operation, involving more than 20,000 United States forces,[76] overly broad presidential rhetoric proclaiming the inadmissibility of another Communist government anywhere in this hemisphere obscured the real strengths of the United States–O.A.S. action and, subsequently, the differences between the United States action in the Dominican Republic and Soviet action in Czechoslovakia. According to international law, there is a great difference between unilateral claims to impose a particular form of government on a foreign country and regional claims to protect self-determination against minority seizure of control.[77] The Dominican intervention would have remained controversial, however implemented, but opposition might have been minimized if public justification had been narrowly related to regional peacekeeping and the prevention of minority seizure of control by force. There might, for example, have been an early pledge to abide by the outcome of internationally supervised elections, subsequently held.

The Indochina war provides a host of examples in which failure systematically to include an international legal perspective in the national security process has imposed an unnecessary cost. The Pentagon Papers explore the decision to begin the bombing of North Vietnam in 1965 and to designate the initial raids as "sustained reprisals" for attacks on the American military advisors' compound at Pleiku and an Army base at Camp Holloway in which nine Americans were killed and seventy-six wounded. Although almost every other consideration was exhaustively briefed, legal considerations seem not to have entered into the planning.[78] A good case can be made that the raids were lawful defensive action against an intervention by North Vietnam in South Vietnam amounting to an armed attack.[79] There is substantial authority, however, that reprisals, which are a technical legal concept for forceful action in response to a prior breach of international law not amounting to an armed attack, are barred by the Charter of the United Nations.[80] By their failure to take account of international legal considerations, American policymakers inadvertently chose a justification for the action which seems to have led to international condemnation.

The 1970 Cambodian incursion provides another example in the Indochina context. Though the incursion was lawful, its implementation was insensitive to international legal considerations. The principal legal basis for the action is that a belligerent may take proportional action on the territory of a neutral state if necessary to offset prior belligerent action in such territory. The important presidential speech announcing the action did not mention this principle. Moreover, though advance Cambodian assent probably could have been secured, it was not, thus creating the erroneous impression of a United States invasion of a small country against its will. It is understandable that national policymakers should have been leery of sacrificing Cambodian neutrality or stirring up congressional hostility by obtaining an open-ended invitation to defend Cambodia. There also was concern for Cambodian sensitivity to an open-ended invitation to the South Vietnamese, a traditional enemy whether Southern or Northern. But these objectives would have been furthered, rather than hindered, if the United States had secured in advance a narrowly drawn Cambodian recognition of the international legal right of the United States and South Vietnam to take proportional military action on neutral Cambodian territory against the prior North Vietnamese violation of Cambodian neutrality. Such an advance agreement seemed particularly important in view of Article IV, paragraph 3 of the SEATO Treaty, which provides that no action on the territory of a Protocol state such as Cambodia "shall be taken except at the invitation or with the consent of the government concerned." The implementation of the Cambodian incursion might also have been strengthened by first laying a groundwork in the United Nations, as was done during the Berlin and *Pueblo* crises. The Cambodian complaint to the Security Council on April 22 probably would have been a particularly opportune time to press a complaint in the Security Council. The North Vietnamese presence and attacks presented about as clear a case of unlawful action as is ever possible in complex world order disputes.[81]

The United States response in the Indochina crisis demonstrates also how more adequate consideration of the legal tradition could have insured greater sensitivity to the constitutional aspects of the use of the armed forces abroad. The Tonkin Gulf Resolution did provide congressional authorization for the Indochina involvement.[82] But it would have passed just as decisively if a careful record had been prepared making the breadth of the authorization sought and obtained unmistakable and if the Resolution had not been closely linked with the Tonkin Gulf attacks. Both President Truman in the Korean War and President Johnson in the Vietnam war were aware of the desirability of congressional authorization. Both, however, underestimated the importance of unambiguous congressional assent.

Similarly, though the United States is committed to enforcing the laws of war and has made genuine efforts at compliance, the Indochina crisis has shown how the problem of enforcement is a continuing one calling for vigorous and imaginative supervision from an international law perspective. It seems likely that such supervision would have gotten off to an earlier start during the Indochina war if representatives of the international legal tradition who had specialized in these problems had participated systematically in the national security process. Thus, possibly through the establishment of a joint interagency task force charged with implementing the Conventions and surfacing problems of compliance, one response might have been to increase training in the laws of war and to emphasize the importance of compliance. It might also have been possible to police more closely the gap between the promulgation of newer modalities, such as "specified strike zones," and their field implementation in a manner consistent with the laws of war. The national uproar over Calley's conviction demonstrates the importance of readily available international legal advice concerning the laws of war and the system of military justice for enforcing them. The occasion also would seem to have provided an invaluable opportunity for popular education as to the national interest in compliance with the laws of war.

Finally, placing greater stress on the legal tradition in the Indochina context might also have provided a useful range of options for increasing the pressure on North Vietnam to comply with the Geneva Conventions in the treatment of Allied prisoners of war. For example, it might have been possible to launch a campaign to increase third state diplomatic pressure on North Vietnam by urging the legal obligation of all signatory states under Article 1 of the Conventions, not only to respect the Conventions, but to ensure respect for the Conventions by others. Another possibility might have been to seek Security Council or General Assembly resolutions requesting an advisory opinion from the International Court of Justice as to North Vietnamese obligations under the Conventions and the consequences of North Vietnamese noncompliance for other signatories. Such a submission to the International Court of a discrete issue of compliance with the Geneva Conventions is of course light-years away from expecting the Court to resolve the war itself.[83]

None of these examples as to how a legal perspective might have improved the national response is intended as a panacea for the enormous difficulties of policy planning. Admittedly, it is easier to make suggestions after the fact than it is to suggest viable options under the pressures of time and circumstance which usually accompany national security decisions. Nevertheless, these examples, taken together, strongly suggest that the failure systematically to include an international legal perspective in the national security process has been costly.

Quite apart from the utility of an international legal perspective in crisis management, there is also a need for more systematic representation of the legal tradition in formulating a coherent and intellectually powerful foreign policy for the 1970s and 1980s. Under the pressures of the Cold War, the United States has drifted away from a consistent vision of world order. Yet a more milieu-oriented foreign policy which focuses on the importance of system stability and cooperative solution of global problems seems strongly in the national interest. Internationally, such a focus might enable the United States to regain world leadership, particularly with the uncommitted nations; nationally such a focus may be a prerequisite to the broad foreign policy support which will be necessary to deal with the enormous problems of security, development, and environmental protection which confront us.

The present neo-isolationist tendencies within the United States are qualitatively different from the isolationism of the "America First" movement preceding World War II, when the predominant strain was to avoid involvement in the affairs of Europe, whatever the moral cost. In contrast, the predominant strain today seems to involve a pronounced concern for the moral dimensions of American foreign policy. If such concern can be channeled into a coherent vision of world order, it may provide a renewed national strength. The international legal tradition, though hardly possessing a monopoly vision on world order, is specialized to the normative aspects of state conduct as well as global organization for minimum order and social justice, and is a particularly valuable tradition in such planning.

Proposals for Change in the Structure of the National Security Process to Take a Legal Perspective into Account More Adequately

In the preceding sections, I have sought to indicate why a legal perspective is a useful, if not indispensable, tradition in the management of national security and to illustrate that such a perspective is not now adequately considered. One reason for this lack is attitudinal, an assumption that the legal tradition is of little importance. A second and more immediate cause which reflects this attitudinal myopia is that the structure of the national security process is inadequate to ensure systematic consideration of the legal components of policy. For example, there is no international legal specialist on the important National Security Council staff, even though it comprises over fifty substantive officers. As this deficiency suggests, and as a reading of the Pentagon Papers confirms, the national security process does not now take the legal tradition systematically into account, despite a variety of offices providing international legal advice.

The principal international legal advisor to the United States Government is the Legal Adviser to the Department of State. The Office of the Legal Adviser is of relatively recent origin within the Department. Although the Office of Solicitor of the Department of State was created in 1891, the Solicitor remained on the payroll of the Department of Justice, and it was not until 1931 that the Office of the Solicitor was abolished and the Office of the Legal Adviser was established in its place. Gradually, most of the legal positions within the State Department came under the direct supervision of the Legal Adviser. At the present time the Office includes about fifty attorneys specializing in a wide variety of international legal matters.[84]

Another legal office within the Government which has had major impact on international law is the Office of General Counsel of the Department of Defense, comprising a branch for International Affairs. Similarly, the General Counsel of the Arms Control and Disarmament Agency plays an important role within its area of competence. In addition, there are a variety of other offices engaged to some degree in international or national security law, including the United States Mission to the United Nations, the Office of Legal Counsel of the Department of Justice, the Office of Solicitor of the Department of the Interior, the Offices of General Counsel of the Departments of Commerce and Transportation, the Legal Adviser to the Chairman of the Joint Chiefs of Staff, the Offices of the Judge Advocates General of the Army, Navy and Air Force, the Office of the Chief Counsel of the Coast Guard, and the General Counsels of the Atomic Energy Commission, the Federal Aviation Administration, the Agency for International Development, and the Central Intelligence Agency.

There are, however, a number of structural difficulties which prevent full utilization of the international legal talent available within this plethora of legal offices. The most important of these is that, increasingly, a major role in the management of national security is played by the National Security Council staff which, as noted, has no in-house international legal representation.[85] This lack is particularly acute in the management of crises such as the Cambodian incursion or the *Mayaguez* incident, which, because of the need for speed and secrecy, tend to be handled by a small group of Cabinet and White House advisors. Of course, there are a variety of reasons for the growth in size and importance of the White House portion of the national security process since the establishment of the National Security Council in 1947. Since there are no international legal specialists on either the White House or National Security Council staffs, however, one perhaps inadvertent consequence of this development has been to minimize an international legal input. This lack of in-house international legal input in the most sensitive area of national security planning is a central reason for many of the past failures to utilize fully an international legal perspective in national security decisions. This is not to suggest that the National Security Council is unaware of the importance of a legal dimension.[86] But in the absence of international legal specialists on the staff, it is unlikely that nonspecialists will be as sensitive to the potential of an international legal input as is required. As Roger Fisher has observed, "the degree to which a government decision reflects a given interest often corresponds to the degree to which a vested lobby exists."[87] The record would seem to bear this out.

A second structural difficulty preventing full utilization of an international legal perspective is the difficulty of coordinated planning on international legal issues and the need to centralize responsibility for general development and oversight of the international legal aspects of national security decisions. The press of day-to-day business within each legal office and the lack of clear lines of responsibility between offices have hindered vigorous efforts at strengthening and developing international law. To be sure, there are some highly successful examples of coordinated planning, such as the NSC Interagency Task Force on the Law of the Sea. Moreover, the Nixon and Ford Administrations have added a new position called Counselor on International Law in the Office of the Legal Adviser, with the principal responsibility of the Counselor being to take a long view in promoting the implementation and development of international law. Despite such excellent innovations, however, there is no continuing machinery to encourage comprehensive governmental planning in the implementation and development of international law. To the extent that such responsibility should be further centralized, the Legal Adviser of the Department of State should be confirmed as the principal international legal adviser to the Government. The Legal Adviser's Office already is substantially more than a house counsel to the Department of State, and the Office has a major resource base and tradition in international law which should be fully utilized.

A third structural defect is that the status of the principal international legal offices within the Government generally is not what it should be if these offices are to be as effective as they should be. An increase in organizational rank in agencies where this is a problem would serve both to increase the influence of international legal considerations within each unit and perhaps somewhat to moderate ingrained attitudinal skepticism about the role of international law in the national security process.

In recent years there have been a variety of proposals as to how best to strengthen the role of international law in the national security process. These have included a Cabinet level Attorney General for International Law,[88] upgrading the State Department Legal Adviser to Under Secretary rank and placing him on the National Security Council,[89] creating an Assistant to the President for International Legal Affairs,[90] creating a federal International Law Commission, creating international legal subcommittees of the Senate Foreign Relations Committee and House Foreign Affairs Committee or a Joint Committee of both Houses, adding an Assistant Attorney General for International Law, providing a staff and additional responsibilities to the Advisory Panel on International Law of the Department of State, adding international-constitutional legal advisors to the staffs of the Senate and House International Relations Committees, and a greater contracting out of international legal studies.[91]

Although it would be a mistake to overemphasize the importance of structural changes as opposed to attitudinal and personnel factors, it seems likely that a coordinated series of structural changes might work a substantial improvement in the present inadequate input of international legal considerations into the national security process. In recommending any such changes, however, a number of criteria seem pertinent. First, the changes should be both responsive to the attitudinal and structural problems contributing to the difficulty and effective in ensuring systematic consideration of the legal aspects of national security decisions. Second, the changes should not detract from the authority of the Legal Adviser of the Department of State. Third, the changes should not contribute to further growth in bureaucratic structure unless there is a compelling reason therefor. And finally, the changes should be compatible with the present NSC–State division of the national security process. The following interrelated suggestions for strengthening the role of international law in the national security process, because they are consistent with these criteria, would seem useful:

1. Make the Legal Adviser of the Department of State a member of the National Security Council and any crisis action group (such as the Washington Special Action Group);

2. Create a new Counselor on National Security Law within the staff of the National Security Council;

3. Create a permanent Interdepartmental Group on International Legal Affairs, chaired by the Legal Adviser of the Department of State;

4. Within the Department of Defense, upgrade the Office of Assistant General Counsel for International Affairs to Deputy General Counsel for International Affairs; and

5. Add consultants on international law to the staffs of the Senate and House International Relations Committees.

Another structural change which would seem useful would include maintaining a Senior Adviser for International Law on the staff of the United States Mission to the United Nations and perhaps increasing the legal staff of the Mission as well. It might also be useful to encourage increased use by all international legal offices of outside consultants and research contracts.

Although these suggestions are no more than tentative formulations, there are a variety of reasonable variations possible to achieve the same ends. Accordingly, they are not suggested as rigid formulas. In fact, any one or more of these suggestions or variations thereof could be adopted with some benefit. Nevertheless, it would seem helpful to explore briefly each of the principal suggestions made.

1. The first change recommended is to make the Legal Adviser of the Department of State a regular member of the National Security Council and any crisis action group (such as the Washington Special Action Group). The purpose of this change is to increase the involvement of the principal international legal advisor to the Government in the work of the National Security Council and its crises action group. One of the main structural problems in systematically including an international legal input in the national security process is the NSC–State division of the process. Placing the Legal Adviser to the Department of State on the National Security Council would serve to secure an international legal input on the NSC side. It would have also the benefit of introducing international legal considerations into crisis management where it is most needed (to the extent that the National Security Council or its crisis action group is used in this capacity) and of reinforcing the opportunity of the Legal Adviser to influence the policy which subsequently he may be called upon to defend. As a regular member of the National Security Council, the Legal Adviser would provide legal advice to the President as well as to the Secretary of State.

This first proposal should not present an insurmountable obstacle. An obvious precedent is that of the Chairman of the Joint Chiefs of Staff, who has had the dual role of advising both the President and the Secretary of Defense. In any event, it could best be implemented by amending the National Security Act of 1947 so as to include the Legal Adviser as a regular member of the Council. If the Office of Legal Adviser were upgraded to Under Secretary rank, the proposal also could be implemented by the President with the advice and consent of the Senate. Existing law provides that Under Secretaries may become members of the National Security Council to serve at the pleasure of the President "when appointed by the President [to the National Security Council] . . . with the advice and consent of the Senate. . . ."[92]

2. The second change recommended is to add a Counselor on National Security Law to the staff of the National Security Council.[93] The purpose of this proposal is to increase the consideration of international legal perspectives in the day-to-day work of the NSC staff portion of the national security process, as well as to introduce such considerations into crisis management not employing the formal machinery of the NSC. One of the principal mechanisms for coordinated foreign policy planning is the National Security Study Memorandum supervised by the National Security Council staff. Judging from the titles of 138 such memoranda prepared from the beginning of 1969 through October 2, 1971, some twenty to thirty have had, or should have had, a significant legal component.[94] These include memoranda on Indochina, Cyprus, the Middle East, southern Africa, the Non-Proliferation Treaty, the Nuclear Test Ban Treaty, tariff preferences, chemical-biological agents, the Seabeds Treaty, toxins, and Chinese admission to the U.N. Though legal considerations are included in most of these memoranda, before they complete their interdepartmental consideration, in-house legal experts on the NSC staff could assist in recognition, analysis, and coordination of the legal components of such policy planning. The formal machinery of the NSC is sometimes bypassed for reasons of speed and secrecy. Hence, it is important for this reason alone to build an international legal staff into the structure of this Executive Office portion of the national security process.

This could be accomplished in a variety of ways. One possibility would be to create an Assistant to the President for International Legal Affairs, a precedent for such a position being the present office of Assistant to the President for International Economic Affairs. In view of the dual role of the Assistant to the President for National Security Affairs as both the principal presidential foreign affairs advisor within the Executive Office and the Director of the NSC staff, however, it would seem preferable to create the new position within the NSC staff. By so doing, the Counselor would be brought into the day-to-day work of the NSC staff, where he is most needed. The new Office might be called that of Counselor on National Security Law, a title which captures both the international and constitutional legal dimensions of the Office, and gives a rank equivalent to that of a Deputy Assistant to the President for National Security Affairs.

The Office of the Counselor on National Security Law would be provided with a small staff of international and constitutional legal specialists and would perform a variety of roles in securing adequate consideration of international legal issues. First, the Counselor and his staff would be available to the President in a crisis to provide advice on the legal dimensions of national security issues when, for reasons of speed or secrecy, the President chooses not to utilize the formal machinery of the National Security Council. Second, the Counselor would serve to alert the President and the NSC staff to the legal dimensions of issues in the policy-planning process supervised by the NSC staff. Third, the Counselor could provide an input at the White House–NSC level as to the importance of, and opportunities for, implementation and development of international law by the United States. Finally, the Counselor would serve as a liaison with other governmental legal advisors, particularly the Legal Adviser of the Department of State and the General Counsel of the Department of Defense, on the legal aspects of national security decisions.

In creating the Office of Counselor on National Security Law there are, however, two pitfalls to be avoided. Each deserves special attention.

The first possible pitfall is that of adding new structures in competition with the Assistant to the President for National Security Affairs. If the relationship is one of competition, or is perceived as one of competition, it seems likely that the Counselor, who would lack access to the ongoing work of the national security staff, would be ineffective. On the other hand, if the new Office is integrated into the staff of the Assistant to the President for National Security Affairs, it could prove beneficial to both Offices. And if it is created at a Deputy Assistant level, it should pack sufficient clout to drive the international legal input home.

The second possible pitfall is that of undercutting the role of the Legal Adviser of the Department of State as the principal international legal advisor to the Government. If the size of the Counselor's Office is kept small and the Legal Adviser is made a regular member of the National Security Council and Chairman of a permanent Interdepartmental Group on International Legal Affairs (which would include the Counselor), this danger seems small. Moreover, by providing a vigorous liaison with the Legal Adviser's Office, as is done between other NSC staff and counterpart offices, the Counselor might substantially strengthen the role of the Legal Adviser and other governmental international legal counsel in the work of the White House–NSC staff portion of the national security process. On balance, the importance of structuring international legal advice into the White House–NSC staff portion of the national security process on a regular basis outweighs any pitfalls which might inhere in the new position.

3.   The third change in the recommended program is to create a permanent Interdepartmental Group on International Legal Affairs, chaired by the Legal Adviser of the Department of State.[95] The purposes of the new Interdepartmental Group would be to coordinate and promote the implementation and development of international law. More specifically, the Group would have at least four functions.

First, it would coordinate the Executive position on international legal issues. An example would be coordination of the position on adherence to the 1925 Geneva Protocol on gas and bacteriological warfare.

Second, it would identify international legal problems in current foreign policy and prepare position papers for consideration by the National Security Council. An example would be the United States obligation under Article 25 of the Charter to accept and carry out the United Nations sanctions against Southern Rhodesia—sanctions which the United States supported and could have vetoed—by refusing to import Rhodesian chrome once such sanctions had been decided by the Security Council. Another example would be the United States obligation to pay its assessed contributions to the International Labor Organization, despite congressional disenchantment with ILO policies and appointments.[96]

Third, it would have responsibility for continuing supervision of internal compliance with international legal obligations binding on the United States. This would include, for example, continuing appraisal of the implementation of the laws of war during the course of hostilities. In the long run, the Group might also promote increased training in the laws of war in all of the National Staff and War Colleges and in the basic training of enlisted men, and promote greater public understanding of the Conventions, all of which is required by the 1949 Geneva Conventions.[97] A second example would be the implementation of recent Conventions, such as the Refugee Protocol, by ensuring procedures that would take account of such Conventions at a working level—for instance, with respect to the Refugee Protocol, by changes in the applicable Coast Guard and Navy regulations to reflect the requirement of an appropriate determination of status prior to the return of defectors.[98]

Fourth, the Group would have responsibility for promoting the progressive development of international law by the United States. In this capacity the Group might identify and promote areas in which United States leadership could strengthen international law. It might also encourage better training in international law for government officials—for example, by strengthening the existing program in international law at the Foreign Service Institute and by instituting such programs in other pertinent government training. Similarly, it might identify and sponsor research in areas of international law which are unclear and of potential importance. In this respect it might cooperate with existing nongovernmental international law associations such as the American Society of International Law, the American Branch of the International Law Association, and the International and Comparative Law Section of the American Bar Association. Such associations incorporate a wealth of talent but sometimes lack the means of problem identification available to the Government's legal advisors.

In its composition, the new Interdepartmental Group would be chaired by the Legal Adviser of the Department of State. It would include at least the General Counsel of the Department of Defense and, if the proposal to create the position of Counselor were adopted, the newly created Counselor on National Security Law as well. In addition, the Group would include any governmental legal counsel deemed important for the effective functioning of the Group, or a functional task force established by the Group. The Group might in some respects resemble the successful NSC Interagency Task Force on the Law of the Sea. It would, however, be structured as a permanent interdepartmental group. As a tentative formulation, the Legal Adviser of the Department of State, as Chairman of the Group and representative of the Department of State, should have the power of final decision subject to appeal to the Under Secretary level committee chaired by the Assistant to the President for National Security Affairs.

4.   The fourth change in the recommended program is to upgrade the Office of Assistant General Counsel (International Affairs) within the Department of Defense to Deputy General Counsel for International Affairs. The Office of the Assistant General Counsel (International Affairs) has the primary responsibility for international legal affairs within the Department of Defense. The Office is particularly knowledgeable on, and influential in, legal aspects of defense-related issues such as the laws of war and military assistance. The proposed change to upgrade the Office to Deputy General Counsel for International Affairs would put the Office immediately below that of the Deputy General Counsel. Upgrading the Office in this fashion would be a useful means for recognizing the importance of an increased international legal input within the Department of Defense. Moreover, the increased burden on the Legal Adviser's Office imposed by the new duties associated with membership on the National Security Council and the chairmanship of the new Interdepartmental Group might also require an additional Deputy Legal Adviser and additional staff within the Legal Adviser's Office of the Department of State.

5.   The final principal recommended change is to add consultants on international law to the staffs of the Senate and House International Relations Committees. Congress as well as the Executive should be structured to take an international legal perspective adequately into account.[99] Possible changes to accomplish this goal would include creating subcommittees of the Senate Foreign Relations and House Foreign Affairs Committees or creating a Joint Committee of both Houses similar to that of the Joint Committee on Internal Revenue Taxation, which maintains a substantial staff available for general assistance to Congress. Since most foreign affairs and national security issues have a legal component, the principal need would seem to be to integrate international legal considerations into the ongoing work of the International Relations Committees, rather than to create any new machinery. As such, it would seem most effective to add

international legal consultants to the staffs of both Committees. Such consultants could assist in recognition and analysis of the legal component of policy, in the implementation and development of international law, and in providing a liaison with the international legal community.

In considering these proposals it should be remembered that the question is not whether international law will always be controlling, but the far more modest one of whether it will be taken into account. On final analysis, taking the legal tradition into account is a prerequisite to improved control as well as to an improved national security process.

Conclusion

The legal tradition is an important tradition in the management of national security. As Stanley Hoffmann, one of the most perceptive international relations theorists, observes: "a comprehensive analysis of world politics and foreign policy cannot afford to neglect the law, both because of its *actual* importance and because of its *potential* importance for a better order . . . ."[100] Regrettably, we have far too frequently neglected the law, and the resultant cost to American foreign policy has been great. The causes of the failure are largely attitudinal (rooted in misconceptions about law and the utility of a legal perspective in the national security process) and structural (rooted in inadequate machinery for policy coordination and long-range international legal planning and in the separation of the principal sources of international legal advice from an important segment of the national security process). These and similar difficulties are not unique to the United States. They are shared by most, if not all, nations. By structuring our national security process to take law more systematically into account, however, the United States could take the lead in improving its own crisis performance while contributing to the growth of law in the common interest of all nations.

Notes

1. *See* N. GRAEBNER, IDEAS AND DIPLOMACY 54–65 (1964).

2. Interestingly, Jefferson spoke of morality as a branch of international law and indicated that as so conceived international law was determinative.

> The Law of nations, by which this question is to be determined, is composed of three branches. 1. The Moral law of our nature. 2. The Usages of nations. 3. Their special Conventions. The first of these only, concerns this question. . . . (*Id.* at 55.)

3. *Id.* at 59.

4. *See* Mahan, *The Deficiencies of Law as an Instrument of International Adjustments*, 194 N. AM REV. 674 (1911); Mahan, *II. Diplomacy and Arbitration*, 194 N. AM. REV. 124 (1911), *in* A. MAHAN, ARMAMENTS AND ARBITRATION (1912).

5.   Root, *The Sanction of International Law,* 2 AM. J. INT'L L. 451 (1908). *See also* Gross, *Preface* to THE AMERICAN SOCIETY OF INTERNATIONAL LAW, INTERNATIONAL LAW IN THE TWENTIETH CENTURY at ix–xi (1969) (concerning the emphasis on the development of arbitration as a technique of international conflict management evident in the first few issues of the AMERICAN JOURNAL OF INTERNATIONAL LAW).

6.   *See* H. MORGENTHAU, IN DEFENSE OF THE NATIONAL INTEREST: A CRITICAL EXAMINATION OF AMERICAN FOREIGN POLICY (1951); Morgenthau, *Diplomacy,* 55 YALE L. J. 1067 (1946).

7.   *See* G. KENNAN, REALTIES OF AMERICAN FOREIGN POLICY (1954); G. KENNAN, AMERICAN DIPLOMACY 1900–1950 (1951).

8.   McDougal, *Law and Power,* 46 AM. J. INT'L L. 102 (1952). *See also* McDougal, *International Law, Power and Policy: A Contemporary Conception,* 82 HAGUE RECUEIL 133 (1953).

9.   *See* P. JESSUP, A MODERN LAW OF NATIONS (1948); Jessup, *The Reality of International Law,* 18 FOREIGN AFFAIRS 244 (1940).

10.   H. DILLARD, SOME ASPECTS OF LAW AND DIPLOMACY (1957); in 91 RECUEIL DES COURS (Hague Academy of International Law) 447 (1957).

11.   *See* G. KENNAN, REALITIES, *supra* note 7, at 16–30.

12.   A. MAHAN, THE INFLUENCE OF SEA POWER UPON HISTORY 1660–1783 (18th ed. 1904).

13.   S. Res., 51st Cong., 1st Sess., 21 CONG. REC. 1325 (1890). For the background of this resolution, see J. B. MOORE, AMERICAN DIPLOMACY: ITS SPIRIT AND ACHIEVEMENTS 200, 216–18 (1905).

14.   *See* Root, note 5 *supra*

15.   *See* Mahan, note 4 *supra.*

16,   One contemporary example is the authority of the International Court of Justice pursuant to Article 39(2) of the Statute of the Court "to decide a case *ex aequo et bono,* if the parties agree thereto."

17.   Mahan, *supra* note 4, 194 N. AM. REV. 674, 677–78.

18.   G. KENNAN, *supra* note 11, at 18–19. Kennan goes on to point out that only "two disputes were actually arbitrated on the basis of any of these instruments; and there is no reason to suppose that these disputes would not have been arbitrated anyway, on the basis of special agreements, had the general treaties not existed." *Id.* at 19.

19.   *See* Finch, *The American Society of International Law, 1906–1956,* 50 AM. J. INT'L L. 293, 296 (1956). To some extent this extraordinary interrelation may have reflected the influence and persuasive powers of Elihu Root more than government fidelity to law. Nevertheless, the period undoubtedly was one of dynamic growth in ideas of arbitration and dispute settlement on the basis of law. The very founding of the American Society of International Law in 1906 is some indication of this.

20.   A strong flavor of this shift in emphasis through time is evident in L. SOHN, CASES ON UNITED NATIONS LAW (2d ed. rev. 1967). *See also* Gross, *Collective Security and American Diplomacy in the 1970's,* 12 VA. J. INT'L L. 1 (1971).
    For a superb analysis of the shifting balance between "realist" and "idealist" approaches to American foreign policy, see R. OSGOOD, IDEALS AND SELF-INTEREST IN AMERICA'S FOREIGN RELATIONS (1953). Osgood emphasizes that the early American realists, led by Alfred Thayer Mahan and Theodore Roosevelt, were motivated more by "an aggressive national egoism and a romantic attachment to national power" than genuine national security interests. But after Pearl Harbor, realism achieved enormous momentum from the popular recognition that events abroad could pose a genuine threat to national security. *Id.* at 28, 429–30. This analysis has, I believe, its parallel in the realist–jurist debate and largely accounts for the sweeping victory of the realists and the neglect of the legal tradition in American foreign policy after World War II. Just as a balance in the realist–idealist mix is more productive of a successful foreign policy, so, too, balance in the related realist–jurist mix is likely to be more productive.

21. G. KENNAN, AMERICAN DIPLOMACY 1900–1950 95–96 (1951).

22. McDougal, note 8 *supra.*

23. *Id.*

24. *Id.* at 113.

25. DILLARD, note 10 *supra.*

26. DILLARD, *supra* note 10, at 452.

27. Oliver, *Reflections on Two Recent Developments Affecting the Function of Law in the International Community,* 30 TEXAS L. REV. 815, 824 (1952). *See also* Oliver, *Relation of International Law to International Relations,* 1954 PROCEEDINGS AM. SOC'Y INT'L L. 108.

28. Oliver, *supra* note 27, 30 TEXAS L. REV. 815, 830.

29. Aron, *The Quest for a Philosophy of Foreign Affairs,* in CONTEMPORARY THEORY IN INTERNATIONAL RELATIONS 79, 82 (S. Hoffman ed. 1960).

30. *See, e.g.,* Holton, *Peace in Vietnam Through Due Process: An Unexplored Path,* 54 A.B.A.J. 45 (1968).

31. M. KAPLAN & N. KATZENBACH, THE POLITICAL FOUNDATIONS OF INTERNATIONAL LAW (1961). This excellent study was significantly influenced by the theoretical work of Myres S. McDougal.

32. *See* Hoffmann, *International Law and the Control of Force,* in THE RELEVANCE OF INTERNATIONAL LAW 21 (K. Deutsch & S. Hoffmann eds. 1968); Hoffmann, *International Systems and International Law,* in THE INTERNATIONAL SYSTEM (K. Knorr & S. Verba eds. 1961), in S. HOFFMANN, THE STATE OF WAR 88 (1965); Hoffmann, *The Study of International Law and the Theory of International Relations,* 1963 PROCEEDINGS AM. SOC'Y INT'L L. 26, in S. HOFFMANN, THE STATE OF WAR 123 (1965); Hoffmann, *Introduction* to INTERNATIONAL LAW AND POLITICAL CRISIS at xi–xix (L. Scheinman & D. Wilkinson eds. 1968); Hoffmann, *Henkin and Falk: Mild Reformist and Mild Revolutionary,* 24 J. INT'L AFFAIRS 118 (1970).

33. M. McDougal, H. Lasswell & M. Reisman, *The World Constitutive Process of Authoritative Decision,* 19 J. LEGAL ED. 253, 403 (2 pts. 1967), in THE FUTURE OF THE INTERNATIONAL LEGAL ORDER 73 (R. Falk & C. Black eds. 1969). This two-part article is the prelude to a book on the same subject.

34. *See e.g.,* INTERNATIONAL LAW AND POLITICAL CRISIS (L. Scheinman & D. Wilkinson eds. 1968); E. HOYT, NATIONAL POLICY AND INTERNATIONAL LAW: CASE STUDIES FROM AMERICAN CANAL POLICY (1966–67); E. Hoyt, *The United States Reaction to the Korean Attack: A Study of the United Nations Charter as a Factor in American Policy-Making,* 55 AM. J. INT'L L. 45 (1961). A variety of such studies on Cyprus, the Cuban missile crisis, and other foreign policy decisions currently are under way under the auspices of the American Society of International Law.

35. *See e.g.,* W. GOULD & M. BARKUN, INTERNATIONAL LAW AND THE SOCIAL SCIENCES (1970); K. DEUTSCH & S. HOFFMANN, THE RELEVANCE OF INTERNATIONAL LAW (1968), W. COPLIN, THE FUNCTION OF INTERNATIONAL LAW: AN INTRODUCTION TO THE ROLE OF INTERNATIONAL LAW IN THE CONTEMPORARY WORLD (1966).

36. *See e.g.,* P. CORBETT, LAW IN DIPLOMACY (1959): R. FALK, LEGAL ORDER IN A VIOLENT WORLD (1968); C. FENWICK, FOREIGN POLICY AND INTERNATIONAL LAW (1968); R. FISHER, INTERNATIONAL CONFLICT FOR BEGINNERS 151–77 (1969); L. HENKIN, HOW NATIONS BEHAVE (1968); J. N. MOORE, LAW AND THE INDO-CHINA WAR (1972); E. ROSTOW, LAW, POWER AND THE PURSUIT OF PEACE (1968); Falk, *Law, Lawyers, and the Conduct of American Foreign Relations,* 78 YALE L.J. 919 (1969); Malawer, *Review of The Relevance of International Law: Essays In Honor of Leo Gross,* 8 COLUM. J. TRANSNAT'L L. 343 (1969).

37. *See* J. N. MOORE, *supra* note 36, at ch. 1.

38. *See, e.g.,* Gerberding, *International Law and the Cuban Missile Crisis,* in L. Scheinman & D. Wilkinson, *supra* note 34, at 175.

39. The "empirical" studies in L. Scheinman & D. Wilkinson, *supra* note 34, are a

good example. For an interesting scheme for classifying the utilization of international law in the foreign policy process, see Malawer, *A Juridical Paradigm for Classifying International Law in the Foreign Policy Process: The Middle East War, 1967,* 10 VA. J. INT'L L. 348 (1970).

40.   *See, e.g.,* H. MORGENTHAU, *supra* note 6, at 144, where Professor Morgenthau speaks of the "iron law of international politics: that legal obligations must yield to the national interest." Morgenthau's "iron law" may sometimes be true, but it is surely an incomplete version of the truth. It fails to consider the situations in which law may inform the national interest or the cost from law violation even when it does not. *See also* Morgenthau, *Another "Great Debate": The National Interest of the United States,* 66 AM. POL. SCI. REV. 961 (1952).

41.   Aron, *supra* note 29, at 89.

42.   *See* H.L.A. HART, THE CONCEPT OF LAW (1961).

43.   Gerberding, *supra* note 38, at 209–10.

44.   *See,* for example, the opposing views expressed on the legality of United States participation in the Vietnam war in 1–3 THE VIETNAM WAR AND INTERNATIONAL LAW (R. Falk ed. 1968, 1969, 1972).

45.   *See* Mahan, *supra* note 4, 194 N. AM. REV. 674.

> This is the form of the contention—"Law in place of War"—which is attempted to be imposed by those who favor Arbitration, not only general but unlimited, on the ground that, as they conceive, all disputes between nations can be brought under the category of legal, by being ranged and classified under a system of laws. My insistence is that this is not possible, because under any classification there cannot but remain always cases in which the right is one of morals and expediency—in other words of policy—not susceptible of legal definitions, because the preciseness of these deprive them of the elasticity necessary to successful international adjustments. (*Id.*)

46.   *See generally* W. RUMBLE, AMERICAN LEGAL REALISM (1968); Rostow, *American Legal Realism and the Sense of the Profession,* 34 ROCKY MT. L. REV. 123 (1962); Dworkin, *The Model of Rules,* 35 U. CHI. L. REV. 14 (1967).

47.   Kennan adverted to "the immense and vital value of international law in assuring the smooth functioning of that part of international life that is not concerned with such things as vital interest and military security." He also said: "In general, I think, you will find that foreign offices and professional diplomatists are very much attached to international law as an institution, and cling to it as one of the few solid substances in their world of shifting, unstable values." G. KENNAN, *supra* note 11, at 38, 39.

48.   *Id.* at 47.

49.   *Id.* at 49.

50.   *See generally* D. BRAYBROOKE & C. LINDBLOM, A STRATEGY OF DECISION (1962); NOMOS VII: RATIONAL DECISION (1964); P. WASSERMAN & F. SILANDER, DECISION-MAKING: ANNOTATED BIBLIOGRAPHY (1958) (with SUPPLEMENT, 1957–1963 (1964)); Cowan, *Decision Theory in Law, Science, Technology,* 17 RUTGERS L. REV. 499 (1963); Mayo & Jones, *Legal-Policy Decision Process: Alternative Thinking and the Predictive Function,* 33 GEO. WASH. L. REV. 318 (1964); Miller & Howell, *The Myth of Neutrality in Constitutional Adjudication,* 27 U. CHI. L. REV. 661 (1960).

51.   Common interests are those shared by all nations. Such interests can be either inclusive, *i.e.,* shared jointly, or exclusive, *i.e.,* allocated to individual states in the common interest. An example of an inclusive common interest is the shared interest in freedom of the high seas. An example of an exclusive common interest is the competence of each state to choose its own form of government. Special interests are those which are neither inclusive nor exclusive common interests. They represent an effort at personal or national aggrandizement.

52.   REINHOLD NIEBUHR ON POLITICS 334 (H. Davis & R. Gould eds. 1960).

53.   D. LITTLE, AMERICAN FOREIGN POLICY AND MORAL RHETORIC: THE EXAMPLE OF VIETNAM 19 (Council on Religion and International Affairs Special Studies No.

206, 1969). On the need for balance between realism and idealism in foreign relations see also the excellent study by R. OSGOOD, note 20 *supra*. Osgood points out:

> If the United States is to have a stable and effective foreign policy, neither egoism nor altruism must interfere with the rational, objective assessment of the real long-run conditions of American self-interest; but this does not mean that Americans should forsake their traditional idealism and relapse into cynicism or moral apathy, any more than that they should renounce their self-esteem. It does not mean that American foreign policy should be guided solely by the goal of self-preservation. This is neither necessary nor desirable. America's task is to be realistic in its view of the actual conditions of international politics without sacrificing its allegiance to universal ideals as an ultimate standard of conduct. (*Id.* at 441.)

> Woodrow Wilson and other American idealists understood the profound moral and psychological bond between America's international and her national behavior. Their mistake was in confusing what was ideally desirable with what was practically obtainable. (*Id.* at 444.)

54.   For example, the 1971 uproar over the conviction of Lieutenant Calley would have provided an ideal opportunity to educate the American people in the importance of national adherence to the laws of war.

55.   See the authorities collected in J. N. Moore, *The Control of Foreign Intervention in Internal Conflict,* 9 VA. J. INT'L L. 209 (1969).

56.   U.N. Doc. A/C.1/946 (1967); U.S. ARMS CONTROL AND DISARMAMENT AGENCY, PUB. No. 46, DOCUMENTS ON DISARMAMENT, 1967, at 69–83 (1968).

57.   These issues are also pertinent for long-range policy planning, as well as for crisis management.

58.   THE FORRESTAL DIARIES 451 (W. Millis ed. 1951).

59.   *See* L. HENKIN, *supra* note 36 at 186–205.

60.   *See* J. N. Moore, *The Geneva Agreements of 1954: A Preface,* 8 VA. J. INT'L L. 1 (1967); R. RANDLE, GENEVA 1954, THE SETTLEMENT OF THE INDOCHINESE WAR (1969).

61.   For development of this point, see J. N. Moore, *Legal Dimensions of the Decision to Intercede in Cambodia,* 65 AM. J. INT'L L. 38, 72–75 (1971).

62.   2 A. CHAYES, T. EHRLICH & A. LOWENFELD, INTERNATIONAL LEGAL PROCESS 1113 (1969).

63.   For development of the importance of a constitutional legal input in the national security process, see J.N. Moore, *supra* note 36, pt. 4.

64.   Falk, *The Cambodian Operation and International Law,* 65 AM. J. INT'L L. 1, 2 (1971).

65.   In his May 2, 1965, report to the American people on the situation in the Dominican Republic, President Johnson declared: "The American nations cannot, must not, and will not permit the establishment of another Communist government in the Western Hemisphere." *See* 2 A. CHAYES, T. EHRLICH & A. LOWENFELD, *supra* note 62, at 1169. The more persuasive point which should have been made was the impermissibility of minority seizure of control by any faction in the armed anarchy then prevailing in the Dominican Republic.

66.   Measures taken by members in the exercise of defensive rights must, pursuant to Article 51, be "immediately reported to the Security Council . . . ." The Cambodian operation of April 30 was reported by the United States to the Security Council on May 5.

67.   *See International Law Aspects of Attempted Defection of Lithuanian Seaman at Martha's Vineyard,* enclosure 12 to Memorandum to the President from the Department of State Concerning the Attempted Defection by a Crew Member of the Sovetskaya Litva from U. Alexis Johnson, Under Secretary for Political Affairs, Dec. 6, 1970, in *Hearings on Attempted Defection by Lithuanian Seaman Simas Kudirka Before the Subcomm. on State Department Organization and Foreign Operations of*

House Comm. on Foreign Affairs, 91st Cong., 2d Sess., at 246 (1971) [hereinafter cited as *Memorandum*]; Goldie, *Legal Aspects of the Refusal of Asylum by U.S. Coast Guard on 23 November, 1970,* 23 NAVAL WAR C. REV. 32 (1971). *See also* SUBCOMM. ON STATE DEPARTMENT ORGANIZATION AND FOREIGN OPERATIONS OF THE HOUSE COMM. ON FOREIGN AFFAIRS, 91ST CONG., 2D SESS., REPORT ON HEARINGS ON ATTEMPTED DEFECTION BY LITHUANIAN SEAMAN SIMAS KUDIRKA HELD BY SUBCOMMITTEE ON DEC. 3–29, 1970 (Comm. Print 1971).

68. *See, e.g., Summary Interim Procedures for the Handling of Requests for Political Asylum by Foreign Nationals,* enclosure 11 to *Memorandum, supra* note 67, at 245.

69. *See* Holton, *Peace in Vietnam Through Due Process: An Unexplored Path,* 54 A.B.A.J. 45 (1968); Bassiouni, *The Middle East in Transition: From War to War, A Proposed Solution,* 4 INT'L LAWYER 379, 387–89 (1970).

70. *See* the remarks by Dean Acheson at the 1963 Annual Meeting of the American Society of International Law in 57 PROCEEDINGS AM. SOC'Y INT'L L. 13, 14 (1963).

71. *See* Kissinger, *The Viet Nam Negotiations,* 47 FOREIGN AFFAIRS 211, 222–23 (1969).

72. Just as the legal tradition is sometimes self-policing as to its own weaknesses, so, too, may the realist tradition be self-policing. Apparently, goal-oriented policy planning is a major emphasis of Secretary of State Kissinger.

73. *See* Scheinman, *The Berlin Blockade,* in INTERNATIONAL LAW AND POLITICAL CRISIS, *supra* note 34, at 1; Jessup, *The Berlin Blockade and the use of the United Nations,* 50 FOREIGN AFFAIRS 163 (1971).

74. *See* 2 A. CHAYES, T. EHRLICH & A. LOWENFELD, *supra* note 62, at 1057–1149. *But see* Gerberding, *International Law and the Cuban Missile Crisis,* in INTERNATIONAL LAW AND POLITICAL CRISIS, *supra* note 34, at 175. Professor Chayes is preparing a book on the importance of law in the Cuban missile crisis which reportedly shows that the legal tradition played a highly useful role in the crisis.

75. *See* J.N. Moore, *supra* note 55, at 261–64.

76. *See* Nanda, *The United States' Action in the 1965 Dominican Crisis: Impact on World Order,* 43 DENVER L. REV. 439 (1966).

77. *See* J.N. Moore, *supra* note 55, at 280–82.

78. *See* THE PENTAGON PAPERS 343 (1971).

79. *See, e.g.* J.N. MOORE, note 36 *supra.*

80. *See, e.g.,* Lillich, *Forcible Self-Help Under International Law,* 22 NAVAL WAR C. REV. 56 (1970).

81. For a fuller discussion of the legal dimensions of the Cambodian case, see J.N. Moore, note 61 *supra.*

82. For a compilation of excerpts from the congressional debate supporting a broad interpretation of presidential authority under the Tonkin Gulf Resolution, see J.N. Moore & J. Underwood, *The Lawfulness of United States Assistance to the Republic of Vietnam,* 112 CONG. REC. 14,943, 14,960–67, 14,983–89 (daily ed. July 14, 1969). *But see* Velvel, *The War in Vietnam: Unconstitutional, Justiciable, and Jurisdictionally Attackable,* 16 KANS. L. REV. 449 (1968). To resolve the controversy, a careful reading of the full congressional debate is suggested.

83. It might also have been helpful publicly to request North Vietnam to agree to an inquiry concerning their compliance with the Convention pursuant to the obligation contained in Article 132 of the Geneva Convention Relative to the Treatment of Prisoners of War.

With respect to legal review of the conduct of hostilities in the Indochina war, the exchange of letters between Senator Fulbright and J. Fred Buzhardt, General Counsel of the Department of Defense, concerning legal review of the crop destruction program, is instructive. Apparently, the last legal review was made in the closing days of World War II. *See* 10 INT'L LEGAL MATERIALS 1303–06 (1971).

84. For a description of the work of the Legal Adviser's Office, see Bilder, *The*

Office of the Legal Adviser, 56 AM. J. INT'L L. 633 (1962); Gross, *Operation of the Legal Adviser's Office,* 43 AM. J. INT'L L. 122 (1949); Woolsey, *The Legal Adviser of the Department of State,* 26 AM. J. INT'L L. 124 (1932). *See also* LEGAL ADVISERS AND FOREIGN AFFAIRS (C. Morillat ed. 1964).

85.   On the role of the National Security Council, see generally THE PRESIDENT AND THE MANAGEMENT OF NATIONAL SECURITY (K. Clark & L. Legere eds. 1969) (report by the Institute for Defense Analyses); THE NATIONAL SECURITY COUNCIL (H. Jackson ed. 1965); Leacacos, *Kissinger's Apparat,* 5 FOREIGN POLICY 3 (1971–72).

86.   See the remarks of Mr. Winston Lord of the National Security Council staff in the proceedings of the Round Table on "New Proposals for Increasing the Role of International Law in Government Decision-Making," in 65 PROCEEDINGS AM. SOC'Y INT'L L. 285, 291 (1971) [hereinafter cited as *Round Table*].

87.   *Id.* at 285. And, more specifically, Theodore Sorensen says: "International Law will thus not be important until someone representing it gains access to the group of the President's close advisers." *Id.* at 288.

88.   *See* Falk, *Law, Lawyers, and the Conduct of American Foreign Relations,* 78 YALE L.J. 919, 930 (1969).

89.   *See* J.N. Moore, *supra* note 55, at 310–14.

90.   *See* J. N. Moore, *supra* note 55, at 310–14; J. N. Moore, *supra* note 61, at 72–75.

91.   For an informed discussion of this range of proposals to increase the consideration of the legal components of foreign policy, see *Round Table,* note 86 *supra.*

92.   50 U.S.C. § 402(a)(7) (1964).

93.   I initially suggested this change in the form of a new Assistant to the President for International Legal Affairs. Though I am persuaded more than ever that there must be a regularized input of international legal considerations in the NSC–White House staff portion of the national security process, I am now convinced that the input would be more effective if integrated into the NSC staff rather than as another Assistant to the President. In any event, the important point is, as Theodore Sorensen points out, that

> [i]t is clear that the State Department's Legal Adviser and Counselor are not at the situs of decision-making and the question is how to get someone responsible present. Inasmuch as a foreign economic policy assistant equivalent to Kissinger and Ehrlichman, has been deemed necessary, a similar international law aide or at least a top assistant to Dr. Kissinger is needed. (*Round Table, supra* note 86, at 288–89.)

94.   For a listing of the titles, see Leacacos, *supra* note 85, at 25–27. The Under Secretary Memorandum or "USM," is another important mechanism for coordinated policy planning. The systematic input of legal considerations on USMs can perhaps be best handled through the State Department Legal Adviser's Office, rather than the National Security Council staff.

95.   For a general discussion of the Senior Interdepartmental Group, the Interdepartmental Regional Groups, and other mechanisms for coordinated foreign policy planning, see K. CLARKE & L. LEGERE, *supra* note 85, at 125–72.

96.   For a brief discussion of these and other recent examples in need of coordinated international legal supervision, see Schwebel, *United States Nears Front Ranks of Treaty-Breakers,* Washington Post, Oct. 19, 1971, at A18, col. 3.

97.   The Geneva Convention Relative to the Treatment of Prisoners of War, Aug. 12, 1949, art. 127, [1955] 6 U.S.T. 3316, 3418, provides:

> The High Contracting Parties undertake in time of peace as in time of war, to disseminate the text of the present Convention as widely as possible in their respective countries, and, in particular, to include the study thereof in their programmes of military and, if possible, civil instruction, so that the principles thereof may become known to all their armed forces and to the entire population.

This provision is representative of roughly similar provisions in the Geneva Convention for the Amelioration of the Condition of the Wounded and Sick in Armed Forces in the Field, Aug. 12, 1949, art. 47, [1955] 6 U.S.T. 3114, 3146; the Geneva Convention for the Amelioration of the Condition of Wounded, Sick and Shipwrecked Members of Armed Forces at Sea, Aug. 12, 1949, art. 48, [1955] 6 U.S.T. 3217, 3248; and the Geneva Convention Relative to the Protection of Civilian Persons in Time of War, Aug. 12 1949, art. 144, [1955] 6 U.S.T. 3516, 3616.

98.   Although such changes have now been made, the point is that a better mechanism for coordinated legal planning might have made them *before* the *Vigilant* incident and thus prevented the incident. For the applicable Navy regulation in force at the time of the *Vigilant* incident see Goldie, *supra* note 67, at 37.

99.   According to Congressman Jonathan B. Bingham: "A relevant subcommittee in the House does not exist now, and they are not disposed to be active. Senator Muskie leads such a Senate subcommittee. Members of Congress participating voluntarily in Peace through Law, an informal group, may be more effective in pressuring the Administration. This group is divided into subcommittees." *Round Table, supra* note 86, at 289.

100.   Hoffman, *Henkin and Falk: Mild Reformist and Mild Revolutionary*, 24 J. INT'L AFFAIRS 118, 120 (1970). Hoffman also explicitly rejects an extreme realist approach. He writes: "[T]he *realist* theory of world politics had introduced an excessively rigid and *un*realistic distinction between law and diplomacy, legal obligation and the national interest, legal fiction and reality." *Id.* at 119. Unfortunately, this rejection has not yet been popularly accepted either among international relations theorists or government policymakers.

Chapter 11

Toward a General Theory of International Customary Law

K. VENKATA RAMAN

Introduction

Custom refers generally to the unformulated component of prescription. "Prescription" of law, in its most fundamental sense, refers to a preferred policy about value allocation accompanied by expectations that it is authoritative in context and controlling in effect. The prescribing function is, thus, a comprehensive and continuing *process of communication* comprising primarily an agreement process, a process of formal enunciation through parliamentary organs, and the customary process. While in the first two categories legal prescription is communicated in some stylized linguistic form, in the customary process it is communicated through uniformities of behavior.

Even within highly organized communities, where legislative and adjudicative functions are formally the prerogative of centralized institutions, it generally is recognized that legislation and adjudication do not exhaust the process by which "law" is prescribed. It is familiar knowledge that in applying prescriptions to any complex interaction there is a continuing interplay between the formulated and the unformulated components—evident whether a decisionmaker is concerned with interpreting a business contract or the constitution of the community itself—and custom generally is seen as a dependable guide for ascertaining what is truly regarded as "authoritative" at any given time. Even in societies structured to look to formal institutions for guidance, the lawmaking process cannot be described adequately without acknowledging the part played by customary practice. This is not just because of the reverence with which societies regard tradition in their social interaction. What is often treated functionally as prescription may not be readily traceable to any formal official source, just as a significant part of what is popularly termed "legislation" may have little or no relevance to community expectations of authority and control. Mistaking the structure for the function, many assume that custom is a technique of "primitive" societies and legislation a technique of "civilized" societies.

The pejorative assumption about "custom" has been carried into international law.[1] But the assumption is wrong. The reference to custom or practice is to the unformulated component of legal prescription, and in this sense it always is important. Customary practice is a dependable guide for ascertaining the continuing scope and meaning of commitments reduced to writing in treaties and international agreements. Moreover, since the multilateral convention method, often believed to be the nearest approach to "legislation" in the international community, is recognized to be generally inadequate and too cumbersome to accomplish prescription in the required detail, the customary process has an indispensable part to play in the development of international law. Custom is of obvious importance not only for maintaining stability and security in the community; it also is of indispensable value for accomplishing changes informally. In custom, prescription and application may merge (since custom is created as it is being applied), and built-in sanctions of reciprocity and retaliation are present. Customary prescription also can be democratic, for the customary process allows wide participation of important segments of the community —official as well as nonofficial, composite as well as individual—in proportion to the degree of interest and resource affected by a practice.

Custom assists in making rational inferences about legal prescription. Since it is based upon collaborative behavior, it is most likely to be representative of the common interests of the community. Customary law thus has crucial importance to a workable system of public order, whether it be local, national, or, indeed, global.

The Inadequacy of Past Approaches

Given the pervasive influence of custom in the development of international law in general, including a substantial part of its specific rules, it is surprising to find how much confusion persists about its relevance to contemporary international law. The criteria for its determination and the policies governing its evaluation and application still remain obscure and controversial.

Traditionally, the requirements for establishing customary international law have been stated thus:

> There should be two factors in the formation of custom: (1) a material fact—the repetition of similar acts by States, and (2) a psychological element usually called the *opinio juris sive necessitatis*—the feeling on the part of States that in acting as they act they are fulfilling a legal obligation.[2]

Doctrinal expositions, however, generally have failed to provide adequate analytical guidance for establishing or appraising the presence of *opinio juris* in the various situations of international practice. Indeed, there is an unending debate about both the empirical content of *opinio juris* and its manifestation in social contexts. The concept has been variously described as referring to such diverse notions as "feelings of legal necessity," "acceptance as legally binding," and "implied consent" to some "preexisting law," etc. Some have insisted that it is necessary to establish evidence of these elements independently of the practice itself.[3]

According to one view, customary law can be inferred from practice, provided that it is shown to have been followed under a conviction that some superior law so requires. The majority opinion of the International Court in the *Continental Shelf Cases* illustrates this approach:

> Not only must the acts concerned amount to a settled practice, but they must also be such, or be carried out in such a way, as to be evidence of a belief that this practice is rendered obligatory by the existence of a rule of law requiring it. The states concerned must therefore feel that they are conforming to what amounts to a legal obligation. The frequency, or even habitual character of the acts is not in itself enough. There are many international acts, e.g., in the field of ceremonial and protocol, which are performed almost invariably, but which are motivated only by considerations of courtesy, convenience or tradition and not by any sense of legal duty.[4]

The difficulty with this traditional characterization, however, is that it obscures the real problem of providing methods and criteria for determining perspectives of authority. Not only is the Court implying a narrow conception of "legal duty," but it is also overlooking that the so-called preexisting rule of law, entailing legal obligation by customary practice, is itself a product of customary practice. The alleged requirement of perspectives of obligation invoked by the Court is rendered nugatory by the habitual practice of appliers' finding the necessary perspectives of the parties in past uniformities of behavior.

International doctrine traditionally has used a highly general formula of behavior and attendant expectations as criteria for discerning prescriptions generated by customary process. In laying down a guide, Article 38(1)(b) of the Statute of the International Court of Justice directs the Court to apply international custom "as evidence of a general practice accepted as law." Although the Court has invoked and applied general practice on a number of occasions as evidence of customary law, the criteria and standards the Court has enunciated for establishing customary law in the several contentious cases brought before it suggest an extremely rigid and unworkable concept of custom and an inadequate appreciation of its role in creating international law.[5] The opinion of publicists is sharply divided on the crucial aspects of practice which create perspectives of authority, exhibiting considerable confusion about the relation between the specific features of a practice and the degree of authority thereby established.

Another aspect of prescription by customary practice in respect of which publicists evince confusion concerns the interrelation of perspectives and their manifestation through uniformities of behavior. Far from clarifying the nuances inherent in this interdependence, scholars unfortunately have been diverted into discovering *the* criterion allegedly transforming customary practice into customary law.[6] The futility of such an approach is apparent in the efforts to "prove" *opinio juris* independently of the material practice of which it is an integral part. Such efforts, like the alchemist's dream, never have really succeeded in establishing a single criterion valid for all contexts.[7] There are doubtless some well-known indices, such as repetition and uniformity, which generally are relied upon for ascertaining the degree to which a given pattern of conduct can be recognized "as evidence of practice accepted as law." But while these indices are useful, they are not adequate to catch prescription in all its rich detail, especially in the present rapidly expanding processes of global interaction.

Delineation of the Problem

In social process, global or otherwise, people are in constant communication with one another through the medium of behavior in very much the same manner as they are in communication through the written and spoken word. When cooperative behavior attains a certain stable pattern of uniformity, it creates expectations among those who are directly involved or affected and thus begins to anticipate the shape of events to come. Hence, customary international law is the process by which expectations appropriate to legal prescription are communicated implicitly through the modality of collaborative behavior. Merely invoking custom emphasizes that actual practice in a given situation and the perspectives thereby created in the community as a whole are of direct relevance for ascertaining legal prescription.

Analysis of customary behavior must delineate the whole range of state practice and relate the numerous features of social interaction examined to the final determination of the outcome—the aggregate finding about the content, authority, and control features relevant to legal prescription. Investigation of past practice generally proceeds first from a detailed identification of the whole sequence of events seen in their total context and interrelationship, and material evidence is then evaluated for ascertaining the degree to which participants share perspectives of authority and control.[8] The primary objective is to identify both the subjectivities accompanying the behavior of these directly engaged in the practice and the perspectives of authority and control engendered by that practice in the concerned community as a whole. The events of global consequence in social interaction which shape communitywide perspectives of authority and control affecting legal prescription occur, sometimes simultaneously, at different levels and involve a wide variety of actors and institutions. When the participants in the community process engage in controversies concerning the content or authority of a purported prescription in relation to the particular facts of a specific controversy, they appeal to authoritative decisionmakers of the community for its resolution.

Challenging problems arise when decisionmakers engaged in the task of interpreting the culminating outcome of a sequence of operations find themselves responding to particular claims alleged to be supported or contradicted by a legal prescription. In order to establish their respective claims, the contending parties generally invoke a whole sequence of events alleged to have occurred in the past and claimed to have a direct bearing upon the context of inquiry ranging from those which are most formal, direct, and explicit with respect to prescription to those which are less deliberate and nonformal (being implicitly communicated by behavior). Some of this "evidence" may bear directly upon the specific questions at issue between the parties; part of the past practice directly relevant to the controversy may be obtained from the parties' own past behavior. Establishing perspectives of authority generated by past behavior, however, involves more than ascertaining the intentions of those who initially are engaged in the activity. It is equally important to examine how in fact the past practice affected the common interests of the community as a whole. In the final analysis, the characterization of the culminating outcome of a sequence of interaction as legal prescription, or its rejection as such, is a function of the overall perspectives of the community as a whole about the "reasonableness" and "lawfulness" of such an inference in the particular context.

The frame of reference most helpful to the study of such patterns of interaction must take into account the relevance of every phase of the world social process and not just some selected features of those processes specialized to legal prescription. Both contextuality and comprehensiveness are realized if the temporal and frequency dimensions of inquiry are viewed along with possible complementarity in a communication. Since no two fact situations ever can be identical, the determination of the aggregate impact of a flow of events on perspectives of authority and control will accordingly vary with time and the intensity and diversity of interaction in any given context. For example, a proper analysis of the whole sequence of behavior is likely to disclose that at different periods of time different features in context have a significant part to play in consolidating the expectations of the community, and the differing levels of expectation created at different time periods must be noted for a proper accounting of the importance of the several events in context. The "importance" of an event is understood to be a matter of the magnitude of the social consequences involved.

In other words, whether it is for the purpose of determining the adequacy of past uniformities of behavior for inferring a legal prescription or for the purpose of determining the degree of compatibility or incompatibility of an asserted claim, it is essential to consider the nature of the interests at stake. From the standpoint of an observer, the objectives of the participants in regard to a given social situation may be characterized as a set of value demands and expectations about the conditions under which they may be realized, identified as the *interests* claimed by the parties. The aggregate interests of the community, for whose protection the system of public order is maintained, may be conveniently categorized as *common interests,* and all others as *special interests.* The common interests are those demanded by the generality of the community, maintained for the common benefit of the community as a whole. Special interests are those identified by the demands of a single member whose recognition can benefit only that member, to the detriment of the community as a whole. Of course the common or special character of interest cannot always be determined merely on the basis of the number of states claiming protection. A large group of states may claim an interest which still may be "special" in nature because its recognition by the community may result in serious impairment of common interests. Common interests may be *exclusive* interests if their recognition as such is beneficial to the promotion of the aggregate common interests of the community, even though their impact is restricted to the resource base of the claimant state alone; they are *inclusive* if their recognition has an impact on the resource base of all states.

Such distinctions are functionally useful for identifying the scope and operation of custom in the various types of situations involving varying intensities of practice.[9] The characterization of perspectives in terms of the different types of interests demanded in any given situation would also assist in explaining the *relevance of general practice* to particular usages or the permissibility of deviations from generally followed patterns of conduct.

The Principal Features of a Legal Prescription

Whatever the degree of formal or informal organization leading to a decision, a prescription is the outcome of a *process of communication* in which expectations are created both about the content of a given policy and its attendant authority and control.[10] When the prescribing processes are relatively formal and specialized, the principal events leading to a prescription can be easily identified. However, when the process is mostly informal, comparatively unorganized, and little specialized, and when the parties (often not even officials) have the least deliberate and explicit intent to prescribe, it is traditional to refer to the expectations they create as customary law. In the process we call customary law the principal events and their bearing on the final outcome are more difficult to identify. Policy that is relevant to the community's public order system is conveyed implicitly, by the manner in which, in varying degrees, preferences are expressed when situations present a choice for acting one way or another. To be sure, some prescriptions belong to the public order of the community, while others, properly speaking, are part of its civic order. Not all mores affect the public order of a community, especially value processes with minimal social consequences. But to say this is not to concede that the events of the social process affecting the expectations of a community are susceptible of classification into "legal" and "extralegal" events.[11] Since almost all the features of social process affect perspectives about law, virtually no event can claim complete immunity from some law-creating function.

A legal prescription is a multiple communication. In addition to its policy core it also conveys expectations about the contingencies of application, authority, and intentions of effectiveness. Indeed, three components are prerequisites for any prescription. First, expectations about the *content* of an alleged prescription must be such that they reflect sufficiently the optimum demands or preferred policies of the community. Second, the preferred policies must carry expectations of *authority,* whose principal connotation is the appropriateness of the policies in relation to every phase of the prescriptive process. And third, the policies of a certain content, disregarding their appropriateness, must entail expectations that they will be *effective* in context. Of course, for a legal prescription to be created, there must be some stability and certainty in these expectations.

Discussions about customary law often raise the question of "how general and uniform a practice is required before it can be recognized as evidence of customary law." This is of course a very vague way of asking whether there is some threshold of expectations of authority and control necessary for inferring a prescription. For purposes of ascertaining whether past practice has engendered expectations appropriate for resolving a given controversy, there is no minimum criterion equally suitable to all situations. As will be demonstrated subsequently, the process of application requires relating the prescription to the controverted facts and weighing it against the community expectations and other relevant considerations.[12] When we look at law as process, it becomes clear that inferring a prescription from past practice is a function of context, including analysis of the anticipated and acceptable consequences of whatever choice one is willing to make.

The response of those affected by an event provides one index of the presence or absence of shared expectations; continuity and uniformity of responses are often invoked as indications of expectations of authority. However, it cannot be assumed that no expectations of authority exist merely because overt concordance is lacking. Communitywide expectations of authority, generated by a sequence of events, are a function of the total context of the social process; it is to the sociological perspective of authority that the term *opinio juris* usually refers in the customary process of law creation. While more direct features such as repetition, long duration, and acquiescence are recurrent and important (and one can proceed by underlining any or all of them in a behavior sequence as relevant for ascertaining authority expectations), only by a contextual analysis of *all* features can the full import of any one be appropriately identified. Unfortunately, the doctrine of *opinio juris sive necessitatis* is too often discussed in terms of theories of consent that do not take all features into consideration but, rather, commingle descriptive and normative conceptions in ways that make it difficult to extract clear propositions. The implication of law or no law merely on the basis of repetition, frequency, or duration, therefore, cannot be accepted as satisfactory, particularly since it tends to disregard events which, though sporadic, have significant social consequences and thus are of enormous importance to the entire body politic.

If, therefore, it is recognized that authority is derived from the total context of practice and that it arises from a variety of factors such as the arena of decision, the role of the decisionmaker, and the base values brought in support of policy, it is clear that insofar as customary prescriptions are concerned expectations of authority and expectations of their controlling effect are impossible to separate. One cannot assume from this, however, that the indices are the same. A realistic analysis of authority expectations generated by people's collaborative behavior often will disclose that although there may be verbal difference on the scope of a practice or on its characterization, there is great deference paid to the practice itself. Indeed, the whole process of prescription may be regarded as an effort to stabilize expectations so that people's behavior, in certain institutional settings, also can be standardized. Cooperative behavior which appears to arise on grounds of "expediency"—for reasons of "reciprocity" or "mutual interest"—may still generate authority expectations. The mutual perception of people's interdependence enables them to identify their common interests and to overcome diversity in behavior through the medium of legal prescription. The prescribing act is incomplete, however, unless at the same time a sufficient level of control or sanction expectations also is created. Not only must the norm in question be regarded as necessary for implementing the preferred policy in a given context, it also must be accompanied by control intentions that adequate sanctions will result if the norm is violated.[13]

It is, in any event, important to locate precisely which features of a social situation indicate the presence or absence of shared expectations of authority and control. If the psychological element, or *opinio juris,* is to be inferred from the manifest evidence of practice, it is important to ask how each phase of a flow of behavior affects its formation. Hence, it is appropriate to identify the essential features of the process of prescription and to indicate briefly the various types of claims advanced with respect to each of its phases. The policies pertinent under each claim and the degree to which past trends in decision approximate or deviate from such policies may be briefly noted to illustrate the potential importance of custom to the law-creating processes of the global community. Traditional theory, emphasizing the requirement of control expectations through the different interpretations of the psychological element, generally has failed to make explicit whether, in a given situation, its reference is to the perspectives of the actors engaged in the practice or to the communitywide expectations of authority and control created by their behavior or, as it should be in most cases, to both dimensions.

The Processes of Interaction, Claim, and Decision as Context

The frame of reference most helpful to the study of legal prescription is that of the comprehensive social process, involving processes of interaction, claim, and decision. A brief consideration of the key elements of each of these processes is thus appropriate.

The Process of Interaction

A convenient way to begin analysis of the process of interaction is to look into *whose* behavior is in fact affecting the value process in question. The "who" includes not only the officials of nation-states, but a great variety of other parties as well. Attention should be focused not only on who has the formal authority to create law, but also on whose behavior is in fact having the controlling effect and creating expectations of authority in the community.

While the *objectives* of the parties are to cooperate in some kind of productive activity, they may have differing subjectivities about the relation of their actions to the requirements of future behavior. Is there a discernible policy projected by relatively nondeliberate patterns of behavior?

There may be several interrelated features in the *situation* of interaction such as the degree of organization and the temporal, geographic, and crisis characteristics which can affect perspectives of authority. While customary international law generally is expected to develop in unorganized arenas, expectations created by communications arising from other situations necessarily affect the attitude of the parties.

The degree to which participants are willing to expend whatever *bases of power* they may have at their command, to support or oppose a given policy, is a relevant index for assessing the extent to which a norm is accepted as law by the community. Widely differing resource bases must be taken into account, and the impact of resources other than power, wealth, and skill must be considered while appraising the presence or absence of a "general practice accepted as law."

The *strategies* of communication through collaborative behavior range from such tacit symbols as acquiescence and absence of protest through a wide variety of collaborative acts. All degrees of explicit and implicit communication must be taken into account.

The *outcome* of an ongoing process of interaction is the determination of whether or not there is a communication of policy and whether expectations of authority and control are thereby created. Hence, the outcome phase of interaction may be said to relate to that moment when the expectations of the participants engaged in the process (and the relevant general community affected by it) become identified with those requirements for decision which are both authoritative and controlling in the given context. The reference to final outcome is to the continuing predisposition of the parties about the requirements for decision, including their expectations that the lawful authority of the community will be made available for securing compliance.

The Process of Claim

Many types of controversies arise between directly engaged participants or between them and the general community concerned with their behavior; the same type of analysis briefly described previously may be applied to analyze these controversies and the relation between the process of advancing the claims defining them and the process of authoritative decision resolving them. The claim process has a special bearing on prescription of law by customary practice, for the recurrence of certain types of claims with respect to a legal prescription may strengthen or weaken the expectations created by the prescription. The absence of a controversy does not necessarily prove that a given practice is not considered authoritative by the community.

The Process of Authoritative Decision

When participants in community process disagree as to what is an appropriate prescription governing the particular facts in a controversy, they appeal to authoritative decisionmakers for application of a prescription that will resolve their dispute. We distinguish the process of prescription from the process of application because the latter functions only when a controversy arises that requires the determination of public order policies as they refer to a concrete case; then participants either assert or deny the invoked policies as authoritative prescriptions. An evaluator or applier must perform three categories of interpretative tasks for identifying community expectations about the content, authority, and control of a policy communication.

ASCERTAINING AND INTERPRETING EXPECTATIONS ABOUT AUTHORITY AND CONTROL

This task requires a comprehensive examination of the whole flow of prescriptive communication and analysis of all the features in the context of the various communications which may affect the aggregate general community expectation about the content, authority, and control of alleged prescriptive communications. The emphasis here is not merely upon the various patterns of behavior and their intensity and sequential occurrence through time, but also upon the interrelations between the several communcations which may differ in degree of explicitness. The ascertainment function is substantially the same whether the expectations in question are those of the general community, a regional community, a number of participants, or even the immediate parties to a controversy.

SUPPLEMENTING AND CLARIFYING AMBIGUITIES

Community decisionmakers are keenly aware that the effort to achieve the closest possible approximation to aggregate community expectations of authority can only be tentative since they are called upon to make contextual appraisal of widely differing, incomplete, incompatible, and vague communications presented as "evidence" of the practice in question. The decisionmaker has to supplement the inevitable gaps and ambiguities by reference to more general basic community policies about the shaping and sharing of values. The presumption here is that authoritative community decisionmakers seek to bring all specific practices into harmony with the goal values of the community.

Community decisionmakers must constantly anticipate discrepancies between the articulated value goals and specific events or trends in behavior, and interpretation is one of the techniques which permits the evaluator or applier to supplement expectations which are contradictory, incomplete, or vague. Sometimes what appear to be different types of prescriptive communication may be revealed as no more than complementary communications in the various arenas of social interaction. In such a situation it is artificial to distinguish one type of prescriptive communication from all others as the only relevant proof of customary law; all prescriptions have a customary component and inquiry must be addressed to the whole flow of behavior. In appraising ambiguities among the various communications, the decisionmaker must attempt an overall assessment of of the value consequences at stake, both for the immediate parties involved and for the aggregate community. Approached systematically, the supplementing and gap-filling functions can be regarded as opportunities for affecting the particular value goals of the community and for shaping the system of public order as a whole. Systematic performance involves: (1) specification of each of the claims and counterclaims made by the parties about prescription in terms of the interests sought to be protected and the particular demands for authoritative decision; (2) formulation of the different options available for decision, which may be even more extensive in scope than what is demanded by the immediate parties; (3) estimation of the consequences for the shaping and sharing of community values of each of the several courses of action open to him (the probable impact upon the inclusive interests of the general community and the exclusive interests of the particular parties); and (4) choosing the course of action that is best for promoting the long-term common interests, inclusive and exclusive, which the parties immediately involved share with the larger community of which they are a part.

INTEGRATING AND POLICING EXPECTATIONS IN ACCORDANCE WITH BASIC COMMUNITY POLICIES

The application context makes clear that it is to the general system of international law, as interpreted and applied by the community at large, that the claimants address their controversy. In its most comprehensive sense, the general international law to which reference has been made itself comprises fundamental constitutive policies which are in part established by customary practice. The constitutive process is the process by which the community establishes authoritative decisionmakers for the various value processes, and the general objectives they should pursue to maintain the process itself, certain protected features of the public order system as a whole, and the most basic community policies as they relate to each of the several value processes.

The task of integration requires coordination of the particular decision with these larger processes. No matter how directly and explicitly a practice may reveal the expectations of the parties, it should be rejected if it is incompatible with the most intensely demanded and comprehensive of community policies. From the standpoint of world public order, all practice, no matter what its intensity and duration, is not ipso facto prescription. Both Roman and international law are familiar with the doctrine of *jus cogens,* whose policy implication is a fundamental postulate of all societies. The constitutive prescription of *jus cogens* is a fundamental norm for integration of all prescriptions, including those established by customary practice. In unorganized processes of decision, these threefold functions of ascertaining, supplementing, and integrating communications influencing legal prescription are constantly performed by the specific attitude which participants adopt in practice. Through modalities of reciprocal tolerance and retaliation, the aggregate value indulgence or deprivation resulting from specific practices inimical to the overriding community goals finds itself manifested.

Trends in Decision About Customary Prescription

Having briefly reviewed the essential features of the process of customary prescription, it is now appropriate to consider how a few claims arising in respect of each of the phases of the process of prescription by customary practice have been resolved. Limitations of space and time call for restricting discussion to the most significant of the claims advanced in each phase.[14]

Claims Concerning Participation

In ascertaining the expectations of authority and control, whose past uniformities of behavior are to be examined? The practice appropriate for ascertaining customary law usually is the aggregate uniformities of behavior prevailing on the matter and not just the behavior of only the officials of nation-states. The question as to who are the proper participants whose behavior is relevant for such determination may not arise directly, although it is implicit in many of the controversies concerning either the "existence" of a practice or its "legal" character. On the other hand, the question always arises with respect to participants whose behavior is under appraisal in particular cases.

It is not without significance that paragraph (b) of Article 38(1) of the Statute of the International Court of Justice, referring to international custom, is silent as to "whose" behavior the decisionmaker should take into account in determining customary international law. Moreover, there is little evidence of any serious consideration given to this problem in the writings of publicists who advocate the view that customary international law, like any other form of lawmaking, is the product of nation-state practice. Thus, Professor Tunkin wrote:

> Customary norms of international law being a result of agreement among States, the sphere of action of such norms is limited to the relations between the States which accepted these norms as norms of international law, i.e., the States participating in this tacit agreement.[15]

Because the empirical reference of "agreement among States" is not broad enough to include the entire sphere of action of customary law, this formula cannot focus on authoritative and controlling prescriptions resulting from international practice involving actions of nonofficials, private associations, pressure groups, and, indeed, individuals.

One cannot adequately resolve the question of whether past practice is "adequate" or "relevant" for drawing inferences about a prescription without recognizing that the crucial issue is whose behavior has been of controlling effect in fact, and regarded as such by the community affected by the practice in question. The emphasis here is, accordingly, upon the actual degree of authority and control attending conduct exhibited in practice, rather than upon the numerical strength or formal authority of the participants. Furthermore, the role of the actors and the level of deliberateness with which they seek to create expectations appropriate for prescription also tend to vary from one situation to another. Accordingly, it is necessary to emphasize the role of nonofficial actors and the relevance of their participation in the creation of customary law. Such an approach not only permits a comprehensive view of the "material element" in its total context, but it provides also a balanced view of the verbal and actual attitude prevailing at the given time.

One of the important characteristics of a legal prescription, already mentioned, is the degree of stability and certainty in expectations created by it. Stability and predictability in people's expectations about customary laws are promoted when the postulated norms are grounded in actual practice and are inferred from such practice. Custom is believed to be the most democratic form of lawmaking because all whose interests are affected —irrespective of their formal authority or status—can participate in it. It is only by honoring customary practice in its entirety that the community ever will arrive at the greatest assurance that the law by which its values are shaped and shared is both dependable and predictable. By including the customary component as a basis of inference, prescription of international law is able to rescue itself from a formalistic frame to the functional and operational realm of reality and effectiveness.

The openness of the customary process and the relatively unorganized procedures by which people create expectations break through the traditional assumptions as to who can affect perspectives of authority and control. Obviously, there are varying degrees of authority attending communications of actors in different roles, situations, and power positions. The questions as to whose behavior and what type of behavior are proper evidence for inferring a legal prescription must necessarily be answered, therefore, in empirical terms: who is making effective value allocations, and does this effective decisionmaker have empirical authority?

Traditional theories tend to place greater, if not almost exclusive, emphasis upon perspectives of actors in official positions, and not enough on the expectations of the community at large (which includes a wide variety of participants other than the officials of nation-states). Of course, there may be greater probability that uniformities of official behavior will create stable expectations in a relatively short period of time; in some circumstances, a longer duration and uniformity in practice may become necessary to evidence perspectives of authority in the case of nonofficial behavior. Similarly, since there is greater probability that communications in judicial and parliamentary roles will create communitywide expectations of authority more rapidly than communications in diplomatic or administrative roles, the actor's role also may affect perspectives of authority in diverse ways.

But these points are subject to empirical verification in each case. The importance of "practice" developed in the executive arena, for example, is commented upon by the World Court in the case of *Judgments of the Administrative Tribunal of the I.L.O. upon complaints made against UNESCO*,[16] wherein the Court was called upon to interpret the meaning of "fixed term contracts" issued in UNESCO's hiring practices. The Court pointed out that the expression cannot be taken in isolation, but must be understood in relation to the attitude assumed in the matter by the Director-General. It was successfully argued that administrative memoranda issued by the Director-General were in practice construed as complementary to the contracts and staff regulations governing the tenure of the officials of the organization. It was held that this practice was a relevant factor in the interpretation of the contracts in question.

Writing in 1937, Dr. Kopelmanas raised the question of whether "there [are] subjects of law other than States whose acts constitute international custom,"[17] and the International Law Commission, in its *Ways and Means of Development of International Customary Law,* expressly recognized that not only executive actions but also decisions of national and international courts constitute evidence of customary international law.[18] In most instances, the issue of what past practice is appropriate evidence for inferring prescription is generally subsumed under claims about the "sufficiency" or "adequacy" of past practice, although the empirical reference is to the qualitative character of such a practice. Positing customary practice in a functional frame points up the fact that nonofficials, private associations, pressure groups, and individuals constitute the bulk of the community which is vitally concerned with prescriptive outcomes. Hence, expectations of authority and control appropriate for legal prescription must include uniformities of nonofficial as well as official behavior.

The role of private behavior in the formation of customary rights was pointed out in the *Anglo-Norwegian Fisheries* case.[19] Thus, commenting on the question of Norway's historic title's constituting an exception to general customary practice, Judge Hsu Mo separately observed:

> In support of her historic title, Norway has relied on habitual fishing by the local people and prohibition of fishing by foreigners. As far as the fishing activities of the coastal inhabitants are concerned, I need only point out that individuals, by undertaking enterprises on their own initiative, for their own benefit and without any delegation of authority by their government, cannot confer sovereignty on the state, and this despite the passage of time and the absence of molestation by the people of other countries.[20]

This observation, however, is an unduly restrictive interpretation of the role of private participation and the scope of acquiescence in international customary law. While adverse possession affecting the interests of other states may appropriately occasion protest and governmental regulation, thus requiring a stricter interpretation, there is no reason why governmental authority cannot and should not give effect to expectations which are created by uniformities in nonofficial behavior. There is, indeed, considerable authority for the proposition that expectations created in nonofficial interactions constitute valid evidence of state practice for purposes of inferring customary law. In its advisory opinion in the *International Maritime Safety Committee* case,[21] the World Court relied upon the practice of private shipping corporations while interpreting the scope of certain controversial provisions of the IMCO Constitution. Similarly, in the *South-West Africa* cases,[22] Judge Jessup's dissenting opinion traces the nongovernmental origins of "the norm of non-discrimination" invoked before the Court. Nevertheless, it may be necessary to distinguish situations in which private practice is a material factor affecting the determination of *opinio juris* from situations in which the absence of official participation in such a practice excites a presumption against the formation of customary law.[23]

Expectations of authority concerning certain oil company practices, for example, were the subject of controversy in the *ARAMCO* arbitration.[24] This dispute arose between the Arabian–American Oil Company (ARAMCO) and the government of Saudi Arabia with respect to the scope of certain provisions in ARAMCO's Concession Agreement of 1933, relating to "the modalities of maritime transport of oil." The Arbitral Tribunal took the view that, in the absence of an express provision indicating the intentions of the parties, the right claimed by ARAMCO for disposing of the oil must be decided in accordance with the custom and practice of the oil industry:

> The Arbitral Tribunal cannot overlook the practices and usages of commerce, known to both parties at the time the Agreement was signed, unless it be prepared to content itself with abstract reasoning and to lose sight of reality and of the requirements of the oil industry.[25]

On the other hand, in the *Barcelona Traction Company* case,[26] wherein the World Court was asked to recognize the international procedural rights of shareholders indirectly injured by damage caused to their company, a different view was taken. By an overwhelming majority, the Court concluded that only the state in which the company is incorporated has the right to claim damages. Holding the rules of diplomatic protection traditionally known to international law as the only principles applicable in this regard, the Court refused to consider as relevant the arbitral practice and lump-sum settlement agreements of the past fifty and more years. These indicia, the Court maintained, were special situations not creative of international customary law.[27] The fact of the matter is that during the postwar era (as also under the new World Bank Convention on the Settlement of International Investment Disputes) private international claims have been decided almost exclusively through lump-sum agreement procedures. Characterizing such practice as being of "special character" or motivated by "political" considerations ignores the general practice which is the source for inferring customary international law.[28]

Claims Concerning Perspectives

Among the numerous claims concerning whether or not past uniformities in behavior are accompanied by expectations of authority and control, the most popular is the claim that a given practice is (is not) considered "legally necessary" or "legally binding." Theorists generally identify this claim in terms of the principle *opinio juris sive necessitatis*. They disagree, however, on what the principle means.[29]

The subjective attitudes or perspectives which are entertained by all members of a concerned community are a crucial element of prescription; in general, they determine the stability and effectiveness of the public order they establish. Hence, *opinio juris* must include references to shared community expectations and not just to the expectations entertained by the parties involved in a dispute. Depending upon the nature of the controversy in question, that is, depending on whether a claim refers to the common inclusive and/or exclusive interests of the community or to some special interests of the participants, the expectations of authority and control appropriate for resolving the dispute must be ascertained from the whole flow of past behavior itself. Indeed, the expectations of the participants about the requirements for future decision are influenced in part by the aggregate of past uniformities in behavior *and* the contingent factors upon which they are based.

A functional, in contrast to a formalistic, approach to the identification of perspectives enables the observer or interpreter of a sequence of events to note that many features in context explain both the level and the intensity of the perspectives accompanying practice. Perspectives, moreover, are significantly affected by events in an ongoing process of interaction since initial insights are constantly revised and reinforced in the process. There is unanimous agreement that when practice is extensive and uniform, the related perspectives are likely to be relatively certain and unambiguous. Frequency and intensity may reinforce initial perspectives and allow for the revision of expectations which are unrealistic.[30] Undoubtedly, the more people interact, the higher will be the probability of identifying the common interests of the community. But more practice may not always reflect a greater consensus as to what are the common interests of the community. In fact, expectations may be vivid when a new variety of initiatives is taken. Reciprocity can be a matter of expectation, and sometimes even the absence of reciprocity can create expectations.

Weighing perspectives in context allows one to distinguish special interests claims from those which reflect the common interests of the community, and to ascertain the degree to which these demands are projected in past behavior. This is done by looking into, among other things, the intensity, duration, repetition, and geographic range of participation. It is not so much the physical magnitude of asserted demands or the extent to which the major participants in a community assert them, but the effect such demands have on community interests that should determine the response of authoritative decisionmakers. Testing these demands involves ascertaining what bearing any of their manifest perspectives, whether articulated by utterances or deeds, have upon the final outcome. In addition, it is necessary to note expectations about the conditions under which they are to be realized. In order to be explicit about the basis of expectations it may be useful to inquire, among other things, if any opportunity for their expression was presented and if an inference can be made that expectations were present when initiatives were taken in a variety of comparable situations. Moreover, a contextual examination of the manifest attitude of the parties requires the decisionmaker to inquire if alternative choices were presented for decision. Where alternatives for future action are available, the expectations of the parties are that there is no specific requirement in the terms alleged by one of them. Thus, it is by a systematic examination of the patterns of demand (claim) and response (decision), of their recurrence in a given period of time, and of the bearing each phase of this process of claim and decision would have on the final outcome that one can ascertain in a responsible manner the perspectives of authority (*opinio juris*) for the particular situation. And even then the finding will be only tentative.

Community perspectives about the appropriateness, validity, or lawfulness of prior practice influence in large measure the outcome of choices leading to prescriptions or decisions applying them in specific contexts.

The doctrine of *jus cogens* and its descriptive illustrations generally referred to as "peremptory norms" of international law refer to basic fundamental policies of the community. That there is so wide a consensus on the concept and so little agreement on its specific content need not arrest consideration of the permissible effects of any generally observed behavior in a given situation, or its recognition as legal prescription.

In most cases involving claims of custom, what the decisionmakers actually accomplish appears generally more satisfactory than the explanations they give for arriving at those decisions. But this is hardly a reason for solace. Very often the particular outcomes of a decision are of fleeting interest to the community at large, while the analysis and reasoning of a court of law affects the development of international law by custom and the future of the process of value shaping and sharing to which the decision is related.

It is not without significance, thus, that the two much quoted decisions of the World Court concerning *opinio juris,* the *Lotus* [31] and *Asylum* cases,[32] both were changed by subsequent legislative developments. After defining the requirements for establishing a customary law which had only a special regional significance, the Court in the *Asylum* case noted that there was no uniform and consistent practice in this connection and added that, since "political considerations" had prevailed over past decisions, even a fair degree of uniformity could not make the claimed practice legally binding.[33] But this was an irrelevant consideration, for the critical question in the generation of expectations of authority through practice is *not* the motive animating the practice, but the expectations established by it. The same baffling type of reasoning was applied, for example, in the *South-West Africa* cases [34] and the *Barcelona Traction Company* case [35] to rebut the presence of *opinio juris*. It is, however, essential to recognize that custom results from tacit and informal behavior in social interaction. There is no international law, either customary or conventional, which is not simultaneously affected by political, social, economic, or humanitarian considerations; from a functional point of view, it would be difficult to place any reliance upon customary law if its relevance to a particular context were always made to depend upon proof of its acceptance as law independently of the practice itself.

Writers who take individual consent (or its varied manifestations) as the sole basis for inferring customary law have found it difficult to explain the role of custom in the creation of law. Since custom is derived from past uniformities in behavior, the reference in specific controversies to the consent of the parties is more appropriately to the claim that the perspectives of the immediate parties did (did not) include expectations of authority and control. While sporadic instances of prior acquiescence, protest, or collaboration may be adduced to support or rebut a claim, it is more appropriate to look into the whole pattern of behavior for ascertaining perspectives of authority.[36] Article 38(1)(b) of the Statute of the World Court requires neither unanimity nor universality for establishing law by customary practice, and the standard assertion that expectations necessarily are subjective and, hence, are not open to empirical verification is rebutted by the most cursory survey of contemporary social science techniques.

Sometimes attempts are made to delineate the scope of the expression "general practice accepted as law" on the grounds that it is necessary to have the consent of the states against whom the practice is sought to be applied if the practice is of recent creation. The late Judge Lauterpacht wrote:

> It would seem . . . that to regard the will of States as the exclusive source of the validity of international law is to confuse the creation, by treaty or custom, of new law . . . for which, in general, the consent of States is required . . . with, in the wider sense, the establishment and the binding force of international law as a whole.[37]

If the thrust of Lauterpacht's statement is that the processes of prescription and application call for different sets of criteria for appraisal, then it is necessary to make explicit how the competence to create law is regulated by the collective processes of the community. If, however, a distinction in terms of consent is sought to be made between "new" law and that which is not, the logic of his argument appears scarcely compelling. If customary international law is the result of a uniform and consistent "general practice," the question of whether or not consent is given, withheld, or refused is no longer relevant even in the narrow cases when a special custom is alleged to operate "between no more than two states,"[38] as the International Court observed in the *Rights of Passage* case. To interpret the "general practice" concept differently is to equate customary law with contract or agreement. Furthermore, it makes little difference whether the custom is of recent origin or from the remote past, and equally irrelevant is the issue of whether the state invoking such a prescription is a newly independent state or part of "the Establishment." But Lauterpacht's stand appears quite categorical:

> To require general consent, as distinguished from universal consent, is not to admit that consent is a mere fiction. It is a requirement of substance—though it does not go to the length of exacting articulate consent to participate in the creation of a rule of law. It is a requirement of substance

inasmuch that, although it is not necessary to prove the consent of every State, express dissent in the formative stage of a customary rule will negative the existence of custom in relation to the dissenting State.[39]

The relation between the competence of individual participants to initiate prescription (with the resultant diversity of practice in matters which relate to the common exclusive interests of the community) and the common inclusive interests thereby served can be determined only by a multiple factor analysis in each context. Although the party adopting a particular course of conduct may, on occasion, successfully justify its attitude to the community on facts—on the ground of the special circumstances in which it is placed—it does not on that account follow that the exercise of such competence is beyond the control of the community as a whole. The inclusive competence of the community to assert its common interests prevails and affects the validity of such claims of special recognition. The recognition of "preferential rights" by the Court in the *Fisheries Jurisdiction* case is illustrative of this point.

In actual practice the controversy is posed in more equivocal form. The party which relies on its own exclusive competence, in the name of sovereignty and independence, asserts itself against the rest of the community by claiming that the matter in dispute is one that is within its exclusive competence ("domestic jurisdiction") or that the general practice on the matter is not so settled or uniform as to override its competence. The apparent conflict in such situations is resolved by external decisionmakers, after careful analysis of all the relevant facts in context, according maximum deference to the genuine shared expectations of the parties insofar as these are not incompatible with the common interests of the community. The empirical reference to compatibility calls for determining, in each case, the available options open to the decisionmaker to perform the task incumbent upon him, namely to decide whether communitywide support should be given to the realization of the specific goals sought by the parties and the limits within which they can be achieved. It is required of him explicitly to examine what value consequences he sees in accepting or rejecting the relevance of general practice to the specific controversy before him. When the scope of the substantive rule is examined in this manner, it becomes evident that a determination of whether or not a particular practice is contrary to international law cannot be based solely on the criterion of "consent." While the preferences made by the parties should receive maximum consideration, it is largely in terms of the aggregate value consequences of these preferences to the community that the relevance of its conformity or deviation can be determined in specific contexts.

As holders of formal authority, nation-states advance claims that their challenged conduct is not proscribed by any established principle of international law. The state challenging inferences of legal prescription from past uniformities of behavior would not only deny the significance attributed to that practice but would assert that even to relate the present context to past practice is contrary to its "sovereignty and independence." Its own past conduct may even disclose some formal protest to the events shaping that practice, or its own nonparticipation may be advanced to rebut the assertion that the present situation is governed by past practice. When claims such as these are advanced before third party decisionmakers, "proof" of the relevant "law" becomes somewhat complicated. It is easier to demonstrate the detailed features of the claimant's own past conduct than it is to demonstrate the degree of authority implied by general practice for governing the situation in question. The correlation between the freedom of action of a state and the aggregate demands and expectations of the organized community is such a delicate matter that the balancing of interests involves more than mere manipulation of the particular attitudes alleged to have been taken by the parties in *their* past practice.

From the perspective of participants engaged in cooperative behavior, it is less the "objective validity" of a given principle than the concrete effects they perceive and the goals they desire to realize that matter most. The parties are in controversy about the value consequences which they expect will result from the specific actions taken in the given situation. Perspectives about the law in question refer to the permissibility of the impugned act, for whose justification or denial the collective demands, identifications, and expectations are cited as authority. Each resolution of controversy builds up experience and opens alternatives for more effective means of accomplishing the desired goals. In short, in a *process* of authoritative decision, perspectives about "authority" are located in the general expectations of the community taken as a whole, and it is to this conception of perspectives that *opinio juris sive necessitatis* must refer.[40]

The judgment of the International Court of Justice in the *Anglo-Norwegian Fisheries* case[41] vividly demonstrates these considerations. In that case, Great Britain contended that the Norwegian legislation under which exclusive fishery rights were claimed contravened principles of international law relevant to the delimitation of territorial waters established by customary practice. Norway contended that the legislation in question was not contrary to international law. Supporting the Norwegian contention, the Court pointed out that the decrees in question constituted permissible deviation from the generally established practice. It is worth recalling that Norway did not rest her claim on historic title, but chose to argue the particular geographic and economic factors as justifying deviation from the generally established practice. The Court correctly asserted that the permissibility of such deviation is a matter of international concern and not subject to the sovereign of each state. Viewing the judgment as a whole, it might even be interpreted that the Court performed an important "legislative" function in the sense of permitting changes in the existing customary law for the purposes of meeting the changing needs of the community for a greater share of the resources of the oceans.[42]

Claims Concerning Situational Features

The relative lack of organization characteristic of the arenas of customary prescription permits the process of prescription by custom much flexibility and adaptability. Arenas vary significantly in the relative degree of their organization; specialization to prescription; centralization in structure; composition, in terms of official or nonofficial character; interaction, in terms of the impact of a practice on the geographic range; local, regional, or global interests affected; and in the temporal, institutional, and crisis factors in context which both individually and in conjunction with other variables mold community expectations of authority and control at any given time. If "law" is to be authoritative and effective, it must reflect the realities of the social context. It is therefore only by honoring the customary component of prescription that decision processes can ever take advantage of the whole range of arenas in which consequential expectations of authority are generated. What custom does is to provide to every human interaction a wide range of alternative solutions, some of which may not be explicitly or formally recognized. In a decentralized and unorganized world this is especially important, for the unstructured patterns of interaction can and often do open up new arenas and new opportunities for alternative solutions. Custom offers alternatives to closed social systems whether or not the arena is characterized by a high degree of reciprocity.

The situational dimension of prescription by custom has occupied an important place in studies on customary law. Indeed, some writers purport to see in one or a few of the integral features conclusive evidence of the existence or absence of customary law, without attempting to interpret those features contextually or to ascertain their significance in reference to other, equally valuable features in context.

Take the time factor. Expressions such as "continuous and uniform practice" or "immemorial usage" or "instant customary law" do little to clarify the significance and the content of the customary practice in terms of the features of the context prevailing at any given time.[43] While the elements of duration and frequency are significant, their importance is relative to the degree of official involvement and formal organization, as well as the subject matter of the practice. Moreover, in a scientific and technological age of communication, a relatively short duration may suffice to create stability in expectations. The premise of the traditional doctrine which interprets *opinio juris* only in terms of the duration and repetition of a practice confuses socially relevant time with chronological time. In the socially relevant sense of time, which is the only pertinent index for ascertaining perspectives, what is to be noted is how the participants themselves have come to realize and react to the passage of time, to get a sense of social reality.[44]

In the *Continental Shelf Cases*,[45] the issue was whether the "equidistance method" for delimiting continental shelf between adjacent states had become a principle established by customary practice.

> The principle of equidistance as it now figures in Article 6 of the Convention, was proposed by the Commission with considerable hesitation, somewhat on an experimental basis, at most *de lege ferenda* and not at all *de lege lata* or as an emerging rule of customary international law.[46]

The Court recognized that such a method can develop; such a process "constitutes indeed one of the recognized methods by which new rules of customary international law may be formed. At the same time this result is not lightly to be regarded as having been attained."[47] Irrespective of the merits of the Court's holding in the instant case, the Court viewed the numerous individual and collective acts both before and after the agreed formulation in Article 6 of the Continental Shelf Convention, but never collectively, for examining a discernible trend in this practice.

If custom is to be accepted as an autonomous procedure in itself, caution must be exercised to avoid mechanical interpretation of the requirements of either duration or general practice. The relevance of the time factor indicated briefly here and its social relevance in context merely illustrate the role a variety of other important situational features' would have on expectations created by practice.

Claims Concerning Bases of Power

The insistence upon unanimity of participation is merely a camouflage for what really is an undeclared preference for the unilateral veto of prescriptions, even when these are demanded by the widest segment of the community. Such a view of "general practice" is surely as objectionable as the opinion occasionally advanced that acceptance by "major powers" is an essential requirement for recognizing practice as evidence of customary law. Both contextuality and comprehensiveness in participation require that the alleged prescription reflect the common interests of the whole community. Of course, not all members of the community find it necessary, possible, or opportune to participate in the entire range of prescriptions that constitute the legal system. Nor can all those whose attitudes shape practice participate in the same manner or to an identical extent.[48] In a great many situations, such opportunities come only to a few, although it is with the general attitude of the community as a whole that perspectives of authority and control are associated. For purposes of appraisal, therefore, it is necessary to take into account not so much the numerical strength of those who accept or reject a practice, but the bases of power expended in support of it. The seriousness and intensity with which demands are pressed and realized in social processes often is indicated by the resources mustered in support of, or opposition to, a certain behavior.

These resources include not only power, but all other values, and the focus is as much on the disposition to use them to make decisions effective as it is on their physical magnitude. In some instances, the commitment of symbols of authority may be just as effective and controlling as a commitment carried by the use of resources. The differential access of various participants to material resources requires consideration to the effect of inequality in bases of power. In making inferences about shared expectations, a modest presumption in favor of the party with fewer resources may be indulged.

Explicit consideration was given to this aspect of practice in the *International Air Transport* arbitration between the United States and France.[49] Consideration of the resources brought to bear upon the expectations engendered by past behavior also influenced the arbitral award in the *ARAMCO* arbitration, which included findings of customary law, as well as the interpretation of a concession agreement made in 1933 between the government of Saudi Arabia and the Arabian–American Oil Company.[50] And, in appraising the extent of ratifications obtained for the Continental Shelf Conventions, the International World Court, in the *Corfu Channel* case, commented upon the attitude of states not having a continental shelf.[51]

While examining the question of the resources and bases of power which participants bring to bear on the shaping of expectations, it is important to strike a desirable balance between community expectations of authority and control created by practice. As the International Court of Justice pointed out in the *Corfu Channel* case with reference to the permissibility of intervention, external decisionmakers may reject expectations of authority if their recognition is believed to be incompatible with the common interests of the community.[52] In the same vein, many of the new nations have questioned the continuing validity of international law not generally supported by them. As Castañeda has pointed out:

> In all that vast body of law having to do with the responsibility of States, the rules now in force, molded by a practice repeated a thousand-fold throughout the last century and a half, were not only created independently of the interested small States, but even against their desires and interests. These norms reflect the relations that were established between two groups of States; on the one hand, the investor countries, generally industrialized and militarily strong, and on the other, the underdeveloped and weaker countries that import capital. Many of the rules that, in the opinion of numerous European authors, are still in force, such as the one enabling foreigners to claim greater rights than nationals, reflect the unequal situation existing between these two groups of countries.[53]

Some of the dissenting opinions in the *Temple of Preah-Vihear* case point out that it is also important to consider the social, in contrast to the formal, competences of the participants to employ resources at their disposal.[54] All these factors are useful for ascertaining the level and the nature of expectations of authority generated by past uniformities of behavior.

Claims Concerning Strategies

Since the subjectivities of contesting parties cannot be verified in a direct scientific manner, every effort must be made toward inferring the genuine shared expectations of the participants by reference to oral and written words, overt deeds, and other acts of collaboration. When one examines a sequence of behavior over a given period of time, it is possible to find outright contradiction or inconsistency of a lesser degree. Often it may not be possible to discern unequivocal acceptance; hence, it is necessary to note the sequential pattern of conduct and to verify the trend for general uniformity or consistency of word and deed over the period in question. In certain contexts, however, inaction may be as significant as action; the absence of practice inconsistent with community expectations may be just as relevant to the clarification of the general practice as positive conduct congruent with community expectations. When people are engaged in the exchange of goods and services they interact under a set of expectations; "absence of practice" occurs only in the phase of initiation of a prescription.

Whatever the strategy, however, it has significance only in terms of all the other features of the context of which it is a part. Consider duration. Repetition may indicate the degree of certainty about the expectations which the repetitious behavior carried with it. On the other hand, in areas where there are no prior competing prescriptions, practice within a relatively short period of time can generate expectations of authority and control. Initially, the participants may not have any definitive expectations, or they even may entertain doubts about the lawfulness of a certain act (although its repetition may, in course of time, shape their expectations). And in some instances, a mere lapse of time and absence of protest, even without any significant recurrence, can provide added significance. For example, an important piece of evidence such as a boundary map drawn by experts, although it may not be intended as an "official document" or an authentic agreement, may acquire a peculiar importance with the lapse of time.[55] It is the continued acquiescence and tacit acknowledgment by the parties in their subsequent conduct that imparts authority to such evidence. The necessary degree of approximation between deeds and declarations of intent is that which is adequate to give effect to the goal values sought in context, and it is for this reason that priority should be given to communications arising in contexts specialized to prescription. This is the comprehensive standpoint adopted here, and includes all arenas, not just those specialized to the formulation of prescriptions.

It is, however, misleading, and simplistic at that, to suggest "the binding qualities" of custom emerge only when the underlying principle is reduced to writing. Karol Wolfke suggests:

> An international custom comes into being when a certain practice becomes sufficiently ripe to justify the presumption that it has been accepted by states as an expression of law. At that moment the custom is regarded as *formed* and the corresponding customary rule of international law, which may at any time be *formulated* begins to have binding effect. Custom as a kind of practice, hence actual qualified conduct, can exist, develop, become extinct, etc., but only the corresponding right and obligation, hence a rule of law which at any time may be *expressed in words,* can bind and be applied.[56]

Nor do the vaguely defined notions of "consensus" or "consent" help clarify what are the empirical references in practice to perspectives of authority. Anthony D'Amato, for one, has advanced the view that the content of international law is a function of the psychology of the participants and that this psychology is said to have been "rooted in the strategic calculation rather than in simple beliefs about norms."[57] But to suggest that "international consensus is manifested objectively as a result of strategic calculations of the States" is not to say much. The important questions are what are the criteria for ascertaining consensus and how are these criteria to be applied to uniformities of past behavior? Coming close to Wolfke's notion of customary law, D'Amato states that "the qualitative element of custom is the articulation of a rule of international law," by which he means that "there must be a characterization of legality," and the "legality must be international, not domestic law." He concludes that "consensus generally occurs with respect to rules that were already well-established!"[58]

Such an approach ignores the fact that customary law is concerned not only with the "strategic calculations" of the participants but also with the expectations they generate in the community as a whole. The increasing demand for conformity between authority and effective control usually is met by taking a balanced view of perspectives and obligations. It is with the commonly shared expectations that customary law is concerned, and its prescriptive significance cannot be attributed to the "consent" or "will" of individual participants. It is a matter of common experience that, on occasion, participants may not be consciously aware that they are creating law by their conduct; yet past practice may conclusively establish where the law can be found for decision. And conversely, even assuming that they did consciously "agree" on what the law ought to be, there is no reason to hold that participants still agree and that external decisionmakers will necessarily honor that commitment irrespective of its consequences.

As a matter of international policy there should be a presumption against inferring prescription from a flow of behavior which is coercive and unlawful in context, although distinctions may have to be drawn between the degree to which the outcome is coercive and the degree to which the strategies are coercive in context. Under certain circumstances, it may be found necessary to administer mild coercions to support the outcome in the interests of maintaining minimum public order. It is the common experience of every working polity that coercion in general is a highly ineffective technique for establishing enduring stability and order. The technique of customary prescription which extends over a long period of time tends to focus upon collaborative behavior.

There are a number of aspects involved in considering the implications of the differing modalities by which participants communicate a policy, sometimes the same policy, in different situations. The degree to which past uniformities of behavior provide a communication, its consistency, degrees of conformity and uniformity in behavior—all are relevant factors in determining expectations. Very often the claims may relate to the relevance of inaction as against action, or to the relative influence of words and behavior, or to the adequacy of the practice for purposes of inferring a communication. The presumptive significance of any feature in this regard must be a function of the total context, and no rules can be suggested for making a priori inference. While it is not possible to provide here a comprehensive and systematic account of the relevance of all the features of this phase, a few aspects raised in current decision practice may briefly been mentioned to emphasize the general trend.

In the current practice of the International Court of Justice, there is considerable insistence upon explicit and direct evidence for proof of custom, an insistence which has created an impression that the relatively informal and implicit method of customary law creation is of no importance to contemporary world public order. Such an attitude is evident in the majority findings of the Court not only in the notorious *South-West Africa* cases but also, to some extent, in the *Continental Shelf* and *Barcelona Traction Company* cases. It is, at any rate, very much to be regretted. The process of development of international law by customary practice differs in some respect from the formal treaty and convention method. Multilateral conventions and agreements proceed generally from a specialized arena subject to previously agreed procedures. As the Vienna Convention on the Law of Treaties indicates, customary practices affect and are in turn affected by multilateral conventions.[59] At times the explicit treaty method, the multilateral convention procedure, and other forms of declaration may have specific functions to perform. The point is, however, that in a rapidly changing context of social interaction, no single method ever can be presumed to accomplish legal prescription in the required detail and comprehensiveness. A multilateral treaty may be a high water mark in progressive development, but it is hard to envisage one which does not explicitly or by implication indicate its relation to prior practice and its dependence on subsequent interpretations and implementation. In short, it is essential to look at all the diverse forms of action as elements in a continuous flow of behavior, rather than as independent events.

It is, moreover, incorrect to assume that merely because all or part of a communication is expressed in verbal form, however hortatory its tenor, it is for that reason irrelevant as an index for ascertaining expectations relevant to prescription. In many areas of common interest to the global community at the present time, a substantial bulk of states find hortatory exercises the only means of influencing expectations of authority within a relatively short period of time. Tracing the history of the concept of "self-determination" in the *Namibia* opinion, for example, the majority of the World Court recognized that the relevant United Nations resolutions constituted evidence of state practice.[60] Endorsing this view, Judge Ammoun pointed out that "if there is any general practice which might be held beyond dispute to constitute law within the meaning of Article 38, paragraph 1(b), of the Statute of the Court, it must surely be that which is made up of conscious action of the peoples themselves, engaged in a determined struggle."[61] In other words, that the legislative competence of the General Assembly is controversial, and consistently disputed by some, need not keep external decisionmakers from recognizing the existence of the verbal communications which they make. They are no less relevant than any other criteria for demonstrating the general expectations of the community on a given matter.

Finally, while evaluating the relevance of prior "protest" and "acquiescence" in collaborative behavior, attention is too often focused on the adversarial postures of the parties and too little emphasis on the importance of acts of collaboration. The latter do communicate even if they are shown to have been voluntarily done.[62]

Claims Concerning Outcomes

Depending on the precise nature of the issues raised in controversy, the final outcome of a decision on customary international law refers to the relevance of past uniformities of behavior to the controversy at hand. It is a finding about the degree to which perspectives of authority about relevant content are communicated by that practice. The principle of contextuality of interpretation, mentioned previously with respect to all phases of behavior, imports that characterization of the final outcome of a certain sequence of events as prescription will depend upon the particular issues in context and the extent to which the choices made are likely to promote the overriding goals of the community, including the common interests of the immediate parties in dispute.

A useful technique for analyzing prescriptive processes is to observe the sequential pattern of prescription. It may be recalled that the precipitating events in a controversy are the facts (demands and expectations) which give rise to specific claims. The decisionmaker, in responding to those claims, interprets these facts in terms of community goals. The view taken of the facts and the premises from which they are interpreted are complementary aspects of the decision process. Both claimants may tender the same factual date in their effort to seek recognition or rejection of an alleged requirement for decision (on the ground that such a requirement has or has not been established by past practice). Sometimes the parties do not question facts. When they are in controversy, however, the context is analyzed by examining the sequence, similarity, and relative uniformity of the actions taken in prior practice. The technique of identifying, with relative accuracy, the factual circumstances which have precipitated the controversy requires a skilled analysis of the whole context.

Beyond the processing of evidence is the more subtle function of relating the facts to the context at hand, in order to deduce the shared expectations of the parties about the requirements for decision. There are some well-known indices employed for determining perspectives of authority and control—*e.g.*, frequency, repetition, long usage—which, together with the attitude taken by the parties as expressed by way of acquiescence or protest, provide insights into the *nature* of the transaction under investigation. However, the strategies employed for interpreting the *scope* of the communication also include other substantive principles whose clarification is necessary to promote the desired stability and certainty of the process by which customary prescriptions of international law are determined. We have noted that the analyst addressing himself to the outcome of a sequence of events is concerned with determining the authority and control expectations engendered by past practice and the content of the prescription. He may find, for example, that it is very artificial to talk about customary law and all the other modes of prescription in sharply exclusive terms (because all prescriptions have a customary component) and that even when the process is least explicit there are enough indications of a deliberate choice to reveal shared expectations of authority and control. Characteristically, the principal elements of prescription may not be revealed in a uniform pattern in the various types of legal prescription. A close examination of the respective practices may reveal, for example, that the principal strategies employed (words and/or deeds) do not always have the same degree of importance in every prescriptive context, but acquire their importance in reference to the nature of the functions expected to be served by the prescription. Depending upon the functions they perform, legal prescriptions may be classified as supervisory, regulatory, enterprisory, corrective, or constitutive in character. It is not merely the duration of a practice or clarity in communication which is important in a particular context; many of the other features of the process will also have relevance in the context.

It will be recalled that the final outcome of a decision is a response to the community demand for a prescription. Considerations of rationality and effectiveness may influence the decisionmaker's response as to when an area of activity should be brought under inclusive public order regulation and when these interests are best promoted by leaving the matter to private ordering and initiative. A public order of human dignity has as its main objectives the protection of the maximum freedom of the individual, by securing a dynamic and progressive civic order as a way of maintaining an effective public order system. On the other hand, even when strictly "domestic," controversies may have serious consequences to public order, affect the common interests of the community, and give rise to intensive demands for regulation through the public order system of the community. Considerations such as these will influence the decisionmaker's response to questions of sufficiency or adequacy of a practice in particular contexts and further the interpretation to be given to the other material features in a situation claimed by both parties as significant evidence of their shared expectations. For instance, it may be asked, as a preliminary matter, whether the situation under inquiry presented any alternative choices for decision. If there were some alternative choices presented for decision but the parties adopted a uniform and consistent attitude, then the elements of repetition, frequency, duration, and so forth can be interpreted as evidence of the subjectivities of the parties. In other words, those features here indicate that some commitment—a deliberate and conscious choice—is expressed in the parties' conduct.

If in furtherance of their desired objectives the parties previously have taken certain steps to meet situations similar to the one under consideration, such past conduct can be analyzed to determine the level of expectations shared by them. For example, if a past decision was arrived at after one of the parties invoked the desirability or necessity of deciding the matter the way it was in fact decided, that constitutes an important event indicating some commitment actually made by the parties. On the other hand, it may turn out that rival claims were advanced as possible solutions to the problem but that the problem was left unresolved, or that the matter was passed over without seriously attempting to arrive at a settlement, or that the settlement itself was expressly understood to be an ad hoc arrangement. All these various possibilities merely reflect the different levels of agreement or disagreement between the parties. The recurrence of these events accordingly throws considerable light on the subjectivities of the parties; with the passage of time and repetition of these actions, the initial differences between the parties may be composed or result in a controversy. If a compromise arrived at is reinforced by the resources at the disposal of the parties, there is further indication that some element of authority has been applied to sustain the choices made. On the other hand, if it is apparent that in a given situation there were no other alternatives open to the parties, then something more than mere repetition and uniformity would be necessary to show that the parties intended to establish a requirement for future behavior. Very often the particular aspects of the practice other than duration and repetition furnish the required evidence for making the appropriate inferences. Traditionally it is in this area that the decisionmaker is supposed to determine whether the practice is merely a "usage" or is accompanied by expectations of authority and control.

Note also that intervention of a third party decisionmaker enables the import of the practice to be either strengthened or weakened, depending upon how he conceives his role in the decision process and disposes his bases of power to affect the future course of events. For example, if he starts from the premise that his task is no more than to ascertain whether the parties are ad idem as to what is lawful and, hence, required in the context, he may proceed to derive his conclusion from some particular feature or features of the behavior itself, such as the official character of the engagement, the relative degree of participation in the practice, the failure to protest, and so on. Or he may approximate the expectations of the parties to what is, in his estimation, lawful and necessary, and interpret accordingly the manifest features of the conduct in the situation under consideration. If the claim pertains to the exclusive interests of the parties, their own prior conduct—to the extent that it is compatible with the overriding community policies—would provide the necessary guidance for decision. If the claim pertains to inclusive interests, the consensus of the community, employing precisely the same indices, is interpreted to relate it to the controversial facts under consideration. The decision, whether it is arrived at in an unorganized arena by the parties themselves or by external decisionmakers, constitutes a significant event and enters the main channels of prescriptive communication affecting the communitywide perspectives of authority and control for future decision.

The general trend of decision affecting the culminating phase of the process of prescription has been extensively commented upon by text writers. The treatises of Wilfred Jenks and Hersch Lauterpacht succinctly document the generally unsatisfactory character of the World Court's handling of claims based upon customary international law—unsatisfactory because of the excessively limited perspective from which the goals of application are set by the World Court. The "supplementing" and "integrating" functions expected of authorized decisionmakers no doubt arise only during the phases of application, but they are of crucial importance to legal prescription and they are equally relevant to the function of ascertaining expectations of authority created by customary practice. A future historian might well wonder why, in the *Right of Passage* case, the Court let pass a creative opportunity to clarify the common interests of the world which the General Assembly a decade later authoritatively incorporated in a general declaration.[63] Notwithstanding the juristic overtures of the Court in its *Namibia* opinion, the irreparable damage of its earlier *South-West*

Africa cases and the jurisprudential outlook reflected in the several other cases mentioned previously have cast doubts on the usefulness of relying on custom. It is worth noting that the general trend of decision outside the World Court during this period appears relatively more responsive to claims based upon customary law.[64]

The Factors Conditioning the Decision Process

In this rapidly changing process of interaction the observer will notice that at any point in time the probable impact of these interrelated "authority functions" on the perspectives of those who have an enduring interest in the subject matter of that decision will depend not on any single event, but on a multiplicity of factors. The intensity with which such demands were made and affirmed, the extent of official involvement in such decisions, the degree of specificity obtained in clarifying the underlying policy preferences, and the willingness of the community to sanction their observance are some of the variants affecting continued compliance with such a requirement, as well as its prescriptive character. A resolution of the General Assembly may "affirm" a particular policy, the International Court of Justice may confirm by "deciding" it as a legal requirement, or a later multilateral convention may "reaffirm" the faith of the signatories in its continued observance (or may rephrase the policy thereunder with requisite subtleties demanded by the occasion); yet the continuing phenomenon of "progressive development" never is at a standstill. Shifting one's focus from interaction and the claim context, to the process of decision, it is further pertinent to inquire into the doctrinal predispositions of the decisionmaker, observer, or other evaluator. These are the factors associated with the theory of international jurisprudence which have a significant effect upon determinations of custom as a principal source of international law in the contemporary world.

Appraisal

Custom is ubiquitous and socially positive. "A social order based on custom provides the individual with optimal guarantees that his human environment is foreseeable."[65] Whatever one's political ideologies, there is no escaping from the vast unformulated component of prescriptive processes at every level of social organization. The inevitability of this phenomenon does not, however, signal passive acceptance. The challenge to the contemporary scholar and decisionmaker is how to make custom optimally responsive to the needs of a world order of human dignity. To achieve this goal, we need a complete picture of the community expectations deemed to be "law."

At any rate, it is necessary that the theory of custom be made coherent and, in particular, that arcane notions, the residue of ancient theories, be purged. Unfortunately, the conceptual tools and specific research techniques which international lawyers continue to use in this period of abundant customary prescription are of the past. That customary prescription nevertheless has contributed to world order is thus less attributable to doctrines and more to the intelligence and intuitive grasp of the practicing lawyer. In view of the increasing role custom will play in the future, the old methods no longer can be relied upon. Furthermore, it is becoming increasingly clear that customary processes require decisionmakers who are equipped with a better cognitive map of social reality, with a more explicit conception of the intellectual tasks of decision, and, in particular, a more sophisticated notion of nonformulated communication. Scholars must provide an expanded conception of prescription in which unformulated elements are recognized as regularly present and often decisive components of prescriptive communication. The ranking of Article 38(1) of the Statute, if it ever employed priorities, clearly is obsolete. In collaboration with social scientists, international lawyers should develop an extremely detailed model of transnational and cross-cultural communication. On the basis of such a model, appropriate monitoring techniques could be established so that participants, decisionmakers, and scholars could be regularly equipped with a complete picture of the prescriptive processes in the world community.

Notes

1. Scholarly opinion appears sharply divided on the continuing relevance of customary practice to contemporary international law. For instance, Professor O'Connell writes:

> The substance of international law is custom, together with the general principles of law, which may be the inspiration of custom or may be resorted to in order to give content to the law when practice is insufficient to create custom. (1 D. P. O'CONNELL, INTERNATIONAL LAW 8 (1965).)

On the other hand, Professor Friedman has taken the view that

> [i]t is an obvious reflection of the radically different character and methods of international relations in our time that custom can no longer be as predominant or important a source of law as it was in the formative period of international law . . . . custom is too clumsy and slow-moving a criterion to accommodate the evolution of international law in our time . . . . (W. FRIEDMAN, THE CHANGING STRUCTURE OF INTERNATIONAL LAW 121–23 (1964).)

See also 1 H. LAUTERPACHT, INTERNATIONAL LAW 14–15 (1970); I. PATON: A TEXT BOOK OF JURISPRUDENCE 165 (1964), where it was said: "Custom is useful for situations that have already occurred, but cannot create a rule to deal with a future difficulty." In a more general vein, Justice Cardozo observed, "International Law . . . has at times, like the Common Law . . . a twilight existence during which it is hardly distinguishable from morality or justice, until at length the *imprimatur* of a court attests its jural quality." New Jersey v. Delaware, 291 U.S. 383 (1934). Noting the inadequacy of customary methods of law creation, Professor Falk wrote:

Rules of customary norms *arise* in an uncertain manner, there is no way to reform or repudiate their *content*, and there is a tendency not to regard their *validity* as dependent upon changes in the character of international society however fundamental. (Falk, *The Complexity of Sabbatino,* 58 AM. J. INT'L L. 935, 939 n.18 (1964) (emphasis added).)

2. Kopelmanas, *Custom as a Means of the Creation of International Law,* 18 BRIT. Y.B. INT'L L. 129 (1937); Silving, *"Customary Law": Continuity in Municipal and International Law,* 31 IOWA L. REV. 614, 626 (1946).

3. *See* Kunz, *The Nature of Customary International Law,* 47 AM. J. INT'L L. 622 (1953); K. WOLFKE, CUSTOM IN PRESENT INTERNATIONAL LAW 60, 18 (1964); Tunkin, *Coexistence and International Law,* 3 RECUEIL DES COURS 34 (1958); A. D'AMATO, THE CONCEPT OF CUSTOM IN INTERNATIONAL LAW (1971); H. THIRLWAY, INTERNATIONAL CUSTOMARY LAW AND CODIFICATION 50–57 (1972).

4. [1969] I.C.J. 44. The same jurisprudential conundrum is exhibited by conceptions of law that seek to locate the "authority" of custom in sources outside the context of the practice itself. See Onuf, *Professor Falk—on the Quasi-legislative Competence of the General Assembly,* 64 AM. J. INT'L L. 349 (1970).

5. H. LAUTERPACHT, THE DEVELOPMENT OF INTERNATIONAL LAW BY THE INTERNATIONAL COURT (1958); C. W. JENKS, THE PROSPECTS OF INTERNATIONAL ADJUDICATION 225, 263 (1964).

6. K. WOLFKE, *supra* note 3, at 60, 18.

7. *See* A. D'AMATO, *supra* note 3, at 60, 76, 87; MacGibbon, *Customary International Law and Acquiescence* 33 BRIT. Y.B. INT'L L. 115, 117–19 (1957).

8. A useful model for interpretation of agreements is provided in M. MCDOUGAL, H. LASSWELL, & J. MILLER, THE INTERPRETATION OF AGREEMENTS AND WORLD PUBLIC ORDER 13–27 (1967).

9. The technique of "proof of custom" will, of course, vary from forum to forum, but the criterion of common interests as a requisite for behavior to be customary law will apply without regard to the local, regional, or global dimension of the behavior in question; *cf.* Colombian–Peruvian Asylum Case, [1950] I.C.J. 266. On this regard I am most critical of the thesis developed by D'Amato and Baxter which argues for inclusive recognition of local illegality; *cf.* authorities cited note 3 *supra.*

10. *See* H. BERLO, THE PROCESS OF COMMUNICATION 23–28 (1960); INTERNATIONAL BEHAVIOR (H. Kelman ed. 1954); Deutsch, *Effect of Events on National and International Images,* in *id.* at 134; Parsons, *The Theory of Symbolism in Relation to Action,* in T. PARSONS, WORKING PAPERS IN THE THEORY OF ACTION 31 (1953).

11. *See, e.g.,* Stone, *Problems Concerning Sociological Inquiries of International Law,* 89 HAGUE RECUEIL 60, 73, 79 (1956-I); MacGibbon, *supra* note 7.

12. For a comprehensive analysis of the policies governing the procedure and content of the principles governing interpretation of agreements, see the Convention on the Law of Treaties (1969); M. MCDOUGAL, H. LASSWELL & J. MILLER, *supra* note 8.

13. For the relevant discussion on the role of sanctions in social processes in general and in the legal process in particular, see W. REISMAN, NULLITY AND REVISION 647–792 (1970).

14. For a brief general outline of the process of prescription by customary practice, see Raman, *The Role of the International Court of Justice in the Development of International Customary Law,* 1965 PROCEEDINGS AM. SOC'Y INT'L L. 169.

15. Tunkin, *Coexistence and International Law,* 95 HAGUE RECUEIL 6, 19, 23 (1958-III). *See also* Tunkin, *Remarks on the Juridical Nature of Customary Norms of International Law,* 49 CALIF. L. REV. 419, 428 (1961).

16. [1956] I.C.J. 77.

17. Kopelmanas, *supra* note 2.

18. *See* U.N. DOC. A/CN. 4/6 (1949).

19. [1951] I.C.J. 4.

20.   *Id.* at 133. See, however, MacGibbon, *supra* note 7, at 136.

21.   [1960] I.C.J. 150.

22.   [1966] I.C.J. 6.

23.   Thus, in the *Right of Passage* case, claims concerning both the "particular" and the "general" law bearing on the right of passage were advanced, although the use of the word "custom" appears somewhat misleading in this connection. *See* [1960] I.C.J. 43–44. *See also* Fitzmaurice, *The Law and Procedure of the International Court of Justice,* BRIT. Y.B. INT'L L. 183 (1959).

24.   27 I.L.R. 117 (1958).

25.   *Id.* at 117–18.

26.   [1970] I.C.J. 3, 35.

27.   *Id.* at 39–40, 47.

28.   There may be evidence of varying degrees of complementarity and diversity between the official and nonofficial actions and, in terms of the other features in context, priorities may be accorded to the official, as against unofficial, behavior unless the latter is extensive and shown to have been acquiesced in despite formal disclaimer by the officials. But where the official participation is absent, it is imperative to look into any expectations created by nonofficial behavior in such situations. *See* in this regard K. V. RAMAN, THE WAYS OF THE PEACEMAKER: A STUDY OF UNITED NATIONS INTERMEDIARY ASSISTANCE IN THE PEACEFUL SETTLEMENT OF DISPUTES, UNITAR, P.S. No. 8 (1975).

29.   *See* H. Kelsen, *Theorie du droit International Coutumier,* 1 REVUE INTERNATIONAL DE LA THEORIE DU DROIT 253 (1939); Guggenheim, *Les deux éléments de la coutume en droit,* 1 ETUDES EN L'HONNEUR DE GEORGES SCELLE 275–84 (1950); Visscher, *Coutume et traité en droit international public,* 1955 REVUE GENERALE DE DROIT INTERNATIONAL PUBLIC 353; note 3 *supra.*

30.   *See* Silving, *supra* note 2.

31.   [1927] P.C.I.J., ser. A, Nos. 9 & 10.

32.   [1950] I.C.J. 266.

33.   *See* H. LAUTERPACHT, *supra* note 5, at 368–93.

34.   [1966] I.C.J. 6.

35.   [1970] I.C.J. 38.

36.   This includes, first, ascertaining the expectations created by past uniformities of behavior both of the parties directly involved in dispute as well as of the general community involved with the practice and, second, determining in the context the appropriate authority of these communications for resolving the specific issues raised by the parties.

37.   H. LAUTERPACHT, *International Law* (COLLECTED PAPERS 57–58, E. Lauterpacht ed. 1970).

38.   [1960] I.C.J. 6, 39.

39.   H. LAUTERPACHT, *supra* note 37, at 66.

40.   This Latin expression has historically been used in Roman law to refer to communitywide expectations of authority and not as it has subsequently come to be identified, with the will or consent of the individual disputing the scope of customary law derived from the practice. *See* H. JOLOWICZ, HISTORICAL INTRODUCTION TO ROMAN LAW 99–105, 363 (1939); 7 V. SUAREZ, A TREATISE ON LAWS AND GOD THE LAW GIVER 441–646, 442 (J. Scott ed. 1944).

41.   These interpretations are further borne out in the responses of the International Law Commission in the Geneva Conventions on the Law of the Sea which make specific references to the opinion of the Court in the *Anglo-Norwegian Fisheries* case [1951] I.C.J. 4.

42.   It may be of interest to note in this regard that under a U.S.–Brazil Agreement of 1972, the U.S. agreed to license and control American shrimp boats fishing within

the 200 miles claimed by Brazil and for which the U.S. agreed to pay Brazil $200,000 annually. *See* N.Y. Times, May 6, 1972 (editorial).

43. *See* Bin Cheng, *The United Nations Resolutions on Outer Space: Instant Customary Law?*, 1965 INDIAN J. INT'L L. 1 (1965).

44. This has been amply demonstrated by the recent developments in the United Nations, for example, in the fields of outer space, seabed, disarmament, and decolonization. See K. V. RAMAN, THE WAYS OF THE PEACEMAKER, *supra* note 28.

45. [1969] I.C.J. 3.

46. *Id.* at 38.

47. *Id.* at 41.

48. The criticism about this aspect of customary law continues to be made. In a 1970 debate in the Sixth Committee of the General Assembly of the United Nations, Dr. Jagota, the representative from India, asserted:

> Major political changes had taken place in the international community over the past twenty years and new States were reluctant to accept obligations and apply laws with which they were not familiar or which were not based on equity and justice. Further efforts should therefore be made to codify international customs and State practice and to develop law, with the co-operation of the new States. (25 U.N. GAOR, U.N. Doc. A/C. 6/SR. 1215 (1970).)

On the question of the differences in approach between the newly independent states and of the earlier Soviet approach toward customary international law, see Raman, *The Role of Customary Practice in the Development of Universal International Law,* in ASIAN STATES AND THE DEVELOPMENT OF UNIVERSAL INTERNATIONAL LAW 212–25 (R. P. Anand ed. 1972).

49. 3 INT'L LEGAL MATERIALS 688 (1964). *See also* authority cited note 50 *infra*.

50. 27 I.L.R. 117 (1958).

51. [1969] I.C.J. 3, 40. The reference to the practice of nonshelf states is presumably to determine the extent of general practice in support of the respective claims advanced by the practice. But on the face of it, such an interpretation does not seem justifiable since the general practice relevant for ascertaining the expectations created by the Convention are those of the parties who have continental shelf. The nature of the "interests" which these two groups have and which are affected by the Convention are not identical.

52. [1949] I.C.J. 4, 30.

53. Castañeda, *The Underdeveloped Nations and the Development of International Law,* 15 INT'L ORG. 38 (1961).

54. [1962] I.C.J. 6.

55. *Id.* at 34, 35.

56. K. WOLFKE, *supra* note 3, at 18, 60.

57. *Id.* at 60, 76.

58. *Id.* at 87. *But see* H. THIRLWAY, *supra* note 3, at 53–56:

> What counts is the view held by a State of its own conduct in relation to the law, not the absolute social desirability of their conduct. The difficulty once again is by what standards or criteria is such a view to be determined when challenged?

59. U.N. DOC. A/3972 (1969).

60. [1971] I.C.J. 16, 31.

61. *Id.* at 74.

62. The distinction suggested here is implied in the passage quoted above from the opinion of the International Court in the *Continental Shelf Cases, supra* note 4, and reflects a restricted view of the "actions" or "behavior" appropriate as evidence of practice. There is no reason for assuming that merely because certain requirements

of social conduct are habitually complied with or voluntarily observed that they are not evidence of shared expectations in that situation.

63.   [1957] I.C.J. *Pleadings,* Vol. 2. The submissions and rejoinder of India in the *Right of Passage* case explicitly referred to the incompatibility of colonial claims under the contemporary international law, exemplified by the Charter of the United Nations. While this aspect has been dealt with in the individual and dissenting opinions of some members of the court, the majority opinion surprisingly failed to accord sufficient response. *See* in this regard the United Nations Declaration on Colonialism, [1960–1961] YEAR BOOK OF THE UNITED NATIONS.

64.   Most of the arbitral awards rendered during the postwar period acknowledge the importance of the role of customary practice quite explicitly. *See,* for example, the unanimous award in the *U.S.–France International Air Transport Agreement* arbitration, *supra* note 45; Raman (comments), in OBSERVATIONS ON INTERNATIONAL NEGOTIATIONS 121–29 (transcript of the Greenwich Conference of the Academy for Educational Development, June 1971).

65.   B. DE JOUVENEL, THE ART OF CONJECTURE 301 (1967).

Chapter 12

Recognition and Social Change in International Law: A Prologue for Decisionmaking

W. MICHAEL REISMAN AND EISUKE SUZUKI

Change at every level of biological and social experience mocks man's quest for stability:[1] *il n'est plus provisoire que le permanent.* The point is dramatized in social institutions which connote in their very name a stereotypical stability. An institution is a recurring pattern of thought and behavior, established by human beings in order to maximize what they perceive to be their own interests. As soon as other human beings begin to believe that the institutions do not serve *their* interests, they may undertake to modify or destroy them. Inherent in every authoritative situation,

This essay is a tentative formulation of research in progress on recognition in international law. For present purposes, we have tried to capsulate the trend material and concentrate instead on the detailed presentation of a different theoretical approach to recognition. Colleagues in the World Public Order Program at Yale Law School discussed many of the problems treated here, and we are grateful to them for criticism and advice.

then, is "the potential illegitimacy of all relations of authority," for "[t]here always is one aggregate of positions and their incumbents which represents the institutionalized doubt in the legitimacy of the status quo of the distribution of authority."[2] In certain historical periods, there may be comparatively wide support in different classes, strata, and groups for major social institutions; in other periods, institutions may be perceived as no more than instruments for the benefit of certain strata or groups rather than for inclusive community benefit. Hence the pressure for institutional change may equal or exceed the support for institutional maintenance. But in all periods, institutional stability is a tense balance in which authoritative coercion often plays a significant role.

The most pervasive experience *within* an institutional process is, of course, the expectation of stability: the general belief held by a significant number of participants within that institutional process that it will continue through time; indeed, that it is "real." On the basis of this expectation, regular value investments are made: people buy, sell, and save, educate their children, seek certain enjoyments and shun or defer others. The expectation of continuous stability is one of the critical struts on which the institutional process rests. From a broader, disengaged perspective, however, the seeming inner stability of a process gives way to a picture of major institutional changes. Consider the nation-state, the archetypal institution of the first half of this century. If one indicated in heavy lines on a Mercator's projection the political boundaries of states, stacked these maps at ten-year intervals, and then flipped through them quickly, the cinematographic effect would produce lines of almost erotic sensuality. And if the ideologies of each state were indicated with color equivalents, the chromatic whirl of changes would suggest a psychedelic experience. Stability, to paraphrase Heraclitus, rests by changing.

Changes in group institutional practices for territorially as well as nonterritorially based groups may include any of the following components:

1. Changes in patterns of participation: new groups or strata may become politicized or enfranchised; other groups may be disenfranchised or liquidated. In the aggregate, power may be more widely shared or it may be concentrated in a smaller group, with or without the disguise of cooptation. Outsiders may be brought in for key positions or they may be expelled and so on.
2. Changes in patterns of myth, demand, and alignment: the group myth may change from democracy to communism, from monarchy to fascism, and so on. New demands in novel patterns of intensity may emerge. Changes in myth and demand may be accompanied by changes in regional or global alignment and by new policies toward others.

3. Changes in aggregate situations: boundaries may be revised. Existing internal institutions may be modified or razed or new institutions may be created. Limitations of access to internal situations, markets, fora, affection circles, and so on may be changed. Externally the group may associate itself with new organizations or withdraw from other associations.

4. Changes in the distribution of values: power, wealth, enlightenment, skill, affection, well-being, respect, and rectitude may be reallocated in patterns of greater dispersal or concentration.

5. Changes in strategy use: group processes may resort increasingly to coercion or to persuasion, and there may be shifts toward or away from the use of military, economic, ideological, and diplomatic or inter-elite strategies.

6. Changes in outcomes: any significant changes in any phases of a group's process will be indicated by changes in the outcomes of the group process; more or less will be produced, patterns of sharing will change, and so on.

Many of the changes within a group have obvious and at times critical ramifications for outsiders. For example, if the comprehensive arena of intergroup exchange is dominated by a high expectation of violence, the change of myth and alignment within a particular group or territorial community may represent a portentous security deprivation for groups that had formerly depended on support, while creating a political windfall for other groups. Thus there will be a strange symmetry of effects on the great powers from a nationalist *cuartelazo* by leftist officers in Latin America and a democratic uprising in an Eastern European republic. The point should be obvious. In a world composed of groups that are both separate and interdependent, changes in the institutional practices of one group may have enormous effects on other groups; at the very least, sectors of their own institutional practices may rest on expectations of continuing practices of a certain sort in the other groups. At the very most, the changes may destroy them. Grotius was simply not correct when he stated *"civitates esse immortales."*[3]

In an interactive system, one may find oneself inextricably involved in the process of change of another component group. It is much more than a matter of *cognition* of changes in some other group. Interdependence makes it necessary to take account of, and in effect to make decisions about, those changes and, thus, in a dynamic social process to influence them in different ways. If state A introduces an expropriatory program, how will the courts of state B react to this change in social practices when an expropriated party seeks to reclaim goods brought into B's jurisdiction? When rebels in state X secure control of segments of a country and their representatives seek control of X's embassy in state Y, how will decisionmakers in Y respond? However they respond, they are involved in the process of change in states Y and X. And this is the crux of the recognition problem.

Recognition in Context

In most comprehensive perspective, recognition involves the modulation of attitudes and of resultant behavior of one or more participants vis-à-vis other participants. The modulation is precipitated by social events deemed to be "change." Change, as we have seen, may involve any perceived variations in projected trends in social process: variations in participation, in perspectives and myth, in situations of interaction, in the allocation of authority and controlling bases of power, in social strategies, and in value outcomes. Of course, everything changes. The transnational or transgroup significance of a particular change will depend on the perspectives and values of the perceiver and the extent to which the new trends will harm or indulge him. The response to change is recognition or the modulation of attitudes and behavior. The response acquires transgroup significance when it, in turn, will have significant impacts on the group or community in which the changes have taken place.[4]

In any interactive process, participants' attitudes and the behavior thereby shaped are a critical component in the multivalue bases of power of any other participant toward whom they are directed. Thus an elite group, to choose one example, is a "government" not only because of the effective control it disposes in some sector, but also because other internal and external participants choose to view it as a state and to act accordingly: to give it all the crucial perquisites which make the status of government worth seeking.[5] Even if the refusal to accord recognition to a particular elite does not degovernmentalize it in terms of effective control within its arena of operation, it nonetheless deprives it of powers which it would otherwise have.[6] Indeed, as the level of interaction and interdependence in any sector increases, the importance of the positive sentiments of others as a base of effective power increases at least proportionately. Recognition, as broadly understood here, is not restricted to the recognition of states: it relates to the process of responding to any formal status with which legal consequences are associated: hence, recognition as a human being, as an ethnic group member, a member of a sex group, a spouse, as a special skill group, as a partnership, a corporation, a regional organization, and so on replicates the basic dynamics of social recognition.[7]

Recognition, in its social scientific sense, is not a single event. Attitudes about the status of others change and are changed over time, in some cases by formalities, in others by a slow, often informal process. In the case of state relations, a state or group of states may withdraw recognition from another state or protostate in a formal ritual or they may signal a slow process of "derecognition" by a flow of minor activities, each of which singly is of minimal import, but which cumulatively strip a territorial elite of the incidental benefits of "recognition."[8] Conversely, the extension of recognition may be a single ceremonial event or a long complex process whose outcome need not be signaled by ceremony.

Consider the case of "Goumhouriya," a fictitious state. Goumhouriya is a monarchy in North Africa, with vast oil reserves currently being harvested by a Western oil consortium and guarded by a large American military base. In 1956, a group of eight Goumhouriyan students, studying in Cairo, met in a café and agreed to mount a revolution which would overturn the monarchy and create a democratic social republic in Goumhouriya. In 1962, after an extensive campaign conducted primarily abroad, a provisional government is formed and bases itself in Algiers.[9] In 1966, after two years of urban terrorism in Goumhouriya, the king flees, the republic is formally declared, and a large number of states proceed to extend "recognition."

In terms of accurate social observation and relevant law, the moment or moments of recognition did not occur in 1962 or 1966. Official and private decisionmakers located in diverse structures in different polities about the globe were obliged to make decisions about the Goumhouriyan republic from the moment it became the official dream of eight students in a Cairo café. These decisions may have ranged from such seemingly trivial matters as extending the residence visa of a Goumhouriyan, to permitting an alien's political activity, to permitting (or at least not vigorously prosecuting) the establishment of a trade office which might purchase or arrange transshipment of weapons, to permitting the establishment of an "embassy" with some diplomatic privileges such as coded communications, and so on.[10] A broad spectrum of recognition responses is available, applied over an equally extensive time span. Simultaneously, decisionmakers will be making claims on the Goumhouriyan national movement for conformity to a variety of international or regional norms, even though the movement is not, or is at least not yet, a state. Thus the protostate is integrated into the international authority system.

Because institutional change is a dominant characteristic of social process, a study of the authoritative response to that change—recognition—is important. A relevant conception of the international recognition of states and governments must focus on all of these claims and decisions, as well as on prescriptions about the complex international decision process which responds to them. In a system of dynamic change, recognition of states and governments includes, perforce, recognition of pre-governments or protostates, as well as entities which do not seek to organize territorially but claim some benefits from international decision processes. Claims must, moreover, encompass all of the *authoritative and controlling* responses of national and international decisionmakers if a realistic and accurate picture of the flow of international decision is to be gained. Studies of recognition in the past have decorously restricted themselves to the formal responses of foreign offices as if they, by definition, were international law. But as foreign offices plod through their rituals, many other agencies, acting overtly or covertly, make choices and implement highly indulgent or deprivatory decisions which are aimed at influencing the processes of structural and personal change in other territorial and nonterritorial communities. Guardians of the myth may choose to overlook these decisionmakers, but scholars and earnest policy appraisers cannot.

Claims must also address themselves to allocation of recognition competence and specification of the beneficial incidents of recognition. Claims for recognition, then, extend over a spectrum as follows:

I.   Claims regarding allocation of competence to recognize (competence in the constitutive process)
  A.   Claims to an inclusive recognition competence
    1.   Security Council competence
    2.   General Assembly competence
    3.   Competence within functional areas by specialized agencies
    4.   Competence of the International Court of Justice
  B.   Claims to an exclusive recognition competence
    1.   Claims regarding executive monopoly
    2.   Claims regarding judicial independence
  C.   Claims to an exclusive competence to restrain recognition
    1.   Claims regarding premature recognition
    2.   Claims to demand withholding recognition
II. Claims to specific statuses of recognition
  A.   Claims to recognition as an aspirant[11]
  B.   Claims to recognition as an insurgent
  C.   Claims to recognition as a belligerent
  D.   Claims to recognition as a provisional government
  E.   Claims to recognition as a government in exile
  F.   Claims to recognition as a de facto government
  G.   Claims to recognition as a de jure government
  H.   Claims for withdrawal of recognition
III. Claims regarding internal access and benefits of recognition
  A.   Claims regarding acquisition of internal "legal personality"
  B.   Claims regarding beneficial tax and revenue status
  C.   Claims regarding standing as plaintiff before domestic courts
  D.   Claims regarding immunity as defendant
  E.   Claims regarding acts of state
  F.   Claims regarding enjoyment of treaty benefits

IV. Claims against prerecognized entities for conformity to international norms
  A. Claims affecting third states
    1. Claims to comply with norms regulating the use of force
    2. Claims to comply with norms facilitating and protecting transnational wealth activities
    3. Claims to comply with norms protecting and facilitating diplomatic and other inter-elite communications
    4. Claims to comply with norms relating to ideological communication across political boundaries
  B. Claims affecting the internal organization of prerecognized entities
    1. Claims regarding the structuring of internal participation
    2. Claims regarding the pattern of internal identification, demand, and myth
    3. Claims regarding the structuring of internal institutions
    4. Claims regarding patterns of mobilization of values for power purposes within the entity
    5. Claims regarding the strategies by which values are officially used within the entity

Each of these general claim categories may be crushed into clusters of more detailed claims. The claim to recognition as a belligerent, for example, involves claims to a certain participatory status, claims of access to certain arenas, as well as a demand for recognition of an authority to prescribe and apply for the access by others to certain sectors, claims to acquire and to use certain values, claims to use certain strategies, and so on. Conversely, the recognized status of a belligerent involves being subject to a large number of claims for distinct forms of behavior conforming to customary and conventional prescriptions and lodged by other participants. The point of emphasis is that, in an interdependent system, virtually every recognition type claim is a situation in which acts by others occasion some choice of response; this is, in a very real sense, a decision.

In an earlier study, our colleagues detailed the most comprehensive world constitutive process.[12] As a part of it, the decision process which responds to the diversity of recognition claims may involve many different participants with different perspectives, located at different points in institutional structures about the globe, equipped with different power bases, and able to resort to different types of strategy programs. A recognition decision may fall to the lot of a local police chief who must decide whether or not to extend some immunity for mundane traffic violations to the "representative" of a provisional government. Or it may move from this *de minimis* plane to a decision by an international organization to withdraw its recognition of the provisional government of a liberation movement. Traders, making shrewd assessments of which among a number of contending parties has the greater chance of winning, make recognition decisions when they extend credit to one side or the other or grant other types of favorable terms to one of a number of contending parties. And, of course, each of these decisions may be—and it is often hoped will be—as Merton put it, a self-fulfilling prophecy.[13]

Courts are regularly faced with different types of recognition problems, and their decisions comprise a rich literature. Many critical decisions are, as we have mentioned, taken by government officials. Political parties, interest groups, and kin and language groups may be important participants. The media play significant roles in many of these decision processes, and in many cases constitute functional decisionmakers. Individuals acting with the authority of different governmental agencies are involved in many of the more conventional recognition activities which are discussed in international legal texts. A detailed breakdown of the world process of recognition would, thus, recapitulate the complex of authoritative and controlling decision processes which comprise the contemporary international law system.

The perspectives which animate decisionmakers in recognition activities reflect the patterns of diversity and conformity in the world arena. While there are, as we shall see, many shared patterns of authority expectations, there are many divisions in identifications and demands for the structuring and restructuring of world order.

Participants in recognition decisions draw on diverse power bases which can affect their prominence in the decision. A contextual view indicates that many geographical features can be decisive. Whether or not the United States positively recognizes a governmental change in Eastern Europe will not decide the issue. The current structuring of the effective power process of the world enfranchises the U.S.S.R. in this hypothetical case to create or destroy a nascent government or state by its "recognition." The U.S. may acquire a parallel potential for changes in this hemisphere. Many other factors can be important bases of power; the capacity to extend aid, for example, may be crucial in the continued existence of a new territorial organization.

Against these rich variations, there are striking patterns of shared authority which can be traced over time. It should be obvious that a matter so integral to the fundamental postulate of international law—the reciprocal deference between territorial elites—would generate much law. Indeed, the very idea of recognition in international law is charged with legalism. Principles of nonrecognition, such as the Tobar [14] and Bryan [15] and Stimson [16] Doctrines, were at one time rather widely shared. In certain periods, prescriptions about recognition of belligerency or insurgency appear to have been widely supported.[17] Doctrines of conditional recognition, such as that attributed to President Wilson but actually practiced since

Jefferson,[18] draw on what are deemed to be appropriate international conceptions of authority. The Rhodesian case, in which the United Nations proscribed recognition of Rhodesia,[19] and the *Namibia* case [20] show the extent to which the international community can be mobilized for unified application of recognition decisions. More generally, the criteria for admission to the United Nations,[21] applied collectively by the organs of that entity, involve regular recognition type evaluations.[22] There are, of course, discrepancies. The very existence of a pluralistic community assures the complementarity of all norms. What is critical is the authority system within which they are applied.

Modes of extending recognition range from the most explicit diplomatic exchanges to tacit communications and may involve, in conjunction with, or distinct from, these symbols, the extending or withholding of military and economic material. There are noisome arguments among legal scholars as to what amounts to tacit recognition: participation in multilateral treaties, in international organization, diplomatic contacts, and so on. These arguments are, it should be clear, rather circular, for the participation in question is often an outcome of recognition as a socially referential concept. The confusion arises from the normative ambiguity of the legal notion of recognition.

The outcomes of recognition can be traced on various planes for the status connotes not a single effect, but a complex of "legal" incidents. Internally, recognition may reinforce a contender for power and weaken the opposition. A recognized government can, it would appear, lawfully ask for aid from another state.[23] On the international plane, recognition opens the way for participation in international organizations and conferences, institutions which are used to maximize the interests of the state in question. Within other states, recognition permits diplomatic representatives a high degree of immunity.[24] While it does not assure formal diplomatic relations, it is usually a precondition for their establishment. In national courts, a rather complex code has been developed for dealing with states enjoying different degrees of recognition and appearing as plaintiff or defendant.[25] Perhaps the most important result of recognition in adjudicative arenas is the effect given to the public acts of a foreign government by the courts of another state: the act of state doctrine.[26] As interdependence increases, deference abroad to the public acts of a state becomes a coordinately more important part of their total effectiveness. Nonrecognition may, in certain contexts, entail many deprivations, though this status, like its counterpart, must itself be viewed as a bundle of legal incidents.

In the aggregate, the whole flow of recognition decisions will itself shape aspects of the constitutive process. Expectations about competence for deciding recognition problems—about criteria which ought to be applied; about the institutional arrangements for such decisions; the resources which can be lawfully used; and the methods for making decisions—are all products of the decision process itself. Their long-range effect can be so important that some recognition decisions may turn on these prescriptive consequences rather than on the merits of the case at hand.

Goals and Policies for Recognition Problem-Solving

We have now identified the recognition problem in context and pointed out the many manifestations in which it can present itself to decision-makers. We have also noted that recognition, in an interdependent system, is not an empty formality but is a politically significant, and in some circumstances a decisive, event. The modulation of attitude and resultant behavior, intentional or otherwise, may affect, in varying degrees, the vectors of success or failure of competing public orders and social changes in a community. In an interdependent system, outsiders are often participating architects in designing and building internal social structures. Let us now turn to the goals or principles or objectives which ought to guide decisionmakers confronted with a recognition problem. There is a rich body of inherited doctrine and practice which seems to have some syntactic coherence. Can it really aid decision?

Many of the inherited prescriptions of international law are tacit and express agreements between the territorial elites about the globe regarding the minimum reciprocal practices they deem necessary for existence. A recurring aspect of these prescriptions is the reciprocal deference for the primary power base of elites: the nation-state as a territorial unit.[27] Thus Article 2(4), one of the fundamental principles of the United Nations Charter and of contemporary international law in general, provides that

> All Members shall refrain in their international relations from the threat or use of force against the territorial integrity or political independence of any state, or in any other manner inconsistent with the Purposes of the United Nations.

A necessary socially empirical reference for the syntactics of international law is, thus, who or what is a state, able to claim this fundamental deference from the elites of other states and be made subject to comparable claims for deference by other states of the world. "Recognition," as Lorimer put it, "in its various phases, constitutes the major premise of the positive law of nations, when stated as a logical system."[28]

Most international writers have agreed upon three or four minimum characteristics of a "recognizable" state: territory, people, political organization, and, of late, the capacity to fulfill international obligations.[29]

Most international writers have disagreed on the modalities for applying these criteria to actual cases. One group, the declaratory school, insists that recognition is automatic upon the "objective" existence of the three or four requisite facts.[30] A second group, the constitutive school, contends that recognition and hence official existence as a state entity occurs only when other states recognize the candidate; in other words, statehood is created by an international ritual of recognition performed by other states.[31]

In the light of our analysis, it should be obvious that the traditional theory of recognition as a discrete doctrine is not workable in either of its constructions. The declaratory school, anxious to facilitate social change by "depoliticizing" recognition, must still make value choices about whether the requirements of territory, people, political organization, and international capacity have in fact been fulfilled. A moment's consideration should make clear that each of these criteria has an unmanageably wide reference to facts and international policies; each is, in short, a complex decision outcome whose antecedents have not been expressed.[32] Declarationists are declaring nothing. They are making a decision; precisely because of the ambiguity of the indices of decision, each decisionmaker retains an enormous discretion.

Of course, the avowed declarationist may aver that he is doing no more than acknowledging the "power realities" of whatever state he turns his attention to. In a deeper sense, he is arguing that authority is an epiphenomenon of power. It was Tawney who remarked drily:

> [I]f scrofula is not cured by the king's touch, neither is power conferred by kissing the king's hand. It is not the legal recognition which makes the power, but the power which secures legal recognition.[33]

The concise answer to this argument is not that power is irrelevant. Plainly, power is a critical component of authority. But in an interdependent world, a necessary component of the power base of a would-be local elite is the attitudes and resultant behavior of outsiders disposing of varying degrees of effective power. When outsiders insist that they are merely "recognizing" a fact, they are really ignoring a decision which they made and which contributes via their "recognition" to the effective power of the local elite.

There is often an implicit policy in the declaratory school's position: a preference for a comparatively high toleration of social change in other states.[34] Yet the declaratory theory cannot even ensure this outcome, for its very ambiguity permits it to be used restrictively if the applier should so desire.

The constitutive school, tending against change and toward old-fashioned legitimacy, readily concedes the enormous discretion reserved to each nation-state in recognizing others and admits candidly that recognition is an instrument of policy. But it overlooks the inevitable collaboration with others in recognizing states and prevents any joint exploration of common criteria which might be used and may, in fact, have been used in this enterprise. In its more extreme forms, the constitutive school leads to a legal strabismus, in which one can perceive no more than one's own objectives, which projected, animated and idolized populate one's private world. From the standpoint of decisionmaking, the constitutive theory is really no theory at all.

All theories of recognition in international law are intensely constricted in their temporal focus. Recognition, as we have seen, is not a single act, but a continuous response by officials as well as by private participants, to claims made by aspiring elites and their adversaries in different situations and with different power bases at their disposal. Neither of the traditional theories of recognition relates that institution to the major thrusts of contemporary international law. Yet this must be done if recognition is to be an instrument of order in a coherent international legal system. Nor does either theory provide any procedural principles by which critical factors relevant to recognition can be located in the vast flow of events comprising the world social process and be rendered applicable to decisions contributing to the realization of community goals.

Law is a process for making decisions. It is distinguished from coordinate political processes in that it seeks to conform in high degree to the expectations of authority of community members regarding who should make decisions, and by what criteria decisions ought to be made, and in that it insists that reasons for those decisions relating them rationally to community goals be made explicit. Legal application involves conformity but, at the same time, creativity; auhority is, in short, a process of both conformity and conformation.

> [E]xpectations of what is substantively and procedurally right, shared by politically relevant strata about the globe, are critical components and inescapable products of behavior. Response options and priorities which an official inventories in a specific case have been influenced, in part, by what was done and aggregately evaluated in the past. The choices which that official makes in the instant case will contribute to perspectives of what is appropriately lawful behavior in the future and will provide the authority environment within which that same official and those with whom he identifies must later operate. Thus the role of international law or, more broadly, authority in decisions involves both conformity with expectations derived from the past as well as a conformation of authority perspectives for the future. Processes of conformity and conformation provide enormous possibilities for disjunction, as decision-makers, under the press of events, select what they deem most worthwhile from the past and project it into radically new contexts in the future.[35]

A comprehensive theory of recognition must be related to the fundamental goals of contemporary international law. Hence, decisions about recognition should select those elements of past decisions which contribute to minimum order and the conditions of human dignity in the future and reject those elements of the past which never have or will no longer contribute to the minimum and optimum goals of the world community. Law is, after all, an instrument of social control. It is only reasonable to use it to fashion a system of world order which we want and not to use it to perpetuate a system we repudiate.

There are a number of substantive and procedural guidelines which may be recommended. As a preliminary to them, one caveat about self-scrutiny is in order. The ultimate instrument of individual observation and choice is the self-system. Hence the importance, as a decision task, of the self-identification of mental rigidities, stereotypes, and other residues of past experience and the attempt to minimize, neutralize, or purge them in decision functions.[36] Unconscious identifications with a particular set of social arrangements may result in an irrational commitment to keep things as they are, even though changes might in fact be more conducive to the realization of the individual's goals. It is possible to generate ego involvements or investments in complex situations and to find oneself ineluctably ranged against change. This is a dynamic which must be identified, for, from a disengaged standpoint, it is readily apparent that neither "change" nor "stability" has any innate value; the rational question is always whether alternatives move one closer or further from preferred goals. Certainly, the personality which straps itself to a corset of rigidity will receive no ultimate support from international law. Like any authoritative decision system in a pluralistic society, international law presents itself in complementary sets in which paired norms call on the one hand for change and on the other, for stability.

In the light of these observations, we may note the substantive goals and the procedural principles which are recommended for recognition.

Substantive Goals

Because systematic coherence imports the accommodation of many choice implementations with the fundamental goals of the comprehensive system, goal clarification, of necessity, starts with an inclusive and high-level goal formulation which is applicable to the entire social system under consideration. While many second level goals may have value in themselves, all must contribute, in application, to the realization of the major systemic goal. The demand for comprehensiveness requires an initial formulation at a level of high abstraction. By subsequent intellectual operations, lower level goals are formulated and programs for implementation in context are designed in each decision situation so that, of the available alternatives, that one is chosen which most approximates the fundamental goals of the social or community system concerned. Note the emphasis on the *coherence of the system*. No "problem" is ever defined in terms of the violation of a single prescription, but rather in terms of the impact of a flow of behavior on the aggregate of goals and policies of the system.

MINIMUM AND OPTIMUM ORDER

The basic substantive preferences are for minimum order most closely approximating preferred goals of human dignity. Minimum order means the minimization of unauthorized violence over an extended period of time, within a public order system which approximates preferred goals. An order of human dignity is one which, in word and deed, is committed to the individual and the optimal realization of his potentialities and, on the macrosocial scale, is committed to an order which secures a wide production and sharing of all values.

Recognition cases arise from an agitated discrepancy in these goals. An aspiring group asserts that minimum order or human dignity can be better realized through community recognition of their claim to exercise authority for the shaping and sharing of diverse values in a certain arena. Their claim may arise from, initiate, or be accompanied by violence. Paradoxically, the very circumstances of violence present decisionmakers with an opportunity to improve public order and, in particular, to minimize future violence.

ESTABLISHMENT OF IMPROVED COMMUNITIES

Recognition, at whatever stage, should be employed as a means for establishing an improved community at the local, national, regional, and international level, in the minimum and optimum terms developed in the preceding section. Whether the question is one of recognizing a political party within an established state or recognizing an entirely new state, the critical question is always whether the result of according or withholding the recognition sought will contribute to these preferred goals.

RENEWING INTERNATIONAL TITLES

The social changes which precipitate recognition problems are further complicated by the problem of international title.

Territorial organization has a slower metabolism of change in international law than the movements of peoples and the fashions of ideology and legal theory. A comparatively high degree of stability for political boundaries has been considered necessary for effective resource exploitation and more generally, for the continuing viability of an international political system organized primarily in territorial nation-state units. Hence the tendency of international decision-makers to prefer a higher degree of stability in matters of boundaries and title.[37]

Over time, however, law and policy change. When recognition questions raise title problems, questions of intertemporal law arise. The general response is to perfect challenged or imperfect titles by contemporary norms. Since unchallenged perfected titles are given regular deference, the result of these two dynamics is a patchwork of international law from different periods. This result is unfortunate and in itself can be tension producing, but it is inevitable so long as territory utilized by institutionalized processes remains a basic feature of value production and is deemed to require highly stable legal regimes.

The U.N. Charter and the human rights declarations and resolutions introduce a new component in perfecting title; it is the uncoerced support of the indigenous population for whatever authoritative institutions seek title.[38] Other nation-state elites who are called upon to accede to a claim for recognition must take this into account.

Procedural Principles

OPERATIONAL SUSPENSION OF PAST RECOGNITION

In many cases, a claimant for recognition has ranged himself against a participant already enjoying the benefits of recognition. Obviously, recognition in the manner suggested here cannot be a meaningful activity unless there is an operational suspension of past recognition and an evaluation de novo of the competitive merits of the contenders.[39]

CONTEXTUAL IDENTIFICATION OF CONTENDERS
FOR RECOGNITION

Evaluation of contending parties involves much more than a cursory or anecdotal survey. What is recommended is a detailed consideration of each phase of the processes involved and a consideration of the probable effects of alternative recognition options available to the decisionmaker.

CONTEXTUAL PROJECTIONS

What are the probable outcomes, insofar as discernible, if decisionmakers do nothing? If they accede to the claim for recognition? If they reject it? What do these outcomes mean in terms of all values for

a. the individuals in the community most immediately affected;
b. surrounding communities;
c. the encompassing region; and
d. the world constitutive process.

ALTERNATIVES STRESSING INTEGRATION

To what extent can a recognition type response act to integrate contending parties or establish new patterns of structured interaction in which former antagonists will share interests in maintenance? The point of emphasis is that though a claim creates an attention focus for decisionmakers, the decisionmaker's response should rise above the parameters set by the conflict and innovate, where possible, new solutions which are superior to the disjunctive formulations put forward by contenders.[40]

Trends in Decision

Claims Regarding Allocation of Competence to Recognize (Competence in the Constitutive Process)

Traditionally, recognition has been viewed as an exclusively national function.[41] The few instances of collective recognition in the nineteenth century were, in effect, decisions by separate states to coordinate their individual recognition policies for specific cases.[42] In the twentieth century, collective recognitions, for example those following peace treaties, are comparable phenomena, with one important distinction: a high moralistic tone was adopted and the supposed reasons for the joint recognition were given.[43] The residue of these reasons has become at least persuasive international precedent for recognition.

Although there is no formal inclusive recognition procedure, many of the incidents of recognition may be accorded by admission to an international organization when that organization's membership is universal and compulsory.[44] If the organization's membership is less than universal, the incidents of recognition would appear to decrease proportionally thereto and proportionally to the range of activities in which the organization is involved. On the other hand, many of the domestic incidents of recognition, e.g., access to domestic courts as a plaintiff, would not necessarily flow from admission to a universal or near universal organization.

CLAIMS TO AN INCLUSIVE RECOGNITION COMPETENCE

Security Council Competence   The United Nations Charter does not accord the Security Council a manifest recognition function. Yet the primary security powers of the Council may, under certain circumstances, lead to decisions of recognition. If the Council determines that a "situation" constitutes a "threat to the peace," for example, and concludes that the appropriate international response is recognition or nonrecognition of a new regime, such a decision would be binding upon all members of the United Nations under Article 25 of the Charter.[45] In effect, an inclusive decision regarding recognition would have been made.

In the Rhodesian case, the white minority elite of a nominal colony of the United Kingdom was about to sunder relations with the metropolitan in order to avoid restructuring the political order to share power with the black majority.[46] Concerned with the problem of colonialism and with the ongoing and quite likely greater deprivation of human rights in Rhodesia, the General Assembly, in a series of resolutions, requested member states not to accept a Rhodesian Unilateral Declaration of Independence (UDI).[47] When, on November 11, 1965, the Rhodesian government proclaimed UDI, [48] the Security Council resolved to condemn the UDI and called upon all states "not to recognize this illegal racist minority regime."[49] It was, however, only in April 1966 that the Security Council characterized the Rhodesian situation as a "threat to the peace" and introduced mandatory sanctions.[50] It was, at this point, that its resolutions became "binding" in the strict sense under Article 25 of the Charter.

An action, comparable in many ways to the Rhodesian case, can be found in the General Assembly's and Security Council's decisions regarding Namibia. The case is considered in detail subsequently.[51]

The Security Council can, then, perform an inclusive and decisive recognition function in those circumstances in which it deems that a "threat to the peace" can best be responded to by recognition or nonrecognition. This decision will be binding within the meaning of Article 25 of the Charter. This ancillary recognition function could institutionalize itself into a regular inclusive recognition process by fictitious extension of the device of "threat to the peace." In short, every recognition situation would automatically be characterized as a "threat to the peace," confirming in each case the Council's plenary jurisdiction, a development parallel to the growth of common law courts' jurisdiction through the patent fictions in writs.[52] The criteria for such inclusive recognition decisions would presumably be found in Article 4 of the Charter.[53] Unfortunately, both the Security Council and the General Assembly, as well as the International Court, have been reluctant to develop the policies in these provisions into effective guidelines for decision.[54]

While the potential for agreement among permanent members of the Security Council seems rare, there have been significant collaborations between the powers which have used the authority of the Security Council. Rhodesia is, of course, the principal case in point; early treatment of the Spanish problem is also instructive. In the current international context, agreement regarding recognition would appear to be likely in cases of decolonization in regions over which no power has established hegemony. Agreement over inclusive recognition would appear to be least likely where governmental changes stimulating recognition decisions have occurred in regions over which one power has established an effective hegemony. We hypothesize that the propensity of state elites to act with primary regard to short-range self-interest increases as the degree of institutionalization of the arena in which they operate decreases.

General Assembly Competence   The Charter provides that the General Assembly will admit states to membership in the United Nations on the recommendation of the Security Council.[55] When a controversy between the Council and Assembly erupted over admissions, the International Court of Justice resolved it in favor of the Council.[56] The Court decided, in effect, that each of the permanent members of the Council should have a veto power over the admission of a new member. The legal device was interpretation of the words "recommendation of the Security Council" as a *requisite* condition precedent for admission by the General Assembly. Thus, while a majority of the General Assembly is needed to deny membership to a state candidate, a single permanent member of the Security Coucil may achieve the same result. The net effect is that the composition of the General Assembly can be a subject of bargaining between the powers, that the political balance of the Assembly will approximate the balance in the international political arena, and that the operation of the objective criteria for membership set out in the Charter will be suspended. This situation will continue as long as membership in the General Assembly is deemed of real international political significance. If that significance wanes, the members of the Security Council will, presumably, relinquish admissions to the General Assembly and to the Charter criteria, if the Assembly is disposed to apply to them.

Thus, the General Assembly of the United Nations cannot participate in that quasi-recognition function of the Security Council implicit in admission to a near universal international organization.[57] It could, of course, recommend to the Council that a particular regime be recognized or subjected to nonrecognition, but this recommendation would be hortatory only. Conceivably, a bloc of Assembly members could seek to influence a recalcitrant permanent member of the Council by offering reciprocating support in the Assembly for a program desired by the Council member. But this would appear to be the outer limit. Though in theory the Assembly can exercise the plenary competence of the Security Council under "Uniting for Peace,"[58] it is difficult to imagine a case in which the exercise of these powers would include the admission of a state. On the other hand, the Assembly could conceivably mandate recognition or nonrecognition of a regime, if, under "Uniting for Peace," it were exercising the plenary powers of the Security Council. And, of course, the Assembly may accord some of the incidents of recognition if individual member states inscribe certain matters of interest to an unrecognized regime on the agenda or otherwise promote such interests.

The *Namibia* case provides us with some insight into the particulars of the role of the General Assembly in recognition. South Africa had refused to convert its League of Nations mandate over South West Africa into a trusteeship under the United Nations regime.[59] Nonetheless, the General Assembly insisted, from 1946 on, that obligations owed by South Africa to the Council of the League of Nations devolved to the Assembly of the United Nations. A series of advisory opinions by the International

Court of Justice confirmed this jurisdictional claim.[60] Yet South Africa continued to reject what it claimed was an unlawful extension of U.N. power. Eventually, the Assembly voted to terminate the mandate over South West Africa and to vest the supervision of the evolution to self-determination of the territory of Namibia, as it was henceforth called, to a United Nations committee.[61] Subsequently, the Security Council adopted the position which had been taken by the General Assembly.[62] When South Africa continued to ignore repeated United Nations calls to vacate Namibia, the Security Council requested of the International Court an advisory opinion regarding "the legal consequences for States of the continued presence of South Africa in Namibia, notwithstanding Security Council resolution 276 (1970)."[63] The Court concluded, in part, by a vote of eleven to four, that

> States Members of the United Nations are under an obligation to recognize the illegality of South Africa's presence in Namibia and the invalidity of its acts on behalf of or concerning any dealings with the Government of South Africa implying recognition of the legality of, or lending support or assistance to, such presence and administration.[64]

It is, as yet, too early to attempt to gauge the effectiveness of this decision.[65]

Recognition Competence of Functional Agencies   Insofar as a functional agency has the exclusive competence to determine its membership, some of the incidents of recognition may be accorded to a new regime by its admission to such an agency. Even if the incidents are not consequential, membership in a peripheral organization may nonetheless constitute the thin edge of the wedge: the new regime may use a single membership to work its way into other, more significant international organizations.

The General Assembly has resolved that the specialized agencies should seek to coordinate their membership policies so that there is a uniform membership in the Assembly and in the agencies.[66] In one instance, in the past, a new regime was admitted to a peripheral agency's regional committee, but it was subsequently forced to withdraw under pressure from elites within the Security Council and the General Assembly.[67] In a multipolar arena, the possibilities of diverse memberships in functional agencies is considerably enhanced, particularly if the decision dynamics of the agencies differ. Hence, the recognition function of specialized agencies in the future may be said to depend upon the degree of fractionalization of the power process.

Recognition Competence of the International Court of Justice   Because the I.C.J.'s membership is contingent upon membership in the

United Nations, the Court itself may not permit a regime to adhere to its Statute if it has not first been admitted to, or recommended by, the General Assembly.[68] In this respect, the Court may not perform the incidental recognition function available to specialized agencies. On the other hand, the Court has some discretion in permitting one state to bring a claim on behalf of an entity which does not enjoy the privilege of direct access to the Court.[69] And though it would stretch the Statute, it is not unlikely that the Court might admit a regime, with the characteristics of a state, to appear as an affected third party (1) if it is likely to be affected by the outcome of the case and (2) if its collaboration is anticipated as necessary to the implementation of alternate decision options available to the Court. Furthermore, insofar as specific recognitions or nonrecognitions are mandated by general international norms, the Court could, in advisory or contentious jurisdiction, conclude as an ancillary matter that a regime should or should not be recognized.[70] The Court has not yet done this.

The Court may be incorporated into the inclusive recognition process by a request from an international organization for an advisory opinion regarding the recognition of a regime or some incident thereof. In the *Namibia* case,[71] it will be recalled, the Court was asked by the Security Council to determine whether third states should act in ways which might involve recognition of the continued illegal presence of South Africa in Namibia.

CLAIMS TO AN EXCLUSIVE RECOGNITION COMPETENCE: THE AMERICAN EXPERIENCE [72]

The traditional theory of recognition as a unilateral act by the executive of a nation-state, acknowledging the existence of a foreign state or government and thereby signaling the granting to the foreign state of the many perquisites of statehood in its own domestic institutions, is an oversimplification of contemporary American political reality. The complexities of recognition in current American practice can be understood only in the perspective of coordinate changes in governmental structures and international politics. American conceptions of recognition took shape in a simpler era of international politics, in which one department of the federal government was in fact, as well as name, *the* Department of State and regularly processed virtually all foreign affairs matters.[73] In these circumstances, courts naturally took their cues from the Department of State regarding executive policies of recognition of foreign states; the cues were usually unequivocal.[74] The proliferation of the federal government from the 1930s on, the burgeoning role of many other government departments in foreign affairs matters since that time,[75] the slow consolidation of foreign affairs' direction in the White House, and the increase in direct elite diplomacy have broken the comparative monopoly of the

Department of State and have contributed to the decline of its formerly preeminent influence in foreign affairs.[76] This trend is manifest in many foreign policy areas, and quite dramatically evident in regard to recognition. Under contemporary practice, the Department of State may be charged with maintaining a policy of nonrecognition of state *X*, while White House aides deal openly with the state, the Department of Commerce issues licenses for trade in strategic items, and the President and his *familia* even visit the unrecognized state.

In circumstances such as these, courts in the United States can no longer take peremptory cues from the Department of State, with the justification that recognition is an executive prerogative and that the efficiency of the U.S. foreign affairs program requires that courts follow the executive lead and present a united front. In a complex and highly interdependent modern world, many official and quasi-official contacts and indeed stabilized relationships are established with territorial communities which the Department of State, on behalf of the government, has not officially recognized. Interdependence has generated a number of functional international communities or integrated transnational exchange sectors which ignore the formal politics of recognition. In these circumstances, contacts with many unrecognized governments may receive either tacit approval or real support from some agency of the federal government. When the inevitable controversies and conflicts regarding these functional relationships come before federal courts, the courts must perforce develop a set of independent guidelines for responding to recognition problems. American courts are, in fact, in the process of doing this; the outlines of a judicial code of recognition are beginning to emerge.

Who Decides Recognition　Foreign policy is often considered a prerogative of the Executive,[77] yet the coordinate branches of the federal government do participate in its formulation and implementation. Allocations of competence for different foreign affairs matters regularly occasion major constitutional confrontations in the United States.[78] The traditional conception held that matters of recognition were the exclusive prerogative of the political branches, that federal courts would not diverge from executive holdings (though they might anticipate or interpret them), and that other constitutional rights notwithstanding, state courts would be obliged to follow executive and federal court rulings on recognition.[79]

Because the formal international institution of recognition has become a rather secondary diplomatic instrument, with nonrecognition often maintained despite the growth of functional transnational communities in which the nonrecognized state or government participates, United States courts have tended in the past two decades to take somewhat more independent stands regarding recognition. In the *Upright* case,[80] for example, a New York court came close to according full adjudicative privileges to an unrecognized government, despite the fact that the formal (if not manifest) policy of the Executive was to the contrary. In the future, one can expect this practice to continue, with the result that a common law of recognition will develop independent of the executive for many recognition cases.

Claims to Specific Statuses of Recognition

CLAIMS TO RECOGNITION AS AN ASPIRANT

Contemporary international law raises human rights within states to the level of international concern for two reasons: human rights are important per se and their deprivation in an interdependent world can constitute a threat to the peace. A fundamental human right, recognized in many of the international codes of human rights, is the right of the individual to form associations and, in particular, groups with political objectives. Where the effective elites of a state interfere and prevent the establishment of internal political groups, an international deprivation takes place.

Article 20 of the Universal Declaration of Human Rights provides: "Everyone has the right to freedom of peaceful assembly and association."[81] The same policy is upheld in Articles 21 and 22 of the International Covenant on Civil and Political Rights.[82] The European Convention on Human Rights provides in Article 11 that: "Everyone has the right to freedom of peaceful assembly and to freedom of association with others, including the right to form and to join trade unions for the protection of his interests."[83]

By "aspirants," we mean groups which seek to participate in authoritative processes of a community with the aim of achieving influence or lawful control. They may be parties or pressure groups, interest groups, or the comparatively new phenomenon of citizen action type groups. They do not project strategic programs of high coercion. In totalitarian states or states in which ascendant elites are unwilling to risk losing incumbency by referendum, these groups are often suppressed and participation in them is severely sanctioned. In many cases, the activities of suppression attract international attention.

The prevention of the formation of parties has been protested in diplomatic exchanges and has been raised in organized international processes.[84] Nongovernmental international organizations concerned with political democracy have been quite active in protesting these deprivations [85] and, of course, the press frequently editorializes against suppressions of parties and thereby influences opinion at the elite and rank and file levels.[86] It is difficult to measure the effects of such responses with anything approaching accuracy, but it seems safe to say that if the protests have rarely succeeded in vindicating the position of aspirants, they have nonetheless sustained a general international demand for the continuation of this norm.

The extent to which elites about the globe will respond positively to invocations of this norm will depend upon three factors: first, general cultural ideologies about the "normality" or "social pathology" of pluralistic societies in which many subgroups interact and compete; second, the political structure, composition, and permeability of the elite; and third, the level of crisis which prevails at the time aspirants lodge claims for recognition.

The optimum international policy would appear to be the strongest and most explicit support for claims for recognition as aspirants. Frenetic political activity is often an alternative to violence; when access to the civic arena is blocked, the probability increases that agitation will take a more coercive turn. From the standpoint of minimum order, political agitation itself is often a catharsis. We hypothesize that the more aspirants believe that they have some chance of success in a civic arena, the greater their commitment to that arena and the less likely they will be to resort to higher levels of violence. The greater the participation in the civic arena, the greater the sharing of power.

CLAIMS TO RECOGNITION AS AN INSURGENT

Insurgency involves political revolt within a country; the revolt has not, for whatever the reasons may be, secured attribution, by the established government and/or by outside governments, of the status of belligerency.[87] Professor O'Connell, representing one European position, argues that there is no legal status of insurgency comparable in any way to that of belligerency.[88] In fact, it was American diplomatic practice to recognize the condition of insurgency since, at least, President Cleveland's Proclamation of June 12, 1896.[89] Professor Hyde writes:

> Recognition of a condition of insurgency within a foreign country is an official reckoning with a state of facts. In one sense such action does not strengthen the legal position already attained by the insurgents; it does not necessarily manifest a design to aid them; it does not impose upon the outside State the technical burdens of a neutral or serve to increase the load of obligations already resting upon it in consequence of the contest. That action does, however, appear to deprive such a State of freedom to question the existence of the fact of insurgency which in itself is productive of certain obligations towards the country disturbed by such a condition. Thus, the former cannot thereafter well regard the efforts of the insurgents to prevent military aid from reaching their enemy as necessarily unlawful conduct, or their belligerent activities at sea as private ventures for private ends savouring of piracy. Moreover, the State that recognizes the condition of insurgency is hardly in a position to deny that its own subsequent acts by way of military assistance to either contestant consti-

tute intervention for the justification of which solid and convincing excuse must be given.[90]

Insurgency, as we shall shortly see, does not convey the important privileges which are set in operation by recognition of the status of belligerency. Nonetheless, it may have significant consequences,[91] and these argue strongly for a general policy of recognition of insurgency for every violent political revolt against an established government.

1. Recognition of insurgency focuses international attention on the insurrection and may thereby provide some restraint on the severity of the conflict and assure greater conformity to the laws of war. One might call this a de facto "internationalization" of the conflict.
2. Recognition of insurgency by outsiders may press the parties to incorporate substantive and procedural international norms in the resolution of the conflict. Conversely, ignoring insurgency is almost a tacit invitation to the contending parties to ignore international standards.
3. Recognition of insurgency forces any third state which wishes to provide aid to the established government to concede openly that it is aiding *one* side in the conflict and hence to justify itself in terms of the *merits* of each contender for political power.
4. Recognition of insurgency identifies, in addition to the local government, a local force which can be held accountable for harm caused to nationals of the recognizing state.

Despite these positive consequences, recognition as an insurgent has comparatively few formal legal consequences. Therefore it can hardly be stigmatized as an intervention in the affairs of a sovereign state.[92]

CLAIMS TO RECOGNITION AS A BELLIGERENT

"Belligerent" is a term of art referring cumulatively to (1) an organized group within a nation-state (2) which seeks control by force of arms within that state and (3) which has already acquired stable control over a significant segment of territory and (4) which has undertaken the operations of a regular government in that sector.[93] Until recently, an additional requisite component for according the status of belligerent was prosecution of the war by the putative belligerent with organized troops which were, in the language of the Institute of International Law, "subject to military discipline and conforming to the laws and customs of war."[94] While a number of writers still insist on this latter component, it is questionable if general expectations require it for purposes of acquiring belligerent status.[95]

Belligerent status is, for the most part, a preferred status for insurgent groups, for it conveys many of the international incidents of statehood and can often aid in the prosecution of an internal war. A belligerent has the right of visit and search and seizure of contraband articles on the high seas, the right of blockade, a right to establish prize courts to condemn merchantmen for carriage of contraband, and so on.[96] There are other advantages. Dana's edition of Wheaton's *International Law* records that

> [t]he recognition of belligerent rights is not solely to the advantage of the insurgents. They gain the great advantage of a recognized *status,* and the opportunity to employ commissioned cruisers at sea, and to exert all the powers known to maritime warfare, with the sanction of foreign nations. They can obtain abroad loans, military and naval materials, and enlist men, as against everything but neutrality laws; their flag and commissions are acknowledged, their revenue laws are respected, and they acquire a *quasi* political recognition. On the other hand, the parent government is relieved from responsibility for acts done in the insurgent territory; its blockade of its own ports is respected; and it acquires a right to exert, against neutral commerce, all the powers of a party to a maritime war.[97]

And there are advantages accruing to the party recognizing a belligerent. The act may be realistic and provide for continuing or reestablishing trade patterns and for establishing minimum political contacts for purposes of protecting the recognizer's own interests. As the United States Supreme Court stated bluntly in *The Three Friends* (1897): "Belligerency is recognized when a political struggle has attained a certain magnitude and affects the interest of the recognizing power."[98]

Past decisions regarding the recognition of belligerency indicate that a wide ambit of discretion was in operation; a great many policies seem to have been brought to bear in each single decision. A rather mechanical formula has been attributed to Mr. Canning: "a certain degree of force and consistency acquired by a mass population engaged in war entitled that population to be treated as a belligerent."[99] This formula would imply that once these facts are ascertained, recognition of belligerency is automatic. Not surprisingly, practice has been at variance. The experience in the American Revolution was mixed and points up many of the political dilemmas of possible recognizers. Most European states tried to evade choice when presented with American prizes. The Danes complied with British demands and delivered prizes to them, a matter which was the subject of diplomatic protest by the U.S. for many years afterward.[100] The Dutch granted the rebellious American colonies belligerency status and found themselves embroiled in a state of war with Britain.[101] The French, of course, were open secret allies.[102]

Since independence, American diplomatic behavior has been just as mixed. In *Rose v. Himely,* Chief Justice Marshall noted that "A war de facto then (1804) unquestionably existed between France and St. Domingo."[103] But the U.S. Executive refused to recognize the insurgents as belligerents and proscribed contact with them.[104] By 1817, the U.S.

was in effect granting belligerent status to all contestants in the Spanish colonial wars in Latin America; after the Spanish expulsion, U.S. policy regarding belligerency in Latin America more or less conformed to its practice elsewhere.[105] For the Latin American cases, the formal self-characterization of the United States was neutrality, as it was in the Texas war of independence of 1836.[106] The U.S. probably recognized the Confederacy as a belligerent during the Civil War.[107] On the other hand, there was great reluctance to extend recognition of belligerent status to the insurgents in Cuba for some thirty years because of the comparative insignificance of the insurgent effort and the difficulties which might have ensued to U.S. interests by such a move.[108]

In this century, American practice has tended toward restraint in recognizing belligerent status, which may reflect a general preference for established governments. The U.S. recognized the belligerency of the Czechoslovaks in 1918,[109] followed the general accord in Europe regarding an embargo on both sides during the Spanish Civil War,[110] but refused to recognize the belligerent status of the nationalist government.

Recognitions of belligerency involve claims by insurgents and by the established government. There seems to be no international prescription requiring other states to grant the status of belligerent, but practical factors might move other states to accord the status when the activities of an insurgency have reached a certain level of intensity.

We recommend that decisions regarding recognition as a belligerent be guided by the same considerations relevant to recognition of any entity as an authoritative community. In brief, does the belligerent represent, in incipient form, the better of the two emerging communities vying for power? What will the aggregate consequences be if belligerent status is recognized? What will the consequences be if it is not?

CLAIMS TO RECOGNITION AS A PROVISIONAL GOVERNMENT

The term "provisional government" has been used with a number of different references. We use it here to refer to a group of individuals organized as a government and exercising effective administration *within* a territory. Such a provisional government could characterize itself as a de facto or even a de jure government. It chooses not to do this because the legitimating myth it invokes in order to pretend to power involves the performance of certain principles and procedures which have not yet been completed. Thus a counterrevolution which sought power in order to bring a monarch's family back to the country to reestablish a monarchy would consider it more appropriate to characterize itself as a provisional government until the return of the monarch. More common in the present era is a group which aims to establish a republic or a democracy and which characterizes itself as provisional until there have been elections.[111]

In addition to conformity with a myth, local factions may settle on the term "provisional government" to permit cooperation inter se without freezing temporary patterns of subordination.

A number of advantages may accrue to the recognizing state from use of the term "provisional government." For one thing, it permits the establishment of fuller political contact and greater opportunities for influencing a belligerent without extending full recognition. It permits the recognizer effectively to condition recognition on the performance of certain activities without the infelicities of conditional recognition. Where governments themselves have sought the characterization "provisional," international recognition in these terms reinforces commitments to whatever rituals may have been promised in the future.[112]

The status of "provisional government" is a useful recognition instrument. It should be used so as to encourage elites that have seized power to provide for procedures assessing the desires of the population in accordance with peremptory norms of international law. Where recognition of a provisional government will have this effect, it should be given. Where it will not, it should be withheld until a meaningful self-characterization of provisionality assures, with a fair degree of probability, conformity with substantive and procedural international standards.

CLAIMS TO RECOGNITION AS AN EXILE GOVERNMENT

A government in exile is one which claims all the attributes of a government except for (hopefully) a temporary, shortly to be remedied loss of effective control over the territory of its state.[113] It usually invokes international authority to be the government of its state, claims the support of the vast majority of its people, and manifests the capacity and will to regain control of its territory. Although it may be involved in overt conflict in its claimed territory, it is not a belligerent in the international legal sense of having stable control over part of its territory. Nevertheless, it frequently seeks the coordinate status of belligerent.[114]

In the past, governments in exile have usually been governments which have been expelled from their territory, but whose pretensions to power are still supported by other states which often host them.[115] Since World War II, however, many groups involved in wars of self-determination or decolonization have formed exile governments but called them provisional governments. The leading example of this phenomenon is found in the protostatehood of Algeria; the revolutionary elite declared itself a government in 1958, several years before it in fact achieved control of Algeria.[116] In the interim, it participated in regional organizations and received accreditation of sorts from many governments. During this period, Algeria was a government in exile, though it styled itself a provisional government and a belligerent.[117] Since its own independence, Algeria has been quite liberal in according the same status to other incipient nation-states.[118] With less success, the Vietcong tried to emulate the Algerian precedent.[119]

Under some classical theories of international law, support of this latter-day type of government in exile would have constituted a highly unfriendly act, under certain circumstances a casus belli. The contemporary reaction is more muted. One reason is the division of the world along certain ideological and power lines. Another reason is the ephemeral character of many soi-disant governments in exile. If ignored, they may wither; if focused on, they acquire an illusion of importance which becomes self-fulfilling.

The internal orders maintained by many governments about the world are abhorrent to those subjected to them and are often incompatible with peremptory norms of international law. Fantastic technologies of social control make it increasingly difficult for those espousing alternative orders to mount resistance or to mobilize latent dissatisfaction *within* the operational arena of the established government. In these circumstances, the institution of government in exile, as it has developed in the postwar period, may be an important instrument for securing human dignity. It provides dissident groups with an opportunity to organize, to seek international scrutiny of the conditions within a state, and to provide alternative symbols for individuals within the state to identify with. At the same time, it provides repositories of responsibility for the acts of regular or irregular forces of the exile government. Governments in exile can, of course, be abused, particularly by becoming enslaved, in turn, to their host states and being rendered an instrument of foreign intervention: choosing a host for a government in exile is obviously a choice of momentous destiny. We suggest that claims for recognition of this institution be granted in all those cases in which aspirant status within the state in question is denied or in which real political activity is severely sanctioned. The mere fact that international decisionmakers accept the institution of government in exile may deter precisely those human rights deprivations which spur their creation.

CLAIMS TO RECOGNITION AS A DE FACTO AND DE JURE GOVERNMENT

American practice has tended to merge de facto and de jure recognition. Jefferson established a theoretical distinction between the two, intimating that de jure recognition by the United States implied acknowledgment not only of the control of the recipient but also of its popular support, a facet he deemed virtually peremptory under his natural conception of international law.[120] The distinction was gradually dropped, and for most of the nineteenth century the United States granted recognition to de facto governments only. The general explanation was that de jure evaluations were infringements of the sovereignty of others and hence inappropriate under international law.[121] In 1829, Secretary of State van Buren stated unequivocally that "[s]o far as we are concerned, that which is the Government de facto is equally so de jure."[122] On the other hand, the older tradition is drawn upon from time to time. Thus, the United States recognized Israel de facto on May 14, 1948.[123] Some eight months later, Syria contended that this de facto, as opposed to de jure, recognition was of legal significance.[124] Ambassador Jessup proceeded to tell the Security Council that this recognition had been unconditional and plenary and recalled that earlier, in October 1948, President Truman had stated that de jure recognition would be promptly given when a permanent government was elected in Israel.[125] In contrast, the U.S.S.R. immediately granted de jure recognition on May 17, 1948.[126]

There is a great scholarly controversy over whether there is such a legal creature as de facto recognition. But the critical question is whether it is at all useful for policy purposes to establish a practice of de facto recognition. We believe that, in the appropriate circumstances, it is.

Contemporary international law does establish certain clear standards for legitimate statehood. Elsewhere an attempt has been made to indicate why the application of these standards is sporadic and necessarily a function of extraconstitutional power changes within states.[127] If recognition practice is to serve as an instrument for achieving the sort of world order envisaged in the U.N. Charter and the other grand documents of international law and yet prove itself sufficiently realistic so that it can survive in the world of grim political reality, it should be able to concede the effective power of an elite group in a state without extending the sanction of approval. The communication of de facto recognition permits this to be accomplished and should be retained.

CLAIMS TO WITHDRAWAL OF RECOGNITION

Doctrinal views about the lawfulness of withdrawal of recognition turn upon basic premises about the international system. Those who believe that states are hermetically sealed units between whom the highest norm must be noninterference in internal affairs insist upon the irrevocability of recognition. Thus, Article 6 of the Montevideo Convention of 1933 declares that recognition is "unconditional and irrevocable."[128] Those who believe that the legitimacy of elite exercise of power within states depends upon conformity with standards shared by the larger community argue that recognition is revocable. From the standpoint of the social observer, it is obvious that attitudes held by other elites can gradually change, in effect "derecognizing" an established state or government. States such as South Africa and perhaps Israel have elicited changing attitudes akin to recognition and derecognition.[129]

Recognitions have been formally withdrawn for different reasons. The United States withdrew recognition from Nicaragua in the nineteenth century [130] though the context of the case may deprive it of some value as a precedent. In this century, both France and the United Kingdom have formally withdrawn recognitions.[131] Many of the doctrines of nonrecognition which we have surveyed can be applied analogically to this claim.

Repudiating the lawfulness of incumbency of a particular territorial elite by formal derecognition is not a promising unilateral strategy. Moreover, there are strong authoritative policies militating against "derecognition" of stable territorial arrangements which have been given prior recognition.[132] As a multilateral strategy it could be extremely useful if its use is explicitly correlated with fundamental international norms. Some sort of formal procedure within an organizational context would appear fair and practicable.

Claims Regarding the Incidents of Recognition

ACQUISITION OF "LEGAL PERSONALITY" WITHIN ANOTHER STATE

Activities within other states offer innumerable power and power-related opportunities for the elites of unrecognized states or protostates. Toleration of the representatives of an insurgent or a belligerent by a third state may be a technique for low-level intervention in the conflict between an incumbent government and its counterforce. For convenience, we will use the term "acquisition of legal personality" to refer to the entry and activity of representatives of an unrecognized political group in internal civic processes of the state which has refused their claim for a formal recognition on the interstate level. Representatives of an unrecognized political group will encounter three categories of governmental response to their claims for legal personality: the "corporate state" response, the "liberal democratic" response, and the "progressive" response.

The Corporate State Response   In any political system in which formation and operation of groups is permitted only with formal official permission and under stringent supervision, the unrecognized government can expect to gain entry and a degree of activity only if the elite of the host state anticipates some policy gain from the invitation.

The Liberal Democratic Response   In political systems in which the formation of lesser groups is deemed an ordinary personal power or privilege, representatives of an unrecognized government will ordinarily be able to enter and to operate as any other nonofficial entity. In the United States, for example, barring extraordinary wartime legislation, representatives of an unrecognized government of a group aspiring to this minimal status would be permitted to operate in conformity with United States law, registering under the Foreign Agents Registration Act.[133] Significantly, that instrument construes "government of a foreign country" to include "any faction or body of insurgents within a country assuming to exercise governmenal authority whether such faction or body of insurgents has or has not been recognized by the United States." [134] Registration may be waived if the Attorney General of the United States determines "that such registration, or the furnishing of such information, as the case may be, is not necessary to carry out the purposes of this subchapter." [135] Nor is registration necessary in regard to

> Any person engaging or agreeing to engage only (1) in private and non-political activities in furtherance of the bona fide trade or commerce of such foreign principle; or (2) in other activities not serving predominantly a foreign interest; or (3) in the soliciting or collecting of funds and contributions within the United States to be used only for medical aid and assistance, or for food and clothing to relieve human suffering, if such solicitation or collection of funds and contributions is in accordance with and subject to the provisions of sections 441, 444, 445, and 447–457 to this title, and such rules and regulations as may be prescribed hereunder.[136]

In addition, the Act allows for manipulation by the Executive, in a manner parallel to the corporate state response. Thus, an exemption may be granted if the President of the United States deems the operations of the foreign representative "vital to the defense of the United States."[137] The constitutionality of parts of the Act has been upheld.[138]

Other restraints on the entry and activities of representatives of an unrecognized government or political group could derive from immigration regulations, conditions of residence, and so on.[139] Nonetheless, the liberal democratic response may be said, on the whole, to provide a wide range of opportunities for the acquisition of legal personality domestically by unrecognized entities.

The Progressive Response   States which have recently secured independence through revolution and retain the experience and states which incorporate in their myth a doctrine of transnational aid in the change of governments in other states will, as a matter of course, extend facilities to unrecognized entities if they deem these entities to be part of the "historic" or "ideological" struggle in which they continue to participate vicariously. Thus France and the United States were sympathetic and hospitable to other nascent national revolutions shortly after their own revolutions.[140] States such as Mexico and Algeria, in which the elites and, as in the case of Mexico, the national myth have been decisively shaped by the experience of revolution, routinely accord many of the benefits of recognition to aspiring protogovernments.

CLAIMS FOR BENEFICIAL STATUS UNDER TAX AND REVENUE LAWS

Liberal democracies which, as a matter of policy, seek to encourage the proliferation of many different groups in social process, resort to a number of strategies of encouragement in proportion to the official desire to facilitate the emergence and operation of groups with certain scope values. Institutions specialized to rectitude or to enlightenment, for example, may benefit from direct allocations or from indirect grants such as preferred statuses for tax and revenue purposes. An interest group within such a democracy may seek to aid the emergence of a new government or state and may seek to gain whatever governmental aid may be available; such interest groups may collaborate in various ways with the elites of the protostates which they seek to aid. Where the domestic pressure group can mobilize sufficient political influence, it may lobby for special tax and revenue exemptions for its activities.[141] Where it cannot do this, it may nonetheless resort to the general provision of 26 U.S.C. § 501 (1954), which can confer certain benefits on a protostate.[142]

RECOGNITION FOR STANDING AS PLAINTIFF: UNITED STATES PRACTICE

It has been venerable judicial principle that an unrecognized sovereign might not sue as plaintiff in American courts.[143] The doctrine was clearly enunciated in *Russian Republic v. Cibrario*,[144] where it was held that a foreign government had no inherent right of litigating in American courts for its privilege rested solely on comity. The operation of comity, in turn, depended upon recognition, both of which were held to be the exclusive prerogative of the political branches of the U.S. government. Absent recognition by the Executive, a court, it seemed, could not take judicial notice of the "objective" existence of the state in question.

The vigor of the *Cibrario* doctrine was quickly diminished by other cases. Courts avoided the rigidity of *Cibrario* by construing recognition implicitly or inferentially. For example, a treaty between the United States government and a nonrecognized government was held by one court to be sufficient indication of recognition to allow suit by the other nation in an American court.[145] Where executive recognition of a new government was deemed highly probable in the near future, an unrecognized government was permitted to sue in U.S. courts.[146] In another, more far-reaching case, a corporation directly controlled by a nonrecognized government, but organized under the laws of New York, was permitted to sue.[147] Although a state of war between the United States and a foreign state would block that state from suing in an American court,[148] the mere breaking of diplomatic relations between the U.S. and a foreign state does not deprive that other state of the privilege of suit in U.S. courts.[149] Moreover, the continuing privilege of suit does not depend upon reciprocal treatment for the U.S. in the courts of that foreign nation.[150]

Cibrario, though doctrinally criticized[151] and precedentially eroded, was not challenged directly for nearly forty years. In 1961, another New York decision, *Upright v. Mercury Business Machines*,[152] revised and, indeed, inverted the rule. *Upright* involved an action by the assignee of a trade acceptance drawn on and accepted by the defendant in payment for products which the defendant had purchased from a foreign corporation controlled by the nonrecognized East German government. *Cibrario,* the court held, did not foreclose suit by the assignee of a nonrecognized government, but such suits could be barred if the underlying transaction or the assignment itself violated public policy.

In dicta, the New York court asserted that a nonrecognized government could not bring suit in the U.S., but it left open the question of a suit by a corporation controlled by such a government. In terms of results, however, the court seemed to open the way for such suits. The point seemed to be that citizens and corporations of a nonrecognized government or state should not face an absolute bar to access to U.S. courts because of the often unrelated reasons for U.S. executive nonrecognition.[153]

A nonrecognized government can easily move the paper necessary for assignment to a third party or for the creation of a state corporation; the assignee or corporation can then sue in place of the government. Artifice need not motivate such transactions. State corporations are becoming a rather mundane instrument for supervising foreign trade, and paper arrangements such as discounted assignments are normal incidents of interstate credit transactions in international trade. As international trade increases, they will become pervasive phenomena reflecting the division and specialization of complex social arrangements. In the context of such emergent changes, *Upright* inverts the *Cibrario* doctrine: in ordinary commercial cases, an American court, according to *Upright,* will ignore the question of recognition in situations in which suit is brought on behalf of an unrecognized state, if such action is not judicially determined to be repugnant to public policy or *semble* is not expressly reproved by the Executive.[154]

RECOGNITION AND IMMUNITY FROM SUIT

The procedural immunity of a foreign government in U.S. courts poses a dilemma for the American judiciary. On the one hand, courts are committed to the vindication of private rights, particularly where they are challenged by a powerful government agency. On the other hand, courts, as a branch of the federal government, are mindful of the Executive's primary responsibility for the conduct of foreign affairs; judges have shown themselves to be sensitive to the diplomatic complications which may arise from suits against foreign governments in U.S. courts, particularly when broader issues are involved or when many other cases are pending and the Executive may be involved in, or anticipate, commencing direct negotiations toward an aggregate agreement.

Current American practice does not recognize an absolute right of immunity for foreign governments from suit in American courts. The foreign nation invoking the privilege may initiate the claim in the Department of State or in the court seized of the basic controversy. If the claim is brought to the Department of State, a procedure based on certain customary and prescribed principles may result in certification of the sovereignty of the impleaded state or agency thereof, coupled with a recommendation by the Department of State to the court that immunity be extended to the impleaded state for that case.[155] Since 1952, the Department of State claims to follow a "restrictive" approach to sovereign immunity, distinguishing between *acta jure imperii* and *acta jure gestionis;*[156] yet it is probable that the Department reserves a broad discretion to request sovereign immunity in cases of *gestio,* should it deem such recommendation to be in the national interest.[157] Although there is no express constitutional or statutory directive mandating a court addressed by the Department of State to accept a request for immunity, courts do in fact accept them.[158] This is part of the general withering of the original structured competition and anticipated friction of the branches of government under the American constitutional system and, particularly in foreign affairs, the increasing subservience of the courts to the Executive. Nonetheless, it is not inconceivable that courts may yet repossess a review function over State Department requests.[159]

If the impleaded state or agency thereof has not turned to the Department of State or has not succeeded in securing a recommendation for immunity from the Department, it may turn directly to the court. In this eventuality, the court will apply the "restrictive" theory of sovereign immunity, in conjunction with a number of other exceptions, and determine whether or not to extend immunity.[160]

Because the underlying rationale of the sovereign immunity doctrine is judicial deference to a primary executive responsibility for foreign affairs and avoidance of disruption to executive programs regarding a particular state, the variable of prior executive recognition *vel non* should, in theory, have nothing to do with the question of whether or not to extend immunity in a particular case. Procedurally, of course, there must be differences. The Department of State would not ordinarily certify the sovereign immunity of an unrecognized state, yet it is not inconceivable that in the future the Department might request such extension of immunity in particular cases. The more common procedure will involve a court itself deciding whether to extend immunity to an unrecognized state which has been impleaded before it. The decisive precedents, established half a century ago, and not reconsidered in the light of other salient jurisprudential developments, paradoxically extend a more absolute immunity to an unrecognized state than to a recognized state. In *Wulfsohn v. R.S.F.S.R.,*[161] it was held that the privilege of sovereign immunity did not require the status of being recognized by the United States. The force of the precedent is somewhat limited by the fact that it involved acts by the unrecognized government in its own territory, where it was conceded to be sovereign. The reasoning of the decision was that immunity was based upon actual sovereignty, which was apparently defined as control of political processes within the nation's territory, a fact which could be judicially established without regard to recognition by the Executive. Once this fact was established, a state or government could not be sued in a U.S. court without its consent. The policy undercurrent of the opinion was the court's conviction that regardless of recognition, a suit against another state touched on all of the problems implicit in any sovereign immunity case.[162]

RECOGNITION AND ACTS OF STATE
Executive recognition imports the acknowledgment of the recognized state's primary competence to prescribe for matters which are deemed by international law to be within the "territorial jurisdiction" of a state.[163] Hence, acts relating to events or persons within the foreign state's jurisdiction will not be reviewed or questioned by U.S. courts as long as *semble* the acts do not violate international law.[164] In earlier practice, the fact of nonrecognition was deemed to be a crucial factor in extending acts of state, though subsequent recognition could be applied retroactively.[165] But the proliferation of revolutions and the growing disparity between executive recognition policy and international "facts of life" generated a spectrum of judicial exceptions. In a number of New York decisions in the 1920s concerned with Soviet nationalizations, acts of an unrecognized government were accorded a "quasi-governmental" status if such a judicial response would avoid "violence to fundamental principles of justice or to our own public policy."[166] This judicial approach necessarily involved a detailed consideration of the milieu of each case and the aggregate consequences of the alternative judicial responses available to the court.[167]

Insofar as a particular nonrecognition was a manifest diplomatic policy aimed at weakening or securing concessions from the elite of an unrecognized state, the New York approach could conflict with executive policy and, indeed, New York courts indicated that they were aware of this possibility. Yet they insisted that their responsibility was different from that of the Executive; as against the political concerns of the Executive, courts were charged with considering the *meum* and *tuum* of private, nonpolitical interests which did not relate to foreign affairs issues. To defer completely to the political aspects of recognition policy would be "to give to fictions an air of reality which they do not deserve." [168]

This constitutional challenge was resolved by the Supreme Court in favor of the Executive in *United States v. Pink,* the culmination of a series of decisions which wrestled with the complex of policies involved.[169] *Pink* confirmed the supremacy of the Executive in foreign affairs matters including recognition and the invalidity of state action which might run counter to an executive decision in these areas. But *Pink* does not destroy judicial independence in this area. A court may, it would seem, accord the incidents of act of state to the governmental acts of an unrecognized entity if, cumulatively,

1. to do otherwise would offend the court's sense of justice and lead to results inconsistent with public policy; and
2. to do so would not be counter to an important diplomatic objective of the Executive.

This development seems to have been reinforced in the *Upright* decision.[170] There the court reaffirmed the earlier Russian nationalization cases, but with a modification. The *Sokoloff* case had placed the burden of proof on the party asking the court to give effect to the acts of the unrecognized regime by showing affirmatively that justice or public policy would be violated if an act of state effect were not allowed. In contrast, *Upright* seems to shift the burden to the party seeking to deny any effect to the acts. That party must demonstrate that giving effect to the acts of state would violate public policy.[171] Thus the judicial presumption after *Upright* is that the acts of an unrecognized government are given effect in U.S. courts, until a party arguing against the acts can show affirmatively that such a judicial response would be against public policy. The result is the increasing assimilation of the acts of state of both recognized and unrecognized governments and a move toward greater judicial independence of executive decisions of nonrecognition. But because of the confusion and, it is submitted, incorrect application of the act of state doctrine in recent American decisions, the full vigor of this trend has not yet been felt.

RECOGNITION AND TREATIES

Questions involving the continuing validity of treaties to which one of the parties has undergone a significant governmental change are exceedingly complex. Such questions arise in American courts when a treaty has been invoked, but the foreign party has since been supplanted by a state or government not recognized by the United States government: the judicial response has been one of wary restraint.[172] In *Clark v. Allen*,[173] the Supreme Court held that without evidence that the political departments deemed Germany incapable, after surrender in 1945, of performing its treaty obligations, the 1923 Treaty with Germany was still valid and in force. The assessment of a state's capacity to perform its treaty obligations was "essentially a political question."[174] In contrast to other recognition problems, there were to be no independent judicial assessments of executive decisions, no matter how discordant international political reality might be. Thus, the U.S. court of claims in 1959 held that the U.S. government's refusal to recognize the Soviet annexation of Latvia meant that the 1928 Treaty between the United States and the Republic of Latvia was still in force.[175] Tentative moves by state courts toward a more independent judicial position on these matters have been blocked by the Supreme Court.[176]

MUNICIPAL RESPONSE TO INTERNATIONALLY PRESCRIBED NONRECOGNITION

Internationally mandated nonrecognition, primarily a product of this century, occurs when an international organization or group of nations establishes an international prescription barring recognition under certain circumstances or decides upon nonrecognition as an international strategy.[177] The phenomenon may arise in a number of arenas, but it has proved most problematic in the United Nations system. When the Security Council of the United Nations declares a complex of events to be a "threat to the peace, breach of the peace or act of aggression," its plenary powers under Chapter VII of the Charter are activated. These powers include decisions regarding the refusal to extend recognition to a nascent regime. Decisions made under these powers are binding on all members states of the United Nations and, in varying ways, on the specialized agency network of the U.N. system.[178] The impact of such decisions on the domestic courts of member states of the United Nations will depend on a number of factors.

If the member state has enacted domestic implementing legislation for Security Council decisions, domestic courts will comply with that legislation. If the member state enacts a special implementing decision for that specific case, courts will comply with it. If the member state's courts have developed a theory of automatic incorporation, the courts themselves will implement the Security Council decision, but if their theory distinguishes between "self-executing" and "non-self-executing" agreements, then their response to the particular decision cannot be gauged from institutional aspects for the distinction itself is susceptible to quite contradictory interpretations.[179] With the exception of states whose courts have developed a theory of independent and automatic incorporation of international agreements and decisions made under them into domestic law, all courts will presumably enforce later domestic legislation as against a Security Council decision on the principle of *lex posterior derogat*. All of these responses, quite inconsistent with the purposes of the U.N. Charter, are part of the problem of the failure to integrate effectively domestic courts into the grid of international decision.

The United Nations has resolved that the Smith regime in Rhodesia is not a lawful government and that member states of the U.N. must not recognize it or trade with it.[180] Although the U.S. government observed the sanctions imposed by the U.N. from their inception,[181] it has changed its policy and since 1972 allows the importation of Rhodesian chrome into the U.S.[182] This action does not amount to a de jure recognition of the

Smith regime, but by frustrating the purpose of the international policy of nonrecognition, it represents a direct challenge to the Security Council's competence to play a role in the recognition process.[183] Earlier U.S. decisions did in fact comply with the Security Council's decision, though their formal reasoning invoked executive recognition policy rather than a U.N. decision.[184]

Variables Accounting for Recognition Responses of American Courts: A Tentative Assessment

The cases which have been surveyed suggest that the complex of responses of domestic courts in the United States which involve significant benefits for foreign states cannot be accounted for by the traditional unilinear theory. According to that theory, it will be recalled, the initial decision regarding the appropriate attitude of all American governmental agencies—federal and state—is to be determined by the Department of State on behalf of the Executive; once this determination has been made, all other agencies will implement it. Structural changes within the United States government, as well as within the world arena, have made that theory obsolete. The formerly preeminent role of the Department of State in the recognition process has become a coordinate role and courts seem to be responding to a range of factors. A fairly detailed set of hypotheses can be formulated, by suspending for the moment psychopersonal factors which inevitably influence decisions, as well as idiosyncratic links of loyalty, affection, or obligation which may subordinate certain judges to political leaders or predispose them for certain cases.

1. An unequivocal executive and legislative policy of nonrecognition will minimize judicial independence in according some incidents of recognition to an unrecognized state. The degree of judicial independence would appear to be inversely proportional to the degree of clarity and intensity of executive and legislative policy. *But*
2. If there is a sharp divergence between executive and legislative policy regarding the recognition or nonrecognition of a particular foreign state, courts will tend to be more independent in according some incidents of recognition.
3. If there is a manifest diversity of approach among coequal executive departments and agencies, courts will tend to be more independent in according some incidents of recognition, but the courts' manifest reasoning in opinions will seek to accommodate itself to the divergent policies of the different agencies in question. *But*
4. If the general understanding of the policy of nonrecognition is that it is motivated by urgent considerations of national security or defense, courts will be increasingly obedient to executive cues of nonrecogni-

tion. In crisis, it is hypothesized, courts tend to obey the Executive rather than to seek to check and balance it by independent judicial criteria.[185]

5. The degree of judicial independence of executive policies of nonrecognition will be directly proportional to the length of the period during which the unrecognized government has exercised effective power. In other words, if courts believe that, nonrecognition policy notwithstanding, state X is permanent and, inferentially, that the U.S. Executive will come to terms with it at some point, the courts are more likely to extend some of the incidents of recognition to a foreign state, even though this diverges from, or is in defiance of, executive policy.[186]

A number of other factors will contribute to the type of recognition incidents a court extends to a nonrecognized state.

1. If the unrecognized state is a member of a functional transnational community of which the United States is a part, courts will be more likely to accord it incidents of recognition. An unrecognized government and/or its citizens and commercial entities within its jurisdiction may have regular commercial relations with Americans. This factor will probably weigh heavily on an American court if its refusal to extend some of the incidents of recognition to the foreign government will impair these exchanges and the commercial interests of the United States.[187]
2. If the effect of refusing to extend particular incidents of recognition to an unrecognized state is the deprivation of American nationals, courts will probably lean toward extending those incidents.
3. If nonrecognition seems to have been exploited by Americans in ways repugnant to general commercial morality, courts may secure a remedy by partial incidents of recognition.[188]

Implications for the Future

The American constitutional scheme was designed to generate competition and, indeed, some friction between the branches of the government through the device of overlapping competences of politically coordinate branches. Because the animating conception of this scheme was the "rule of law," an independent judiciary applying legal criteria to the acts of the Executive was particularly crucial. In the realm of foreign affairs, the checks and balances system has not worked with optimum efficiency for a number of reasons. The United States system took shape at the dawn of the modern nation-state system. This international system was characterized by a persisting expectation of violence and, hence, the ongoing mobilization of component states for defense. Because foreign affairs involved security, courts tended to subordinate themselves to the policies of the Executive in this area, even though international law was the law of the land and many foreign affairs decisions had major impacts on citizens and on aspects of domestic social processes. Furthermore, because the American constitutional system was novel and likely to be misunderstood by the elites of other regimes, there was salience to the court's concern to avoid "embarrassing" the Executive in critical foreign affairs.

The embarrassment factor is no longer real; notice of the peculiarities of the American system is more than constructive. Indeed, the pattern of judicial deference to the Executive in foreign affairs matters for purposes of maintaining the integrity of our system of government begins to erode the very integrity of the domestic constitutional system when the level of interaction between American citizens and groups and foreigners passes a certain threshold. Beyond that threshold, domestic and foreign matters merge and become increasingly indistinguishable as American social and economic processes become integrated in functional transnational communities. If the judiciary continues to defer to the Executive when the signal "foreign affairs" is flashed, the separation of powers shifts into a new sociopolitical configuration of executive superordination.

The most probable judicial trend in international law cases at this time is one of increasing subservience to the Executive.[189] But recognition cases indicate an incipient countertrend, for they indicate that domestic courts are yet capable of testing executive policies against international law and of extending the guarantees of American law to functional transnational communities in which Americans participate.

Claims Against Prerecognized Entities for Conformity to International Norms

Groups which have not yet been formally recognized as states but whose activities may have significant impacts on the international system are subjected to claims by others for conformity to critical international standards.[190] We next consider, in programmatic fashion, claims on prerecognized entities to conform to international standards in the fundamental strategies of behavior.

CLAIMS AFFECTING THIRD STATES

Claims to Comply with Norms Regulating the Use of Force   The most fundamental principles of the conventional international law of force of this century apply equally to state and nonstate entities.[191] While many more specific norms are phrased in terms of national command structures, their normative marrow can be applied as well to prerecognized entities.

Customary principles about the use of force which applied to *hostes humani generis* never, of course, required a real or fictitious link between the deviant and some nation-state apparatus in order to subject the deviant to international law.[192] While private groups have often espoused clear codification of principles applicable to prerecognized entities, official elites have been somewhat ambivalent. On the one hand, they recognize their own interest in subjecting prerecognized belligerents to fundamental rules of war. On the other hand, such overt application may be tantamount to a degree of recognition.[193] Moreover, prescription of certain norms may deprive prerecognized entities of some field advantages, *e.g.*, the requirement of uniforms as a precondition for the application of other norms. Prescriptions such as these, of course, are vigorously resisted by forces of prerecognized entities.

Claims to Comply with Norms Facilitating and Protecting Transnational Wealth Activities Customary and conventional international law include numerous prescriptions facilitating transnational wealth activities and, in particular, limiting the authority of official territorial elites to interfere with these exchanges. Nonetheless, exceptions are allowed for periods of belligerency.[194] These exceptions are not formally extended to the forces of prerecognized entities. However, if these entities succeed, the latitude granted to official elites is extended retroactively.[195] Nor are the many strategic maritime advantages which involve disruption of wealth flows allowed to prerecognized elites without extending recognition of belligerent status.[196]

On a more informal level, however, it seems clear that official and unofficial participants in the transnational wealth process bring a variety of pressures to bear on prerecognized entities to conform to international prescriptions protecting wealth processes.

Claims to Comply with Norms Protecting and Facilitating Diplomatic and Other Inter-Elite Communications Prescriptions protecting elite communication are among the most venerable and fundamental of the international system.[197] One of the most important perquisites of state recognition is the complex of privileges surrounding use of the diplomatic instrument. Official elites have regularly demanded of prerecognized entities a full compliance with these norms. On the other hand, prerecognized elites have not been granted, as of right, any of the benefits of diplomatic communication. Functional immunities do seem to be granted when conditions of recognition are being negotiated between an official elite and an as yet unrecognized elite.[198] Where the controlling situation is less favorable to the prerecognized elites, more limited safe-conducts may be promised. Recent experience instructs, however, that such concessions are "safe" only in proportion to the bona fides of the grantor.

In the past decade, prerecognized entities have increased their assaults on the formerly inviolable institutions of diplomatic communication and personal and *familial* immunity.[199] Official elites have responded by codification of customary norms and attempts to prescribe more effective sanction programs.[200] If the normative structure of the diplomatic instrument is based ultimately on reciprocity, however, the better strategy would appear to be an extension of functional benefits to prerecognized elites as a means of securing their positive interest in maintaining the integrity of the institution.

Claims to Comply with Norms Relating to Ideological Communication Across Political Boundaries   Both practice and expectations about the transnational use of the ideologic instrument are considerably less uniform than those relating to the diplomatic instrument. Elites that enjoy great technological capacity and that, accordingly, see in the ideological instrument a strategic device which they can use more effectively than others, will demand of the world constitutive process facilitation of world "freedom of information." Elites that have no such technological capacity will construe "freedom of information" as little more than a fig leaf for subtle interventions by alien elites in the communities over which they wish to consolidate control. An international policy of maximum enlightenment is not easily specified, for the content of mass communications may be weighted against the sheer quantity of information made available: the capacity to discriminate between truth and falsehood presupposes a reservoir of prior experience and enlightenment which may not in fact exist in the target audience.

Prerecognized elites regularly claim access to ideological modalities. In a liberal democratic system in which doctrines of "fair representation" operate,[201] a case can be made for access to media by alien aspirants and prerecognized groups.[202] On the other hand, prerecognized groups rarely have the capacity to interfere with the ideological communications of their adversaries.

Claims Affecting the Structuring of Internal Participation   General international prescriptions provide a rather detailed code for the appropriate internal organization· of component communities which aspire to some recognition from others in the internationl system. There are, in short, prescriptions about patterns of participation, about appropriate perspectives on the elite and rank and file levels, about the appropriate structuring of power and other arenas, about the appropriate distribution of authority and control, and about how control is actually to be used. Because of the current organization of the international system, these complex norms are ordinarily invoked only when an event has become "internationalized," *e.g.,* during a belligerent occupation or a succession or self-determination followed by claims for recognition.

Conditions and Projections

Recognition presents itself as a problem to decisionmakers because, in any interdependent system, a change in one part affects others. The inevitable responses, intended and unintended, will in turn affect the vector and intensity of change. Even if the nation-state system could some-how be frozen in its current configuration, recognition problems would continue to plague decisionmakers, for internal changes—in participation, group myth, community structures, authority and control patterns, and procedures for the use of values—would continue to precipitate effects external to the group in a degree commensurate with the level of inter-dependence in the system.

But the political structure of the nation-state system is not frozen; it changes constantly. Part of the change can be attributed to the political machinations of the competing elites of the larger powers, who contend, among other things, by proxy struggles in, and realignments of, smaller states. Part of the change is attributable to activities of indigenous political elites that may reshape political and other value communities—for ex-ample, through the formation or dissolution of federations or other stable collaborations—because it maximizes their own or their community goals. The most volatile cause for change and hence for recognition problems arises from a fundamental social phenomenon: the ongoing formation of groups by individuals as a means of maximizing their preferred values. Max Weber called this a process of consociation; international law has referred to it generally as self-determination. Elsewhere the social and psychological factors which may facilitate the transition of a consociation to a territorial community [203] have been examined in some detail. In the present context, our concern is not with these factors but rather with the phenomenon itself, for it is one of the basic sources of that type of change which is deemed internationally critical and which regularly engages international constitutive decision.

Our cursory trend study suggests that while the constitutive process has prescribed a rather complex code to guide recognition decisions, actual decision trends are significantly conditioned by the structure of the world power arena. As the level of crisis increases, it would appear, the pre-disposition of major powers to accord or withhold certain incidents of recognition turns increasingly on security considerations. As crisis abates, factors such as wealth, affection, and human rights considerations may become more prominent. The ideology of shared public order does not appear to be a decisive factor for it seems that major powers will support ideological incompatibles if strategic or tactical gains are to be made; international, like national, politics makes strange bedfellows.

The basic syndrome will presumably continue if the current structure of the world arena persists. Different recognition patterns can be projected for alternative constructive futures. Consider a number of alternatives:

1. *An Organized World Power Oligarchy.* If the five or six largest communities, with the greatest capacity for the use of violence, choose to coordinate policies in a tight power oligarchy, they may establish, in concert, recognition policies either in general or for specific cases which will presumably be followed by all other official and nonofficial decision-makers. The factors which will govern the oligarch powers themselves will, at least initially, be based on naked power alone, the lesser oligarchs in each case following the recognition policy set by the stronger in the interest of maintaining the cabal. Although sporadic violence may continue, elites and counter-elites in the more peripheral communities will be less likely to succeed in bringing about those social changes which have generated international recognition decisions. Over time, of course, the world power oligarchy will generate a complex of norms which will influence recognition decisions. At the same time, elites and counter-elites in the smaller states will lodge claims either with the concert or with individual oligarchs, invoking these norms; insofar as they identify themselves as momentarily critical components in their oligarch's base of power, they may bargain with it for favorable recognition responses. Paradoxically, the organized oligarchy may accelerate the codification of an inclusive recognition law.

2. *A Decentralized World Power Oligarchy.* The five or six largest communities may coordinate policy simply by demarking "spheres of influence" in which the preferences of the sphere's hegemon are deferred to by the other oligarchs. In this construct, five or six laws of recognition would develop within each sphere of influence, with decision processes in each dominated by a regional satrap.

3. *A Disintegrated World System.* Certain technological innovations, for example, a radical lowering of the unit cost of energy, could lead to a slackening of the links which have been forged to provide easy access to raw materials and to markets. The ultimate result might be the development of many comparatively autarkic communities about the globe. In this construct, the fact of interdependence would diminish, and social changes within the communities would excite relatively little interest in other communities. The international law of recognition would wither away.

4. *An Integrated World System.* In an effectively integrated world system, in contrast, consociation would presumably assume patterns roughly comparable to incorporation or the establishment of noncommercial entities in contemporary nation-states. The outcome of such a process would be the ascription of a "legal personality" of varying incidents to a claimant group. A high degree of official control would then attend each phase of the establishment or termination of existing social structures. Decision responses could increasingly emphasize optimum community goals.

Notes

1.   Darwin's theory, of course, postulated the ongoing production of variants, but it is only recent genetic inquiry which has vindicated the formulator of modern evolutionary doctrine. DNA research has established the probability of mutation and some of its effects. The greater randomness of this process, as opposed to the almost mystical progress of evolutionary "orthogenesis," should have enormous impacts on social as well as philosophical and religious theories. For the impact of this doctrine on contemporary metatheory, see T. S. KUHN, THE STRUCTURE OF SCIENTIFIC REVOLUTION (1962). But *cf.* Davis, *Toward a Theory of Revolution,* 27 AM. SOCIOLOGICAL REV. 6 (1962). *See also* Davis, *The Circumstances and Causes of Revolution: A Review,* 11 J. CONFLICT RESOLUTION 247 (1967).

2.   R. DAHRENDORF, CLASS AND CLASS CONFLICT IN INDUSTRIAL SOCIETY 176 (1959).

3.   H. GROTIUS, DE JURE BELLI AC PACIS bk. II, ch. IX, para. III.

4.   The doctrine of "domestic jurisdiction," it should be noted, can provide no more than a pious flutter of protest in the face of the facts of social interstimulation. Significantly, the Permanent Court, in its *Tunis-Morocco Nationality Decrees* opinion, emphasized the necessary relativity of the concept of domestic jurisdiction: "The question whether a certain matter is or is not solely within the jurisdiction of a state is an essentially relative question; it depends upon the development of international relations." [1923] P.C.I.J., ser. B. No. 4, at 23–24.

5.   For a useful examination of many of the benefits which ensue on recognition or which are withheld in cases of nonrecognition, see Alexy, *Die Beteiligung an Multilateralen Konferenzen, Verträgen und internationalen Organisationen als Frage der indirekten Anerkennung von Staaten,* 26 ZEITSCHRIFT FÜR AUSLANDISCHES OFFENTLICHES RECHT UND VÖLKERRECHT 495 (1966). *See also* Bindschedler, *Anerkennung in Völkerrecht,* 1962 ARCHIV DES VÖLKERRECHTS 392, 394. *See also* Zellweger, *Anerkennung und Nichtanerkennung Neuer Staaten (nachkriegsaspekte),* 24 ANNUAIRE SUISSE DE DROIT INTERNATIONAL 9 (1966). The modulation of attitudes simultaneously proceeds in response to the sequence of events. The Greek Cypriot coup of 1974 and the U.S. response provide a dramatic recent example of the interfaces of the processes of recognition and change. *See* the sequence of the attitude change in N.Y. Times, July 18, 1974, at 1, col. 8; *id.,* Aug. 6, 1974, at 2, col. 4.

6.   Thus, the Hallstein Doctrine of Non-Recognition must be distinguished from that of Stimson. As early as 1949, Adenauer had stated that his government alone was authorized to represent the entire German people. In 1955, Foreign Minister von Brentano formally declared that Bonn would immediately sever diplomatic relations with any government which recognized East Germany. And, indeed, in a significant number of instances, the Federal Republic either severed relations or brought considerable pressure on other states not to recognize. For a critical survey of some of these cases, see Bierzanek, *La Non-Reconnaissance et le Droit International Contemporain,* 8 ANNUAIRE FRANCAIS DE DROIT INTERNATIONAL 118, 119–121 (1962).

For some consideration of the Hallstein Doctrine as an overt strategy for undermining the D.D.R., see Kroger, *Das Demokratische Völkerrecht und die Grundlagen der Bonner "Hallstein-Doctrin,"* 10 STAAT UND RECHT 963 (1962). Hallsteinian nonrecognition does not relate to collective responses to what is widely perceived to be a violation of an important international norm. Rather, it is a technique in which a diplomatically powerful state deploys its bases of power to influence the recognition policies of smaller states in a matter which it deems to be its concern. Professor Bierzanek argues that Hallsteinian nonrecognition is violative of international law for it is used to deprive third states of the free exercise of the right of recognition. In an irony characteristic of the world arena, it is now the People's Republic of China which is using Hallstein-nonrecognition most effectively.

For a review of West German recognition practice through the early 1960s, see Klein, *Zur Praxis der Anerkennung neuer Staaten durch die Bundesrepublik Deutsch-*

land, in RECHT IM DIENSTE DER MENSCHENWÜRDE: FESTSCHRIFT FÜR HERBERT KRAUS 191 (Göttinger Arbeitskreises ed. 1964).

7.   The fundamental character of "recognition" as a social event is reflected in the codification of appropriate norms even for the simplest interactions. Individuals are emotionally wounded if not "recognized"; the failure in a face-to-face situation to acknowledge the existence of a person is thus deemed a serious affront and a real breach of the operational social code. E. GOFFMAN, BEHAVIOR IN PUBLIC PLACES (1968). Indeed, repeated failures to recognize may lead to emotional disorders of ego diffusion, for a significant part of the self's sense of being derives from reassurances through acknowledgments in encounters with others. The directive of the Bundesrepublik to its diplomats during the vigor of the Hallstein Doctrine, *supra* note 6, to avoid recognition and even to avert eyes in encounters with East Germans was, of course, a complex prescription but may have included some shrewdly conceived cruelty. *See also* Williams, *Some Thoughts on the Doctrine of Recognition in International Law,* 47 HARV. L. REV. 776 (1934).

8.   *See* Lauterpacht, *De Facto Recognition, Withdrawal of Recognition, and Conditional Recognition,* [1945] 22 BRIT. Y.B. INT'L L. 164. *But cf.* TI-CHIANG CHEN, THE INTERNATIONAL LAW OF RECOGNITION 8 (L. C. Green ed. 1951) [hereinafter cited as TI-CHIANG CHEN, RECOGNITION]; P. JESSUP, A MODERN LAW OF NATIONS 57–58 (1948); S. R. PATEL, RECOGNITION IN THE LAW OF NATIONS 105–10 (1959).

The most dramatic recent example of this transformation is, of course, Taiwan, which was quickly and inclusively derecognized and stripped of many of the benefits of statehood and, indeed, of putative great-powerhood. G.A. Res. 2758, U.N. DOC. A/8429 (1971), 26 U.N. GAOR. Supp. 29, at 2. *See also* N.Y. Times, Oct. 26, 1971, at 1, col. 8. For further detail, see Chen & Reisman, *Who Owns Taiwan: A Search for International Title,* 81 YALE L.J. 599 (1972). A more subtle change can be found in the case of Israel. M. REISMAN, THE ART OF THE POSSIBLE: DIPLOMATIC ALTERNATIVES IN THE MIDDLE EAST 9 (1971).

On the forms and consequences of indirect recognition as treated in the socialist doctrinal literature, see Frenzke, *Stillschweigende Anerkennung durch Vertagsschluss in der ostlichen Völkerrechtslehre,* 14 OSTEUROPA-RECHT 113 (1968).

9.   On the role of "progressive" states in extending early recognition, see p. 433 *infra.*

10.   *See, e.g.,* the "embassy" of the Black Panther party in Algeria. Gramont, *Our Other Man in Algiers,* N.Y. Times, Oct. 1, 1970, at 30–31 (Magazine). The sequence of events was followed by the African Party for the Independence of Guinea and Cape Verde. *Id.,* Nov. 8, 1971, at 1, Col. 1; *id.,* No. 5, 1972, at 10, col. 1; U.N. DOC. A/RES/3061 (XXVIII), Nov. 2, 1973. *See generally* A. CABRALLY, REVOLUTION IN GUINEA (R. Handyside transl. & ed. 1969); Note, *Recognition of Guinea (Bissau),* 15 HARV. INT'L L.J. 482 (1974).

11.   Aspirant refers to a group which seeks authoritative control of, or participation in, the authoritative process of a territorial community. It is clear that the democratic manifestos of the United Nations Charter and the human rights declarations and conventions have rendered as matters of international concern the access to, and participation in, national authoritative processes by groups not affiliated with an established government.

12.   McDougal, Lasswell & Reisman, *The World Constitutive Process of Authoritative Decision,* 19 J. LEGAL ED. 253, 403 (1967), *reprinted in* 1 THE FUTURE OF THE INTERNATIONAL LEGAL ORDER 73 (C. Black & R. Falk eds. 1969).

13.   R. K. MERTON, SOCIAL THEORY AND SOCIAL STRUCTURE 182–83, 475–90 (enl. ed. 1968).

14.   In 1907 Dr. Tobar, Minister of Foreign Affairs of Ecuador, proposed that Latin American countries conclude an agreement not to recognize a government which came into power by extraconstitutional means. The Tobar Doctrine was adopted by the Republics of Central America in the Central American Convention of 1907, which adopted the General Treaty of Peace and Amity of 1907. 2 AM. J. INT'L L. SUPP. 219

(1908). For a specific provision, see Additional Convention to the General Treaty, *id.* at 229–30. Subsequently, the Doctrine was further strengthened in the General Treaty of Peace and Amity of 1923. *See* 1 G. HACKWORTH, DIGEST OF INTERNATIONAL LAW 187–88 (1940) [hereinafter cited as 1 G. HACKWORTH, DIGEST]. The Convention of 1923 was, however, denounced as from January 1, 1934, by Costa Rica and El Salvador. *See* Woolsey, *The Recognition of the Government of El Salvador,* 28 AM. J. INT'L L. 325 (1934). The text of the convention may be found in 17 AM. J. INT'L L. SUPP. 118 (1923). While the Tobar Doctrine was not used extensively beyond Ibero-America, it was advanced and practiced by President Wilson. *But cf.* Buell, *The United States and Central American Stability,* 7 FOR. POLICY REP. 161 (1931); Buell, *The United States and Central American Revolution, id.* at 187.

15. Secretary of State Bryan issued a note of nonrecognition to China and Japan when Japan successfully presented a twenty-one-demand ultimatum to China. For a full text of Bryan's note, see [1915] FOREIGN REL. U.S. 146. A similar declaration was made by China in 1917 when the Lansing-Ishii Agreement was concluded: [1917] FOREIGN REL. U.S. 270. The nonrecognition policy practiced by Secretary Bryan was adopted by Secretary Stimson, but the philosophical underpinnings were quite different. The former nonrecognition policy was primarily based on President Wilson's Tobarist test of constitutionality. *See* note 14 *supra.* A shift from the Jeffersonian emphasis on the "will of the nation substantially declared" as a basis for recognition regardless of the modality of change, to the Wilsonian orientation which denies recognition for change by extraconstitutional means has been linked to the increasing expansion of American economic control in the Western Hemisphere, necessitating the "stability" of the existing institutions. *See* S. A. MACCORKLE, AMERICAN POLICY OF RECOGNITION TOWARD MEXICO 22–23, 91 (1933). The Wilsonian Doctrine was applied most prominently to the Huerta regime of Mexico and the Tinoco government in Costa Rica. *See* Baker, *Woodrow Wilson's Use of the Non-Recognition Policy in Costa Rica,* 22 AMERICAS 3 (1965). *See* Wilson's statement on December 2, 1913, with respect to Huerta's government. [1913] FOREIGN REL. U.S. x. *See also* P. E. HALEY, REVOLUTION AND INTERVENTION: THE DIPLOMACY OF TAFT AND WILSON WITH MEXICO, 1910–1917, at 82–94 (1970). In the Tinoco case, the Department of State informed American merchants that they could not expect diplomatic protection if they invested in Costa Rica.

Wilson's test of constitutionality as a prerequisite to recognition was abandoned by Hoover. *See* 2 M. WHITEMAN, DIGEST OF INTERNATIONAL LAW 69 (1963) [hereinafter cited as 2 WHITEMAN, DIGEST]; DEPT. OF STATE, THE UNITED STATES AND OTHER AMERICAN REPUBLICS 8 (Latin American Series No. 4, 1931). Judge Lauterpacht writes critically: "The practice emphasized, though not inaugurated, by President Wilson was . . . fully in keeping with the Jeffersonian tradition." H. LAUTERPACHT, RECOGNITION IN INTERNATIONAL LAW 128 n.2 (1947) [hereinafter cited as LAUTERPACHT, RECOGNITION]. Lauterpacht plainly assumes that an expression of "the will of the nation substantially declared" can be achieved only by "constitutional" change. The briefest consideration should make patent that this is neither generally nor necessarily the case and is, in fact, a *petitio principii,* presupposing that a "constitutional" government is per se an expression of the will of the people.

Wilson, anxious to encourage the constitutional development of Latin American republics, pursued the nonrecognition policy vis-à-vis governments created by extraconstitutional means. Wilson's policy, like Tobar's, was a comparatively undiscriminating instrument for it might easily reinforce a tyrannical status quo against popularly demanded change. *But see* D. P. O'CONNELL, INTERNATIONAL LAW 149 (1965). In fact, its normative ambiguity allowed it to be employed for contradictory purposes. *Compare,* for example, two statements made by Secretaries of State Bryan and Stimson about Wilson's policy, regarding Huerta. Speech made Feb. 6, 1931, *quoted* in W. LIPPMAN & W. SCROGGS, THE U.S. IN WORLD AFFAIRS 1931, 333 (1932). *See generally* S. A. MACCORKLE, *supra.* For the contemporary U.S. practice, see Cochrane, *U.S. Policy Towards Recognition of Governments and Promotion of Democracy in Latin America since 1963,* 4 J. LAT. AM. STUD. 275 (1972); Dozer, *Recognition in Contemporary Inter-American Relations,* 8 J. INTER-AM. STUD. 318 (1966). For criticism of this practice, see McNair, *The Stimson Doctrine of Non-Recognition*, [1933] 14 BRIT. Y.B. INT'L L. 73; TI-CHIANG CHEN, RECOGNITION, *supra* note 8, at 131.

Europeans viewed Stimson's Doctrine not as a forceful and positive technique for policing international morality, but as a cheap, safe, and innocuous "out." On the eve of World War II, a popular French journal surveyed the Stimson Doctrine and noted its increasingly inconsistent application by the United States. That the U.S. felt that more than ignoring *faits accomplis* would be necessary was indicative of the termination of American isolationism. L'EUROPE NOUVELLE, May 25, 1940, at 568.

16. Secretary of State Stimson's identical notes to Japan and China may be found in [1932] 3 FOREIGN REL. U.S. 7–8. *See also* H. STIMSON, THE FAR EASTERN CRISIS 93 (1936) for the background of his decision. *See* the League of Nations resolution of March 11, 1932. League of Nations Off. J., Spec. Supp. 101, at 87–88 (1932). *But cf.* Japanese perspectives: S. Tachi, a Japanese professor of international law at the then Imperial University of Tokyo, asserted in his JIKYOKU KOKUSAIHO RON (Essays on International Law of Current Issues) 80–101 (1934) that states are not obliged to recognize a new state, but the Stimson Doctrine, which proclaimed that a territorial acquisition in violation of a certain treaty should not be universally recognized, was not compatible with contemporary international law. *See also* Yokota, *Recent Development of the Stimson Doctrine*, 8 PAC. AFF. 133 (1935). *But cf.* Wright, *Reply to K. Yokota, Legal Foundation of the Stimson Doctrine, id.* at 439; Wright, *Some Legal Aspects of the Far Eastern Situation*, 27 AM. J. INT'L L. 509 (1933). *See also* Baty, *Abuse of Terms: "Recognition": "War"*, 30 AM. J. INT'L L. 377 (1936); Borchard, *Recognition and Non-Recognition*, 36 AM. J. INT'L L. 108 (1942); Briggs, *Non-Recognition of Title by Conquest and Limitations on the Doctrine*, 1940 PROCEEDINGS AM. SOC'Y INT'L L. 72–82; Cavare, *La Reconnaisance de l'Etat et la Manchukuo* 42 R.G.D.I. 16–39 (1935); McNair, *The Stimson Doctrine and Non-Recognition*, [1933] 14 BRIT Y.B. INT'L L. 65. *But cf.* Lauterpacht, *The Principle of Non-Recognition in International Law*, in LEGAL PROBLEMS IN THE FAR EASTERN CONFLICT 129–56 (Q. Wright ed. 1941). *See also* R. LANGER, SEIZURE OF TERRITORY: THE STIMSON DOCTRINE AND RELATED PRINCIPLES IN LEGAL THEORY AND DIPLOMATIC PRACTICE 50–74 (1947); 1 HACKWORTH, DIGEST 334–38; Current, *Stimson Doctrine and the Hoover Doctrine*, 59 AM. HIST. REV. 513 (1954). For the then prevailing policies of nonrecognition, see generally Hill, *Recent Policies of Non-Recognition*, INTERNATIONAL CONCILIATION, No. 293, at 9 (1933); Rea, *Probing the Issues: Recognition of Manchukuo*, 31 FAR EAST REV. 449 (1935); Rea, *Adhering to Fictions*, 32 *id.* at 18 (1936); Garner, *Non-recognition of Illegal Territorial Annexations and Claims to Sovereignty*, 30 AM. J. INT'L L. 679 (1936); Rea, *On Recognition*, 32 FAR EAST REV. 201 (1936).

17. For a classic statement, see G.G. WILSON, INSURGENCY (Naval War College Stud., 1900); Wilson, *Insurgency and International Marine Law*, 1 AM. J. INT'L L. 46 (1907); Wilson, *Recognition of Insurgency and Belligerency*, 1937 PROCEEDINGS AM. SOC'Y INT'L L. 136. *See also* R. OGLESBY, INTERNATIONAL WAR AND THE SEARCH FOR NORMATIVE ORDER (1971).

In the case of *The Three Friends*, 166 U.S. 1, 63–64 (1897), the Court distinguished between "recognition of existence of war in a material sense and war in a legal sense." *See also* the Prize Cases, 67 U.S. (2 Black) 635, 667 (1862). Erick Castren observed a trend toward recognition of a state of insurgency. *See* E. CASTREN, CIVIL WAR 207 (1966). *But cf.* R. OGLESBY, *supra*, at 113. H. LAUTERPACHT, RECOGNITION 270–71, 276–78; C. DE VISSCHER, THEORY AND REALITY IN PUBLIC INTERNATIONAL LAW 238 (1957); P. JESSUP, *supra* note 8, at 53–54; Jessup, *The Spanish Rebellion and International Law*, 15 FOREIGN AFFAIRS 260, 270–73 (1937).

18. The United States Supreme Court held in *United States* v. *Pink* that: "Recognition is not always absolute; it is sometimes conditional." 315 U.S. 203, 229 (1942). *See* LAUTERPACHT, RECOGNITION 186. *But cf.* TI-CHIANG CHEN, RECOGNITION 8. *See also* Article 6 of the Montevideo Convention on Rights and Duties of States, 6 M. HUDSON, INTERNATONAL LEGISLATION 620, 623 (1937).

19. S.C. Res. 217 (1965), Nov. 20, 1965, U.N. Doc. S/NF/20/Rev. 1, at 8 (1965) Nov. 20, 1965; 60 Am. J. Int'l L. 924 (1966). *See generally* McDougal & Reisman, *Rhodesia and the United Nations: The Lawfulness of International Concern,* 62 Am. J. Int'l L. 1 (1968). *Cf.* a Rhodesian response by Devine, *Rhodesia and the United Nations: The Lawfulness of International Concern—A Question,* 2 Comp. & Int'l L. J. So. Africa 454 (1969). *See also* the judgment of the Appellate Division of the High Court of Rhodesia in Madzimbamuto v. Lardner-Burke N.O., 1968(2) S.A.L.R. 284, 234–326. *See also* Devine, *Status of Rhodesia in International Law,* Acta Juridica 39 (1967). As for the constitutional crisis created by Rhodesia's Unilateral Declaration of Independence, see Molteno, *The Rhodesian Crisis and the Courts,* 2 Comp. & Int'l L. J. So. Africa 254, 404 (1969) and 3 *id.* at 18 (1970); Devine, *Rhodesia: A Duty Not to Recognize?,* 33 J. Contemporary Roman-Dutch L. 152 (1970).

20. G.A. Res. 2145 (XXI), 21 GAOR Supp. 16, at 2, U.N. Doc. A/6316 (1966). *See also* Legal Consequences for States of the Continued Presence of South Africa in Namibia (South West Africa) Notwithstanding Security Council Resolution 276 (1970), [1971] I.C.J. 1, 51.

21. *See* U.N. Charter art. 4(1) and (2); *id.* art. 5 for criteria for withdrawal of membership privileges; Admissions Case, [1947] I.C.J. 57.

22. The nexus between a vote for admission and recognition was sufficiently obvious to disturb admission procedures. In 1950, the Secretary-General issued a memorandum that, with some double-talk, established a *modus vivendi*: "a member could properly vote to accept a representative of a government which it did not recognize, or with which it had no diplomatic relations . . . such a vote did not imply recognition or readiness to assume diplomatic relations." U.N. Doc. S/1466 (1950).

23. *See* Moore, *The Control of Foreign Intervention in Internal Conflict,* 9 Va. J. Int'l L. 205, 272 (1969).

For the traditional view, see Borchard, *Neutrality and Civil Wars,* 31 Am. J. Int'l L. 304, 306 (1937); Garner, *Question of International Law in the Spanish Civil War,* 31 Am. J. Int'l L. 66, 68 (1937); O'Rourke, *Recognition of Belligerency and the Spanish War, id.* at 398, 410. (1937). *But cf.* Farer, *Intervention in Civil War: A Modest Proposal,* 67 Colum. L. Rev. 266 (1967); Farer, *Harnessing Rogue Elephants: A Short Discourse on Foreign Intervention in Civil Strife,* 82 Harv. L. Rev. 511 (1969); and Boals, *The Relevance of International Law to the Internal War in Yemen,* in The International Law of Civil War 303, 333 (R. Falk ed. 1971).

24. *See* M. Kaplan & N. deB. Katzenbach, The Political Foundations of International Law 121 (1961). Recognition has "common law" marriages. The recent United States experience with China shows that diplomatic ritual will be dispensed with if elites find that their interests are served by other arrangements. Thus members of the Chinese "liaison office" in Washington were given diplomatic status and immunities by special congressional legislation. 22 U.S.C. § 288i, note, Ex. Ord. No. 11771 (1976 Supp.). *See* N.Y. Times, Apr. 19, 1973, at 3, col. 4.

25. *See* pp. 434–37 *infra.*

26. *See* pp. 437–38 *infra.*

27. Reisman, *Private Armies in a Global War System: Prologue to Decision,* 14 Va. J. Int'l L. 1 (1973).

28. 1 & 4 J. Lorimer, The Institutes of the Law of Nations (1883).

29. Motevideo Convention art. 1, 165 L.N.T.S. 19; 6 M. Hudson, International Legislation 620 (1937). *See also* Lauterpacht, Recognition 26–30; 1 D.P. O'Connell, International Law 303–18 (1965); G. Schwarzenberger, International Law 55–56 (5th ed. 1967). *But cf.* the U.S. observations about the qualification of statehood with respect to the admission of Israel to the United Nations. 3 U.N. S.C.O.R. No. 128, at 10–11; the U.S. policy regarding recognition of Guinea-Bissau, *reprinted in* 68 Am. J. Int'l L. 309 (1974).

Liechtenstein was denied admission to the League of Nations because of a presumed lack of capacity to discharge international obligations. *See* 1 Hackworth,

DIGEST 48–49. However, it was permitted to adhere to the Statute of the I.C.J. *See* 4 U.N. SCOR, 432d meeting 4–5 (1949). *But cf.* the argument against it in 4 U.N. SCOR 6th Comm. 214 (1949). *See generally* Kohn, *The Sovereignty of Liechtenstein*, 61 AM. J. INT'L L. 547 (1967). *See also* Cohen, *Concept of Statehood in United Nations Practice*, 109 U. PA. L. REV. 1127 (1961).

30. On criteria for recognition, see J. H. VAN ROIJEN, DE RECHTSPOSITIE EN DE VOLKENRECHTELIJKE ERKENNING VAN NIEUWE STATEN EN DE FACTO-REGEER-IGEN 13 (1929). For a contemporary perspective of the declaratory school, see TI-CHIANG CHEN, RECOGNITION 259. *See also* J. BRIERLY, THE LAW OF NATIONS 138–39 (6th ed. 1963); Borchard, *Recognition and Non-Recognition,* 36 AM. J. INT'L L. 108 (1942). Though Kelsen subsequently converted to the constitutive school, he was a principal proponent of the declaratory school in his earlier writing. *See, e.g.,* H. KELSEN, GENERAL THEORY OF LAW AND STATE 223 (1945).

31. *See* LAUTERPACHT, RECOGNITION 78. *But cf.* Kelsen, *Recognition in International Law,* 35 AM. J. INT'L L. 605, 609 (1941). *See also* Borchard, *supra* note 30; TI-CHIANG CHEN, RECOGNITION 74–75.

32. The enormous discretion concealed in the allegedly "objective" criteria of the declaratory school is neatly underlined by Sabir in his consideration of the "effective internal government" criteria:

> The rule is that recognition granted before an effective internal government has been established constitutes intervention. But the many interpretations given to the term "effective internal government" permit a very broad approach; a government which suppresses all opposition through terror tactics may be called an effective internal government. On the other hand, one can say that it is not an effective international government for it does not represent the will of the people as expressed by a majority. It is doubtful if there is an answer to this conundrum. (Sabir, *Recognition of New Governments* [the authors' transl.], 16 HAPRAKLIT 119 (1960).)

33. R. H. TAWNEY, EQUALITY 175 (4th & rev. ed. 1952).

34. Note, however, that there is a declaratory *school* and not necessarily declaratory states. Elites who favor a certain pattern of changes will presumably resort to the declaratory method as long as the changes are to their liking and will revert to a constitutive position when changes are deemed against their interests. Thus, Lauterpacht concedes that there is "the dual position of the recognizing States as an organ administering international law and as a guardian of its own interests. . . ." H. LAUTERPACHT, RECOGNITION 67 n.28. For further discussion see pp. 445–46 *infra.*

35. Reisman, *supra* note 27, at 46.

36. *See* S. Shapiro, Goal Clarification (unpublished manuscript in Yale Law Library, 1971).

37. Chen & Reisman, *supra* note 8, at 601–02.

38. *Id.* at 654–60.

39. Operational suspension is an intellectual operation and not necessarily an overt communication. What is required is that the appraiser succeed in suspending, in his own mind, that attribution of legitimacy (in part, a function of his own attitudes) to one of the contenders in a recognition problem. If he fails to do this, recognition becomes no more than a certification of naked power, on the one hand, or a continuation of past attitudes without reappraisal, on the other.

40. M. FOLLETT, CREATIVE EXPERIENCE (1930).

41. H. LAUTERPACHT, RECOGNITION 4; Garner, *Executive Discretion in the Conduct of Foreign Relations,* 31 AM. J. INT'L L. 289, 291–92 (1937).

42. J. WESTLAKE, INTERNATIONAL LAW 47–48 (1910).

43. *See, e.g.,* 1 HACKWORTH, DIGEST 260. For collective "nonrecognition," see Woolsey, *supra* note 14, at 325; Buel, *supra* note 14, at 193 (1931).

44. The notion that every state should be a member of the inclusive international

organization unless it voluntarily withdraws seems to have been raised in its earliest form by Argentina in the first Assembly of the League. For a review of the events, see BOLLINI-SHAW, EL RECONOCIMIENTO EN EL DERECHO INTERNACIONAL PÚBLICO 155 (1936).

45. S.C. Res. 276 (1970), Jan. 30, 1970, U.D. Doc. S/INF/25, at 1 (1970). *See also* the Namibia judgment, [1970] I.C.J. 16, 58; U.N. Charter arts. 39 & 25.

46. *See generally* Special Committee on the Situation with regard to the Implementation of the Declaration on the Granting of Independence to Colonial Countries and Peoples (1965) U.N. Docs. A/5800/Rev. 1 and A/6000/Rev. 1). *See also* text and citation in McDougal & Reisman, *supra* note 19, at 4.

47. *See especially* G.A. Res. 2022 (XX), 22 GAOR Supp. 14, at 54, U.N. Doc. A/6014 (1965).

48. For text, see 5 INTL'L LEGAL MATERIALS 230 (1966).

49. S.C. Res. 217 (1965), Nov. 20, 1965, U.N. Doc. S/INF/20/Rev. 1, at 8 (1965).

50. S.C. Res. 232 (1966), Dec. 16, 1966, U.N. Doc. S/INF/21/Rev. 1, at 7 (1966).

51. *See* pp. 420–22 *infra*.

52. 1 F. POLLOCK & F. MAITLAND, THE HISTORY OF ENGLISH LAW 150–51 (2d ed. 1952).

53. For historical surveys of the application of Article 4(1) of the Charter, see L. GOODRICH, E. HAMBRO & A. SIMON, CHARTER OF THE UNITED NATIONS 72–93 (3d & rev. ed. 1969).

54. Conditions of Admission of a State to Membership in the United Nations (Article 4 of the Charter), [1948] I.C.J. 57.

55. U.N. Charter art. 4(2). Tabata, *Admission to the U.N. and Recognition of States,* 5 JAPAN. ANNUAL INT'L L. 1 (1961); Liang, *Recognition by the United Nations of the Representative of a Member State: Criteria and Procedures,* 45 AM. J. INT'L L. 689 (1951); Rosenne, *Recognition of States by the United Nations,* [1949] 26 BRIT. Y.B. INT'L L. 437. The Canadian vote in the General Assembly on May 11, 1949, in favor of admitting Israel to the U.N. was considered as its *de jure* recognition of Israel following its *de facto* recognition on December 14, 1948. Dai, *Recognition of States and Governments under International Law with Special Reference to Canadian Postwar Practice and the Legal Status of Taiwan (Formosa),* [1965] 3 CAN. Y.B. INT'L L. 290, 294.

56. Competence of the General Assembly for the Admission of a State to the United Nations, [1950] I.C.J. 4.

57. In fact, an attempt was made to confer on the General Assembly the competence to recognize one government to represent a state in cases of contending claims. In the midst of the fifth session's fury concerning the Chinese representation question, the Cuban delegation proposed that "in virtue of its composition, the General Assembly is the only organ of the United Nations which is in a position to express the general opinion of all Member States in matters affecting the functioning of the Organization as a whole." U.N. Doc. A/AC.38/L.6. The Cuban proposal recommended that the question be decided in the light of (1) effective authority over the national territory; (2) the general consent of the population; (3) ability and willingness to achieve the purposes of the Charter, to observe its principles, and to fullfill international obligations of the state; and (4) respect for human rights and fundamental freedoms. But it specifically declared: "Decisions taken by the General Assembly in accordance with this resolution shall not affect the direct relations of individual Member States with the State, the represenation of which has been the subject of such decisions." U.N. Doc. A/AC.38/L.6. A majority of the representatives to the Ad Hoc Political Committee were in favor of some set of criteria to solve the representation question. U.N. Docs. A/AC.38/SR.18; A/AC.38/SR.19; A/AC.-38/SR.20; 9 U.N. BULL. 734–37 (1950). *See, e.g.,* the proposals made by the U.K. representative. U.N. Doc. A/AC.38/SR.18, para. 57; U.N. Doc. A/AC.38/L.21/Rev.1.

The final resolution adopted by the General Assembly took an intermediate position between the objective test and the exclusive discretionary test. *See* G.A. Res. 396 (V), 5 GAOR Supp. 20, at 24, U.N. Doc. A/1775 (1950). For appraisal, see Schachter, *Problems of Law and Justice,* [1951] ANN. REV. U.N. AFF. 190, 204.

58.   Uniting for Peace, G.A. Res. 337A (V), 5 GAOR Supp. 20, at 10, U.N. Doc. A/1775 (1950). *See also* Certain Expenses Case, [1962] I.C.J. 151.

59.   G.A. Res. 2145 (XXI), 21 GAOR Supp. 16, at 2, U.N. Doc. A/6316 (1966). *See generally* Dugard, *The Revocation of the Mandate for South Africa,* 62 AM. J. INT'L L. 78 (1968).

60.   *See* Advisory Opinion on International Status of South West Africa, [1950] I.C.J. 128; Advisory Opinion on South West Africa—Voting Procedure, [1955] I.C.J. 67; Advisory Opinion on the Admissibility of Hearings of Petitioners by the Committee on South West Africa, [1956] I.C.J. 23; South West Africa Cases Preliminary Objections, [1962] I.C.J. 319; and Advisory Opinion on Legal Consequences for States of the Continued Presence of South Africa in Namibia (South West Africa) Notwithstanding Security Council Resolution 276 (1970), [1971] I.C.J. 6, 34. *See* Dugard, *Namibia (South West Africa): The Court's Opinion, South Africa's Response, and Prospects for the Future,* 11 COLUM. J. TRANSNAT'L L. 14 (1972); Lissitzyn, *International Law and the Advisory Opinion on Namibia, id.* at 50; Rovine, *The World Court Opinion on Namibia, id.* at 202; Gross, *The United Nations, Self-Determination and the Namibia Opinions,* 82 YALE L.J. 533, 548–57 (1973); Higgins, *The Advisory Opinion on Namibia: Which U.N. Resolutions are Binding under Article 25 of the Charter?,* 21 INT'L & COMP. L.Q. 270 (1972); Murphy, *Whither Now Namibia?,* 6 CORNELL INT'L L.J. 1 (1972). *But cf.* Acheson & Marshall, *Applying Dr. Johnson's Advice,* 11 COLUM. J. TRANSNAT'L L. 193 (1972). As for the advisory jurisdiction of the International Court of Justice, see generally D. PRATAP, THE ADVISORY JURISDICTION OF THE INTERNATIONAL COURT (1972).

61.   G.A. Res. 2372 (XXII), 22 GAOR Supp. 16A, at 1, U.N. Doc. A/6716/Add. 1 (1968).

62.   S.C. Res. 276 (1970), Jan. 30, 1970, U.N. Doc. S/INF/25, at 1 (1970).

63.   S.C. Res. 284 (1970), July 29, 1970, U.N. Doc. S/INF/25, at 4 (1970).

64.   [1971] I.C.J. 6, 58.

65.   The Secretary-General may also play a significant recognizing role. In 1963, Indonesia, Malaya, and the Philippines agreed to accept as final a U.N. examination, under the auspices of Secretary-General U Thant, as to the wishes of the population of North Borneo and Sarawak regarding federation with Malaysia. The U.N. report concluded that there was substantial popular support for federation. Political groups within the Philippines argued that adherence to the modified arbitration procedure bound the Philippines to extend recognition to Malaysia. *See* Sumulong, *Should the Philippines Grant Immediate Recognition to Malaysia?,* 11 FAR EASTERN L. REV. (1963).

66.   G.A. Res. 396 (V), 5 GAOR Supp. 20, at 24, U.N. Doc. A/1775 (1950). For a prerecognized entity which seeks to establish an observer status in the United Nations, membership in functional agencies may be a useful stepladder. On March 13, 1973, the Provisional Revolutionary Government of the Republic of South Vietnam announced that Nguyen Van Tien, head of its mission in Hanoi, had been appointed as its chief observer at the U.N. N.Y. Times, Apr. 1, 1973, at 3, col. 2. This announcement was obviously made before the formal decision to accord the observer status to the Vietcong representative at the U.N., although a request to that effect had been formally made through Secreary-General Waldheim while he was in Paris. *Id.* Apr. 3, 1973, at 7, col. 1. But the request was rejected ostensibly because the Revolutionary Government was not a member of any specialized agency of the United Nations. In addition, the United States government made it clear that it would not issue visas to Vietcong representatives on the ground that they do not represent a government. *See id.* Apr. 10, 1973, at 1, col. 6. The Vietcong's Provisional Government also lost a bid to gain recognition as a "sovereign state" in an interna-

tional conference on the law of war. *Id.*, Mar. 1, 1974, at 3, col. 7. For an exposition on recognition and international organizations, see Lachs, *Recognition and Modern Methods of International Co-operation,* [1948] 25 Brit. Y.B. Int'l L. 254; B.R. Bot, Nonrecognition and Treaty Relations 156–57 (1968). On the role of the Secretary-General, see Schachter, *supra* note 57, at 214–15.

67. In the midst of the Chinese representation question in the United Nations and its related agencies, the Executive and Liaison Committee of the Universal Postal Union admitted for its session in Montreux, Switzerland, for May 16, 1950, as "the sole qualified representative of China" the delegate of the People's Republic of China. 8 U.N. Bull. 498, 505 (1950). But that decision was subsequently reversed by a proposal to reseat Nationalist China.

Franco's Spain, an original member of the International Civil Aviation Organization, was subsequently expelled from it. First, the General Assembly endorsed an agreement reached among the U.K., U.S.A., and the U.S.S.R. that they would not favor any application for membership by Spain and recommended that "the Members of the United Nations should act in accordance with" these statements with respect to Spain. G.A. Res. 39 (I), U.N. Doc. A/64 (1946). The Assembly then recommended that the "Franco Government of Spain be debarred from membership in international agencies established by or brought into relationship with the United Nations." *Id. See also* G.A. Res. 50 (I), U.N. Doc. A/64/Add. 1, at 78, and ICAO Assembly Proc. 237 (1952); Sohn, *Expulsion or Forced Withdrawal from an International Organization,* 77 Harv. L. Rev. 1381, 1401–04 (1964).

68. U.N. Charter arts. 93(1) & 93(2).

69. M. Reisman, Nullity and Revision: The Review and Enforcement of International Judgments and Awards 90 (1971).

70. The lawfulness of a chattel transfer which is under litigation might turn on whether the "authorities" who transferred it in a certain place were, in fact, internationally recognized. This would require argument and ancillary decision on the question of international recognition. Presumably, an international court would apply international criteria to this question. *See also* B.R. Bot, *supra* note 66, at 163–66.

71. S.C. Res. 284 (1970), July 29, 1970; U.N. Doc. S/INF/25, at 4 (1970).

72. The following claim surveys only American practice.

73. *See* the discussion in S. Simpson, Anatomy of the State Department 48–50 (1967).

74. Because recognition has generally been considered a formal, explicit action of a government which allows for no subtleties, courts, in their implementing role, have expected the cues to be unequivocal. This notion can be inferred from such judicial dicta as: "Who is the sovereign, *de jure* or *de facto,* of a territory is not a judicial, but a political question, the determination of which by the legislature and executive departments of any government conclusively binds the judges. . . ." Jones v. United States, 137 U.S. 202, 212 (1890). *But compare* the early case Consul of Spain v. The Conception, 6 F. Cas. 359, 360 (1819): "Courts exercising jurisdiction of international law may often be called upon to deduce the fact of national independence from history, evidence, or public notoriety, where there has been no formal recognition."

75. *See* S. Simpson, *supra* note 73, at 51–69; T. McCamy, The Administration of Foreign Affairs (1950); J. F. Campbell, The Foreign Affairs Fudge Factory (1971).

76. *See* I.M. Destler, Presidents, Bureaucrats, and Foreign Policy (1972).

77. The often quoted source for this independent presidential power is *United States v. Curtiss-Wright Corp.,* 299 U.S. 304 (1936), a case involving a challenge to legislative and executive acts prohibiting the sale of munitions in the U.S. to countries engaging in warfare in the Chaco. The Court held that the presidential power had to be consistent with the Constitution. For comment, see L. Henkin, Foreign Affairs and the Constitution 64–65 (1972). For historical assessment without policy considerations, see Lofgren, *United States v. Curtiss-Wright Export Corporation: An Historical Reassessment,* 83 Yale L.J. 1 (1973).

78. Such confrontations should not necessarily be considered dysfunctional. The American system is based upon "checks and balances" which provide barriers to one branch's attempting to achieve hegemony. THE FEDERALIST Nos. 47, 49, 51 (A. Hamilton). Recent years have seen dramatic confrontations over foreign affairs and war powers between the Executive and the Judiciary and between the Executive and the Congress. In the contest between the courts and the Executive, the Supreme Court gave way rather eagerly. Banco Nacional de Cuba v. Sabbatino, 376 U.S. 398 (1964). Congress restored some balance through the so-called Hickenlooper Amendment, 22 U.S.C. §2370(e)(2) (1970), held constitutionally valid in Banco Nacional de Cuba v. Farr, 383 F.2d 166 (1967). See McDougal, Act of State in Policy Perspective: The International Law of an International Economy, in PRIVATE INVESTORS ABROAD 327 (Southwestern Legal Foundation ed. 1966). Regarding the Executive-congressional contest, see War Powers Resolution of 1973, 50 U.S.C. §1541 et seq. (1970), reprinted in 68 AM J. INT'L L. 372 (1974).

79. Russian Republic v. Cibrario, 235 N.Y.S. 255 (1923); United States v. Palmer, 16 U.S. (3 Wheat.) 610 (1818); Rose v. Himely, 8 U.S. (4 Cranch) 241, 272 (1808); The Hornet, 12 F. Cas. 529 (1870).

80. Upright v. Mercury Business Machines Co., 213 N.Y.S.2d 417 (1961).

81. G.A. Res. 217 (III), U.N. DOC. A/810 at 71 (1948), reprinted in I. BROWNLIE, BASIC DOCUMENTS OF HUMAN RIGHTS 106 (1971).

82. G.A. Res. 2000A, 21 GAOR Supp. 16, at 52, U.N. Doc. A/6316 (1966), reprinted in I. BROWNLIE, supra note 81, at 211, 219. See generally Robertson, The United Nations Covenant on Civil and Political Rights and the European Convention on Human Rights, [1968–69] 43 BRIT. Y.B. INT'L L. 21.

83. 213 U.N.T.S. 221.

84. See resolution adopted by the Standing Committee of the Consultative Assembly of the Council of Europe regarding the Greek case. Council of Europe Directorate of Information, Doc. B (67) 37 (26.6.67). In accordance with Article 24 of the European Convention of Human Rights, Denmark, Norway, and Sweden initiated action against Greece before the European Commission of Human Rights on September 20, 1967, as did the Netherlands on September 27, 1967. Council of Europe Directorate of Information, Doc. C (67) 33 (20.9.67), Doc. C (67) 33 (20.9.67) & Doc. C (67) 36 (27.9.67), respectively.

85. Amnesty International, the International Commission of Jurists, the International Federation for the Rights of Man, and the International League for the Rights of Man are active, in varying degree, in gathering information and reporting and protesting deprivations. See, e.g., in regard to Greece, N.Y. Times, Apr. 22, 1972, at 8, col. 3; id., Sept. 21, 1972, at 18, col. 1.

86. Thus a N.Y. Times editorial urged U.S. pressure for fair presidential elections in South Vietnam after President Thieu made it virtually impossible for other candidates to contest him. N.Y. Times, June 3, 1971, at 1, col. 7; id., June 13, 1971, § 4, at 12, col. 1; id., Aug. 23, 1971, at 28, col. 1; id., Aug. 22, 1971, at 3, col. 5.

87. The Three Friends, 166 U.S. 1, 63–64 (1897). See also A. ROUGIER, LES GUERRES CIVILES ET LE DROIT DES GENS 29, 34–35, 167–68 (1903); C. WEISSE, DROIT INTERNATIONAL APPLIQUÉ AUX GUERRES CIVILES 28 (1898); H. HERSHEY, ESSENTIALS OF PUBLIC INTERNATIONAL LAW 201 (1912). See 1 C. C. HYDE, INTERNATIONAL LAW CHIEFLY AS INTERPRETED AND APPLIED BY THE UNITED STATES 202–04 (2d rev. ed. 1945). There is little consistency in the use of the terms. One distinction may lie in the fact that the insurgent has not yet established a territorial base which involves effective control over the population. See E. STOWELL, INTERNATIONAL LAW: A RESTATEMENT OF PRINCIPLES IN CONFORMITY WITH ACTUAL PRACTICE 41 (1931); T.J. LAWRENCE, THE PRINCIPLES OF INTERNATIONAL LAW 332 (7th ed. 1928). See also H. KELSEN, PRINCIPLES OF INTERNATIONAL LAW 291–92 (1952).

88. 1 D.P. O'CONNELL, supra note 29, at 164–65. See also Commissioner Nielsen's opinion in Oriental Navigation Co. v. United Mexican States, Claims Commission—United States and Mexico, 23 AM. J. INT'L L. 434, 450–51 (1929). But for useful

distinctions between insurgency and belligerency, see G.G. Wilson, *supra* note 17; N. PADELFORD, INTERNATIONAL LAW AND DIPLOMACY IN THE SPANISH CIVIL STRIFE 307 (1939); McNair, *The Law Relating to the Civil War in Spain,* 53 L.Q. REV. 490 (1937); H. LAUTERPACHT, RECOGNITION 270–71; S. R. PATEL, RECOGNITION IN THE LAW OF NATIONS 92–96 (1959).

89. 29 Stat. 870–71. *See also* President Cleveland, Annual Message, Dec. 7, 1896, [1896] FOREIGN REL. U. S. at xxix-xxxv. Compare the shift in the need for some U.S. action from his previous message on Dec. 2, 1895, [1895] FOREIGN REL. U.S. at xxxii; 1 J. MOORE, DIGEST OF INTERNATIONAL LAW 242–43 (1906) [hereinafter cited as 1 MOORE, DIGEST].

90. 1 HYDE, *supra* note 87, at 203–04.

91. Hence the practice of counterclaims protesting "premature" recognition. *See,* for example, U.S. outrage during the Civil War. G. BEMIS, HASTY RECOGNITION OF REBEL BELLIGERENCY, AND OUR RIGHT TO COMPLAIN OF IT (1865). *See generally* H. H. TEUSCHER, DIE VORZEITIGE ANERKENNUNG IM VÖLKERRECHT (1939), concluding that it is an increasingly unworkable doctrine.

92. *See* H. KELSEN, *supra* note 87, at 292. *But cf.* the decision in The Three Friends, 166 U.S. 1, 65–66 (1897). *See also* 1 MOORE, DIGEST 184–85. On the very real impacts of characterizations by third parties, see H. LAUTERPACHT, RECOGNITION 272–74.

93. The Institute of International Law adopted the regulation on September 8, 1900. *See* Article 8, "Droits et devoirs des puissances étrangères, au cas de mouvement insurrectional, envers les gouvernements établis et reconnus, qui sont aux prises avec l'insurrection," 18 ANNUAIRE DE L'INSTITUT DE DROIT INTERNATIONAL 227, 229 (1900). *See* C. C. HYDE, *supra* note 87, at 198–202; W. HALL, INTERNATIONAL LAW 36–39 (7th ed. 1917); E. STOWELL, *supra* note 87, at 40. For the conditions for recognition of belligerency, see L. OPPENHEIM, INTERNATIONAL LAW 249–50 (8th ed. Lauterpacht 1955). *See also* H. LAUTERPACHT, RECOGNITION 175–85; H. KELSEN, *supra* note 87, at 291–92; C. C. HYDE, *supra* note 87, at 201. *See* Canning's reply of 1825 to a complaint of Turkey about the Greek rebellion, *quoted in* Walker, *Recognition of Belligerency and Grant of Belligerent Rights,* 33 TRANSACTIONS OF THE GROTIUS SOC'Y 117, 180–81 (1938).

94. Art. 8(3) of the regulation adopted on September 8, 1900, by the Institute of International Law, *supra* note 93.

95. Art. 3 of all four Geneva Conventions of 1949: Convention for Wounded in the Field, Aug. 12, 1949, [1955] 6 U.S.T. 3115, 3116; Geneva Convention for Wounded at Sea, Aug. 12, 1949, *id.* at 3219, 3220; Geneva Convention Relating to Prisoners of War, Aug. 12, 1949, *id.* at 3316; 3318; Geneva Convention Relating to Civilians, Aug. 12, 1949, *id.* at 3516, 3518.

Lauterpacht states that while "[r]ecognition of belligerency brings about the normal operation of the rule of war proper" (L. OPPENHEIM, *supra* note 93, at 140), Article 3 of the Geneva Conventions applies irrespective of recognition of belligerency and indicates that the general state of "armed conflict" between the two contending groups is sufficient for the acquisition of insurgent status. *See also* G.I.A.D. DRAPER, THE RED CROSS CONVENTIONS 11 (1958). *But cf.* J. SIOTIS, LE DROIT DE LA GUERRE ET LES CONFLITS ARMÉS D'UN CARACTÈRE NON-INTERNATIONAL 223 (1958). *See* note 192 *infra.*

It has been argued that the Algerian F.L.N. was in effect recognized as a belligerent group. M. BEDJAOUI, LAW AND THE ALGERIAN REVOLUTION 138 (1961). Greenberg, *Law and the Conduct of the Algerian Revolution,* 11 HARV. INT'L L. J. 37, 47 (1970); Fraleigh, *The Algerian Revolution as a Case Study in International Law,* in THE INTERNATIONAL LAW OF CIVIL WAR 179, 210–13 (R. Falk ed. 1971). *But cf.* Jean Charpentier, who argued in light of criteria set by the Institute of International Law in 1900 that a recognition of belligerents could not be legally accorded to the F.L.N. Charpentier, *La reconnaissance du G.P.R.A.,* 5 ANNUAIRE FRANÇAIS DE DROIT INTERNATIONAL 789, 803 (1959); Flory, *Algérie et droit international, id.* at 817, 826–27.

96. H. WHEATON, INTERNATIONAL LAW 34, 35–36, n.15 (Recognition of Belligerency) (8th ed. Dana 1866).

97. *Id.* at 37.

98. 166 U.S. 1, 63. *See also* United States v. Palmer, 16 U.S. (3 Wheat.) 610 (1818); The Divina Pastora, 17 U.S. (4 Wheat.) 52 (1819). H. WHEATON, *supra* note 96, at 35, n. 15. *See also* J. WESTLAKE, INTERNATIONAL LAW 51–52 (1910); R. OGLESBY, *supra* note 17, at 33.

99. *Quoted in* J. KENT, COMMENTARY ON INTERNATIONAL LAW 94 (J. T. Abdy ed. 1878).

100. 1 MOORE, DIGEST 169; 5 J. B. MOORE, INTERNATIONAL ARBITRATIONS 4572 (1898) [hereinafter cited as MOORE, ARBITRATIONS].

101. 1 MOORE, DIGEST 169.

102. *Id. See also* R. MORRIS, THE AMERICAN REVOLUTION 74–75 (1955).

103. 8 U.S. (4 Cranch) 239, 272 (1809).

104. MOORE, ARBITRATIONS 4476–77.

105. 1 MOORE, DIGEST 170.

106. *Id.* at 176.

107. *Id.* at 184–86. Though the United States did not formally employ the term "recognition of belligerency" in the President's proclamation of blockade on April 19, 1861, the proclamation of blockade was taken as official and conclusive evidence of recognition of the state of belligerency. G. G. WILSON, INTERNATIONAL LAW 43 (1910). Thus the proclamation deprived the U.S. of the right to claim that the other foreign states' subsequent recognition of the belligerency of the Confederacy was illegal. *See* 1 MOORE, DIGEST 184–98; R. OGLESBY, *supra* note 17, at 48–51. The Supreme Court held that the proclamation was tantamount to an official act of recognition that a state of war existed. The Prize Cases, 67 U.S. (2 Black) 635 (1910). *See also* J. WESTLAKE, *supra* note 98, at 53–54. C. C. HYDE, *supra* note 87, at 200–01. In the Nigerian civil war, Biafra was allegedly accorded an implied belligerent status. Ijalaye, *Some Legal Implications of the Nigerian Civil War,* 1969 PROCEEDINGS NIGERIAN INST. INT'L AFF. 70, 76–80 (1969). As for implied recognition of belligerent rights, see R. OGLESBY, *supra* note 17, at 35–39.

108. 1 MOORE, DIGEST 193–200. President Grant's Annual Message, Dec. 7, 1875, [1875] FOREIGN REL. U. S. at ix-x. *See also* President Cleveland's Annual Message, Dec. 7, 1896, [1896] FOREIGN REL. U. S. at xxxii.

109. 1 HACKWORTH, DIGEST 203–08, 319. The United States extended a recognition of belligerency to the Czecho–Slovak National Council on September 3, 1918, in the form of a public announcement. *Id.* at 203–04.

110. N. Padelford, *supra* note 88, at 187–88; Padelford, *International Law and the Spanish Civil War,* 31 AM. J. INT'L L. 226 (1937); Finch, *The United States and the Spanish Civil War,* 31 AM. J. INT'L L. 74 (1937). *But cf.* Borchard, *"Neutrality" and Civil War,* 31 AM. J. INT'L L. 304, 306 (1931).

111. M. BEDJAOUI, *supra* note 95, at 76.

112. Extending *de facto* recognition to the Provisional Government of Israel on May 14, 1948, President Truman stated: "When a permanent government is elected in Israel it will promptly be given *de jure* recognition." 19 DEP'T STATE BULL. 582 (1948). A few months later the United States extended *de jure* recognition after it was informed of the election of a government. 20 DEP'T STATE BULL. 205 (1949).

113. Thus, the U.S. was cool to the Cuban exiles' suggestion that it set up a provisional government on landing at the Bay of Pigs. A. SCHLESINGER, A THOUSAND DAYS 245 (Fawcett Premier Book ed. 1965). The two groups of Cuban exiles which formed the Cuban Revolutionary Council in the United States agreed that the Council "will assume the functions of the Provisional Government when it moves to Cuba." The full text of the agreement may be found in T. DRAPER, CASTRO'S REVOLUTION: MYTHS AND REALITIES 97 (1962). *See* note 116 *infra.*

114.   Where host country support is continued, governments in exile in the traditional sense may continue to perform many functions associated with effective and authoritative control, including diplomatic and consular offices, granting of passports, etc. *See, e.g.,* Pusta, *Du Statut des Etats Baltes,* [1960] INTERNATIONALES RECHT UND DIPLOMATIE 93.

115.   After the occupation of metropolitan France by Germany, General de Gaulle's London-based French National Committee was "recognized" in Britain as representing a politically relevant segment of the French community. *See* Oppenheimer, *Governments and Authorities in Exile,* 36 AM. J. INT'L L. 568 (1942); Brown, *Sovereignty in Exile,* 35 AM. J. INT'L. L. 666 (1941); as to the effect of a decree issued by a government in exile, see, *e.g.,* Boguslawski v. Gdynia-Ameryka Line, [1950] 1 K.B. 157 (1949), *aff'd* [1951] 1 K.B. 162 (C.A.), *aff'd sub nom.* Dgynia Ameryka Line Zeglugowe Spolka Akcyjana v. Boguslawski, [1953] A.C. 11 (1952). *See* LAUTERPACHT, RECOGNITION 91–92 n.1, *But cf.* TI-CHIANG CHEN, RECOGNITION 63–64, 292–99. Unlike de Gaulle's Committee, the Polish government in exile participated in numerous diplomatic activities, which included, among other things, the Lend-Lease Agreement, the U.N. Declaration, the U.N. Food and Agricultural Conference, the Agreement for the U.N. Relief and Rehabilitation Administration, and the Bretton Woods Agreement. KRYSTYNA MAREK, IDENTITY AND CONTINUITY OF STATES IN PUBLIC INTERNATIONAL LAW 93–94, 439–40 (1968). For a detailed review of the recognition of Latvia, see Towson, La Reconnaissance de l'independence de le Lettonie, [1968] INTERNATIONALE RECHT UND DIPLOMATIE 39.

   While visiting Moscow, Cambodia's Sihanouk was ousted by Lon Nol, his Premier-designate, on March 18, 1970. Sihanouk sought refuge in Peking while Lon Nol's government assumed control. Sihanouk was then removed as Chief of State by unanimous vote of the Cambodian Parliament. The Staff Report, Cambodia: May 1970, 91st Cong., 2d Sess. 6, *reprinted in* 9 INT'L LEGAL MATERIALS 858, 860 (1970). For detailed account of Lon Nol's coup, see Shaplen, *Letter From Indo-China,* THE NEW YORKER, May 9, 1970, at 130. The United States quickly indicated its intention to "continue to deal with that government as long as it [appeared] to be the government of the nation." 62 DEP'T STATE BULL. 437 (1970). Sihanouk established a government in exile in Peking as a Royal Government of National Union on May 5, 1970. It was recognized by China the same day and by North Vietnam and the Provisional Revolutionary Government of South Vietnam the following day. 9 INT'L LEGAL MATERIALS 862 (1970). For a contemporaneous argument in favor of U.S. recognition of Sihanouk's government in exile as the legitimate Cambodian regime, see Barnes, *United States Recognition Policy and Cambodia,* 50 BOSTON U. L. REV., Special Issue 117, 125 (1970), *reprinted in* 3 THE VIETNAM WAR AND INTERNATIONAL LAW 149, 156 (R. Falk ed. 1972).

116.   The Co-ordinating and Executive Committee proclaimed the establishment of the Algerian Republic and the Provisional Government of the Algerian Republic on September 19, 1958. M. BEDJAOUI, *supra* note 95, at 73–80.

   Note the difference in sequential pattern of formation of a government in exile where a group has been expelled from incumbency which it seeks to regain and where a group seeks, as a protostate, to establish a government. The former was represented by numerous "sovereignties in exile" during World War II, and the latter is the contemporary phenomenon in the midst of the wave of national liberation. The contemporary government in exile is often not a "refugee" government deposed by a later regime, but a "government abroad" in the process of establishing a new government in a given target territory. *See* J. DAY, INTERNATIONAL NATIONALISM: THE EXTRATERRITORIAL RELATIONS OF SOUTHERN RHODESIAN AFRICAN NATIONALISTS 88–89 (1967). Activities to establish such a government may be undertaken concurrently in that territory where the formal regime still operates. A government in exile may lead to a provisional government in the target territory. For the interactions between the "interior group," which is engaged in activities within the territory, and the "exterior group," which campaigns from without, see W. QUANDT, REVOLUTION AND POLITICAL LEADERSHIP: ALGERIA, 1954–68, at 87–107 (1969).

117.   *See* M. BEDJAOUI, *supra* note 95, at 111. *But cf.* Flory, *supra* note 95, at 817;

Charpentier, *supra* note 95, at 799. Compare the striking differences in the operational patterns between General de Gaulle's "Provisional Government of France" and Ben Bella's "Provisional Government of Algeria." Both men employed the same symbol, "provisional government," with different contents. For a more detailed analysis of the refugee governments, see M. FLORY, LE STATUT INTERNATIONAL DES GOUVERNEMENTS REFUGIES ET LE CAS DE LA FRANCE LIBRE, 139–45 (1952). *See also* 1 M. WHITEMAN, DIGEST 358–78.

118. One Algerian official commented: "We support all liberation movements which conduct an armed struggle. . . . Of course, we will give asylum to anyone who wants it, even President Nixon." *Quoted in* Gramont, *Our Other Man in Algiers,* N.Y. Times, Dec. 1, 1970, at 30, 116 (Magazine).

119. The National Liberation Front of South Vietnam announced on June 10, 1969, the establishment of a "provisional revolutionary government" to rule South Vietnam. According to a spokesman for the NLF's delegation to the Paris peace talks, the All-South Vietnam Congress of Peoples' Representatives from all over South Vietnam met in a "liberated area" on June 6, 7, and 8, 1969, and decided to create the Provisional Revolutionary Government of the Republic of South Vietnam "in order to push forward the struggle of the population of South Vietnam against American aggression, for the national salvation." The Congress of eighty-eight representatives supposedly represented all resistance groups in South Vietnam including the NLF, the Alliance of National, Democratic and Peace Forces, and other "patriotic organizations." The Alliance was formed with a view to mobilizing the support of the urban middle class and the intellectuals in the South. Hard data on the reality or effectiveness of the "provisional revolutionary government" was not available. *See* N.Y. Times, June 11, 1969, at 1, col. 6. *See also* an interview with the Vietcong representative at Paris, LE MONDE DIPLOMATIQUE, June, 1969, at 15. For the text of the Declaration of the Provisional Revolutionary Government of the Republic of South Vietnam, see N.Y. Times, June 12, 1969, at 13, col. 1. The reactions of the U.S. and South Vietnam appear in *id.* at 12, col. 1. As for the effect of the establishment of the Provisional Government, see Minister to the Office of the Chairman, Tran Buu Kiem's statement, *id.,* June 15, 1969, at 1, col. 3.

The Provisional Revolutionary Government was accorded recognition by Cuba, Syria, Rumania, Algeria, Poland, and North Vietnam as of June 12, 1969. N.Y. Times, June 13, 1969, at 9, col. 1. Prior to the creation of the Provisional Government, the NLF of South Vietnam was recognized by Cuba, which announced that it had established formal diplomatic relations with the Vietcong on March 17, 1969. *Id.,* Mar. 18, 1969, at 3, col. 1. It also was alleged that Raul Valdes Vivo, Havana's first Ambassador to the NLF, presented his credentials to Chairman Nguen Huu Tho of the Central Committee somewhere in "liberated South Vietnam" on March 4. *Id.,* Mar. 19, 1969, at 5, col. 1. The Cuban Embassy was assertedly established in the jungle of South Vietnam. Photographs appeared in *id.,* Mar. 23, 1969, at 3, col. 1. *See also* Frank & Rodley, *Legitimacy and Legal Rights of Revolutionary Movements with Special Reference to the Peoples' Revolutionary Government of South Viet Nam,* 45 N.Y.U. L. REV. 679 (1970), *reprinted in* 3 THE VIETNAM WAR AND INTERNATIONAL LAW 724 (R. Falk ed. 1972).

120. *See* Jefferson's letter to Morris, the U.S. Minister to France, in 3 T. JEFFERSON'S WORKS 489 (Washington ed. 1853). *Quoted in* 1 MOORE, DIGEST 120. As for the Jeffersonian doctrine, see J. GOEBEL, JR., THE RECOGNITION POLICY OF THE UNITED STATES 97 (1915).

Confronted with a series of secessions of Latin American republics in the early nineteenth century, the British government sought a practical solution in "a measure of *de facto* recognition, the distinguishing feature of which was that it did not purport to express an attitude with regard to the legal merits of the claim to independence and of the title of the parent State." Lauterpacht, *supra* note 8, at 165. Some define *"de jure"* as a government which came into power in conformity with the internal constitution of a body politic and *"de facto"* in violation of the constitution. *See* 4 ANN. DIG. 1927–1928 204 (No. 136). *See also* Great Britain v. Costa Rica (the

Tinoco Arbitration), 18 Am. J. Int'l L. 147 (1924); Luther v. Sagor, [1921] 3 K.B. 532. The employment of both terminologies has been a source of confusion with respect to the qualification of governments. Briggs, *De Facto and De Jure Recognition: The Arantzazu Mendi,* 33 Am. J. Int'l L. 689–99 (1939). *See also* Cochran, *The Development of an Inter-American Policy for the Recognition of de facto Governments,* 62 Am. J. Int'l L. 460 (1968); Williams, *supra* note 7, at 776.

121.   *See* in this regard the Estrada Doctrine, enunciated on September 27, 1930. 25 Am. J. Int'l L. Supp. 203 (1931). *See also* Jessup, *The Estrada Doctrine,* 25 Am. J. Int'l L. 719 (1931); Cochran, *The Estrada Doctrine and United States Policy,* 5 Lawyer of the Americas 27 (1973). The critique of the Estrada Doctrine is found in P. Jessup, *supra* note 8, at 60–62. An interesting collection of contemporary Latin American comments about the Estrada Doctrine is found in the Instituto Americano de Derecho y Legislación Comparada, La Opinión Universal sobre La Doctrina Estrada (1931).

The frequent usage of the term *"de facto* governments" in U.S. practice actually involved full recognition of *"de facto* governments" firmly established in accordance with the will of the people. *See* 1 Moore, Digest 142, 148, 156. Marjorie Whiteman writes: "In prevailing practice, when the United States extends recognition, it is recognition *per se* not *'de facto'* recognition." 2 M. Whiteman, Digest, *supra* note 15, at 3. She later explained: "I had hoped to make it clear in the *Digest* that in the past the United States has extended *de jure* recognition to both *de jure* and *de facto* governments, as the case may have been. It is the government that is *de facto,* not the U.S. recognition. I used the expression recognition *'per se'* meaning that the recognition was 'recognition,' not a tenuous or qualified recognition, not a *de facto* recognition." Letter to Professor Charles L. Cochran, *quoted in* Cochran, *De Facto and De Jure Recognition: Is There a Difference?* 62 Am. J. Int'l L. 457 (1968).

122.   1 Moore, Digest 137.

123.   H. Briggs, The Law of Nations 125 (2d ed. 1952).

124.   *Id.*

125.   *Id. See also* Brown, *The Recognition of Israel,* 46 Am. J. Int'l L. 620 (1948).

126.   *Id.*

127.   Reisman, *supra* note 27. *But cf.* Ijalaye, *Was 'Biafra' at Any Time a State in International Law?* 65 Am. J. Int'l L. 551 (1971). On the capacity of unrecognized and *de facto* regimes to operate internationally, see van Roijen, *supra* note 30, at 159. *See also* J. Viret, La Portée Extra-territoriale des Actes de Souveraineté Interne d'un Gouvernement non-reconnu 98 (1951).

128.   Convention on Rights and Duties of States, 165 L.N.T.S. 19.

129.   In contrast, Rhodesia might be viewed in this respect as a community which is gradually being recognized. A more dramatic example is found in the case of the People's Republic of China and the United States; while the latter has not formally recognized China as of this writing, it has progressively increased many of the incidental benefits of recognition, including many of the rights of legation and of coded communication. *See* N.Y. Times, Apr. 19, 1973, at 3, col. 4.

130.   In that case, the U.S. resident Minister Wheeler had recognized as the new government a group which had violently seized power. In November 1855, Secretary of State Marcy instructed Wheeler to withdraw recognition, but to remain in the country. The reason for the withdrawal, in Marcy's words, was that the alleged government was "no more than a violent usurpation of power, brought about by irregular self-organized military force, as yet unsanctioned by the will or acquiescence of the people of Nicaragua." 1 Moore, Digest 140. Thereafter Marcy rejected two proffered credentials from the new government. But in May 1856, he did receive the credentials of an envoy from the new Nicaraguan government. On May 15, 1856, President Pierce, in a special message to Congress, stated as U.S. policy the recognition of effective control "accepted by the people of the country" without evaluation of the means by which power was secured. Nonetheless, in July 1856, the government

of Nicaragua was derecognized once again because of the "troubled state of affairs" there. *Id.* at 141–43. As in the case of many other recognition cases, factors which do not appear in the record of diplomatic correspondence seem to have been in operation. Though the conditions of power transfer in Nicaragua were reproduced in many other Latin American countries during the nineteenth century, there does not appear to be another case in which recognition via acceptance of the credentials of an envoy was thereafter removed from the recognized government without the simultaneous recognition of a new government. Perhaps the appropriate characterization of U.S. recognition policy in this period would be as follows: where the power process of a state with which the U.S. dealt was unsettled over an extended period, the U.S. would extend a type of provisional recognition to whoever was performing certain indispensable public services for the period in which that person did in fact perform those services. The U.K. example is extremely instructive as to the suppleness of the instrument of recognition. The U.K. apparently recognized certain Italian rights in regard to Ethiopia, as part of an agreement, tacit or otherwise, to assure Italy's ambitions and keep it from the Axis. When Italy declared war against the U.K., the Under Secretary of State for Foreign Affairs, responding to a question in Commons, said: "In view of Italy's unprovoked entry into the war against this country, His Majesty's Government hold themselves entitled to reserve full liberty of action in respect of any undertakings given by them in the past to the Italian Government concerning the Mediterranean North or East African and Middle Eastern areas." 362 PAR. DEB. (5th ser.) 139–40 (1940). Several months later, in a case brought before the Palestine Supreme Court, where Italy claimed property by reason of its conquest of Ethiopia, the Palestine Supreme Court ruled that "the title of the Italian Government to the property in question can no longer be recognized as existent," for the High Commissioner of Palestine had informed the Court that "I have been acquainted by the Secretary of State for the Colonies that the *de jure* recognition by His Majesty's Government of the Italian conquest of Ethiopia has been withdrawn." 7 P.L.A. 597; [1938–1940] ANN. DIG. 93 (No. 36).

131.   Apparently the British chose to construe their recognition of Italian overseas claims as continuously conditional, *i.e.,* we will continue to "recognize" your claims as long as you continue to behave in a certain prescribed way. For all its effectiveness, there is some question as to whether this *unilateral* strategy is lawful. For further discussion, see pp. 416–417 *supra.*

In rather comparable circumstances, the French government withdrew its recognition of Finland in 1918, because Finland accepted a German prince. 1 P. FAUCH-ILLE, TRAITE DE DROIT INTERNATIONAL PUBLIC 239 (1921), *cited in* 1 D. P. O'CONNELL, *supra* note 29, at 159, n.18. Both of these cases took place in wartime contexts in which derecognition was used rather overtly as a weapon. The Nicaraguan case, in contrast, seems to have been occasioned by more general principles of effectiveness.

132.   Decision trends, as well as doctrinal opinion, are comparatively uniform in concluding that war does not justify a belligerent in denouncing prior title to territory. *See* Society for the Propagation of the Gospel v. New Haven, 21 U.S. (8 Wheat.) 464, 494 (1823); A. McNAIR, LAW OF TREATIES 705 (1961); 2 L. CAVARÉ, LE DROIT INTERNATIONAL PUBLIC POSITIF 175–76 (1962); and *see generally* Chen & Reisman, *supra* note 8, at 634. For an indication of general resistance of international tribunals to changes in territorial allocation, see Temple of Preah Vihear, [1962] I.C.J. 6, 34.

133.   The Foreign Agents Registration Act regulates against acting for, or on behalf of, "a foreign principal," *i.e.,* "a foreign government, a political party, or an association organized under the law of or having its principal place of business in a foreign country." 22 U.S.C. §611 (1940). Agents regulated by the Act are acting for a foreign group which does have, by and large, its lawfully established base in a body politic of foreign origin and seeks to change the policy or public perspective of the U.S. with a view to enhancing its value position. The requirement for registration under the Act is not limited to agencies by an express contract, but the true test is

whether agency in fact exists. United States v. German-American Vocational League, 328 U.S. 833, 834 (1946).

134. *Id.* 611(e).

135. *Id.* 612(f) (2).

136. *Id.* 613(d).

137. *Id.* 613(f). On the other hand, if the elite of a body politic considers the group seeking "recognition" in the former's territory inimical to its own fundamental interests, it may not allow the entry of such groups into the territory; once discovered, the group will, as a rule, be deported. *See* Latva v. Nicholls, 106 F. Supp. 658 (1952); Harisiades v. Shaughnessy, 342 U.S. 580 (1952). Freedom of association cannot be invoked by the group, though such rights and freedoms are normally safeguarded by the state's constitution. Thus, the dictum in Latva v. Nicholls, *supra*: "Protection of the freedom of speech does not . . . necessarily involve a complete parallel protection of freedom of association." *Id.* at 601.

Inter-elite collaboration to defend shared interests may deprive a group of constitutionally safeguarded rights. The British government requested the Nixon administration to regulate the flow of arms from the United States to Northern Ireland on behalf of the I.R.A. *See* N.Y. Times, July 17, 1972, at 1, col. 8. *See also* Kenneth Tierney et al. v. United States, *cert. denied,* 410 U.S. 914 (1973) (Douglas, J., dissenting). For facts and opinion, see In re Tierney, 465 F.2d 806 (1972).

138. *See generally* Note, *The Status of Anti-Communist Legislation,* 1965 DUKE L. J. 369.

139. 18 U.S.C. 956. *See also* Kliassas v. Immigration and Naturalization Service, 361 F. 2d 529 (1966). *See* Dietz, *Deportation in the United States, Great Britain and International Law,* 7 INT'L LAWYER 326 (1973).

The deportation of aliens due to the nullification of a passport is another technique. *See* Judgment of Nov. 8, 1969, Tokyo District Court, Case No. 662 (1968), *reprinted in* 15 JAPAN. ANNUAL INT'L L. 188 (1971). The case deals with the deportation of Liu Wey Chin, a Taiwanese member of the United Formosans for Independence, to Taipei, where he was *ipso facto* prosecuted. *See also* Lynd v. Rusk, 389 F.2d 940, 945 (1967). Regarding the passport in general, see D. C. TURACK, THE PASSPORT IN INTERNATIONAL LAW (1972).

140. And indeed the U.S. in its early years manifested this "pro-change" stance in recognition policy. *See* Rie, *Die Entwicklung der Anerkennungspolitik der Vereinigten Staaten von America im 18. und 19. Jahrhundert,* 11 ARCHIV DES VÖLKERRECHTS 265, 284–85, (1964).

The first test came when Toussaint L'Ouverture in Haiti led his private armies of blacks against the Spanish colonial government. American reactions were ambivalent toward a black republic. R. B. MORRIS, THE EMERGING NATIONS AND THE AMERICAN REVOLUTION 122 (1970). Despite such occasional ambivalence, the U.S. was generally sympathetic and encouraging to Latin American uprisings. *Id.* 135–36, 152–72.

141. Zionist organizations are classified as "charitable organizations" and contributions or gifts thereto are tax deductible. *See* 26 U.S.C. §170(c) (1954). Note the significant roles played by the Zionist organizations as protostate groups prior to the creation of Israel and their continuing support of the security of that state. J.J. LADOR-LEDERER, INTERNATIONAL NON-GOVERNMENTAL ORGANIZATIONS AND ECONOMIC ENTITIES 126–27 (1963). The Zionist Organization is the prime example of what Lador-Lederer calls "a state-preparing NGO," but similar cases are the irredentist Irish who formed Ireland; the Internal Macedonian Revolutionary Organization, which contributed to establishing Bulgaria and eventually Yugoslavia. *See generally* J.J. LADOR-LEDERER, *supra,* at 117. As for numerous African groups, see generally R. GIBSON, AFRICAN LIBERATION MOVEMENTS (1972).

142. 26 U.S.C. §501(c) (1954). *See also* Debs Memorial Radio Fund, Inc. v. Commissioner of Internal Revenue, 148 F.2d 948 (1945). *But cf.* 50 U.S.C. § 790(b) (1950) for nonexemption of Communist-controlled organizations.

In order for a protostate group to receive favorable treatment, it is essential to acquire a sufficient base of power in a state in which the group operates so as to influence the domestic political process of that state. *See* Judge Jessup's remark about recognition of Israel: Jessup, *Book Review,* 82 YALE L.J. 611, 616 (1972). For detailed exposition of the process of recognizing Israel, see J. SNETSINGER, TRUMAN, THE JEWISH VOTE, AND THE CREATION OF ISRAEL (1974); P. JESSUP, THE BIRTH OF NATIONS 225–303 (1974). Such domestic political pressures were manifested in the Democratic presidential candidate's speech in 1972. With the exception of Vietnam, Israel was the only country mentioned in Senator McGovern's speech accepting nomination for the candidacy. N.Y. Times, July 14, 1972, at 11, col. 1.

143.   The Sapphire, 78 U.S. 164, 168 (1870); The Hornet, 12 F. Cas. 529 (1870); The Penza, The Tobolsk, 277 F. 91 (1921); Guaranty Trust Co. v. United States, 304 U.S. 126, 136 (1938). *Cf.* Consul of Spain v. The Conception, 6 F. Cas. 359 (1819); United States v. Insurance Cos., 89 U.S. (22 Wall) 99 (1875). *See also* Alder, *The Unrecognized Government in the Courts of the United States,* 5 VA. J. INT'L L. 36 (1964); Borchard, *Unrecognized Government in American Courts,* 26 AM. J. INT'L L. 261 (1932). J. G. HERVEY, THE LEGAL EFFECTS OF RECOGNITION IN INTERNATIONAL LAW AS INTERPRETED BY THE COURTS OF THE UNITED STATES 54–81 (1928).

144.   Russian Republic v. Cibrario, 235 N.Y. 255 (1923); Preobazhenski v. Cibrario, 192 N.Y. 275 (1922); Lehigh Valley R. Co. v. State of Russia, 21 F.2d 396, 400–01 (1927).

145.   Republic of China v. Merchants Fire Assur. Corp., 30 F.2d 279 (1929).

146.   United States of Mexico v. Fernandez, *reported in* [1923] 2 FOREIGN REL. U.S. 773.

147.   Amtorg Trading Corp. v. United States, 71 F.2d 524 (1934).

148.   Ex parte Don Ascanio Colonna, 314 U.S. 510 (1942).

149.   Banco Nacional de Cuba v. Sabbatino, 376 U.S. 398, 410 (1964). The "incongruity" of "judicial" recognition was not present in a case of broken diplomatic relations.

150.   *Id.* at 411–12 (distinguishing the principle of reciprocity in the recognition of foreign judgments).

151.   *See* Borchard, *supra* note 144, at 261, 265–66. *See also* Dickinson, *The Unrecognized Government or State in English and American Law,* 22 MICH. L. REV. 29, 118, 122–24 (1923); L. JAFFE, JUDICIAL ASPECTS OF FOREIGN RELATIONS 155 (1933). For a favorable attitude to *Cibrario,* see Tennant, *Recognition Cases in American Courts, 1923–1930,* 29 MICH. L. REV. 708, 713 (1931).

152.   213 N.Y.S. 2d 417 (1961). (Supreme Court, Appellate Division, First Dep't.; Breitel, P.J.). No appeal was taken.

153.   *Id.* at 422.

154.   For an excellent, extensive treatment of *Upright,* see Lubman, *The Unrecognized Government in American Courts: Upright v. Mercury Business Machines,* 62 COLUM. L. REV. 275 (1962).

155.   For discussion of State Department practice and the different degrees of conclusiveness given by courts to State Department suggestions, see Lyons, *The Conclusiveness of the "Suggestion" and Certificate of the American State Department,* [1947] 24 BRIT. Y.B. INT'L L. 116. Ex parte Muir, 254 U.S. 522 (1921); The Pasaro, 255 U.S. 216 (1921).

156.   *The "Tate Letter,"* 26 DEP'T STATE BULL. 984–85 (1952). *See* Victory Transport v. Comisaria General, 336 F.2d 354 (1964), *cert. denied,* 381 U.S. 934 (1965).

157.   Isbrandtsen Tankers, Inc. v. President of India, 446 F.2d 1198 (1971), *cert. denied,* 404 U.S. 985 (1971). *See also* New York and Cuba M.S.S. Co. v. Korea, 132 F. Supp. 684 (1955).

158.   Ex parte Peru, 318 U.S. 578, 589 (1943). *See also* Knocklong Corp. v. Kingdom of Afghanistan, 167 N.Y.S. 2d 285 (1957), and Rich v. Naviera Vacuba, S.A., 197 F. Supp. 710 (1961).

159.   *See, e.g.,* Stephen v. Zivnostenska Banka, 199 N.Y.S. 2d 797, 802–03 (1960). *See also* The Katingo Hadjipatera, 40 F. Supp. 546 (1941).

160.   Compania Espanola v. Navemar, 303 U.S. 68, 75 (1938). *See also* Republic of Mexico v. Hoffman, 324 U.S. 30 (1945); Victory Transport v. Comisaria General, *supra* note 156; Heaney v. Government of Spain, 445 F.2d 501 (1971).

The lack of State Department suggestion can be a conclusive factor. The Benton Park, 65 F. Supp. 211 (1946). *But cf.* National City Bank v. Republic of China, 348 U.S. 356 (1955); First National City Bank v. Banco Nacional de Cuba, 92 S.Ct. 1808 (1972). *Compare* Dexter and Carpenter v. Kunglig Jarnvagsstyrelsen, 43 F.2d 705 (1930) *with* Coale v. Societé Co-Operative Suisse des Charbons, Basle, 21 F.2d 180 (1921).

It should be noted that a foreign government can waive immunity by appearing and failing to make a timely plea for immunity. Wacker v. Bisson, 348 F.2d 602 (1965).

161.   234 N.Y. 372 (1923).

162.   For decisions following the *Wulfsohn* rationale, see Nankivel v. Omsk All Russian Government, 237 N.Y. 150 (1923); Voevodine v. Government of Commander-in-Chief, 249 N.Y.S. 645 (1931); and Telkes v. Hungarian National Museum, 38 N.Y.S. 2d 419 (1942).

163.   Underhill v. Hernandez, 168 U.S. 250, 252 (1897). *See also* the stress on equal sovereignties and territoriality in the classic Schooner v. McFadden, 11 U.S. (7 Cranch) 116 (1811).

164.   In *Sabbatino,* 376 U.S. 398 (1964), the Supreme Court held that the act of state rule would be applied even if the foreign government's act were alleged to violate international law. The Court's principle of complete deference to the Executive was changed by Congress; the act of state doctrine will be applied to alleged violations of international law only if the President so requests. 22 U.S.C. §2370(e)(2) (1970). This legislation, however, covers only those cases in which claims are made to property which has been taken by a foreign government. In a more recent decision involving another situation, the Supreme Court has used another principle as a corollary to the act of state rule. First National City Bank v. Banco Nacional de Cuba, 92 S.Ct. 1808 (1972). See also Dunhill v. Cuba 96 S.Ct. 1854 (1976).

For earlier expressions of the act of state rule, see American Banana Co. v. United Fruit Co., 213 U.S. 347 (1909); Oetjen v. Central Leather Co., 246 U.S. 297 (1918); Richard v. American Metal Co., 246 U.S. 304 (1918); Shapleigh v. Mier, 299 U.S. 468 (1937); Bernstein v. Van Heyghen Frères Societé Anonyme, 163 F.2d 246 (1947). For the rule that the act of state doctrine does not include the extraterritorial acts of a foreign government, see Republic of Iraq v. First National City Bank, 353 F.2d 47 (1965); Zwack v. Kraus Bros., 237 F.2d 255 (1956); Vladikavkazsky Ry Co. v. N.Y. Trust Co., 237 N.Y. 369 (1934); Petrogradsky M.K. Bank v. National City Bank, 253 N.Y. 23 (1923).

165.   Oetjen v. Central Leather Co., *supra* note 164, at 302–03; United States v. Belmont, 301 U.S. 324, 330 (1937).

166.   Sokoloff v. National City Bank, 239 N.Y. 158, 166 (1924); James & Co. v. Second Russian Ins. Co., 239 N.Y. 248 (1925); Russian Reinsurance Co. v. Stoddard, 240 N.Y. 149 (1925); Petrogradsky M.K. Bank v. National City Bank, 253 N.Y. 23 (1930); Salimoff & Co. v. Standard Oil Co., 262 N.Y. 220 (1933); Banque de France v. Equitable Trust Co., 33 F.2d 202 (1929).

After the Civil War the U.S. Supreme Court indicated that not all of the acts of the rebelling states would be considered invalid; those acts of a de facto government "necessary to peace and good order among citizens" would be upheld. Texas v. White, 74 U.S. (7 Wall.) 700, 733 (1868); Horn v. Lockhart, 84 U.S. (17 Wall.) 570, 580 (1873); Sprott v. United States, 87 U.S. (20 Wall.) 459, 464 (1874).

The Soviet annexation of the Baltic republics has resulted in considerable litigation in New York courts, which have split on the question of the validity of the *de facto* Soviet authorities (the U.S. never having recognized the annexations). Denying the validity of the acts of the Soviet authorities: In re Adler's Estate, 93

N.Y.S. 2d 416 (1949); In re Mitzkel's Estate, 233 N.Y.S. 2d 519 (1962); In re Luks' Estate, 256 N.Y.S. 2d 194 (1965). Upholding their validity: Matter of Luberg, 19 A.D.2d 370 (1963); In re Estate of Bielinis, 284 N.Y.S. 2d 819 (1967), aff'd 292 N.Y.S. 2d 363 (1968). Other cases involving the Baltic republics: The Kotkas, 35 F. Supp. 983 (1940); The Regent, 35 F. Supp. 985 (1940) (both giving effect to U.S. nonrecognition of annexations); The Denny, 127 F.2d 404 (1942) (validity of decree of de facto Lithuanian authorities upheld). See also In re Alexandravicus' Estate, 172 A.2d 641 (1961). For a commentary: Briggs, Non-Recognition in the Courts: The Ships of the Baltic Republics, 37 Am. J. Int'l L. 585 (1943). A successor government of a nonrecognized government can be held liable for the latter's obligations. The Tinoco Arbitration, 18 Am. J. Int'l L. 147 (1924).

167.　See Russian Reinsurance Co. v. Stoddard, 240 N.Y. 149 (1925).

168.　Salimoff & Co. v. Standard Oil Co., supra note 166, at 227. See also Russian Volunteer Fleet v. United States, 282 U.S. 481 (1931).

Courts in the U.S. have shown a keener sense of the equities of private parties involved in recognition questions than English courts. See Luther v. Sagor & Co., [1921] 1 K.B. 456; [1921] 3 K.B. 532; Carl-Zeiss Stiftung v. Rayner and Keeler, Ltd., [1966] 2 All E.R. 586; Adams v. Adams, [1970] 3 All E.R. 572 (PDA) (note the court's apology at 592). Cf. Legal Consequences for States of the Continued Presence of South Africa in Namibia (South West Africa) Notwithstanding Security Council Resolution 276 (1970), Advisory Opinion, [1971] I.C.J. 16, 56.

In a companion case, the Swiss Supreme Federal Tribunal ruled in the Swiss Zeiss case that Swiss nonrecognition of East Germany would not prevent it from considering East German law. Such consideration could not be taken as recognition since the tribunal was not competent to extend recognition; conflicts of law rules, however, indicated that East German law had to be considered. VEB Carl Zeiss Jena v. Firma Carl Zeiss Heidenheim, 91 II Entscheidungen des Schweizerischen Bundesgerichtes 117 (1965). Contrary to the practice of U.S. courts in deferring to other branches, the Swiss court felt able to hear the merits.

In the American Zeiss litigation, the courts were willing to consider East German law, but the consideration given was limited and colored by ideological hostility. Carl Zeiss Stiftung v. V.E.B. Carl Zeiss Jena, 293 F. Supp. 892, 906–08 (1968), aff'd as modified 433 F.2d 686 (1970), cert. denied, 403 U.S. 905 (1971).

See also Bank of China v. Wells Fargo Bank and Union Trust Co., 194 F. Supp. 59 (1959).

169.　U.S. v. Pink, 315 U.S. 203 (1942); Pink in effect overruled Moscow Fire Ins. Co. v. Bank of New York, 280 N.Y. 286 (1939), aff'd, 309 U.S. 624 (1940) (evenly divided Court). For significant decisions following the Pink line, see The Maret 145 F.2d 431 (1944); Latvian State Cargo and Passenger S.S. Line v. McGrath, 188 F.2d 1000 (1951).

The New York Court of Appeals did not, however, defer to the Pink ruling (at least verbally). In Anderson v. N.V. Transandine Handelmaatsschappij, 289 N.Y. 9, 15 (1942), it stated that State Department certification of recognition settled the political question but not judicial questions such as the "scope and effect within this State of a decree promulgated by the recognized government."

170.　213 N.Y.S. 2d 417, 421–22 (1961).

171.　The Sabbatino decision, 376 U.S. 398 (1964), represents a judicial abdication of competence in international legal disputes. The Court there felt that "[e]ven if the State Department has proclaimed the impropriety of the expropriation, the stamp of approval of its view by a judicial tribunal, however impartial, might increase any affront and the judicial decision might occur at a time, almost always well after the taking, when such an impact would be contrary to our national interest." Id. at 432. The same fear of "frustrating" the conduct of foreign relations is the keystone of Justice Rehnquist's plurality opinion in First National City Bank v. Banco Nacional de Cuba, 92 S.Ct. 1808, 1813 (1972) (but see Justice Powell's concurring opinion at 1816–17). See also Dunhill v. Cuba 96 S.Ct. 1854 (1976).

The Upright approach requires greater judicial independence in determining the limits of the political effects of nonrecognition. Following the Supreme Court's lead, however, a judge would be tempted to indulge his imagination in the possible complications which the treatment of a nonrecognized government in his court might raise for U.S. foreign relations. But the basic *Upright* rule has taken firm roots for future growth. *See* RESTATEMENT, SECOND, FOREIGN RELATIONS LAW OF THE UNITED STATES, § 113 (1965).

172. Cardozo, for instance, thought that courts must "play a humbler and more cautious part" than invalidating a treaty when the will of the political branches was "unrevealed"; if war had erupted between the parties to the treaty, a court should invalidate, in an actual controversy before it, only that which is "inconsistent with the policy of safety of the nation in the emergency of war." Techt v. Hughes, 229 N.Y. 222 (1920). Foley Bros. v. Filardo, 336 U.S. 281, 293–94 (1949) (Frankfurter, J., concurring). *Cf.* U.S. v. Louisiana, 363 U.S. 1, 64 (1960). *See generally* the discussion in BOT, *supra* note 66, at 212 ff.

173. 331 U.S. 503 (1947).

174. *Id.* at 514.

175. Zalemanis v. United States, 173 F. Supp. 355 (1959), *cert. denied,* 363 U.S. 917 (1959).

176. In 1955 a California court was confronted with the question of whether a 1946 treaty between the U.S. and the Republic of China held with respect to individuals residing in 1949 in Manchuria, which was then controlled by the Communist Chinese. The court ruled that, in the context of a "fluid civil war," the treaty was still in force with respect to the entire state of China. The Chinese Communists were waging a civil war for control of that state, but they were not seceding from it. Thus, in the court's view, there remained only one sovereign Chinese state. The court gave no significance to the fact that the Communists had declared after the treaty was signed and before it was ratified that they would not recognize it. In re Nepogodin's Estate, 285 P.2d 672 (1955) (Dist. Ct. of App.).

In 1964 another California court considered a very similar case. It held that the 1946 treaty was no longer in force with respect to mainland China. It distinguished *Nepogodin* as set in a time of "fluid civil war." In re Eng's Estate, 39 Cal. Rptr. 254 (1964) (Dist. Ct. of App.).

This ruling appears to be a more vigorous judicial action than Cardozo and the U.S. Supreme Court had advised; the U.S. government had not declared the treaty terminated. The court had based its decision on such U.S. governmental acts as refusals to allow U.S. citizens to visit or trade with the Chinese mainland. The State Department, however, had previously indicated that transfers of property, including inheritances (at issue in both *Nepogidin* and *Eng*), were prohibited if they involved Communist-controlled areas of China. The right to an inheritance was not affected, but enjoyment of the right could be postponed (apparently indefinitely). State Dep't. Letter, Feb. 21, 1964, 58 AM. J. INT'L L. 1005 (1964). When review of the *Eng* case was sought in the U.S. Supreme Court, a memorandum for the U.S. indicated that the State Department viewed the 1946 treaty as currently inoperative with respect to areas not conrolled by the Republic of China. 59 AM. J. INT'L L. 921 (1965). Certiorari was denied. 381 U.S. 902 (1965).

See also the Oregon case, In re Kasendorf's Estate, 353 P.2d 531 (1960) (a 1925 treaty between U.S. and Estonia still in force) (Supreme Ct. of Oregon).

The Supreme Court of Oregon, in Zschernig v. Miller, 412 P.2d 781, *rehearing denied* 415 P.2d 15 (1966), held that the State Department's indication that it viewed the 1923 treaty with Germany as still in force with respect to the territory of East Germany was controlling on that point. The decision in the case was reversed by the U.S. Supreme Court on the ground that the Oregon law (an inheritance law requiring reciprocity in the treatment of U.S. citizens by the foreign state the citizens of which were claiming an inheritance in Oregon) involved was an unconstitutional intrusion into the federal domain of foreign relations. Zschernig v. Miller, 389 U.S. 429 (1968). The Treaty question itself was thus not touched.

See the discussion in B.R. BOT, *supra* note 66, at 46, 212–39. *See id.* at 26–28

and 143–46 (with respect to the League of Nations nonrecognition of Manchukuo).
177. The I.C.J. has found the South African presence in Namibia to be unlawful
and has advised the world (whether or not members of the U.N.) of their duties of
nonrecognition of that presence. [1971] I.C.J. 54–56.

178. *See* Sei Fujii v. California, 242 P.2d 617 (1952).

179. *See* S.C. Res. 202 (1965), May 6, 1965, U.N. Doc. S/INF/20/Rev.1, at 6
(1965); S.C. Res. 216 (1965), Nov. 12, 1965, *id.* at 8; S.C. Res. 217 (1965), Nov.
20, 1965, *id.*; S.C. Res. 221 (1966), Apr. 9, 1966, U.N. Doc. S/INF/21/Rev.1, at 5
(1966); S.C. Res. 232 (1966), Dec. 16, 1966, *id.* at 7 (1966); S.C. Res. 253 (1968),
May 29, 1968, U.N. Doc. S/INF/23/Rev.1, at 5 (1968); S.C. Res. 277 (1970),
Mar. 18, 1970, U.N. Doc. S/INF/25, at 5 (1970); S.C. Res. 288 (1970), Nov. 17,
1970, U.N. Doc. S/INF/25, at 7 (1970).

180. United Nations Participation Act, 22 U.S.C. 287 (c) (1971); Exec. Order No.
11322, 3 C.F.R. 441 (1971); Exec. Order No. 11419, 3 C.F.R. 452 (1971) (actions
taken by the President in 1967 and 1968 to fulfill sanctions policy); Prohibition of
Transportation by Vessel of Commodities and Products from and to Southern Rhodesia, 15 C.F.R. 11 (1971) (regulations issued by Commerce Dep't); Rhodesian
Sanctions Regulations, 31 C.F.R. 530 (1971) (regulations issued by Treasury Dep't).

181. The "Rhodesian Chrome Statute," an amendment to the Military Procure-
ment Act of 1971, Pub. L. No. 92–156, 503 (Nov. 17, 1971).

182. Subsequent to this writing, a federal court ruled that the matter of conformity of U.S. action to Security Council decisions would not be reviewed in U.S.
courts. Diggs v. Schultz, 470 F.2d 461 (1972), *cert. denied,* 411 U.S. 931 (1973).
See also Executive Orders 1132 and 11419, *reprinted in* 6 INT'L LEGAL MATERIALS
100 (1967) and 7 *id.* at 1088 (1968). *See also* the Byrd Amendment to the Strategic
and Critical Materials Stock Piling Act, 50 U.S.C. § 98–98(h)(10). *Cf.* U.N. Doc.
S/RES/314 (1972) and Statement by Ambassador Phillips of the U.S. to the U.N.,
11 INT'L LEGAL MATERIALS 680 (1972). *See generally* Note, *Security Council Resolutions in United States Courts,* 50 INDIANA L.J. 83 (1974).

183. The United Nations was swift in condemning the shift in U.S. policy. *See* G.A.
Res. 2765 (XXVI), 26 GAOR Supp. 29, at 97, U.N. Doc. A/8429 (1971), and U.N.
Doc. S/RES/314 (1972).

184. Ngai Chi Lam v. Esperdy, 411 F.2d 310 (1969); Shyu Jeng Shyong v. Esperdy,
294 F. Supp. 355, 356 (1969): "Which government has sovereignty over Rhodesia is
a political question not within the competency of this court to decide; this is left to
the President and the Secretary of State."

On this Rhodesian situation, see Note, *The Rhodesian Chrome Statute: The
Congressional Response to United Nations Economic Sanctions Against Southern
Rhodesia,* 58 VA. L. REV. 511 (1972); Note, *Congressional Power to Abrogate the
Domestic Effect of a United Nations Treaty Commitment: Diggs v. Shultz* (D.C. Cir.
1972), 13 COLUM. J. TRANSNAT'L L. 155 (1974).

The opinion by Justice Douglas in United States v. Pink, *supra* note 169, can
be understood as a "crisis" decision. Written in 1942 in the early, dark days of World
War II, its great stress on executive prerogatives is a manifestation of a general feeling that strong central authority is mandatory during wartime. The case also involved
Soviet–American relations, a touchy point throughout that war. It is of doubtful
benefit to read *Pink,* and to give it power as law, in conditions other than general
wartime mobilization.

185. The New York decisions in the 1920s and 1930s are clearly understandable
in these terms. It was obvious that the U.S. would have to adjust to the Soviet reality
at some point.

186. The passport cases of recent years are indications of this trend. Courts have
resisted attempts by the Executive to control the increased travel by American citizens. Zemel v. Rusk, 381 U.S. 1 (1965); United States v. Laub, 385 U.S. 475 (1967);
Lynd v. Rusk, 389 F.2d 940 (1967). *Cf.* Kent v. Dulles, 357 U.S. 116 (1958), and
Aptheker v. Secretary of State, 378 U.S. 500 (1964). Lynd v. Rusk, *supra,* shows

the limits of judicial action in the area; the U.S. government is not required to give certain incidents of recognition to a nonrecognized government in a restricted area; it can refuse to extend diplomatic aid to U.S. citizens in that area.

187. *Upright*, 213 N.Y.S.2d 417 (1961), would appear to prevent Americans from taking unfair advantage of U.S. recognition policy in their private business dealing with citizens or residents of nonrecognized governments.

188. *See* note 7 *supra.*

189. This trend is exemplified by the *Sabbatino* and *First National City Bank* cases, note 171 *supra*, by the *Zschernig* decision and by the unwillingness of the U.S. Supreme Court to consider the constitutionality of U.S. military activity in Vietnam. Mitchell v. United States, *cert. denied*, 389 U.S. 934 (1967) (Douglas, J., dissenting), Mora v. McNamara, *cert. denied*, 389 U.S. 934 (1967) (Stewart, J., dissenting), *rehearing denied*, 389 U.S. 1025 (1967). *Cf.* Orlando v. Laird, 443 F.2d 1039 (1971), *cert. denied*, 404 U.S. 869 (1971).

190. On the principle of the obligations of unrecognized states in international law, see ERDMANN, NICHTANERKANNTE STAATEN UND REGIERUNGEN: FORMEN UND GRENZEN INTERNATIONALER BEZIEHUNGEN 27 (1966).

191. *See especially* Article 3 of the Geneva Conventions of 1949; and Paust, *Law in a Guerrilla Conflict: Myths, Norms and Human Rights*, [1973] ISRAEL Y.B. HUMAN RIGHTS 39. *See also* T. Yingling & Ginnane, *The Geneva Conventions of 1949*, 46 AM. J. INT'L L. 393 (1952). Draper, *Human Rights and the Law of War*, 12 VA. J. INT'L L. 326 (1972); Draper, *The Implementation of the Modern Law of War*, 8 ISRAEL LAW REVIEW 1 (1973); G.I.A.D. DRAPER, THE RED CROSS CONVENTIONS OF 1949 (1958); Kahn, *The Private Armed Groups and World Order*, NETHER. Y.B. INT'L L. 32 (1970).

192. *See* Draper, *The Geneva Conventions of 1949*, 114 HAGUE RECUEIL 63, 94 (1965). G.G. WILSON, INTERNATIONAL LAW 41 (3d ed. 1939). *Cf.* In re Karpler (the Ardeatine Cave case), [1948] ANN. DIG. 471, 472–73. *See also* Peeterbroek v. Assurance Générales de Paris [1946] ANN DIG. 230–31 (No. 98). *But cf.* in X v. Cie d'Assur. Z., [1946] ANN. DIG. 229–30 (No. 95); The Military Prosecutor v. Omar Mahmud Kassem and others, LAW AND THE COURTS IN THE ISRAEL–HELD AREAS 17, 48 (Faculty of Law of the Hebrew Univ. ed. 1970). *See also* Zorgbibe, *Le sort des combattants palestiniens*, LE MONDE DIPLOMATIQUE, June 1969, at 1; Note, *The Geneva Convention of 1949: Application in the Vietnamese Conflict*, 5 VA. J. INT'L L. 243 (1965), *reprinted in* 2 THE VIETNAM WAR AND INTERNATIONAL LAW 416 (R. Falk ed. 1969).

193. Organizational structure may determine the extent to which prescriptions of the conduct of warfare become applicable. *See* the Geneva Convention of 1949, Article 4(2). 75 U.N.T.S. 135, 138 (1950); Kahn, *supra* note 191 at 47–48; the French government's rationale to the Algerian claim that the Algerian Provisional Government would adhere to the Geneva Conventions. Note of July 25, 1960, from the French Ministry of Foreign Affairs to the Swiss Federal Political Department, *quoted in* Fraleigh, *The Algerian Revolution as a Case Study in International Law*, in THE INTERNATIONAL LAW OF CIVIL WAR 79, 195 (R. Falk ed. 1971) *But cf.* M. BEDJAOUI, LAW AND THE ALGERIAN REVOLUTION 217–20 (1961) and Fraleigh, *supra*, at 194–97. As for the Palestinian Organization, see Zorbibe, *Le sort des combattants palestiniens*, LE MONDE DIPLOMATIQUE, June, 1969, at 1, 5. For the relations between the recognition of an entity and the Geneva Conventions, see B.R. BOT, NONRECOGNITION AND TREATY RELATIONS 160–163 (1968). As for the Vietcong, the I.C.R.C. communicated to the United States that "the National Liberation Front too is bound by the undertakings signed by Viet Nam." 4 INT'L LEGAL MATERIALS 1171 (1965). *See also* I.C.R.C. Rep. 1965, at 53.

194. For example, in a proclamation of August 9, 1941, President Roosevelt declared the suspension of the International Load Line Convention of 1930 insofar as the United States was concerned "for the duration of the present emergency." 6 Fed. Reg. 3999 (1941). No state presumably protested the United States action. 5 DEP'T STATE BULL. 114 (1941).

195.   Williams v. Bruffy, 96 U.S. 176, 186 (1877); Salimoff & Co. v. Standard Oil Co. of New York, 262 N.Y. 220, 223 (1933); A.M. Luther v. James Sagor & Co., [1921] 3 K.B. 532; C.C. HYDE, *supra* note 87, at 184–86.

196.   2 MOORE, DIGEST 1113; State Dept. Communication to Secretary of Navy, Dec. 15, 1902, *quoted in* NAVAL WAR COLLEGE, INTERNATIONAL LAW SITUATIONS 80 (1902). *Cf.* U.S. v. Ambrose Light, 25 F. 405 (1885).

197.   The Vienna Convention on Diplomatic Relations, 500 U.N.T.S. 95; Garreston, *The Immunities of Representatives of Foreign States,* 41 N.Y.U.L. REV. 67 (1966); *Harvard Research in International Law, Diplomatic Privileges and Immunities,* 26 AM. J. INT'L L. SUPP. 15 (1932). *See also* Hurst, *Diplomatic Immunities— Modern Developments,* [1929] 10 BRIT. Y. B. INT'L L. 1; Preuss, *Capacity for Legation and the Theoretical Basis of Diplomatic Immunities,* 10 N.Y.U.L.Q. REV. 170 (1932–33); H. REIFF, DIPLOMATIC AND CONSULAR PRIVILEGE, IMMUNITIES AND PRACTICE (1954); H. NICHOLSON, DIPLOMACY (1939).

The interests of states in the protection of diplomatic communication are such that even political demonstrations can be restricted around the diplomatic premises. Jewish Defense League, Inc. v. Walter Washington, 347 F. Supp. 1300 (1972). *See also* Jews for Urban Justice v. Wilson, 311 F. Supp. 1158 (1970).

198.   *See* note 24 *supra.* Should a recognizing state's interests permit, functional immunities may include the use of coded communications, quasi-diplomatic privileges, and, sometimes, the establishment of a private army.

199.   In March 1973 the U.S. Ambassador and his chargé d'affaires were captured in the Saudi Arabian Embassy in Khartoum by Black September commandoes, a Palestinian guerilla organization, and held in exchange for several hundred prisoners in Israel. Subsequently, the American diplomats were killed in the Embassy. N.Y. Times, Mar. 2, 1973, at 1, col. 5; *id.,* Mar. 3, 1973, at 1, col. 8; *id.,* Mar. 4, 1973, at 1, col. 8. In May 1973, the People's Revolutionary Armed Forces of Mexico kidnapped the United States Consul General in exchange for the release of thirty prisoners and $80,000 ransom. *Id.,* May 6, 1973, at col. 1; *id.,* May 7, 1973, at 1, col. 1.

200.   *See* draft articles concerning crimes against persons entitled to special protection under international law. U.N. DOC. A/CN.4/L.182, *reprinted in* 11 INT'L LEGAL MATERIALS 493 (1972). *See* draft articles on the prevention and punishment of crimes against diplomatic agents and other internationally protected persons. 11 INT'L LEGAL MATERIALS 977 (1972); U.S. Protection of Diplomats Act, Public Law 92–539, *reprinted in* 11 INT'L LEGAL MATERIALS 1405 (1972). *See also* 1973 PROCEEDINGS AM. SOC'Y INT'L L. 87.

201.   47 U.S.C. §315(a) (1934). *See* Columbia Broadcasting System, Inc. v. Democratic Nat'l Committee, 412 U.S. 94 (1973); Brandywine-Maine Line Radio, Inc. v. F.C.C., 473 F.2d 16 (1972); Columbia Broadcasting System, Inc. v. F.C.C., 454 F.2d 1018 (1971); Neckritz v. F.C.C., 446 F.2d 501 (1971).

202.   Insofar as changes in other communities will have significant effects on domestic policies and insofar as national behavior will, in turn, influence the changes in these other communities, internal democratic principles will require increasing information flows about politics in other states and about the contending forces there. Hence, there are compelling reasons for extending the fairness doctrine in U.S. media to contending groups in other states as well as in the United States.

203.   Reisman, *supra* note 27; E. Suzuki, Self-Determination and World Public Order: Community Response to Group Formation (unpublished J.S.D. thesis at the Yale Law School, 1974).

IV
Resources

Chapter 13

The International Law and Politics of Marine Science Research

WILLIAM T. BURKE

In the past few years, government officials' and observers have called attention to the increasing restrictions being placed on scientific investigation of the oceans [1] and sometimes have briefly mentioned the remedial measures that can assist in alleviating or removing these restrictions.[2] Although most concerned persons, including marine scientists, agree that these restrictions are a serious impediment warranting international action, still there appears to be a body of opinion that this matter has been greatly exaggerated and that, hence, it requires little or no remedial international action. The purpose of this essay is to discuss the magnitude of the problem, both actual and potential, and to elaborate somewhat on the various alternatives that might help in rectifying it.

This essay, drafted in January 1971, was prepared before the convening of the Third United Nations Conference on the Law of the Sea.

The Magnitude of the Problem

To understand that restraints on scientific exploration and investigation of the oceans do constitute an important problem it is useful, first, to take note of the vital role of marine science research to a national ocean program. Second, it is essential to realize that this exploration and investigation must extend to all parts of the oceans in both horizontal and vertical planes. Finally, it is important to describe briefly the legal framework within which marine research must take place and to summarize the various ways in which this framework inhibits, prevents, or otherwise deleteriously affects the conduct of science at sea. It will be assumed that there is no need to elaborate on the important, and in some ways critical, contributions that productive national ocean programs may make to the interests of individual states and of the world community generally.[3]

Vital Role of Research

No elaborate discussion is required to emphasize the critical role that marine science research occupies in the development of the oceans for national and international objectives. In the First Report of the Marine Resources Council, Chapter XII is entitled "Research—The Base of the Marine Science Effort." [4] After noting the Council's concern for the application of ocean science and technology to meet national needs, the Report declared that "[t]he possibility of meeting each need depends on a strong scientific base" [5] and that funds for research total 30 percent of the total marine science budget.[6] The President's Science Advisory Committee, in the 1966 Report of its Panel on Oceanography, made a similar appraisal:

> Although the Panel recommends pursuing scientific investigation for describing and understanding marine phenomena, processes and resources as a separate goal of the national ocean program, it is apparent that increased knowledge and greater understanding are fundamental to achievement of all our objectives in use of the oceans.[7]

Further and more specific indications of the recognized significance of scientific research are contained in the Council's First Report. Referring to ocean data needs, the Council identified the wide range of uses for, purposes served by, and information derived from research:

> Vast quantities of marine environmental information are required to support virtually all the purposes of marine science and technology discussed in this report. Scientists, commercial fisheries experts, meteorologists, military planners and operators, and ocean engineers are naturally concerned with the collection and interpretation of materials in a manner

suited to their own particular needs. . . . Officials in Government and executives in business management increasingly depend on quantitative scientific information and objective analysis to make policy decisions.[8]

Equally strong assertions of the importance of marine science for ocean use are found on the international level. *International Ocean Affairs,* the so-called Helio Cabala Report, by a joint working party of the Scientific Committee on Oceanic Research (SCOR) of the International Council of Scientific Unions (ICSU), the Advisory Committee on Marine Resources Research (ACMRR) of the Food and Agriculture Organization (FAO), and WM-AC observes that "[a]ll marine activities and uses of resources of the sea can benefit from research. Indeed a few of these can be expected to develop further without it."[9]

If scientific research in the oceans is by general agreement essential to the achievement of national and international goals and needs, it is important to ask whether the international legal framework is, and will continue to be, favorable for activities necessary to productive research. The critical nature of this question arises from the fact, perhaps not self-evident, that fundamental scientific and other research must be prosecuted on a global basis if the complexity of marine phenomena is to be properly investigated and understood.[10] Reaching into all areas and regions of the world's oceans, effective and fruitful research cannot be excluded arbitrarily from the waters near the coasts of any state. Accordingly, the existence of effective legal and political restraints upon the conduct of research which operate to deter, hamper, or prevent ocean research projects impose costs which may be reflected in an inability to further national ocean objectives and needs.

Requirement of Widespread Investigation

The global ambit of marine science research, either in terms of a requirement for investigation in all parts of the oceans or in selected regions, can be illustrated by reference to some research needs in the major disciplines of physical oceanography, marine geology and geophysics, and biological oceanography.

PHYSICAL OCEANOGRAPHY

The physical oceanographer, who is "concerned with the physical properties and motions of the ocean waters and with the transport of energy, momentum, and matter," has for one task that of describing the "circulation and distribution of properties and their time changes *in different parts of the ocean or in all of it.*"[11] It is especially important to understand, however, that ocean waters are not homogeneous (*i.e.,* that the properties of such waters vary from place to place and through time)[12] and since this means that measurements of properties made in one place cannot be extrapolated to others, the only feasible investigative method is that of direct access to the waters to be studied. The scope of the task is succinctly described in the draft of a General Scientific Framework for World Ocean Study: "Because of the size, complexity, and variability of the oceans, a great many measurements are required to fix the distribution of properties in time and space. The magnitude of the necessary effort in oceanography is equal to the task of meteorology in describing weather and climate." [13] The enormity of the task of investigating ocean circulation and ocean–atmosphere interaction is vividly illustrated by passages in the Ponza Report, produced by another joint working party from SCOR, ACMRR, and WMO–AGOR. In delineating examples of worthwhile projects, the Ponza group identified studies to be carried out concerning the North and Equatorial Pacific, the California Current region, West Africa between Gibraltar and Dakar, the Arabian Sea, the Brazil Current in the South Atlantic, and oceanic areas observable from island stations on Tahiti, Bermuda, or Hawaii.[14]

The study of motions of ocean water demands also investigation throughout the volume of the sea, as is illustrated by reference to the sampling requirements for observation of currents. The 1967 Report of the Committee on Oceanography, National Academy of Sciences–National Research Council (NASCO), states:

> If we wish to study seasonal or other variations in the circulation, we are confronted . . . with the problem of the geographical and time spacing of the observations. The difficulty arises from our lack of knowledge of the spectrum of variations in the motions in the sea.
>
> The classical oceanographic cruise is inadequate to sample the high-frequency and small-scale phenomena, and oceanographic expeditions are generally not long enough or extensive enough to sample the low-frequency or large-dimension phenomena.[15]

The solution required appears to be that of "[b]uoy arrays maintained for periods of a year or longer. . . ." [16] These difficulties in large-scale observation are responsible in part for the notion of an Integrated Global Ocean Station System (IGOSS). The Comprehensive Outline of the Scope of the Long-Term and Expanded Program of Oceanic Research and Exploration as explained to the Twenty-fourth General Assembly describes IGOSS as follows:

> IGOSS, which is being developed on the basis of scientific principles, includes the modern technical means for observation, radio-communication and data processing and is intended to provide, together with WWW, the synchronous and undelayed oceanographical and meteorological information *from the whole ocean.*[17]

It seems reasonably clear that the criteria for emplacement of buoys and instrumentation for these purposes do not include the location of claimed political boundaries, such as the extensive claims made by states on the western coast of South America. Better understanding of turbulent motions in the deeper ocean is said to be necessary for development of an "adequate theory of the general circulation of the ocean," [18] and a variety of devices is useful for this task, among them moored instrument stations and bottom-mounted instruments in the deep ocean.

Wave instruments, both internal and surface, also call for widespread investigation and use of instrumented, unmanned, anchored, and drifting stations and bottom-mounted instruments. Speaking of internal waves, NASCO states that "[t]he most promising approach . . . is probably the use of arrays for buoys with sensors for temperature and velocity at various depths from near the bottom of the mixed layer to the bottom of the ocean." [19] And with respect to surface waves, NASCO observes: "A major remaining obstacle to our knowledge of the wind generation of waves, and consequently of the predictions of waves at sea, is absence of good observations or predictions of the wind field. Improvement of good observations or predictions might be accomplished by use of stable platforms, submarines, and possibly unmanned buoys." [20]

MARINE GEOLOGY AND GEOPHYSICS

A number of projected studies illustrate the wide-ranging investigations required in the area of marine geology and geophysics. Inquiry into deposition of sediments by turbidity currents involves experiments on the sea floor as well as in the laboratory. The previously mentioned draft Framework identified certain regions for such experiments: "Suitable regions for field experiment and surveys of turbidity current phenomena are numerous. Ideal areas are in the Mediterranean, the Caribbean, off Melanesia, and off eastern Asia. These areas are relatively shallow, and instrumentation should be comparatively easy." [21]

One of the most important regions of interest to this field of study is the continental terrace which embraces the coastal plain, the continental shelf, continental slope, and the underlying sediment and rock mass. A facet of the importance of investigation in this region and the state of knowledge are summarized in the draft Framework: "Any speculation on the structure, permanency, drift and history of continents and ocean basins must necessarily involve consideration of the structure and history of the continental terrace; but these are as yet poorly known and understood." [22]

The NASCO Report made reference to more utilitarian considerations:

Knowledge of the deep-sea floor and of the continental margins overlain by the ocean is basic to many present and future uses of the sea. Among these are the extraction of minerals and other materials from the sea floor, navigation of both surface and submarine vessels, the design and construction of engineering works on the sea-bottom and along the margin of the sea, the development of undersea recreation facilities, and ocean farming.[23]

The observations and recommendations of the draft Framework, however, are of special interest for present purposes:

> Preliminary exploration of continental terraces, particularly around North America, has revealed a wide variety of structures [both deep and sedimentary]. It had been anticipated that there would be no typical continental terrace, and that terraces, like mountain ranges, are regionally different. This has proved true.[24]

> Unexplored terraces of the world should be investigated oceanographically, biologically, and geologically, and the results compared with other terraces. Surface sediment distribution should be evaluated in the light of present and past supply, agents of distribution, and control by eustatic and local sea level fluctuations. The sub-surface should be investigated geophysically, especially by acoustic reflection, and by deep sampling, if possible by drilling. Terrace sediments and structure should be compared between regions and eventually on a worldwide basis.[25]

The point of this excerpt is of course the identification of the need for regional and comparative studies if generalizations are to be made. Continental shelf studies for purely scientific purposes cannot be confined to the shelf off the United States or any other state.

It should be noted in this connection that the study of sediments on the continental shelf as a means of discovering environmental conditions of the past few thousand years is "difficult on most parts of the shelf because the sediments have been disturbed by slumping and by reworking by organisms." [26] Among the "deep oxygen-poor basins" in which such study is feasible, the NASCO Report mentions deep basins off southern and Baja California, the north central coast of Peru, the basins of the Caribbean Sea, the Black Sea, the Norwegian fjords, and the Baltic. Again, it is evident that worldwide activity is required if research is to accomplish scientific goals.

BIOLOGICAL OCEANOGRAPHY

Studies in biological oceanography illustrate perhaps most dramatically the need for extensive research in every part of the oceans. In investigations of the food chain in the ocean "[w]e need to learn the routes, rates, and reservoirs of organic matter in the sea from the phytoplankton, which originally synthesize it, through the ramifications of the web of herbivorous and carnivorous animals, to its eventual decomposition to inorganic elements." [27]

One aspect of the study of phytoplankton is especially noteworthy for the emphasis on spatial distribution and, hence, on access to different areas of the sea. The NASCO Report states:

> From a new understanding of nutritional requirements of marine phytoplankton, however, we now know that probably more than half the species in the sea are not truly autotropic but require for growth the presence of at least some small amounts of organic substances such as vitamins. There is evidence that the spatial and time distribution of those growth substances may determine not so much the magnitude of plant production, rather the particular species present at any time. Because different phytoplanktons may have quite different food value to grazers (depending on their size, shape and chemical composition), the subsequent steps of the food chain may also be altered, regardless of the physical environment. Thus, in addition to the biomass, the species composition of the primary producers is of considerable importance to the total productivity.[28]

If these differences carry far enough up the food chain to affect commercial fishery population, it seems evident that such research might come under the general appellation of "fisheries research" and that studies of phytoplankton could be affected by controls asserted over such research. In further reference to ocean productivity, the Report states:

> Enough understanding of plankton production may be developing to make possible a general estimate of ocean productivity at the phytoplankton and, perhaps, the zooplankton level. Before the estimate can be made, much more knowledge is required of seasonal variation in productivity nearly everywhere and especially in such poorly studied areas as the South Pacific.[29]

Another phase of the food web that requires study is the benthos inhabiting the bottom of the continental shelf.

> Research on benthic organisms, particularly animals, is hampered even more than research on plankton by the great number of species, most of which are not well known. Since the species are not usually as widely distributed as planktonic organisms, each geographic region must be studied separately from even a taxonomic viewpoint.[30]

In further comment upon biological oceanography, it is important to observe that commercial fishing vessels are a critical adjunct to regular research vessels, especially in the research on the dynamics of harvestable organisms:

> The widespread and intensive commercial fisheries for some species in various parts of the ocean have made possible studies that could not

have been carried out by research vessels alone. In these studies, the biomass of the commercial species has been assessed and the rates of growth, mortality, and reproduction have been measured. These rates determine both the flux of organic matter through the population and the relations among biomass harvesting rates, and sustained yields. The extensive research conducted on these matters for several decades has recently been much accelerated, primarily to gain knowledge for the management of the fisheries in order to conserve commercial-fish populations. The research has also helped significantly in understanding the dynamics of the populations of these organisms at or near the top of the food chain. Much of the theoretical framework of competitor and predator-prey relationships in the ocean has been developed and supported from studies of the commercial fisheries and applied subsequently to other groups of marine organisms.[31]

In a number of ways, the contribution of commercial fleets has been so effective that our knowledge of relationships between populations and various oceanographic conditions is further advanced for commercial fish species than for most other marine organisms. The impact of new and further restraints on the movement of commercial fishing vessels is thus seen to have a harmful effect on their research activities.

The International Legal Framework and Impediments to Marine Science Research

Although most concerned persons probably are familiar with the prescriptions affecting research, a brief reminder of these prescriptions is desirable. Of course, their actual impact, in terms of their effect upon the behavior of state officials and private groups and individuals, requires more elaboration.

THE FRAMEWORK

Internal Waters The region of internal waters, comprised of the waters immediately adjacent to the coast of a state, is subject to the complete and unfettered authority of the coastal state. This means that access to such waters, for scientific or other purposes, generally is not a matter of right and that the coastal state, apart from contrary agreement, is entitled to exclude access as a matter of discretion and to assert such control as it chooses, should entry be granted. In many instances, provision for access is made in bilateral agreements, but this usually extends, in so many words, only to normal commercial transportation and does not embrace investigation for scientific purposes. Such investigation therefore should be preceded by a request for coastal consent, such request to be made through the normal channels available for such purposes. The exception referred to arises from Article 5(2) of the Convention on the Territorial Sea and Contiguous Zone: "Where the establishment of a straight baseline in accordance with article 4 has the effect of enclosing as internal waters areas which previously had been considered as part of the territorial sea or of the high seas, a right of innocent passage, as provided in articles 14 to 23, shall exist in those waters." The extent, if any, to which this provision permits scientific investigations in internal waters during the course of innocent passage awaits clarification, however, since the question has not yet arisen.

Should entry into internal waters be effected without the knowledge or consent of the coastal state and should the intruding object (such as a research buoy) be discovered later, it would be subject to local regulation. There usually are local regulations for buoys within national territory, such as for marking, lighting, and damage (to or by the buoy), and it is conceivable that such regulations would be applied to research buoys that drift into national territory. The responsibilities of buoy owners or operators would be fixed by the local rules, including those allocating liability for harm caused to or by the buoy. It should be noted, however, that local regulations are not likely to extend explicitly to research buoys, but that interpretations could be adopted which would bring them within the reach of such regulations. A reasonable surmise is that this probably would be the case for marking and lighting regulations and that improper marks and lights would be sanctioned by local law.[32]

In view of the comprehensive nature of permissible coastal control over internal waters, it is plain that the extent of the geographic area claimed is itself of immediate relevance to the conduct of scientific research. The larger the area claimed, the larger the area within which a coastal state may demand advance consent for the conduct of research. Whether or not the claim to enclose an area as internal waters is recognized either generally or specifically by the United States, the effect may be to interfere with research in the area. It also may be noted that enlarging the region of internal waters has the consequence of expanding the outer limit of the territorial sea, which affects the necessity of consent for scientific research in that region. Furthermore, the location of baselines as geometric constructs crossing water may have an impact in certain circumstances on locating the line or lines allocating the submarine region of the continental shelf. In this latter instance, the baseline location may not affect the need for consent to research, but it might determine the state to whom a request for consent to continental shelf research should be directed.[33] Finally, the location of baselines could affect the delimitation of specific zones of authority beyond the territorial sea (the so-called contiguous zones), since measurement of these zones begins usually from the baselines for the territorial sea.[34] This has special significance for biological oceanography; in recent times, numerous states, including the United States, have established contiguous zones for fishery purposes in which the concerned state claims the same right over fisheries as it exercises within territorial waters. Research aimed at fisheries for commercial purposes, therefore, could be affected by baselines which create new areas of internal waters.

Expansion is the most descriptive term applicable to events of the past decade affecting the limits of internal waters. Numerous states have made new delimitations of such waters, either in particular areas or on the entire coastal frontier. Moreover, the Convention on the Territorial Sea embodies prescriptions which establish the lawfulness of certain expansions of this area. In some states, agitation continues for the government to adopt new baseline systems and new baselines. In certain instances the claims of particular states could affect extremely large high seas areas, and the impact on research could be extremely detrimental.[35]

It is not proposed here to examine the international law principles established to regulate the assertion of claims to delimit internal waters, since the relevant considerations are not unique to scientific research. It suffices to note that these claims vary greatly around the world and that as questions of permissibility arise their impact on research, as noted earlier in regard to various specific ocean areas, should be taken into account in responding to such claims.

Territorial Sea   The territorial sea, the marginal zone each coastal state possesses under international law, is located seaward of the limit of internal waters where such waters exist; where they do not exist, the territorial sea is delimited solely from base points located on, or associated with, the adjacent land mass. Coastal authority over the territorial sea commonly is described as "sovereignty," subject to the right of innocent passage for foreign vessels. Under certain circumstances even innocent passage may be forbidden, except in those areas of the territorial sea which fall within the conception of a strait. (It should be noted that submarines may transit the territorial sea, but that such passage is innocent only if the submarine is on the surface. This principle, which probably is universally accepted, was formulated when the general assumption, not then inaccurate, was that all submarines are military vehicles.)

There appears to be general understanding that all scientific research in the territorial sea of a foreign country, including the use of research buoys, calls for the consent of the host state. Addressing the question of research vessels, Interagency Committee on Oceanography (ICO) Pamphlet No. 25 (prepared by the State Department) states flatly that "[n]o vessel may conduct research in foreign territorial waters without clearances from the host government." [36] With respect to research buoys, the Preliminary Report of UNESCO and the Intergovernmental Maritime Consultative Organization (IMCO) on the Legal Status of Unmanned and Manned Fixed Oceanographic Stations asserts:

1. The coastal state may exercise its sovereign rights in governing the use of oceanographic research buoys.

2. The coastal state may freely permit or deny permission to employ such devices.

*   *   *

4. No one may claim an absolute international right to place oceanographic buoys in the internal or territorial waters of any state without the express or implied permission of the government of that state.[37]

It seems likely that these propositions are in general accord with the expectations of national officials.

One universally accepted component of coastal authority over the territorial sea is that the coastal state has complete and unlimited authority over access to fishery and other extractive resources of the area. This apparently implies that "fisheries research" within this area is subject to the consent of the coastal state concerned. The statement quoted from ICO Pamphlet No. 25 is sufficiently broad to include fisheries research, as well as any other.

States parties to international conservation agreements frequently have given permission in the basic constitutive treaty to the conduct of fisheries research within their respective territorial seas.[38] I am not familiar with the practice of states in their relations with each other, apart from agreement. So far as is known, however, no study has been made of this subject. In any event, there is no doubt about the authority of the coastal state in the absence of agreement.

As was noted with respect to the limit of internal waters, the width claimed for the territorial sea has obvious impact upon the extent of the regions freely available for scientific research. The United States continues to maintain a three-mile territorial sea and refuses to recognize wider claims, but the fact is that there exist claims to greatly differing widths and that research within these disputed areas is subject to potential interference if coastal state consent is not obtained. If any trend is discernible in this connection, it is in the direction of the eventual establishment, as permissible under international law, of a territorial sea of twelve miles, perhaps wider.

Contiguous Zone   The ocean regions covered by the label "contiguous zones" are the high seas areas contiguous to the territorial sea over which coastal states exert limited authority for particular purposes. The limits of the various contiguous zones vary from state to state and also within one state since the geographic reach of coastal laws frequently is made to vary with the requirements of the situation which the law is supposed to control.

Insofar as is known no state asserts specific control over scientific research activities on the high seas by means of extending its law beyond the territorial sea, except in the case of fisheries research. Even this latter extension of control is relatively recent because it is only since about 1960–65 that the pattern of state claims to a special exclusive fishing area beyond the territorial sea crystallized to the point that such zones came to be considered permissible under international law.[39] Accordingly, Article 24(1) of the Convention on the Territorial Sea and Contiguous Zone, which provides for the permissible purposes and scope of coastal state controls in the contiguous zone, no longer reflects (if ever it did) the state of international law. The reason is that fisheries matters are not listed by Article 24 as one of the purposes for which states may exert limited controls in the contiguous zone. In addition, the kind of control asserted in prohibiting foreign fishing in an exclusive fishing zone goes well beyond the limited authority Article 24 would permit. Similarly, coastal assertion of authority to prohibit fisheries research in the exclusive fishing zone is inconsistent with the circumscribed control provided for in Article 24. The conclusion is, therefore, that exclusive fishery zones represent a new type of contiguous zone recognized in customary international law and that Article 24 cannot properly be considered an obstacle to creation of lawful contiguous zones for purposes not enumerated in that Article.[40]

One problem in determining the scope of permissible control over fisheries research in an exclusive fishing zone arises because of the need to distinguish research directly relevant to fishery exploitation from research which may benefit such exploitation but which is aimed basically at other purposes. Although it has been suggested that the control exercised by the United States over fisheries research in its territorial sea is now extended to the exclusive fishing zone, it is doubtful whether this can be accepted as in accordance with international law without further clarification. Within its territorial sea the United States may exercise control over all research however indirectly related to, but valuable for, fisheries. In the contiguous zone for fisheries, however, the authority exercised must relate to the purpose the zone was created to serve, i.e., the protection of fishing rights. It would seem apparent, therefore, that the carry-over of controls over research relating to fisheries is not coextensive with those lawfully exercised in the territorial sea. The latter are fully comprehensive; the former are not.

One possible definition of fisheries research is: "Fishery research is the study of the biology, environment, abundance, availability, and exploitation of fish or other aquatic organisms *for the purpose of* facilitating the utilization of those organisms for sport or commercial purposes."[41] This formulation would not require consent for research into marine organisms, which still might be valuable for fisheries, so long as that research is aimed at other purposes. The chief determinant of the necessity for requesting consent for research is in this conception one of the purposes of the conduct. One caveat is already on record concerning such a definition. Dr. M. B. Schaefer writes:

> I submit that this definition is not operationally very useful, because of the difficulties of determining the motives of the scientific complement of any particular research vessel. I doubt, therefore, whether I can rely upon it to determine whether or not I should request permission from any given foreign country before conducting any research in biological oceanography or related subjects, in its exclusive fisheries zone.[42]

Whether or not the definition in terms of purpose still is too comprehensive calls for decision by scientists, not lawyers. But even the latter may raise a question about one seeming ambiguity. Exclusive fishing rights in the contiguous zone extend only to fish exploited in the zone. Yet, because of the many interrelationships between conditions and animals in the zone and those outside, research in the zone could relate to exploitation of fish largely, if not wholly, exploited outside the zone.[43] Even the taking of fish otherwise protected in the zone could further research into exploitation of still other species not so protected. If administratively feasible, the distinction drawn on the basis of "facilitating utilization" might be further refined to take account of this possibility.

Continental Shelf It is not improbable that the provisions of the 1958 Continental Shelf Convention that place previously unknown restraints on scientific research have inspired all the difficulties now posed for science throughout the world's oceans since it is these provisions which have called most attention to the possible commercial significance of scientific exploration and investigation at sea. Be this as it may, the critical articles of this Convention are articles 2 and 5, which are excerpted here.
According to Article 2:

> 1. The coastal State exercises over the continental shelf sovereign rights for the purpose of exploring it and exploiting its natural resources.
> 2. The rights referred to in paragraph 1 of this article are exclusive in the sense that if the coastal State does not explore the continental shelf or exploit its natural resources, no one may undertake these activities, or make a claim to the continental shelf, without the express consent of the coastal state.
>
> *   *   *

Article 5 provides:

> 1. The exploration of the continental shelf and exploitation of its natural resources must not result in any unjustifiable interference with navigation, fishing or the conservation of the living resources of the sea,

nor result in any interference with fundamental oceanographic or other scientific research carried out with the intention of open publication.

* * *

8. The consent of the coastal State shall be obtained in respect of any research concerning the continental shelf and undertaken there. Nevertheless the coastal State shall not normally withhold its consent if the request is submitted by a qualified institution with a view to purely scientific research into the physical or biological characteristics of the continental shelf, subject to the proviso that the coastal State shall have the right, if it so desires, to participate or to be represented in the research, and that in any event the results shall be published.

The negative coastal control authorized by Article 5(8) has significance beyond the parties to the Convention. The United States and an uncertain but probably large number of other states consider that every state has such control over research simply by virtue of the admitted control every state has over the exploration and exploitation of the resources of its shelf. It is perhaps ironic that the United States has taken the initiative to affirm the existence of this aspect of customary international law since it is widely recognized that United States scientists suffer most from the existence of such control. Very few, if any, foreign scientists are affected vis-à-vis research on the United States shelf since there is no evidence of any interest in the United States shelf on the part of such scientists, except for the living resources thereof.

In light of subsequent restraints on shelf research, it is important to recognize that the 1958 Conference acted with ample opportunity to be aware of possible harm to marine science. Even before the Conference convened, the International Law Commission had been made aware of the disquiet among marine scientists over this matter, and the Commission took note, if not account, of this concern. The 1958 Conference itself heard from the International Council of Scientific Unions via UNESCO and from expert consultants retained by the United Nations Secretariat, but these warnings were to no avail.[44] It seems probable that then, as now, the state representatives, to the extent that they considered the problem at all, were too apprehensive over supposed connections between marine science research and commercial prospecting. It also is likely that concern over military implications influenced some states, including the United States, to approve restrictions on shelf research.

The most explicit warning from a state at the Conference itself came from the Soviet Union, which stated (and, as it turned out, predicted) that "if no kind of scientific research into the continental shelf could be undertaken there without the consent of the coastal state, much valuable purely scientific work would be stopped."[45] Fairness requires observing that this prognosis turned out to be prescient partially because the Soviet Union has availed itself of Article 5(8) to refuse consent to some purely scientific work on the Soviet shelf. In 1967, 1969, and 1970, the Soviet Union refused a permit to the University of Washington research vessel *Thomas G. Thompson* to do scientific work on the Soviet shelf. No satisfactory explanation ever has been offered for this behavior by a state which otherwise strongly insists upon freedom of scientific investigation.

A major substantive problem arising from Article 5(8) is the kind of research embraced by the clause "any research concerning the continental shelf and undertaken there." It would be possible to interpret this as all-embracing and to require prior consent for all research into shelf characteristics, features, and resources no matter how such research is conducted. Another possible interpretation, and the one urgently advanced by states strong in marine science, places emphasis on the qualifying phrase "and undertaken there." This phrase seems to connote some kind of physical relationship between the investigative actions and the seafloor constituting the shelf. Additional plausibility is lent to such an interpretation by the communication to the Conference from the Secretary-General of the ICSU, who pointed out that scientific investigation of the seabed, as apart from the " 'exploration and exploitation of its natural resources' does not necessarily involve actual operational contact with the ocean floor." [46]

These alternatives in interpretation and the major policies and factors relevant thereto are discussed in more detail elsewhere.[47] It suffices to note here that the United States (and other states) usually acts upon the restrictive interpretation mentioned previously. The document *U.S. Oceanic Research in Foreign Waters* states:

> Research on the continental shelf includes the removal of the shelf samples (such as by coring and dredging) and of living resources which are unable to move at the harvestable stage except in constant physical contact with the shelf. Research on waters above the shelf or on swimming creatures is not affected.[48]

This definition would exclude measurements of magnetic fields, the taking of sub-bottom acoustic measurements, and the taking of water samples. It is to be noted, however, that this definition is enumerative; it does not restrict the defined research to that having physical contact.

High Seas   Although there is no explicit statement in any of the Geneva Conventions on the Law of the Sea, it is firmly fixed in general expectation that freedom of research on and in the high seas constitutes one element of the freedom of the seas. Article 5 of the Shelf Convention comes closest to explicit recognition in the statement that there must be no interference with fundamental oceanographic and other scientific research. Article 2 of the Convention on the High Seas enumerates four elements of freedom of the seas and then declares that "[t]hese freedoms, and others which are recognized by the general principles of international law, shall be exercised by all states with reasonable regard to the interests of other states in their exercise of the freedom of the high seas." The acceptance of freedoms other than those listed is generally (but not universally) understood to include freedom of scientific research.[49]

Assessing these various general principles, the joint UNESCO–IMCO report on fixed oceanographic stations offered the following "tentative conclusions":

1. Freedom of the high seas includes the "freedom of research in the high seas."
2. No State may exercise exclusive sovereign rights of the high seas for the conduct of research by means of fixed oceanographic stations.
3. No State may restrict the reasonable conduct of such research by other governments or by individuals over whom it has no personal jurisdiction.
4. States are under a duty to ensure that such research undertaken by them or by their nationals is conducted with reasonable regard to their exercise of the freedom of the high seas.
5. A State is permitted by international law to place additional restrictions on the conduct of research on the high seas for its own nationals and vessels, but not for persons over whom the State has no jurisdiction.[50]

These conclusions were offered in the context of the use of buoys or data stations, but they offer a generally accurate summary of international law decisions relating to the conduct of research by any method or device. One caveat may be in order: conclusion 2 refers to a prohibition against "exclusive sovereign rights of the high seas for the conduct of research." Whether or not intended to raise the issue, this reference recalls the controversy generated by the conduct of nuclear weapons tests on the high seas, an activity in which four major states have engaged, and the contention that the preemption of ocean areas involved violated the concept of freedom of the seas. This controversy need not be ventilated further at this stage except to note that one consequence of the controversy was that increased emphasis was placed upon the notion that the rights protected by the concept of freedom of the seas must be exercised with reasonable regard for the activities of others also protected by the same doctrine. It appears to be implicit in this reemphasis that some exclusive use of the high seas is compatible with freedom of the seas. Admittedly, it is highly subjective to identify such permissible exclusive use as that which is "reasonable," but it is surely significant that the notion of "reasonableness" is now expressly incorporated into Article 2 of the Convention on the High Seas.

Except for the continuing contraction of the high seas area itself, which occurs through claims to expansion of various national boundaries irrespective (in practice) of whether or not the claims are lawful,[51] the principal restraint on marine science in this region is prospective at this writing, arising from potential restrictions on science which might be incorporated in a regime for the seabed beyond national jurisdiction. At least four types of problems might emerge: first, increased difficulty in preserving selected high seas areas from human activity or intervention, with the aim of maintaining wholly natural phenomena for baseline and other scientific purposes; second, physical interference with scientific operations by prospecting and exploitive activities, ranging from complete displacement of science to varying lesser degrees of obstruction; third, imposition of conditions precedent to the conduct of research; and fourth, a demand that scientific exploration and investigation comply with the same or similar rules as are applied to such activities for commercial purposes, including application and payment for a license or permit. This last difficulty seems the most formidable and is the subject of later discussion in connection with remedial measures.

Instability in Boundaries   As emphasized in connection with specific areas subject to coastal state control over research, it is obvious that the larger the area of such control, the greater the potential restrictions on such research.[52] Accordingly, two features of the process of boundary claim have great importance for marine science research: the lack of firm agreement on a specific limit for the territorial sea and other limits which makes it easier for states to promulgate successive and differing extensions of this limit (creating uncertainty); and this same lack of agreement seized upon by some states to make extravagant claims to extremely large areas of sea.

Uncertainty attends not only territorial sea limits but also exclusive fishing zones and the continental shelf, a fact that is bound to have a hampering effect upon scientists who conscientiously seek to comply with the requirements of law in the planning of investigations many months ahead of their execution. Cruise tracks conceivably could require alteration to conform with sudden boundary changes and the content of the investigative program may also be affected.

As will be noted later in more detail, the consequences of extreme claims which are seldom recognized formally by other states are especially serious for marine scientists. Indeed, it is probable that proposed investigations within unrecognized areas of internal waters, the territorial sea, or the continental shelf are more substantially affected than are plans for areas admittedly within coastal authority. For this reason, the new 200-mile claims from 1965 to 1971, added to those already existing, are especially notable for the probable negative effect they will have on research at sea.

IMPEDIMENTS CREATED BY THE INTERNATIONAL
LEGAL FRAMEWORK

It does not necessarily follow that because coastal states may lawfully control scientific research in areas under their jurisdiction that such research will be hampered. Beyond the existence of such controls it is necessary to consider how this framework of authority, including the uncertainties of boundary delimitations, actually operates detrimentally upon research. The following discussion concerns, first, internal waters, and, then, all other areas of coastal control. Control over access to internal waters is in some respects a separate problem since entry is more often sought (and sometimes denied) for reasons of logistic support than for investigation. Hence this separate discussion.

Internal Waters The major importance of internal waters arises because ports are virtually always within internal waters, and for public vessels entry usually must be preceded by a request for a port call. Private research vessels are permitted entry into ports as a matter of routine, with arrangements made by the ship's agent in the normal course of events.

As in any instance in which affirmative action by the coastal state may be required for a vessel to enter an area, the need for consent for a port call or other entry into internal waters can be a hindrance simply because the coastal officials may delay consent until so late that approval can no longer be assumed, and alternative or contingency plans must be acted upon. When the contrary assumption is acted upon, to wit, that timely consent has been granted but in fact has not been granted, the consequence can be (and has been) harmful both for the immediate operation (as in penalties for unauthorized entry) and for future operations of the same research ship and even, perhaps, of any research ships with a record of past infractions of law or of unwarranted presumptions of coastal hospitality.

The harmful effects of refusal of clearance for a port call are significant partly because alternative plans could involve large added costs of additional running time for diversion to another port of call. Furthermore, the very possibility of a refusal, often a very real one, means that the entire scientific program must be planned to take this into account. On voyages of long duration at great distances from home port, it obviously is essential for logistic purposes to make port calls, and it is desirable to build in alternatives at the planning stage. When refusals do occur, however, the shift to another port, whether or not pursuant to contingency plans, can and does diminish the scientific effectiveness of the cruise when the alternate port is not equally convenient.

Entry into internal waters is sometimes sought for purely scientific, rather than logistic, purposes, and consent always is required irrespective of the public or private nature of the vessel. In such instances refusal of clearance obviously completely prevents the investigation. Such investigations are occasionally of critical scientific importance (as, for example, the inquiries into the Amazon, which is wholly within Brazilian internal waters) and refusals are serious setbacks to marine science. The detrimental effect of refusals is compounded if the investigation has some time-dependent quality about it, as occasionally is the case.

One final point about port call clearances is that they seem peculiarly subject to extraneous political considerations, considerations which lend added complexity to the problem. Relations between the flag and port states may be strained for reasons having no connection with the ship or its investigations. Sometimes relations between the port state, the flag state, or a third state have such strong, even if momentary, political implications that a port call seems undesirable to coastal officials. Occasionally such tense feelings prevail between rival political factions within the host state that visits by foreign vessels are temporarily forbidden.

Other Areas Requiring Consent for Research   The purpose of this discussion is to indicate the nature of the impediments that emerge from the requirements of consent for research that are common to the territorial sea, the contiguous fishing zone, and the continental shelf. In any particular instance, of course, there is the preliminary question of whether the specific research contemplated does require clearance, and the question and its answer can differ with the region concerned. But for each of these regions, clearances are required, however the circumstances may differ. Hence it is appropriate to speak generally of the effect of this requirement.

The evidence for the degree of obstruction to marine science presented by the present legal framework is, unfortunately, more fragmented and less direct than is desirable.[53] Nonetheless the conclusion can fairly be reached on the basis of this evidence that marine science now is substantially impeded by legal barriers to research and that, when the future is considered, these barriers are likely to increase. A number of factors suggest the dimensions of the difficulty for marine scientists including:

Diversion of Time, Resources, and Money
Deterrence of Projects and of Requests for Clearances
Influence upon Nature, Scope, and Methods of Marine Research
Denials of Clearances
Indications of Private and Public International Concern
The Creation of a Regime for the Deep Seabed

Diversion of time, resources, and money   Although no comprehensive measuring stick or gauge exists, it is believed by U.S. government personnel, on the basis of their experience in working with scientists and research vessel operators, that the latter are required to devote substantial time and planning effort to the task of complying with foreign laws governing research. For operators of public vessels in the United States (this includes the several universities and laboratories that conduct research using vessels owned by the federal government) research clearances must be secured through the State Department and private vessel operators are advised that this avenue is highly desirable. Whether operators utilize this route or not, it is necessary for the applicant seeking a clearance to provide the host state with the information required by its legislation and to comply with any other conditions imposed by the coastal state. Types of information and conditions are increasing in number and complexity, and institutions are finding them increasingly difficult to meet. The Brazilian requirements are probably the most onerous to date (1971), and include a great deal of information.[54]

Other conditions involve both the execution of cruise plans and certain steps to be taken on completion of the expedition. An increasingly common demand is that a coastal representative be on board during the stay in or over areas subject to coastal jurisdiction. This alone is hardly objectionable, especially if the representative is a scientist; but too frequently valuable time is diverted from the research operation in order to take the representative aboard and then to return him to a convenient place. After completion of the cruise it is expected that a report on the investigation will be forthcoming. More recently, this wholly reasonable condition has been expanded to a demand that a duplicate of all data and all samples be given to the coastal state. While all data can be produced, this turns out to be expensive in the case of large computer printouts, and there is some doubt that in its raw form the data is of much use to coastal state officials (as distinguished from coastal scientists, who most often are nonexistent). The demand for samples can be particularly vexing since some cannot be shared without giving them up altogether. Since this could defeat the purpose of part or all of an investigation, this condition alone creates concern over the value even of engaging in the operation.

In sum, the burden of complying with coastal state conditions to grant a clearance diverts both time and money in sometimes substantial amounts from use in the major purpose of the enterprise—scientific investigation. On occasion, the demands are so onerous that many research operators are said to have been forced to cancel previously planned cruises into the areas claimed to be within the jurisdiction of certain states.[55]

Deterrence of projects and of requests for clearances   It is reasonable to speculate that because of anticipated clearance difficulties often the decision is made not to seek a clearance for a project and, accordingly, to decide not to undertake the project. Such instances probably exceed cases of denial of clearances. The frequency of this behavior obviously is difficult to establish except by directly interrogating scientists and so far as is known such an inquiry has not been undertaken. Situations do come to light for one reason or another to indicate that deterrence does take place. Some instances of this occur when the prospects of securing a clearance are so patently dim or even nonexistent that proceeding with a clearance request clearly is not worth further effort. The easiest situation to document occurs when the Department of State advises a research operator that a clearance either cannot or should not be requested, and the applicant makes no request. This is known to happen, but, understandably, the frequency of occurrence is not publicly available. It is not difficult to imagine, either, why such advice is sometimes given. To take the most innocuous instance, for example, when an institution does not make its request in a timely fashion, it may be reasonable to conclude on the basis of past experience that it is useless to initiate an application to the particular coastal state. Even when the request is timely it may happen that preliminary inquiries to coastal state officials elicit such discouraging responses that there is no point in pursuing the matter. Such negative reaction can be associated, for example, with unhappy past experiences with a particular institution.[56]

Various kinds of political situations, perhaps wholly extraneous to the investigation, also may account for discouragement of a clearance request. For example, in the case of port calls, it is United States policy not to make requests to South Africa due to the policy and practice of that state in regard to discriminatory treatment of nonwhite crew members of visiting vessels. But sometimes the political overtones do relate more or less directly to a question concerning the investigation. One of the more common situations involves United States policy toward clearance requests for research in an area claimed by the coastal state but not recognized by the United States. In the case of states claiming a 200-mile territorial sea, a claim rejected by the United States in common with about 95 percent of the world, it would be wholly inappropriate to seek a clearance for research since the area is widely considered part of the high seas. The pamphlet *U.S. Oceanic Research in Foreign Waters* qualifies for the understatement-of-the-decade award in offering the following advice to operators contemplating research in such waters: "[t]he Department of State can advise operators of research vessels of claims to offshore jurisdiction and explain the difficulties vessels may encounter because of such claims." [57] Since the explanation presumably points out the possibility of being fired upon by armed ships and aircraft of the coastal state, followed by arrest and delay of the vessel, confiscation of data and perhaps equipment, and, finally, heavy fines, it is not inconceivable that the roster of "difficulties" would have the effect of discouraging the conduct of research without a clearance. The dilemma is perhaps seen more clearly by the operator when he understands that it is not known to be United States practice to offer active assistance at sea to a vessel in these circumstances (although diplomatic assistance is given). As Dr. Schaefer so elegantly put it, scientists "ignore such extended claims at their own peril." Since virtually the entire South American continent is enveloped by 200-mile claims (though not all to territorial sea), the possible frequency of this situation is evident. Extraneous political considerations can affect clearance requests no matter what particular region is concerned, *i.e.,* no matter whether a port, the territorial sea, or the continental shelf. Plainly the absence of a requirement for a clearance would remove or substantially alleviate the influence of such factors in preventing research.[58]

Another set of circumstances, resembling the foregoing, arises when the research vessel operator inquires at the State Department (or other clearance agency) and, on discovering the obstacles (including the numerous conditions some states impose), decides not to request a clearance. This instance differs from the previous one in that the Department does not seek to discourage the operator, merely to inform him. Nonetheless, the operator determines that the project does not merit the expenditure of time, effort, and money entailed by complying with the clearance procedure and its aftermath. By the nature of the circumstances, it is next to impossible to establish the frequency of this occurrence. Generally the only indicia are the inquiry and a failure to act. Since the latter could result from a great variety of causes, this combination alone is not particularly revealing. State Department officials believe, nonetheless, that some operators do decide to forego a particular project after being informed of the requirements of a clearance. The difficulties, red tape, and delays occasioned by clearance requirements have by now become so clear to some scientists and research institutions that they decide on their own not to undertake some projects. Again, no one can know, short of formal inquiry to scientists and institutions, how often projects are deterred by this consideration, but it is certain that such decisions have been made.[59] It is highly probable that if the continental shelf is extended as far as the edge of the continental rise, especially if this occurs by way of unilateral action, the deterrence effect probably will become rather common. The reason is, simply, that as sometimes onerous coastal state conditions are extended to increasingly larger areas, scientists will be even less inclined to undertake projects subject to such conditions. Projects involving drilling into the seabed will be particularly affected.

A final instance of deterrence, which cannot be documented satisfactorily, involves inquiry directly from scientist to coastal state. Again, facts such as these do not normally and easily come to light, but situations are known to have occurred when the response from coastal officials has been sufficiently discouraging that no clearance request has been subsequently made.

Influence upon nature, scope, and methods of marine research
It is more pernicious than shocking to realize that plans for research

cruises and projects are sometimes importantly, if not wholly, determined by legal requirements, rather than by scientific criteria and judgment. Speaking of the effects of coastal state regulations, Ambassador Donald L. McKernan stated that "[m]any cruises are altered after substantial planning has taken place and, in several instances within the past two years, early consultations have led to substantial changes in plans which undoubtedly reduce the effectiveness of research cruises." [60] It is perhaps equally significant to note that even initial planning may sometimes take into account that legal/political factors override valid scientific judgment. For example, investigators may realize that it is not possible to permit the vessel to take advantage of investigative opportunities revealed or discovered by virtue of research previously carried out during the same cruise, assuming this opportunity requires entry by the vessel into an area claimed by the coastal state but unrecognized by the flag state. As indicated, in such a situation the vessel will not have a coastal clearance and therefore proceeds at its own risk. Accordingly, even in the initial planning the cruise track may be laid out rigidly and without allowance for opportunistic investigations indicated by contemporary research.

Methods of investigation also are influenced by clearance requirements. As suggested previously, bottom sampling on the continental shelf probably requires a clearance no matter how distant the samples may be from providing commercially useful data. In order to avoid the difficulty of securing a clearance and particularly of complying with the conditions attached to it, planners may and do decide to forego research involving bottom contact and consequently limit themselves to other methods of inquiry.

The need for a clearance even in disputed areas may force an investigator to do research merely to secure one. This happens because the Department of State will not request a clearance for a disputed area (such as a territorial sea claim greater than three miles). This may be illustrated by the procedures employed by some scientists in securing a clearance when they wish to work in the outer reaches of a claimed 200-mile territorial sea. To avoid difficulties in the disputed area, a clearance is requested for research within three miles of the coast, this being the territorial sea by any criterion. In using this device, the scientist must do the proposed research, even though this may entail the unnecessary expenditure of many hours of the ship's operational time to move near the coast in order to do scientific work for nonscientific purposes. In addition to doing unwanted research, which may or may not be useful, the money cost of such extensive diversion of ship time runs into several thousand dollars per day. This costly procedure has the effect of not giving recognition to a disputed claim.

Finally, it follows from what already has been said about deterrence that the choice of entire investigative opportunities is now occasionally determined by the need to get a clearance. Plans for surveys of shelf areas

adjacent to numerous states have been dropped simply because of anticipated clearance difficulties. In sum, the choice of research projects already
is decisively affected, perhaps in substantial degree, simply by the recently
created or emphasized need for clearances in certain coastal regions.

Denials of clearances   Outright rejection of a clearance for a proposed project certainly is the most drastic barrier that coastal states may
erect to marine science research, but, as has been indicated, this probably
is not the most significant measure of the impediments to such research.
Unfortunately, there are no reliable data on the frequency of rejection on
a worldwide basis, and the data for the United States have not been fully
analyzed. However, we do have the testimony of Ambassador Donald L.
McKernan (as of November 1968 and more recently in a letter he has
made public) that, since 1967, the problem for United States scientists
has noticeably worsened. In November 1968, at a State Department brief-
ing, Ambassador McKernan stated that after January 1967 there was a
very significant increase in the number of requests rejected. From January
1967 to November 1968, there were twelve known cases of refusal of
clearances of United States public and private vessels (although undoubtedly there were more, as private vessels sometimes deal directly with
the foreign government). This contrasts sharply with the experience of
earlier years, when grant of a clearance was virtually automatic and the
conditions for the grant were seldom demanding.

Since 1968, the number of outright rejections has declined somewhat,
with but six outright refusals from January 1968 to mid-April 1970. Of
course, as already suggested, this diminution does not mean that, in overall
perspective, marine research is any less impeded; the other factors already
discussed suggest that the problem is more, not less, severe. Moreover, the
decrease in the number of rejections must be understood in the context of
a vastly increased effort by the Department of State to assist in formulating
acceptable clearance rejects and in cutting losses by advising researchers
when it is futile to make a request.

It may be emphasized that the preceding figures on rejections are also
conservative interpretations of the records. For example, these figures do
not include instances in which a favorable reply to a request is received
too late to be of any use. Such replies are rejections for all practical purposes, since often the vessel has been diverted to an alternative operation.
Similarly, the imposition of virtually impossible conditions is not here
labeled a rejection, though it might well be considered such. If these and
similar instances were considered refusals, the number would be considerably larger.

Indications of private and public international concern   There is
ample evidence from a number of sources that the difficulties for marine
science research are shared by scientists and states around the world. The

principal international private organization of marine scientists is the Scientific Committee on Oceanic Research (SCOR) of the International Council of Scientific Unions, and in June 1968 the Executive Committee of SCOR made the following statement to demonstrate the worldwide concern of scientists over impediments to certain research:

> Evidence is accumulating that the Convention on the Continental Shelf, now ratified by many maritime nations, is on occasion being applied so as to hinder scientific investigation of the circulation of ocean waters, the biology of the sea floor, the origin and movements of continents, and other problems of considerable .scientific importance. Accordingly, SCOR decided to ask its Members, National Committees and their parent organizations, to urge their governments to adopt liberal interpretations of the articles of this Convention in order to facilitate the carrying out of oceanographic research.[61]

Even before the 1958 Geneva Conference adopted the Shelf Convention—indeed before the International Law Commission finally formulated its draft rules on this subject in 1956—the ICSU had warned of the dangers to marine science implicit in this Convention.[62] The SCOR statement thus records the fulfillment of these early expressions of apprehension.[63]

Somewhat more recently the joint working party on the Scientific Aspects of International Ocean Research, composed of scientists nominated by SCOR, ACMRR, and the Advisory Group on Ocean Research of WMO, appeared to go out of its way to take note of the difficulties for marine science caused by coastal state regulation. In its report entitled *Global Ocean Research* (the so-called Ponza Report), the group addressed certain questions posed by the Bureau of the Intergovernmental Oceanographic Commission (IOC), among which was: "In what geographical areas of the world's oceans will increased research efforts make the best contributions in solving these problems (*i.e., the most important research problems that should receive particular attention in the near future*)?" In answering this query, the Ponza group recognized, albeit obliquely, that coastal states sometimes are not hospitable to research and that the effect is to hamper scientific understanding of natural phenomena:

> While ocean research activities can be carried out on the high seas by suitably manned and equipped ships of any nation, in coastal waters there may be imposed some restrictions on research. Yet the distribution of the natural phenomena usually bears no relation to the limits established by man. Full understanding of these phenomena cannot be obtained if their investigation is unduly impeded.[64]

The record of misgivings over coastal state impediments to research is written much larger, naturally, in the proceedings of public international bodies. Fittingly, the IOC, which was established for the express purpose of promoting scientific investigation of the ocean, serves as the principal forum for this expression. In January 1967, after earlier discussion in the IOC, the U.S.S.R. took the initiative and proposed that the IOC seek, *inter alia,* to elaborate a general convention embodying principles for safe-guarding marine science research. At the fifth session of the IOC in the following October, the Commission reacted to this initiative and gave expression to its concern by creating a Working Group on Legal Questions Related to Scientific Investigations of the Oceans. The Working Group's function was not to prepare draft treaties, but essentially to prepare the way for resolution of the problems by

> preparing documentation concerning the effect of the law of the sea on scientific research and proposals relating both to the contribution of scien-tific knowledge to the development of the law of the sea, and to the par-ticipation of the IOC in the deliberations of the United Nations and ap-propriate specialized bodies to assist them in taking proper account of scientific interests and scientific knowledge in the consideration of the further development of the law of the sea.[65]

The Working Group has met *twice* as of this writing and its actions, which have been controversial within the IOC, establish beyond peradventure that states regard marine science and legal restraints thereon as of major importance to them.

The most striking demonstration of international concern over this problem in the IOC came during its sixth session in September 1969, which witnessed the first major confrontation between the developing states, who often are opposed to freedom of research, and the states advocating such freedom. As will be discussed shortly, this group clashed over the issue of an IOC procedure [66] (embodied in a proposal formulated at the first meet-ing of the Working Group) by which states might be aided in securing and in granting clearances for research in areas subject to coastal jurisdiction. For present purposes, however, the more significant clash came about because of the proposal to revise the Statute of the IOC to provide that one of the organization's purposes is to promote freedom of scientific in-vestigation. The controversy engendered by this proposal has dual signif-icance since it reflects both the deep concern of the developed states over the plight of marine science and the apprehensions of the developing states that the conduct of such research prejudices their interests. Both groups felt so intensely about this issue that the invariable practice of making decisions in IOC plenary sessions by means of a consensus and without a formal ballot was cast aside on this occasion in favor of a roll-call vote on this revision. It so adequately measures the intensity of the disagree-ment that, when the developed states prevailed and the revision was adopted, some of the developing states declared their intention to carry the opposition to the October–November 1970 session of the UNESCO General Conference, which has the ultimate authority to dispose of proposed amendments to the statutes of its subsidiary bodies, including the IOC.[67]

The creation of a regime for the deep seabed   As is well known, the question of a legal regime for exploitation of the seabed beyond the limit of national jurisdiction has been before various bodies of the United Nations since 1967 and has led to the creation of the Committee on the Peaceful Uses of the Seabed and the Ocean Floor beyond the Limits of National Jurisdiction. For present purposes, the importance of the Seabed Committee discussions lies in their indication of inhospitable state attitudes toward research. (In the next section we examine the substantive problems involved in subjecting research in this area to a control system.) Although directed at high seas areas beyond national control, the concerns expressed by various states in Seabed Committee discussions over supposed undesirable consequences of scientific research are almost certainly applicable to, and probably derive from, research executed in areas subject to national jurisdiction. The 1969 Report of the Legal Subcommittee of the Seabed Committee demonstrates that this attitude was made explicit by some states:

> 64. The view was set forth that, since the marine environment constituted a whole, some rights of coastal States should be recognized with regard to research carried out in areas of the seabed which are adjacent to their national jurisdiction, so that research in the seabed is not used as a pretext for research on the continental shelf without the consent of the coastal State, as required by Article 5, paragraph 8, of the Geneva Convention.[68]

If this attitude is translated into law, the present controls over research on the continental shelf may be extended far beyond that area out into the deep seabed.

Remedial Measures

The principal means by which impediments to research might be lessened or removed include governmental actions on both the national and international levels. Measures within a nation-state, mostly as supplementary to international action rather than exclusive in nature, include unilateral measures designed to lessen restraints on research within the context of assurances to safeguard coastal interests. International actions may be concerned solely with marine science research or only with such research as is ancillary to other problems of ocean use.

Nation-state measures embrace arrangements varying in inclusiveness of participation and in comprehensiveness of subject matter. At one end of the spectrum is a general international convention embodying prescriptions for all the legal problems involved in the conduct of marine science, while at the other pole are the bilateral agreements providing for research in a specific subject area of marine science. Between these extremes are agreements among varying numbers of participants, regional or worldwide, but limited to specific problems, such as the proposed Treaty on Ocean Data Acquisition Systems, or specific procedures, such as the arrangement for using the good offices of the IOC to facilitate the securing of clearances.

The ancillary type of international action concerns the inclusion of specific provisions about scientific research in agreements dealing with other substantive matters in ways which could or do have negative implications for research. Examples of this are the 1958 Continental Shelf Convention and the impending international negotiations regarding the policies and principles applicable to mineral exploitation in the seabed and ocean floor beyond national jurisdiction.

Multilateral Agreement

GENERAL AGREEMENT ON A CONVENTION ON SCIENTIFIC RESEARCH IN THE OCEAN

The earliest proposal for a general international agreement for safeguarding the community interest in marine science inquiry in the ocean appears to have originated with the Soviet Union. At the meeting of the Bureau and Consultative Council of the IOC in 1967, the Soviets proposed a two-pronged approach to what it believed were imminent legal problems of ocean use: the development of a treaty for ocean mineral exploitation and an agreement on legal principles for scientific research. Although members of the IOC did not respond favorably to these proposals (except as this Soviet initiative led to the IOC Working Group on Legal Questions), it was echoed in somewhat more detail within the United States by the National Commission on Marine Science, Engineering, and Resources. In *Our Nation and the Sea* the Commission recommended in January 1969 that the United States take the initiative in pursuit of a general international agreement embodying the following:

> (1) Scientific research in the territorial waters or on and concerning the continental shelf of a coastal nation may be conducted without its prior consent, provided that it is notified of the objectives and methods of the research and the period or periods of time during which it will be conducted, in sufficient time to enable the coastal nation to decide whether it wishes to participate or be represented in all or part of the research; and provided that the investigators agree to publish the results of the research.

(2) Fisheries research (including the limited taking of fish specimens) may be conducted in the exclusive fisheries zone of any coastal nation under the same conditions.

(3) Research submersibles may be used in the conduct of authorized scientific research in territorial waters, even if they do not navigate on the surface as the Convention on the Territorial Sea and Contiguous Zone now requires them to do, provided that the coastal nation is also notified of the time, place, and manner of their use sufficiently in advance to assure safety of navigation.

(4) Research buoys may be placed in any coastal nation's territorial waters. Buoys so placed, as well as those placed in the superjacent waters of the continental shelves or in the high seas beyond the continental shelves, shall be protected against unwarranted interference from any source. The coastal nation, however, may specify reasonable requirements for location, lighting, marking, and communications with respect to buoys placed in its territorial waters.[69]

At this writing it is extremely doubtful whether states generally, perhaps even the United States and the U.S.S.R., are inclined to seek a treaty of this type. There is very little evidence that the general community of states places any particular weight on resolving this set of problems in this fashion. There is, on the other hand, very persuasive evidence that most states do wish to convene a conference to deal with numerous other problems attending development of the ocean and its resources. At this writing, the results of the Secretary-General's survey of states on this issue, a survey called for by General Assembly Resolution 2574 (passed in December 1969 at the Twenty-fourth Assembly), are not available, but it would come as a small surprise if a majority of states do not call for the rather early convening of such a conference.[70]

In these circumstances some cautionary comments on the proposed general treaty on scientific research in the oceans are worthwhile. Although such an agreement would seem highly desirable if it did in fact safeguard research in a satisfactory manner, the prospects for realization of this goal are not bright if a proposed agreement were on the agenda of a general international conference to revise the Law of the Sea. For example, it is quite doubtful, at least under the present state of affairs, that the principles proposed by the Marine Science Commission for such an agreement will find easy acceptance by states generally and by developing states in particular. It is more likely that, given a two-thirds voting requirement to approve proposed treaty provisions, a blocking third of states would be rather easily constituted whereby provisions allowing genuine freedom of research would be effectively opposed at such a conference. Indeed, the most likely result is that two-thirds of the states at such a conference would succeed in agreeing on new and severe restrictions on research.

The rather obvious course is to refrain from any effort to negotiate an agreement of this sort in the same meeting that attempts to resolve other ocean problems, since to proceed in this manner probably would be near disastrous for marine science. The better course of action is to continue to pursue such an agreement in the more limited forum of the IOC, where the prospects are better for meaningful protection at least among the member states. Even here, of course, there will be strong opposition by some states to effective measures to facilitate research, but, generally speaking, all members of the IOC realize the value of research to all states (developed and developing), and the possibilities of meaningful compromise are better in this context. Where such compromise proves impossible, the chances also are better that the necessary votes will be there for overriding the opposition, for whatever value this might have.

GENERAL AGREEMENT ON A PROCEDURE TO FACILITATE SCIENTIFIC RESEARCH IN THE OCEAN

A more specialized and limited international action for facilitating research consists of the creation of a mechanism for simplifying the task of getting consent for research in areas over which a coastal state exercises jurisdiction. It was to this task that the first meeting of the IOC Legal Working Group devoted special attention, culminating in a proposed resolution setting out a procedure by which the IOC might supplement individual state efforts to secure clearances for research. This resolution (Resolution VI–13) came before the sixth session of the IOC, and after lengthy and detailed consideration the Commission modified the proposed procedures but still agreed that its Secretariat could be called upon to assist states in obtaining clearances. Some scientists in the United States are reported to have expressed alarm over what they regard as an additional level of unnecessary bureaucracy being introduced into the clearance process. The following comments on Resolution VI–13 hopefully will provide some clarification, however, indicating that the IOC Resolution authorizes but minor involvement by the IOC Secretariat and suggesting also some interpretations of the Resolution (attached hereto as the Appendix).

Compulsory Nature of IOC Procedure   The reported apprehension about the IOC involvement in securing clearances apparently rests on the belief that because of Resolution VI–13 a requesting state always must enlist the aid of the IOC, thus making the IOC procedure compulsory. Both the Resolution itself and the nature of the IOC establish that the Resolution has no such effect. First and most basic, the IOC has no authority to adopt regulations binding on member states. Indeed, it is believed by some states that the IOC does not even have the authority to draw up a draft treaty dealing with this or any other topic for later action by states. Whether or not this view has merit, the fact is that the Resolution is not a "treaty" or "international agreement" imposing a binding obligation on states to comply with its terms. Second, one of the preambular paragraphs of Resolution VI–13 was adopted for the express purpose of affirming the primacy of the usual bilateral methods: "Taking into account that specific cases of obtaining consent for conducting scientific research in areas falling under the national jurisdiction of coastal states are usually resolved between the interested states. . . ." Participants in the discussion understood this paragraph to mean that the IOC procedure "was not intended to supersede the usual bilateral arrangements on such matters. . . ." [71]

The only potential compulsory effect of Resolution VI–13 would come if some coastal states insisted that this IOC procedure must be employed by requesting states instead of by taking a direct route. It is of course not inconceivable that some states might insist on the former course, but to complain of this possibility seems fruitless, since a coastal state always could insist on outside assistance whether or not Resolution VI–13 had made an IOC procedure available. Even now, any coastal state, IOC member or not, can require that clearance requests be appraised by some designated third party as a condition to favorable consideration by the coastal state. In light of this possibility, also by no means inconceivable, requesting states might well prefer compulsory use of the IOC procedure, which has the advantage of establishing conditions found acceptable to coastal states and states heavily engaged in scientific investigation at sea. It should be said, of course, that presently there are no indications that any coastal state desires to make the IOC procedure compulsory.

At the same time it is reasonable to expect that some states, particularly developing ones, will take advantage of this procedure to obtain IOC assistance. As noted by the IOC Working Group on Legal Questions Related to Scientific Investigations of the Ocean, the guidelines it recommended for use in implementation of Resolution VI–13 would have a "tendency . . . to enhance the role of the Commission in facilitating the conduct of scientific investigations by its Members, and the participation of coastal states in such investigations." [72]

Notice Requirement The key provisions of IOC Resolution VI–13, spelling out the notification procedures to be employed, call for the following:

(a) As soon as a tentative decision to carry out a research programme is made, the coastal State shall be informed in a preliminary manner to ensure that it may, if it so desires, be associated, from the preliminary steps, with the planning of the programme and arrange for early contact between interested scientists;

(b) A formal description of the nature and location of the research programme shall be submitted to the coastal State and to the Commission as soon as possible in order to enable the coastal State to respond formally as far in advance as possible and in order to enable the coastal State to participate effectively in the research programme. . . .

The Legal Working Group proposed, in contrast, but one notice to the coastal state, and solely for the purpose of setting in motion the coastal state's machinery for processing clearance requests. IOC Resolution VI–13 now calls for a two-step notification, one very early and preliminary and designed to facilitate coastal planning for participation in the research program, and a second designed both to elicit a response consenting to the proposal and to permit effective participation by coastal state scientists. In sum, the emphasis has shifted from involving the coastal state primarily for securing the necessary consent (with secondary importance attached to scientific cooperation) to facilitating a genuine participation and involvement by coastal scientists in all or some of the proposed program of research. If the states concerned, both requesting and requested, do act in light of this apparent change, the consequences could be salubrious for science and for political relations generally. Genuine participation by coastal scientists would add to the store of their knowledge of adjacent regions, which could have beneficial effects upon resource development at least over the long run and might help to alleviate some of the suspicion and distrust which have tainted political considerations of ocean problems.

The evidence for this shift consists of (1) the requirement for informing the coastal state as soon as a tentative decision is made to carry out a research program and (2) the omission, in this instance and in the later detailed notice requirement, of any specific timetable for advance notice. It is reasonable to infer, however, that the preliminary information should be forwarded at least six months prior to the cruise, preferably earlier, and that the formal description should be forwarded at least sixty days in advance. Compliance with a schedule of this order, if not in exact detail, should facilitate clearances by giving coastal authorities ample time both to permit planning for desired participation and to allow officials to check as needed into the nature of the proposed program.

That this timetable requiring early notice will introduce difficulties for some vessel operators is not inconceivable, and in this connection two comments are pertinent. First, it may well be that cruise planners, by devoting particular attention to the matter, can significantly accelerate the time at which a tentative decision on a research program can be communicated to affected coastal states with some assurance that the program will be executed. It also is conceivable that some complaints by scientists about early notice requirements are not wholly justifiable and that the additional attention to this matter is not an unreasonable request at all.

Second, even if some inconvenience or added administrative burden results from these notice provisions, it is a very small price to pay for securing a clearance. It is not at all improbable that no consent would be forthcoming unless some such notice provisions were observed.

The Role of the IOC   According to paragraph (c) of IOC Resolution VI–13, upon receiving a formal description from the requesting state of the nature and location of the research program, "[t]he Secretary of the Commission, shall transmit the formal description so received to the coastal State within twenty days of receipt together with the Commission's request for favourable consideration and, if possible, with a factual description of the international scientific interest in the subject prepared by the requesting State, supplemented, if he considers this desirable, by the Secretary." The primary object of this terminology appears to be to establish a means for certifying the bona fides of a particular investigation without imposing simultaneously a great and probably impossible burden on the IOC Secretariat by requiring it to engage in an evaluation of each research request sent to it. In this sense the IOC Resolution satisfies, and even improves upon, the recommendation of the United States National Committee to SCOR that "the most useful role for the Intergovernmental Oceanographic Commission in facilitating clearances for research vessels undertaking fundamental scientific research would be passive in nature." [73] The National Committee spelled out what it meant by "passive" in suggesting that "the IOC, upon receipt of requests from member states for research clearances, would immediately transmit them to the concerned coastal state, certifying (when such is found to be the case) that statements are included in compliance with" enumerated conditions concerning handling of data and samples, publication of results, and participation in the research by the coastal state.[74] The IOC Resolution seems to be more satisfactory than the U.S. recommendation since it calls for an automatic favorable recommendation, justifying that by requiring the requesting state to submit a statement of the international scientific interest in the research program described. This statement, supplemented by the IOC Secretary if he thinks it necessary, is then quickly transmitted to the coastal state, thus providing an additional element of support for the bona fide scientific nature of the proposed program.

One of the guidelines recommended by the Legal Working Group at its second meeting dealt with the role of the Secretariat:

It would be desirable for the Secretary, if requested by the coastal State, to supplement the factual description prepared by the State planning the scientific programme. In preparing such a supplement the Secretary should draw on the resources and skills available to the Secretariat, including the assistance of the Commission's scientific advisory bodies and when

necessary, if time and funds permit, the assistance of experts in the subject of the research in question.[75]

The report of the meeting further reflects the Working Group's awareness
of the risk that these procedures could be unduly time-consuming. Thus:

> The Working Group felt that while the effective application of Reso-
> lution VI–13 would place increased responsibilities on the Secretariat, this
> must not result in delays in obtaining the Commission's assistance, where
> sought. The Secretary stated that everything possible would be done to
> avoid delays.[76]

Quite plainly, the IOC Resolution calls for minimal but meaningful involvement by a central international agency and is thus but a small step
away from the normal route of direct state-to-state interaction. When and
if the guidelines become effective, this involvement may become more
intense. As international institutions evolve, growing in experience, capability, and depth of resources and skill, it will be worth a new appraisal to
determine whether a more positive role might better facilitate marine
science research.

Data Handling   Another significant feature of Resolution VI–13 is
that dealing with the method of handling data and samples as between the
investigators and the coastal state, as per paragraph (e):

> The coastal State will have available to it as soon as possible all data from
> such research, including data and samples not feasible to duplicate; special
> arrangements shall be made regarding the custody of data and samples not
> feasible to duplicate.

Initially, of course, it is the researcher who obtains the data and samples
and who uses them for the purposes of the inquiry being undertaken. But
in recognition of the coastal state's interest in the materials acquired during the investigation, including the data about the environment and samples from it, the investigator must make these available to the coastal
state. In instances of data or samples which can be replicated, the matter
is merely one of the timing of furnishing copies. For items not feasible to
duplicate, the Resolution anticipates that normally they will remain in the
hands of the investigator while still being made available to the coastal
state. That this arrangement would be expected seems to flow rather
naturally from the fact that data and samples normally are in the possession of the investigator who acquires and examines them and, further,
from paragraph (e): "special arrangements shall be made regarding the
custody of data and samples not feasible to duplicate." In the absence of
special arrangements, the investigator would retain possession and in any
event would retain ownership even if custody is granted to the coastal

state in accordance with a special arrangement. The important point is not these technical details but support of scientific research whoever is carrying it out.

It merits special note that no specific time period is mentioned in this provision—merely that data be made available, as per paragraph (f), "as soon as possible." As they should in regard to all other aspects of Resolution VI–13, scientists would be well advised to assure as far as they can that data is made quickly available. Legalistic insistence on the lack of a precise timetable should not be used to justify tardiness in this phase of cooperation with the coastal state. Continued laxity in this regard is virtually certain to result in continued or new restraints on research. Developing coastal states already are exceedingly sensitive to the way they are treated by governments and research institutions of states doing research off their coasts. Many are aware that IOC Resolution VI–13 emerged as a consequence of efforts by developed states to ease restrictions on marine research. Those developing states responded to this initiative by acquiescing in the procedure of IOC Resolution VI–13, apparently hopeful of gaining from the research so facilitated. If these procedures are not substantially complied with, the resulting disappointment could well take the form of further interference with research.

Publication Paragraph (f) of Resolution VI–13 provides that "[t]he results of such research programmes shall be published as soon as possible in an open internationally distributed scientific publication." Again, no timetable is established, but genuine effort to accelerate publication of results may turn out to be critical in encouraging coastal states to agree to research.

REGIONAL ARRANGEMENTS

Less inclusive arrangements than those just discussed would also be useful, including remedial measures for application on a regional basis or among a limited number of states. The only attempt in this direction thus far is that of the International Council for the Exploration of the Sea (ICES). It has not been a resounding success, though efforts continue to take some cooperative action designed to facilitate certain research.

Initial discussion within the ICES of potential difficulties for some continental shelf research occurred in 1964, immediately after the Shelf Convention came into force. As a result of this discussion "[t]he Council decided to seek the cooperation of its member governments in ensuring that the work of research vessels of member countries should not be impeded, and it offered, if that should be the wish of the members, to assist by compiling a register of vessels regularly engaged in scientific investigations on behalf of member countries." [77] After the responses of all members were reviewed, "it became clear that, while they were not prepared to waive their rights under the provisions of Article 5, paragraph 8, of the

Convention, they all would wish to see that conventional and traditional research should not be impeded." [78] Accordingly, the Council, at its 1967 Statutory Meeting, adopted the following proposal:

> 1. The International Council for the Exploration of the Sea will provide a list of research vessels of the member countries, regularly engaged in scientific investigations. The list will contain such data for each vessel that are needed for identification.
> 2. Annual cruise programmes will be exchanged between member countries, with the understanding that any member country is free to require a change to be made in the proposed programme of work on its Continental Shelf, if it so wishes.
>   The cruise programmes will indicate, as far as possible, where they will impinge on the Continental Shelf and mention specifically any proposed research on the sea floor.
> 3. On the basis of the List of Research Vessels and the Cruise Programmes, the member countries are prepared to give, through a national office or agency which they will authorize to act on their behalf, general permissions in cases of routine scientific sampling and other probing of the seabed and subsoil and of the bottom fauna by means of grabs and dredges and similar devices.
> 4. In the case of seismic tests and research involving the use of seismic charge, specific application to undertake such research will continue to be required in each case, and such research will always be dependent upon prior permission.
> 5. This Agreement is without prejudice to the provisions of the Article 5(8) of the Geneva Convention on the Continental Shelf, 1958, and it is on the understanding that recourse may be had to a stricter interpretation at any time.
> 6. Copies of Cruise Programmes and the general permissions will be deposited in the office of the General Secretary of the International Council for the Exploration of the Sea.[79]

Unfortunately, even this extremely cautious, albeit potentially helpful, approach was not acceptable to all members. Before the 1969 Statutory Meeting, the Soviet Union notified the Council that it could not accept the Council's proposal, quoting the Decree of the Supreme Soviet dated February 6, 1968, from which the conclusion apparently was drawn that "to seek the permission for conducting research on the USSR continental shelf it is required [that there be] application to the Soviet competent authorities through appropriate channels for each case." [80] At the 1969 Statutory Meeting itself, the 1967 proposal did not secure approval, but plainly there is a rising concern among ICES members about this problem:

> Some delegates said that they felt the situation with respect to conventional research activities on the continental shelf was gradually getting

worse. This means that the efficiency of such joint efforts which have become traditional in the Council's area, will be impeded. They said that this introduced a note of urgency in the matter and that those of the member countries which would wish to collaborate along the lines indicated earlier by the Council, should find a way to do so.[81]

In the end, it was agreed that the Council's services would be offered "to those members who would be in a position to adopt a standard procedure. . . ."[82] Thus, though the ICES apparently is unable to undertake joint action among all its members, it is possible that some of them will join to adopt measures to remedy impediments to their research.

Bilateral Agreements

Although the conclusion of bilateral agreements is among the least inclusive of international remedial actions, such a course may be particularly useful at the present stage. Relations between states of course vary from one bilateral relationship to another. Hence, there are special advantages to agreements that can be fashioned to take these nuances into account. Furthermore, since there is some urgency to removal (or prevention) of undue restraints, the conclusion of bilateral agreements initially may be most desirable because of the length of time necessarily involved in achieving more inclusive understandings. A further advantage of bilateral agreements is that of acquiring the knowledge and experience that assist in dispelling the suspicion and distrust which sometimes hamper broader agreements.

One particular element of the proposed bilateral agreements on marine science research that might be particularly worthwhile is agreement on a definition of marine science research. One such formulation conceives marine science research as comprehending "scientific programs of observation, collection and measurement intended to permit a description of the oceans, their physical interfaces and their contents, or to improve understanding of processes operating in the marine environment." Additional elements of the bilateral agreement might include provisions for, *inter alia,* making data and samples available or accessible, timing of notification for various purposes, port calls, participation or representation in the research program and its planning, and publication of the results of the investigation. Hopefully, a pattern of agreement on both a substantive definition and these procedural aspects might contribute to achieving broader international agreement on an appropriate conception of marine science research.

The United States already has employed this bilateral method in facilitating one specific type of marine research—namely, fisheries. In a series of agreements with Poland, the U.S.S.R., Mexico, and Japan, provision is made for cooperation in expanding marine science research on both a national and joint basis with respect to fisheries of common concern or in particular regions. In implementation of these general provisions, some foreign research vessels operate in areas subject to United States jurisdiction from which they would otherwise be forbidden entry for this purpose. Some of these agreements also contain provisions for facilitating entry of foreign public vessels into United States ports, within the limits of applicable laws and regulations.

Unilateral Action by the United States

Not all remedial measures depend upon negotiations to persuade other states to cooperate. The United States can and should take certain actions unilaterally, actions which could assist in freeing scientific research in the ocean.

The Committee on Oceanography of the National Academy of Sciences formulated a recommendation for such unilateral action, as recorded in the following position paper of April 28, 1970:

> The Committee on Oceanography and its International Marine Science Affairs Panel have been concerned with the problem of maintaining freedom of scientific research and exploration of the sea and the seabed. The Committee and the Panel have actively cooperated with the federal agencies in pursuing certain limited international actions which might facilitate such research and exploration. The Committee and the Panel believe that other governmental measures must be initiated for this purpose and propose that the United States government announce that henceforth it will freely permit scientific research in areas subject to U.S. jurisdiction and that no permit will be required except for investigations in internal waters. In order to be satisfied, however, that research vessels in these areas do properly conduct bona fide scientific activities and that the results of their work are available to the U.S., the following assurances should be observed so that the United States shall:
> (1) Be given reasonable advance notice, a period of 60 days probably being adequate.
> (2) Have the opportunity to participate in the research and exploration and have access to all equipment, compartments and instruments aboard the vessel.
> (3) Have the right to receive copies of all data on request, and the right of access, for study, to all samples not feasible to duplicate.
> (4) Be assured that significant research and exploratory results will be published in the open scientific literature.
> (5) Be assured that the scientific exploratory activities will present no hazard to the resources or uses of the sea or seabed (e.g., seismic explorations that could damage fish stocks, or exploratory drilling that could result in petroleum pollution).
> The Committee and the Panel believe that bold unilateral action sub-

stantially similar, but not necessarily identical, to this recommendation could well be effective in demonstrating the advantages to all states of encouraging free and open scientific research and exploration. We hope that appropriate officials in our government will consider this recommendation and explore the possibilities of such an initiative by the U.S. government.[83]

Unilateral action of this type, perhaps with alterations in the detailed conditions or assurances, might provide a dramatic demonstration by the United States of its recognition of the importance of free ocean research. It is particularly fitting that the United States take this initiative since its position of world leadership in the actual conduct of ocean science should be paralleled by equivalent leadership in general support of freedom of scientific inquiry and, specifically, in removing or lessening restraints on such research. In any event, urging developing nations to take this action seems unlikely to be successful in view of their deep suspicions of the motives of the more developed states. A demonstration by the United States, wholly without regard to any advance commitment of reciprocal action, would appear to be the best approach, since a number of desirable consequences might reasonably be expected to follow from action of this type.

In the first place, such a bold unilateral initiative could be extremely effective in demonstrating the advantages, both to the United States and any other states so acting and to states generally, of encouraging free and open scientific research and exploration. If one or two states take this means of welcoming scientific research and exploration in areas under their jurisdiction, it might soon become more widely apparent that this is a very economical means of acquiring information of especial value to the coastal state. Whether or not any other state takes similar action, the removal of restraints would be beneficial to the United States and to other states if other states take advantage of this action to expand their research into the areas concerned.

A further initial impact, hopefully lasting, could be a dissipation of the suspicions attached to American scientific expeditions operating in areas subject (or allegedly so) to the jurisdiction of other states. If the United States demonstrates its willingness to enable foreign scientists to operate in similar areas of the United States, subject only to minimum and nearly universally accepted safeguards, this might well create a greater trust in our own activities abroad.

Although not conditioned on reciprocal action by others, it is of course conceivable, and certainly to be welcomed, that American unilateral action might induce similar action by other states, opening up regions now either closed completely or restricted by vexing conditions and uncertainties. Unilateral action by the United States might provide a substantial argument to foreign scientists who may wish to persuade their governments to reduce national obstructions to foreign research. Most marine scientists, if not their governments, are entirely aware of the high value to be placed on freedom of inquiry and also are cognizant of the substantial benefits to be gained from foreign scientists' working in adjacent waters. The opportunity to participate in the planning and implementation of such work provides real benefit to local scientists, and whether or not participation is feasible, the information and data thus made available can be a measurable contribution to the scientific work of coastal state scientists.

It also is not inconceivable that unilateral action could encourage the conclusion of bilateral agreements between the United States and other states. Some states may feel themselves unable to take unilateral action of their own but still be inclined to make formal arrangements to the same end. Given a display of United States goodwill toward foreign scientists, some states might well believe that by agreement with the United States a coastal state could assure itself of procedures and principles that satisfactorily meet its interests and requirements and, at the same time, reduce obstructions to scientific efforts in its waters.

A further consideration, more long run than others, is that unilateral action of the kind described here could bolster the general position the United States should assume in the future, as usually it has in the past, of genuine commitment to, and vigorous support of, the concept of freedom of the seas. It continues to be in the interest of the United States and the entire world, including developing states, to maintain the oceans open to utmost freedom of use, with restraints imposed only when reasonable exercises of freedom are less productive of values than imposition of a form of exclusive control by a nation-state or international agency. Leading American international legal scholars concur in urging that the United States reaffirm its support of freedom of the seas and are specific in advocating the widest possible freedom for marine science research. Unilateral action by the United States to promote freedom of scientific investigation would lend credibility and substance to its voice and influence in confronting the coming challenges to a meaningful freedom of the seas.

Another, not inconsiderable, advantage of unilateral action is in the flexibility it permits in adjusting ongoing policy to unfolding experience. If for some reason another nation somehow abuses the freedom accorded by the policy of liberalizing access, it would be relatively simple for the United States either to change or retract completely its unilateral action. In particular, if the various assurances should prove inadequate to protect reasonable exclusive interests, it would be wholly a domestic, not an international, decision to supplement them by other or different safeguards. In this sense, unilateral action is more advantageous to the United States than international agreement.

In assessing the merit of proposed unilateral moves by the United States, it obviously is necessary to weigh potential disadvantages. Three in particular stand out.

The major category of possible liabilities of this action may be subsumed under the notion that the response of other states will be unsatisfactory and actually inhibit the removal of restraints on United States research in foreign waters. Thus, it might be suggested, in opposition to unilateral action, that such action would forfeit a bargaining position of value to the United States in seeking bilateral agreements to remove impediments to research. The contention would be that another state has nothing to gain in agreeing to permit United States research in its waters if the United States already has conceded free entry to foreign scientists to areas under U.S. jurisdiction. However, this objection appears far more formidable than actually it is since consideration of the actual negotiating situation reveals that the U.S. bargaining position would be unaffected by unilateral action. So far as the United States is concerned, the reason for negotiating with other states is not, for practical purposes, to enable foreign scientists to do research within regions subject to U.S. jurisdiction (since most states do not have that capability) but, rather, to secure access for American scientists to foreign waters. In such a context, the United States forfeits nothing by unilaterally permitting foreign scientists to operate free of a permit. On the other hand, for those states having the capability of doing research adjacent to the United States, negotiations would in all probability be between states with the same interest, *i.e.,* freeing research from coastal state impediments. In this context, the problem would be that of resolving some relatively specific details, not that of securing agreement on the basic policy of freedom of scientific inquiry. Hence, a unilateral move to promote such freedom does not hamper negotiations or prejudice a bargaining position since probably there would be no fundamental difference of opinion or attitude on this matter and therefore no real bargaining situation.

Another possible unsatisfactory response is that unilateral moves would constrain foreign scientists preferring bilateral agreements as devices to pressure their own governments to adopt more liberal policies with regard to foreign scientists. It is difficult to answer this concretely in the absence of information about the preferences of foreign scientists. On the other hand, it is not unlikely that they resemble those of U.S. scientists who are known to recommend that their government take unilateral action to promote freedom of research for all scientists. United States marine scientists who have been heard on this matter thus far apparently believe that it is desirable to move on all fronts to enhance this freedom. In particular, they believe that unilateral action will not remove pressure on the U.S. government to negotiate bilateral agreements to resolve the problem.

Another suggested undesirable response that some might anticipate is that unilateral action will generate suspicion of United States motives. Of course, this would be directly contrary to the intended effect of United States unilateral action. While it is true that few states are capable of doing research off U.S. shores, there are some that are nonetheless so capable and do such research, although now usually beyond U.S. jurisdiction. Accordingly, there is no basis for assuming that the United States actually is trying to get something for nothing. In the end, the existence of suspicion about motives probably does not get one very far. Some states already are highly suspicious of U.S. motives in conducting research and in using various avenues for removing restraints on research. Some states also may react with suspicion to a unilateral move. Others, however, may see in this an expression of commitment to the value of freedom of research and perceive that the United States now generally recognizes the particular usefulness of this freedom.

On balance, none of these objections appears sufficiently weighty to justify rejection of liberalizing United States policy along the lines proposed by NASCO.

A New Law of the Sea Conference: Negotiations About Marine Science

There probably are very few people left who do not now believe that a new Law of the Sea (LOS) Conference will be convened relatively soon to consider some new legal problems of ocean use and, probably, to renegotiate some problems previously resolved.[84] So far as marine science is concerned, we already have noted the expectation that it would be hazardous for continued meaningful freedom of exploration to attempt negotiation of a general treaty on this subject at such a conference. Even if such an agreement could be concluded in a form acceptable to the developed states, the likely prospect is that the parties to it would be predominantly those states with a capability for undertaking such research, leaving the waters surrounding entire continents without treaty protection for scientific activity. It is distinctly possible, too, that developing states could conclude an agreement imposing severe restrictions on marine research.

It is virtually certain that the agenda of a new LOS Conference will contain items that raise some specific questions about interference with marine science. Accordingly, there really is no way to avoid confronting the need for devising prescriptions which minimize (or even remove) obstruction or interference with scientific research at sea. The following comments consider revision of the Continental Shelf Convention, revision of the High Seas Convention, and creation of a seabed regime. In each instance we are concerned with impacts upon marine science.

REVISION OR REPLACEMENT OF THE
CONTINENTAL SHELF CONVENTION

There are two features of the Shelf Convention that have special significance for science: first, the expanding boundary definition, with the prospect that through time coastal controls over resources will continue to move outward; and second, the confusing provisions concerning sovereign rights over exploration and exploitation of the natural resources of the shelf, the prohibition of "any interference with fundamental oceanographic and other scientific research carried out with the intention of open publication," and the requirement for consent to research concerning the shelf and undertaken there.

There can be little serious question that marine science research would benefit if states agreed to place a narrow limit on the continental shelf and did not concurrently extend coastal authority in some other manner over ocean floor resources beyond such a limit. Unfortunately, nearly every important proposal on this matter within the United States either projects a "wide" shelf (such as to the edge of the continental margin) or recommends a narrow shelf coupled with extension of some coastal control beyond the shelf for purposes of exploration and exploitation of natural resources.

Certainly a landmark pronouncement within the United States regarding the shelf was that of President Nixon on May 23, 1970, proposing a new agreement (supplementing, but not replacing, the 1958 agreement) which would provide for a very narrow shelf but which would permit the coastal state to exercise certain unspecified authority as trustee for the international community in a further area out to the edge of the continental margin.[85] The President's statement itself did not expressly address the scope of coastal control over marine science in the trusteeship zone (hereinafter designated as TZ), and at a news conference the Legal Adviser to the Department of State reportedly was unable to clarify this matter, stating that while the Department was zealously concerned to protect freedom of scientific inquiry, this matter was one of many details not provided for in the presidential statement. Subsequently, however, this omission was sought to be remedied, or so it seems. In testimony on May 27, 1970, before the Special Subcommittee on the Continental Shelf of the Senate Interior Committee, then Under Secretary of State Elliott L. Richardson apparently implied that in the TZ, in the United States view, the coastal state would not have the same controls over scientific research as over the shelf. In explaining the rationale for the 200-meter shelf limit proposed by the President, Mr. Richardson characterized the proposal as one for "narrow limits of national sovereign rights." [86] He added that "[f]or the United States to propose a concept of broad extension of national jurisdiction would have indirect, but serious, national security implications, and *would impede the freedom of scientific research* and other uses of the high seas." [87] Accordingly, it seems fair to conclude that the United States will propose that scientific research in the TZ should not require coastal consent as it does on the continental shelf.[88]

A 200-meter limit on the shelf proper is of course as narrow as could be proposed with any prospect of acceptance, and in this sense marine science would benefit. However, it is very difficult to understand how the United States proposes to persuade other nations to permit research in the TZ without the necessity of a permit. On the face of it at least, the same considerations which are adduced to support a consent requirement for shelf research appear available for a similar requirement in the TZ. It is difficult to see why merely crossing the magic 200-meters depth line suddenly will dispel coastal concern (however unwarranted) over research activities in an area subject to coastal control over exploration and exploitation. To the contrary, since coastal and international revenues still would be affected by activity in the TZ, it would be surprising if both coastal and noncoastal states did not insist on extending the consent requirement to this additional area. This conclusion is only reinforced by considering that the coastal state may be especially interested in assuring itself that research activities present no hazard to the environment or living resources therein. In sum, the likely outcome of the United States proposals for a 200-meter limit plus a trusteeship zone extending to the continental margin is that coastal controls over research will be extended at least to the latter limit and conceivably beyond.

If, however, the United States is to oppose a mandatory permit for certain research in the TZ, it also should be the overriding policy of the United States to eliminate entirely or to minimize substantially this requirement as regards shelf research. On the same reasoning as above, if a permit ought not be required at 201 meters' depth, there is no justification for it at 200 meters. Deletion of Article 5(8) of the Shelf Convention obviously would contribute to this end but would not be sufficient. In providing that each coastal state has exclusive rights of exploration of its shelf, it is reasonably plain that even without Article 5(8) some, perhaps many, coastal states would forbid even bona fide scientific research on their shelves on the ground that it was inconsistent with that state's exclusive right to explore (which, it would be claimed, is indistinguishable from scientific research). Accordingly, the only certain way of freeing scientific research is to abolish the coastal state's exclusive right of exploration. Unfortunately, it does not seem at all likely that coastal states are prepared to relinquish their newly acquired sovereign rights of exploring and exploiting the natural resources of the shelf. The question, thus, is how to acknowledge this right while minimizing its impact on bona fide scientific research.

One desirable alternative would be to secure the deletion of Article 5(8), with its express requirement of consent, and to substitute therefor a requirement for notice of certain intended research. The coastal state would continue to be authorized to refuse to allow the research, but affirmative objection would be required. In the absence of objection within a stated period after timely notice, the particular research would be considered authorized. It might be helpful in this connection to insert a provision in the revised Convention recognizing the importance and value of freely conducted scientific research regarding the shelf.

Another alternative is to maintain the present formulation of Article 5(8), but to continue to improve on the procedures by which clearances for research are obtained. As experience develops with the use of the IOC procedure discussed earlier, ways for strengthening this avenue should be explored with a view to improving it. Observations on this matter were made previously.[89]

REVISION OF THE HIGH SEAS CONVENTION

A principal improvement in the High Seas Convention is to remedy the failure to mention "freedom of scientific research" as one of the freedoms expressly embraced by "freedom of the seas" (as defined in Article 2 of this treaty). There can be no serious question, despite the contentions by a few of the developing states, that the conduct of research has been regarded in the past as an exercise of one of the protected freedoms. Nor can it be reasonably doubted that it is in the genuine common interest of all states, developed or developing (or whatever), to promote the utmost freedom of access to the ocean for this purpose. Accordingly, it may be beneficial to emphasize the high value of this particular freedom by its express provision in a new convention on the High Seas.

REGULATION OF SCIENTIFIC RESEARCH ON THE SEABED BEYOND NATIONAL JURISDICTION OR CONTROL

The two primary considerations which account for the contemporary concern over research over the deep seabed are, first, the expectation that such research will provide economic benefit only to developed states while inflicting economic loss upon developing states, and, second, the apprehension that research will cause damage to the ocean environment, including the resources therein. The former arose earlier and is primarily responsible for the agitation surrounding the topic of ocean resources, but concern for the environment adds a new dimension of importance for certain restricted types of research operation.

The principal problem in this instance is not to devise remedial measures for unfettering research, since research is now free in this vast region, but to safeguard deep sea research while at the same time promoting and protecting other uses of the area. The objective should be to provide for maximum freedom of investigation consistent with reasonable protection of other uses and the environment. Highest priority attaches to freedom of research; hence, restrictions on such freedom should require demonstration of their necessity for protecting other uses. No restrictions should be imposed on research unless a strong case is established for its necessity. At the present time, no one, whether representing a state, international organization, or private entity, has made a case for any restrictions on scientific research in order to safeguard mining operations in the area beyond national jurisdiction. The only restriction which thus far seems reasonably well supported by social need pertains to the conduct of research activities which might pose some threat of harm to the ocean environment or resources, and it requires emphasis that only very few such activities have any implication of harm. Scientists are of course as concerned as anyone else to avoid environmental damage, and there can be no serious doubt that reasonable regulations to this end would be welcomed in the scientific community.

Despite the lack of justifiable concern over the incompatibility of scientific research with commercial operations, there are suggestions that research should no longer be unrestricted and should, instead, be subject to a number of conditions. The 1969 Report of the Seabed Committee suggests the scope of some of these restrictions which are spelled out in more detail in the annexed Report of the Informal Drafting Group. The latter's Report states:

Item 5. Freedom of scientific research and exploration.
26. After consideration of the several formulations it was decided to separate the main elements which are:
    (i) Freedom of scientific research (for peaceful purposes) without discrimination and avoidance of interference with such research;
    (ii) Communication beforehand of programmes of scientific research. Different methods were mentioned in the proposals: (a) publication; (b) accessibility; and (c) dissemination;
    (iii) Communication of results of scientific research. The different methods mentioned under (ii) were also suggested for (iii);
    (iv) Promotion of international co-operation. Two suggestions were made: (a) participation of nationals of different States in common research programmes; and (b) strengthening of the research capabilities of the developing countries;
    (v) Encouragement by States of their nationals to follow the practices concerning communication of information regarding programmes and results;
    (vi) No rights of sovereignty or exploitation are implied in the carrying out of scientific research.
27. The examination of the proposals indicated the existence of three different approaches as to the relationship between element (i) and other elements. The first approach would state independently the freedom of scientific research and such other elements as may be agreed upon. The second approach predicted that these other elements should

be stated as necessary consequences of the freedom of scientific research. The third approach would make freedom of scientific research conditional upon publication beforehand of research programmes and upon the accessibility of the results of these programmes with the least possible delay.[90]

The following comments consider the impact of the first four of these elements in terms of their possible effects on scientific research if they were imposed as obligations to be discharged by states or research institutions.

Freedom of Scientific Research As formulated by the Informal Drafting Group, this "element" does not appear as an obligation which might impose restrictions on research. Appearances, however, are often deceptive, and the appearances here should inspire caution among unwary observers. What seems an unexceptionable statement of unquestioned principle may have a harmful effect. Accordingly, it should occasion no surprise that in the Legal Committee some delegations were able to endorse freedom of research and also to point out that freedom does not mean license and, hence, that imposition of a number of restrictions on research is not really incompatible with freedom of research. Indeed, according to the Legal Committee Report, these delegations observed that "no freedom was absolute" and that, one may imply, to impose preconditions on research was merely to assure that the exercise was not "abused" and was "exercised with reasonable regard to the interests of other states." In other words, the unquestioned existence of freedom of research establishes that certain conditions on such research also must be accepted since they inhere in the principle of freedom of research.

It must be readily conceded that freedom of use never has meant the complete absence of conditions on engaging in an activity. However, in the Law of the Sea the conditions on freedom of use are those required to make such use reasonable. Whether any particular condition has this effect depends on assessing its impact on the activity in question in relation to the social goal it purports to achieve, the degree to which it might achieve such a goal, and the cost involved. It seems reasonably obvious that a priori reasoning such as described in the previous paragraph is no substitute for such an appraisal. Similarly, insistence that other exercises of freedom of the sea are subject to certain conditions prescribed by treaty does not demonstrate that freedom of research must be subject to still other different conditions. There is no escape, if minimum rationality in inquiry is to be preserved, from a deliberate weighing of the need and value of restrictions on scientific investigation.[91]

Prior Communication of Programs of Scientific Research Apparently the object of this "element" is to create a system whereby states, on behalf of public and private agencies, would give notice of some kind that a particular program of investigation would be undertaken. In the view of some, according to the Legal Committee Report, notification would be an obligation to be discharged as a condition to the freedom to engage in research. The Report does not indicate any means for enforcing this condition, such as by limiting investigations not preceded by notice of the required kind, although presumably some such sanction was in mind.

It is clear from the portion of the Legal Committee Report already quoted that some of the delegations opposed this suggested condition as a considerable obstacle both to the conduct of research and to international cooperation in this effort. The effect of this type of condition also has been assessed by the International Marine Science Affairs Panel (IMSAP) of the Committee on Oceanography of the United States National Academy of Sciences. The Panel concluded:

> The condition of advance notice constitutes a significant reduction in the flexibility of research planning. If coupled with the necessity for specific consent to be granted upon receipt of the advance notice, this restriction could serve to eliminate some useful research programs. If a detailed requirement for advance notice is strictly enforced, it will be impossible to conduct many types of investigations envisioned for the International Decade of Ocean Exploration and other international cooperative investigations.[92]

In short, the cost of imposing an advance notice requirement for scientific investigation would be to hamper planning of future programs. Such a requirement also could completely prevent certain research if strictly enforced or if coupled with a consent requirement. On the other hand, the gains from such notice seem highly problematical unless some additional steps by the agency or group notified are anticipated, such as participation in the program. Even if participation were made theoretically possible by this requirement, the effects of such an obligation would constitute a high cost in relation to the frequency of actual participation, since the latter probably would be minimal. In sum, there is reason for grave doubt that the problematical gain from being notified of deep sea research comes anywhere near justifying the detrimental effects of a notification system.[93]

Communication of Results of Scientific Research   Not many scientists, if any, would be prepared to argue against open publication of the results of a research cruise, but a great many would urge rejection of a proposal that publication of results be made a compulsory obligation. As desirable as publication of results usually is, there are instances in which the outcome of an investigation does not warrant the effort and expense required to publish. Anyone who has done research of any kind is aware that the fruits of the labor involved often are so insubstantial that their exposure would do more harm than good, including of course harm to the investigator.

There is the additional question of what is embraced by the term "results." It is not at all inconceivable to include in this concept the raw data and samples that are acquired by the research operator. In this situation, implementing a compulsory disclosure requirement becomes both costly and complicated. Modern research ships collect data and samples very rapidly, and processing them requires considerable time and money. The result is that there are likely to be delays in disseminating the data, and the cost of doing so can become a burdensome expense. In its assessment on this point, IMSAP points out, additionally, that "the inevitable delays in meeting these conditions may be interpreted as indicating bad faith on the part of the operating institutions." Samples are a special problem since, obviously, they cannot always be duplicated for sharing with others. The solution is to make them accessible to those interested, but this, too, may pose considerable difficulties in implementation.

The sum of the foregoing is that the detrimental impact of a publication requirement is not insubstantial and suggests that distribution of results of cruises might better be left to the discretion of the individual operator. At the same time the latter should be strongly encouraged to publish his results and data as fully and as soon as practicable.

Promotion of International Cooperation   No one openly opposes international cooperation in marine science, and, so, the members of the Legal Committee understandably found this element "unquestionable." Presumably, such unquestioning acceptance implies that the reference to participation in research does not imply any obligation upon the researcher to seek out and accept participants from other states. However, the earlier element calling for notification of planned research suggests the possibility that permitting participation might be regarded by some as the obligation of the researcher. Required participation has, however, several substantial drawbacks. IMSAP called attention to the following:

> The opportunity to participate in research may cause a reduction in the number of scientists from the supporting institutions because most research vessels are relatively small and overcrowded. This relates to the problem of advance notice in that LDC's, while wishing to participate, have very limited numbers of qualified scientists and observers, and accordingly request the greatest possible lead notice in order to arrange their participation. The logistic requirements involved in embarking and disembarking observers or visiting scientists may reduce significantly the ship time available for conducting research.[94]

The latter point particularly deserves some emphasis. Diversion from the ship's cruise track to take on participants can sometimes be substantial, calling for loss of a day or more of extremely expensive operating time. An obligation to permit participation in deep seabed cruises may be an onerous burden also because of the delays and administrative complexities that would very likely ensue in implementing the scheme. In addition to delays in picking up participants, it is not unlikely that the process of arranging for such participation would occupy an extended period.

OTHER PROPOSALS

Other suggestions, not embraced in the Seabed Committee Report, include the proposal that a scientific research activity should be registered with an international agency and a nonexclusive permit obtained. The precise details of such registration might of course vary over a considerable range. Some suggest that the procedure would be the same as for commercial operations, including the payment of a fee. The thought underlying this suggestion is that so far as hazard to the environment is concerned scientific research into the deep seabed does not differ from commercial operations. Similarly, it is suggested that if a commercial operator should be required to disclose the information he gathers, after a delay to protect him, the same obligation should apply to a scientific researcher a fortiori.

The difficulty with these proposals is that they threaten to add administrative inconvenience and delay to all kinds of scientific research involving the seabed even though only a minor segment of such research poses any threat of damage to the environment and though almost none has any significant potential for conflict with other uses. At present, for example, only one state, the United States, has any capability for drilling into the deep seabed, and this activity is only one (but highly important) form of conducting deep seabed research. In view of the current agitation over environmental harm, U.S. scientists can be expected to take every precaution to avoid activities that might harm the environment. It is probable that scientists of other states will share and act upon this concern in similar fashion. A general requirement for registration and the securing of a permit would contribute very little, if anything, to protecting against damage but would complicate the task of investigation.

Suggestions for requiring registration plus a nonexclusive permit sometimes do not provide that the registering authority will have discretion to refuse to issue a permit, except as the applicant may fail to meet standards of operation related to environmental protection. In such a conception, the authority could not refuse a permit because of the area involved or the methods to be employed or the type of program selected, but it might refuse a permit if the research vessel were not properly equipped for safeguarding the environment from the effects of its planned research operations. Other suggestions, however, seem to anticipate that the registering authority should be able to review the proposed scientific program and deny the permit if, for example, the authority deemed the program "suspect" as a possibly disguised commercial operation.

It hardly needs to be stated that a system of the latter kind is far too restrictive of research to be desirable in the community interest. Even the

Economic and Technical Subcommittee of the Seabed Committee appeared to recognize that the initial phase in mineral resource development, which is termed "acquisition of basic knowledge," should be governed by the principle of freedom of research. To subject research activities to a discretionary international authority would in practical effect hand over marine research to the control of an international agency. Even if the discretion so conferred were carefully circumscribed by conditions for its exercise, the possibilities of interference appear far too great to commend this arrangement.

Conclusion

The preceding discussion is incomplete without at least brief reference to the draft Convention on the International Seabed Area, tabled by the United States at the United Nations Seabed Committee meeting in August 1970 as a working paper for discussion purposes. With one exception, the provisions in this treaty seem satisfactory insofar as they are concerned specifically with marine science research at sea. The "basic principles" seem to be directed at assuring that all activity beyond the 200-meter isobath, which generally is the inner limit of the International Seabed Area (ISBA), is free and open with the exception of exploration–exploitation activities for natural resources of the ISBA and, so far as science is concerned, except for deep drilling, which is subject to special regulations. Ocean inquiry would thus be left as unrestricted as any other activity in the ISBA.

Among the "general rules" in the draft, Article 24 is specifically directed at scientific research:

1. Each Contracting Party agrees to encourage, and to obviate interference with, scientific research.
2. The Contracting Parties shall promote international cooperation in scientific research concerning the International Seabed Area:
   a. By participating in international programs and by encouraging cooperation in scientific research by personnel of different countries;
   b. Through effective publication of research programs and the results of research through international channels;
   c. By cooperation in measures to strengthen the research capabilities of developing countries, including the participation of their nationals in research programs.[95]

This provision, if accepted, would appear to provide for freedom of scientific investigation at sea. It is perhaps pedantic to note, therefore, that it does not affirm that freedom in so many words. At the same time, research also is not subjected to any conditions (precedent or subsequent).

A good deal could be said by way of detailed commentary on this Convention from the viewpoint of scientific research. By way of conclusion, however, it is worthwhile to question whether the freedom for research that would be permitted by this draft can be expected to survive the negotiations that will be required to reach eventual agreement. The draft itself, of course, does not supply any reason to believe that coastal states will refrain from demanding certain controls over research in the trusteeship zone proposed herein.

But beyond the uncertainties attendant upon the inevitable bargaining over the innumerable details of the regime proposed in this draft, there is uneasiness about a related matter. Sooner or later, states generally may begin to realize that the United States is proposing for the region beyond 200 meters what is, in essence, a complete vacuum of political authority except as may be exercised pursuant to this treaty or pursuant to subsequent treaties. The idea apparently is to eliminate any evolution of law by customary methods and also to refrain from establishing any organized international means for timely creation of any needed regulation. Inasmuch as the direct regulatory authority permitted by this treaty, whether to the trustee state or to the International Seabed Resource Authority, is limited completely to activities of exploration–exploitation of certain extractive resources, it appears that all other activities are removed from the authority of any political body except as subsequently may be agreed upon or as individual states may control their own nationals. This means, for example, that in the TZ, the coastal state will be unable to regulate activities by non-nationals which involved installation of structures on the seabed so long as they do not unreasonably interfere with exploration and exploitation. It is hardly open to serious doubt that such structures can be built within this limitation; hence, under the present draft the structure, its inhabitants, and the activities thereon could be beyond any political authority whatsoever.

It is at least possible that nations and perhaps some of the component states of the United States will not be enthusiastic about a proposal which so firmly ties their hands from dealing with activities in nearby waters which could have a harmful impact in the coastal zone. If states do begin to question the desirability of the regulatory vacuum which would appear to exist if this draft Convention were made effective, it is not inconceivable that they will insist on more extensive coastal authority in the proposed trusteeship area. Once this process begins, it would not be an overwhelming surprise if controls over seabed research were included in demands for more comprehensive coastal authority.

These few concluding remarks are limited to the draft treaty and marine science. They suggest, however, some of the incongruity of a Convention proposal that creates an extremely elaborate institutional structure to deal only with a single use of an area, parts of which may well be subjected in the near future to relatively intense multiple uses. In these days of common recognition of the utility of multiple use regulation, the draft treaty seems an anomaly indeed. Fortunately, the United States intended the draft as a basis for discussion. Such gaps as exist can be remedied, and, in the process, this draft very likely will have to be modified considerably if it is to provide an adequate body of law for activities in the regions adjacent to land.

Appendix

Promoting Fundamental Scientific Research (Previously Dr. 19)

The Intergovernmental Oceanographic Commission,

Recognizing that in accordance with Article 1, Para. 2, of the Commission's Statutes its main function is: ". . . to promote scientific investigation . . . of the oceans, through the concerted action of its members,"

Taking into account that physical, chemical, biological and geological phenomena are closely interrelated throughout the ocean and observe the laws of nature,

Bearing in mind the interests of mankind in the field of scientific research, with particular reference to the interests and needs of the developing countries,

Taking into account that specific cases of obtaining consent for conducting scientific research in areas falling under the national jurisdiction of coastal States are usually resolved between the interested States,

Taking note of the Summary Report of the IOC Working Group on Legal Questions Related to Scientific Investigations of the Ocean, established by Resolution V–6,

Being of the opinion that it is desirable that the procedures to obtain the consent of a coastal State for carrying out of fundamental scientific research in the areas over which jurisdiction is exercised be simple and effective,

Observing that any steps which might be taken in this regard are not intended to impair the sovereign rights of States,

Considers that the Commission should assist in promoting fundamental scientific research that is carried out either in the framework of the Long-Term and Expanded Programme of Oceanic Research or within Declared National Programmes. This assistance regarding areas of national jurisdiction will be subject to the following principles:

(a) As soon as a tentative decision to carry out a research programme is made, the coastal State shall be informed in a preliminary manner to ensure that it may, if it so desires, be associated, from the preliminary steps, with the planning of the programme and arrange for early contact between interested scientists;

(b) A formal description of the nature and location of the research programme shall be submitted to the coastal State and to the Commission as soon as possible in order to enable the coastal State to respond formally as far in advance as possible and in order to enable the coastal State to participate effectively in the research programme;

(c) The Secretary of the Commission shall transmit the formal description so received to the coastal State within twenty days of receipt together with the Commission's request for favourable consideration and, if possible, with a factual description of the international scientific interest in the subject prepared by the requesting State, supplemented, if he considers this desirable, by the Secretary;

(d) The coastal State, if it so desires, will participate in such research programmes as arranged between the interested States;

(e) The coastal State will have available to it as soon as possible all data from such research, including data and samples not feasible to duplicate; special arrangements shall be made regarding the custody of data and samples not feasible to duplicate;

(f) The results of such research programmes shall be published as soon as possible in an open internationally distributed scientific publication;

Invites interested Member States to act in a spirit of international cooperation, to consider favourably and to facilitate within the framework of national laws and regulations the requests for vessels conducting fundamental scientific research to make port calls;

Recommends that the Working Group continue examining the question in the terms of the above-mentioned resolution, and report back on it at the VIIth session.

Notes

1. *See* Brown, *Freedom of Scientific Research and the Legal Regime of Hydrospace,* 9 INDIAN J. INT'L L. 327 (1969); Schaefer, *The Changing Law of the Sea— Effects on Freedom of Scientific Investigation,* in THE LAW OF THE SEA: THE FUTURE OF THE SEA'S RESOURCES, PROCEEDINGS OF THE SECOND ANNUAL CONFERENCE OF THE LAW OF THE SEA INSTITUTE 113 (L. Alexander ed. 1968); Sullivan, *Freedom of Scientific Inquiry,* in THE LAW OF THE SEA: NATIONAL POLICY RECOMMENDATIONS, PROCEEDINGS OF THE FOURTH ANNUAL CONFERENCE OF THE LAW OF THE SEA INSTITUTE 364 (L. Alexander ed. 1970). *See also* W. BURKE, INTERNATIONAL LEGAL PROBLEMS OF SCIENTIFIC RESEARCH IN THE OCEANS (1967); Burke, *Law and the New Technologies,* in THE LAW OF THE SEA: OFFSHORE BOUNDARIES AND ZONES, PROCEEDINGS OF THE FIRST ANNUAL CONFERENCE OF THE LAW OF THE SEA INSTITUTE 204 (L. Alexander ed. 1967).

The most authoritative "observers" have been the members of the Marine Science Commission, composed mostly of private citizens. The Commission concluded that a new international framework for marine science inquiry is required and, in addition to recommendations for such a framework, proposed interim steps for facilitating research. *See* COMMISSION ON MARINE SCIENCE REPORT, ENGINEERING AND RESOURCES, OUR NATION AND THE SEA, H. R. DOC. NO. 42, 91st Cong., 1st Sess. 201–05 (1969).

2. *See* text following note 82 *infra* for recommendations of the National Academy of Sciences and its Committee on Oceanography.

3. A brief statement on this point is to be found in COMMISSION ON MARINE SCIENCE REPORT, *supra* note 1, at 1–4.

4. U.S. NATIONAL COUNCIL ON MARINE RESOURCES AND ENGINEERING DEVELOPMENT, MARINE SCIENCE AFFAIRS, A YEAR OF TRANSITION, THE FIRST REPORT OF THE PRESIDENT TO THE CONGRESS ON MARINE RESOURCES AND ENGINEERING DEVELOPMENT 97 (Feb. 1967) [hereinafter cited as 1967 MARINE SCIENCE COUNCIL REPORT].

5. *Id.*

6. *Id.* at 98.

7. PRESIDENT'S SCIENCE ADVISORY COMMITTEE, REPORT OF THE PANEL ON OCEAN-OGRAPHY, EFFECTIVE USE OF THE SEA 91 (1966).

8. 1967 MARINE SCIENCE COUNCIL REPORT, *supra* note 4, at 65.

9. INTERNATIONAL OCEAN AFFAIRS 2 (1967).

10. The following is a particularly vivid expression of this notion:
    The concepts of the entirety of the ocean, the great complexity of ocean-ology as a science, the interaction and interdependence of all the phenomena and processes which take place in the ocean must be basic to long-period oceanic and oceanological research programs. The concept of the entirety of oceanology follows from the entirety of the work substance—the World Ocean—from the entirety of its waters with their physical and chemical properties, the entirety of its floor and the life which populates it. (NA-TIONAL COMMITTEE OF SOVIET OCEANOGRAPHERS, THE SCIENTIFIC BASIS OF THE 10-YEAR GLOBAL OCEANIC RESEARCH PROGRAM.)

11. COMMITTEE ON OCEANOGRAPHY, NATIONAL ACADEMY OF SCIENCES–NATIONAL RESEARCH COUNCIL, OCEANOGRAPHY 1966, at 18 (1967) (emphasis added) [herein-after cited as 1967 NASCO REPORT].

12. The same may be said of virtually everything else in the oceans, especially of plant and animal life.

13. UNESCO, Intergovernmental Oceanographic Comm'n, Draft of a General Scientific Framework for World Ocean Study 37, U.N. Doc. IOC/89/k (1964) [here-inafter cited as Draft Framework]. Part One of this document was prepared for the IOC by the Scientific Committee on Oceanic Research of the International Council of Scientific Unions. Part Two was prepared for the IOC by the Advisory Committee on Marine Resources Research of FAO.

14. GLOBAL OCEAN RESEARCH 3–9 (1969) (a report prepared by the Joint Work-ing Party on the Scientific Aspects of International Ocean Research of ACMRR, SCOR, and WMO–AGOR).

15. 1967 NASCO REPORT, *supra* note 11, at 24. *See also* Draft Framework, *supra* note 13, at 36.

16. 1967 NASCO REPORT, *supra* note 11, at 25.

17. Note by the Secretary-General, Long-term and Expanded Program of Oceano-graphic Research, 24 U.N. GAOR, Annexes, Agenda Item No. 12, at 31, U.N. Doc. A/7750 (1969) (emphasis added).

18. 1967 NASCO REPORT, *supra* note 11, at 27.

19. *Id.* at 29.

20. *Id.* at 30.

21. Draft Framework, *supra* note 13, at 52.

22. *Id.* at 56.

23. 1967 NASCO REPORT, supra note 11, at 38.

24. Draft Framework, *supra* note 13, at 56–57.

25. *Id.* at 57–58.

26. 1967 NASCO REPORT, supra note 11, at 47.

27. *Id.* at 52.

28. *Id.* at 54–55.

29. *Id.* at 59.

30. *Id.* at 60. *See also id.* at 80–81.

31. *Id.* at 61.

32. For a preliminary draft of a treaty on Ocean Data Acquisition Systems, see UNESCO, Summary Report of the Third Meeting of the IOC Group of Experts on the Legal Status of Ocean Data Acquisition Systems, 27 Oct.–17 Nov. 1969, Annex IV, U.N. Doc. SC/IOC.EG–1/7 (1969). The IOC Legal Working Group com-mented on this draft. *See* UNESCO, Summary Report of the Second Session of the

Working Group on Legal Questions Related to Scientific Investigations of the Ocean, Annex V, U.N. Doc. SC/IOC/WG–4/2 (1970).

33.   That this consequence may follow is derived from the method for delimiting the shelf as between states. Article 6 of the Continental Shelf Convention provides for measurement of median lines from the nearest points of the baselines of the territorial sea of each state concerned.

34.   Article 24(2) of the Convention on the Territorial Sea and the Contiguous Zone provides for delimitation of the contiguous zone from the baseline.

35.   Happily, the Office of the Geographer of the Department of State is contributing to man's welfare by issuing studies of some baseline claims around the world in its Series A, "Limits in the Seas," international boundary studies. To 1971 the baseline studies include Ireland, Mexico, Dominican Republic, Yugoslavia, Albania, Mauritania, Faeroes, Burma, Madagascar, Denmark, Venezuela, and the United Kingdom.

36.   INTERAGENCY COMMITTEE ON OCEANOGRAPHY, U.S. OCEANIC RESEARCH IN FOREIGN WATERS 6 (I.C.O. Pamphlet No. 25, 1966).

37.   UNESCO, Intergovernmental Oceanographic Comm'n, U.N. Doc. NS/IOC/INF/34, at 6 (1962). Article 4 of the draft ODAS Convention affirms the complete control of the coastal state in the territorial sea and in internal waters.

38.   See W. BURKE, INTERNATIONAL LEGAL PROBLEMS OF SCIENTIFIC RESEARCH IN THE OCEANS 133 n. 37 (1967).

39.   On the extent of use of these zones, see FAO, LIMITS AND STATUS OF THE TERRITORIAL SEA, EXCLUSIVE FISHING ZONES, FISHERY CONSERVATION ZONES, AND THE CONTINENTAL SHELF (1969). Proposals advanced at the 1958 and 1960 Geneva Conferences on the Law of the Sea sought to provide for exclusive fishing zones (with conditions attached) as part of a strategy for securing general international agreement on a specific (six-mile) width for the territorial sea. These proposals did not succeed at that time, but in the intervening period the accumulation of unilateral claims by states led to the general expectation that exclusive fishery zones were lawful. Eventually, in 1966, the United States Congress enacted legislation creating a twelve-mile fishery zone and, in so doing, received the advice of the Department of State that this was compatible with international law.

40.   Mr. Brown comments that it invites "confusion" to describe an "exclusive fishing zone" as a "contiguous zone," since the Geneva Convention thereon involves a quite different concept. See Brown, supra note 1, at 341 n.41. This latter observation is true, but the point is that the concept of the contiguous zone in international law is not limited to that defined in the 1958 Convention. The concept existed prior to the Geneva Conference and, in functional terms, referred to the exercise of limited authority beyond the bounds of comprehensive coastal control. The notion of an exclusive fishing zone is precisely this. In choosing to incorporate a more limited contiguous zone concept in the Convention, the contracting parties could not and did not prevent further limited extensions of state authority as new needs arose for which international measures were not provided. Unless states act to provide reasonable protection for coastal interests from emerging uses in adjacent waters, it is amply clear that further extensions of authority will occur. One of the shortcomings of the current consideration of a seabed regime is that it is focused almost entirely on the single use of mineral resource extraction and ignores the other developing uses of regions now beyond coastal (and other) control. Further unilateral extensions of coastal control undoubtedly will result from this piecemeal approach to ocean regulation. To recommend a new label for each of these extensions as they occur merely obscures that what is happening has a respectable ancestry, stemming from when the organized community of states also refused to establish a more comprehensive, inclusive system for governing interactions on the ocean. Until the world community does confront this problem, I prefer to use the term "contiguous zone" and see no reason for confusion about it. In passing, it is worth noting that barely over one-third of coastal states around the world are parties to the Convention on the Territorial Sea and Contiguous Zone.

41. Schaefer, *supra* note 1, at 115. Dr Schaefer was quoting an unnamed State Department official as the source of this proposed formulation.

42. *Id.* at 115–16.

43. The observations of Dr. Schaefer are pertinent:
> Indeed a doctrine of exclusion with respect of fisheries research since it obviously includes studies of the life history and ecology of the exploitable organisms, can seriously militate against the conservation of the living resources of the high seas, in instances where the organism which occurs on the high seas also occurs in an exclusive fishing zone, and the researchers are unable to do their work in such zone. (*Id.* at 116.)

44. The late Dr. Schaefer was one of the experts retained by the Secretariat, and he participated in these and other related events. *See* Schaefer, *supra* note 1, at 116, for an account of these events.

45. U.N. Conf. on the Law of the Sea, Official Records, Vol. II: Plenary Meetings, U.N. Doc. A/Conf. 13/38, at 15, para. 4 (1958).

46. U.N. Doc. A/Conf. 13/28, at 6 (1958).

47. *See* authorities cited note 1 *supra*.

48. INTERAGENCY COMMITTEE ON OCEANOGRAPHY, *supra* note 36, at 7.

49. The debate in the U.N. Seabed Committee strongly suggests that a considerable number of states will resist recognizing unrestricted freedom of research.

50. UNESCO, Intergovernmental Oceanographic Commission, *supra* note 37, at 11.

51. The contraction occurs only in the sense that research can be hampered by an exercise of control by the claimant state. For U.S. practice in this situation, see text accompanying note 56 *infra*.

52. It is of course possible that the restrictions imposed by an international seabed agency will be nearly or equally as onerous in the high seas region as those created by coastal states, in which case the text statement would be incorrect or require qualification.

53. The records on clearances in the Department of State are voluminous and in a few days could be only partially examined by me. This examination occurred in April 1970. Accordingly, the following section is based, in addition to the data in the files, on conversations over a period of several days with personnel in the Office of the Special Assistant to the Secretary of State for Fisheries and Wildlife, especially Mr. William L. Sullivan, Jr., and LCDR Karl Keininger. Any errors of assertion or interpretation are, of course, my own.

54. The Brazilian Government, in Decree No. 62.837 (June 6, 1968), requires the following categories of information:
> I—Name of the entity responsible for the exploration or research and a list of its previous activities.
> II—Name of the entity which will finance the exploration or research and list of previous activities financed by the entity in Brazil.
> III—Name of explorers, researchers, and technicians, mentioning their specialties and providing their curriculum vitae.
> IV—Proposed route for the exploration or research, on which working sites are marked (positions of oceanographic stations, location or course on which geophysical prospecting will be carried out). Such route must be presented in nautical chart in easily readable scale.
> V—Plans and objectives governing the exploration or research.
> VI—Description of all equipment to be used during the exploration or research.
> VII—Description of the type of navigation to be utilized when foreign ships or aircraft will be used.
> VIII—Proposed duration of activities.
> IX—Proposed dates for stop at national ports or airports.

X—Proposed dates for stop at the last foreign port or airport before the beginning of activities in the national territory and at the first foreign port or airport after the end of the activities, in case the exploration or research is carried out by foreign entities.

XI—Technical, scientific, and structural specification of any ship or aircraft to be utilized, as well as their photograph.

XII—Declaration that space on board the ship or aircraft which intends to carry out the activities will be reserved, so that observers to be indicated by the Ministry of the Navy may partially or totally accompany those activities.

XIII—Promise to provide the Directory of Hydrography and Navigation of the Ministry of the Navy, which now will become the national institution designated by Brazil to the Intergovernmental Oceanographic Commission sponsored by UNESCO, a copy of all information obtained during the activities to be carried out on the country's submarine shelf, oceanic territorial waters, or interior waters.

XIV—Declaration by the responsible entity for the activities that it will comply with the country's laws, regulations, and the present decree.

55.   Letter from Ambassador Donald L. McKernan to Dr. John A. Knauss, Apr. 10, 1970, referring specifically to Brazil and Ecuador.

56.   This situation emphasizes the need for responsible behavior on the part of investigators and institutions.

57.   INTERAGENCY COMMITTEE ON OCEANOGRAPHY, *supra* note 36, at 6.

58.   The influence of political considerations deserves emphasis. State officials may not have any substantive or genuine objection to an investigation, but because of politics (local as well as international, and the former may frequently be far more important) they feel unable to respond affirmatively to a clearance request. The whole procedure of deciding upon clearances is part of the internal politics of bureaucratic structures and it hardly should occasion surprise that these influences play a major part in some negative clearance decisions. One of the advantages of a system of notification with consent assumed unless objection is made is that local officials are not required to take affirmative action, and part of the influence of internal politics can be avoided.

59.   Dr. K. O. Emery reports that he abandoned "an effort to learn about the topography of part of the Mediterranean shelf because permission to enter claimed territorial waters was delayed by suspicion about possible military motives." Emery, *Geological Aspects of Sea-Floor Sovereignty,* in THE LAW OF THE SEA: OFFSHORE BOUNDARIES AND ZONES, PROCEEDINGS OF THE FIRST ANNUAL CONFERENCE OF THE LAW OF THE SEA INSTITUTE 139, 156 (L. Alexander ed. 1967).

60.   Letter from Ambassador Donald L. McKernan, *supra* note 55.

61.   Circular letter from Warren S. Wooster, President of SCOR, to SCOR members and National Committees, June 24, 1968.

62.   The ICSU, in 1954, not only expressed alarm over detrimental consequences to marine science, but also recommended that the General Assembly so amend the Articles then before the International Law Commission "as to ensure that such fundamental research at sea may proceed without vexatious obstruction." François, *Report on the Regime of the High Seas and Regime of the Territorial Sea,* [1956] 2 Y.B. INT'L L. COMM'N 1, 10, U.N. DOC. A/CN.4/97 (1956). For the text of the ICSU Resolutions of 1954 and 1955, see *id.*

63.   The SCOR again took note of the research problem at its Tenth General Meeting in Tokyo, September 13–25, 1970. In order better to focus attention on the problem, SCOR members agreed that the Executive Committee should solicit the views of SCOR members and National Committees, as well as of other scientists, on the necessary conditions for effective scientific research in the oceans. After compilation by the Executive Committee, these views would be made available for use by National Committees and scientists. Circular letter from SCOR to members and

National Committees, Necessary Conditions for the Effective Conduct of Ocean Research, Dec. 28, 1970.

64. GLOBAL OCEAN RESEARCH, *supra* note 14, at 49.

65. Resolution V–6 also provides that the Working Group was to indicate "legal principles which should facilitate and guide such research." The Working Group did a small amount of work in this respect at its first meeting but had insufficient time to do anything at its second meeting.

66. IOC Resolution VI–13 spells out the procedure ultimately agreed upon. *See* the Appendix, pp. 525–26 *supra*.

67. Making good on their promise, a strong coalition of developing states combined efforts at the November 1970 General Conference of UNESCO, overcame the objections of the developed states, and succeeded in rejecting the provision approved by the IOC. Although retaining the reference to "freedom of scientific investigation," the new provision emphasizes only the interests of the coastal states. The new IOC statute now provides that the IOC is to "promote the freedom of scientific investigation of the oceans for the benefit of all mankind, taking into consideration all the interests and rights of coastal states relating to scientific investigation in areas under their jurisdiction." New statutes of the Intergovernmental Oceanographic Commission art. 2(1), UNESCO Doc. No. 16/C/108 Add. 2 (1970).

68. Comm. on the Peaceful Uses of the Seabed and the Ocean Floor Beyond the Limits of National Jurisdiction, Report, 24 U.N. GAOR Supp. 2, at 24, U.N. Doc. A/7622 (1969).

69. H.R. Doc. No. 42, *supra* note 1, at 203.

70. In December 1970, the General Assembly agreed on a procedure for convening a comprehensive Law of the Sea Conference in 1973, provided that the Twenty-seventh General Assembly did not decide to postpone the Conference because of inadequate preparatory work.

71. Report of the United States Delegation to the Sixth Session of the IOC, Paris, France, Sept. 2–13, 1969, at 50 (1969). The tortuous, prolonged debate on Resolution VI–13 is admirably summarized in this Report. The "summary" occupies thirteen single-spaced pages, giving some idea of the intensive examination that entered into production of Resolution VI–13.

72. IOC, Summary Report of the Second Meeting of the Working Group on Legal Questions Related to Scientific Investigations of the Ocean, at 4, para 14, IOC Doc. SC/IOC/WG-4/2 (1970).

73. Letter from John C. Calhoun, Jr., Chairman, U.S. National Committee to SCOR, to Warren S. Wooster, President of SCOR, Jan. 8, 1969.

74. *Id.*

75. Suggested Provisional Guidelines for the Application of IOC Resolution VI–13 with respect to Assistance Regarding Areas of National Jurisdiction, IOC, Summary Report, Annex IV, *supra* note 72. The Guidelines are to be considered by the IOC Bureau and Consultative Council "with a view to their eventual endorsement by the Commission." *Id.* at 3.

76. *Id.* at 4.

77. IOC, Summary Report of the First Meeting of the Working Group on Legal Questions Related to Scientific Investigations of the Ocean, Annex IV, IOC Doc. AVS/9/89 M(8) (Dec. 1968).

78. *Id.*

79. *Id.*

80. Letter from S. A. Studenetsky, Deputy Minister of Fisheries of the U.S.S.R., to the ICES, Addendum to ICES Doc. C.M. 1969/Del: 3.

81. ICES Doc. C.M. 1969/Del:3, supp. 3.

82. *Id.*

83. This paper was forwarded in May 1970 to the Department of State along with

a resolution by the Council of the Academy recommending serious study by the Government of the possibility of a U.S. initiative to allow scientific research without a permit, but with adequate safeguards, in areas subject to its jurisdiction outside internal waters. Text available on request from Ocean Affairs Board, National Academy of Sciences, 2101 Constitution Avenue, Washington, D.C.

84. As noted in note 70 *supra,* the decision by the General Assembly in December 1970 to hold a conference in 1973 is not necessarily final. The Resolution makes clear that the agenda for the conference will very likely include all Law of the Sea issues, including those thought resolved in the 1958 Conventions and other, new ones.

85. The conclusion to this essay contains some observations on the draft seabed treaty, developed subsequent to the presidential pronouncement, which the United States tabled as a working document at the August 1970 session of the Seabed Committee. At one time in the evolution of this treaty it was planned to table it as a United States proposal, but the introductory page of the draft states that it does not represent the definitive views of the United States.

86. Hearings on Issues Related to Establishment of Seaward Boundary of United States Outer Continental Shelf, Senate Interior Committee, 91st Cong., 2nd Sess. 430 (1970).

87. *Id.*

88. As indicated below, the United States draft seabed treaty does not provide for such consent.

89. *See* text at and following note 71 *supra.*

90. Comm. on the Peaceful Uses of the Seabed and the Ocean Floor Beyond the Limits of National Jurisdiction, Report, *supra* note 68, at 38–39.

91. The General Assembly adopted a Declaration of General Principles in December 1970, concerning the seabed beyond national jurisdiction. G.A. Res. 2749 (xxv), 25 U.N. GAOR Supp. 28, at 24, U.N. Doc. A/8028 (1970). Among these was the following on scientific research:

> 10. States shall promote international cooperation in scientific research exclusively for peaceful purposes:
> (a) By participation in international programmes and by encouraging co-operation in scientific research by personnel of different countries;
> (b) Through effective publication of research programmes and dissemination of the results of research through international channels;
> (c) By cooperation in measures to strengthen research capabilities of developing countries, including the participation of their nations in research programmes.

No such activity shall form the legal basis for any claims with respect to any part of the area or its resources.

92. Text available on request from Ocean Affairs Board, National Academy of Sciences, 2101 Constitution Avenue, Washington, D.C.

93. It may be asked why it is unreasonable to impose requirements for deep sea research which are now regarded as reasonable when imposed in areas subject to coastal jurisdiction. If it is proper to require advance notice as a condition to research in the latter instance, why is not the same requirement appropriate in areas beyond coastal jurisdiction? One answer to this question is that once legal impediments in the form of a consent requirement came to be established as lawful, it seemed reasonable to accept the restrictions of a notice requirement as a means of gaining access for research. But in the deep sea area there are now no consent requirements or any other impediments to bona fide research. Introduction of restrictions such as the notice requirement thus has no compensating gain in this area. This same calculus applies to any new restriction on research in the deep sea area. In addition, the creation of an international structure for administering regulation of

research may well involve substantial administrative complexities for both states and scientists.

94.   Text available on request from Ocean Affairs Board, National Academy of Sciences, 2101 Constitution Avenue, Washington, D.C.

95.   The United States draft Seabed Convention, which includes the above article, is set forth, with numerous other proposed statements of principle and draft articles in Comm. on the Peaceful Uses of the Seabed and the Ocean Floor Beyond the Limits of National Jurisdiction, Comparative Table of Draft Treaties, Working Papers, and Draft Articles, U.N. Doc. A/AC.138/L.10 (1972).

Chapter 14

Facts and Value in the Prevention and Control of Marine Pollution

DOUGLAS M. JOHNSTON

The 1970s will be remembered, perhaps above all, as the decade of crisis in resource and environmental management. As the prediction suggests, I share the general concern at the mounting evidence of environmental deterioration, but assume optimistically that there will be succeeding generations to remember our folly. Some of this optimism may come too easily from the assumption that legal regulation will bring such management increasingly under scientific restraint. Certainly scientists and lawyers are collaborating more than ever before in the process of environmental policymaking.

The collaboration between environmental lawyer and scientist might usefully begin with an exchange of gifts: the scientist's talent for hypothesis on the basis of uncertain facts, and the lawyer's dexterity in the reformulation of social norms. Curiously, the layman tends to imagine the scientist as a man of certainty and the lawyer as a man of rigidity. Yet it is the former's art of hypothesis and the latter's art of innovation which best exemplify their contribution to the genius of man. In the making of international environmental law, each must acquire something of the other's special skill. The lawyer involved in this creative task needs to appreciate the value of working assumptions when the scientific facts are still uncertain. The scientist's inquiry is futile without the lawyer's engagement in word battles for the design of new commitments that will enlarge the scope of authoritative action.

The environmental phase of international law might be regarded as dating from 1970, when the United Nations began to prepare systematically for the first intergovernmental conference charged with confronting the threat to the global environment.[1] Before 1970, many governments and organizations had initiated studies of particular environmental problems shared by two or more states, and several international agreements dealing with environmental protection had been signed.[2] But it was the decision to convene the 1972 United Nations Conference on the Human Environment at Stockholm which first expressed the environmental concern of the organized world community and signaled the start of widespread intergovernmental consultation and cooperation.[3] It was also in 1970 that realistic doubts about the efficacy of existing international machinery for environmental protection were translated into bolder assertions of national authority over extensive offshore areas. The Arctic Waters Pollution Prevention Act,[4] adopted by the Canadian Parliament in the summer of 1970 and promulgated two years later, was the first national maritime claim of its kind. Protective rather than acquisitive, the Act applied to a distinguishable ocean environment (or subenvironment), rather than to a maritime region or marine resource.

The significance of the advent of the environmental period of international resource law is less likely to be underestimated if the development of international law is seen in historical perspective.[5] Between 1945 and 1970, many of the most spectacular developments in international lawmaking arose from the application of technology to unoccupied spaces (the sea, Antarctica, outer space) and from the need to regulate the development of shared or sharable resources (marine resources, international lakes and rivers, nuclear capability). Indeed, in the postwar period, acquisitive national claims to independence and increased wealth were so frequent that it is tempting to refer to these years as an economic or developmental phase of international law.

Before World War II, by contrast, the prevailing attitude toward international law was preservative rather than developmental, reflecting the interest of the dominant states and their allies to safeguard the political status quo and to ensure the highest degree of certainty that could be imposed on the affairs of states. In the law of the sea, for example, the dominant maritime powers preserved the legal status quo resting on the classical distinction between territorial waters and the high seas. The ocean was regarded simply as space rather than as a resource, and interests of the maritime powers were thought of as reciprocal, rather than competitive. For 300 years a suitable accommodation was maintained in the clear-cut classical formula which acknowledged the coastal state's comprehensive and exclusive authority over territorial waters (by analogy with the "sovereignty" it exercised over its land territory), as well as the world community's inclusive interest in the "freedom of the high seas" beyond. What this freedom in these spaces ensured was, of course, the right of any state to carry its exclusive and comprehensive authority around the world in every vessel flying its flag. In spatial terms, it was an ideal compromise between inclusive and exclusive regimes. In functional terms, it was an ingenious arrangement that suited the interests of the dominant flag states, all of which shared the same interest in the maximum freedom of movement for commercial and military purposes.

Now, rather suddenly, the sea has begun to be viewed as part of the global or human environment, a distinct environment on its own or, alternatively, a complex of related subenvironments. There is a danger that some international lawyers, reacting against the facile use of fashionable jargon, may prefer to revert to spatial or resource authority concepts; however, it is unlikely that familiar but conceptually irrelevant terminology will provide a useful vocabulary for the study of environmental protection. Marine problems that are admittedly environmental in nature and scope—such as the problems of marine pollution—surely are best treated by those willing to adopt an explicitly environmental approach to the law of the sea. This would involve not merely a new "perspective," but an emphasis on the urgency of the new situation.

It should also be asserted that if the lawyer is to play a creative role in marine pollution prevention, he will have to attempt a systematic approach to the problem. Until a comprehensive framework for marine environmental policy studies can be devised, inquiry into the legal problems of allocating authority over the preservation of the marine environment will be tentative at best. At this early stage in the "evolution" of international environmental law, of this kind an inquiry might be divided into five parts: the characterization of problem situations; the identification of claims and counterclaims; the clarification of policy; the description of trends in decisionmaking; and recommendations for international action.

Characterization of Problem Situations

As the current debate on the law of the sea demonstrates, nothing is more difficult than to secure widespread agreement on how to characterize the problems that need to be solved. The scope of preventive and remedial action permitted under a new treaty law of the sea will be limited chiefly by the kind of language in which authoritative concern is expressed. If environmental concerns were expressed in truly planetary terms—for example, by reference to the need to postpone the death of the human species[6]—the scope of action would be potentially much wider than if the general reference were to "environmental pollution" or to more specific problems such as "marine pollution." The term "pollution" is almost as imprecise as "environment," and the range of scientifically credible meanings that could be given to it in different contexts is broad.[7] Under any one scientifically credible definition, "pollution" assumes different forms, varying in intensity from area to area and from one period of time to another. No one type of marine pollution has uniform effects in changing hydrographic conditions. Even the physical process of marine environmental deterioration is not yet fully understood, and the technology of marine pollution prevention and control is in its infancy.[8]

The most meaningful focus of marine pollution concern is no less difficult to define than the nature of such concern. To focus on the sea as a whole, in the spirit of global environmentalism, seems likely to ensure the unmanageability of a regulatory system for the prevention and control of marine pollution. If we move away from the scientific ideal, which usually assumes the need for an effective universal authority, how far do we have to go in accepting the reality of political limits in the sea? Both present and prospective national boundaries extending seaward cut across ecologically related marine areas and make no sense to the environmental scientist.[9] Is it possible, then, to characterize marine pollution situations— that is, to define the nature and focus of marine pollution concerns—in a way that is both politically and scientifically meaningful?

In attempting to answer this fundamental question confronting scientists and lawyers together, we might take cognizance of four kinds of relevant factors: scientific judgment, scientific fact, legal norm, and legal fact.

Scientific Judgment

In the characterization of marine pollution situations requiring regulation, the factor of scientific opinion is almost always present. At one extreme is the situation of allegedly irreversible deterioration, which usually means a situation in which the cost of rehabilitation is deemed to be "prohibitive" under present conditions. Such a characterization, therefore, usually is based on a value judgment, and on one which is not likely to be the product of a careful comparison of policy options. Scientific opinions of lesser gravity—"serious pollution hazard," "unacceptable level of effluence," "dangerous to health"—are even more likely to be based on unacknowledged assumptions about social choices. But even if all actual marine pollution situations *seem* still to be capable of remedy, at some cost level, it would be extremely foolish to discount the scientific judgment that a particular body of water such as Lake Erie is in a state of technically irreversible deterioration. Unfortunately, there is nothing weightier than counteropinion against the scientific judgment that the oceans of the world are rapidly approaching the same state. Obviously, the assumption of prohibitive cost must be taken seriously if we accept the view that the entire ocean environment must be brought under a single universal system of regulation in order to be preserved.

Sometimes, however, scientific judgment is pressed into the service of advocacy for a particular kind of preventive or remedial action. There is, for example, a respectable scientific opinion that mercury in its present quantities is not one of the most serious pollutants of the ocean and that mercury dumping need not yet be "blacklisted" as it is under the 1972 Convention on the Prevention of Marine Pollution by Dumping of Wastes and Other Matter.[10] It should not be surprising that this opinion is expressed frequently in the scientific circles of Japan, which is the world's leading user and dumper of mercury. Similarly, many governments that participated in the 1973 International Conference on Marine Pollution convened by the Intergovernmental Maritime Consultative Organization (IMCO) used scientific opinion, much like legal opinion in other contexts, as a means of justifying a policy preference motivated chiefly by political and economic considerations of competitive advantage.[11] Government policy aside, scientific judgment that 80 percent of the ocean's pollutants are airborne or river discharged may owe something to the scientist's own conscious or unconscious preference for a more "heroic" approach to marine pollution prevention and control than the present 20 percent approach through the regulation of shipping practices.[12]

Unlike most other opinions, scientific judgments (or hypotheses) have the virtue of being subject more or less constantly to attempts to diversify them. Venturesome scientists have to be on guard especially against the fallacies inherent in "conventional wisdom." Among marine scientists today, the theory of ecosystems is much less scorned than it was in the 1950s, when it was invoked unsuccessfully by a number of Latin American delegations at the First U.N. Conference on the Law of the Sea. The prevailing view now is that it is not so much fallacious as it is in need of further corroborative data. It may turn out to be valid after all, like John Hanning Speke's claim to have discovered the source of the Nile, unsupported as it was by the indisputable data and vigorous logic demanded by more scientific explorers such as Richard Francis Burton.

Scientific Fact

Most scientific facts about the threat to the marine environment are uncertain; that is, they tend to be unverified, unconfirmed by comparative studies, incomplete, unsystematically collected, or of limited or temporary usefulness. Since the marine environment is constantly changing, even the most reliable facts about yesterday's pollution trends may be relatively useless tomorrow. There is, however, an order of scientific fact that cannot be disputed or changed, such as the simple factual distinction between open and closed hydrological systems, which might be regarded as presenting fundamentally different pollution problem situations. In a "closed hydrosystem," the cost of water resource management can be estimated with greater accuracy, investing predictions with almost the reliability of certain facts. But marine pollution occurs in an "open hydrosystem," where the managerial approach would be extraordinarily complicated even if a global marine pollution agency could be brought into existence. It is likely that this will be the course of action in the more distant future, but to characterize marine pollution situations according to the kinds of managerial techniques to which they can be subjected is now visionary and premature.

Of course, in every marine pollution situation there always is a substratum of certain scientific facts. There almost always is, for example, a high degree of certainty about the chemical composition of a marine environment and the agents introduced into it. Above this primary level, there also may be a high degree of certainty about the interaction of these chemical elements in varying proportions. But above this secondary level of facts, knowledge about the actual chemical effects of human activity within a given environment may be quite skimpy. At this third level, which is crucial for operational decisions, scientific fact may drift imperceptibly into scientific opinion. Yet it is at this third level of fact that marine pollution concerns evolve and that informed recommendations to authoritative decisionmakers must be made.

Legal Norm

Most lawyers are likely to begin the characterization of marine pollution situations within the framework of existing legal concepts. The worst method of characterization by legal norm would be one that begins with the traditional concept of state sovereignty, which assumes that pollution in the territorial sea and pollution on the high seas are fundamentally distinct situations. To combat this arbitrary, unscientific approach, it is necessary to emphasize that responsibility, not right, is the primary juridical component of environmental authority, since environmental powers, properly regarded, are essentially nonacquisitive in purpose. Nothing is gained juridically by blurring the distinction between a claim to exploitation authority over, say, a fishery resource and an undertaking to exercise the powers that are necessary to discharge one's responsibility for preserving the adjacent marine environment. If a state is genuinely willing to accept exclusive or special responsibility for environmental protection within the adjacent marine environmental area, it is difficult to see the need for introducing the fiction of territoriality. *Non entia debenda sunt praeter necessitatem.* Although the outcome of the Third U.N. Conference on the Law of the Sea (UNCLOS III) is not known at the time of writing, there is evidently an irreversible trend toward general acceptance of a 200-mile "economic zone" which would lie beyond relatively modest territorial limits and within which the coastal state would accept, among other things, special, if not exclusive responsibility for the prevention and control of marine pollution.[13]

Legal Fact

In light of these developments in the law of the sea and the considerations discussed above, the characterization of marine pollution situations should take the following four "legal facts" into account:

1. That there are marine areas which generally are recognized as falling within the exclusive or special authority of one state (by virtue of "sovereign or limited jurisdiction");
2. That there are marine areas which are the focus of contested claims and counterclaims;
3. That there are marine areas in which an internationally shared resource is located, sometimes under international regulation, sometimes not; and
4. That there are marine areas for which no exclusive or special authority is claimed by any state and in which no internationally shared resource is located.

Assuming that the meaning of marine pollution in a particular situation can be agreed to on the basis of scientific fact and opinion, the legal task of allocating marine environmental authority should be approached in light of these four basic legal facts, rather than by reference to existing legal norms. In this way, it appears that there are at least thirty-nine distinguishable policy-relevant situations:

1. Where pollution is confined within recognized limits of exclusive or special authority of one state;
2. Where pollution originating within recognized limits of exclusive or special authority of one state
    a. spreads or may spread into areas over which the state's claim to exclusive or special authority is contested,
    b. spreads or may spread into areas within the recognized limits of exclusive or special authority of another state,
    c. spreads or may spread into areas to which one or more other states make claims to exclusive or special authority that are contested by the state in whose area the pollution originated ("the state of origin"),
    d. spreads or may spread into areas in which the state of origin shares a marine resource with one or more other states,

    e. spreads or may spread into areas of an internationally shared resource in which the state of origin does not participate, and

    f. spreads or may spread into areas over which no exclusive or special authority is claimed by any state and in which no internationally shared resource is located;

3. Where pollution is confined to areas to which only one state makes a contested claim to exclusive or special authority;

4. Where pollution originating in an area to which one state makes a contested claim to exclusive or special authority

    a. spreads or may spread into areas within the recognized limits of that state's exclusive or special authority,

    b. spreads or may spread into areas within the recognized limits of exclusive or special authority of another state,

    c. spreads or may spread into areas to which one or more other states make claims to exclusive or special authority that are contested by the state of origin,

    d. spreads or may spread into areas in which that state shares a marine resource with one or more other states,

    e. spreads or may spread into areas of an internationally shared resource in which the state of origin does not participate, and

    f. spreads or may spread into areas over which no exclusive or special authority is claimed by any state and in which no internationally shared resource is located;

5. Where pollution is confined to areas to which two or more states make conflicting claims to exclusive or special authority;

6. Where pollution originating in an area to which two or more states make conflicting claims to exclusive or special authority

    a. spreads or may spread into areas within the recognized limits of exclusive or special authority of one of these states of origin,

    b. spreads or may spread into areas within the recognized limits of exclusive or special authority of another state,

    c. spreads or may spread into areas to which only one of the states of origin makes a contested claim to exclusive or special authority,

    d. spreads or may spread into areas to which another state makes a contested claim to exclusive or special authority,

    e. spreads or may spread into areas in which one or more of the states of origin participate in an internationally shared resource,

    f. spreads or may spread into areas in which two or more other states participate in an internationally shared resource,

    g. spreads or may spread into areas over which no exclusive or special authority is claimed by any state and in which no internationally shared resource is located, and

    h. spreads or may spread into areas to which two or more other states make conflicting claims to exclusive or special authority;

7. Where pollution is confined within areas in which an internationally shared resource is located;

8. Where pollution originating within an area of an internationally shared resource
   a. spreads or may spread to areas in which another internationally shared resource is located,
   b. spreads or may spread into areas within the recognized limits of exclusive or special authority of one of the participating states,
   c. spreads or may spread into areas within the recognized limits of exclusive or special authority of a nonparticipating state,
   d. spreads or may spread into areas to which one of the participating states makes a claim to exclusive or special authority that is contested by one or more of the other participating states,
   e. spreads or may spread into areas to which one of the participating states makes a claim to exclusive or special authority that is contested by one or more nonparticipating states,
   f. spreads or may spread into areas to which two or more of the participating states make conflicting claims to exclusive or special authority,
   g. spreads or may spread into areas to which two or more nonparticipating states make conflicting claims to exclusive or special authority,
   h. spreads or may spread into areas to which a nonparticipating state makes a claim to exclusive or special authority that is contested by one or more of the participating states,
   i. spreads or may spread into areas to which a nonparticipating state makes a claim to exclusive or special authority that is contested by one or more nonparticipating states, and
   j. spreads or may spread into areas over which no exclusive or special authority is claimed by any state and in which no internationally shared resource is located;

9. Where pollution is confined within areas over which no exclusive or special authority is claimed by any state and in which no internationally shared resource is located; and

10. Where pollution originating within an area over which no exclusive or special authority is claimed by any state and in which no internationally shared resource is located
    a. spreads or may spread into areas within the accepted limits of exclusive or special authority of one state,
    b. spreads or may spread into areas to which one state makes a contested claim to exclusive or special authority,
    c. spreads or may spread into areas to which two or more states make conflicting claims to exclusive or special authority, and
    d. spreads or may spread into areas in which an internationally shared resource is located.

All of these situations refer to legal facts, not to norms or judgments. It is a verifiable fact that a state's claim is or is not contested (by interested parties); that an internationally shared resource is or is not located in an area; that a state does or does not participate in exploiting such a resource. Of course, two or more of these situations can overlap, say, when three or more of the areas previously designated are affected by pollution. Also, it should be observed that this scheme or characterization does not account for the phenomenon of pandemic pollution of accumulative origin carried to the sea through the air over great distances. Pollution in this form, it is assumed, cannot be dealt with effectively by the allocation of state authority over marine areas.

The characterization is based on two dominant principles: (1) that a state may be entitled to exclusive or special authority over marine environmental protection beyond narrow territorial limits and (2) that the existence of an internationally shared resource may be crucial to issues of allocation of state authority over marine environmental protection.

Claims and Counterclaims

It is characteristic of the present early stage of international environmental law that states scarcely have begun to formulate specific claims to environmental authority beyond their land territory. Even within land territory, most national governments are just beginning to develop the concept of public responsibility for protection of the environment. The chief reason for the slow rate of such claim making in the context of marine pollution prevention and control is, of course, that what essentially is involved is the acceptance of new forms of responsibility involving incalculable costs of administration and highly uncertain benefits. It is possible, however, to discern the emergence of at least eleven types of such claims.

Claim to Exclusive Authority Within Territorial Limits

The right to protect the territorial marine environment is certainly included within the concept of sovereignty traditionally applied to the territorial sea. Unfortunately, it is not yet clear that most states are prepared to accept "sovereign responsibility" for the consequences of pollution originating in their territorial sea, at least not in a degree commensurate with the commonly accepted notion of sovereign rights.

Claim to Exclusive Authority over the Environment of the Continental Shelf (Slope, Rise)

The "doctrine of the continental shelf" still is fashionable. In the 1950s, the shelf became the focus of coastal state claims to "sovereign rights" for the limited purpose of exploring and exploiting the resources on, under, and attached to the bed of the shelf. The 1958 Convention on the Continental Shelf is entirely economic (acquisitive) in motivation, but it is possible nevertheless to infer from the text anticipatory obligations of marine pollution prevention falling on the coastal state.

Claim to Exclusive Protective Authority over Particularly Vulnerable Areas Where Ecological Hazards Are Exceptional

The rationale of this type of claim is that the exceptional vulnerability of certain areas creates an obligation for the nearest adjacent state to exercise exceptional powers to secure the areas from unnecessary ecological dangers. The nearest adjacent state is presumed to have the best opportunity to take effective preventive or remedial action. This consideration was part of the official claim underlying the enactment by Canada of the Arctic Waters Pollution Prevention Act, applied to an extensive offshore area of the Arctic Ocean which faces the prospect of exceptional ecological risks associated with the exploitation and transportation of mineral resources.[14] It also underlies 1971 British legislation, and the joint policy of Indonesia, Singapore, and Malaysia with respect to the straits of Malacca and Singapore.[15]

Claim to Exclusive Protective Authority over Particularly Susceptible Areas Where Environmental Rehabilitation Is Especially Difficult

This was an implicit part of the official rationale of the Canadian legislation referred to in the preceding section. It is potentially a more limited kind of assertion based on special circumstances since it purports to be capable of invalidation by scientific evidence. But, unlike the previous claim, it is not implicitly confined to a particular range of economic activities which give rise to the ecological hazards.

Claim to Exclusive Protective Authority over a Threatened Marine Species or Resource Area in Which the Claimant State Has an Exclusive Special Interest

The logic of exclusive coastal fishing zones and special coastal fishing privileges sustains not only the argument for exclusive managerial authority on the part of the fishing state, but also, by extension, the argument for exclusive authority over the marine environment on which the resource is immediately dependent. It would seem to apply especially to potentially polluting activities which might threaten the life cycle of the species. Of special significance is the current trend at UNCLOS III toward claiming exclusive coastal authority over fishing, fishery conservation, marine pollution regulation, and control of oceanographic research, all within a single multipurpose "economic zone" which would extend a considerable distance beyond modest territorial limits.[16]

Claim to Exclusive Authority over an Extraterritorial Area on the Ground of Adjacency

The claim of the nearest adjacent state, as such, to exceptional rights beyond its territorial limits often has been made in the past, sometimes by reference to the practice of exercising certain administrative acts within a contiguous zone, sometimes by reference to the right of hot pursuit, sometimes by reference to the doctrine of self-defense, and otherwise. There were intimations of the self-defense or self-help doctrine in the presentation of the case supporting Canadian and British marine pollution legislation, as well as in the joint communiqué of the Malacca Strait states. And since 1971 there has been steadily growing support, as noted previously, for the proposal to establish beyond the territorial sea an "economic zone" within which the coastal state, as the nearest adjacent state, would be entitled to exclusive control over activities creating the risk of marine pollution. At the 1972 United Nations Conference on the Human Environment, the Third United Nations Conference on the Law of the Sea, and other conferences dealing with marine pollution problems, Canada suggested a different version of the same adjacency-type claim, whereby the coastal state, as the nearest adjacent state would have exclusive authority over marine pollution prevention and control over extensive offshore areas as a trustee of the international community. It has been added that coastal state authority of this kind might be rationalized by reference to a fictitious or implied delegation of powers.[17]

Claim to Special Protective Authority over a Threatened Marine Species or Resource Area Adjacent to the Claimant's Territorial Sea

This claim is spelled out in the 1958 Convention on Fishing and Conservation of Living Resources of the High Seas, which refers specifically to the coastal state's special interest in the maintenance of the productivity of the living resources of the high seas adjacent to its territorial sea.[18] The case is all the stronger if the adjacent resource is deemed to be threatened, whether by pollution, overfishing, or otherwise.

Claim to Special Protective Authority over an Internationally Shared Resource Which Is Subject to an Effective Conservation Program in Which the Claimant Has Invested Substantially

Some states, notably the United States and Canada, have tried to convert a fishery claim of this kind into a duty of other fishing states, such as Japan, to abstain from fishing stocks so regulated.[19] By an obvious kind of extension, a coastal state which has undertaken considerable marine pollution prevention costs beyond its territorial limits could be likened to a coastal state which has accepted the major share of fishery management costs.[20]

Claim to Special Protective Authority over the Regional Marine Environment on the Basis of an International Agreement Establishing Joint Authority with Adjacent or Coregional States

Regional agreements on marine pollution prevention and control do not yet make explicit provision for the special interest of the nearest adjacent regional state in nonterritorial coastal waters. This is, however, a likely development, especially if UNCLOS III is unable to agree on the establishment of an economic zone and if future IMCO conferences on marine pollution continue to reject the argument that the coastal state has a primary and prior jurisdiction over pollution control in nonterritorial coastal waters. Even with a global treaty establishing an economic zone, two or more neighboring states in certain semi-enclosed marine areas, such as the Caribbean, may be willing to establish a "regional economic zone," as proposed in some of the Conference debates.[21]

Claim to Shared Protective Authority over a Threatened Marine Species or Resource Area in Which the Claimant Has Developed a Significant Commercial Interest

This is the general claim by user states to have an interest in the protection of a resource which they exploit with other users and in the protection of the environment on which the resource is dependent. Ideally, it should be spelled out in terms of an international resource management or conservation agreement. At the global level it is unlikely that UNCLOS III will result in a treaty that reflects any significant development of the doctrine of state responsibility along the lines anticipated in the Stockholm Declaration on the Human Environment [22] and the accompanying recommendations. It can be predicted, however, that some marine resource management arrangements at the regional level will make provision for the allocation of regulatory authority over activities that might pose a pollution threat to the resource.

Claim to Shared Protective Authority over the Global Marine Environment on Behalf of Mankind As a Whole

This claim already is established on the universal level by derivation from more general invocations in the 1972 Stockholm Declaration on the

Human Environment.[23] It is the minimal and most basic principle of international responsibility for the protection of the marine environment.

Counterclaims

Counterclaims against the claims to *exclusive* or *special* authority take the form of either of the last two claims to *shared* authority, although more often they are couched in terms of the enumerated freedoms of the high seas contained in the 1958 Convention on the High Seas [24] or in the doctrine of the freedom of the high seas that evolved in customary international law. Claims to *special* authority on the basis of a treaty—an international resource agreement or a regional (or bilateral) agreement for marine environmental protection—are, of course, opposed by the counterclaim that third parties are not bound by such treaty arrangements.

Clarification of Policy

The fundamental policy objective for the international community is to provide the most *effective* forms of protective authority over the marine environment. As emphasized in the preceding discussion, claims to this kind of authority are essentially nonacquisitive. The chief problem is, therefore, to decide how *state responsibility* is to be allocated in marine areas so as to provide the most effective safeguards against the various forms of marine pollution.

One of the major difficulties is that the interest of marine environmental protection is sometimes seen as running counter to the short-term user interest, especially that of the shipping trade and the dumpers of waste materials. A reasonable accommodation needs to be made with the age-old freedom of navigation, but it is now fairly clearly established by scientific evidence that the world community no longer can grant the luxury of a license to pollute, even to vessels in mid ocean. It is necessary also to distinguish between permissible and nonpermissible dumping, according to material and locality; however, in the absence of wholly reliable scientific facts, the line between the two can be expected to shift as new data become available.[25]

Since lack of sufficient knowledge is a barrier to the establishment of rational schemes for environmental protection, the allocation of state authority for this purpose must not be allowed to impair seriously the effectiveness of scientific investigation of the marine environment. The best safeguard for effective marine research may not be through an absolute concept of the freedom of scientific investigation outside territorial limits but, rather, through larger regimes of regulatory authority supported by global investment on a cooperative basis.

If the effectiveness is accepted as the prime criterion for the allocation of state authority for pollution prevention and control, logic will support national claims and initiatives by the coastal state that clearly are motivated by genuine fears about threats to the marine areas in which it has the most to lose (in a broad socioeconomic sense) from severe ecological damage. Even if it cannot be proved statistically that the nearest adjacent coastal state would lose most from a particular form of pollution in a specific area, that state might be entitled to assume that it would be the first in line if pollution occurred. As the first state required to act in self-defense, it should be recognized to have the primary right to exercise authority for preventive purposes and the primary obligation to take appropriate measures, on behalf of the world community.

It may be unwise, however, to place the sole responsibility for the protection of the coastal environment in the hands of the coastal state. Most coastal states are developing states. Even if it can be assumed that coastal states have the highest motivation to take effective action, effectiveness depends equally on opportunity and capability. By these latter criteria, it is more difficult to pinpoint where responsibility ought to be assigned, for it seems to depend on the type of marine pollution in question. In the case of the discharge and dumping of ship-generated wastes, it clearly is the shipping states which have the best opportunity, if a low motivation, to introduce preventive measures, especially under the organizational auspices of IMCO. The capability for implementing shipping controls varies enormously from state to state, and one can only take notice that many developing coastal states are making significant progress in this area of technical sophistication. The fact that most pollution-causing vessels are owned by a few industrially advanced nations will tend to stiffen the resolve of developing coastal states to make vessels in the vicinity comply with fairly rigorous coastal safeguards.

But in the case of shore-generated emissions and effluents, which supposedly contribute 80 percent of the pollutants in the ocean, the criteria of opportunity and capability draw attention to the serious flaw in any scheme of regulation which leaves important initiatives to the discretion of developing coastal states. The curtailment of shore-generated wastes, whether or not they lead to marine pollution, is seen by most developing states as an additional cost and hindrance to their development policies and programs.[26] The proper objective is, surely, to improve the opportunity and capability of developing coastal states to reduce the incidence of marine pollution from these sources, not to persuade them that development and environmental control are wholly compatible goals. One looks for new, improved forms of development aid from advanced countries that take into account the environmental needs and dangers of the recipient countries at the same time that one expects a heightened degree of environmental awareness from the recipient countries. An appropriate balance of these concerns was struck in the Stockholm Declaration on the Human Environment.[27]

It also should be underlined that nonadjacent, even distant, user states with a legitimate and established interest in a marine resource also have a legitimate interest in the preservation of the marine environment on which the resource is dependent. This kind of interest is the more deserving of protection if the user states have formed an international resource management authority able and willing to help the adjacent or nearest coastal state in implementing commonly acceptable measures for preserving the shared marine environment. In light of the coastal state's special interest, a heavy onus rests upon the distant, noncoastal user states to help establish effective conservation procedures.

Trend in Decision

The organized world community is just beginning to map out the general principles for the prevention and control of marine pollution. Municipal law—normally a fruitful source of analogies for the development of international law—abounds in developed doctrine on liability and has potential value for remedial action.[28] But we still are at a very early stage in the development of principles of prevention. Nevertheless, scattered "precedents" in international environmental law can be found.

It is de rigueur to refer to the *Trail Smelter* arbitration in which the Arbitral Tribunal affirmed Canada's liability for air pollution originating in British Columbia and causing injury in the State of Washington, though the matter was not an issue between the parties. "No state," the Tribunal asserted, "has the right to use or permit the use of its territory in such a manner as to cause injury by fumes in or to the territory of another . . . when the case is of serious consequence." [29] The Tribunal, however, could find no international judicial decision dealing either with air or water pollution, and it resorted instead to an examination of decisions of the Supreme Court of the United States which, it stated,

> may legitimately be taken as a guide in this field of international law, for it is reasonable to follow, by analogy, in international cases, precedents established by that Court in dealing with controversies between States of the Union or with other controversies concerning the quasi-sovereign rights of such States, where no contrary rule prevails in international law.[30]

It is necessary also to cite the dictum of the International Court of Justice in the *Corfu Channel* case that every state has an obligation "not to allow knowingly its territory to be used contrary to the rights of other states." [31]

International treaty obligations to prevent marine pollution have been emerging over several years. The most general of earlier statements was contained in Articles 24 and 25 of the 1958 Convention on the High Seas, which now has been ratified by most maritime states. Article 24 reads:

> Every State shall draw up regulations to prevent pollution of the seas by the discharge of oil from ships or pipelines or resulting from the exploitation and exploration of the seabed and its subsoil, taking account of existing treaty provisions on the subject.[32]

And Article 25 reads:

> 1. Every State shall take measures to prevent pollution of the seas from the dumping of radio-active waste, taking into account any standards and regulations which may be formulated by the competent international organizations.
> 2. All States shall co-operate with the competent international organizations in taking measures for the prevention of pollution of the seas or air space above, resulting from any activities with radio-active materials or other harmful agents.[33]

In the 1958 Convention on the Continental Shelf, also now widely adopted, it was provided in Article 5(1) that exploitation of shelf resources by the coastal state "must not result in any unjustifiable interference with navigation, fishing or the conservation of the living resources of the sea";[34] and in Article 5(7) it was provided that the coastal state was obliged, in safety zones established in waters over the shelf, to undertake "all appropriate measures for the protection of the living resources of the sea from harmful agents." [35] Ecologically relevant provisions were also included in the 1958 Convention on Fishing and Conservation of the Living Resources of the High Seas: e.g., Article 1(2) ("All States have the duty to adopt, or to co-operate with other States in adopting such measures for their respective nationals as may be necessary for the conservation of the living resources of the high seas");[36] and Article 6(1) ("A coastal State has a special interest in the maintenance of the productivity of the living resources in any area of the high seas adjacent to its territorial sea").[37]

Another advance in the formulation of state responsibility for environmental protection is contained in the 1963 Nuclear Test Ban Treaty, Article 1(1) of which reads as follows:

> Each of the Parties to this Treaty undertakes to prohibit, to prevent, and not carry out any nuclear weapon test explosion, or any other nuclear explosion, at any place under its jurisdiction or control:

(a) in the atmosphere; beyond its limits, including outer space; or underwater, including territorial waters or high seas; or

(b) in any other environment if such explosion causes radioactive debris to be present outside the territorial limits of the State under whose jurisdiction or control such explosion is conducted . . . .[38]

In addition to these and other general treaty provisions concerning marine pollution, there are, of course, numerous other provisions related to pollution problems in regional agreements for the conservation of marine resources and the management of water resources in international lakes, rivers, and river basins.[39]

At a lower level of relevance to marine pollution, there also is evolving in state practice an acceptance of the doctrine of equitable utilization applied to international drainage basins. The essence of this doctrine has been described in the nonbinding Helsinki Rules adopted by the International Law Association in 1966. Article IV reads:

Each basin State is entitled, within its territory, to a reasonable and equitable share in beneficial uses of waters of an international drainage basin.

Article V reads:

What is a reasonable and equitable share within the meaning of article IV is to be determined in light of all the relevant factors in each particular case. The weight to be given to each factor is to be determined by its importance in comparison with that of other relevant factors.[40]

Whatever may be thought of the "reasonable man test" in international law, the acknowledgment of a multifactoral, situational approach to water resource management policy may prove to be precursor of a similar approach to the development of "international environmental law."

For the *control* of marine pollution, a remedial, liability approach has been attempted by the shipping states, mostly under the auspices of the Intergovernmental Maritime Consultative Organization (IMCO), a specialized agency of the United Nations. The first of these agreements, adopted at a conference convened in 1954 at the invitation of the British government, was called, somewhat misleadingly, the International Convention for the Prevention of Pollution of the Sea by Oil.[41] In fact, the Convention dealt, in a limited and tentative way, only with the problem of oil pollution caused by deliberate discharges from ships at sea.[42] In 1962, it was revised under IMCO auspices, but its scope was not extended. Further amendments were adopted in 1969, but before these came into force they were superseded by a wholly new, more preventively oriented treaty, the International Convention for the Prevention of Pollution from Ships, which was opened for signature at the end of 1973.[43]

Also in 1969, other initiatives were taken through IMCO: a public law convention, the International Convention relating to Intervention on the High Seas in Cases of Oil Pollution Casualties,[44] and a private law convention called the International Convention on Civil Liability for Oil Pollution Damage.[45] Both conventions represent limited approaches to the problem of marine pollution.

The public law Convention does permit the coastal state to take preventive measures beyond the territorial limits, but only after a maritime casualty and only in the case of oil pollution. Its major purpose is to allow states signatory to it to resort to reasonable self-help in major oil spill situations that might assume emergency proportions. Although the principle of self-help on the high seas is not new, this was the first International Convention to apply it to the purpose of environmental protection.

The private law Convention imposes strict, not absolute, liability on shipowners (but not cargo owners) and provides compensation to persons who have suffered damage caused by pollution resulting from the escape or discharge of oil from ships. It applies, however, only to pollution damage caused in the territory, or in the territorial sea, of a contracting state. Moreover, actions for compensation have to be brought in the courts of the contracting state within whose territory or territorial sea the pollution damage has occurred or where measures have had to be taken to prevent or minimize pollution damage. Compulsory insurance provisions make the insurer directly answerable, however, to any claim for compensation for pollution damage.

In December 1971, the states signatory to the 1969 Liability Convention established a compensation and indemnification system supplementary to that created by the earlier agreement. Under this new Convention—the International Convention on the Establishment of an International Fund for Compensation for Oil Pollution Damage[46]—the Fund exists to pay compensation to any person suffering oil pollution damage who has been unable to obtain full and adequate compensation under the Liability Convention. The Fund may be wholly or partially exonerated from its obligations to provide relief if it proves that, as a result of the actual fault or privity of the owner, the ship causing the damage did not comply with the requirements laid down in specified conventions and the incident or damage was caused wholly or partially by such noncompliance. To this limited extent, then, the Fund operates as an external sanction of these Conventions—the 1954 International Convention for the Prevention of Pollution of the Sea by Oil (as amended in 1962), the 1960 International Convention for the Safety of Life at Sea,[47] the 1966 International Convention on Load Lines,[48] and the 1960 International Regulations for Preventing Collisions at Sea.[49]

The legislative initiatives taken by Canada and the United Kingdom in 1970 and 1971, respectively, are familiar examples of the trend in state practice toward the acceptance of coastal state responsibility for the prevention of marine pollution in extensive offshore areas. The introduction of the Arctic Waters Pollution Prevention Act by Canada [50] seems to have provoked a more negative reaction than that of the Oil in Navigable Waters Act by the British.[51] It was feared, especially in the United States, that the Canadian legislation would be widely copied by those favoring the trend toward the unilateral extension of maritime jurisdiction by coastal states,[52] and by those preferring the preventive, rather than the remedial, approach to marine pollution risks in offshore areas. In practice, the developing coastal states have not yet found it necessary to follow the Canadian legislative example and have been content to ride out the economic zone proposal down to the finishing post at the Third United Nations Conference on the Law of the Sea.[53] In conference diplomacy leading up to the 1972 Stockholm Conference on the Human Environment, Canada had mixed success in attracting support for the principles underlying its Arctic legislation.[54] At UNCLOS III, however, there has been a trend toward new forms of equity which would permit the preferential treatment of "special circumstances," such as the ecologically vulnerable environment of the Arctic Ocean.[55]

Whether or not UNCLOS III adopts a new coastal regime for the protection of the marine environment, we can expect a continuation of important regional initiatives. Reference already has been made to the attempt by the Malacca Strait states to create a pollution prevention zone in these hazardous, tanker-infested waters.[56] But it is still uncertain whether this can be settled on a regional basis.[57] It is safer to predict further cooperation by the North European states on the basis of existing arrangements such as the 1969 Bonn Agreement Concerning Pollution of the North Sea by Oil (signed by eight North Sea countries)[58] and the 1972 Oslo Convention on the Control of Marine Pollution by Dumping from Ships and Aircraft (signed by most of the Northeast Atlantic states).[59] The Oslo Convention played an important role outside the region in preparing the way for the global London Convention on Ocean Dumping,[60] which was opened for signature in December 1972.[61] In the case of marine pollution from land-based sources, however, regional treaty making is not likely to have an immediate impact at the global level, because of the widespread fear in the developing world that this kind of pollution control would add substantially to the costs of economic development.[62]

Recommendations 86 to 94 of the Stockholm Conference on the Human Environment[63] deal directly with marine pollution. Some of them call upon governments to cooperate in various ways with one another and with international organizations such as the Joint Group of Experts on the Scientific Aspects of Marine Pollution (GESAMP), the Food and Agriculture Organization (FAO), the World Health Organization (WHO), the

Intergovernmental Oceanographic Commission (IOC), the International Atomic Energy Agency (IAEA), the World Meteorological Organization (WMO), the Intergovernmental Maritime Consultative Organization (IMCO), the International Hydrographic Organization (IHO), and the International Council for the Exploration of the Sea (ICES). Special reference is made to the need for full participation in the 1973 IMCO Conference on Marine Pollution and the Third United Nations Conference on the Law of the Sea. It is recommended that "any mechanism for coordinating and stimulating the actions of the different United Nations organs in connection with environmental problems include among its functions overall responsibility for ensuring that needed advice on marine pollution problems shall be provided to Governments."[64]

More important, it is recommended that the governments collectively endorse the principles set forth as guiding concepts for the Third Law of the Sea Conference and 1973 IMCO Conference. These principles, based on those adopted at the second session of the preparatory Intergovernmental Working Group on Marine Pollution held at Ottawa in November 1971, declare that every state has a duty to protect and preserve the marine environment (in particular, to prevent pollution that may affect areas in which an internationally shared resource is located) and that each should ensure that its national legislation provides adequate sanctions against those who infringe existing regulations on marine pollution. States also should assume joint responsibility for the preservation of the marine environment beyond the limits of national jurisdiction. In addition to its responsibility for environmental protection within the limits of its territorial sea, a coastal state has responsibility to protect adjacent areas of the environment from damage that may result from activities within its territory. All states should ensure that vessels under their registration comply with internationally agreed upon rules and standards relating to ship design and construction, operating procedures, and other relevant factors. States should cooperate in the development of such rules, standards, and procedures in the appropriate international bodies. Following an accident on the high seas which may be expected to result in serious pollution, or the threat of serious pollution, of the sea, a coastal state facing grave and imminent danger to its coastline and related interests may take appropriate measures as may be necessary to prevent, mitigate, or eliminate such danger, in accordance with internationally agreed upon rules and standards.

The Stockholm Conference also recommended that governments take note of the principles discussed, but neither endorsed nor rejected, at the Ottawa meeting.[65] The proposals submited to that meeting by the host government of Canada were as follows:

(1) A State may exercise special authority in areas of the sea adjacent to its territorial waters where functional controls of a continuing nature are necessary for the effective prevention of pollution which could cause dam-

age or injury to the land or marine environment under its exclusive or sovereign authority.

(2) A coastal State may prohibit any vessel which does not comply with internationally agreed rules and standards or, in their absence, with reasonable national rules and standards of the coastal State in question, from entering waters under its environmental protection authority.

(3) The basis on which a State should exercise rights or powers, in addition to its sovereign rights or powers, pursuant to its special authority in areas adjacent to its territorial waters, is that such rights or powers should be deemed to be delegated to that State by the world community on behalf of humanity as a whole. The rights and powers exercised must be consistent with the State's primary responsibility for marine environmental protection in the areas concerned; they should be subject to international rules and standards and to review before an appropriate international tribunal.

It also should be noted that the Stockholm Declaration on the Human Environment[66] contains principles of international environmental policy that have both direct and indirect relevance to the treatment of marine pollution. Principle 7, for example, declares that states shall take all possible steps to prevent pollution of the seas by substances that are liable to create hazards to human health, to harm living resources and marine life, to damage amenities, or to interfere with other legitimate uses of the sea. Principle 21 recognizes that states have, in accordance with the Charter of the United Nations and the principles of international law, the sovereign right to exploit their own resources pursuant to their own environmental policies, and the responsibility to ensure that activities within their jurisdiction or control do not cause damage to the environment of other states or of areas beyond the limits of national jurisdiction. And Principle 22 declares that states shall cooperate to develop further the international law regarding liability and compensation for the victims of pollution and other environmental damage caused by activities within the jurisdiction or control of such states to areas beyond their jurisdiction.

Since the adoption of all the Stockholm recommendations by the General Assembly in December 1972 (and their referral for implementation to the newly established United Nations Environment Secretariat in Nairobi), it seems fairly safe to anticipate that most of these principles will soon be regarded as expressive of international environmental policy. In the immediate future, however, treaty developments designed to implement these principles are likely to come mostly from regional initiatives in the developed world.[67]

Appraisal

The future of international environmental law needs to be secured chiefly through the development of state responsibility. The right kinds of measures for the prevention and control of marine pollution are not likely to emerge if legal development is conceived wholly in acquisitive terms, such as an extension of coastal rights. The essence of environmental policy is obligation, and one wishes that this were reflected more clearly in current claims to authority over the preservation of the coastal and noncoastal marine environments. The current proposals for an exclusive "economic zone" or "patrimonial sea" are not necessarily detrimental to the environmental cause, but one hopes that there is a real understanding that the exclusive or special economic rights which the coastal state claims to exercise in its zone are more likely to be respected if the claimant state faithfully tries to discharge its environmental obligations within the limits of its opportunity and capability. No part of the sea "belongs" to any one portion of humanity, to be abused at pleasure.

Perhaps it is historically unfortunate that the first systematic efforts to preserve the ocean environment are being taken at the same time that many of the developing coastal states have the first opportunity to focus their economic aspirations on attainable marine resources at a considerable distance from the shoreline. But at present it still is the industrially developed and maritime countries that pose the most serious threat to the ocean environment. It is to their law-making initiatives that we must look for the most important correctives, and a judgment of their efforts so far must be a mixed one. The shipping states deserve credit for recent reforms to combat the dangers of pollution by oil and to curb dumping practices at sea. Recent changes in the membership of IMCO are likely to make that technically competent body better suited for the formulation of international initiatives directed at the welfare of the ocean environment, albeit at a time when technical agencies are threatened by over-politicization of issues. The pollution prevention role of IMCO is likely to be extended and clarified with the adoption of a comprehensive law of the sea treaty at UNCLOS III, and indeed even if the law-making conference fails.

It is still too early to pass final judgment on UNCLOS III from the perspective of environmental law and policy, but clearly the opportunity to develop state responsibility for marine pollution to a higher level is strictly limited by the need to reconcile the imposition of international standards in Committee III with the grant of national jurisdiction in Committee II. Those drafts most likely to be influential in the final stages of the Conference, such as the Informal Single Negotiating Texts produced by the chairmen of the three Main Committees in May 1975, fail to reflect the imprint of the best available scientific facts and judgments. A comprehensive treaty on marine pollution would have to go far beyond the formulation of general principles by taking into account the most relevant "legal facts," such as the four outlined earlier, and the variety of pollution situations that might occur, such as the thirty-nine identified in this essay. Only a few of these situations are likely to be dealt with directly in any final text emerging from UNCLOS III.

The most crucial improvements that need to be effected are in the control of shore-generated waste emissions and effluents, which account for 80 percent of the problem of marine pollution. Unfortunately, these sources of marine pollution contribute also to air and water pollution within each state, and international proposals for effective control can be expected to open a Pandora's box of objections about interference with the internal affairs of "target" states. The international development of controls over these land-based sources of marine pollution cannot be expected to take place in a single conference of plenipotentiaries, or even in a series of law-making conventions, but only through the gradual absorption of internationally recommended standards and safeguards in national and regional environmental law and policy. Fortunately, the United Nations Environment Program seems to be aware of the environmental shortcomings of UNCLOS III,[68] and it may be hoped that some of these deficiencies may be remedied at the Second U.N. Conference on the Human Environment.[69]

Notes

1. For a review of the United Nations Conference on the Human Environment preparations, see Johnston, *International Environmental Law: Recent Developments and Canadian Contributions,* in CANADIAN PERSPECTIVES ON INTERNATIONAL LAW (R. Macdonald, G. Morris & D. Johnston eds. 1973), at 555–611.

2. The range of environmental treaty making is reviewed in Bleicher, *An Overview of International Environmental Regulation,* 2 ECOL. L.Q. 1, 31–51 (1972). For a collection of texts, see J. BARROS & D. JOHNSTON, THE INTERNATIONAL LAW OF POLLUTION (1974). General studies on international environmental law are beginning to appear: see, for example, LAW INSTITUTIONS AND THE GLOBAL ENVIRONMENT (J. Hargrove ed. 1972); and R. FALK, THIS ENDANGERED PLANET: PROSPECTS AND PROPOSALS FOR HUMAN SURVIVAL (1971).

3. *See* United Nations Conference on the Human Environment, Stockholm, 1972, Report, U.N. DOC. A/Conf. 48/14/11, and Declaration and Principles of the United Nations Conference on the Human Environment, U.N. DOC. A/AC. 138/CS III/L. 17. *See also* Johnston, *The United Nations' Institutional Response to Stockholm: A Case Study in the International Politics of Institutional Change,* 26 INT'L ORG. 255 (1972).

4. Rev. Stats. Can., 1970, c. 2 (1st supp.).

5. *See* Johnston, *Recent Canadian Marine Legislation: An Historical Perspective,* in CANADIAN–U.S. MARITIME PROBLEMS 63–67 (L. Alexander & G. Hawkins eds. 1972) (Law of the Sea Workshop, June 1971).

6. For a discussion of environmentalism as concept, mood, and perspective, see Johnston, *supra* note 1, at 555–59.

7. *See* examples given in J. BARROS & D. JOHNSTON, *supra* note 2, at 6–8.

8. On technological developments in the control of oil spills see Hoult, *Marine Pollution, Concentrating on the Effects of Hydrocarbons in Seawater,* in CANADIAN–U.S. MARITIME PROBLEMS, *supra* note 5, at 29–31. *See also* Knauss, *Ocean Pollution–Status and Prognostication,* in LAW OF THE SEA: THE EMERGING REGIME OF THE OCEANS (J. Gamble & G. Pontecorvo eds. 1974), at 313–28.

9. The Canadian government has been accused, quite fairly, of arbitrariness in seeking to create "shipping safety control zones" in the Arctic which are not to exceed 100 miles in extent. *See, e.g.,* the debate in THE UNITED NATIONS AND OCEAN

MANAGEMENT, PROOCEEDINGS OF THE FIFTH ANNUAL CONFERENCE OF THE LAW OF THE SEA INSTITUTE 321–23 (L. Alexander ed. 1971). The "reasonableness" of this claim is defended by many writers. *See, e.g.,* Pharand, *Oil Pollution Control in the Canadian Arctic,* 7 TEXAS INT'L L.J. 45, 67–71 (1971). But the truth is perhaps that any uniform boundary limits for the purposes of environmental management are likely to be somewhat arbitrary and difficult to justify, either in scientific or managerial terms. The exercise of national functional jurisdiction over extensive offshore areas may not result in significant improvements in the efficiency of ocean management if it is not accompanied by a rising level of environmental consciousness. The "mystique of the frontier," in Richard Falk's phrase, might simply have moved further out to sea. A uniform 200-mile "economic zone" might attract much the same kind of myths as a three-mile territorial sea.

10.   This Convention was opened for signature at the end of 1972, at the conclusion of the Intergovernmental Conference on the Convention on the Dumping of Wastes at Sea. For text, see 11 INT'L LEGAL MATERIALS 1291 (1972). "Mercury and mercury compounds" are included in the prohibited list contained in Annex I and referred to in Article IV of the text. Paragraph 9 of Annex I provides, however, that the prohibition does not apply to the listed matters when they are found to be only "trace contaminants." For a discussion, see de Mestral, *La Convention sur la prevention de la pollution resultant de l'immersion de dechets,* 11 CAN. Y.B. INT'L LAW 226, 232–35 (1973). For a more general study, see Johnston, *Marine Pollution Control: Law, Science and Politics,* 28 INT'L J. 69 (1972–73).

11.   This Conference, which ended in November 1973, opened for signature the International Convention for the Prevention of Pollution from Ships. For text, see 12 INT'L LEGAL MATERIALS 1319 (1973). The politically selective use of scientific opinion was also a feature of the 1972 Stockholm Conference on the Human Environment. Knelman, *What Happened at Stockholm,* 28 INT'L J. 28, 46–49 (1972–73). Unfortunately, the same abuse has been evident at the Third U.N. Conference on the Law of the Sea in contexts such as fishery management and pollution control where one would have wished for a high degree of dependency on enlightened scientific opinion.

12.   On the "20 percent approach," see Johnston, *supra* note 10, at 69–74. But not all characterizations based on scientific judgment and directed at practical solutions countenance the "heroic" approach. The following fourfold characterization, for example, has been proposed by Yates, *Unilateral and Multilateral Approaches to Environmental Problems,* in THE INTERNATIONAL LEGAL ASPECTS OF POLLUTION (1971), *reprinted in* 21 TORONTO L.J. 173, 186–89 (1971).

> 1. A situation which tends "to be domestic in scope, such as air pollution in the neighborhood of cities, or inland water pollution. Though it is true that over a period of time there may be international ecological consequences these situations are dealt with on a national level."
> 2. A situation which tends "to be international but remains regional in scope; for example, international rivers or water basins that are international" (*e.g.,* the Great Lakes).
> 3. A situation which "is national or regional in scope for most purposes, but because of special ecological sensitivities requires a large measure of international cooperation for conservation" (*e.g.,* the Canadian Arctic).
> 4. "Those areas of the biosphere which by their nature can only be viewed as resources that that are the common heritage of mankind, including the ocean, certain areas of the seabed and subsoil thereof, and outer space. These areas can only be protected from ecological damage by acceptance of international standards and creation of multi-national agencies to oversee activities that must be regulated."

13.   For an analysis of this trend, see D. JOHNSTON & E. GOLD, THE ECONOMIC ZONE IN THE LAW OF THE SEA: SURVEY, ANALYSIS AND APPRAISAL OF CURRENT TRENDS (Occasional Papers Series No. 17, Law of the Sea Institute, Kingston, Rhode Island, 1973). The Informal Single Negotiating Text produced at the Geneva ses-

sion of the Conference in May 1975 envisages that within the proposed zone the coastal state would have, *inter alia,* "jurisdiction with regard to the preservation of the marine environment, including pollution control and abatement." This grant of jurisdiction is not characterized as "exclusive" or "special"; in exercising it, the coastal state would be required to have "due regard to the rights and duties of other States"; and this language may have to be further modified in order to be reconciled with other provisions in the treaty. Compare Article 45 in U.N. Doc. A/Conf. 62/WP. 8/Part II, p. 19, with the ten chapters on "Protection and Preservation of the Marine Environment" in Part III, pp. 2–14, of the same text. But the existence of "special" coastal authority, at the least, seems central to the concept of an economic zone.

14. Until an international regime for the protection of all vulnerable areas can be brought into existence, "Canada must take steps to ensure that irreparable harm will not occur in the interim." Trudeau, *Canada Leads Fight Against Pollution,* STATE-MENTS AND SPEECHES, No. 70/3, at 3 (1970). For a proposal along these lines made at the Third U.N. Conference on the Law of the Sea, see U.N. Doc. A/Conf.62/WP.8/Part III, p. 8 (Art. 2065).

15. *See* Oil in Navigable Waters Act 1971, c. 21 (U.K.); and Joint Communique of Indonesia, Malaysia, and Singapore, issued Oct. 16, 1971, in the Singapore newspaper *Sing Tao Ri Bao,* Oct. 17, 1971. In this latter text, however, the special coastal responsibility of the claimant states is said to be necessary to maintain the "safety of navigation." With respect to the Strait of Malacca, Indonesia and Malaysia now seek to encompass the coastal areas with extended territorial claims and, unlike Singapore, deny that the strait has international status. *See* Shaw, *The Juridical Status of the Malacca Straits and its Relation to Indonesia and Malaysia,* 3 NANYANG U. L. J. 284 (1969).

16. U.N. Doc. A/Conf.62/WP.8/Part II, 19 (Art. 45).

17. *See* Statement by Mr. J.A. Beesley, Canadian delegate to the U.N. Seabed Committee, Plenary Session, Aug. 5, 1971.

18. Art. 6(1), 559 U.N.T.S. 285.

19. *See* D. JOHNSTON, THE INTERNATIONAL LAW OF FISHERIES: A FRAMEWORK FOR POLICY–ORIENTED INQUIRIES 275–82 (1965).

20. This type of claim is unlikely to be made explicitly by developing coastal states which lack the capability to take effective measures for the prevention and control of marine pollution in extensive offshore areas beyond relatively modest territorial limits.

21. This concept of a regional economic zone may be limited to the sharing of living resources. *See* U.N. Doc. A/Conf.62/WP.8/Part II, 24–25 (Articles 57–59).

22. U.N. Doc. A/Conf. 48/C.R.P. 26.

23. Especially Principles 7, 21, and 22. *See* p. 555 *infra.*

24. Art. 2, 450 U.N.T.S. 82, 84.

25. On efforts to distinguish between permissible and nonpermissible dumping and discharge, see Johnston, *supra* note 10, at 93–101.

26. *See Founex Report on Development and Environment,* INT'L CONCILIATION, No. 586, at 7 (1973).

27. U.N. Doc. A/AC. 138/SC III/L. 17. Part 4 of the Declaration reads, for example:

> In the developing countries most of the environmental problems are caused by under-development. Millions continue to live far below the minimum levels required for a decent human existence, deprived of adequate food and clothing, shelter and education, health and sanitation. Therefore, the developing countries must direct their efforts to development, bearing in mind their priorities and the need to safeguard and improve the environment. For the same purpose, the industrialized countries should make efforts to reduce the gap between themselves and the developing countries.

In the industrialized countries, environmental problems are generally related to industrialization and technical development.

28. *See* J. BARROS & D. JOHNSTON, *supra* note 2, at 18–66.

29. *See* situation 2b in the list at p. 540 *supra*. Trail Smelter Arbitration (United States v. Canada), 3 U.N.R.I.A.A. 1905, 1965 (1949).

30. *Id.* at 1964.

31. *See* situation 1 in the list at p. 540 *supra*. [1949] I.C.J. REP. 4, 22.

32. 450 U.N.T.S. 82, 96.

33. *Id.*

34. 499 U.N.T.S. 311, 314.

35. *Id.* at 316.

36. 559 U.N.T.S. 285, 286–88.

37. *Id.* at 290.

38. 480 U.N.T.S. 43, 45.

39. *See, e.g.,* J. BARROS & D. JOHNSTON, *supra* note 2, at 83–173. *See also* Bourne, *International Law and Pollution of International Rivers and Lakes,* 21 U. TORONTO L.J. 193 (1971); Bleicher, *supra* note 2, at 31–35.

40. J. BARROS & D. JOHNSTON, *supra* note 2, at 77–82.

41. 327 U.N.T.S. 3. *See* Gold, *Pollution of the Sea and International Law: A Canadian Perspective,* 3 J. MARITIME L. & COM. 13 (1971).

42. Moreover, the provisions, as amended in 1962, exempt tankers from the prohibition against the deliberate discharge of oil when they are more than fifty miles from the nearest land and nontankers or when the discharge is made "as far as practicable from land" (Article III). Nor does the prohibition apply to "the escape of oil or of oily mixture resulting from damage to a ship or unavoidable leakage if all reasonable precautions have been taken after the occurrence of the damage or discovery of the leakage for the purpose of preventing or minimizing the escape" (Article IV(b)). For further deficiencies of the 1954 Convention, see Johnston, *supra* note 10, at 75–76.

43. *See* note 11 *supra*. The coming into force of this Convention has been delayed by the tendency of many governments to await the outcome of UNCLOS III on related jurisdictional issues.

44. 9 INT'L LEGAL MATERIALS 25 (1970).

45. *Id.* at 45.

46. 11 INT'L LEGAL MATERIALS 284 (1972).

47. 536 U.N.T.S. 27.

48. 18 U.S.T. 1857, T.I.A.S. No. 6331.

49. The text of the Regulations is reproduced in 1 F. ARZT, MARINE LAWS: NAVIGATION AND SAFETY 443–65 (1963). For other features of the 1971 Convention and of the public and private conventions of 1969, see Bleicher, *supra* note 2, at 38–42; Johnston, *supra* note 10, at 74–80. *See also* Healy & Paulson, *The C.M.I. and IMCO Conventions on Civil Liability for Oil Pollution,* 1 J. MARITIME L. & COM. 93 (1969); Healy, *The International Convention for Civil Liability for Oil Pollution Damage, 1969,* 1 J. MARITIME L. & COM. 317 (1970).

50. For an explanation and defense, see Beesley, *Rights and Responsibilities of Arctic Coastal States: The Canadian View,* 3 J. MARITIME L. & COM. 1 (1971–72); Legault, *Canadian Arctic Waters Pollution Prevention Legislation,* in THE UNITED NATIONS AND OCEAN MANAGEMENT, *supra* note 9, at 301. *See also* Wilkes, *International Administrative Due Process and Control of Pollution—The Canadian Arctic Waters Example,* 2 J. MARITIME L. & COM. 499 (1971); Gotlieb & Dalfen, *National Jurisdiction and International Responsibility: New Canadian Approaches to International Law,* 67 AM. J. INT'L L. 229, 240–47 (1973).

51. Much comparative study needs to be made of different national approaches to

oil pollution problems. *See* Swan, *International and National Approaches to Oil Pollution Responsibility: An Emerging Regime for a Global Problem,* 50 ORE. L. REV. 506 (1971).

52. *See* Bilder, *The Canadian Arctic Water Pollution Prevention Act: New Stresses on the Law of the Sea,* 69 MICH. L. REV. 1 (1970); Clingan, *Third Party Limitations of Canadian Legislation and the Implications for International Law Development,* in CANADIAN–U.S. MARITIME PROBLEMS, *supra* note 5, at 68–74; Henkin, *Arctic Anti-Pollution: Does Canada Make or Break International Law?,* 65 AM. J. INT'L L. 131 (1971).

53. *See* D. Johnston & E. Gold, *supra* note 13, at 28–33.

54. Johnston, *supra* note 1, at 581–593.

55. The rationale for the Canadian legislation has been put forward in the Informal Single Negotiating Text prepared in May 1975. *See* Art 20(5) in U.N. DOC. A/Conf. 62/WP. 8/Part III, at 8.

56. *See* pp. 544–545 *supra.*

57. For a general review of the regional maritime issues in the North Pacific, see Johnston, *Development, Environment, and Marine Resources in the North Pacific* (unpublished manuscript).

58. 9 INT'L LEGAL MATERIALS 359 (1970).

59. 11 INT'L LEGAL MATERIALS 262 (1972).

60. *Id.* at 1294.

61. For a description of the Bonn Agreement, the Oslo Convention, and the Ocean Dumping Convention, see Johnston, *supra* note 10, at 76–77, 86–89.

62. Note, for example, that the Conference held in February 1974 which adopted the Convention for the Prevention of Marine Pollution from Land-Based Sources was attended by only 14 European participants and two European observers, 13 INT'L LEGAL MATERIALS 352 (1974). Regional developments are especially conspicuous in the Baltic and Mediterranean. *See* 1974 Convention on the Protection of the Marine Environment of the Baltic Sea Area, 13 INT'L LEGAL MATERIALS 546 (1974); and Draft Convention for the Protection of the Marine Environment against Pollution in the Mediterranean, and related protocols, 14 INT'L LEGAL MATERIALS 481 (1975).

63. U.N. DOC. A/Conf. 48/14.

64. *Id.* at 48.

65. U.N. DOC. A/Conf. 48/IWGMP II/5, 7.

66. U.N. DOC. A/Conf. 48/14, 2–65. For a recent commentary, see Sohn, *The Stockholm Declaration on the Human Environment,* 14 HARV. INT'L L. J. 423 (1973).

67. The Governing Council of UNEP is disappointed at the slow rate of accession to existing international conventions in the environmental field. *See* Decision 24 (III), 14 INT'L LEGAL MATERIALS 1076 (1975).

68. Maurice Strong, Secretary-General of UNEP, made this clear in an address to the Caracas session of UNCLOS III in July 1974. For views on the need for environmental improvements at UNCLOS III, see R. Hallman, *Towards an Environmentally Sound Law of the Sea* (International Institute for Environment and Development, 1974); and CRITICAL ENVIRONMENTAL ISSUES ON THE LAW OF THE SEA (International Institute for Environment and Development, R. Stein ed. 1975); and A. d'Amato and J. Hargrove, ENVIRONMENT AND THE LAW OF THE SEA (American Society of International Law, Studies in Transnational Legal Policy, No. 5, 1974).

69. The Governing Council of UNEP has recommended the convening of such a conference "not earlier than 1980" after the completion of a series of related conferences including UNCLOS III. Decision 43 III of the Governing Council, 14 INT'L LEGAL MATERIALS 1087 (1975).

Afterword

EUGENE V. ROSTOW

On July 1, 1975, under the immemorial and immutable rules of Yale University, Myres S. McDougal became Sterling Professor of Law Emeritus, at the peak of his creativity.

This splendid Festschrift is witness to McDougal's place in the realm of legal scholarship. My afterword will attempt a simple, preliminary sketch of his person and his work.

The facts are not in doubt, and may be stipulated: born and brought up in Mississippi; graduated from the University of Mississippi, where he taught classics for two years; a Rhodes Scholar, who had studied to advantage with Holdsworth and Brierly; a Sterling Fellow and J.S.D. during vintage times at Yale. His youthful frolic in the classics aside, McDougal's whole working career, thus far at any rate, has been rooted in the Yale Law School, save for a lively apprenticeship (1931 to 1934) at the Law School of the University of Illinois and a season in the foreign affairs bureaucracy during World War II. His wartime experiences shifted the focus of his immediate concern from the law of real property, which he called Land-Use Planning, to international law, which he identifies as the Public Order of the World Community.

The facts, however, do not begin to suggest the magnitude of the task of accounting for the phenomenon of Myres Smith McDougal.

Reprinted by permission of The Yale Law Journal Company and Fred B. Rothman & Company from THE YALE LAW JOURNAL 84 (1975) 704.

I.

Myres McDougal is not a complex personality, as many students of the subject have supposed. Scholars in the field, writers of theses and learned monographs, have created a mystery where there is none. Confused by McDougal's diversity, they have missed the key point because it is too simple for their solemn methods. The Grand Cham is not one man, but three remarkable men contained in one man's skin.

The first of the three McDougals—perhaps we should identify him as Senator McDougal—is a consummate Mississippi politician of the old school, wordly, perceptive, and persuasive—principled, to be sure, but above all an artist in power. There is not a trace of Senator Claghorn in Senator McDougal—no fustian, no bombast, nothing of the demagogue. But he knows about power, gathers it, cultivates it, and uses it, with a grace Senator Russell and Mr. Sam Rayburn would have understood, and appreciated. Senator McDougal has been the innovative President of the American Association of Law Schools and of the American Society of International Law. For many years, he was a Baron of the Yale Law Faculty, Chairman of its Graduate Committee, and mover and shaker in its vehement political life, which occasionally became internecine warfare. From time to time, he has advised lawyers, government departments, and corporations, served on committees, and proved to be the architect of victory in international arbitrations and legislative contests, like that which reversed the Supreme Court's first decision in *Sabbatino*.[1] And, above all, he is the spider at the center of a worldwide Old Boy network which is the marvel of the age. It deals with the very stuff of power—appointments, promotions, honors, the makeup of key committees, assistance to a brother or a sister in difficulty for the moment. A sabbatical, let us say, in Bangkok? The Deanship, hypothetically, at Freiburg, or Florida, or Cornell? A grant and a visiting appointment to tide over a period of political turbulence at home? Appointment to the staff or even higher reaches of a federal department? Nothing could be simpler. Nor could any set of decisionmaking processes be managed with greater elegance or discretion.

Mac has never given Senator McDougal his head, of course. He has interests and goals which have commanded priority. The other McDougals have required too much even of Mac's titanic energies to allow the Senator domination in his life. But in one realm the Senator has been permitted full sway. Professor McDougal was thrice Chairman of the Yale Law School's Faculty Committee on the selection of a Dean.

The Yale bylaws provide that the University President place the names of prospective professors before the Yale Corporation for appointment "upon the recommendation" of each School's Board of Permanent Officers—a body which at Yale consists of the full professors. The naming of Deans, however, is a different matter. The statutes say that the President nominates Deans to the Corporation "after consultation" with the Board of Permanent Officers of the School concerned, although on this issue the Board may graciously allow the rest of the faculty to participate in the ritual. At Yale, the entire law faculty has a voice in selecting its Dean. For as long as the memory of man runs, this bylaw has had a special gloss of usage in the life of the Yale Law School. The Yale law faculty, proud of its autonomy, insists that it elect its own Deans. Indeed, it is hard to imagine that a Dean could lead our stiff-necked faculty unless he had a mandate running directly from it. On the other hand, the Presidents of Yale are proud and stiff-necked, too, and jealous of their prerogatives. They insist that Deans are their representatives to the faculty, just as the faculties insist on the obverse proposition. And Yale Presidents have a tendency to recite the literal words of the University bylaws on these occasions, and sometimes they try to avoid collective action by the faculty, which could be interpreted as an election.

The independence of the Yale law faculty goes beyond electing its own Deans. On one celebrated occasion, Dean Henry Wade Rogers was appointed Judge of the United States Court of Appeals for the Second Circuit. In those comfortable days, the judge thought it would be nice to remain Dean of the Law School as well. The faculty soon disabused him of that idea. Vigorous action led by Arthur Corbin induced Rogers to resign and obtained the appointment of Tom Swan as Dean. Judge Swan was a great Dean, and his consulship marks the true beginning of the modern Yale Law School.

In fact, a Dean recommended by a majority of the Yale law faculty has only once been rejected by the President of Yale in modern times—in 1939. All other Deans appointed to the post have first been chosen and anointed by the faculty, through a tribal rite I once described as "a procedure so arcane that only a few initiates understand it, and for most of them the postpartum trauma is so great that they forget, quickly and with relief, what really did happen." [2] It is an exercise which requires tolerance, forbearance, and humor on the part both of the faculty and of the President, and a high measure of diplomacy on the part of the Chairman of the Faculty Committee. He is placed squarely between Scylla and Charybdis and exposed to slings and arrows from every side.

Senator McDougal discharged these delicate duties on three occasions, each time to the grateful acclaim of jealous faculty and jealous President alike. Each time, needless to say, the Dean of Mac's choice was elected by the faculty, and appointed, more or less meekly, by the President and Fellows of the Yale Corporation.

The second McDougal is the kindest and most generous of friends and teachers. I have never witnessed a finer human relationship than that of McDougal's enlarged family—the web of interest, concern, and affection which links him to present and former students and colleagues all over the world. The skills of Senator McDougal helped to place and promote many of them. But Professor McDougal has remained a living force in their lives, helping them to fulfill their highest potential as lawyers, government officials, scholars, or teachers by his encouragement and example. It is an extraordinary comment on McDougal's spirit and character that his former students, much as they respect him and use his methods, remain free to disagree with him comfortably, and without strain. He has established a school, not a sect.

II.

McDougal III—McDougal the scholar and theorist of law—is the most remarkable and important of all—the McDougal whose substance gives meaning to the activities and achievements of Senator McDougal and Professor McDougal the teacher. The third and ultimate McDougal is a formidable man, altogether different in personality from both his siblings. Where the Senator is suave, and the teacher generous, sympathetic, and supportive, the intellectual McDougal is fierce. An argument he regards as shallow or erroneous arouses his righteous wrath. The world of ideas is the passionate heart of his universe. In that realm, there is only one criterion, and his devotion to it is complete.

McDougal's achievement as a scholar is so original, and bulks so large in our world, that we find it nearly impossible to realize its scope, power, and significance. This is especially the case in his own school, where all the normal factors of family life inhibit the acceptance of such judgments. It is fair to say, I believe, that no American scholar save Story has built a house to compare with McDougal's. His vision is not international law, or the law of property, but the process of law itself. Having translated his vision into a theory, and a methodological scheme, he has applied it with stunning power to panel after panel of the misty field of international law. Among the modern writers of treatises, Corbin is the only one whose work compares with McDougal's in coherence and in quality. Like McDougal, Corbin developed a sophisticated and analytical method for studying law as part of the social process, and he used it superlatively well in his classic treatise. For all its sophistication, however, Corbin's way of identifying the issues at stake in the development of social policy through law is not nearly so complete as McDougal's, so systematic, nor so far-reaching. As a consequence, his analysis is not so fundamental.

It is impossible, and would be unfair, to contemplate Mac's accomplishment as a scholar without recalling his partnership with Harold Lasswell. Before the McDougal–Lasswell firm was established, Lasswell was well known as a pioneer in political and social science. He was one of the first scholars to use Freudian insights in the study of political behavior and was a key figure in the serious literature of propaganda and a number of other features of modern political life. The collaboration of McDougal and Lasswell has certainly been one of the most important, and most fruitful, in modern intellectual history. It has been developing over a period of nearly forty years and embodies an achievement which is changing the way we think about law.

III.

McDougal came to Yale from Oxford at a definite stage of the revolution in jurisprudence which had become manifest fifty years before, with the publication of *The Common Law*. McDougal's work can be understood only in the context of the American realist movement, the soil in which it was nurtured.[3]

Holmes' great book, and the intellectual process which produced it, were typical of the intellectual climate of the late nineteenth century. In every body of knowledge, from economics and political theory to literary criticism, two tendencies were at work and often at war. One group of knights carried the banner of science, the other of history. The first school stressed the importance of "reason" and "theory," the second of "nature" and "fact." Both claimed the nearly magical prestige of natural science and its methods as authority for what they were doing. The theorists invoked the example of Newton, the historical school that of Darwin and the classifiers. In the din of battle, few of the protagonists ever perceived that both schools were right—that organized knowledge requires both facts and theories, both a static and a dynamic view, both logic and experience.

In law, or at least in American law, the late nineteenth century was a time when the rationalizing, system-building component of law was becoming oppressive. The judges and the lawyers tended to treat precedent—or at least to speak of precedent—as a rigid and nearly absolute rule governing the development of law. At Harvard, Langdell preached the gospel of a science of law, to be distilled by professors from the law library as a set of clear, symmetrical, and logically consistent propositions or rules. If the professors were good enough, the law could be reduced to a code, or restatement, that would end the sprawling confusion of the common law. Then judgment could be found, not made, and society could at long last enjoy a stable, certain, and perfectly predictable legal order.

To this view, the opening page of *The Common Law* was a challenge direct:

> The object of this book [Holmes wrote] is to present a general view of the Common Law. To accomplish the task, other tools are needed besides logic. It is something to show that the consistency of a system requires a particular result, but it is not all. The life of the law has not been logic:

it has been experience. The felt necessities of the time, the prevalent moral and political theories, intuitions of public policy, avowed or unconscious, even the prejudices which judges share with their fellow-men, have had a good deal more to do than the syllogism in determining the rules by which men should be governed. The law embodies the story of a nation's development through many centuries, and it cannot be dealt with as if it contained only the axioms and corollaries of a book of mathematics. In order to know what it is, we must know what it has been, and what it tends to become. We must alternately consult history and existing theories of legislation. But the most difficult labor will be to understand the combination of the two into new products at every stage. The substance of the law at any given time pretty nearly corresponds, so far as it goes, with what is then understood to be convenient; but its form and machinery, and the degree to which it is able to work out desired results, depend very much upon its past.

In Massachusetts to-day, while, on the one hand, there are a great many rules which are quite sufficiently accounted for by their manifest good sense, on the other, there are some which can only be understood by reference to the infancy of procedure among the German tribes, or to the social condition of Rome under the Decemvirs.[4]

Holmes' intellectual formation showed the influence of English, French, and German historical studies, and the influence of William James and Charles Peirce as well, with their insight into the methods of science and the role of theory in the structure of knowledge. Holmes saw the social process as a historian—indeed, as a participant in history. The professor and then the judge never forgot that he had been a Brevet-Colonel in the Civil War. But he knew, too, that facts do not exist apart from the ideas we hold about them—that a flag is more than a bit of bunting.

The American debate about the nature and purpose of law developed as an integral theme in the formation of modern American intellectual life as a whole, starting eighty-five or ninety years ago. Holmes' essays and speeches, and his example, had influence. But he was hardly alone. The debate had all the characteristics of American intellectual life generally. It was vigorous, colorful, not very learned, insular, and often naive; it was also, of course, curious, creative, and endlessly drawn to reality. Few of the participants, except for Holmes, Pound, and a number of later exceptions, had read much beyond the more obvious Anglo-American classics. Our legal literature was almost universally crippled—as so large a part of American intellectual life has been crippled—by philosophical ignorance, and especially by ignorance about the nature of discovery, and the relationship between hypotheses and evidence—between "theory" and "fact"—in any system of organized knowledge. Most of us were content to proclaim our faith in "pragmatism" or "institutionalism" and our undying opposition to "abstract theory."

The role of rules in the law was the most active front in the continuing battle, for reasons basic to the philosophical issues at stake. And it has remained a central one, with some shift in emphasis, ever since.

The rules of law, however awesome in appearance, are tentative hypotheses advanced from time to time by judges, lawyers, legislators, and others who write law, or write about it, in order to explain the changing patterns of social decision embodied in the law. The impulse to formulate rules is not simply a measure of the obsessive tendencies in the legal mind. It derives from an ethical imperative basic to every legal system—the principle that like cases should be decided alike.

Some of those who participated in the battle as "realists" attacked the rules root and branch. They were genuine nihilists and denied the legitimacy—or indeed the presence—of a generalizing element in law altogether. For them, the rules of law were fig leaves of deception. Decisions were in fact based on unstated interests or value preferences—on the judge's state of mind, his bourgeois prejudices, or the state of his digestion. The reasons he offered for decisions were afterthoughts, cynical rationalizations, representing the judge not as a conscientious lawyer, working within the permissible limits of his craft, but as a willful autocrat.

Others among the realists concentrated not on the existence, but on the intellectual quality, of the rules of law. They were content to demonstrate that what passed for orthodox rules of law no longer corresponded to reality; that they were meaningless, or circular, or self-contradictory, like the concept of "implied malice" which drew Holmes' scorn.[5]

A third party within the realist camp was fascinated by the fact that the judge often has a significant possibility of choice in deciding a case— choice in finding the facts, which Jerome Frank stressed, or choice among the rules which might be taken as major premise for the case. While nearly all the realists agreed with their opponents that most cases which reach appellate courts can be decided one way only, they realized that many of the remaining cases are settled by the judge's "qualification" or "classification" of the controversy—his nearly instinctive decision to treat it in one perspective rather than another. The rest of the cases are decided by changes in the rules of law: by the conscious determination of the judge or other lawmaker that one or another of the social interests at stake in the controversy should now be given a different weight in the balance, even at the expense of continuity in the law. This was the feature of the lawmaking process to which Holmes and Cardozo had given so much attention—the fact that judges, like legislators, had to make policy choices. There was no way for them to escape from their share in the sovereign prerogative.

IV.

How and on what grounds were such choices to be made? Cardozo had said that the judge must "get his knowledge just as the legislator gets

it, from experience and study and reflection; in brief, from life itself." [6]
Holmes had preached with fire in his pen that the law must reach into
economics, sociology, philosophy, and history, into all the sciences of man
and of society, to help make its policy choices rational. But singularly little
had been done to carry out Holmes' gospel by the early thirties, when
Myres McDougal entered the fray, fresh from Mississippi and Oxford. He
came to Yale at a particularly heady time in the life of that institution. He
had benefited greatly from his tutelage with Holdsworth. He already had a
strong sense of law as part of history and a clear perception of the central
fact that law is the instrument of society for fulfilling its ideal of justice.
But he had much to unlearn, too. His year as a Sterling Fellow was filled
with the delightful crash of breaking icons. Sturges and Arnold were there,
hooting at the very possibility of law. Others helped to demonstrate, in
every class, and at every cocktail party, that the rules the young Rhodes
Scholar imagined were so clear and so settled were in fact nonsense—that
they had ceased to correspond to the law-in-fact or had lost contact with
the mores of the community.

The young McDougal plunged into the pond with zest and enthusiasm.
He never joined the camp of the nihilists, but he ranks with the best of the
realists in an effort which has characterized his work ever since—the scrupu-
lous and critical reformulation of the rules of law in the light of the tests
and tenets of realism. One could pick illustrations at random. I have
worked recently with his masterful reformulation of the principle of self-
defense in international law, in which he shows that a dozen seemingly
different rules and categories accepted in the older literature are simply
instances along a spectrum of permissible self-help in time of peace to
remedy a breach of international law for which there is no other feasible
remedy. The essence of McDougal's argument is that the identification both
of the wrong and of the permissible limits of the remedy must be made in
the context of all the facts, and of the conditions essential to the peaceful
functioning of the state system, in accordance with a set of policies which
embodies the community's goals for that system. [7]

But while good, sinewy legal analysis of this order has always been a
strong feature of McDougal's work, it has not been its central or most
important thrust.

From the beginning, McDougal perceived the main intellectual gap in
the realist movement and addressed himself to curing it.

With few exceptions, both the realists who would drive rules out of
the law and those who devoted themselves to clarifying and improving the
articulation of the rules, stopped short of developing explicit criteria for
judging the goodness or badness of law, beyond the single issue of the
correspondence between the law in the books and the law in action: that is,
between positive law and custom. Reading their books and articles, one
got the impression that the whole task of legal scholarship was to see to it

that the law discover itself accurately and realistically, as the mirror of custom.

Professor Ackerman has recently commented on this aspect of the realist movement, writing particularly of Jerome Frank:

> According to Frank, the fundamental problem for the legal profession was not intellectual but emotional. The basic task for lawyers, and especially judges, was not to articulate an extrapersonal standard of judgment on the basis of history and social philosophy, but to look within themselves and seek to understand the nonrational wellsprings of their own conduct. Once he attained a mature self-understanding, a judge would have the personal strength to understand that neither legal tradition nor social philosophy had the coherence so readily attributed to them by the dominant legal culture. Once they accepted the broad range of conflicting ideals that coexisted within the received legal tradition, neither lawyers nor judges would be victimized by the illusion that a difficult case could be decided by reasoning from asserted legal principles. Instead, by creatively combining the disparate elements of the legal tradition, they would seek to fashion a legal solution which could serve as a just resolution of the conflicting interests involved in the case before them. Frank's book, however, made very little effort to define the substantive outcomes which would best accommodate social conflicts. To embark upon this task would be to commit the same old fundamental legal error, and Frank would not play Father Knows Best.
>
> Frank's whole-hearted embrace of Freudianism was atypical even among the Realists. Others did, however, use the tools of political science, anthropology, and statistics to engage in institutional studies which denied the autonomy of legal science and sought to expose it as a smokescreen disguising the realities of human motivation and interaction among legal decision-makers. More traditional Realist studies contented themselves with demonstrating that supposedly fundamental principles did not in fact explain the existing patterns of decision. Like Frank, however, the other Realists did relatively little to formulate new criteria by which substantive legal outcomes could be evaluated. At the core of Realism was an extraordinary optimism, a belief that once men were free from all the damaging myths of the past, they would have little difficulty understanding the proper shape of a just society.[8]

One of McDougal's first significant contributions to the literature addressed this criticism, which was advanced at the time by Lon Fuller. Fuller charged that by concentrating on the law that is, the realists were neglecting the problem of what the law ought to be.

McDougal commented on the charge in these terms:

> The American legal realism which Professor Fuller attacks is . . . a bogus American legal realism. John Austin, Kelsen, and others, from abroad and at home, may have done their bit to "separate the inseparable," but most of the men whose names appear upon Professor Llewellyn's

famous list of American legal realists are innocent men. So also are most of their followers. They do not deny that the law-in-fact (rules and behavior) embodies somebody's ethical notions (how absurd it would be to deny it!); on the contrary, they are the people who have been most insistent that it has too often embodied an ossified ethics, inherited from previous centuries and opposed to the basic human needs of our time. More clearly than any of their critics, the realists have appreciated that legal rules are but the normative declarations of particular individuals, conditioned by their own peculiar cultural milieu, and not truths revealed from on high. Most of their writing has, in fact, been for the avowed purpose of freeing people from the emotional compulsion of antiquated legal doctrine and so enabling them better to pursue their hearts' desires. Not bothering to explain how judges can legislate, it is they who have insisted that judges do and must legislate, that is, make a policy decision, in every case. The major tenet of the "functional approach," which they have so vigorously espoused, is that law is *instrumental* only, a means to an end, and is to be appraised only in the light of the ends it achieves. Any divorce they may at times have urged between *is* and *ought* has been underscored always as *temporary,* solely for the purpose of preventing their preferences from obscuring a clear understanding of the ways and means for securing such preferences. Directly contrary to Professor Fuller's charges, they have sought to distinguish between the *is* and the *ought,* not for the purpose of ignoring or dismissing the *ought,* but for the purpose of making a future *is* into an *ought* for its time.[9]

McDougal's famous reply to Fuller is full of brio; in retrospect, I conclude that while I still agree with its basic argument, the youthful combatant was perhaps too kind to many of his teachers, friends, and natural allies. They were indeed among the most devoted and effective reformers of their time. Many of them did use more or less explicit criteria for choosing one path rather than another in reshaping the law. But most of them merited Fuller's criticism, which Ackerman has now repeated. Some were indeed genuinely nihilist, or nearly so, and devoted their time only to the cheerful toil of smashing idols. Many, perhaps most of the others, as Ackerman justly remarks, did singularly little "to consider in a sophisticated way the relationship between the legal order and the ends of social life." [10] But McDougal's paragraph on Fuller, written thirty years ago, accurately describes the major theme of his own work ever since.

Holmes had put his definition of law into the future tense. It was never enough, he said, to discover what the law really was at a given moment. What would it become tomorrow? What forces would influence the law to change, and what fruit would come of the process of change? To answer that question, Holmes had urged, the lawyer had to understand and consider the ideas playing on the formation of law—the pressures for social change in many areas, from banking and bankruptcy to labor law and the law of torts. He had to master all the sciences of society, from anthropology to statistics. And he had to know the judges, their prejudices and predilections, their zeal to participate in the growth of the law, or to resist it. After all, Holmes spoke of law not only as a prediction of what the judges would in fact decide, but also as the "witness and external deposit of our moral life," and of its history as "the history of the moral development of the race." [11]

Several of McDougal's contemporaries perceived with him that the success of the icon-breaking period of the American realist movement had cleared the ground for an indispensable next stage in the development of American legal thought—the quest for standards and values in terms of which one could judge the goodness or badness of the living law and guide the evolution of "the law that is"—"the living law"—toward the law we think it ought to become. McDougal's contemporaries Felix Cohen and Alexander Pekelis wrote with distinction about the moral element in law.[12] Others dealt with the problem of policy goals in the context of particular areas of law—economic regulation, policies toward freedom of expression and of the press, equality for blacks. These men—and they were a small band within the American legal professoriate—realized that the events of the thirties and forties demanded a conscious renewal of interest in the relationship between law and ethics. An interest in the moral content of law had seemed derisory to the sophisticates of the twenties. In the thirties, confronting Hitler and Stalin, a Great Depression, and the apparently endless prospect of war and revolution, ethics had ceased to be a laughing matter. A number of sensitive writers about the philosophy of law began to declare that it had been neglected too long. Thus it was not an accident that McDougal and others of similar views took an abiding interest in the modern revival of natural law, led by some of the law schools of Roman Catholic orientation. McDougal and his associates were seeking to build a secular democratic "natural law" for modern America and the modern world community. They recognized their kinship with those who were seeking the same or cognate goals within a religious tradition.

How did it come about that McDougal and Lasswell emerged not simply as leaders and prophets of this movement, but as the creators of an analytic method whose purpose is to teach people how to think systematically about what the law is seeking to accomplish, and what it should seek to accomplish?

Whenever one investigates an important creative act, one is always left with an unanswerable question: why this man? It is not hard to identify the issues which agitated the intellectual world McDougal inhabited, and the place of the problems he chose to study in the array of those issues. But short of psychoanalysis, it is impossible to explain how and why the young McDougal, fresh from Mississippi and Oxford, became the monument we know.

I shall not attempt here to put the McDougal–Lasswell system for clarifying, identifying, and criticizing the policy goals of particular social policies, and of particular communities, into the proverbial nutshell. Those who have not yet mastered those guides and checklists of the problems any student of social policy must deal with in a comprehensive analysis of a particular problem of law should repair at once to one or another of their classic essays in method and perspective.[13] I shall comment here on two features of their methodology which seem to me of major importance to legal and social science scholarship at the moment and for the foreseeable future.

First, the McDougal–Lasswell approach treats all lawmaking as of equal significance. It is completely free of myopic concentration on what judges do—a concentration which makes so much of our traditional legal literature trivial. McDougal and Lasswell have fully accepted and digested the lesson taught by Holmes and Cardozo—that judges cannot help making law. They should of course make law as judges, and not as legislators or Constitution-makers, within the real if necessarily impalpable boundaries imposed on the judges by the nature of their duties. But the McDougal–Lasswell method deals with law as the product of a social process in which many institutions and groups, beyond the courts, must participate responsibly: legislatures and corporations; foreign offices and other agencies of national states; elites and nonelites; transnational "private" bodies like churches and political parties; and organs of the United Nations. The McDougal–Lasswell taxonomy is comprehensive enough to take account also of the effect on law of events themselves—wars, for example. For McDougal and Lasswell, law is a pattern of behavior deemed right by a society at a particular time in its evolution, and a set of peaceful and not so peaceful procedures for determining what that pattern of behavior is. In scope, it encompasses the whole process of making decisions of social policy, as it should.

Second, the McDougal–Lasswell approach rests on a disciplined distinction of the utmost importance to all social science scholarship—the distinction, often blurred in the literature, between the ethical norms of a particular society at a particular time and those of the scholar himself. Their stress on the necessity to define and clarify the observational standpoint of the detached scholar is one of the most useful features of the McDougal–Lasswell method. It liberates the scholar to be conscious of the fact that he need not—indeed that he should not—always accept the moral code of his own or any other society at any given moment of time, since one of his highest responsibilities as a scholar is to offer an independent and rigorously ordered criticism of that code. It is distressing to realize how many serious scholars mistake their own standards of judgment for those of a given society at a given time, or indeed for standards of universal validity.

What McDougal and Lasswell have done, on a majestic scale, is to transform the sociological-functional jurisprudence of the realist generation into a jurisprudence of values. The most striking feature of their method is a scheme for classifying, clarifying, and evaluating the variables necessarily involved in the analysis of any body of law in terms of the social policies the community wishes to see fulfilled by its law. The purpose of each such analysis is to discover (1) whether the law-in-fact corresponds to existing standards of social morality; (2) whether the existing standards of social morality correspond to the aspirations of that society for its law; and (3) whether the prevailing aspirations of the society for its law match those which McDougal and Lasswell believe should prevail over the long run.

As students of society imbued with a strong sense of history, McDougal and Lasswell never confuse their own value system with that of the social order they are studying and criticizing. They are developing a reasoned and fully articulated social philosophy of their own—a humane and democratic vision of the social order they wish to see realized through law. But the passion of their dedication to that ideal is never allowed to distort their examination of the relationship between the living law and the moral code of the society it purports to govern.

McDougal's retirement marks a date of consequence in a splendid academic career—not its end, but nonetheless a transition we are forced to remark. He has genuinely done what every professor is supposed to do: he has created, or recreated, his own version of the intellectual and moral universe which has been the nominal subject matter of his lifelong scholarly effort. And he has been throughout his career a supremely generous and human teacher and colleague.

McDougal's work is not finished. Four or five books are in process. More gleam in his eyes. But what has been done already is grand, and good.

Notes

1. Banco Nacional de Cuba v. Sabbatino, 376 U.S. 398 (1964), Pub. L. No. 88–633, 78 Stat. 1009, 1013 (1964); First National City Bank v. Banco Nacional de Cuba, 406 U.S. 759 (1972).

2. 11 YALE L. REPORT, No. 3, at 7, 8 (1965).

3. I have commented on this movement in *The Realist Tradition in American Law*, in PATHS OF AMERICAN THOUGHT 203 (A. M. Schlesinger, Jr. & M. White eds. 1963), from which some phrases are borrowed, and at greater length in my forthcoming book THE IDEAL IN LAW.

4. O. W. HOLMES, JR., THE COMMON LAW 1–2 (1881).

5. Holmes, *Privilege, Malice, and Intent*, 8 HARV. L. REV. 1 (1894), *reprinted in* COLLECTED LEGAL PAPERS 117–18 (1920).

6. B. N. CARDOZO, THE NATURE OF THE JUDICIAL PROCESS 114 (1921).

7. M. McDOUGAL & F. FELICIANO, LAW AND MINIMUM WORLD PUBLIC ORDER chs. 2–3 (1961), *discussed in* Rostow, Book Review, 82 YALE L. J. 829 (1973).

8. Ackerman, Book Review, 103 DAEDALUS 119, 122 (1974) (review of J. FRANK, LAW AND THE MODERN MIND).

9. *Fuller v. American Legal Realists: An Intervention*, 50 YALE L. J. 827, 834–35 (1941).

10. Ackerman, *supra* note 8, at 126.

11. COLLECTED LEGAL PAPERS, *supra* note 5, at 170.

12. *See,* e.g., F. COHEN, ETHICAL SYSTEMS AND LEGAL IDEALS (1933); F. COHEN, THE LEGAL CONSCIENCE (1960); A. PEKELIS, LAW AND SOCIAL ACTION (1950).

13. McDougal & Lasswell, *Legal Education and Public Policy: Professional Training in the Public Interest,* 52 YALE L.J. 203 (1943), *reprinted in* M. S. MCDOUGAL & ASSOCIATES, STUDIES IN WORLD PUBLIC ORDER 42 (1960); McDougal & Lasswell, *Criteria for a Theory about Law,* 44 S. CAL. L. REV. 362 (1971); McDougal, Lasswell & Reisman, *Theories about International Law: Prologue to a Configurative Jurisprudence,* 8 VA. J. INT'L L. 188 (1968).

Bibliography of Works by and Relating to Myres S. McDougal

COMPILED BY
FREDERICK SAMSON TIPSON

Works by Myres S. McDougal*

Jurisprudence

BOOKS

LAW, SCIENCE, AND POLICY: THE JURISPRUDENCE OF A FREE SOCIETY (forthcoming) (with Harold D. Lasswell).

ARTICLES

Trends in Theories About Law: Comprehensiveness in Conceptions of Constitutive Process, 41 GEO. WASH. L. REV. 1 (1972) (with Harold D. Lasswell).

Criteria for a Theory About Law, 44 S. CAL. L. REV. 362 (1971) (with Harold D. Lasswell).

Jurisprudence in Policy-Oriented Perspective, 19 U. FLA. L. REV. 486 (1967) (with Harold D. Lasswell).

Jurisprudence for a Free Society, 1 GA. L. REV. 1 (1966).

The Ethics of Applying Systems of Authority: The Balanced Opposites of a Legal System, in H. LASSWELL & H. CLEVELAND (eds.), THE ETHICS OF POWER 221 (1962).

The Identification and Appraisal of Diverse Systems of Public Order, 53 AM. J. INT'L L. 1 (1959), *reprinted in* M. McDOUGAL & ASSOCIATES, STUDIES IN WORLD PUBLIC ORDER 3 (1960) and L. GROSS (ed.), INTERNATIONAL LAW IN THE TWENTIETH CENTURY 169 (1969).

Law as a Process of Decision: A Policy-Oriented Approach to Legal Study, 1 NATURAL LAW F. 53 (1956).

The Comparative Study of Law for Policy Purposes: Value Clarification as an Instrument of Democratic World Order, 1 AM. J. COMP. L. 24 (1952), *reprinted in* 61 YALE L.J. 915 (1952) and M. McDOUGAL & ASSOCIATES, STUDIES IN WORLD PUBLIC ORDER 947 (1960).

Fuller vs. the American Legal Realists: An Intervention, 50 YALE L.J. 827 (1941) (an extensive review of L. FULLER, THE LAW IN QUEST OF ITSELF (1940)).

MISCELLANEOUS

Foreword to W. WEYRAUCH, THE PERSONALITY OF LAWYERS at xi (1964) (with Harold D. Lasswell).

Book Review, 45 AM. J. INT'L L. 399 (1951) (a review of S. SIMPSON & J. STONE, CASES AND READINGS ON LAW AND SOCIETY (1948–49)).

Book Review, 34 ILL. L. REV. 109 (1939) (a review of J. HALL, READINGS IN JURISPRUDENCE (1938)).

Book Review, 87 U. PA. L. REV. 495 (1939) (a review of M. RADIN, THE LAW AND MR. SMITH (1938)).

Book Review, 5 U. CHI. L. REV. 702 (1938) (a review of S. CHASE, THE TYRANNY OF WORDS (1938)).

Book Review, 46 YALE L.J. 1269 (1937) (a review of T.V. SMITH, THE PROMISE OF AMERICAN POLITICS (1936)).

UNPUBLISHED MATERIALS

The Constitutive Process and Principles of Interpretation (preliminary outline, 1966).

*For a bibliography of the works of Harold D. Lasswell to 1969, see the compilation by J. Gaston in A. ROGOW (ed.), POLITICS, PERSONALITY AND SOCIAL SCIENCE IN THE TWENTIETH CENTURY: ESSAYS IN HONOR OF HAROLD D. LASSWELL 407 (1969).

The Community Power Process: An Outline for Policy-Oriented Inquiry (preliminary outline, 1962) (with Harold D. Lasswell & Mary Ellen Caldwell).

The Study of Decision (preliminary materials, 1958).

Law, Science, and Policy: The Jurisprudence of a Free Society (materials periodically revised since 1946) (with Harold D. Lasswell and others).

Legal Education

ARTICLES

Beware of the Squid Function, 1 LEARNING & THE LAW 16 (Spring 1974).

The Objectives of Professional Training in Community Interest, in S.K. AGRAWALA, LEGAL EDUCATION IN INDIA: PROBLEMS AND PERSPECTIVES 62 (1973).

The Teaching of International Law, 2 GA. J. INT'L & COMP. L., Supp. II, at 111 (1972).

In Dedication to Dean Dillard: Man of Depth and Style, 54 VA. L. REV. 585 (1968) (with Harold D. Lasswell).

Reflections of a Fellow Teacher, 17 CATH. U. L. REV. 291 (1968).

Education for Professional Responsibility, 12 STUDENT LAWYER 6 (1966).

Legal Education for a Free Society: Our Collective Responsibility, 1 PROCEED. ASSOC. AM. LAW SCHOOLS 33 (1966), reprinted in A. ROGOW (ed.), POLITICS, PERSONALITY AND SOCIAL SCIENCE IN THE TWENTIETH CENTURY: ESSAYS IN HONOR OF HAROLD D. LASSWELL 383 (1969).

The Law School of the Future: From Legal Realism to Policy Science in the World Community, 56 YALE L.J. 1345 (1947).

Aims and Objectives of Legal Education, in HANDBOOK ASSOC. AM. LAW SCHOOLS 125 (1945).

Legal Education and Public Policy: Professional Training in the Public Interest, 52 YALE L.J. 203 (1943) (with Harold D. Lasswell), reprinted in M. MCDOUGAL & ASSOCIATES, STUDIES IN WORLD PUBLIC ORDER 42 (1960) and H. LASSWELL, THE ANALYSIS OF POLITICAL BEHAVIOR: AN EMPIRICAL APPROACH 21 (1948).

Policy-Making as the Center of Emphasis, in HANDBOOK ASSOC. AM. LAW SCHOOLS 47 (1943).

MISCELLANEOUS

Comment [on a paper by Justice Abe Fortas], in T. COWAN (ed.), THE LAW SCHOOL OF TOMORROW 201 (1968).

Remarks [on a panel of the Association of American Law Schools], 13 PRACTICAL LAWYER, No. 6, at 107 (1967).

Statement on National Foundation for Social Sciences, Hearings on S. 836 Before the Subcomm. on Government Research of the Senate Comm. on Government Operations, 90th Cong., 1st Sess., at 508 (1967).

Remarks [on current issues in legal education], 8 CLEV.-MAR. L. REV. 199 (1959).

Book Review, 46 YALE L.J. 1433 (1937) (a review of R. HUTCHINS, THE HIGHER LEARNING IN AMERICA [1936]).

World Constitutive Process

BOOKS

WORLD CONSTITUTIVE PROCESS AND PUBLIC ORDER: INTERNATIONAL LAW IN A COMPREHENSIVE COMMUNITY CONTEXT (2 vols., forthcoming) (with Harold D. Lasswell & W. Michael Reisman).

ARTICLES

The Intelligence Function and World Public Order, 46 TEMPLE L. Q. 365 (1973), reprinted in WORLD CONSTITUTIVE PROCESS AND PUBLIC ORDER: INTERNATIONAL LAW IN A COMPREHENSIVE COMMUNITY CONTEXT ch. 5, supra.

International Law and Social Science: A Mild Plea in Avoidance, 66 AM. J. INT'L L. 77 (1972) (a response to Young, *International Law and Social Science: The Contributions of Myres S. McDougal, id.* at 60).

Theories About International Law: Prologue to a Configurative Jurisprudence, 8 VA. J. INT'L L. 188 (1968) (with Harold D. Lasswell & W. Michael Reisman), *reprinted in* WORLD CONSTITUTIVE PROCESS AND PUBLIC ORDER: INTERNATIONAL LAW IN A COMPREHENSIVE COMMUNITY CONTEXT ch. 1, *supra.*

The World Constitutive Process of Authoritative Decision, 19 J. LEGAL ED. 253, 403 (1967) (with Harold D. Lasswell & W. Michael Reisman), *reprinted in* WORLD CONSTITUTIVE PROCESS AND PUBLIC ORDER: INTERNATIONAL LAW IN A COMPREHENSIVE COMMUNITY CONTEXT ch. 4, *supra,* and 1 R. FALK & C. BLACK (eds.), THE FUTURE OF THE INTERNATIONAL LEGAL ORDER 73 (1969).

The Changing Structure of International Law: Unchanging Theory for Inquiry, 65 COLUM. L. REV. 810 (1965) (an extensive review of W. FRIEDMANN, THE CHANGING STRUCTURE OF INTERNATIONAL LAW (1964)) (with W. Michael Reisman).

Some Basic Theoretical Concepts About International Law: A Policy-Oriented Framework of Inquiry, 4 J. CONFLICT RESOLUTION 337 (1960), *reprinted in* 2 R. FALK & S. MENDLOVITZ (eds.), THE STRATEGY OF WORLD ORDER 116 (1966).

The Impact of International Law Upon National Law: A Policy-Oriented Perspective, 4 S. DAK. L. REV. 25 (1959), *reprinted in* M. MCDOUGAL & ASSOCIATES, STUDIES IN WORLD PUBLIC ORDER 157 (1960).

Perspectives for an International Law of Human Dignity, 1959 PROCEED. AM. SOC'Y INT'L L. 107, *reprinted in* M. MCDOUGAL & ASSOCIATES, STUDIES IN WORLD PUBLIC ORDER 987 (1960).

International Law and Contending World Orders, 1958 PROCEED. INST. WORLD AFF. 11 (1959).

Jurisdiction, 9 NAVAL WAR COLLEGE REV. 1 (1957).

The Policy Science Approach to International Legal Studies, in INTERNATIONAL LAW AND THE UNITED NATIONS (Eighth Summer Institute, U. Michigan Law School, 1955).

International Law, Power, and Policy: A Contemporary Conception, 82 RECUEIL DES COURS 133 (Hague Academy of International Law, 1953).

The Role of Law in World Politics, 20 MISS. L.J. 253 (1949).

MISCELLANEOUS

Remarks [on the moral foundations of international law], 1959 PROCEED. AM. SOC'Y INT'L L. 135–36, 168.

Comments [on the nature of international law], PROCEED. SECOND SUMMER CONFERENCE ON INTERNATIONAL LAW 65–86, 162–64, 182–203 (Cornell Law School, June 23–25, 1958).

The Realist Theory in Pyrrhic Victory, 47 AM. J. INT'L L. 376 (1955) (a review of H. MORGENTHAU, POLITICS AMONG NATIONS (2d ed. 1954).

Remarks [on the recognition of the People's Republic of China], 1955 PROCEED.. AM. SOC'Y INT'L L. 106–08.

Book Review, 48 AM. J. INT'L L. 680 (1954) (a review of Q. WRIGHT, PROBLEMS OF STABILITY AND PROGRESS IN INTERNATIONAL RELATIONS (1954)).

Remarks [on "domestic jurisdiction" v. "international concern"], 1954 PROCEED. AM. SOC'Y INT'L L. 120–22.

Book Review, 47 AM. J. INT'L L. 340 (1953) (a review of O. LISSITSYN, THE INTERNATIONAL COURT OF JUSTICE (1951)).

Dr. Schwazenberger's Power Politics, 47 AM. J. INT'L L. 115 (1953) (a review of G. SCHWARZENBERGER, POWER POLITICS: A STUDY OF INTERNATIONAL SOCIETY (2d rev. ed. 1951)).

Law and Power, 46 AM. J. INT'L L. 102 (1952) (comments on H. MORGENTHAU, IN DEFENSE OF THE NATIONAL INTEREST (1951) and G. KENNAN, AMERICAN DIPLO-

MACY 1900–1950 (1951), *reprinted in* L. GROSS (ed.), INTERNATIONAL LAW IN THE TWENTIETH CENTURY 104 (1969).

Remarks [on the nature of international law], 1950 PROCEED. AM. SOC'Y INT'L L. 92–93; 1947 *id.* at 47–50.

UNPUBLISHED MATERIALS

The Public Order of the World Community: A Contemporary International Law (course materials, 1964) (with Harold D. Lasswell & William T. Burke).

The World Community and Law (assorted materials and outline, 1951) (with Harold D. Lasswell).

International Organization*

ARTICLES

Response by Professors McDougal and Reisman, 3 INT'L LAWYER 438 (1969) (a response to a "Comment" by Charles B. Marshall, *id.* at 435, criticizing positions taken on United Nations sanctions against Rhodesia).

Rhodesia and the United Nations: The Lawfulness of International Concern, 62 AM. J. INT'L L. 1 (1968) (with W. Michael Reisman).

Chinese Participation in the United Nations: The Legal Imperatives of a Negotiated Solution, 60 AM. J. INT'L L. 671 (1966) (with Richard M. Goodman).

The Veto and the Charter: An Interpretation for Survival, 60 YALE L.J. 258 (1951) (with Richard N. Gardner), *reprinted in* M. MCDOUGAL & ASSOCIATES, STUDIES IN WORLD PUBLIC ORDER 718 (1960).

MISCELLANEOUS

Remarks [on revolution as a United Nations concern], 1961 PROCEED. AM. J. SOC'Y INT'L L. 40.

Book Review, 47 AM. J. INT'L L. 351 (1953) (a review of L. BRYSON ET AL., FOUNDATIONS OF WORLD ORGANIZATION (1952).

UNPUBLISHED MATERIALS

International Organization and World Public Order (assorted materials for a seminar given at various times with Harold D. Lasswell, Oscar Schachter, Egon Schwelb, Richard M. Goodman, and others).

Treaties

BOOKS

THE INTERPRETATION OF AGREEMENTS AND WORLD PUBLIC ORDER: PRINCIPLES OF CONTENT AND PROCEDURE (1967) (with Harold D. Lasswell & James C. Miller).

ARTICLES

Third-Party Decision, 63 AM. J. INT'L L. 685 (1969) (statement before Asian-African Legal Consultative Committee, 10th Sess., Karachi, Jan. 22, 1969, as "observer" from the American Society of International Law).

Vienna Conference on the Law of Treaties: Statement of Professor Myres S. McDougal, United States Delegation, to the Committee of the Whole, April 19, 1968, 62 AM. J. INT'L L. 1021 (1968).

The International Law Commission's Draft Articles Upon Interpretation: Textuality Redivivus, 61 AM. J. INT'L L. 992 (1967).

The Treaty Power and the Constitution: The Case Against the [Bricker] Amendment, 40 A.B.A.J. 203 (1954) (with Brunson MacChesney and others).

---

*Senator James Eastland (D–Miss.), in reference to McDougal's views on the United Nations Charter: "Mr. McDougal was a schoolmate of mine. He is a very distinguished professor at Yale University, and I think a very misguided liberal." 101 CONG. REC. 3017 (daily ed. Mar. 16, 1955).

The Treaty-Making Power, 1952 PROCEED. INT'L L. ASSOC. (American Branch) 13, *reprinted in Hearings on S.J. 130 Before the Subcomm. of the Senate Comm. on the Judiciary,* 82d Cong., 2d Sess. (1952).

Treaties and Congressional-Executive or Presidential Agreements: Interchangeable Instruments of National Policy, 54 YALE L.J. 181, 534 (1945) (with Asher Lans), *reprinted in* M. MCDOUGAL & ASSOCIATES, STUDIES IN WORLD PUBLIC ORDER 404 (1960).

MISCELLANEOUS

Letter to Senator Barry Goldwater, Jan. 12, 1973, *quoted in* Goldwater, *The President's Constitutional Primacy in Foreign Relations and National Defense,* 13 VA. J. INT'L L. 463, 472 (1973).

Remarks [on treaty interpretation], 1969 PROCEED. AM. SOC'Y INT'L L. 131–33, 136–39.

Remarks [on the draft Articles of the International Law Commission], 1967 PROCEED. AM. SOC'Y INT'L L. 204–05, 208–09.

Footnote, 57 AM. J. INT'L L. 383 (1963) (a response to Anderson, *A Critique of Professor McDougal's Doctrine of Interpretation by Major Purposes, id.* at 378).

Remarks [on constitutional limitations and the treaty power], 1959 PROCEED. AM. SOC'Y INT'L L. 323–24.

Remarks [on the Bricker Amendment], 1954 PROCEED. AM. SOC'Y INT'L L. 153–55.

Remarks [on treaties and executive agreements], 1951 PROCEED. AM. SOC'Y INT'L L. 30–32, 101–03.

Remarks [on the constitutionality of the Pepper Bill], 21 CONG. DIG. 272 (1942).

Minimum Order

BOOKS

LAW AND MINIMUM WORLD PUBLIC ORDER: THE LEGAL REGULATION OF INTERNATIONAL COERCION (1961) (with Florentino P. Feliciano).

ARTICLES

Authority to Use Force on the High Seas, 20 NAVAL WAR COLLEGE REV. 19 (1967).

The Soviet-Cuban Quarantine and Self-Defense, 57 AM. J. INT'L L. 597 (1963), *reprinted in* L. GROSS (ed.), INTERNATIONAL LAW IN THE TWENTIETH CENTURY 716 (1969).

Community Prohibitions of International Coercion and Sanctioning Processes: The Technique of World Public Order, 35 PHILIPPINE L.J. 1256 (1960) (with Florentino P. Feliciano), *reprinted in* M. MCDOUGAL & F. FELICIANO, *supra* at 261–383.

Legal Regulation of Resort to International Coercion: Aggression and Self-Defense in Policy Perspective, 68 YALE L.J. 1057 (1959) (with Florentino P. Feliciano), *reprinted in* M. MCDOUGAL & F. FELICIANO, *supra* at 121–260.

The Initiation of Coercion: A Multitemporal Analysis, 52 AM. J. INT'L L. 241 (1958) (with Florentino P. Feliciano), *reprinted in* M. MCDOUGAL & F. FELICIANO, *supra* at 97–120.

International Coercion and World Public Order: The General Principles of the Law of War, 67 YALE L.J. 771 (1958) (with Florentino P. Feliciano), *reprinted in* M. MCDOUGAL & F. FELICIANO, *supra* at 1–96, and M. MCDOUGAL & ASSOCIATES, STUDIES IN WORLD PUBLIC ORDER 237 (1960).

The Hydrogen Bomb Tests in Perspective: Lawful Measures for Security, 64 YALE L.J. 771 (1958) (with Norbert A. Schlei), *reprinted in* M. MCDOUGAL & ASSOCIATES, STUDIES IN WORLD PUBLIC ORDER 763 (1960).

Peace and War: Factual Continuum with Multiple Legal Consequences, 49 AM. J. INT'L L. 63 (1955).

MISCELLANEOUS

Foreword to J.N. MOORE, LAW AND THE INDO-CHINA WAR at vii (1972).

Foreword to R. HULL & J. NOVOGROD, LAW AND VIETNAM at vii (1968).

Letter to President Lyndon Johnson, Feb. 14, 1966, in reply to the Lawyers' Committee on American Policy Toward Vietnam, 112 CONG. REC. 3842 (daily ed. Feb. 26, 1966) (with Neill H. Alford, Jr., Richard R. Baxter, William W. Bishop & Louis B. Sohn).

Remarks [as Chairman of panel on "The International Regulation of Internal Conflict in Developing Countries"], 1966 PROCEED. AM. SOC'Y INT'L L. 82.

Remarks [on self-defense and Vietnam], 1965 PROCEED. AM. SOC'Y INT'L L. 77–78.

Foreword [to Sanctions Symposium]: Sanctions in Context, 49 IOWA L. REV. 229 (1964).

Remarks [on coercion and the Cuban quarantine], 1963 PROCEED. AM. SOC'Y INT'L L. 15–16, 163–65, 169–71.

Remarks [as Chairman of panel on "Recent Technological Developments: Political and Legal Implications for the International Community], 1959 PROCEED. AM. SOC'Y INT'L L. 166–69.

Book Review, 48 AM. J. INT'L L. 525 (1954) (a review of H. STERN, THE STRUGGLE FOR POLAND (1953)).

Remarks [as Chairman of panel on "World Security and International Law at Mid-Century"], 1950 PROCEED. AM. SOC'Y INT'L L. 2–3.

Human Rights

BOOKS

HUMAN RIGHTS AND WORLD PUBLIC ORDER (forthcoming) (with Harold D. Lasswell & Lung-chu Chen).

ARTICLES

The Protection of Respect and Human Rights: Freedom of Choice and World Public Order, 24 AM. U.L. REV. No. 4 (1975) (with Harold D. Lasswell and Lung-chu Chen).

Human Rights for Women and World Public Order: The Outlawing of Sex-Based Discrimination, 69 AM. J. INT'L L. 497 (1975) (with Harold D. Lasswell and Lung-chu Chen).

Human Rights and World Public Order: Principles of Content and Procedure for Clarifying General Community Policies, 14 VA. J. INT'L L. 387 (1974).

Nationality and Human Rights: The Protection of the Individual and External Arenas, 83 YALE L.J. 900 (1974) (with Harold D. Lasswell & Lung-chu Chen), reprinted in HUMAN RIGHTS AND WORLD PUBLIC ORDER, supra.

Human Rights and World Public Order: A Framework for Policy-Oriented Inquiry, 63 AM. J. INT'L L. 237 (1969) (with Harold D. Lasswell & Lung-chu Chen).

Human Rights and the United Nations, 58 AM. J. INT'L L. 603 (1964) (with Gerhard Bebr).

The Genocide Convention and the Constitution, 3 VAND. L. REV. 683 (1950) (with Richard Arens).

The Rights of Man in the World Community: Constitutional Illusions versus Rational Action, 14 LAW & CONTEMP. PROBS. 90 (1949) (with Gertrude C. K. Leighton), reprinted in M. MCDOUGAL & ASSOCIATES, STUDIES IN WORLD PUBLIC ORDER 335 (1960).

MISCELLANEOUS

Remarks, HUMAN RIGHTS: PROTECTION OF THE INDIVIDUAL UNDER INTERNATIONAL LAW (1970) (Proceedings of the Fifth Summer Conference on International Law, Cornell Law School, June 1964).

Book Review, 60 YALE L.J. 1051 (1951) (a review of H. LAUTERPACHT, INTERNATIONAL LAW AND HUMAN RIGHTS (1950).

Remarks [on the international protection of human rights], 1949 PROCEED. AM. SOC'Y INT'L L. 65–68, 83–85.

UNPUBLISHED MATERIALS

Amicus Brief, *Shelley v. Kraemer*, 334 U.S. 1 (1947) (coauthor of brief by the Committee for Collective Security, American Association for the United Nations, in case involving private property agreement with racial discrimination).

Brief for the Respondent, *Ex Parte Quirin*, 317 U.S. 1 (1942) (counsel with others to the Attorney General in a habeas corpus suit involving German saboteurs).

Economic Well-Being and Wealth Transactions

BOOKS

PROPERTY, WEALTH, LAND: ALLOCATION, PLANNING AND DEVELOPMENT—SELECTED CASES AND OTHER MATERIALS ON THE LAW OF REAL PROPERTY (1948) (with David Haber).

THE CASE FOR REGIONAL PLANNING, WITH SPECIAL REFERENCE TO NEW ENGLAND (1947) (Report of Directive Committee on Regional Planning) (with Maurice Rotival).

MUNICIPAL LAND POLICY AND CONTROL (Practicing Law Inst. 1946).

ARTICLES

Act of State in Policy Perspective: The International Law of an International Economy, in V. CAMERON (ed.), PRIVATE INVESTORS ABROAD—STRUCTURES AND SAFEGUARDS 327 (1966).

The Influence of the Metropolis on Concepts, Rules and Institutions Relating to Property, 4 J. PUB. LAW 93 (1955), *reprinted in abridged form as The Impact of the Metropolis Upon Land Law*, in R. FISHER (ed.), THE METROPOLIS IN MODERN LIFE 212 (1955).

Planning and Development for Metropolitan Communities, in AMERICAN PLANNING AND CIVIC ANNUAL 94 (1950).

Regional Planning and Development: The Process of Using Intelligence Under Conditions of Resource and Institutional Interdependence for Securing Community Values, 32 IOWA L. REV. 193 (1947).

Municipal Land Policy and Control, 242 ANNALS 88 (1945).

A Regional Development Administration, 4 NEW ENG. WAR BULL., No. 264, at 14 (June-July 1945).

Future Interests Restated: Tradition versus Clarification and Reform, 55 HARV. L. REV. 1077 (1942).

Public Purpose in Public Housing: An Anachronism Reburied, 52 YALE L.J. 42–73 (1942) (with Addison A. Mueller).

Title Registration and Land Reform: A Reply, 8 U. CHI. L. REV. 63 (1940) (a reply to Bordwell, *The Resurrection of Registration of Title*, 7 id. at 470).

Land Title Transfer: A Regression, 48 YALE L.J. 1125 (1939) (with John W. Brabner-Smith), an extensive review of R. POWELL, REGISTRATION OF THE TITLE TO LAND IN THE STATE OF NEW YORK (1939)).

Bankruptcy, in 3 ENCYCLOPEDIA BRITANNICA (14th rev. ed. 1936) (with William O. Douglas).

MISCELLANEOUS

Testimony on the Sabbatino Amendment, *Hearings on H.R. 7750 Before the House Comm. on Foreign Affairs*, 89th Cong., 1st Sess., at 1033 (1965).

Remarks [on the Act of State Doctrine and *Sabbatino v. Banco Nacional de Cuba*], 1964 PROCEED. AM. SOC'Y INT'L L. 48–52.

Remarks [on the foreign impact of antitrust laws], REPORT OF THE FIFTY-FIRST CONFERENCE OF THE INTERNATIONAL LAW ASSOCIATION 328–32, 347 (1964).

Book Review, 58 YALE L.J. 500 (1949) (a review of C. CLARK, REAL COVENANTS AND OTHER INTERESTS WHICH "RUN WITH THE LAND" (1947)).

Summary and Criticism of Answers to Question 8 of the Property Questionnaire, HANDBOOK AM. ASSOC. LAW SCHOOLS 268 (1941) (report of the Sub-Committee on Property, Committee on Curriculum, American Association of Law Schools).

Book Review, 49 YALE L.J. 1502 (1940) (with Charles Runyon) (a review of vol. 4, ch. 41—on "natural rights" of property holders—of AMERICAN LAW INSTITUTE, RESTATEMENT OF THE LAW OF TORTS. (1939)).

Book Review, 47 YALE L.J. 514 (1938) (a review of R. BROWN, A TREATISE ON THE LAW OF PERSONAL PROPERTY (1936)).

Book Review, 32 ILL. L. REV. 509 (1937) (a review of 1–2 AMERICAN LAW INSTITUTE, RESTATEMENT OF THE LAW OF PROPERTY (1936), *reprinted in abridged form as A Review of the Property Restatement,* in THE LIFE OF THE LAW 161 (J. Honnold ed. 1964).

Book Review, 45 YALE L.J. 1158 (1936) (a review of E. HOLBROOK & R. AIGLER, CASES ON THE LAW OF BANKRUPTCY (3d. ed. T. C. Billig 1936)).

Book Review, 45 YALE L.J. 1159 (1936) (a review of J. HANNA, CASES AND MATERIALS ON CREDITORS' RIGHTS (2d ed. 1935)).

Book Review, 44 YALE L.J. 1278 (1935) (a review of W. WALSH, A TREATISE ON MORTGAGES (1934)).

Book Review, 27 ILL. L. REV. 469 (a review of C. TOOKE, CASES ON THE LAW OF MUNICIPAL CORPORATIONS (1931)).

UNPUBLISHED MATERIALS

The International Law of Private Business Associations (seminar materials).

Report of the Committee on Planning, Rebuilding and Developing Metropolitan Communities (Property Section, American Bar Association, 1946).

Earth–Space Environment

BOOKS

LAW AND PUBLIC ORDER IN SPACE (1963) (with Harold D. Lasswell & Ivan A. Vlasic).

THE PUBLIC ORDER OF THE OCEANS: A CONTEMPORARY INTERNATIONAL LAW OF THE SEA (1962) (with William T. Burke).

ARTICLES

The Protection of the Environment and World Public Order: Some Recent Developments, 45 MISS. L.J. 1085 (1974) (with Jan Schneider).

The Law of the High Seas in Time of Peace, 25 NAVAL WAR COLLEGE REV. 35 (1973), *reprinted in* 3 DENVER J. INT'L L. & POLICY 45 (1973).

Commentary [upon "Prospects for Agreement, the Law of the Sea: a New Geneva Conference"], in PROC. SIXTH ANN. CONF. OF LAW OF THE SEA INST. at 50–51, 68–69, 118–19, 179–83, 201–02 (1971).

Legal Bases for Securing the Integrity of the Earth–Space Environment, 184 ANNALS N.Y. ACAD. SCIENCES: ENVIRONMENT AND SOCIETY IN TRANSITION 375 (1971).

A Footnote [to a clarification of the "genuine link" doctrine by H. van Panhuys], 62 AM. J. INT'L L. 943 (1968) (with William T. Burke).

Revision of the Geneva Conventions of the Law of the Sea—The Views of a Commentator, 1 NATURAL RESOURCES LAWYER 19 (1968).

International Law and the Law of the Sea, in L. ALEXANDER (ed.), THE LAW OF THE SEA: OFFSHORE BOUNDARIES AND ZONES 3 (1967).

The Prospects for a Regime in Outer Space, in M. COHEN, LAW AND POLITICS IN SPACE 105 (1964).

Emerging Customary Law of Space, 58 Nw. U.L. REV. 618 (1963).

Enjoyment and Acquisition of Resources in Outer Space, 111 U. PA. L. REV. 521 (1963) (with Harold D. Lasswell, Ivan A. Vlasic & Joseph Smith), *revised and reprinted in* M. MCDOUGAL, H. LASSWELL & I. VLASIC, *supra* at 749–871.

Law and Public Order in Space, in CONF. PROC. ON SPACE SCIENCE AND SPACE LAW 151 (Univ. of Okla., M. Schwartz ed. 1963).

Claims to Authority Over the Territorial Sea, 1 PHILIPPINE INT'L L.J. 29 (1962) (with William T. Burke).

The Community Interest in a Narrow Territorial Sea: Inclusive versus Exclusive Competence Over the Oceans, 45 CORNELL L.Q. 171 (1960) (with William T. Burke), *revised and reprinted in* M. MCDOUGAL & W. BURKE, *supra* at 446–564.

The Maintenance of Public Order at Sea and the Nationality of Ships, 54 AM. J. INT'L L. 25 (1960) (with William T. Burke & Ivan A. Vlasic), *revised and reprinted in* M. MCDOUGAL & W. BURKE, *supra* at 1008–1140.

Crisis in the Law of the Sea: Community Perspectives versus National Egoism, 67 YALE L.J. 539 (1958) (with William T. Burke), *revised and reprinted in* M. MC-DOUGAL & W. BURKE, *supra* at 1–88.

Perspectives for a Law of Outer Space, 52 AM. J. INT'L L. 407 (1958) (with Leon S. Lipson), *reprinted in* M. MCDOUGAL & ASSOCIATES, STUDIES IN WORLD PUBLIC ORDER 912 (1960).

Artificial Satellites: A Modest Proposal, 51 AM. J. INT'L L. 74 (1957).

The Hydrogen Bomb Tests and the International Law of the Sea, 49 AM. J. INT'L L. 356 (1955).

MISCELLANEOUS

Remarks [as Chairman of a working group on "Decision Process, Conflict Resolution and the Control of War—The Organized Planet, Human Rights and Individual Participation"], 184 ANNALS N.Y. ACAD. SCIENCES: ENVIRONMENT AND SOCIETY IN TRANSITION 612–34 (1971).

Remarks [as Chairman of panel on "Conflicting Approaches to the Control and Exploitation of the Oceans"], 1971 PROCEED. AM. SOC'Y INT'L L. 141–43.

Remarks [on approaches to the environmental crisis], 1970 PROCEED. AM. SOC'Y INT'L L. 233–34.

Remarks [on shared access to space], REPORT OF THE FIFTY-FIRST CONFERENCE OF THE INTERNATIONAL LAW ASSOCIATION 630–32, 769–70 (1964).

Remarks [on the U-2 incident and claims to outer space], 1961 PROCEED. AM. SOC'Y INT'L L. 18, 20–23.

Remarks [on the three-mile territorial limit], 1959 PROCEED. AM. SOC'Y INT'L L. 215.

Remarks [on legal status of air space], 1958 PROCEED. AM. SOC'Y INT'L L. 242–43, 250.

Remarks [on outer space problems], 1958 PROCEED. INST. WORLD AFF. 68–69.

Remarks [on legal problems of spacecraft], 1956 PROCEED. AM. SOC'Y INT'L L. 108–09.

Selected Works About Myres S. McDougal*

Jurisprudence

Blackshield, THE POLICY SCIENCE APPROACH TO JURISPRUDENCE (Australian Society of Legal Philosophy Preliminary Working Paper No. 5, 1964).

D. Daniel, Clarification and Appraisal of the Policy-Oriented Framework for Inter-

*For a set of brief personal tributes by colleagues and students, see 1 DENVER J. INT'L L. & POLICY 8 (1971) and 84 YALE L.J. 704, 961 (1975).

national Legal Analysis: Inquiry into the Work of Myres S. McDougal (unpublished Ph.D. dissertation, Georgetown University, 1971).

Dillard, *The Policy-Oriented Approach to Law*, 40 VA. Q. REV. 626 (1964).

R. FALK, THE STATUS OF LAW IN INTERNATIONAL SOCIETY ch. 1 *(Gaps and Biases in Contemporary Theories of International Law)* (1970).

Granfield, *Towards a Goal-Oriented Consensus*, 19 J. LEGAL ED. 379 (1967).

Little, *Toward Clarifying the Grounds of Value-Clarification: A Reaction to the Policy-Oriented Jurisprudence of Lasswell and McDougal*, 14 VA. J. INT'L L. 451 (1964).

Moore, *Prolegomenon to the Jurisprudence of Myres McDougal and Harold Lasswell*, 54 VA. L. REV. 662 (1968), *reprinted in* J.N. MOORE, LAW AND THE INDO-CHINA WAR ch. 2 (1972).

Pascual, *The Policy Function of the Law: Value Creation, Clarification and Realization*, 20 PHILIPPINE L.J. 431 (1954).

Stone, *Problems Confronting Sociological Inquiries Concerning International Law*, 89 RECUEIL DES COURS 61 (Hague Academy of International Law, 1957).

Suzuki, *The New Haven School of International Law: An Invitation to a Policy-Oriented Jurisprudence*, 1 YALE STUD. W.P.O. 1 (1974).

Tipson, *The Lasswell–McDougal Enterprise: Toward a World Public Order of Human Dignity*, 14 VA. J. INT'L L. 535 (1974).

Young, *International Law and Social Science: The Contributions of Myres S. McDougal*, 66 AM. J. INT'L L. 60 (1972).

Legal Education

Bergin, *The Law Teacher: A Man Divided Against Himself*, 54 VA. L. REV. 637 (1968).

Falk, *New Approaches to the Study of International Law*, in M. KAPLAN (ed.), NEW APPROACHES TO INTERNATIONAL RELATIONS 357 (1968.)

Llewellyn, *McDougal and Lasswell Plan for Legal Education*, 43 COLUM. L. REV. 476 (1943).

Maculey, *Notes on the Margins of "Professional Training in the Public Interest,"* 54 VA. L. REV. 617 (1968).

Speidel, *A Matter of Mission*, 54 VA. L. REV. 606 (1968).

World Constitutive Process

BOOKS AND ARTICLES

Allott, *Language, Method and the Nature of International Law*, 1971 BRIT. Y.B. INT'L L. 79.

Coplin, *Current Studies of the Functions of International Law: Assessments and Suggestions*, 1971 POL. SCI. ANNUAL 149.

Falk, *A New Paradigm for International Legal Studies: Prospects and Proposals*, 84 YALE L.J. 969 (1975).

———, *The Place of Policy in International Law*, 2 GA. J. INT'L & COMP. L., Supp. II, at 29 (1972).

———, *The Relevance of Political Context to the Nature and Functioning of International Law: An Intermediate View*, in K. DEUTSCH & S. HOFFMANN (eds.), THE RELEVANCE OF INTERNATIONAL LAW 202 (1968), *reprinted in* R. FALK, THE STATUS OF LAW IN INTERNATIONAL SOCIETY ch. 2 (1970).

Farer, *International Law and Political Behavior: Toward A Conceptual Liaison*, 25 WORLD POL. 430 (1973).

H. Hernes, Concepts of Community in Modern Theories of International Law, (unpublished Ph.D. dissertation, Johns Hopkins University, 1970).

Higgins, *Policy and Impartiality: The Uneasy Relationship in International Law,* 23 INT'L ORG. 914 (1969).

———, *Policy Consideration and the International Judicial Process,* 17 INT'L & COMP. L.Q. 58 (1968).

S. HOFFMANN, THE STATE OF WAR ch. 5 (*The Study of International Law and the Theory of International Relations*) (1965).

K. KRAKAU, MISSIONSBEWUSSTSEIN UND VOLKERRECHTSDOKTRIN IN DEN VEREINIGTEN STAATEN VON AMERIKA (1967).

Lissitzyn, *Comment* [on a paper by McDougal], in INTERNATIONAL LAW AND THE UNITED NATIONS 62 (Eighth Summer Institute, U. Michigan Law School, 1955).

Meyrowitz, *Droit international et "policy science,"* 97 J. DROIT INT'L 902 (1970).

Ortega, *La Concepcion del Derecho Internacional de Myres S. McDougal,* 36 REV. JURIDICA DE LA UNIV. DE PUERTO RICO, No: 1, at 1 (1967).

B. ROSENTHAL, ETUDE DE L'OEUVRE DE MYRES SMITH MCDOUGAL EN MATIÈRE DE DROIT INTERNATIONAL PUBLIC (1970). (*See* Higgins, Book Review, 66 AM. J. INT'L L. 646 (1972).)

Schachter, *The Place of Policy in International Law,* 2 GA. J. INT'L & COMP. L., Supp. II, at 5 (1972).

G. TUNKIN, TEORIA MEZHDUNARODNOGO PRAVA 304–05, 335–41 (1970).

Wood, *Public Order and Political Integration in Contemporary International Theory,* 14 VA. J. INT'L L. 423 (1974).

———, *History, Thought and Images: The Development of International Law and Organization,* 12 VA. J. INT'L L. 35 (1971).

BOOK REVIEWS

Reviews of M. MCDOUGAL & ASSOCIATES, STUDIES IN WORLD PUBLIC ORDER (1960):

   Brinton, 16 REV. EGYPTIENNE DE DROIT INT'L 157 (1960).

   Buckwalter, 3 WM. & MARY L. REV. 229 (1961).

   Czyzak, 7 NATURAL LAW F. 216 (1962).

   D'Amato, 75 HARV. L. REV. 458 (1961).

   Falk, 10 AM. J. COMP. L. 297 (1961), *reprinted in* R. FALK, THE STATUS OF LAW IN INTERNATIONAL SOCIETY, app. C (1970).

   Fernando, 1 PHILIPPINE INT'L L.J. 178 (1962).

   Fisher, 135 SCIENCE 658 (1962).

   Giannella, 7 VILL. L. REV. 157 (1961).

   Gormley, 55 AM. J. INT'L L. 755 (1961).

   Lissitzyn, 63 COLUM. L. REV. 386 (1963).

   Miller, 10 J. PUBLIC L. 158 (1961).

   O'Connell, 4 SYDNEY L. REV. 318 (1963).

   Wright, 39 U. DETROIT L.J. 145 (1961).

Treaties

BOOKS AND ARTICLES

Anderson, *A Critique of Professor McDougal's Doctrine of Interpretation by Major Purposes,* 57 AM. J. INT'L L. 378 (1963).

Falk, *Charybdis Responds: A Note on Treaty Interpretation,* 63 AM. J. INT'L L. 510 (1969) (a response to Larsen, *infra*).

———, *On Treaty Interpretation and the New Haven Approach: Achievements and Prospects,* 8 VA. J. INT'L L. 323 (1968), *reprinted in* R. FALK, THE STATUS OF LAW IN INTERNATIONAL SOCIETY ch. 11 (1970).

Fitzmaurice, *Vae Victis, or Woe to the Negotiators! Your Treaty or Our "Interpretation" of It?* 65 AM. J. INT'L L. 358 (1971).

Gottlieb, *The Conceptual World of the Yale School of International Law*, 21 WORLD POL. 108 (1968).

Larsen, *Between Scylla and Charybdis on Treaty Interpretation*, 63 AM. J. INT'L L. 108 (1969).

Merrills, *Two Approaches to Treaty Interpretation*, 1968–69 AUST. Y.B. INT'L L. 55 (1971).

J. STONE, OF LAW AND NATIONS ch. 4 *(Fictional Elements in Treaty Interpretation)* (1974).

Weisstub, *Conceptual Foundations of the Interpretation of Agreements*, 22 WORLD POL. 255 (1970) (a response to Gottlieb, *supra*).

BOOK REVIEWS

Reviews of M. MCDOUGAL, H. LASSWELL & J. MILLER, THE INTERPRETATION OF AGREEMENTS AND WORLD PUBLIC ORDER (1967):

> Briggs, 53 CORNELL L. REV. 543 (1968).
>
> Friedmann, 7 COLUM. J. TRANSNAT'L L. 354 (1968).
>
> Holder, 57 KY. L.J. 772 (1969).
>
> Rohn, 63 AM. POL. SCI. REV. 541 (1969).
>
> Weston, 117 U. PA. L. REV. 647 (1969).

Minimum Order

BOOKS AND ARTICLES

Acheson, *The Arrogance of International Lawyers*, 4 INT'L LAWYER 591 (1968).

Falk, *International Legal Order: Alwyn v. Freeman v. Myres S. McDougal*, 59 AM. J. INT'L L. 66 (1965).

Farer, *Law and War*, in 3 R. FALK & C. BLACK (eds.), THE FUTURE OF THE INTERNATIONAL LEGAL ORDER 15 (1971).

Hoffmann, *Henkin and Falk: Mild Reformist and Mild Revolutionary*, 24 J. INT'L AFF. 118 (1970).

BOOK REVIEWS

Reviews of M. MCDOUGAL & F. FELICIANO, LAW AND MINIMUM WORLD PUBLIC ORDER: THE LEGAL REGULATION OF INTERNATIONAL COERCION (1961):

> Bowett, 38 BRIT. Y.B. INT'L L. 517 (1962).
>
> Castren, 15 U. TORONTO L.J. 227 (1963).
>
> Falk, 8 NATURAL LAW F. 171 (1963), *reprinted in* R. FALK, LEGAL ORDER IN A VIOLENT WORLD ch. 3 (1968).
>
> Freeman, 58 AM. J. INT'L L. 711 (1964).
>
> Friedmann, 64 COLUM. L. REV. 607 (1964).
>
> Hambro, 50 CALIF. L. REV. 745 (1962).
>
> Jones, 15 J. LEGAL ED. 341 (1963).
>
> Lissitzyn, 76 HARV. L. REV. 668 (1963).
>
> Mickelwait, 60 MICH. L. REV. 535 (1962).
>
> Nicholson, 39 U. DETROIT L.J. 712 (1962).
>
> O'Brien, 72 YALE L.J. 413 (1962).
>
> O'Connell, 4 SYDNEY L. REV. 318 (1963).
>
> Simpson, 79 LAW Q. REV. 144 (1963).

Economic Well-Being and Wealth Transactions

Reviews of M. MCDOUGAL & D. HABER, PROPERTY, WEALTH, LAND: ALLOCATION, PLANNING AND DEVELOPMENT—SELECTED CASES AND OTHER MATERIALS ON THE LAW OF REAL PROPERTY (1948):

> Bordwell, 1 J. LEGAL ED. 326 (1948).

Cross, 24 WASH. L. REV. 74 (1949).

Dunham, 62 HARV. L. REV. 1414 (1949).

Johnson, 34 VA. L. REV. 629 (1948).

Tugwell, 58 YALE L.J. 809 (1949).

Watts, 34 IOWA L. REV. 384 (1949).

Earth–Space Environment

Reviews of M. MCDOUGAL, H. LASSWELL & I. VLASIC, LAW AND PUBLIC ORDER IN SPACE (1963):

Brown, 36 MISS. L.J. 116 (1964).

Chaumont, 3 COLUM. J. TRANSNAT'L L. 271 (1965).

Cheng, 16 U. TORONTO L.J. 210 (1965).

Dayal, 10 J. INDIAN L. INST. 173 (1968).

Doyle, 10 MCGILL L.J. 197 (1964).

Johnson, 13 INT'L & COMP. L.Q. 1121 (1964).

Leopold, 42 U. DETROIT L.J. 238 (1964).

Lyon, 42 CAN. B. REV. 653 (1964).

Peterson, 18 J. LEGAL ED. 115 (1965).

Pinegar, 43 N. CAR. L. REV. 1032 (1965).

Posner, 77 HARV. L. REV. 1370 (1964).

Rosenblum, 58 AM. POL. SCI. REV. 1052 (1964).

Scarufi, 18 VAND. L. REV. 863 (1965).

Wehringer, 31 BROOKLYN L. REV. 197 (1964).

Woetzel, 61 AM. J. INT'L L. 627 (1967).

Reviews of M. MCDOUGAL & W. BURKE, THE PUBLIC ORDER OF THE OCEANS (1962):

Baldwin, 73 YALE L.J. 727 (1964).

Bowett, 39 BRIT. Y.B. INT'L L. 509 (1963).

Brownlie, 12 INT'L & COMP. L.Q. 1053 (1963).

Dorsey, 57 AM. POL. SCI. REV. 505 (1963).

Ereli, 16 VAND. L. REV. 1009 (1963).

Friedmann, 64 COLUM. L. REV. 607 (1964).

Hyde, 58 AM. J. INT'L L. 1031 (1964).

Johnson, 79 LAW Q. REV. 448 (1963).

Johnston, 15 U. TORONTO L.J. 225 (1963).

Kenney, 32 GEO. WASH. L. REV. 676 (1964).

Lissitzyn, 52 CALIF. L. REV. 447 (1964).

O'Connell, 4 SYDNEY L. REV. 312 (1963).

Peterson, 18 J. LEGAL ED. 115 (1965).

Stern, 56 LAW LIBRARY J. 282 (1963).

Utton, 3 NATURAL RESOURCES J. 208 (1963).

Selected Works Influenced by Myres S. McDougal

BOOKS

A. DAVID, THE STRATEGY OF TREATY TERMINATION: LAWFUL BREACHES AND RETALIATIONS (1975).

R. FALK, A STUDY OF FUTURE WORLDS (1975).

———, THIS ENDANGERED PLANET (1971).

———, THE STATUS OF LAW IN INTERNATIONAL SOCIETY (1970).

———, LEGAL ORDER IN A VIOLENT WORLD (1968).

———, THE ROLE OF DOMESTIC COURTS IN THE INTERNATIONAL LEGAL ORDER (1964).

————, Law, Morality, and War in the Contemporary World (1963).

R. Higgins, The Development of International Law Through the Political Organs of the United Nations (1963).

W. Holder & G. Brennan, The International Legal System—Cases and Materials, with Emphasis on the Australian Perspective (1972).

D. Johnston, The International Law of Fisheries: A Framework for Policy-Oriented Inquiries (1965).

M. Kaplan & N. Katzenbach, The Political Foundations of International Law (1961).

J. Lyon & R. Atkey, Canadian Constitutional Law in a Modern Perspective (1970).

J. N. Moore, Law and the Indo-China War (1972).

B. Murty, Propaganda and World Public Order: The Legal Regulation of the Ideological Instrument of Coercion (1968).

W. Reisman, Nullity and Revision: The Review and Enforcement of International Judgments and Awards (1971).

B. Weston, 1–2 International Claims: Their Settlement by Lump Sum Agreements (1975) (with Richard B. Lillich).

————, International Claims: Postwar French Practice (1971).

W. Williams, Inter-Governmental Military Forces and World Public Order (1971).

ARTICLES

Allen & Caldwell, *Modern Logic and Judicial Decision-Making: A Sketch of One View,* 28 Law & Contemp. Probs. 213 (1964).

Baldus, *State Competence to Terminate Concession Agreements,* 53 Ky. L.J. 56 (1964).

Burke, *Ocean Sciences, Technology, and the Future International Law of the Sea,* in 2 R. Falk & C. Black (eds.), The Future of the International Legal Order 183 (1970).

————, *Aspects of Internal Decision Processes in Inter-Governmental Fishery Commissions,* 43 U. Wash. L. Rev. 115 (1967).

Chilstrom, *Humanitarian Intervention Under Contemporary International Law: A Policy-Oriented Approach,* 1 Yale Stud. W.P.O. 93 (1974).

Colby, *The Developing International Law on Gathering and Sharing Security Intelligence,* 1 Yale Stud. W.P.O. 49 (1974).

Katzenbach, *Conflicts on an Unruly Horse: Reciprocal Claims and Tolerances in Interstate and International Law,* 65 Yale L.J. 1087 (1956).

Note (Lembesis), *The SALT Process and Its Use in Regulating Mobile ICBM's,* 84 Yale L.J. 1078 (1975).

Lung-chu Chen & Reisman, *Who Owns Taiwan: A Search for International Title,* 81 Yale L.J. 599 (1972).

Lyon, *A Fresh Approach to Constitutional Law: Use of a Policy-Science Model,* 45 Can. B. Rev. 554 (1967).

McDougal (Luther L. III), *Land-Use Planning by Private Volition: A Framework for Policy-Oriented Inquiry,* 16 Ariz. L. Rev. 1 (1974).

McWhinney, *Operational Methodology and Philosophy for Accommodation of the Contending Systems of International Law,* 50 Va. L. Rev. 36 (1964).

————, *Soviet and Western International Law and the Cold War in the Era of Bipolarity,* 1 Can. Y.B. Int'l L. 40 (1963).

————, *Peaceful Coexistence and Soviet–Western International Law,* 56 Am. J. Int'l L. 951 (1962).

Miller, *Access to do Business Across International Boundaries,* 42 Tul. L. Rev. 795 (1968).

Moore, *Toward an Applied Theory for the Regulation of Intervention, in* J. N. MOORE (ed.), LAW AND CIVIL WAR IN THE MODERN WORLD 3 (1974).

Nanda, *The United States Action in the 1965 Dominican Crisis: Impact on World Order,* 44 DENVER L.J. 439 (1966); 44 *id.* at 225 (1967).

O'Connor, *Soviet Procedures in Civil Decisions: A Changing Balance Between Public and Civic Systems of Public Order, in* W. LaFAVE (ed.), LAW IN THE SOVIET SOCIETY 51 (1965).

Paust, *An International Structure for Implementation of the 1949 Geneva Conventions: Needs and Function Analysis,* 1 YALE STUD. W.P.O. 148 (1974).

Reisman, *Humanitarian Intervention to Protect the Ibos, in* R. LILLICH (ed.), HUMANITARIAN INTERVENTION AND THE UNITED NATIONS 167 (1973).

———, *Private Armies in a Global War System: Prologue to Decision,* 14 VA. J. INT'L L. 1 (1973), *reprinted in* J. N. MOORE (ed.), LAW AND CIVIL WAR IN THE MODERN WORLD 252 (1974).

———, *Responses to Crimes of Discrimination and Genocide: An Appraisal of the Convention on the Elimination of Racial Discrimination,* 1 DENVER J. INT'L L. & POLICY 29 (1971).

———, *Sanctions and Enforcement, in* 3 R. FALK & C. BLACK (eds.), THE FUTURE OF THE INTERNATIONAL LEGAL ORDER (1971).

Note (Schneider), *New Perspectives on International Environmental Law,* 82 YALE L.J. 1659 (1973).

Vlasic, *The Relevance of International Law to Emerging Trends in the Law of Outer Space, in* 2 R. FALK & C. BLACK (eds.), THE FUTURE OF THE INTERNATIONAL LEGAL ORDER 265 (1970).

Weston, *"Prompt, Adequate and Effective": A Universal Standard of Compensation?,* 30 FORDHAM L. REV. 727 (1962) (with Frank G. Dawson).

———, *Community Regulation of Foreign-Wealth Deprivation: A Tentative Framework for Inquiry, in* R. MILLER & R. STANGER (eds.), ESSAYS ON EXPROPRIATIONS 117 (1967).

———, *L'Affaire Sabbatino: A Wistful Review,* 55 KY. L.J. 844 (1967) (an extensive review of E. MOONEY, FOREIGN SEIZURES AND THE ACT OF STATE DOCTRINE (1967)).

———, *International Law and the Deprivation of Foreign Wealth: A Framework for Future Inquiry, in* 2 R. FALK & C. BLACK (eds.), THE FUTURE OF THE INTERNATIONAL LEGAL ORDER 36 (1970), *revised and reprinted from* 54 VA. L. REV. 1069, 1265 (1968).

———, *Valuation Upon the Deprivation of Foreign Enterprise: A Policy-Oriented Approach to the Problem of Compensation Under International Law, in* 1 R. LILLICH (ed. & contrib.), THE VALUATION OF NATIONALIZED PROPERTY IN INTERNATIONAL LAW 3 (1971) (with Dale R. Weigel).

———, *"Constructive Takings" under International Law: A Modest Foray into the Problem of "Creeping Expropriation,"* 16 VA. J. INT'L L. 103 (1975).

———, *Education for Human Survival: An Immediate World Priority,* 188 ANNALS N.Y. ACAD. SCIENCES 115 (1975).

Note (Wheeler), *World Hunger and International Trade: An Analysis and a Proposal for Action,* 84 YALE L.J. 1046 (1975).

MISCELLANEOUS

Weston & Wolf, *Report of the Working Group on "Decision Processes, Conflict Resolution, and the Control of War—The Organized Planet, Human Rights, and Individual Participation,"* 184 ANNALS N.Y. ACAD. SCIENCES: ENVIRONMENT AND SOCIETY IN TRANSITION 635 (1971).

K. V. Raman, The Prescription of International Law by Customary Practice (unpublished J.S.D. dissertation, Yale Law School, 1967).

L. Schuckinski, Traditional Theories of Inquiry: The Contributions of the Schools of Jurisprudence (unpublished mimeo., Yale Law Library, 1965).

Index